Chaos Theory in Economics

To Ana

*I thank Levent Akdeniz, without whose research
assistance and support this volume would not
have been completed.*

The International Library of Critical Writings in Economics

Series Editor: Mark Blaug

Professor Emeritus, University of London
Professor Emeritus, University of Buckingham
Visiting Professor, University of Exeter

This series is an essential reference source for students, researchers and lecturers in economics. It presents by theme an authoritative selection of the most important articles across the entire spectrum of economics. Each volume has been prepared by a leading specialist who has written an authoritative introduction to the literature included.

A full list of published and future titles in this series is printed at the end of this volume.

Chaos Theory in Economics
Methods, Models and Evidence

Edited by

W. Davis Dechert
Associate Professor of Economics
University of Houston, US

INTERNATIONAL LIBRARY OF CRITICAL WRITINGS IN ECONOMICS

An Elgar Reference Collection
Cheltenham, UK • Brookfield US

Published by
Edward Elgar Publishing Limited
8 Lansdown Place
Cheltenham
Glos GL50 2HU

Edward Elgar Publishing Company
Old Post Road
Brookfield
Vermont 05036
US

British Library Cataloguing in Publication Data
Chaos theory in economics : methods, models and evidence.
    (The international library of critical writings in
    economics ; no. 66)
    1. Economics 2. Chaotic behavior in systems – Economic
    aspects 3. Nonlinear theories – Economic aspects
    I. Dechert, W. Davis
    330'.01

Library of Congress Cataloguing in Publication Data
Chaos theory in economics : methods, models, and evidence / edited by
    W. Davis Dechert.
        p.   cm.— (International library of critical writings in
    economics ; 66)
    Includes bibliographical references and index.
      1. Economics, Mathematical.   2. Chaotic behavior in systems.
    3. Statics and dynamics (Social sciences) 4. Time-series analysis.
    5. Nonlinear systems. I. Dechert, W. Davis, 1942– . II. Series.
    HB135.C447 1996
    330'.01'51—dc20

                                                                    96–5317
                                                                    CIP

ISBN 1 85898 216 2

Printed in Great Britain by Galliard (Printers) Ltd, Great Yarmouth

Contents

Acknowledgements

The editor and publishers wish to thank the authors and the following publishers who have kindly given permission for the use of copyright material.

American Finance Association for article: David A. Hsieh (1991), 'Chaos and Nonlinear Dynamics: Application to Financial Markets', *Journal of Finance*, **XLVI** (5), December, 1839–77.

American Journal of Agricultural Economics for articles: Jean-Paul Chavas and Matthew T. Holt (1991), 'On Nonlinear Dynamics: The Case of the Pork Cycle', *American Journal of Agricultural Economics*, **73** (3), August, 819–28; Jean-Paul Chavas and Matthew T. Holt (1993), 'Market Instability and Nonlinear Dynamics', *American Journal of Agricultural Economics*, **75** (1), February, 113–20.

American Statistical Association for article: E. Scott Mayfield and Bruce Mizrach (1992), 'On Determining the Dimension of Real-Time Stock-Price Data', *Journal of Business and Economic Statistics*, **10** (3), July, 367–74.

Basil Blackwell Ltd for articles: Murray Frank and Thanasis Stengos (1988), 'Chaotic Dynamics in Economic Time-Series', *Journal of Economic Surveys*, **2** (2), 103–33; Cars H. Hommes and Helena E. Nusse (1989), 'Does an Unstable Keynesian Unemployment Equilibrium in a non-Walrasian Dynamic Macroeconomic Model Imply Chaos?', *Scandinavian Journal of Economics*, **91** (1), 161–7; José A. Scheinkman (1990), 'Nonlinearities in Economic Dynamics', *Economic Journal*, **100** (400), Conference, 33–48; M.S. Bartlett (1990), 'Chance or Chaos?', *Journal of the Royal Statistical Society A*, **153** (3), 321–30.

Elsevier Science B.V. for articles: Rose-Anne Dana and Luigi Montrucchio (1987), 'On Rational Dynamic Strategies in Infinite Horizon Models Where Agents Discount the Future', *Journal of Economic Behavior and Organization*, **8**, 497–511; Murray Frank, Ramazan Gencay and Thanasis Stengos (1988), 'International Chaos?', *European Economic Review*, **32** (8), October, 1569–84; Murray Z. Frank and Thanasis Stengos (1988), 'Some Evidence Concerning Macroeconomic Chaos', *Journal of Monetary Economics*, **22**, 423–38; John D. Sterman (1989), 'Deterministic Chaos in an Experimental Economic System', *Journal of Economic Behavior and Organization*, **12**, 1–28; H.E. Nusse and C.H. Hommes (1990), 'Resolution of Chaos with Application to a Modified Samuelson Model', *Journal of Economic Dynamics and Control*, **14**, 1–19; Cars H. Hommes (1991), 'Adaptive Learning and Roads to Chaos: The Case of the Cobweb', *Economics Letters*, **36**, 127–32; Richard H. Day and Giulio Pianigiani (1991), 'Statistical Dynamics and Economics', *Journal of Economic Behavior and Organization*, **16**, 37–83; Steven G. Craig, Janet E. Kohlhase and David H. Papell (1991), 'Chaos Theory and Microeconomics: An Application to Model

Specification and Hedonic Estimation', *Review of Economics and Statistics*, **LXXIII** (2), 208–15; Ramazan Gencay and W. Davis Dechert (1992), 'An Algorithm for the *n* Lyapunov Exponents of an *n*-Dimensional Unknown Dynamical System', *Physica D*, **59**, 142–57; Claire G. Gilmore (1993), 'A New Test for Chaos', *Journal of Economic Behavior and Organization*, **22**, 209–37.

Elsevier Science Inc. for article: Thomas Willey (1992), 'Testing for Nonlinear Dependence in Daily Stock Indices', *Journal of Economics and Business*, **44** (1), February, 63–76.

Elsevier Science S.A. for article: Sergio Invernizzi and Alfredo Medio (1991), 'On Lags and Chaos in Economic Dynamic Models', *Journal of Mathematical Economics*, **20**, 521–50.

Estudios Económicos for article: William A. Brock (1993), 'Pathways to Randomness in the Economy: Emergent Nonlinearity and Chaos in Economics and Finance', *Estudios Económicos*, **8** (1), 3–55.

International Economic Review for article: James B. Ramsey, Chera L. Sayers and Philip Rothman (1990), 'The Statistical Properties of Dimension Calculations Using Small Data Sets: Some Economic Applications', *International Economic Review*, **31** (4), November, 991–1020.

John Wiley & Sons Inc. for articles: Robert Savit (1989), 'Nonlinearities and Chaotic Effects in Options Prices', *Journal of Futures Markets*, **9** (6), 507–18; Steven C. Blank (1991), '"Chaos" in Futures Markets? A Nonlinear Dynamical Analysis', *Journal of Futures Markets*, **11** (6), 711–28.

Journal of Financial and Quantitative Analysis for article: David A. Hsieh (1993), 'Implications of Nonlinear Dynamics for Financial Risk Management', *Journal of Financial and Quantitative Analysis*, **28** (1), March, 41–64.

Oxford University Press for article: William A. Brock (1991), 'Understanding Macroeconomic Time Series Using Complex Systems Theory', *Structural Change and Economic Dynamics*, **2** (1), 119–41.

Review of Economic Studies Ltd for article: William A. Brock and Ehung G. Baek (1991), 'Some Theory of Statistical Inference for Nonlinear Science', *Review of Economic Studies*, **54** (4), No. 196, 697–716.

Springer Verlag GmbH & Co. KG for articles: Mahmoud A. El-Gamal (1991), 'Non-Parametric Estimation of Deterministically Chaotic Systems', *Economic Theory*, **1** (2), 147–67; Venkatesh Bala and Mukul Majumdar (1992), 'Chaotic Tatonnement', *Economic Theory*, **2** (4), 437–45.

Every effort has been made to trace all the copyright holders but if any have been inadvertently overlooked the publishers will be pleased to make the necessary arrangement at the first opportunity.

In addition the publishers wish to thank the Library of the London School of Economics and Political Science, and the Marshall Library, Cambridge University, for their assistance in obtaining these articles.

Introduction
W. Davis Dechert

The theory of chaotic dynamics has opened up a new approach to the analysis of intertemporal economic phenomena. Chaotic dynamics are inherently unstable and characterized by fluctuations that bear a striking resemblance to stochastic data. Nevertheless, chaotic dynamics are purely deterministic phenomena. Superficially, the most obvious question to answer is: Can economic fluctuations be explained as the equilibrium outcome of deterministic dynamics? If so, then the focus of economic analysis should be on deterministic rather than stochastic models. As the works of Benhabib and Day (1981) and Boldrin and Montrucchio (1986) have shown, chaotic dynamics can indeed be the intertemporal equilibrium which results from utility maximization. These results should inspire further research into economic models that lead to chaotic dynamics and should encourage further analysis of the properties of chaos.

There has been a widespread criticism of the application of chaos theory to 'real world' economics and in particular of those that 'trend surf' the new ideas of mathematics. There is a widely held view that economic fluctuations are caused by random shocks, and as such stochastic models are the appropriate tools of analysis. Furthermore, in this view, the characteristics of the fluctuations produced by deterministic models do not match those of economic time series. Similar to the early critique of utility theory, these criticisms are being levelled at dynamic models which are in their nascent stage of development. Although many economists have sought to analyse dynamic economic phenomena, there has been a dearth of both models and tools for the researcher to use. This lack of variety of dynamic models has led to the unrealistic nature of the result from these analyses.

In this century mathematics has become the language of economic research. Its widespread use was brought about by the desire of economists to analyse multivariate problems with which the earlier graphical methods could not cope. This has led to two principal research methods. One has been to develop specific mathematical tools for economic analysis, and the other has been to apply existing theorems in mathematics to economics. In the latter category have been such tools as the Lagrangian representation of constrained optimization problems, the Envelope Theorem, the fixed point theorems of equilibrium theory and the Pontryagin Theorem of optimal control among many others. The most current developments in nonlinear dynamics have been catastrophe theory and the theory of chaos. Whether or not these theories will be as important to economics as the earlier mathematical methods were has yet to be determined. Nevertheless, it is safe to say that they will have a lasting impact on the development of dynamic economic models.

For this volume I have chosen a collection of recently published papers on the continuing research into nonlinear dynamics and economics. I have focused on three primary areas of this research. The first area explores the methodology of nonlinear dynamics as it applies to economic theory; the second area includes the current developments in the modelling of economic dynamics; and the third area combines statistical methods with the theory of nonlinear dynamics to test for the presence of chaos and other nonlinear phenomena in economic time series. These three areas provide a nice overview of the connection between theoretical and practical economic analyses.

Methods

Chapters 1 and 2 by Brock outline in detail his views on the potential for nonlinear dynamics and complex systems theory as analytical methods in economics. In Chapter 1 he borrows from Physics an interactive particle system which he uses as a theoretical model of consumer choice. In this model each agent's choice depends in part on the choices of others. This externality provides a link that results in a multiplicity of (locally stable) equilibria and complex dynamics. In Chapter 2 he outlines several other models that can also lead to chaos. The striking point in these models is that they are intrinsically stochastic. It is the combination of complex dynamics and uncertainty that is at the centre of Brock's view of the role of nonlinear dynamics as a tool of analysis in economics. Scheinkman (Chapter 3), commenting that 'It is extremely unlikely that macroeconomic fluctuations could ever be explained by a purely deterministic model', also believes that mixed systems are the most likely source for better models of intertemporal economics. He focuses on detecting nonlinearities in time series data and reviews the Brock, Dechert and Scheinkman (BDS) test which has been the primary statistical tool used in this literature. Brock, Dechert, Scheinkman and LeBaron (1995) review much of the literature since the Scheinkman article that uses the BDS test.

The presence of time lags is another important component in the analysis of economic chaotic dynamics. Delays in acquiring information and implementing decisions can introduce substantial nonlinearities into the equilibrium process. Using a variety of models, Invernizzi and Medio (Chapter 4) analyse the effects of time lags on the resulting dynamics. They also developed a number of mathematical methods to deal with such models. In a simple tatonnement model Bala and Majumdar (Chapter 5) demonstrate the techniques that are used to prove the existence of ergodic chaos. This is important for models with lags (and all dynamical systems can be thought of as models with lags) because, often it is very difficult to determine whether or not a particular model exhibits chaotic dynamics. Often one has to rely on numerical techniques and statistical tests to show that chaos is likely to present. In Chapter 6 Day and Pianigiani review many of the statistical methods and give some applications to tatonnement processes and to business cycles. Gilmore covers some of the topological methods for identifying chaos in time series analysis in Chapter 10. She also describes the use of several nonlinear time series techniques of analysis including close returns plots and histograms as well as the use of smoothing techniques.

Chaos and other time series nonlineareties can be detected with two primary methods. The first is the use of statistics such as the BDS test mentioned above. The second is to fit a dynamical system to the data first and then to analyse the fitted model for the presence of chaos. The latter is the method of Gencay and Dechert (Chapter 9) who use neural networks to estimate the Lyapunov exponents of an unknown dynamical system. As an alternative to the neural network approach, El-Gamal (Chapter 7) estimates unknown dynamical systems with kernel density estimators. Both of these methods take advantage of the fact that they are very successful at fitting a model to the unknown dynamics. Therefore, they can be used to estimate such measures of chaos as the Lyapunov exponents which are calculated with the derivatives of the dynamical system. In this regard they have proved to provide more stable estimates than direct statistical techniques.

In response to the view that stochastic dynamics are the only source of economic fluctuations, Bartlett (Chapter 11) discusses the fundamental issue of which model – deterministic or stochastic – is the appropriate one for the given process. This has important implications for both theoretical and empirical analyses. For example, in the flipping of a coin, the probability model does quite well in matching the observations, while a deterministic model seems nearly impossible to implement. Perhaps in future explorations, models will be selected not just on the criterion of which ones best fit the observations, but also with a view as to what questions we want to answer with the model. If one wishes to study the nonlinear dynamics of the tossed coin, the stochastic model is a poor one. However, if one wants to analyse the sequence of outcomes of the coin flips, the stochastic model is an excellent one.

Models

In spite of the recent theoretical advances in the theory of chaos, there are few models of economic dynamics that give rise to chaotic fluctuations. This is in part due to the fact that much of economic analysis to date does not truly rely on fully dynamic models. Compared to the collection of models of consumption and production which lead to the supply and demand analyses and the general equilibrium analyses, there are very few similar models of dynamic economic behaviour. The papers in this section reflect both the lack of such models and the current state of building dynamic economic models.

Formal results can be derived in recursive economic models by using a dynamic programming approach. In Chapter 12 Dana and Montrucchio show the extent to which the value function can be used and they describe the current theoretical advances in dynamic economic modelling. Their results apply both to single agent optimal growth problems and to multi-player dynamic games. What is evident from their paper and the papers they cite is that theoretical results are hard to come by. Furthermore, conditions (both sufficient and necessary) for chaos are difficult to apply to practical models. Sorger (1992) has been making advances in this direction.

Because of the difficulty in achieving theoretical results, a number of researchers are turning to computer simulations of models in order to study dynamical phenomena. Judd (1995) argues that computational economics is a complement to rather than a substitute for analytical economic theory. Furthermore, he goes on to show that a much broader class of models can be analysed with simulation methods than those which are analytically tractable. Therefore it is not surprising that simulation methods are the basis for most of the papers in this section. Sterman (Chapter 13) reports results in an experimental setting which appear to be chaotic. With the use of experimental economics he estimates the decision rules of the subjects. He then simulates the model and finds that chaotic solutions occur for parameter values that closely fit the decision rules of the experimental subjects. In a similar vein, Chavas and Holt (Chapter 14) have modelled the supply and demand for dairy products by incorporating the decision rules of dairy farmers in managing their stock of animals. In simulation studies, using parameter values that fit the observed data on dairy herds and dairy prices, they too find that chaotic solutions can occur.

Simulation studies are also being used to analyse purely abstract models. In Chapter 15 by Hommes, Chapter 16 by Hommes and Nusse and Chapter 18 by Nusse and Hommes there is a nice mixture of numerical and theoretical analysis. In a recent study, Brock and Hommes (1995) continue this line of research and show how topological properties of dynamical systems can be derived with simulation studies. These papers serve as a prototype for future research into nonlinear dynamical phenomena in economics.

Traditionally, theories of asset pricing have relied on fundamentally stochastic models. By using a chaotic time series as the 'shocks' to the system, Savit (Chapter 17) shows how to adjust the classical option pricing formula for these shcoks. While it is well understood that the nature of the stochastic shocks affect the value of an option on an underlying asset, Savit's contribution is to show how a mixture of stochastic and chaotic shocks affect the option value. In this interesting application of chaotic dynamics to option pricing, Savit demonstrates a method for analysing mixed stochastic and deterministic systems. These are the types of systems which are likely to play a major role in economic modelling of the near future.

Evidence

A number of statistical tests have been proposed to detect nonlinearities in both stochastic and deterministic time series. The BDS test, which has its roots in the detection of chaos, has been widely applied to economic time series. The advantage of this test is that it is particularly sensitive to nonlinearties in the model that generates the data. In its simplest form it is a test for independence in the data. Since there are often strong correlations in economic data, this test is not usable on raw data. However, most economic models have independent and identically distributed errors at some point in the model, which makes it possible to use the test in a broader fashion as a model specification test. A number of papers in this section show how to use the BDS in this manner. However, as is often the case in empirical work, this is easier said than done. In Chapter 19 by Frank and Stengos there is an excellent review of both the mathematical properties of chaotic dynamics and the econometric methodology of time series analysis in economics.

Several methods have been developed to empirically test for nonlinearties in economic data. Chapter 27 by Frank and Stengos, and Chapter 26 by Frank, Gencay and Stengos are typical of the empirical methods that are currently being used in economic research. They test both raw data, as well as the residual errors after fitting an appropriate model to the series. They also use a technique which is known as shuffling of the data. This technique consists of testing a model on the data in its original order as well as on the same data in a randomly chosen order. By comparing the results they get with this technique they can detect which test results come from serial correlations in the data, and which do not. Frank and Stengos (Chapter 27) analyse Canadian macroeconomic data for the presence of chaos, while Frank, Gencay and Stengos do the same for data from Japan, Italy, Germany and the UK.

Brock, Dechert and Scheinkman (1987) show that the BDS test statistic is asymptotically normal. However, Brock, Hsieh and LeBaron (1991) show that the rate of convergence is quite slow. This means that the size and power of the BDS test needs to be established by such methods as boot strapping or Monte Carlo studies. Chapter 20 by Hsieh is a premier on nonlinear time series methodology. He provides a complete description of the techniques that are currently being used to analyse financial data. In Chapter 22 Hsieh uses these techniques to estimate financial risk and provides a case study in the management of risk.

Along with the correlation interval which is the base of the BDS test there are a number of other important measures of chaos, such as the Lyapunov exponents, the Kolmogorov entropy and the fractal dimension of the data. Chapter 21 by Mayfield and Mizrach, Chapter 23 by Blank and Chapter 24 by Willey all demonstrate how to estimate these measures with economic data. As a technical note of caution, Ramsey, Sayers and Rothman (Chapter 25) describe how measures of dimension can be biased when estimated on small data sets.

All but one of the papers in this section have examined macroeconomic time series for the presence of nonlinear dynamics. However, one of the longest time series which has been recorded is the price and volume data of the pork market. These data exhibit strong cyclical behaviour which nevertheless appears to be unpredictable. In a detailed analysis of this market, Chavas and Holt (Chapter 28) use the BDS test to examine this microeconomic data. They are able to find the clear presence of nonlinearities in the data which are necessarily indicative of the presence of chaos.

The natural application of the nonlinear techniques that are described in this volume is to time series analysis. The reason for this is that the time index provides a natural ordering of the data. Also, from theoretical considerations we would expect to find strong intertemporal correlations in the economic decisions of consumers and produers. Nevertheless, in Chapter 29 Craig, Kolhase and Papell apply the BDS test in a cross-sectional study of housing demand. Their technique is to sort the data set by using a key variable in much the same way that a time series is (naturally) sorted by time. They then test the Ordinarily Least Squares residuals for independence with the BDS statistic. They find that for most of the variables in the regression, the BDS test rejects the independence hypothesis. One conclusion from this study is that the linear model is not a good fit for the data.

There is a widespread interest in academic and other professional circles in the applications of nonlinear techniques to time series analysis. The evidence for this is not only the burgeoning literature on this topic but also the edited volumes by Benhabib (1991), Jarsulic (1993), Creedy and Martin (1994) as well as this one. The direct benefits of this research have been to cause us to examine economic data from a fresh perspective. However, there are other benefits that may have a more far-reaching impact on economic analysis. By developing better tests for the presence of nonlinearities, we are led to constructing better nonlinear models of the causal relationships in the data. This is particularly true in time series analysis where economists have relied on statistical rather than economic models. There is also a spill-over effect in economic theory where the development of better models will provide a firmer foundation for the analysis of intertemporal economic equilibria.

References

Benhabib, J. (1991), *Cycles and Chaos in Economic Equilibrium*, Princeton NJ: Princeton University Press.

Benhabib, J. and R.H. Day (1981), 'Rational Choice and Erratic Behavior', *Review of Economic Studies*, **48**, 459–72.

Boldrin, M. and L. Montrucchio (1986), 'On the Indeterminacy of Capital Accumulation Paths', *Journal of Economic Theory*, **40**, 26–39.

Brock, W.A., W.D. Dechert and J.A. Scheinkman (1987), 'A Test for Independence Based On the Correlation Dimension', University of Wisconsin at Madison, University of Houston and University of Chicago: Department of Economics.

Brock, W.A., W.D. Dechert, J.A. Scheinkman and B. LeBaron (1995), 'A Test for Independence Based On the Correlation Dimension', forthcoming in *Econometric Reviews*.

Brock, W.A. and C.H. Hommes (1995), 'Rational Routes to Randomness', University of Wisconsin and University of Amsterdam: Department of Economics.

Brock, W.A., D. Hsieh and B. LeBaron (1991), *Nonlinear Dynamics, Chaos and Instability*, Cambridge, Mass.: MIT Press.

Creedy, J. and V.L. Martin (1994), *Chaos and Non-linear Models in Economics: Theory and Applications*, Aldershot, UK: Edward Elgar.

Jarsulic, M. (1993), *Non-Linear Dynamics in Economic Theory*, The International Library of Critical Writings in Economics, Aldershot, UK: Edward Elgar.

Judd, K.L. (1995), 'Computational Economics and Economic Theory: Substitutes or Complements?', Stanford University: Hoover Institute.

Sorger, G. (1992), *Minimum Impatience Theorems for Recursive Economic Models*, Lecture Notes in Economics and Mathematical Systems, **390**, Berlin: Springer-Verlag.

Part I
Methods

[1]

PATHWAYS TO RANDOMNESS IN THE ECONOMY: EMERGENT NONLINEARITY AND CHAOS IN ECONOMICS AND FINANCE

William A. Brock*
University of Wisconsin, Madison

Resumen: Este trabajo muestra porqué la teoría no-lineal, incluyendo la del caos, es importante en economía y finanzas. Se presentan dos definiciones de no-linealidad estocástica y se arguye que son útiles no sólo en pruebas de no-linealidad, sino también en la construcción de una nueva clase de modelos de valuación de activos. También se muestra cómo la teoría de sistemas de partículas en interacción puede ser usada para hacer modelos estructurales de valuación de activos que convierten procesos lineales de ganancias en procesos no-lineales de rendimientos en equilibrio.

Abstract: This paper: (1) Gives a general argument why research on nonlinear science in general and chaos in particular is important in economics and finance. (2) Puts forth two definitions of stochastic nonlinearity (IID-Linearity and MDS-Linearity) for nonlinear time series analysis and argues for their usefulness as organizing concepts not only for discussion of nonlinearity testing but also for building a new class of structural asset pricing models. (3) Shows how to use ideas from interacting particle systems theory to build structural asset pricing models that turn IID-Linear or MDS-Linear earnings processes into non MDS-Linear equilibrium returns processes.

* I thank the NSF (SES-9122344) and the Vilas Trust for research support; and Steve Durlauf and Blake LeBaron for very useful comments. I thank Carlos Urzúa for inviting me to present this work at a most exceptional conference. None of the above are responsible for errors, shortcomings, and opinions expressed in this paper. An earlier version of this paper circulated under the title, "Beyond Randomness, or, Emergent Noise: Interactive Systems of Agents with Cross Dependent Characteristics."

1. Introduction

In the past few years a large literature on chaos and nonlinear science has appeared in economics. While the economics literature is large it is dwarfed by the parallel literature on chaos and nonlinear science in the other sciences. Here we will use the term "nonlinear science" to refer to the broader study of nonlinear dynamical systems, not just chaotic ones. More will be said about the domain of "nonlinear science" when we discuss journals and other outlets in the area.

A loose definition is this: "Nonlinear science" studies stochastic and deterministic dynamical systems that lead to "complex" dynamics. A deterministic dynamical system generates "complex dynamics" when "most" trajectories of the dynamical system do not converge to rest points or limit cycles. Here, in the stochastic case, "the dynamical system" refers to the underlying deterministic dynamical system, i.e. the system one obtains when the underlying stochastic forcing is shut off.

The main tasks of the current paper are three: *i)* Give a general argument why research on nonlinear science in general and chaos in particular is important in economics and finance. *ii)* Put forth two definitions of stochastic nonlinearity (IID-Linearity and MDS-Linearity) for nonlinear time series analysis and argue for their usefulness as organizing concepts not only for discussion of nonlinearity testing in time series econometrics but also for building a new class of structural asset pricing models. *iii)* Show how to use ideas from interacting particle systems theory to build structural asset pricing models that turn IID-Linear or MDS-Linear earnings processes into non MDS-Linear equilibrium returns processes.

Although we give a sneak preview here the reader may wish to glance ahead at Section three for the concepts of IID-Linearity and MDS-Linearity. We call stochastic process $\{Y_t\}$ IID-Linear (MDS-Linear) if

$$ Y_t - \mu = \sum \beta_j N_{t-j}, \quad \sum \beta_j^2 < \infty, $$

where the innovations, also called shocks, N_t are Independent and Identically Distributed, abreviated IID, (form a Martingale Difference Sequence, abbreviated MDS). As we shall see in Section three, MDS-Linearity corresponds to the case where the conditional expectation of Y_{t+1} given $\{Y_t, Y_{t-1}, \ldots\}$ is a linear function of $\{Y_t, Y_{t-1}, \ldots\}$. The concept of IID-Linear is more stringent than MDS-Linear. Noisy chaos is a striking example of a process that is not MDS-Linear.

This paper is organized as follows. Section one contains a brief introduction. Section two uses this paper as a "bully pulpit" to make a plea for more research on nonlinear science in general and chaos in particular in economics and finance. During this plea we give a very brief sketch of the literature.

There is a sizable literature in economics on statistical testing for the presence of chaos and other nonlinearity in time series data. Since that has been covered elsewhere by articles in Benhabib (1992), as well as by Brock and Dechert (1991), Brock, Hsieh and LeBaron (1991), Sayers's article in Krasner (1990), and Scheinkman (1990), we shall say little about it here, except to say that many applications of the techniques found strong evidence against linear models driven by IID shocks and weaker evidence against a subclass of MDS-Linear models driven by certain parameterized forms of heteroscedastic shocks.

The techniques of Section three are purely statistical techniques for testing whether a time series sample comes from a linear process or whether a time series comes from a chaotic process. While statistical techniques are useful they are no substitute for a structural model in giving insights into the economic forces that may generate nonlinearity or chaos.

Section four develops structural models which can generate "endogenous" discontinuous changes in equilibrium asset prices. In particular we study a class of asset pricing models that generate returns per share processes that are not linear processes. The intent of these examples is to show how the theory of Section three can be used to build a parsimoniously parameterized econometrically and analytically tractable class of asset pricing models which allow returns data to speak to the presence of economic forces causing abrupt changes in volatility and returns. The models are also structured to have the potentiality of generating equilibrium returns that display GARCH effects (*cf.* Bollerslev *et al.*, 1992) as well as "excess volatility" relative to measured fundamentals.

2. Theoretical Overview

We shall deal with the theoretical part of the literature first. The journals (*i*) *International Journal of Bifurcation and Chaos* (IJBC), (*ii*) *Journal of Nonlinear Science,* (*iii*) *Physica D,* (*iv*) *Chaos,* and (*v*) *Nonlinearity* give a glimpse of impact that research on chaos in particular and nonlinear science in general has had in sciences other than economics. Indeed the term "nonlinear science" could be well defined to be the subject matter treated in the above journals. A good place for the reader to view this type of work in economics is the volume edited by Benhabib (1992).

An informal definition of chaos is this. A deterministic dynamical system is chaotic if it displays *sensitive dependence upon initial conditions* in the sense that small differences in initial conditions are magnified by iteration of the dynamical system. A stochastic dynamical system is *noisy chaos* if it is chaotic when the conditional variance of the stochastic driver (the ultimate source of the uncertainty) is set identically equal to zero.

The Benhabib book gives a guide to the literature on formal definitions of chaos as well as a multitude of theoretic economic models that show chaotic equilibria are theoretically possible and are non pathological. Indeed, in economies with many sectors sufficient conditions needed to obtain chaotic equilibria are not very strong when evaluated by the standards of general equilibrium theory.

Grandmont argues in a recent paper (1992) that: *(i)* The economic time series that display the most volatility, *e.g.*, investment, inventories, durable goods, financial and stock markets, are those for which it appears that expectations play an important role in generating them, *(ii)* markets where expectations play an important role are most likely to be experience learning-induced local dynamic instability, *(iii)* plausible capital market imperfections, adjustment lags and limited substitutability can generate compex endogenous expectations-driven business cycles. He argues that it is important to incorporate nonlinearities to study such fluctuations.

The recent book by Hommes (1991) shows how easy it is to produce chaos in Hicksian type models with lags in investment and consumption. Majumdar and Mitra (1992) locate sufficient conditions for robust ergodic chaos to appear in growth models. The studies cited above raise the key issue of the plausibility of chaos as a generating mechanism of fluctuations in the real economy.

Before we go further, I wish to discuss some issues, especially three common misunderstandings, that have been repeatedly raised to me while lecturing on the area of nonlinear science in general and chaos in particular.

I don't believe there is any disagreement amongst economists on whether exogenous shocks play an important role in astute modeling of economic fluctuations. The issue of contention concerns the relative value of modeling endogenous fluctuations directly to modelling a system driven by exogenous fluctuations, i.e., exogenous shocks. The issue whether chaos is an important source of endogenous fluctuations is especially contentious for the case of aggregative macroeconomics (*cf.* Boldrin and Woodford's discussion of Sims's comment on Grandmont in Benhabib, 1992).

"Calibrationists" have criticised some theoretic models which produce chaotic equilibria for requiring parameter values that conflict with known measurements. Empirical work on testing for the presence of statistically detectable chaos in financial and macroeconomic time series data has not been very supportive of the hypothesis (*cf.* Ramsey, Sayers, and Rothman, 1988). This controversy has lead to some misunderstandings on the importance of research on chaotic and other nonlinear phenomena in economics.

The first misunderstanding is this. Just because evidence for chaos in time series data is weak does not mean that chaos is not a useful lens through which to view economic activity. The joint problem of data quality and weakness of statistical tests make the power of such tests to detect chaos in economic data particularly weak.

Indeed a recent paper by Barnett, Gallant, Hinich, and Jensen (1992) applied three tests for nonlinearity and chaos to monetary data and found inconsistent results across the three tests. They state: "Given the weak nature of that hypothesis and the implausible nature of the alternative –that the explanation of fluctuations lies in supernatural shocks to a linear universe– we find the degree of controversy regarding the existence of nonlinearity or chaos in economic data to be surprising." This statement seems to me to be right on target. Even if the reader does not agree with Barnett *et al.* it seems more productive to adopt a scientific research program that directs one to search for a mechanism that generates the observed movements in time series data which minimizes the role of "exogenous shocks."

The second misunderstanding is to conclude that weak evidence for chaos implies weak evidence for nonlinearity in general. Chaos is a very special species of nonlinearity. Methods inspired by the attempt to detect chaos have turned out to be useful in detecting other types of nonlinearity. There is another reason to be nervous about the use of linear methods in macroeconomics.

The reader should be reminded that the currently available sufficient conditions on stochastic multisector models for convergence to a unique stochastic steady state are severe (*cf.* Marimon, 1989). Much of modern macro economics, including real business cycle theory, is built upon the foundations of models that have a unique globally asymptotically stable stochastic steady state. The cases where linear approximation methods (after appropriate transformations) work well are, for the most part, the cases where attractors are simple points or cycles (when the driving noise is shut off). So theory is no refuge for the linearist.

The third, and probably the most important misunderstanding is to conclude that nonlinearity is unimportant in macroeconomics and finance because out-of-sample prediction of nonlinear models does not appear to be better than linear models such as random walk models in finance. Prominant examples of studies that find no out-of-sample forecast improvement for non-linear models are Diebold and Nason (1990), Meese and Rose (1991). Perhaps, because of these negative results on forecasting, some are lead to question the value of research on nonlinear econometric models in the times series area.

However, LeBaron (1992a, b) has found reliable out-of-sample nonlinear forecast improvements in stock returns by cleverly conditioning on local information such as local volatility. He shows that measures of near future predictability increase when measures of near past local volatility fall. Antoniewicz (1992) obtains forecast improvements on returns for individual stocks by conditioning on local volume by use of certain trading strategies.

The main point is this. Earlier studies examined *unconditional measures* of out-of-sample forecast improvment. Estimates of these measures are an *average* over the sample over periods where the forecast may be doing well and where it may be doing poorly. LeBaron shows that this averaging can make it difficult to discover conditioning information which could help identify periods when out-of-sample forecast improvement is possible.

Since Brock (1991b) gave an heuristic argument that tests in the family studied by Brock, Dechert, Scheinkman, LeBaron (1990) and de Lima (1992a,b) are good at exploring the whole space for local pockets of predictability therefore a rejection of IID-Linearity by one of these tests suggests that effort should be made to detect potential pockets of predictability. LeBaron's work can be viewed as a successful location of such pockets of predictability. The trading rule specification tests of Brock, Lakonishok, and LeBaron (1992) are also designed to locate zones where prediction might be possible.

Since LeBaron is working in the area of finance where the Efficient Markets Hypothesis gives a strong argument that any predictability is going to have to be subtle to prevent traders from exploiting it, therefore success at finding prediction possibilities in this area suggests that search in other areas of economics might be even more fruitful. Having dealt with some concerns about techniques inspired by nonlinear science in economics and finance let me turn to an overview of interest in nonlinear science in disciplines other than economics and finance.

My reading of natural science literature suggests, after initial debate on the claims of having found actual evidence for chaos in Nature, that natural science accepts the usefulness of nonlinear science in general. Evidence for this view follows.

First, a United States National Academy of Sciences report states, "As a consequence of its fundamental intellectual appeal and potential technological applications, nonlinear science is currently experiencing a phase of very rapid growth....In any effort to guide this research, however, it is imperative that nonlinear science be recognized for what it is: An inherently interdisciplinary effort..." (NAS, 1987, p. 14). The report worries about the difficulty of supporting research in this area within the confines of the balkanized U.S. university department system whose reward structure tends to discourage bold interdisciplinary research. They also worry about the large amounts of support of the area in other countries relative to the support in the United States. They conclude that nonlinear science has "...a remarkable breadth of application and the potential to influence both our basic understanding of the world and our daily life".

A second piece of evidence is a dramatic bar graph in Casti (1992, Vol. I, p. viii) where he plots the number of articles on chaos and fractals by year from 1974-1990. The bar graph shows an explosion of interest starting in 1983 which is rapidly growing to a level of almost four thousand articles in 1990. Since nonlinear science covers the general species of complex nonlinearity and since chaos and fractals are subsets of the area, Casti's bar graph understates the true extent of activity in this area.

Here is my attempt at distillation of a general view which has emerged from a huge literature in natural science. Natural science work on chaos leads to the view that dynamical systems which are composed of many locally and/or globally interacting parts with a variety of lag lengths due to adjustment dynamics or other sources of delayed reaction are quite likely to be chaotic where "likely" is measured relative to a population of general dynamical systems.

In practice measurements taken on the output of such systems are usually aggregative and corrupted by noise. Therefore even though the underlying generating mechanism may be chaotic the measurements taken on the system appear to be stochastic or purely random. In order to see how tough it can be for statistical tests to detect patterns in some deterministic dynamical systems take a look at Griffeath's comment (especially his reference to Wolfram's work on cellular automata) in Berliner (1992).

A prototypical example in natural science is fluid flow dynamics (*cf.* Van Atta's article in Krasner, 1990). For an economist fluid flow dynamics may, perhaps, be usefully viewed as a cellular automaton defined on a large dimensional state space. In certain Taylor-Couette fluid flow experiments (where the fluid is "weakly" turbulent) velocity measurements of a small chunk of fluid appear stochastic to many statistical tests but statistical tests based upon chaos theory detect evidence of low dimensional chaos.

Studies in epidemiology are discussed by Schaffer in Krasner (1990). Here, much as in economics, the controversy centers around whether, for example, the time series of measles cases is better described as a low order autoregression with seasonalities associated with the opening and closing of schools or is better described by a periodically forced dynamical system with a delay structure across components, perhaps along the lines of Kuznetsov *et al.* (1992), which can take the torus destruction route to chaos. The working conditions in epidemiology and biology are closer to those in economics where data quality is not so high and where laboratory experiments are expensive or impossible.

It appears that chaos is useful as a lens through which to view the world in epidemiology, biology, and ecology, not because it helps so much in prediction but because it is *suggestive of pathways to complex dynamics.*

This type of viewpoint leads to a paradigmatic shift in thinking about useful methods of study of such fields. Some scientists have been taking the view that in many cases linearization methods are suspect and the only excuse for using them is computational cost. Advances in computation have removed this constraint. Indeed some natural scientists are becoming rather sceptical about linearization. See, for example, Chua's editorial in *International Journal of Bifurcations and Chaos*, March, 1991.

In view of the rapid increase in nonlinear science activity in the other sciences, and, with the dramatic decline of computer costs making nonlinear science research within the realm of any researcher with a PC, one might argue that economics ignores nonlinear science at its peril.

Indeed people of a more practical sort with no incentive to have allegiance to any particular academic methodology have been recently using ideas from nonlinear science such as genetic algorithms and neural nets to design trading strategies for financial assets. Three examples that have recently hit the popular media are Hawley *et al.* (1990), *London Economist*, August 15, 1992, p. 70, and "The New Rocket Science Hits Corporate Finance", *Business Week*, Nov. 2, 1992. Reading between the lines one can see that at least one of the strategies discussed by the *Economist* and *Business Week* was inspired by Holland's (1992) "bottom up" approach to artifical intelligence by creation of an artificial ecology of strategies encoded by bit strings so that evolutionary Darwinistic dynamics can be simulated via computer.

In this system the best strategies are those which survive many generations of simulated evolutionary struggle. The Santa Fe Institute has stimulated research along this line in economics. Prominant examples are Anderson, Arrow, and Pines (1988), Arthur (1992), and Sargent (1992). Arthur (1992) and Sargent (1992) contain elegant statements of this approach to modeling "bounded rationality" in economics.

More on the Santa Fe theme can be found in a recent Scientific American article, "The Edge of Chaos: Complexity is a Metaphor at the Santa Fe Institute", October, 1992. The Santa Fe Institute studies complex dynamical systems and uses them as an organizing theme to study a catalogue of phenomena including the economy. See Anderson, Arrow, and Pines (1988) for an early statement of the Santa Fe approach. While I believe that there is a general consensus in economics that research in economics in the general area of nonlinear science as exemplified by the Santa Fe Institute is valuable, the usefulness of research on the particular area of chaos may not have such a consensus.

Nevertheless I argued above that this kind of research has been important. Other reasons why the research is important are these. First, in models with many sectors with a variety of adjustment lags it is easy to produce chaotic equilibria for plausible parameter values. Yet it is easy to produce examples where the aggregates do not appear chaotic to statistical tests for chaos. So aggregation may be responsible for the lack of evidence of chaos in macroeconomic data.

Second, the article by McNevin and Neftci in Benhabib (1992) argued that a set of aggregate data is less anti-symmetric than the disaggregated data under plausible economic conditions. Anti-symmetry is evidence consistent with nonlinearity because symmetric input into a linear map leads to symmetric output. They argue that the cyclical behavior of major capital goods industries is likely to be out of phase at business cycle frequencies and this would lead to symmetric aggregates even though the components are anti-symmetric. Their evidence is consistent with this story.

This situation is rather similar to the work of Sugihara and May (1990). They exhibit evidence consistent with the view that aggregate data on measles looks like an AR(2) with seasonalities associated with the opening and closing of schools is composed of components which behave in a manner more consistent with chaos (Sugihara, Grenfell, and May, 1990). Indeed when Sugihara, Grenfell, and May (1990) disaggregated the data they found evidence that there was a lag structure in propagation of the disease from area to area which generated dynamical information consistent with chaos. Note that we are not saying they showed the data was chaotic. We are only saying that the disaggregated data exhibited behavior consistent with chaos.

Third, research on chaos has sensitized scholars to pathways for emergent structure such as emergent nonlinearity. It is important to recall that chaos is a very special form of nonlinearity and, hence, the set of nonlinear data generating processes is much larger than the set of chaotic data generating processes.

3. Testing for Chaos and General Nonlinearity

A common method, but certaintly not the only one, of testing for "neglected structure" of any form is to estimate a best fitting model in a given null hypothesis class and pass the estimated residuals through a testing procedure designed to detect "neglected structure". If the null hypothesis class is the linear class this gives a procedure to test for nonlinearity.

In order to discuss this subject we need some definitions which we take from Brock and Potter (1992). For brevity we concentrate on scalar valued processes and q lags in the law of motion (1.b) below.

DEFINITION 1. We say the observed data process $\{A(t)\}$ is generated by a noisy deterministically chaotic explanation, "noisy chaotic" for short, if

$$A_t = h(X_t, M_t), \tag{3.1.a}$$

$$X_t = G(X_{t-1}, \ldots, X_{t-q}, V_t), \tag{3.1.b}$$

where $\{X_t\}$ (when $V_t = 0$) is generated by the deterministic dynamics,

$$x_t = G(x_{t-1}, \ldots, x_{t-q}, 0), \tag{3.1.c}$$

which is *chaotic*, that is to say the largest Lyapunov exponent (defined below) exists, is constant almost surely with respect to the assumed unique natural invariant measure of $G(.)$, and is positive.

Here $\{M_t\}$, $\{V_t\}$ are mutually independent mean zero, finite variance, Independent and Identically Distributed (IID) processes. Here $\{M_t\}$ represents measurement error, $h(x, m)$ is a noisy observer function of the state X_t, and $\{V_t\}$ is dynamical noise.

We warn the reader that positive largest Lyapunov exponent of the underlying deterministic map is not the only definition of chaos which appears in the literature. However this definition, and all definitions we have seen, share the following hallmark of chaos: Sensitive Dependence upon Initial Conditions (SDIC). Turn now to a definition of the largest Lyapunov exponent.

DEFINITION. *Largest Lyapunov Exponent of map $F(x)$.* Let $F : \mathbf{R}^n \to \mathbf{R}^n$. The largest Lyapunov exponent, λ, is defined by

$$\lambda \equiv \lim_{T \to \infty} \ln[D_{x_0} F^t . v] / t, \tag{3.2}$$

where D_{x_0}, ".", v, $\ln$, F^t, denote derivative with respect to initial condition x_0 at time zero, matrix product with direction vector v, natural logarithm, map F applied t times (the t-th iterate of F), and matrix norm respectively.

The following well known scalar valued example, called the tent map,

$$F(x) = 1 - |2x - 1|, \tag{3.3}$$

is a deterministic chaos with the following properties: $F(x)$ maps $[0, 1]$ to itself, and for almost all initial conditions, $x_0 \in [0, 1]$, with respect to, Lebesque measure on $[0, 1]$, the trajectory $x_t(x_0)$ of the dynamics, (1.c) is second order white noise i.e., has flat spectrum, and, the Autocorrelation Function (ACF) is zero at all leads and lags. The largest Lyapunov exponent is $\lambda = \ln(2) > 0$. There are many examples of deterministic chaoses. They share the feature that they are not predictable in the long term but they are predictable in the short term.

The approach of Barnett, Gallant, Hinich, and Jensen (1992) locates sufficient conditions on the above setup such that the method of delays can be used to "reconstruct" the underlying deterministic dynamical system (3.1c) so that nonparametric regression can be used to obtain a consistent estimator of (3.1c) so that a consistent estimator of the largest Lyapunov exponent can be found. Once a consistent estimator of the largest Lyapunov exponent is in hand, they test whether it is positive.

The definition of chaos as positive largest Lyapunov exponent naturally leads to an heuristic suggestion why chaotic dynamics should be expected for the dynamics $x_{t+1} = f(x_t)$, $f: \mathbf{R}^n \to \mathbf{R}^n$ for n large enough. The intuitive idea is this: If a system f is "drawn at random" the chances of getting one with a positive Lyapunov exponent should tend to one as $n \to \infty$.

In order to see why it may be possible to formulate and prove such a result turn to Ruelle's (1989, Chapter 9) treatment of Liapunov exponents. Place enough restrictions on each dynamical system $f(.)$ so that the Oseledec Multiplicative ergodic theorem can be applied to give existence of the limit of the $1/2N$-th root of the product of the derivative of the N-iterate of $f(.)$ with its adjoint. Call this limit Λ_x for initial condition x. The logarithms of the eigenvalues of this limit matrix are the Liapunov exponents. While the limit exists for ρ-almost all initial conditions, the invariant measure ρ which appears in the theorem depends upon $f(.)$. Also the measure ρ may contain "atoms", i.e., may not be absolutely continuous with respect to Lebesque measure. Hence there are obstacles on the route to showing that the story we tell below could serve as a metaphor for the likelihood of drawing a dynamical system whose limit matrix Λ_x exists and which has an eigenvalue with modulus greater than one, i.e., a positive Liapunov exponent, i.e, the dynamical system is chaotic.

Consider the following story which will serve as a kind of metaphor. Let B be a large positive number. Draw n numbers λ_i, $i = 1, 2, \ldots, n$, at random from the set $[-B, B]$ according to acumulative probability density distribution function $P_i(.)$ for the i-th draw. Let these numbers play the role of the eigenvalues of Λ_x above. The probability that at least one λ_i is greater than one (i.e. we have a positive largest Lyapunov exponent for the linear dynamics on $\mathbf{R}^n$ given by $x_{j,t+1} = \lambda_j x_{jt}$, $j = 1, 2, \ldots, n$) is one minus the probability that all λ_i are less than or equal to one. Assuming independent draws we see immediately that $A_n \equiv \prod_{i=1}^{i=n} Pr\{\lambda_i \leq 1\}$ is nonincreasing in n, hence converge to a nonnegative limit L, as $n \to \infty$. If $L > 0$ then taking logs shows us that $\log[Pr\{\lambda_i \leq 1\}] \to 0$, $i \to \infty$; i.e., $Pr\{\lambda_i \leq 1\} \to 1$, $i \to \infty$. This gives us

PROPOSITION. *Let* $\{P_i\}_{i=1}^{\infty}$ *be a family of distribution functions such that* $\lim \inf_{i \to \infty} Pr\{\lambda_i \leq 1\} < 1$. *Then as* $n \to \infty$ *the probability that at least one* $\lambda_i > 1$ *in* n *draws converges to unity.*

We hasten to add that the above argument is only meant to suggest that it is not absurd to expect that chances are high for obtaining a positive Lyapunov exponent for a dynamical system on $\mathbf{R}^n$ "drawn at random" (however "drawn at random" is given precise meaning). We consider it an interesting research project to find sufficient conditions on the space of dynamical systems on $\mathbf{R}^n$ so that the likelihood of a chaotic system could be made precise as n tends to infinity. At this stage we are simply trying to show that it is not implausible to expect that a "lot" of systems are chaotic if n is large enough. Turn now to a treatment of general nonlinearity that goes beyond chaos in particular and nonlinearity of deterministic dynamical systems in general.

3.1. *Some Notions of Stochastic Linearity and Nonlinearity*

For brevity we consider scalar valued strictly stationary stochastic processes. Consider the following stochastic process

$$Y_t - \mu = \sum \beta_j N_{t-j} \, , \ \sum \beta_j^2 < \infty \, . \tag{3.4}$$

where $\{N_n\}$ is a mean zero, finite variance denoted, $(0 \, , \sigma^2)$, strictly stationary stochastic process. In the discussion here $\sum$ ranges from 0 to ∞. It can be generalized.

We discuss two commonly used definitions of stochastic linearity: MDS-Linear and IID-Linear.

DEFINITION (*MDS-Linear*) (Hall and Heyde, 1980, pp. 182, 183). The stochastic process $\{Y_t\}$ *is MDS-Linear* if it can be represented in the form (3.4) above where the "innovations" $\{N_t\}$ are a *Martingale Difference Sequence (MDS)* relative to the sigma algebras $\mathbf{F}_t$ generated by $\{Y_s \, , s \le t\}$.

Hence a stochastic process is "MDS-Linear" if it can be represented as a linear filter applied to MDS innovations. To put it another way, the best Mean Squared Error (MSE) predictor based upon the past is the same as the best linear predictor based upon the past.

De Jong (1992) shows how the Bierens consistent conditional moment test of functional form can can be adapted to create a consistent test of MDS Linearity. The intuitive idea is to consistently estimate (under the null hypothesis of MDS-Linearity) a linear model and pass the residuals through De Jong's adaptation of Bierens's test. We refer the reader to De Jong for the details. Turn now to the definition of IID-Linear.

DEFINITION (*IID-Linear*) (Hall and Heyde, 1980, p. 198). The stochastic process $\{Y_t\}$ is *IID-Linear* if it can be written in the form (4) where the innovations $\{N_t\}$ are *IID* $(0 \, , \sigma^2)$.

The test of Brock, Dechert, Scheinkman, LeBaron (1990) is especially adaptable to testing the hypothesis of IID-Linearity. This is so because Brock and Dechert (1991), Brock, Dechert, Scheinkman, and LeBaron (1990), Brock, Hsieh, and LeBaron (1991) show that the first order asymptotic distribution on the estimated residuals of best fitting linear models are the same as on the true residuals for a large class of IID-Linear processes. The last two references argue this point both by theory and monte carlo work. De Lima (1992a, b) gives the most general and most complete proof of this invariance property for a family of related statistical tests.

Note that the Wold representation theorem says any purely (linearly) nondeterministic stochastic process has a representation of the form (4) for some $\{N_t\}$ innovation process which is *uncorrelated* (HH, p. 182). The two definitions of linearity require much more than *mere uncorrelatedness* of the innovations. That is what gives the definitions content. Futhermore requiring (as in the concept of MDS-Linear) that the best MSE-linear predictor be the best MSE-predictor seems to be as far as one can go in weakening the IID requirement on $\{N_t\}$ without running into the inherent nontestability of the Wold decomposition.

The above exposition gives an heuristic overview of the two main definitions of stochastic linearity. However, in financial applications it is controversial to assume that second order moments exist of outputs and innovations. The reason is simple. There is strong evidence that the unconditional variance of asset returns is infinite and, furthermore, conditional volatility measures are extremely persistent (*cf.* Loretan and Phillips (1992) and their references). For this reason the definitions require relaxation of the moment conditions.

De Lima (1992a, b) provides a general class of tests which can be used to test the hypothesis of IID-Linear under minimal moment restrictions. Essentially de Lima requires no more moment requirements than those needed to consistently estimate linear models. Furthermore the first order asymptotic distribution of his tests on estimated residuals are rigorously shown to be independent of the estimation procedure for a large class of IID-Linear data generating processes. Furthermore he shows by theory and monte carlo work that moment requirements of rival tests matter for correct inference under conditions typical for financial data. We urge the reader who works with heavy tailed data generating processes such as those in finance to read de Lima's two papers.

We hasten to add that the literature on testing for nonlinearity and estimation of nonlinear models is vast and that the point of view exposited here disproportionately represents my own work. The book by Brock, Hsieh, and LeBaron (1991) expounds the point of view taken here and briefly attempts to relate it to other parts of the econometric literature. The books by

Casdagli and Eubank, (1992), Granger and Terasvirta (1992), and Tong (1990) should be consulted by the reader for a more balanced treatment of nonlinear time series econometrics.

Turn now to the development of new classes of structural asset pricing models that generate non MDS-Linear equilibrium processes for returns per share of risky asset.

Recall that MDS-Linearity is equivalent to: The best MSE predictor given the past, i.e., the conditional expectation given the past, is the best linear MSE predictor. Hence any class of models that contain endogenous jumps and discontinuities in response to changes in the variables used for prediction cannot be MDS-Linear because linear predictors are continuous functions of the variables used for prediction.

4. Structural Modeling Using Interacting Particle Systems Theory

In this section we exhibit a class of asset pricing models that show how MDS-Linear earnings processes can be transformed into equilibrium returns per share processes that are not MDS-Linear. While we emphasize that more conventional asset pricing theories such as Lucas (1978) and Brock (1982) can transform linear earnings processes into nonlinear returns processes through the market equilibration equations, in these models small changes in the environment do not lead to large changes in returns or returns volatility. Evidence in articles such as Haugen et al. (1991) suggests that abrupt changes in returns and volatility which are difficult to link to measures of fundamentals are quite common. We want our models to be able to address such evidence. Turn now to a class of models that endogenize discontinuous responses to changes in the environment and history of evolution of the system.

We shall use the probability structure of interacting particles systems (IPS) theory as an input into building our class of asset pricing models. See Durlauf (1989a, b; 1991a, b) and his references, especially to Follmer, for uses of IPS theory in economics. Here we shall complement this work by fusing together ideas from discrete choice theory (*e.g.* Manski and Mc-Fadden, 1981), and IPS by using mean field theoretic arguments to obtain closed form solutions for equilibria in our models in the large economy limit. In this way we can formulate the theory at a level of accuracy sufficent to capture the phase transition behavior emphasized by Durlauf, but still have the convenience of closed form solutions which can be adapted for statistical inference.

Hence, this part of our paper is methodological in the same sense as Lucas (1978). The emphasis will be on finding parsimoniously parameterized, yet flexible, probability structures. The modelling technique offered here will be applied to examples in order to show its usefulness.

The organization of Section four of this paper is as follows. First, in Section 4.1, we state the general probability structure of interacting systems that we shall use. Second, in Section 4.2 we shall apply this probability structure to develop asset pricing models where demands are cross-dependent at a point in time over the set of traders. The large economy limit will be taken and conditions will be located on the strength of the cross dependence for the cross sectional ergodic theorem to hold. We shall then study the temporal evolution of the cross sectional dependence. The models are framed to be econometrically tractible to adaptions of the method of moments.

In Section 4.2 we treat the first example of our type of model. This is a formalization of "noise trader" models in economics and finance, where we find sufficient conditions on the probability structure for the noise traders to matter in the large economy limit. Since, "noise" trader models are controversial we emphasize at the outset that our type of model may be interpreted as a model where traders have heterogeneous beliefs or heterogeneous estimation or learning methods for relevant conditional moments needed to form their demands for assets. The new ingredient that we add is a parameterization of the cross-dependence of the heterogeneity that is econometrically tractable and leads to the uncovering of sufficient conditions for the heterogeneity to matter in the large economy limit.

In Section 4.3 we develop an asset pricing model where dependence of each trader's income on the market portfolio is itself dependent across the set of traders. This model leads to a simple relationship for the equilibrium price of the risky asset and relatively simple equilibrium volume dynamics.

Section 4.4 treats a version of Campbell, Grossman, and Wang's (1991), hereafter, CGW, model of traders with random risk aversion parameters. In our version the temporal movement of risk aversion evolves endogenously in such a way that explosive bursts of volatility are possible in a rational expectations equilibrium. Our model is a nonlinear model that nests the CGW model as a special case. We indicate how the parameters of the model may be estimated using data on price and volume.

None of the above models are rational expectations models with asymmetrically informed agents in the sense of Gennote and Leland (1990), Hellwig (1980 and 1982). In Section 4.5 we briefly show how Hellwig's (1980) large economy limit theorem can be used to produce a model with an equilibrium price relationship which can display abrupt changes to small changes in the environment.

Section 4.6 shows how to build a simple macro finance asset pricing model that "endogenizes" the exogenous shocks in the Lucas (1978), and Brock (1982) models. This example was stimulated by Durlauf (1991a, b).

These models illustrate that interactive systems probability modelling can produce analytically tractable asset pricing and macroeconomic models. The models all share the common property that small input noise into the environment can produce large noisy movements in equilibria. The models suggest economic pathways through which input noise magnification can occur.

4.1. *General Probability Structure*

We exposit the simplest version of our probability structure here. The appendix contains a generalization where the interactions are be considered over disjoint sets $A_1, \ldots, A_K$ where types are homogeneous within each set but heterogeneous across each set. In the Appendix, the large system limit (as $N \equiv$ total number $\to \infty$) is taken by holding the fraction of each type $k = 1, 2, \ldots, K$ constant.

To formalize the simplest version which contains the main ideas, let Ω be a set of real numbers, let Ω_N be its N-fold Cartesian product, $\omega \in \Omega_N$, and put

$$Pr\{w\} = \exp[\beta G] P_N(\omega) / Z,$$

$$G \equiv U(\omega) + (1/2) \sum_i \sum_{(i)} J_{ij} \omega_i \omega_j + h \sum_i \omega_i,$$

$$U(\omega) \equiv \sum u(\omega_i), \qquad\qquad\qquad (4.1.1)$$

where $\sum_i$ is over $i = 1, 2, \ldots, N$, $\sum_{(i)}$ is over "neighbors of i", $Pr\{\omega\}$ denotes probability of social state ω, $u(\omega_i)$ is own utility to agent i of choice $w_i \in \Omega$, $Z \equiv \sum \exp[\beta G(v)] P_N(v)$, $\sum$ is over all v, and β is a parameter whose role will be explained later. Here $P_N(v)$ denotes the product probability on Ω_N induced by the common distribution function F on Ω. We will concentrate on the case where Ω is finite and F is a sum of "*Dirac deltas*" but use $\sum$ and $\int$ interchangeably to suggest the natural extension to a continuous state space.

The best way to think about this structure is to think of (4.1.1) as giving the joint distribution of social states ω of a society of N individuals, each facing a choice from a set of alternatives, Ω. Here J_{ij} is a measure of the strength of interaction between individuals i, j located at sites i, j. We wish to exposit a discrete choice (Manski and McFadden, 1981) interpretation of (4.1.1) because this will be important to our development.

Consider the discrete choice model

$$V(\omega) = G(\omega) + \mu \varepsilon(\omega), \qquad \{\varepsilon(.)\} \text{ IIDEV.} \qquad (4.1.2)$$

Here "IIDEV" denotes Independent and Identically Distributed Extreme Value. The model (4.1.2) represents a stochastic social utility model where the errors $\varepsilon(.)$ are IID extreme value (Weibull) over ω in Ω_N. Manski and McFadden (1981, pp. 198-272) show that the probability that a particular social state ω is social utility maximizing is given by (4.1.1) with $\beta \equiv 1/\mu$, where β is called the "intensity of choice." Note that $\beta = 0$ gives the most random measure across social states, i.e., each social state has probability $1/|\Omega_N| = 1/|\Omega|^N$, where $|\Omega|$ denotes the cardinality of the finite set Ω.

Anderson, de Palma, and Thisse (1993), Chapter 2, hereafter "ADT," review results in the discrete choice literature that show

$$E\{\max G(\omega)\} = (1/\beta)\ln(Z)$$

where ln denotes the natural logarithm and max is over $\omega \in \Omega_N$. This gives a nice connection between the welfare measure, $E\{\max G(\omega)\}$, of discrete choice theory and the free energy function of statistical mechanics. They are the same except for a change in sign. See Kac (1968) for the free energy function. ADT also show how $(1/\beta)$ is related to measures of diversity in differentiated product models as well as to the CES parameter in Constant Elasticity of Substitution differentiated product models. It is helpful to keep these possible interpretations of $(1/\beta)$ in mind while reading the sequel and to keep in mind that it does not have to be interpreted as "inverse temperature" which is the standard interpretation in statistical mechanics.

We wish to relate individual choices to aggregate social choice. We wish to compute long run averages and locate conditions for ergodicity failure for probability systems like (4.1.1) and (4.1.2). The interacting particles systems theory, hereafter "IPS", discussed by Durlauf (1989a, b; 1991a, b), Ellis (1985) and their references is the tool we use. Durlauf's work locates sufficient conditions for ergodicity failure for models with general $\{J_{ij}\}$. We specialize here to a rather coarse level of approximation, called "mean field theory," which replaces the joint probability distribution in (4.1.1) with an approximating product probability.

This level of approximation is accurate enough to *(i)* uncover sufficient conditions for phase transitions which predict phase transition behavior in the more general case, *(ii)* give useful parameterizations for economic modelling that yield econometrically tractable models, *(iii)* give the same equations for limit values of certain bulk quantities such as means as more general structures. We shall explain below.

Let $\langle \omega_i \rangle$ denote expected value computed with respect to the probability structure (4.1.1). Assume "translation" invariance, $\sum_{(i)} J(i-j)\omega_j = \sum_{(k)} J(k-j)\omega_j$, for all i, k. This implies $m \equiv \langle \omega_i \rangle = \langle \omega_k \rangle$ for all i, k. Consider the component of social utility in (4.1.1) that is generated by agent i,

$$V_i(\omega_i; \omega_{-i}) \equiv u(\omega_i) + [\sum_{(i)} J(i-j)\omega_j]\omega_i + h\omega_i + \mu\epsilon(\omega_i), \{\epsilon(\omega_i)\} \text{ IIDEV} \qquad (4.1.3)$$

We remark that in later applications, as in Durlauf (1991a, b), we shall interpret ω_{-i} as the previous period choices of agents other than i. Furthermore the utility function $u(.)$, the parameters $J(i-j)$, h, μ, and the distribution of $\epsilon(.)$ can depend upon the past. For the moment we proceed in an atemporal setting

Mean field theory, hereafter denoted MFT, replaces $\sum_{(i)} J(i-j)\omega_j$ by

$$E\{\sum_{(i)} J(i-j)\omega_j\} = m\sum_{(i)} J(i-j) \equiv mJ$$

in expression (4.1.3) to obtain,

$$V_i(\omega_i, m) \equiv u(\omega_i) + Jm\omega_i + h\omega_i + \mu\epsilon(\omega_i), \{\epsilon(\omega_i)\} \text{ IIDEV.} \qquad (4.1.3')$$

Since $m \equiv \langle \omega_k \rangle$, mean field theory computes the average $\langle \omega_k \rangle'$ with respect to the probabilities (4.1.3') and imposes the self consistency condition,

$$\langle \omega_k \rangle' = m. \qquad (4.1.4)$$

Equation (4.1.4) is a fixed point problem for m.

We shall see below how useful the MFT procedure can be to approximate quantities of interest. The procedure is much more general and can be carried out to higher levels of approximations in many different types of models. See Mezard *et al.* (1987), Ellis (1985), Kac (1968) and their references. However, the linkage of MFT and discrete choice theory presented below appears new to this paper.

Before we go further we wish to exhibit a connection between a Nash type notion of economic equilibrium in a Manski-McFadden world of inter-connected discrete choosers and the MFT procedure.

Equation (4.1.3') leads to probabilities,

$$\hat{P}\{\omega\} \equiv \prod \hat{Pr}\{\omega_i\}, \ \hat{Pr}\{\omega_i\} = \exp\{\beta[u(\omega_i) + (Jm+h)\omega_i]\} / Z_i. \qquad (4.1.5)$$

Here $Z_i \equiv \sum \exp\{\beta[u(v_i) + (Jm+h)v_i]\}$, where $\sum$ is over $v_i \in \Omega_i \equiv \Omega$. Note that when $J = J_{ij} = 0$, all i, j, then the probabilities given by (4.1.1) are identical to those given by (4.1.5). Also note, in our context, MFT may be viewed as the equilibrium generated by a group of individual agents i forming common expectations on the choice $\langle \omega_k \rangle = m$ of their neighbors, making their stochastic choices according to (4.1.3′), and having their expectations confirmed via the self consistency condition (4.1.4). We shall see examples below where the exact large system value of m is a solution to (4.1.4). The Kac method, which is exposited below, will give a theory of solution choice when there are multiple solutions to (4.1.4).

Consider the special case of (4.1.1) where $J_{ij} = J/N$. In this case the interaction strength goes to zero as $N \to \infty$, but every site has interaction strength J/N with every other site, no matter how distant. Hence, we have weak local interaction, but long range interaction.

For future use, for example, as inputs to formation of demand functions for risky assets, we want to find the limiting value of the following statistic: $\hat{m} \equiv M/N$, where $M \equiv \sum \omega_i$. The reader may wish to glance ahead at the next sections of the paper in order to see the key role that the "order parameter" m plays in the asset pricing models. We shall show,

$$\langle \hat{m} \rangle \to m^*, \quad N \to \infty, \tag{4.1.6}$$

Where m^* solves (4.1.19a) below. Here $\langle . \rangle$ denotes expectation with respect to the probability (4.1.1) for the special case, $J_{ij} = J/N$. Details on how to define the object $\langle . \rangle$ will follow in due course. We show now, that the limiting value in (4.1.6) is given by a direct application of Kac (1968, p. 248).

In order to see how the Kac method works, let's do an example. A general treatment is in the Appendix. Put $J(i-j) \equiv J$ in (4.1.1). Let us compute $Pr\{\omega\}$, $Z \equiv Z_N$, and $\langle \omega_i \rangle$. We have

$$Z_N \equiv \sum \exp \{ \beta[\sum u(v_i) + (J/2) (\sum v_i / N^{1/2})^2 + h(\sum v_i)]\} P_N(v), \tag{4.1.7}$$

$\sum$ is over $v \in \Omega_N$. Do the following steps. First, use the identity

$$\exp[a^2] = (1/(2\pi))^{1/2} \int \exp[-x^2/2 + 2^{1/2}xa]dx, \tag{4.1.8}$$

and, second use the change of variable $y = x(\beta J/N)^{1/2}$ to obtain

$$Pr\{\omega\} = (N/2\pi\beta J)^{1/2} \int \exp[-y^2N/2\beta J]\prod \exp[\beta u(\omega_i) +$$

$$+ (y + \beta h)\omega_i]dy P_N(\omega)/Z_N, \tag{4.1.9}$$

$$Z_N \equiv (N/2\pi\beta J)^{1/2} \int \exp[-y^2N/2\beta J]\prod M[(y+\beta h)]dy, \tag{4.1.10}$$

$$M \equiv \int_{\xi \in \Omega} \exp[z\xi + \beta u(\xi)]dF, \quad \prod \text{ is the product over } i = 1, 2, \ldots, N. \tag{4.1.11}$$

Note that we use M to denote "moment generating function" for (4.1.11). Compute, observing that $\langle \omega_i \rangle = \langle \omega_j \rangle$ for all i, j,

$$m = \lim \{ \langle [(1/N)(\textstyle\sum \omega_i)] \rangle \}$$

$$= \lim \{ \textstyle\int g(\beta h + y) [K(y)]^N dy / \int K(\vartheta)^N d\vartheta \}$$

$$\equiv \lim \textstyle\int g(\beta h + y) \mu_N(dy), \qquad (4.1.12)$$

where, $\mu_N(dy) \equiv [K(y)]^N dy / \int K(\vartheta)^N d\vartheta \Rightarrow \delta_{y^*}(dy)$, $N \to \infty$,

$$K(y) \equiv M(\beta h + y)\exp[-y^2/2\beta J], \qquad (4.1.13)$$

$$g(\beta h + y) \equiv \textstyle\int \{ \xi \exp[\xi(\beta h + y) + \beta u(\xi)] dF(\xi) \} / M(\beta h + y)$$

$$= M'(\beta h + y) / M(\beta h + y) \qquad (4.1.14)$$

Apply Laplace's method (*cf.* Kac, 1968, p. 248; Ellis, 1985, pp. 38, 50, 51) to see that, as $N \to \infty$, all probability mass is piled onto

$$y^* \equiv \mathrm{Argmax} \{ M(\beta h + y)\exp[-y^2/2\beta J] \}, \qquad (4.1.15a)$$

i.e., $\mu_N(dy) \Rightarrow \delta_{y^*}(dy)$, $N \to \infty$. Hence, y^* solves

$$\beta J M'(\beta h + y) / M(\beta h + y) = y, \qquad (4.1.15b)$$

and m^* is given by

$$m^* = M'(\beta h + y^*) / M(\beta h + y^*). \qquad (4.1.15c)$$

Note three things. First, (4.1.15a) demands that y^* be chosen to be the solution of (4.1.15b) which, in the case $u(.) \equiv 0$, has the same sign as h when h is not zero. Second, note that $\beta J m^* = y^*$. Third, observe that

$$\beta(\lim_{N \to \infty} E\{\max_{(\cdot)} G(\omega)\} / N) = \lim_{N \to \infty} (\ln(Z_N)/N)$$

$$= \max_y \ln \{ \exp[-y^2/(2\beta J)] M(y + \beta h) \}$$

$$= \max_m \ln \{ \exp[-m^2\beta J/2] M(\beta J m + \beta h) \}, \qquad (4.1.15d)$$

hence, the Kac (1968) method of solution selection amounts to choosing the social optimum solution of the "Nash" condition (4.1.19b) below. The point is this: Minimizing free energy in the thermodynamic limit to find the ground states corresponds to maximizing expected social welfare in the large economy limit to find the socially optimal states.

Now Ellis (1985, p.38) shows, for the case $u(.) \equiv 0$, $c(z) \equiv \log[M(z)]$ is convex in z. Replace the measure $dF(x)$ by $\exp[\beta u(x)]dF(x)$, and follow Ellis (1985, p. 229) to show $c(z)$ is convex for general $u(.)$, β. Therefore $c'(z) = M'(z)/M(z)$ nondecreases in z. Make the modest additional assumption that $c'(z)$ increases in z. Thus $c(.)$ is 1-1 and it follows that

$$m = c'(\beta Jm + \beta h) = M'(\beta Jm + \beta h)/M(\beta Jm + \beta h) \equiv \theta(m). \qquad (4.1.16)$$

In order to study equations (4.1.15), (4.1.16) first look at the special case, $\Omega \equiv \{-1, +1\}$, $u(-1) = u(+1) = 0$, $dF(a) \equiv (1/2)\sum \delta_a$, where δ_a puts mass one on $a = -1, +1$, and mass zero elsewhere. We have, recalling the definitions of hyperbolic cosine, sine, and tangent,

$$M(z) = \cosh(z), \quad M'(z) = \sinh(z), \quad c'(z) = \tanh(z), \qquad (4.1.17)$$

$$m = \tanh(\beta Jm + \beta h). \qquad (4.1.18)$$

Equation (4.1.18) is Ellis's Curie-Weiss mean field equation (Ellis, 1985, pp. 180, 182). Turn now to the discussion of this key equation.

Following Ellis it is easy to graph (4.1.18) and show that for $h = 0$, there is only one solution, $m = 0$; but, two solutions, $m_- = -m_+$, appear as soon as βJ becomes greater than one. For h not zero, (4.1.15a) requires the one with the same sign as h be chosen. A "phase transition" or "spontaneous magnetisation" is said to appear when βJ becomes greater than one. Turn now to the general case which includes the case, $u(-1) \, \upsilon(+1)$.

For this case we have, from (4.1.15), denoting the optimum m by m^*,

$$m^* = \mathrm{Argmax}\left\{ \int \exp[\xi(\beta h + \beta Jm) + \beta u(\xi)]dF(\xi)\exp[-\beta Jm^2/2] \right\}$$

$$\equiv \mathrm{Argmax}\{\Upsilon(m)\}. \qquad (4.1.19a)$$

Hence m^* solves. $m = \theta(m)$ where $\theta(m)$ is given by

$$\int \xi \exp[\xi(\beta h + \beta Jm) + \beta u(\xi)]dF(\xi) \, / \int \exp[\xi(\beta h + \beta Jm) + \beta u(\xi)]dF(\xi), \qquad (4.1.19b)$$

but (4.1.19a) gives the selection rule for the solution of (4.1.19b). We summarize the discussion to this point into

PROPOSITION 4.1. *For the special case of (4.1.1) with* $J_{ij} \equiv J/N$, $\langle (1/N)\sum \omega_i \rangle \to m^*$, $N \to \infty$, *where* m^* *solves (4.1.19a). The solution set to the first order necessary conditions for a maximimum in (4.1.19a) is the same as the solution set to the MFT equations (4.1.3'), (4.1.4), (4.1.5). However the limiting behavior of (4.1.1) gives a selection rule (4.1.19a) whereas the MFT equations do not.*

We remark that the value of $\langle \omega_i \rangle$ with respect to the MFT probabilities is easy to calculate using the product structure of the MFT probabilities. The calculation is similar to, but simpler than, the one carried out above. Turn now to the possibility of phase transition for the economics case $h = 0$, $u(-1)$ not equal to $u(+1)$.

The intuition of the analysis of (4.1.18) suggests β, J large should lead to abrupt changes in m^* if $du \equiv u(+1) - u(-1)$ changes sign. Let us study (4.1.19a) to investigate this possibility. Our approach adapts Pearce (1981, p. 312-313).

Put $k \equiv \beta h + \beta Jm$ and rewrite (4.1.19b) thus

$$\theta(m) \equiv \Phi(k) = \int \xi \exp[\xi k + \beta u(\xi)] dF(\xi) / \int \exp[\xi k + \beta u(\xi)] dF(\xi)$$

$$= \{\exp[k + \beta du] - \exp[-k]\} / \{\exp[k + \beta du] + \exp[-k]\}$$

$$= \tanh[\beta(Jm + h')], \qquad h' \equiv h + du/2. \tag{4.1.20}$$

We shall do a fairly complete analysis for the case,

$$dF \equiv (1/2)(\delta_{-1} + \delta_{+1}),$$

and content ourselves with suggesting possible extensions for general h, dF. Note that the right-hand side of (4.1.20) shows us that replacing h by h' reduces (4.1.20) to an application of (4.1.18).

It is now straightforward to use (4.1.20) to check the following: *(i)* When $du = 0$, $\Phi(k)$ is given by (4.1.18), $\gamma \equiv \beta J > 1$ implies there is a phase transition, i.e., a positive and a negative root to (4.1.18) with the root having the same sign as h chosen by (4.1.19a). *(ii)* For fixed du, $\Phi(K) \to +1$, $K \to \infty$; $\Phi(k) \to -1$, $k \to -\infty$. *(iii)* For $\beta > 0$, for $du > 0$ (< 0) but close enough to zero and $\gamma \equiv \beta J > 1$, the function $\Upsilon(m)$ in (4.1.19a) has two local maxima and one local minimum. The positive (negative) one is the global maximum. The global maximum $m^* = m^*(h', \gamma)$ is discontinuous at $h' = 0$ for $\gamma > 1$. All solution arcs $m(h')$ are anti-symmetric with the local minima rising in h' and the local maxima falling in h'. The local mimimum arc starting at $h' = 0$ satisfies $m(0, \gamma) = 0$ and decreases in h'.

Under regularity conditions the solution properties outlined above can be generalized to the case where $dF(y) \equiv f(y)dy, f(-y) = f(y)$. Let

$$du(x) \equiv u(x^*) - u(x),$$

where $x^* \equiv \text{Argmax}\{u(\omega)\}$. In this case, for $du \equiv 0$, one can show

$$c'(-z) = -c'(z), \quad M'(0) = \int \xi dF = 0,$$

$$M''(0) = \int \xi^2 dF, \quad c'(0) = M''(0),$$

so for $h = 0$ two solutions $m_- = -m_+$ appear for $\beta JM''(0) > 1$, and $m = 0$ is the solution for $\beta JM''(0) < 1$. Some conditions are needed on F to make $c'(z)$ display the qualitative properties of $\tanh(z)$ which were used above. We summarize:

PROPOSITION 4.1.2. *For the case $dF \equiv (1/2) (\delta_{-1} + \delta_{+1})$ phase transition behavior will appear, i.e.,the maximum of (4.1.19a) will change discontinuously from negative to positive as $du \equiv u(+1) - u(-1)$ changes sign from negative to positive provided that $\beta J > 1$. Under regularity conditions this result can be generalized to general $F(.)$.*

Let $\Rightarrow$, and $\Rightarrow^p$ denote convergence in distribution and in probability. For use in further sections we need to show that $\hat{m} \Rightarrow m^*$, $N \rightarrow \infty$. A natural strategy is to use the large deviations approach of Ellis (1985, *cf.* his references to the joint work of Ellis and Newman), but $u(.)$ causes an obstacle in rewriting $Pr\{\hat{m} \in A\}$ as a function of $\hat{m}$ and using large deviations theory to obtain a law of large numbers (*cf.* for example Ellis, 1985, p. 99). This obstacle seems to be a problem even if m^* is a unique global maximum of (1.19a) with locally strongly concave behavior near m^* (*cf.* Ellis and Newman, 1978b,d cited in Ellis, 1985, p. 342). However, it is not difficult to obtain a law of large numbers,

PROPOSITION 4.1.3. *Assume m^* is a unique global maximum of (1.19a) with locally strongly concave behavior near m^*. Then $\hat{m} \Rightarrow m^*$.*

PROOF. Let $\varepsilon > 0$. We use Chebyshev's inequality to prove $\hat{m} \Rightarrow^p m^*$. By Lukacs (1975, p. 33, 37), $\hat{m} \Rightarrow^p m^*$ implie s $\hat{m} \Rightarrow m^*$. By Chebyshev's inequality (Lukacs, 1975, p. 9),

$$Pr\{|\hat{m} - m^*| \geq \varepsilon\} \leq \text{Var}\{\hat{m} - m^*\} / \varepsilon^2, \qquad (4.1.21)$$

so it is sufficient to prove $\text{Var}\{\hat{m} - m^*\} \to 0, N \to \infty$. We must show,

$$\langle [(1/N)\sum\omega_i - m^*]^2 \rangle \to 0, \ N \to \infty.$$

It is sufficient to show $\langle \sum\sum\omega_i\omega_j \rangle / N^2 \to m^{*2}$. Hence, it is sufficient to show $\langle \omega_i\omega_j \rangle \to m^{*2}, N \to \infty$, for i not equal to j. Show this by arguing as in (4.1.12), (4.1.14), (4.1.15) to show $\langle \omega_i\, \omega_j \rangle \to g(\beta h + y^*)^2 = m^{*2}, N \to \infty$.

We have briefly sketched the theory we need and have done a fairly complete job for the two state case, $\Omega = \{-1, +1\}$. Turn now to a very brief sketch of the K-state case for $K > 2$.

The issue concerns construction of an IPS structure that is flexible enough to yield a "landscape" that is tunable to each of K choices. To see the problem look at the expression (4.1.7) copied below,

$$Z_N \equiv \sum\exp\{\,\beta[\sum u(v_i) + (J/2)\,(\sum v_i/N^{1/2})^2 + h(\sum v_i)]\}\,P_N(v), \quad (4.1.22)$$

and note how the convex term $(J/2)\,(\sum v_i/N^{1/2})^2$ rewards going to the extremes of the choice set Ω. Hence, this convex term plays a key role in determining the limit via (4.1.19a), therefore placing more elements into Ω is not likely to give us the flexibility we desire even if we move the mass points of F around at will.

As a tentative proposal to be investigated in more detail in a future paper we encode each of the K elements into a "bit string" of ± 1's. One can encode 2^L elements using bit strings of length L. Let $\omega_i \equiv (\omega_{i1}, \ldots, \omega_{iL}) \in \{-1, +1\}^L$. Define $u : \{-1, +1\}^L \to \mathbf{R}$. Define $u \equiv -\infty$ for some bit strings in order to deal with cases where K is not equal to 2^L for some L. Define Z_N by replacing the term, $(J/2)\,(\sum v_i/N^{1/2})^2$ with

$$\sum(J_1/2)\,(\sum v_i^l/N^{1/2})^2 ,$$

where the sum runs from $l = 1, \ldots, L$. Proceed as in the case $L = 1$ to develop the limit theory.

The solution theory presented above will be used in the applications below. The applications will induce dynamics on the solution for $m \equiv m(\beta J, \beta h; u(.))$ by inducing parsimoniously parameterized functional forms for $u(.), J$ as a function of past information. This, in turn will give us flexible functional forms of dynamics on volume and stock returns, which will be one of our key applications.

4.2. *Applications*

In this section we deliver on the promised applications of the mathematical technology in Section 4.1. But before we get into details of the examples we should be clear about the goals we wish them to serve.

In particular we want the models to have the potential to contribute to explanation of the following stylized facts laid out nicely by the paper of Haugen, Talmor, Torous (1991) (hereafter, "HTT"). *(i)* HTT (1991, p. 987) point out the finding of Roll, Schwert, Cutler, Poterba, Summers as well as their own work that it is difficult to relate "volatility, changes in volatility, and significant price movements to real economic events". *(ii)* HTT (1991, p. 985) find "A majority of our volatility changes cannot be associated with the release of significant information". *(iii)* In studying the reaction of returns to changes in volatility HTT (1991, p. 1001) find there is an asymmetry in the "reaction of prices and subsequent mean returns (which is) consistent with non-linear risk aversion.

(iv) HTT (1991, p. 1003) stress the result of Roll that "much of the variance in the equity return series may be related to either private information or occasional "frenzy" unrelated to concrete information." *(v)* HTT (1991, p. 1003) stress Schwert's finding: "Schwert (1989), in an exhaustive study, finds that the volatility of stock returns are not closely related to the volatility of other economic variables such as long and short term interest rates, the money supply, and inflation rates." *(vi)* HTT (1991, p. 1004) stress "..the fact that we find a highly significant, positive price reaction to volatility decreases...the fact that the price adjustments are followed by directionally consistent adjustments in mean realized returns...further reinforce our confidence that, on average over all events, we are seeing a reaction to changes in risk as opposed to expected cash flow". With this factual background in place let us return to the examples.

Examples 4.2.1-4.2.3 concern equilibrium asset pricing models where all traders have mean variance demands and some traders have biases in their expectations. Example 4.2.1 contains traders with biased expectations where IPS theory is used to parameterize interdependence across biases and to locate sufficient conditions for an effect of biased traders to remain in the large economy limit. The example suggests uses of IPS theory to parsimoniously parameterize interdependence of biased expectations in such a way that econometric techniques based upon orthogonality conditions may be used to estimate the parameters and test for the presence of biased traders. Examples 4.2.2 and 4.2.3 are variations on this theme.

Section 4.3 exposits an example which shows how interdependence across agents in correlations of their own-income with the market leads to an adjustment in conventional asset pricing formulae as well as a source of equilibrium trading volume. Section 4.4 contains a version of Campbell,

Chaos Theory in Economics

Grossman, and Wang's (1991) model with interdependence in trader risk tolerances where the degree of interdependence may depend upon the past. The fifth section, 4.5, contains a version of Hellwig's (1980) model with inderdependence in signal quality. Stephen Durlauf has stressed the point that this kind of model can show how abrupt market movements can be caused by changes in the degree of correlation of information between agents rather than by large changes in information.

Section 4.6 briefly shows how interdependent firms in the Lucas (1978), Brock (1982) asset pricing models can lead to large movements in asset prices. The examples are all unified by showing how parameterization of the degree of interdependence by IPS modeling leads to analytically tractable equilibrium dynamics in the large economy limit which are suggestive of pathways through which small changes can have large impacts. Turn to describing demand functions.

The demand functions stress three channels of heterogeneity: (i) Differing risk aversion parameters, (ii) differing expectations or beliefs, (iii) differing covariance structure of own-income with the marekt. Let trader i have demand

$$D_i(p) = \tau_i E_{it} q' / V_{it}(q') - \text{Cov}_{it}(q', w_i') / V_{it}(q'), \tag{4.2.1}$$

where p is asset price, τ is risk tolerance, E_{it}, V_{it}, Cov_{it} are conditional mean, variance, covariance on information available to i at date t, $q' \equiv p_{t+1} + y_{t+1} - Rp_t \equiv$ excess return at $t+1$, p_{t+1}, y_{t+1} are asset price and asset dividend (or net cash flow) at date $t+1$, $R \equiv 1 + r$ is return on a risk free asset, $w_i' \equiv w_{i,t+1}$ is other sources of income to i at date $t+1$. We shall often denote $x \equiv x_t$, $x' \equiv x_{t+1}$, for any quantity, x, to save typing.

The demand function (4.2.1) can be obtained from a two period overlapping generations setup where each trader gets first period income which is allocated between the risky asset and the risk free asset. Utility is obtained from consumption of all wealth in the second period. Wealth comes from (i) other sources of income, (ii) earnings on the two assets. The demand function (4.2.1) is derived by maximizing conditional expectation of mean-variance utility or, under normally distributed returns, by maximizing conditional expectation of exponential utility.

The assumption of two period lived traders is restrictive, but it should be clear that the methods laid out here can be generalized to handle traders with arbitrary lives.

In (4.2.1) there are three channels by which trader characteristics could be related: (i) Expectational differences; (ii) risk tolerances; (iii) covariances of excess returns with own-income.

First we deal with E_{it}, V_{it}. Nelson (1992) has shown, in a diffusion context, that frequent sampling within a period can produce an estimator of the conditional variance that is much more precise than the best estimator of the conditional mean. For this reason and for simplicity we shall assume $V_{it} \equiv V_t$, is independent of i. It will be apparent as we illustrate our methods that this assumption can be relaxed at the cost of considerable complexity.

Assume, $w_i' = \rho_i(p' + y') + \varepsilon_i'$, and ε_i' conditionally independent of $p' + y'$, divide both sides of (4.2.1) by N, sum over i to obtain (conditional on the history of the economy at date t), suppressing t for ease of notation,

$$(1/N)\sum \{ \tau_i E_i q' / V(q') - \rho_i \} \Rightarrow (1/V(q')) [E^* \{ \tau_i E_i q' \}] - E^* \rho_i \, , \, N \to \infty, \quad (4.2.2)$$

where E^* denotes expectation with respect to the measure, $\mu^*(A)$, defined by

$$(1/N)\sum I [(\tau_i, I_i, \rho_i) \in A] \Rightarrow \mu^*(A), \, N \to \infty. \quad (4.2.3)$$

Here I_i denotes the information set of trader i at date t, A is a set of agent characteristics (which includes choices), $I[(\tau_i, I_i, \rho_i) \in A$ is the indicator function of the event $[(\tau_i, I_i, \rho_i) \in A]$ which is unity if $(\tau_i, I_i, \rho_i) \in A$, zero otherwise, and $\Rightarrow$ denotes weak convergence. The theory of Section 4.1 locates sufficient conditions for the weak convergence of (4.2.3). We shall assume without further mention that these sufficient conditions hold.

Suppose there are x shares outstanding per trader. Then equilibration of demand and supply per trader yields, in the large economy limit, by (4.2.2),

$$(1/V(q')) [E^* \{ \tau_i E_i q' \}] - E^* \rho_i = x \quad (4.2.4)$$

We show the value of the modelling of Section 1 by applying it to a sequence of examples based on the above.

Example 4.2.1

Consider the "noise trader" theory of DeLong, Shleifer, Summers, and Waldman (1990), hereafter "DSSW." Let us use the theory of Section 4.1 to locate sufficient conditions for noise trader risk to matter in the large economy limit and to suggest a method of estimating the effect of noise traders using the methodology of Hansen and Singleton (1982).

For simplicity assume homogeneous conditional expectations on variance and an estimation procedure for the conditional mean with the following structure of errors across the set of noise traders, $\Omega = \{$bear, bull$\}^2 \equiv \{-1, +1\}^2$,

$$E_{it}(p' + y') = b_0 \omega_{0it} + [1 + b_1 \omega_{1it}] E_t(p' + y') , \quad (4.2.5)$$

where at each date t, $E_t(p' + y')$ is conditional expectation on a common information set available to all N traders, $\{\omega_{.it} \equiv (\omega_{0it}, \omega_{1it})\}$ is distributed according to a product form (like Example 4.2.3 below) of (4.1.3′), (4.1.5) where $u(\omega, t)$ is parameterized according to a measure of how well belief ω produced risk adjusted profits (utility) in the past.

In DSSW (1990) the bias in expectation is additive IID so $b_1 = 0$ captures the flavor of DSSW. So let us put $b_1 = 0$ for specificity. But, the reader should keep in mind that we can deal just as easily with multiplicative errors as additive errors. Put $x = \rho = 0$, assume constant risk tolerance across agents, bring back subscripts for clarity in (4.2.4) to obtain, from (4.1.19a,b),

$$Rp_t = b_0 m_t^* + E_t(p_{t+1} + y_{t+1}). \tag{4.2.6}$$

Write (4.2.6) in the form

$$E_t\{b_0 m_t^* + (p_{t+1} + y_{t+1}) - Rp_t\} = 0. \tag{4.2.7}$$

Equation (4.2.7) can be used to generate a set of orthogonality restrictions so that the parameters b_0, and the parameters embedded in m_t^* via (4.1.19) may be estimated (given a specification of behavior of $(\beta, J, h, u(.))$ over time) following the Generalized Instrumental Variables (GIV) used by Hansen and Singleton (1982). We speculate that the parameters of rather elaborate dynamic specifications could be estimated by adapting the simulation estimator methods of Hotz, Miller, Sanders, and Smith (1992). In this way returns data can speak to testing for the presence of noise traders with, for example, additive errors in formation of conditional expectations by testing $H_0 : b_0 = 0$ against the alternative $H_a : b_0$ not zero.

Of course some conditions must be imposed for the GIV procedure to "identify" the parameters of interest. A more serious problem with testing (4.2.7) concerns confusion of movements of the marginal rate of substitution in the CCAPM (Lucas (1978)) context tested by Hansen and Singleton with presence of noise traders in the context (4.2.7). But this problem could be dealt with by a noise trader component into the CCAPM setup of Hansen and Singleton (1982), following a procedure analogous to the above and deriving a general set of orthogonality conditions in which both the "pure" Hansen and Singleton CCAPM and the "pure" noise trader models are "nested."

Example 4.1 shows how a rich class of models may be formulated that *(i)* are econometrically tractable to GIV methodology, *(ii)* can be used to locate sufficient conditions for noise trader effects to survive the washing out effect of the law of large numbers, (There must be aggregate shocks to the $u(., t)$ or

$\beta J > 1$), *(iii)* can be used to locate sufficient conditions for the additive IID errors of DSSW (1990) to appear in the large economy limit, *(iv)* can be enriched by different parameterizations of the $u(. , t)$ in (4.1.3′). We point out in passing that the presence of noise trading effects in the context (4.2.6) can be tested by using the West (1987) test. His procedure tests for the presence of terms like b_0 in linear present value models (4.2.6).

This is a good point to add a few words about justification for study of models with dispersion of beliefs. Antoniewicz (1992) in her work on volume reviews received work on volume dynamics. The consensus of this work is that trading volume is a very persistent series that is difficult to reduce to white noise by standard "detrending" methods.

Sargent (1992) shows how hard it is to preserve volume persistence in settings where the no-trade theorem becomes operative through learning. Therefore it appears that persistence in belief disparity will be needed if one is to get volume persistence out of belief disparity. While we shall exhibit models below that generate volume dynamics from heterogeneity in risk aversion and correlations of own income with the market these models do not seem right for explaining high frequency volume dynamics.

One justification for persistence in belief disparity is the work of Kurz (1990, 1991 and 1992) who develops a theory where all traders see the same data, form bulk quantities such as time averages, all time averages converge for each trader, yet disparity in limiting quantities remain. There is enough stationarity in Kurz's setting so that time averages converge, yet there is enough nonstationarity that each agent may not converge onto the same probability (the true probability). For the context of persistence of belief disparity it may be useful to think of Kurz's setting as a metaphor for a situation where data is arriving fast enough for each individual trader's estimators using time averages to converge but where the underlying system dynamics is changing slowly but fast enough that traders do not "lock onto" common agreement about the underlying probability. I.e. their estimators do not converge onto common limits.

Our type of modeling may have use in the future as a way of locating sufficient conditions on the degree of dependence of individual beliefs so that an aggregative effect remains in the cross sectional large economy limit. Kurz (1992) uses his theory to argue that the Dow was grossly overvalued in 1966. This argument requires that belief bias remain in the large economy limit. It is beyond the scope of our paper to say more about Kurz's stimulating work here. Suffice it to say that we believe that belief disparity plays an important role in volume dynamics and study of such models is justified. The dynamics of such models may be usefully disciplined by evolutionary modeling as in Blume and Easley (1992). Turn now to a related class of examples.

Example 4.2.2

Brock (1991a, p. 136-137) sketches a model where each trader has a choice of two strategies: − 1 equals a chartist "trend chasing" strategy and + 1 equals a "fundamentalist" strategy. Each of these strategies is a recipe for updating their estimate $E_{it}(p' + y')$ at each date t. Traders keep a record of the profits earned by the two strategies. Brock (1991a, p. 136-137) updated the "field" parameter h_t in (4.1.7) as a function of relative profits at t. We improve on this by using the theory in Section 4.1.

It is more natural to put $h_t = 0$ in (4.1.7) and define $u(\omega, t)$ to be the estimated profit for strategy $\omega \in \Omega \equiv \{-1, +1\}$, where the estimate is based upon the common information I_t available to traders at date t.

We define the fundamental strategy by putting

$$E_{+1, t}(p' + y') = E_t y' + E_t p'_{F, t+1}$$

where $\{p_{Ft}\}$ is the forward rational expectations solution process of the equation $Rp_t = E\{p_{t+1} + y_{t+1} \mid I_t\}$. As in Brock (1991a, p. 136), for strategy $\omega = -1$, put, $q_t \equiv p_t + y_t$,

$$E_{-1, t} q_{t+1} \equiv p_{Ft}/R + b_t, \quad b_t \equiv b_{t-1} + \lambda(q_{t-1} - MA(1, t-1)), \qquad (4.2.8)$$

$$MA(l, t-1) \equiv [q_{t-1} + \dots + q_{t-1-(l-1)}]/l \equiv \text{moving average with } l \text{ lags. } (4.2.9)$$

Suppose $\lambda > 0$. Note that $q_{t-1} > MA(l, t-1)$ causes the bias over the fundamental to be increased; vice versa for "<".

Assume, for clarity that $\tau_i = \tau$, $\text{Cov}_{it} \equiv 0$, $x = 0$. Close the model by using the expectation $E_{\omega_{it}}(q_{t+1})$, $\omega_{it} \in \{-1, +1\}$ to form the demands (4.2.1). Assume, at each date t, the probability trader i chooses ω_{it} is given by the MFT-discrete choice model (4.1.3'), (4.1.5).

We have a mixed discrete/continuous choice problem where (4.1.3') serves as the discrete choice model for which strategy (conditional expectation) to use in forming demands. The continuous choice problem is the choice of optimum quantity of stock and bond to purchase given the conditional expectation (strategy). For each fixed date t, the $N \to \infty$ equilibrium (4.2.4) may be rewritten

$$Rp_t = [(1 - m_t^*)/2]E_{-1, t}(q_{t+1}) + [(1 + m_t^*)/2]E_{+1, t}(q_{1+t}), \qquad (4.2.10)$$

where we choose m_t^* to be the largest (in absolute value) solution with the same sign as du to,

$$m = \{\exp[\beta Jm + \beta du] - \exp[-\beta Jm]\} / \{\exp[\beta Jm + \beta du] + \exp[-\beta J]\}$$

$$= \tanh[\beta(Jm + h')] , \tag{4.2.11}$$

where $h' \equiv du / 2$, $du \equiv u(+1, t) - u(-1, t)$ and $u(\omega, t)$ are measures of how well following strategy ω has generated utility for the trader had he followed it in the past. We assume this measure is a matter of public record available to all traders, but choice of ω is governed by (4.1.3'). One may now study the dynamics generated by (4.2.10). Unfortunately we must leave it to future research.

Example 4.2.3 (Based on Arthur, 1992)

Brian Arthur has written an interesting paper where he argues for replacing the deductive mode of theorizing by an inductive mode of theorizing. He shows that inductive modes are analytically tractable by considering a stock market where traders take positions by monitoring a collection of predictors $H_1, \ldots, H_p$. Suppose we encode these using bit strings $\omega \in \{-1, +1\}^L$ of length L as suggested at the end of Section 4.1. Introduce social interaction terms for each slot of the bit string and introduce a record for each predictor on how well it has done in the past. Base the utility $u(\omega, t)$ on this record at t. Let, at each date t, discrete choice occur according to the natural generalization of the discrete choice model (4.1.3'). Then join Arthur's approach and Example 4.2.2 to develop the dynamics. Our modification of Arthur allows "herding" which is induced by the interaction terms $\{J_l\}$.

The dynamics of this modified Arthur model should be very rich. It would be interesting to simulate it and see how easy it is to find parameters such that the output of returns and volume replicate the stylized facts reported by HTT which were discussed above. In principle the parameters of this modified Arthur model could be fitted to a subset of data to replicate relevant moments in sample. Then it could be evaluated by tests out-of-sample. Turn now to an example that generates trading volume via heterogeneity in correlations of own income with the market portfolio.

4.3. A Model with Volume and Price Dynamics

The volume dynamics are complicated in the general model (4.2.4), but they can be worked out and volume data may be used in estimation. However, simple volume dynamics may be obtained from (4.2.4) with

$$w_i' = \rho_i(p' + y') + \varepsilon_i', \tag{4.3.1}$$

where $\{\rho_i\}$ has the probability structure (4.1.1), ε_i' is independent of p', y' and satisfies $(1/N)\sum\varepsilon_i' \Rightarrow 0$.

Assume there is supply of x shares per trader. Assuming homogeneous expectations on conditional mean and variance in (4.2.4), equating demand to supply of shares for N traders yields, introducing a first type of trader which has all ρ_i equal to a constant, we have,

$$x = (1/N)\sum D_i(p) = (1/N)\sum [\tau E_i q' / V_i(q')] - \rho_i]$$

$$= \tau E_i q' / V_i(q') - n_1 \rho_1 - n_2 \hat{\rho}_2 ,\qquad (4.3.2)$$

where

$$\hat{\rho}_2 \equiv \sum_i \rho_i / N_2 \Rightarrow \rho_2(m), \quad N \to \infty, \quad N_k = n_k N, n_k \quad \text{fixed}, k = 1, 2 . \quad (4.3.3a)$$

Note that q' depends upon N but we abuse notation by neglecting this dependence in the notation. Here we suppose ρ_1 is constant across the N_1 type one traders, $\rho_2(\omega_{ii})$ is the state of correlation for type two traders where $Pr\{\omega\}$ is given by (4.1.5).

This raises an issue of interpretation. One interpretation is to put $u(.) = 0$ and simply treat (4.1.5) as a convenient way to parsimoniously parameterize cross dependence of ρ in group two. Equation (4.1.5) may be motivated by placing the traders on a Durlauf (1991a,b) type lattice with probability structure (4.1.3) on the ρ's of (4.3.1). The lattice captures the relatedness of trader own incomes to each other. Equation (4.1.5) is an MFT approximation to (4.1.3) that is rough, but is accurate enough to suggest sufficient conditions for phase transition type behavior to take place (*cf.* Pearce, 1981). In any event this parametrization forces one to realize that *some* measure of cross dependence plays a key role in preventing the law of large numbers from "washing out" the ρ-effect, i.e, preventing $\hat{\rho}_2$ from converging to 0, as $N \to \infty$ unless this is "forced" by putting h not equal to zero. Small changes in h (or $u(.)$) can lead to large effects only when *some* measure of cross dependence is big enough. Equation (4.1.5) seems as attractive a way to capture this kind of effect as any.

Another interpretation is to imagine a discrete menu of funds with the same conditional variance but varying correlation with own income for group two traders. Consider the special case of a low correlation fund, -1 and a high correlation fund $+1$ Let a measure of past performance of each fund $u(\pm 1, t)$ be available at each date t. Then each member of group two picking which fund to buy shares in according to the discrete choice model (4.1.3) will lead to (4.1.5).

In this two state case, at each point in time, the limiting value of $\hat{\rho}_2$ will be

$$\rho_2(m) \equiv [(1-m)/2]\rho_2(-1) + [(1+m)/2]\rho_2(+1). \qquad (4.3.3b)$$

Solve (4.3.2) for $E_t q' / V_t(q')$ to obtain

$$E_t q' / V_t(q') = [x + n_1\rho_1 + n_2\rho_2(m)]/t \equiv z_t. \qquad (4.3.4)$$

In order to simplify the volume dynamics we ignore trading within group two and measure trading across groups one and two. Denote by D_{kt} the equilibrium demand by trader group $k = 1, 2$. With this qualification a natural measure of trading per capita per share can be generated from the following, which must hold in equilibrium,

$$D_{1t} - D_{1,t-1} = n_1\tau(z_t - z_{t-1}) \qquad (4.3.5)$$

Motivated by (4.3.5) we define the turnover measure over the period $[t-1, t]$, denote it by V_t,

$$V_t \equiv n_1\tau(z_t - z_{t-1})/x. \qquad (4.3.6)$$

Equation (4.3.6) can be turned into a useful equation by parameterizing the volume dynamics via parameterization of $\{u_t(.), J_t, h_t\}$ as functions of, for example, past y-innovations and past volume. Given a probability structure on $\{y_t\}$, for example, Autoregressive with Independent and Identically Distributed (IID) or Martingale Difference Sequence (MDS) innovations, and a derived dynamics for $\{m_t\}$, where $m_t \equiv (J_t, h_t; u(.))$; equation (4.3.4) may be solved by forward iteration. This can be written as the conditional expectation of a capitalized sum of "adjusted" earnings where the capitalization factor is $1/R$. Both the price and volume dynamics can display abrupt changes to small changes in $u_t(.)$, h_t when $\beta J_t > 1$. We believe it would be interesting to "calibrate" models like Examples 4.1-4.3 and see how many of the stylized facts listed by HTT can be replicated. More will be said about this and other applications below.

4.4. *A Rational Expectations Models of Trading Volume and Liquidity Providers*

Campbell, Grossman, and Wang (1991) have developed a rational expectations model with two types of traders. Type A have constant risk aversion parameter a and type B have stochastic risk aversion parameter b_t at time t. We use the probability structure of Section 1 to "derive" a stochastic dynamics for b_r. We outline how the model may be "solved" for a closed form solution by a dynamic variational approximation analysis.

We use similar notation as CGW. Put $R \equiv 1 + r$, $r > 0$ equal to return on the risk-free asset which is in perfectly elastic supply. Let X be supply per capita of stock, each share pays $D_t = D + d_t$, $d_t = \alpha d_{t-1} + u_t$, $0 \leq \alpha \leq 1$, u_t IID $(0, \sigma_u^2)$. There are two type of investors A, B with mean variance demands,

$$X_t^k = E[Q_{t+1} \mid I_t] / \psi_k \text{Var}[Q_{t+1} \mid I_t], \ \psi_A \equiv a, \ \psi_B \equiv b_r, \ I_t = (P_t, D_t, S_t), \quad (4.4.1)$$

where $Q_{t+1} \equiv P_{t+1} + D_{t+1} - RP_t \equiv$ excess returns, $u_{t+1} = S_t + \varepsilon_{t+1}$, $\{S_t, \varepsilon_{t+1}\}$ is jointly IID with both means zero, $E[u_{t+1} \mid S_t] = S_t$, $\text{Var}[u_{t+1} \mid S_t] = \sigma_\varepsilon^2$, $\text{Var}[S_t] = \sigma_s^2$. Put

$$Z_t \equiv ab_t / [(1 - \omega)a + \omega b_t], \ \ \omega \equiv \text{fraction type } A, \quad (4.4.2)$$

assume $\{Z_t\}$ satisfies $E[Z_{t+1} \mid Z_t] = \gamma_0 + \gamma_1 Z_t$, $0 \leq \gamma_1 \leq 1$, $\text{Var}[Z_{t+1} \mid Z_t] = \sigma_Z^2$, assume $\sigma_Z^2 \leq (R - \gamma_1)^2 (R - \alpha)^2 / 4\bar{X}^2 (R^2 \sigma_\varepsilon^2 + \sigma_s^2)$. Then CGW show there is an equilibrium price function of the form,

$$P_t = p_0 + p_1 d_t + p_2 Z_t + p_3 S_t, \ p_1, p_3 > 0, \ p_2 < 0, \quad (4.4.3)$$

$$p_1 = \alpha / (R - \alpha), \ p_3 = 1 / (R - \alpha), \ p_0 = (1 / (R - 1)) [\bar{D} + \gamma_0 p_2], \quad (4.4.4)$$

$$p_2 = (1 / (2\bar{X}\sigma_Z^2)) \{ -(R - \gamma_1) + [((R - \gamma_1)^2 -$$

$$- 4(1 / (R - \alpha))^2 (\bar{X}^2 \sigma_Z^2) (R^2 \sigma_\varepsilon^2 + \sigma_s^2)]^{1/2} \}, \quad (4.4.5)$$

$$Q_{t+1} = (\bar{D} - rp_0) + p_2[Z_{t+1} - RZ_t] + (1 / (R - \alpha))S_{t+1} + (R / (R - \alpha))\varepsilon_{t+1}. \quad (4.4.6)$$

Add the demands, use the market clearing condition and the form of the solution price function to obtain

$$E[Q_{t+1} \mid I_t] = (\bar{X}\sigma_Q^2)Z_t, \ \text{Var}(Q_{t+1} \mid I_t) \equiv \sigma_Q^2 = (1 + p_1)^2 \sigma_\varepsilon^2 + p_2^2 \sigma_Z^2 + p_3^2 \sigma_s^2. \quad (4.4.7)$$

Note that (4.4.7) says that excess returns are positive with the size increasing as the measure of average risk aversion, Z_t increases. Excess returns also increase as the conditional variance increases. However, note that conditional variance is constant. Hence the CGW model is not able to explain the well known serial correlation structure of conditional variance, i.e. the Autoregressive Conditional Heteroscedasticity (ARCH) documented by the studies cited by Bollerslev, Chou, and Kroner (1992). This is because the CGW model is a linear model. Turn now to a nonlinear model which nests the CGW model.

Let there be three types of investors, A, B, C. Types A, B are as in CGW. At date t, member i of type C has risk tolerance given by $T_c(\omega_{it})$. Passing to the limit as the number of traders, N, goes to infinity but holding the fractions n_k, $k = A$, B, C fixed we have, equating demand to supply,

$$E[Q_{t+1} \mid I_t] = (\bar{X}\sigma_{Qt}^2)Z_t, \ \sigma_{Qt}^2 \equiv \mathrm{Var}(Q_{t+1} \mid I_t), \ Z_t \equiv 1 / [n_a\tau_a + n_b\tau_{bt} + n_c\tau_c(m_t)] \ (4.4.8)$$

where

$$\tau_c(m) = [(1 - m)/2]T_c(-1) + [(1 + m)/2)]T_c(+1),$$

$m_t = m(J_t, h_t)$, $\tau_{bt} = 1/b_t$, $b_t \equiv$ risk aversion of type B as in CGW. If $\{(J_t, h_t)\}$ is a stochastic process such that $\{Z_t\}$ satisfied $E[Z_{t+1} \mid Z_t] = \gamma_0 + \gamma_1 Z_t$, $0 \le \gamma_1 \le 1$, $\mathrm{Var}[Z_{t+1} \mid Z_t] = \sigma_Z^2$ we could simply copy CGW and find their equilibrium price function.

But we want to parameterize $\{(J_t, h_t; u(.))\}$ as a function of past volume and past returns in such a way that we have the potential to replicate the stylized facts collected by HTT. This requires a nonconstant σ_Z^2 and a natural way to introduce this is to parameterize J_t, h_t as functions of the past. For example, a large "aggregate dividend surprise", $D_t - E_{t-1}D_t$, may be associated with a change in the degree of dependence of risk tolerances in the future, i.e., a change in J_{t+1}.

While it is beyond the scope of this article to develop them, there are two routes to dealing with the third class of traders in the CGW model. The first one is to take a parameter like n and expand the equilibrium in a Taylor series in n_c around the value $n_c = 0$. In this way one can exploit the known CGW solution ($n_c = 0$) to build up an approximation to the unknown solution for positive n_c. The second route is to solve T period problems by backwards "dynamic programming" from a known terminal value p_T at T. A typical value for p_T is zero.

4.5. *An Asymmetric Information Rational Expectations Model*

Hellwig (1980) is a well known paper that derives a closed form solution for the large economy limit for a rational expectations model where N traders each receive signals about the future earnings of an asset. The solution shows how information is aggregated by the rational expectations price function in a competitive market.

Fix date t, suppress "t" in the notation, and append to Hellwig's model the following probability structure of signal quality across the set of N traders. If trader i is in state -1, let her signal variance be $S^2 > s^2$ which is her signal variance in state $+1$. Let $\omega \equiv (\omega_1, \ldots, \omega_N)$, $\omega_i \in \{-1, +1\}$ denote a configuration and let configuration probabilities be given by the Curie-Weiss probabilities treated in (4.1.17), (4.1.18) above. We have positioned ourselves to use Section 5 of Hellwig (1980) where he derives the form of the equilibrium price function in the large economy limit.

Define a trader to be "informed" if she is in state $+1$ so that her signal variance, s^2 is small. Traders in state "-1" are "uninformed". Now check that Hellwig's Assumptions B.1-B.4 are satisfied and take the large economy limit. Assume $(X, Z, \varepsilon_1, \ldots, \varepsilon_N)$ is Gaussian conditional on ω with the same diagonal variance covariance structure as Hellwig. Let f_-, f_+ denote the limiting fractions of uninformed and informed traders.

Look at Hellwig's equations (1980, p. 492), where we use his notation except we suppress the "upper *", write random variables as caps, put A equal to risk tolerance, and $B = A[f_-/S^2 + f_+/s^2]$, where, by (4.1.17), (4.1.18),

$$f_- = (1 - m)/2, \; f_+ = (1 + m)/2, \; m = \theta(m) = \tanh(\beta Jm + \beta h), \qquad (4.5.1)$$

for $u(.) = $ constant,

$$P = \pi_0 + \pi X - \gamma Z, \tag{4.5.2}$$

$$\pi_0 \equiv [\bar{X}\Delta^2 A + \sigma^2 \bar{Z} AB]/D, \tag{4.5.3}$$

$$\pi \equiv [\sigma^2 B\Delta^2 + \sigma^2 AB^2]/D, \tag{4.5.4}$$

$$\gamma \equiv [\sigma^2 \Delta^2 + \sigma^2 AB]/D, \tag{4.5.5}$$

$$D \equiv \sigma^2 B\Delta^2 + \sigma^2 AB^2 + A\Delta^2 \tag{4.5.6}$$

Concentrate first on the case $u(.) = $ constant. If the mean field equation,

$$m = \tanh(\beta Jm + \beta h), \tag{4.5.7}$$

has two solutions, choose the one with the same sign as h to be compatible with (4.1.19a).

The following four points may be made about this version of Hellwig's model. First, the correlatedness of the trader signal quality states may lead to a "phase transition" where the equalibrium price relationship makes an abrupt shift in reponse to small changes in (J, h). Stephen Durlauf has made the important point that this kind of model can be used to show how large market movements may be caused by changes in the degree of correlation of information between agents rather than by large changes in the information itself.

Second, the model raises issues of how to measure factors that might effect the correlation strength of signal quality across agents. This in turn impacts on how rapidly the price function impounds information and impacts on the likelihood of abrupt changes in returns which may appear to be blowoffs and crashes.

Gennotte and Leland (1990) study how the sensitivity of demand of each trader type demands upon relative quality of signals and how this feeds into above changes in the price relationship provided their outside hedging function is upward sloping. The formula above shows how similar behavior can be obtained without the need for such an outside hedging function. Also note that it may be possible to "endogenize" the outside supply of shares, Z, by a community of noise traders modelled as in Section two above. A generalization of Hellwig (1980) to allow a probability structure on signals themselves, rather than just signal variances, like that in Section 1 would allow more abrupt changes in the level of prices to a small amount of "news", but that attempt must await future research.

Third, note the qualitative role of the correlation structure of signal receipts of inducing abrupt changes in the equilibrium price function, and, hence, in equilibrium returns. This feature is likely to remain in more elaborate models.

A fourth point is this. We may introduce a discrete choice decision into the model where we allow agents to choose high signal quality strategy, $\omega = +1$, (for which a fee of F is paid each period) or choose low signal quality strategy $\omega = -1$, (which is free). At each date t, choice is conducted according to the discrete choice model (4.1.3′) where $u(\omega, t)$ is based upon a measure of past performance of strategy choice $\omega \in \{-1, +1\}$. Two separate cases can be treated: *(i)* $u(\omega, t)$ is updated according to a publically kept record of experience with strategy ω; *(ii)* $u(\omega, t)$ is updated according to each individual trader's experience with ω. Discrete choice model (4.1.3), (4.1.3′) governs the probability structure in both cases.

A version of this model under research parameterizes correlation strength J as a function of past volume and past "surprises" at the time slot frequency. This is an attempt to capture the idea that high information channel congestion forces traders to condition on "coarse" information sets such as past prices which should lead to higher J which leads to higher volatility, i.e., larger changes in response to vibrations in h, $u(.)$. During periods of low congestion traders should be able to get better quality signals on X from more independent sources so that J should be lower. Regardless of the loose heuristics, the idea is to parameterize J, h, $u(.)$ a functions of past price behavior, past volume, and past "surprises" (a measure of modulus of past forecast errors) in such a way that the data can speak to the form of this relationship. One version of this model that we have formulated leads to unpredictable first conditional moments of returns but somewhat predictable higher order conditional moments of returns.

The six applications above have been to financial models. We hasten to caution the reader that two period models and incomplete markets models, which we use to illustrate the usefulness of IPS methods are dangerous to apply in practice. This is partly because we have arbitrarily assumed that markets are incomplete in the Arrow-Debreu sense without giving a theory of why these markets are missing.

We have said nothing about the potentiality of options markets and other derivative security markets to ameliorate the potentiality for abrupt changes in returns in response to small events. Longer horizon models typically will lead to more smoothing behavior. More realistic models than those treated above will need to be investigated before it can be claimed that anything said in this paper pertains to financial reality. The point made in the financial section of this paper is simple: Models of this type are tractable to econometric methods such as Hansen and Singleton (1982), and Hotz *et al.* (1992). Indeed Tsibouris (1992) has estimated a version of an IPS model and tested the orthogonality restrictions with a degree of success comparable to received CCAPM theory. IPS models like those sketched above have the potential to help shed light on the puzzling stylized facts of HTT. Turn now to a very brief sketch how MFT/IPS/discrete choice methods may be useful in generating a new class of closed form solutions for simple macro/finance models.

4.6. A Macro-Finance Equilibrium Asset Pricing Model with Interacting Agents

We show off the flexibility of the approach to interactive systems modeling advertised above by exhibiting a macro-finance asset pricing model with a closed form solution. Consider Brock (1982, Example 1.5) where a representative "stand-in" consumer solves

$$\text{Max } E_0\{\sum_{t=0}^{t=\infty}\beta^{t-1}\log(c(t))\} \text{ s.t. } c_t + x_t = y_t \equiv \sum A_{it}x_{it-1}^{\alpha}, \ \sum x_{it-1} \leq x_{t-1}, \quad (4.6.1)$$

where c_t, x_t, x_{it}, A_{it}, y_t, β, α, denote consumption, capital stock, capital stock allocated to process i, productivity shock to process i, total output plus total capital stock carryover (all at date t), discount factor on future utility, and elasticity of production function. It is easy to see that the optimal solution of (4.6.1) is $x_t = \alpha\beta y_t$, $c_t = (1 - \alpha\beta)y_t$, $x_{it} = \eta_{it}x_t$, where the $\{\eta_{it}\}$ solve

$$\text{Max } E_t\log(\sum A_{i,t+1}\eta_{it}^\alpha x_t^\alpha), \text{ s.t. } \sum\eta_{it} = 1 \qquad (4.6.2)$$

Note that (4.6.2) implies the $\{\eta_{it}\}$ do not depend upon x_t. We have now laid the foundation for building and solving an interacting systems model.

First, note that the solution form $x_t = \alpha\beta y$, does *not depend* upon the dynamic structure of $\{A_{it}\}$, hence we may preserve the same form of solution by introducing any pattern of externalities we wish and any number of agents we wish, so long as all of them are log utility maximizers facing problems with the same structure as (4.6.1), and all of them face the externalities parametrically when they solve their optimization problems. However, we wish to be able to compute statistics from aggregate quantities in order to make contact with Durlauf's (1991a, b) work on disparities among income and wealth across sites.

The solution for the $\{\eta_{it}\}$ in (4.6.2) is easy to find under the assumption that $Pr\{\omega_t\}$ is invariant to permutations within ω_t for each t. In this case we have

$$v_{it} = 1/N, \text{ for all } i, t, \qquad (4.6.3)$$

$$x_t = \alpha\beta\sum A_{it}(1/N)^\alpha x_{t-1}^\alpha. \qquad (4.6.4)$$

Given (4.6.3), (4.6.4) there are now two routes to obtaining a class of closed form solutions in the large economy limit, $N \to \infty$. First note that Section 1 locates sufficient conditions on the MFT/IPS probability structure for,

$$\sum A_{it}(1/N) \Rightarrow E^*A_{it}, N \to \infty, \qquad (4.6.5)$$

so there is no problem for $\alpha = 1$. Second, in order to deal with $\alpha < 1$, consider an economy where $A_{it} = N^{1-\alpha}A_{0it}$. With this scaling (4.6.4) reduces to

$$x_t = \alpha\beta\sum A_{0it}(1/N)x_{t-1}^\alpha. \qquad (4.6.6)$$

One may now investigate asset prices following Brock (1982) for specific examples such as simple MFT parameterizations of $A_{it} \equiv A(\omega_{it})$ with $\omega = -1$ for low A, $\omega = +1$ for high A using the simple equations (4.1.17), (4.1.18). In this way one can show how $\beta J > 1$, and an IID process for $\{h_t\}$ with mean zero and small variance can lead to big macro economic flucations.

A closely related type of example would be to replace the probability structure in Durlauf (1991a,b) with one of the MFT/IPS probability structures treated in this paper. The "Curie/Weiss" structure leading to (4.1.18) is simple enough to generate closed form solutions. The version of the discrete choice model reported by Proposition 4.1.2 is simple enough to apply to Durlauf's firms' choice of two technologies. While the resulting model would give something closer to a "closed form" solution, we doubt that it would be as rich as Durlauf's model.

5. Summary, Further Remarks, and Conclusions

This paper has tried to illustrate the usefulness of MFT/IPS methods as an input module into producing econometrically and analytically tractible models of use to finance and macroeconomics. We concentrated on finance and stressed the potentially of MFT/IPS models of addressing stylized facts which stress the apparent lack of connection of movement of stock returns and volume to "fundamentals". This is a natural place to argue for the promise of this type of model in being able to deal with stylized facts such as HTT (1991).

HTT (1991, p. 1006) state: "The large number of volatility shifts that we detect, and the fact that we are unable to find significant, real economic events in the neighborhood of a majority of these shifts, lead us to the conclusion that we may be observing instability in the noise component of volatility stemming from the microstructure of the stock market. Thus while our findings support the notion that changes in risk premia may serve to partially explain the excess volatility observed in stock prices, the apparently excessive volatility of volatility which we observe only serves to raise further questions regarding our ability to account fully for the behavior of stock prices through current financial markets paradigms".

Note that HTT stress the lack of a linkage between real economic events and the volatility shifts, and the asset pricing models sketched above generate large changes in response to small changes in du or h provided $\beta J > 1$. The parameter β is easy to interpret in the models built on the foundation of discrete choice such as (4.1.3). It is simply the intensity of choice and is a measure of the level of sharpness in choice. The parameter J is a measure of the strength of "ties" to a relevant "reference group" for each agent. Note that if intensity of choice is high we do not need much "sociology" for βJ to be greater than one. It is also plausible to think of parameterizing β, J as functions of the past history of the economy and estimating the parameters using, for example, the Generalized Instrumental Variable procedure (Hansen and Singleton, 1982). This is a good time to address a side issue that arises in IPS modeling.

IPS modeling is sometimes criticized in economics because it is said that there is no natural interpretation of the "inverse temperature" parameter β and even if there were the inverse temperature β is set exogenously such as controlling in a laboratory experiment or controlling by outside cooling or heating. Per Bak *et al.* (1992a, b) argue that sandpile models are superior to IPS models because the move to criticality is "self-organizing" rather than being forced exogenously.

While this argument has merit we believe that both types of models should be studied for the following reasons. *(i)* When IPS models are given a foundation in discrete choice random utility theory the interpretation of β becomes natural and we can imagine parameterizing it to capture economic incentives to make sharp or loose choices. *(ii)* The parameters J_{ij} become a tractable way to capture strong and weak ties between agents.

(iii) Since discrete choice econometric theory and IPS theory are well established we can draw on it to generate broad classes of econometrically tractable models as illustrated by the six examples above. Furthermore Anderson, de Palma, and Thisse (1993), show how there is a parallel between CES production functions and discrete choice theory and, hence, β is related to the elasticity of substitution in their CES production function. They show how welfare measures in discrete choice theory relate to production functions. The welfare measures treated in discrete choice theory are essentially the same as free energy expressions in IPS theory. This parallelism between economically interpretable quantities and physically interpretable quantities is beautiful and useful. *(iv)* Sandpile-based models still need an outside source (*e.g.* falling sand) to drive the pile to criticality. *(v)* The sandpile theory is not yet developed enough to conduct estimation and hypothesis testing which is fairly straightforward to do in the six examples laid out above. We conclude that it is wise to pursue both approaches because there are advantages and disadvantages to each.

Appendix

General Probability Structure with K Types of Interacting Agents

The interactions will be considered over disjoint sets $A_1, \ldots, A_K$ where types are homogeneous within each set but heterogeneous across each set. The large system limit (as $N \equiv$ total number $\to \infty$) will be taken by holding the fraction of each type $k = 1, 2 \ldots, K$ constant. To formalize this let Ω be a set of real numbers, let Ω_N be its N-fold Cartesian product, $\omega \in \Omega_N$,

$$Pr\{\omega\} = \exp[\beta G] P_N(\omega) / Z, \ G \equiv (1/2) \sum \sum M_k J_{kl}(N) M_l + \sum h_k M_k. \quad (1)$$

where $M_k \equiv \sum \omega_i$ where $\sum$ is over i in A_k and $Z \equiv \sum \exp[G(v)]P_N(v)$ over all v. Here $P_N(v)$ denotes the product probability on Ω_N induced by the common distribtion function F on Ω. We will concentrate on the case where Ω is finite and F is a sum of "dirac deltas" but use $\sum$ and $\int$ interchangeably to suggest the natural extension to a continuous state space. We shall also assume the utility functions $u(.)$ treated in Section 4 are constant. Once one sees how to generalize Section 4 for this case it will be straightforward to do it for utility functions.

The best way to think about this structure is to partition the vector ω thus: List first the components i in A_1, second the components i in A_2, etc. The probability structure captures homogeneous interactions within each set of entities $i \in A_k$ and captures heterogeneous interactions among entities across sets $A_1, \ldots, A_K$. The strength of interactions within A_k (across A_k, A_l) is measured by $J_{kk}(N)$ (by $J_{kl}(N)$) where the interaction strength will decrease linearly with N in this paper. That is to say the interaction strength becomes uniformly weaker across and within all sets of entities as N increases.

For future use, we want to find limiting values of the following statistics:

$$\hat{m}_k \equiv M_K / N_k \Rightarrow \langle \omega_i \rangle, \ i \in A_k, \tag{2}$$

where $N_k \equiv$ # of elements of A_k, $N_k / N = n_k$, and, $N_k, N \to \infty$ with n_k fixed. Here $\langle . \rangle$ denotes expectation with respect to the limiting probability, as $N \to \infty$, defined by (1) and $\Rightarrow$ denotes convergence in distribution. Details on how to define the object, $\langle . \rangle$, will follow in due course. We show now, that if we put $J_{kl}(N) = I_{kl} / N$, I_{kl} constant, the limiting value of (2) is given by a small generalization of Kac (1968).

At the risk of repeating material in the text, in order to see the Kac method with a minimum of clutter, deal first with the case $K = 1$, $I_{kl} \equiv J$, $h(A) = h$, $N_k = N$, $\hat{m}_k = \hat{m}$. Compute $Pr\{\omega\}$, $Z \equiv Z_N$. We have

$$Z_N \equiv \sum \exp \{ \beta[(J/2) (\sum v_i / N^{1/2})^2 + h(\sum v_i)]\} P_N(v) \tag{3}$$

$\sum$ is over $v \in \Omega_N$. Do the following steps. Put $\beta = 1$ to ease notation. First, use the identity

$$\exp[a^2] = (1/(2\pi))^{1/2}\int \exp[-x^2/2 + 2^{1/2}xa]dx, \tag{4}$$

and, second use the change of variable $y = x(J/N)^{1/2}$ to obtain

$$Pr\{\omega\} = (N/2\pi J)^{1/2}\int \exp[-y^2N/2J]\prod \exp[(y+h)\omega_i]dyP_N(\omega)/Z_N, \tag{5}$$

$$Z_N \equiv (N/2\pi J)^{1/2} \int \exp[-y^2 N/2J] \prod M[(y+h)]dy, \tag{6}$$

$$M(z) \equiv \sum_{\xi \in \Omega} \exp[z\xi]dF, \ \prod \text{ is product over } i = 1, 2, \ldots, N. \tag{7}$$

Note that we use M to denote "moment generating function" for (7). Compute

$$m = \lim\{\langle [(1/N)(\sum \omega_i)]\rangle\}$$

$$= \lim\{\int g(h+y)[K(y)]^N dy / \int K(\vartheta)^N d\vartheta\}$$

$$\equiv \int g(h+y)\mu_N(dy), \tag{8}$$

where, $\mu_N(dy) \Rightarrow \delta_{y*}(dy), N \to \infty$,

$$K(y) \equiv M(h+y)\exp[-y^2/2J], \tag{9}$$

$$g(h+y) \equiv \int\{\xi\exp[\xi(h+y)]dF(\xi)\}/M(h+y) = M'(h+y)/M(h+y). \tag{10}$$

Apply Laplace's method (*cf.* Ellis, 1985) to see that, as $N \to \infty$, all probability mass is piled onto $y^* \equiv \text{Argmax}\{M(h+y)\exp[-y^2/J]\}$, i.e., $\mu_N(dy) \Rightarrow \delta_{y*}(dy)$, $N \to \infty$. Hence,

$$y^* \text{ solves } JM'(h+y)/M(h+y) = y, \ m = M'(h+y^*)/M(h+y^*). \tag{11}$$

Now, Ellis (1985, p.38) shows $c(z) \equiv \log[M(z)]$ is convex, therefore $c'(z) = M'(z)/M(z)$ nondecreases in z. Make the modest additional assumption that $c'(z)$ increases in z. Then it is 1-1 and it follows that

$$m = c'(Jm+h) = M'(Jm+h)/M(Jm+h) \tag{12}$$

In order to study equations (11), (12) look at the special case, $\Omega \equiv \{-1, +1\}$, $dF(a) \equiv (1/2)\sum \delta_a$, where δ_a puts mass one on $a = -1, +1$, mass zero elsewhere. We have, recalling the definitions of hyperbolic cosine, sine, and tangent,

$$M(z) = \cosh(z), \ M'(z) = \sinh(z), \ c'(z) = \tanh(z), \tag{13}$$

$$m = \tanh(Jm+h) \tag{14}$$

Equation (14) is Ellis's Curie-Weiss mean field equation (Ellis, 1985, p. 180, p. 182) where we absorbed his β into J, h. Turn now to the discussion of this key equation.

Following Ellis it is easy to graph (14) and show that for $h = 0$, there is only one solution, $m = 0$; but, two solutions, $m_- = -m_+$, appear as soon as J becomes greater than one. For h not zero the one with the same sign as h is chosen. A "phase transition" or "spontaneous magnetisation" is said to appear when J becomes greater than one.

Before turning to central limit theorems, we remark that the solution properties outlined above can be generalized to the case where $dF(y) \equiv f(y)dy, f(-y) = f(y)$ and some regularity conditions. In this case one show $c'(-z) = -c'(z)$, $M'(0) = \int \xi dF = 0$, $M''(0) = \int \xi^2 dF$, $c'(0) = M''(0)$, so for $h = 0$ two solutions $m_- = -m_+$ appear for $JM''(0) > 1$, and $m = 0$ is the solution for $JM''(0) < 1$. Some conditions are needed on F to make $c'(z)$ display the qualitative properties of tanh which were used above.

Ellis (1985, pp. 187, 207, and reference to work of Ellis and Newman for general J, and h not zero) gives central limit theorems. In particular, for the case $J < 1$, $h = 0$ we have the central limit theorem

$$N^{1/2}(\hat{m} - m) \to N(0, \sigma^2(J, 0)), \ N \to \infty, \ \sigma^2(J, 0) \equiv (1 - J)^{-1}. \qquad (15)$$

Note how the variance tends to infinity as J tends to 1 from below.

Remark: It is easy to show using the same type of argument as that above that the covariances $\langle (\omega_i - m)(\omega_{i+L} - m) \rangle = 0$ in the limit for all integers L. That is why there are no covariance terms in (15). This appears to be a contradiction to the whole theme of this paper which is to show how models with correlated characteristics could be parsimoniously parameterized in such a way that econometric estimation is possible.

In order to explain this apparent contradiction we point out that Kac (1968, p. 258) shows that the Curie-Weiss probability structure we are using here is the limit as $\gamma \to 0$ of a class of structures indexed by γ which contain local interactions which *do give nonzero correlations*. As $\gamma \to 0$ the *range of interactions* becomes longer while the strength decreases in such a way that the Curie-Weiss equation (14) is obtained in the limit. In view of this "Kac bridge" between models with local strong interactions that have nonzero local correlations *whose strength increases with J* and the Curie-Weiss models with long range weak interactions that give the *same* equation (14) for the long run value of $\langle \omega_i \rangle$ we shall speak of an increase in J as an increase of local correlation of characteristics. Kac (1968) develops a series of expansions in γ for solutions for his general model where the Curie-Weiss theory appears as the lowest order of accuracy but accurate enough to display the phase transition behavior that appears in the general model. In our view the analytical advantage of the Curie-Weiss structure and the Kac Bridge justifies the abuse of language we use in associating an increase in *J* with an increase in correlations across characteristics.

Turn now to the general case. We shall use an identity exploited by Kac (1968). In the applications below, inducing dynamics will give us flexible functional forms of dynamics on volume and stock returns, which will be one of our key applications. Another key application will be dynamics of *K* macro aggregates.

General Case: K > 1

Rewrite (1) as follows

$$Pr\{\omega\} = \exp[G]P_N(\omega)/Z, \ G \equiv (1/2)\sum\sum M_K J_{Kl}(N)M_l + \sum h_k M_k. \quad (16)$$

Put $N_j = n_j N$, $n_k^{1/2} J_{kl}(N)n_l^{1/2} \equiv n_k^{1/2} I_{kl} n_l^{1/2}/N \equiv J_{kl}/N$, J_{kl} constant,

$$G(\omega) \equiv (1/2)\sum\sum(M_k/N_k^{1/2})J_{kl}(M_l/N_l^{1/2}) + \sum h_k M_k. \quad (17)$$

Following Kac (1968, p. 254) use the following identity,

$$\exp\{(1/2)\sum\sum\xi_i A_{ij}\xi_j\} = (2\pi)^{-K/2}[\det(A)]^{-1/2}\int\exp[\sum\xi_i x_i - x'A^{-1}x]/2dx, \quad (18)$$

where $\sum$ is from 1 to *K*, bold face letters are vectors and matrices, $\int$ is over the *K*-vector **x**, **A** is $K \times K$.
Put $A = J$, $C \equiv (2\pi)^{-K/2}[\det(A)]^{-1/2}$ and write

$$Pr\{\omega\} = CN[\prod n_j]^{1/2}\int\exp[\sum M_k(h_k + z_k) -$$

$$- (N/2)\sum\sum B_{kl}n_k n_l z_k z_l dz/Z$$

$$z_j \equiv y_j/N_j^{1/2} \quad (19)$$

after making a change of variable from *y* to *z*, letting the product $\prod$ run from $1, 2, \ldots, K$, and putting $B \equiv J^{-1}$. Application of Kac's identity and summing term by term allows one to show that *z* is given by

$$Z = CN[\prod n_j]^{1/2}\int\{[\prod M(h_k + z_k)^{n_k} \exp[-(1/2)\sum\sum B_{kl}n_k n_l z_k z_l]]\}^N dz, \quad (20)$$

We are now in a position to compute the limiting values, as $N \to \infty$, of moments. Consider

$$\langle M_j / N_j \rangle \text{ for set } A_j. \tag{21}$$

Use (19) and (20) to obtain

$$\langle M_j / N_j \rangle =$$

$$= \int [A(h_j + z_j) / M(h_j + z_j)] \{ \prod M(h_k + z_k)^{n_k} \exp[-\sum \sum B_{kl} n_k n_l z_k z_l] / 2 \}^N dz / Z \tag{22}$$

Here $A(y) \equiv \int \xi \exp[\xi y] dF(\xi) = M'(y)$. Use Laplace's method (Ellis, 1985) to observe that, as $N \to \infty$, all probability mass piles onto z^* where z^* maximizes

$$\sum n_k \log M(h_k + z_k) - (1/2) \sum \sum B_{kl} n_k n_l z_k z_l. \tag{23}$$

The first order necessary conditions for a maximum of (23) are given by

$$M'_k / M_k = \sum B_{kl} n_l z_l, \ M_k \equiv M(h_k + z_k). \tag{24}$$

Put $a_k \equiv M'_k / M_k$, $a \equiv (a_1, \ldots, a_K)$, $c_k \equiv n_k z_k$, $c \equiv (c_1, \ldots, c_K)$ and rewrite (24) thus,

$$a = Bc, \ Ja = c. \tag{25}$$

Recall that $J_{kl} = [n_k n_l]^{1/2} I_{kl}$, so (25) becomes

$$\sum_k [n_k n_l]^{1/2} I_{kl} M'_k / M_k = n_l z_l, \ l = 1, 2, \ldots, K. \tag{26}$$

Note that in the diagonal case $I_{kl} = 0$ for k not equal to l, and that n_l cancels from both sides of (26). In general the *relative size* $[n_k / n_l]^{1/2}$ plays a key role in transmitting interactions across different sets of entities as can be seen by dividing both sides of (26) by n_l.

We have

$$\hat{m}_k \equiv M_k / N_k \Rightarrow \langle \omega_i \rangle = M'(h_k + z_k^*) / M(h_k + z_k^*), \ i \in A_k. \tag{27}$$

Similar arguments yield, replacing $M_k \equiv \sum \omega_i$ by $\sum g(\omega_i)$ for any function g,

$$\sum g(\omega_i) / N_k \Rightarrow \int g(\xi) \exp[(h_k + z_k^*)\xi] dF(\xi) / M(h_k + z_k^*), \ i \in A_k. \tag{28}$$

These formulae for computation of limiting moments can be used to extend the applications given in the text.

Maximum Entropy and other Rationales

The probability structures put forth in Section 1 of our paper may appear arbitrary and chosen merely for convenience. There is some justification for the particular parameterization of probability structure that we chose to use. We give several arguments below. First we deal with the idea of modelling error-prone or "noise" traders. Then we show how such probabilities arise naturally from discrete choice theory.

A natural way to model the notion of "noisy beliefs" is to choose the most random probability measure subject to constraints. For example the most random probability measure on $\Omega \equiv \{-1, 1\}^N$ is the uniform measure that assigns $P(\omega) = 1/2^N$ to each $\omega \in \Omega$. Explanation of this idea requires a digression into the subject of maximum entropy measures.

Maximum Entropy Measures

To be precise consider the following optimization problem

$$\text{Maximize } [- \sum p(\omega)\ln(p(\omega))], \qquad (29)$$

subject to,

$$\sum p(\omega)G(\omega) = G, \ \sum p(\omega) = 1, \qquad (30)$$

where $\ln(x)$ denotes the natural logarithm of x, $\sum$ is over all $\omega \in \Omega$, and G denotes a fixed level of group sentiment. Let λ_1, λ_2 be the Lagrange multipliers associated with the two constraints in (29) by order of appearance. Then it is easy to show by differentiating the Lagrangian

$$L \equiv \sum - p(\omega)\ln[p(\omega)] + \lambda_1(G - \sum p(\omega)G(\omega)) + \lambda_2(1 - \sum p(\omega)), \qquad (31)$$

that

$$p(\omega) = \exp[\beta G(\omega)]/Z; \ Z \equiv \sum_{\upsilon \in \Omega} \exp[\beta G(\upsilon)], \ \beta \equiv -\lambda_1. \qquad (32)$$

Using the concavity of the function $H(x) \equiv -\ln(x)x$ on $(0, \infty)$ and the linearity of the two constraints in p, it is straightforward, using standard nonlinear programming theory, to show that β approaches $+\infty$ $(-\infty)$ as G approaches G^* (G_*) where G^* (G_*) denote the maximum (minimum) values of G. Note that $p(\omega)$ collapses to the most uniform measure over Ω, i.e., the IID process over Ω, when $\beta = 0$. Denote this measure by π and note that $\pi(\omega) = 1/2^N$, for all $\omega \in \Omega$, and that (32) may be equivalently written by multiplying the numerator by $\pi(\omega)$ and each term of the denominator by $\pi(\upsilon)$. This is useful in Ellis's (1985) development of the limit theory which we follow. Also note that Ellis's β is absorbed in our J, h. To put it another way, Ellis's βJ, βh correspond to our J, h.

Rationale for Entropy Maximization

At this point we must further digress to discuss the rationale for entropy maximization. The motivation of entropy maximization stems from my own attempt to reformulate the "Harsanyi" doctrine or "common priors" assumption in such a way that some diversity of beliefs is allowed at a cost of a minimal number of free parameters.

The Harsanyi doctrine is controversial. Witness the labor expended defending it by Aumann against the flat statement by Kreps: "This assumption has very substantial implications for exchange among agents; we will encounter some of these later in the book. I leave it to others to defend this assumption −see, for example Aumann (1987, section 5)− as I cannot do so. But the reader should be alerted to this modeling assumption, which plays an important role in parts of modern microeconomic theory; it is called both the *common prior assumption* and the *Harsanyi doctrine*." (1990, p. 111). Kurz (1990), for example, makes a strong argument that diversity of beliefs will remain in the face of learning in a context where one would expect belief convergence.

In view of this conflict in the profession we propose a compromise. Entropy maximization subject to constraints is given a very spirited defense as a useful way to do prediction in statistical mechanics by E. T. Jaynes (1983) and there may be a useful analogy in economics as discussed by Zellner (1991). It may possibly be viewed as a way to allow some diversity in beliefs without emptying the theory of predictive content and in Bayesian literature as a way of giving some "objectivity" to "subjective" beliefs. I use it here to motivate an anaytically tractable model of interactive group formation of beliefs or sentiment. That is to say the group is assumed to have the most random set of group beliefs subject to a given mean level G. This restriction parsimoniously parameterizes the beliefs by three parameters (β, J, h) where β is fixed by G.

A very innovative use of entropy and the methodology of Gibbsian statistical mechanics is in Stutzer's work (*cf.* Stutzer (1992) and references to his earlier papers). He uses this methodology to put forth a concept of financial entropy which he relates to the degree of risk adjustment required of any arbitrage-free asset pricing theory to explain the risk premia of a given set of assets. He applies his theory to data on the stock and bond markets and produces evidence consistent with a secular decline in the influence of risk aversion in the stock and bond markets over the past 65 years. We urge the reader to study Stutzer's work.

If the reader does not care for the maximum entropy argument the same probabilities may be derived, as in Section 4.1, by viewing the group of interactive noise traders as solving the "social discrete stochastic choice problem"

$$\text{Maximize}_{\omega \in \Omega} \; G(\omega) + \mu e(\omega), \; \beta \equiv \mu^{-1} \tag{33}$$

where $\{e(\omega)\}$ is IID extreme value distributed. It is pointed out in Manski and McFadden (1980) that Prob{ choose ω} is exactly equal to the logit probability (32). Since the probabilities are logit we have access to the extensive econometric literature on estimation of logit systems. Indeed this is a main part of the motivation for the type of theory we are building. More will be said about estimation in future work.

References[1]

Antoniewicz, R. (1991). "An Empirical Anaysis of Stock Returns and Volume", PhD Thesis, Department of Economics, University of Wisconsin.

Anderson, P., K. Arrow, and D. Pines (1988). *The Economy as an Evoloving Complex System*, Santa Fe Institute Studies in the Sciences of Complexity, Volume V, California, Addison Wesley.

Anderson, S., A. de Palma, and J. Thisse (1993). *Discrete Choice Theory of Product Differentiation*, Cambridge, MIT Press.

Aoki, M., and Y. Miyahara (1991). "Stochastic Aggregation and Dynamic Field Effects", Department of Economics, University of California-Los Angeles.

Arthur, B. (1992). "On Learning and Adaptation in the Economy", Food Research Institute, Stanford University.

Bak, P., K. Chen, J. Scheinkman, and M. Woodford (1992a). "Self Organized Criticality and Fluctuations in Economics", Santa Fe Institute W.P. No. 92-04-018, Santa Fe, New Mexico.

––––– (1992b). "Aggregate Fluctuations from Independent Sectoral Shocks: Self-Organized Criticality in a Model of Production and Inventory Dynamics", (revised version of 1992a).

[1] Not all of the references are cited in the text. Since part of the purpose of this paper is to provide a guide to the literature, I have listed many references here. The Brock, Hsieh, LeBaron book cited below many references which are not cited here.

Barnett, W., A. Gallant, M. Hinich, and M. Jensen (1992). "Robustness of Nonlinearity and Chaos Test to Measurement Error, Inference Method, and Sample Size", Department of Economics, Washington University, St. Louis, July.

Benhabib, J., ed. (1992): *Cycles and Chaos in Economic Equilibrium*, Princeton, Princeton University Press.

Berliner, L. (1992). "Statistics, Probability, and Chaos", with comments by Cutler, Geweke, Granger, Griffeath, Smith, Tsay, and rejoinders by Chatterjee, Yilmaz, Berliner; *Statistical Science*, vol. 7, No. 1, pp. 69-122.

Blume, L., (1991). "The Statistical Mechanics of Strategic Interaction", Department of Economics, Cornell University, New York.

_____ , and D. Easley (1992). "Evolution and Market Behavior", *Journal of Economic Theory*, vol. 5, pp. 9-40.

Bollerslev, T., R. Chou, and K. Kroner (1992). "ARCH Modelling in Finance: A Review of the Theory and Empirical Evidence", *Journal of Econometrics*, vol. 52, pp. 5-60.

Brock, W. (1982). "Asset Prices in a Production Economy", in J. McCall (ed.), *The Economics of Information and Uncertainty*, Chicago, The University of Chicago Press.

_____ , W. Dechert, J. Scheinkman, and B. LeBaron (1990). "A Test for Independence Based Upon the Correlation Dimension", Department of Economics, The University of Wisconsin, Madison, The University of Houston, and The University of Chicago.

_____ , J. Lakonishok, and B. LeBaron (1990). "Simple Technical Trading Rules and the Stochastic Properties of Stock Returns", *Journal of Finance* (forthcoming), Social Systems Research Institute W.P. No. 9022, The University of Wisconsin, Madison.

_____ (1991a). "Understanding Macroeconomic Time Series Using Complex Systems Theory", *Structural Change and Economic Dymamics*, vol. 2, pp. 119-141.

_____ (1991b). "Causality, Chaos, Explanation, and Prediction in Economics", in J. Casti and A. Karlqvist (eds.), *Beyond Belief: Randomness, Prediction, and Explanation in Science*, Boca Raton, Florida, CRC Press.

_____ , D. Hsieh, and B. LeBaron (1991). *Nonlinear Dynamics, Chaos, and Instability: Statistical Theory and Economic Evidence*, Cambridge, MIT Press.

_____ , and W. Dechert (1991). "Non-Linear Dynamical Systems: Instability and Chaos in Economics", in W. Hildenbrand and H. Sonnenschein, *Handbook of Mathematical Economics*, vol. IV, Amsterdam, North Holland, pp. 2209-2235.

_____ , and S. Potter (1992). "Nonlinear Time Series and Macroeconomics", in C. R. Rao (ed.), *Handbook of Statistics*, New York, North Holland (forthcoming).

Campbell, J., S. Grossman, and J. Wang (1991). "Trading Volume and Serial Correlation in Stock Returns", Princeton University, Wharton School, Sloan School, MIT, *Quarterly Journal of Economics* (forthcoming).

Casdagli, M., and S. Eubank (1991). *Proceedings of The 1990 Nato Workshop on Nonlinear Modeling and Forecasting*, Santa Fe Institute Series, Redwood City, California, Addison-Wesley.

Casti, J. (1992). *Reality Rules*, Volumes I and II, New York, John Wiley and Sons.

Diebold, F., and J. Nason (1990). "Nonparametric Exchange Rate Prediction", *Journal of International Economics*, vol. 28, pp. 315-332.

de Jong, R. (1992). "The Bierens Test Under Data Dependence", Department of Econometrics, Free University, Amsterdam, The Netherlands.

de Lima, P. (1992a). "Testing Nonlinearities Under Moment Condition Failure", Department of Economics, Johns Hopkins University.

_____ (1992b). "On the Robustness of Nonlinearity Tests to Moment Condition Failure", Department of Economics, John Hopkins University.

de Long, J., A. Shleifer, L. Summers, and R. Waldmann (1990). "Noise Trader Risk in Financial Markets", *Journal of Political Economy*, vol. 98, No. 4, pp. 703-738.

Durlauf, S. (1989a). "Locally Interacting Systems, Coordination Failure, and The Behavior of Aggregate Activity", Department of Economics, Stanford University.

_____ (1989b). "Output Persistence, Economics Structure and the Choice of Stabilization Policy", *Brookings Papers on Economic Activity*, vol. 2, pp. 69-116.

_____ (1991a). "Nonergodic Economic Growth", *Review of Economic Studies* (forthcoming), Stanford Institute for Theoretical Economics, TR No. 7.

_____ (1991b). "Path Dependence in Aggregate Output", Stanford Institue for Theoretical Economics, TR #8.

_____ , and P. Johnson. "Local Versus Global Convergence Across National Economies", Department of Economics, Stanford University.

_____ (1992). "A Theory of Persistent Income Inequality", Department of Economics, Stanford University.

Ellis, R. (1985). *Entropy, Large Deviations and Statistical Mechanics*, New York, Springer-Verlag.

Gennotte, G., and H. Leland (1990). "Market Liquidity, Hedging, and Crashes", *American Economic Review*.

Grandmont, J. (1992). "Expectations Driven Nonlinear Business Cycles", forthcoming in Proceedings of Stockholm Conference on Business Cycles organized by the Trade Union for Economic Research, Oxford, Oxford University Press.

Granger, C., and T. Terasvirta (1992). *Modeling Dynamic Nonlinear Relationships*, Oxford, Oxford University Press.

Hall, P., and C. Heyde (1980). *Martingale Limit Theory and Its Applications*, New York, Academic Press.

Hansen, L., and K. Singleton (1982). "Generalized Instrumental Variables Estimation of Nonlinear Rational Expectations Models", *Econometrica*, vol. 50, pp. 1269-1286.

Haugen, R., E. Talmor, and W. Torous (1991). "The Effect of Volatility Changes on the Level of Stock Prices and Subsequent Expected Returns", *Journal of Finance*, vol. XLVI, No. 3, pp. 985-1007.

Hawley, D., J. Johnson, and D. Raina (1990). "Artificial Neural Systems: A New Tool for Financial Decision-Making", *Financial Analysis Journal*, November-December, pp. 63-72.

Hellwig, M. (1980). "On the Aggregation of Information in Competitive Markets", *Journal of Economic Theory*, vol. 22, No. 3 pp. 477-498.

_____ (1982). "Rational Expectations Equilibrium with Conditioning on Past Prices: A Mean-Variance Example", *Journal of Economic Theory*, vol. 26, No. 2, pp. 279-312.

Hommes, C. (1991). *Chaotic Dynamics in Economic Models: Some Simple Case-Studies*, Groningen, The Netherlands, Wolters-Noordhoff.

Holland, J. (1992). *Adaptation in Natural and Artifical Systems*, Cambridge, MIT Press.

Hotz, V., R. Miller, S. Sanders, and J. Smith (1992). "A Simulation Estimator for Dynamic Models of Discrete Choice", NORC W.P. No. 92-1, The University of Chicago.

Hsieh, D. (1987). "Testing for Nonlinear Dependence in Daily Foreign Exchange Rates", *Journal of Business*, vol. 62, No. 3, pp. 339-368.

_____ (1991). "Chaos and Nonlinear Dynamics: Applications to Financial Markets", *Journal of Finance*, vol. XLVI, No. 5, pp. 1839-1877.

_____ (1990). "Implications of Nonlinear Dynamics for Financial Risk Management", Fuqua School of Business, Duke University, forthcoming in *Journal of Financial and Quantitative Analysis*.

Jaynes, E. (1983). *Papers on Probability, Statistics, and Statistical Physics*, R. D. Rosenkrantz (ed.), Boston, D. Reidel Publishing Company.

Kac, M. (1968). "Mathematical Mechanisms of Phase Transitions", in M. Chretien, E. Gross, and S. Deser (eds.), *Statistical Physics: Phase Transitions and Superfluidity*, vol. 1, pp. 241-305. Brandeis University Summer Institute in Theoretical Physics, 1966.

Kreps, D. (1990). *A Text in Microeconomic Theory*, Princeton, Princeton University Press.

Kurz, M., (1990). "On the Structure and Diversity of Rational Beliefs", Department of Economics, Stanford University.

———— (1991). "On Rational Belief Equilibria", Department of Economics, Stanford University.

———— (1992). "Asset Prices with Rational Beliefs", Department of Economics, Stanford University.

LeBaron, B. (1992a). "Some Relations between Volatility and Serial Correlation in Stock Market Returns", *Journal of Business*, vol. LXV, pp. 199-219.

———— (1992b). "Persistence of the Dow Jones Index on Rising Volume", Social Systems Research Institute, W.P. No. 9201, The University of Wiscinsin, Madison.

Lucas, R. (1978). "Asset Prices in an Exchange Economy", *Econometrica*, vol. 46, pp. 1429-1445.

Lukacs, E. (1975). *Stochastic Convergence*, New York, Academic Press.

Krasner, S. (ed.) (1990). *The Ubiquity of Chaos*, American Association for the Advancement of Science, Publication No. 89-15S, Washington, D.C.

Kuznetsov, Y., S. Muratori, and S. Rinaldi (1992). "Bifurcations and Chaos in a Periodic Predator-Prey Model", *International Journal of Bifurcations and Chaos*, vol. 2, No. 1, pp. 117-128.

Loretan, M., and P. Phillips (1992). "Testing the Covariance Stationarity of Heavy-Tailed Time Series: An Overview of the Theory with Applications to Several Financial Datasets", SSRI Working Paper 9208, University of Wisconsin, Madison.

Majumdar, M., and T. Mitra (1992). "Robust Ergodic Chaos in Discounted Dynamic Optimization Models", Department of Economics, Cornell University.

Mandelbrot, B. (1963). "The Variation of Certain Speculative Prices", *Journal of Business*, vol. 36, pp. 394-419.

———— (1972). "Statistical Methodology for Nonperiodic Cycles: From the Covariance to R/S Analysis", *Annals of Economics and Social Measurement*, July, pp. 259-290.

Manski, C. (1992). "Identification Problems in the Social Sciences", SSRI W.P. No. 9217, The University of Wisconsin, Madison.

————, and D. McFadden (1981). *Structural Analysis of Discrete Data with Econometric Applications*, Cambridge, MIT Press.

Marimon, R. (1989). "Stochastic Turnpike Property and Stationary Equilibrium, *Journal of Economic Theory*, vol. 47, pp. 282-306.

McFadden, D. (1981). "Econometric Models of Probabilistic Choice", in C. Manski and D. McFadden (eds.), *Structural Analysis of Discrete Data with Econometric Applications*, Cambridge, MIT Press.

Meese, R., and A. Rose (1991). "An Empirical Assessment of Non-Linearities in Models of Exchange Rate Determination", *Review of Economic Studies*, vol. 58 (3), No. 195, pp. 603-619.

Mezard, M., G. Parisi, and M. Virasora (1987). *Spin Glass Theory and Beyond*, Singapore, World Scientific.

Nelson, D. (1992) "Filtering and Forecasting with Misspecified ARCH Models I: Getting the Right Variance with the Wrong Model", *Journal of Econometrics*, vol. 52, pp. 61-90.

Pearce, P. (1981). "Mean-Field Bounds on the Magnetization for Ferromagnetic Spin Models", *Journal of Statistical Physics*, vol. 25, No. 2, pp. 309-320.

Pesaran, M., and S. Potter (1991). "Equilibrium Asset Pricing Models and Predictability of Excess Returns: Theory and Evidence.

Ramsey, J., C. Sayers, and R. Rothman (1988). "The Statistical Properties of Dimension Calculations Using Small Data Sets: Some Economic Applications", *International Economic Review*, vol. 31, pp. 991-1020.

Ruelle, D. (1989). *Chaotic Evolution and Strange Attractors*, Cambridge, Cambridge University Press.

Sargent, T. (1992). "Bounded Rationality in Macroeconomics", Hoover Institution, Stanford, CA.

Scheinkman, J. (1990). "Nonlinearities in Economic Dynamics", *Economic Journal Conference Papers*, vol. 100, No. 400, pp. 33-48.

Stutzer, M. (1992). "Arbistatics", Department of Finance, University of Minnesota, Menneapolis, Minnesota.

Scheinkman, J., and B. LeBaron (1989). "Nonlinear Dynamics and Stock Returns", *Journal of Business*, vol. 62, pp. 311-337.

Sugihara, G., and R. May (1990). "Nonlinear Forecasting as a Way of Distinguishing Chaos from Measurement Error in Time Series", *Nature*, vol. 344, pp. 734-741.

_____, B. Grenfell, and R. May (1990). "Distinguishing Error from Chaos in Ecological Time Series", Scripps Institution of Oceanography, University of California, San Diego, Department of Zoology, Cambrige University, Department of Zoology, Oxford University.

Theiler, J., S. Eubank, A. Longtin, B. Galdrikian, and J. Farmer (1992)."Testing for Nonlinearity in Time Series: The Method of Surrogate Data", *Physica D*, vol. 58, pp. 77-94.

Tong, H. (1990). *Non-Linear Time Series: A Dynamical Systems Approach*, Oxford, Oxford University Press.

Tsibouris, G. (1992). PhD Thesis, Department of Economics, The University of Wisconsin, Madison.

United States National Academy of Sciences (1987). "Report of the Research Briefing Panel on Order, Chaos, and Patterns: Aspects of Nonlinearity", Washington, D. C., National Academy Press.

Vaga, T. (1990). "The Coherent Market Hypothesis", *Financial Analysts Journal*, November/December, pp. 36-49.

Varian, H. (1985). "Divergence of Opinion in Complete Markets: A Note", *Journal of Finance*, vol. XL, No. 1, pp. 309-317.

_____ (1986). "Differences of Opinion in Financial Markets", in Courtenay Stone (ed.), *Financial Risk: Theory, Evidence and Implications*, Boston, Kluwer Academic Publishers.

Wang, J. (1989). "A Model of Intertemporal Asset Prices Under Asymmetric Information", forthcoming *Review of Economic Studies*, Sloan School of Management, MIT.

_____ (1991). "A Model of Competitive Stock Trading Volume", Sloan School of Managmet, MIT.

Weidlich, W., (1991). "Physics and Social Science: The Approach of Synergetics", *Physics Reports*, vol. 204, No. 1, May, pp. 1-163.

West, K. (1987). "A Specification Test for Speculative Bubbles", *Quarterly Journal of Economics*, August, pp. 553-580.

Zellner, A. (1991). "Bayesian Methods and Entropy in Economics and Econometrics", in W. Grandy and L. Schick, (eds.), *Maximum Entropy and Bayesian Methods*, Kluwer Academic Publishers, pp. 17-31.

[2]

Structural Change and Economic Dynamics, vol. 2, no. 1, 1991

UNDERSTANDING MACROECONOMIC TIME SERIES USING COMPLEX SYSTEMS THEORY

WILLIAM A. BROCK

There has been a lot of recent activity in complex systems theory which is a broad area that includes chaos theory, and a part of statistical mechanics which deals with interacting particle systems, self-organized criticality models, cellular automata theory, spin glass models, simulated annealing learning models, stochastic approximation theory and more. In this paper we briefly review a subset of this area, i.e. interacting particle systems and cellular automata, and ask whether models built from these components can shed light on the structure of macroeconomic time series. In particular we investigate the promise of these models to help us understand the typical spectral shape of economic time series without introducing exogenous outside shocks. We also ask whether tools from statistical mechanics can help us model 'noisy' and 'irrational' agents in a natural way and whether an analytically tractable and economically persuasive model of market equilibrium results. Irrational agents are modelled as entropy maximizers over their choice sets subject to constraints. This captures the idea that their choice is as random as possible given constraints. The paper sketches several 'trial' models in order to give the economist some idea of whether tools from complex systems theory and statistical mechanics might be useful in building models to explain a list of stylized facts which are set out at the beginning of the paper. A model of stock market equilibrium driven by a mixture of fundamentalist and 'Ising' noise traders is sketched. The conclusion is that while the tools are aesthetically beautiful a lot of work will be needed to machine these tools into something useful for serious economic modelling.

1. INTRODUCTION

There has been an explosion of recent research activity in the general area which I will call 'non-linear science' and 'complex systems theory'. The perspective from which I will be writing is influenced by the Santa Fe Institute Volume edited by Philip Anderson, Kenneth Arrow and David Pines (1988). This perspective includes chaos theory, interacting particle systems, self-organized criticality in cellular automata, study of aggregates produced by coupled non-linear maps, spin glass models, simulated annealing stochastic approximation theory and more. There has been recent excitement about the promise of a special class of dynamical system models called self organized criticality models (*cf.* Bak and Chen, 1991) as well as spin glass models (*cf.* Mezard *et al.*, 1987).

The above theories and models have the potential of contributing to the

Address: Department of Economics, The University of Wisconsin, Madison, USA.

120 W. A. BROCK

unifying of explanations of strong persistence in time series data. Strong persistence of time series data is common to fields that range from economics, earthquake studies, fluid turbulence, meteorology and many more. Some of the above models generate steady state dynamics whose time series records display properties of '$1/f$' noise. The term '$1/f$' noise refers to strong persistence as captured by power law temporal/spatial correlation functions and power law spectral density functions for smaller frequencies. The models are of interest to the softer sciences as well as 'harder' sciences because the power law scaling properties of the steady state dynamics appears to be robust to local details of the dynamical updating rules.

In view of the coarseness inherent in economics modelling the possibility of finding such unifying 'universality' as a certain amount of independence from local details of model structure is exciting. The purpose of this article is to describe and probe this fascinating class of models using various economic contexts. We will work in the style of a 'review essay' in the sense of trying to sketch out how economics may make use of some of the ideas in the above theories and models. It will be beyond the scope of this 'review essay' to develop any of these ideas beyond an impressionistic level. Before we begin a caveat on goals and style is in order.

As Mirowski (1990) has written, economists may be too quick to embrace recent developments in an area of natural science such as non-linear science and complex systems theory because they, perhaps, have 'physics envy'. In order to avoid falling into this trap it is well to discipline our activity at the outset by setting forth precise theoretical structures from economics and a list of 'stylized facts' we wish to explain.

The goal of this paper will be to outline how to incorporate some of the new ideas listed above into conventional economic modelling in such a way as to shed light on explanation of a list of stylized facts to be given below.

The theoretical structures we shall use will be (i) stripped down asset pricing versions of the overlapping generations model with heterogeneous agents which are coupled together with a connection structure designed to be plausible economically and (ii) versions of the single agent model of macroeconomics but with a connection structure of external effects in production. Emphasis will be placed upon domino types of effects where diffusion is ignited by threshold effects or by 'magnetization effects' of Ising type (Ellis, 1985). The overall theme will be to outline an impressionistic sketch of some ideas of how to unify standard equilibrium modelling with some models from statistical mechanics and non-linear dynamics.

Unlike some of the physics and non-linear science literature on cellular automata and interacting particle systems we shall stress global connectors as well as local connectors and non-symmetric interactions as well as symmetric interactions. Also the role of conservation principles and invariance principles under symmetries will be minimal in economic applications many of which suggest no natural counterparts to these concepts of central importance in some natural science applications. The models under scrutiny will be probed for their sensitivity to changes in the connection structure and lack of symmetries that economists do not care about that natural scientists do care about.

We shall first start out by listing stylized facts we wish the models to help illuminate. After these are listed we shall move into discussion of models.

*F*1: The autocorrelation function of many economic time series decays rather slowly to zero, i.e. the spectrum has a peak at the origin and displays a downward slope as frequency increases near the origin. That is to say there is a lot of spectral power at the low frequencies. Yet another way to put this fact is that near unit roots are present in levels. The series are:

(i) Measures of asset returns volatility such as squared (or absolute values) of returns on assets such as stocks, commodities, bonds, etc. (Taylor, 1986). Returns volatility series appear to have autocorrelation functions which die off with roughly power law tails in contrast to the exponential die off typical in ergodic stationary processes. One way of describing this kind of behavior is this. It is a mixture of processes, each of which has dependence dying off at an exponential rate, but the distribution of half lives includes lives of all sizes. Haubrich and Lo (1988) show how ideas dating back to Granger and Theil on aggregation can be used to create for example a mixture of stable linear processes whose autocorrelation function of the aggregate has power law tails. Bak and Chen (1991) stress that explaining such autocorrelation patterns is a main goal of their self-organized criticality models. Indeed, they describe some work they are doing with José Scheinkman and Michael Woodford in economics.

(ii) Levels of macroeconomic time series as real GNP per capita, unemployment rate, industrial output per capita and others (Nelson and Plosser, 1982; Sargent, 1987) show evidence of high persistence in levels. See Durlauf (1989a, b) and Haubrich and Lo (1988) for a discussion and context that is especially relevant to the theme we develop here. Durlauf shows how a 'ferromagnetic'/Ising (*cf.* Ellis, 1985) externality structure can generate time series that 'look like' the Nelson and Plosser series. There is some dispute whether fractionally differenced processes describe quarterly real GNP better than the trend stationary or difference stationary models used by Nelson and Plosser (1982). We repeat that one should see Haubrich and Lo (1988) for a discussion of theory that emanates from Granger and others that indicates that aggregation should lead to fractional differenced processes.

Fact *F*1 has been called the 'typical spectral shape' of economic time series by Granger (*cf.* Sargent, 1987a, p. 279). A version of this fact exists in natural science under the name '1/*f*' noise. The term '1/*f*' noise refers to any process whose spectrum scales like 1/*f* for frequencies, *f*, near zero. Loosely used, the term refers to any process whose spectrum scales like $1/f^{-\alpha}$, $\alpha > 0$, for *f* near zero. See Bak and Chen (1991) and Keeler and Farmer (1986) to get some idea of the prevalence of 1/*f* noise in physics. Physicists have joked to me that all you have to do to get a large audience at a physics conference is to whisper '1/*f* noise'. One might say there is a similar intensity of interest in economics. The large 'unit roots' literature in macroeconomics emanating from the Nelson and Plosser

122   W. A. BROCK

(1982) paper is a reflection of similar phenomena in economics (*cf.* Durlauf, 1989a, b).

F2: There is high spectral coherence at business cycle frequencies (3–5 years) among many macroeconomic time series. Many macroeconomists define 'the business cycle' to be this pattern in the cross spectrum. See Sargent (1987a, p. 283) for a description of this finding and use of it to define the business cycle.

F3: There is strong evidence of asymmetry about trend in aggregate measures of activity over the business cycle as captured by measures of relative duration over expansions and contractions about trend. For example, Diebold and Rudebusch (1990) have documented that expansions are twice as long post-World War II in the US in comparison with pre-war expansions. Contractions are about half as long post-World War I compared with pre-war. This asymmetry in duration is inconsistent with a linear model driven by symmetrical distributed innovations. A detailed discussion of such macroeconomic facts that conflict with linear models that are driven by symmetric innovations is in Potter (1990).

F4: Earnings of an individual corporation closely follow a random walk. Levels of stock prices also closely follow a random walk. See Lorie and Brealey (1972) for early evidence, Taylor (1986) for later evidence, and Li (1990b) for evidence that the stock price levels looks more like $1/f^2$ than $1/f$ for small f. Random walks with drift only provide a first order of approximation. There are 'higher order dependencies' such as strong persistence in measures of volatility of asset returns which is stressed in F5 below.

F5: Measures of local volatility are highly autocorrelated in asset returns. Squared returns display an autocorrelation function that decays very slowly. There is some evidence that autocorrelation functions of squared returns on value weighted indexes decay slower than equal weighted indexes which in turn decay slower than individual firms. There is fairly strong evidence that returns are more predictable following periods of relatively low volatility. See LeBaron (1990) for a discussion of these facts.

2. MODELS

2.1. *Coupled Maps, Cellular Automata, Sandpiles*

First, I shall lay out the broad structure of the models as they are given to us by natural science. Then I shall discuss some of their testable hypotheses. To some extent I will relate their testable hypotheses to the stylized facts listed above. After that is done, I shall suggest how the models may be adapted for use in economics if that appears possible.

2.1.1. *Coupled maps*

Coupled maps have been studied by Crutchfield and Kaneko (1987), Keeler and Farmer (1986) and others. Here the system to be studied can be written

$$x_i(t+1) = f(\{x_{N_i}(t)\}), \qquad (1)$$

where N_i is the set of neighboring sites of site i, which may include i itself, $x_i(t)$ denotes the state vector (the state of site i) at date t and $f(.)$ is a function from the vector space whose dimension is the cardinality of N_i times the dimension of x_i to the vector space whose dimension is x_i. Note that the site index i can be a vector of arbitrary dimension. For example, in the popular case of a d-dimensional integer cubic lattice, which we denote by $\mathbb{Z}^d$, site i is a d-dimensional vector of integers. The neighborhood structure is the natural one of nearest neighbors. That is to say the neighbors of site i are the immediate nearest neighbors on the edges of the symmetric hypercube centered at i. However, we stress that neighborhood structures can be much more general than this.

Aggregates are formed by summing x_i over a set S of sites. Component aggregates can be formed, as in Durlauf (1988a, b), summing over subcomponents of i.

For various neighborhood structures, which need not be local, the dynamics of aggregates formed from (1) can be studied. When f is a set of coupled maps, as in Keeler and Farmer (1986), surprisingly simple neighborhood structures can generate aggregates displaying a 'stochastic' appearing structure that looks like the near unit root processes that appear in F1 above.

While we are not going to work with coupled maps in this article we have devoted a short mention of them to make the reader aware of their promise.

2.1.2. *Cellular automata*

'Cellular automaton' is a term used for cases of (1) when the state space is 'coarse grained' for example when $x_i(t)$ is restricted to be in $\{0, 1\}$ and the updating of each site depends only on neighboring sites. A dramatic example is the game of Life (*cf.* Bak and Chen, 1991). Let us briefly describe it.

2.1.3 *The game of Life*

Imagine a square integer lattice on the plane. Site $i = (a, b)$ is 'alive' $x_i(t) = 1$ or 'dead' $x_i(t) = 0$ at date t. Here are the updating rules. The neighbors of i, N_i are the eight nearest neighbors of site i of the smallest square centred at i on the square lattice, $\mathbb{Z}^2$.

 (i) If i is alive at t it will die at $t+1$ if there are less than two or more than three live neighbors.
(ii) If i is dead at t it will be alive at $t+1$ only if there are exactly three live neighbors.

Note that the dynamical system defined by rules (i) and (ii) is a special case of (1). Life may generate power law distributions for measures of activity. For example, Bak and Chen (1991) discuss research (which Bennett and

124   W. A. BROCK

Bourzutschky (1991) question) that shows that the distribution of clusters of size s, $D(s) = ks^{-a}$, $a \approx 1.4$, where cluster size s is measured as the total number of births and deaths following a single perturbation of a randomly chosen site. The distribution, $D(s)$, was estimated over a large number of perturbations.

I shall put the work of Durlauf (1988a, b) on Ising models in the cellular automata class closely related to the game of Life because his updating rules depend only upon nearest neighbors. He studies an economy on a square integer lattice where the producer at i 'comes alive' and produces provided enough of his near neighbors are producing. Congestion, however, does not 'kill' Durlauf's producer, unlike the game of Life, although, of course, one could study such a version. Durlauf's model generates aggregative time series of output that display strong persistence (near unit roots) if the strength of local externality connection at each production site is strong enough.

His model is a direct parallel of the models of magnetism studied in Ellis (1985). Durlauf's model predicts strong persistence in the resulting time series of output provided the strength of connection of external effects of neighbours on production is strong enough. When the connection strength is high enough, i.e. it passes the critical level (*cf.* Ellis, 1985, on criticality), the model generates nonergodic time series.

The work on robustness of scaling laws of temporal/spatial correlation functions at criticality which is discussed by, for example, Ellis (1985, chapter V.8) suggests the rate of decay, i.e. the 'critical exponents' of the temporal/spatial correlations, should be robust to changes in the local details of the connection structure. As Ellis points out this robustness is studied by renormalization group arguments and is one reason for the excitement that the study of criticality causes in physics. Such a study would be a valuable extension of Durlauf's model. Such a study may allow us to show, at the critical level of connection strength, existence of a power law structure in spatio-temporal autocorrelations of output and classify the connection structures into 'universality classes' (*cf.* Ellis, 1985, p. 178) which are widely believed to be robust to changes in local details of the connection structure. Turn now to a discussion of dynamics of Ising models that may be useful for economic modelling.

Grinstein *et al.* (1985, hereafter GJH) study statistical mechanics of cellular automata and relate their dynamic theory to the theory of interacting particle systems as detailed in, for example, Ellis (1985). They show that one can define a quantity which is average magnetization in their context, and is average output in Durlauf's context. By taking the 'thermodynamic limit', i.e. letting the width of the lattice go to infinity they obtain the limiting value of average magnetization for each fixed date t. Then they show that analytically tractable classes of models can be found where the limiting average magnetization evolves over time according to a discrete time difference equation which can be chaotic depending upon the details of the underlying model. Their approach may be very usefully applied to give more dynamic structure to Durlauf's model which is more motivated by economic modelling but lacks the rich dynamical structure of the GJH formulation.

The models of Durlauf, GJH and Ellis (1985) are all 'Ising' type models which

Chaos Theory in Economics

require some exogenous 'tuning' parameter such as temperature, connection strength, or whatever, 'to be increased to a 'critical' level in order to generate the strong persistence and non-ergodicity in time series output that we are after. It would be more persuasive if the 'criticality' needed was endogenous, not exogenous. Turn now to a class of 'Ising' type models, but where the criticality is 'self-organized'.

2.1.4. *Sandpile models*

The sandpile models of Bak and Chen (1991) are used to suggest explanations for '1/f' noise, i.e. spectra that peak at zero and slope down with a power law near zero. They also generate autocorrelation functions with power law tails. These models are a family of cellular automata that are exogenously forced and have a threshold dynamics that works as follows. Recall that a cellular automaton is just a dynamical system like (1), but the state space is discrete as in the game of Life.

Sandpile models, more generally, self-organized criticality models (SOC models) are treated as a rather broad explanation for phenomena that includes earthquakes, extinction of the dinosaurs, avalanches, stock market crashes and many other situations where 'domino' effects are triggered by thresholds. Bak and Chen and their references discuss a variety of models that have a common structure that can be illustrated by the metaphor of a sandpile.

Build a pile of sand on a table and keep dropping grains of sand on it from above. Eventually the pile will reach a critical level where added grains of sand start sandslides of various lengths. These sand avalanches continue until the sand either rolls off the edge of the table or the pile relaxes back to its critical slope. Note how the pile self-organizes itself as the grains of sand are continually added.

One can build a model of the dynamics of the sandpile by first partitioning the surface of the table into small discrete sites to represent it as a square lattice. Then, represent the sand as homogenous discrete grains, putting the state at site i, $x_i(t)$ at date t equal to the number of grains stacked up on that site where the units of the base of the site are chosen to be the size of one grain. Neighbours of each site not on the edge of the table are the nearest neighbours.

Let a critical slope s be given such that if the height difference between two neighbouring sites is greater than s, sand rolls toward the lower height site until the slope is equal to s. Sand that is dropped on each site of the table will build up until s is reached. Sand that exceeds s on the edge of the table rolls off onto the floor below. Hence, the boundary conditions for the dynamics on the edge of the table are defined. We have outlined an example of cellular automaton dynamics that we shall call the Sandpile game, which is an example of dynamics (1).

The term 'self-organized criticality' refers to the sandpile self-organizing itself by releasing sand slides of various lengths in order to relax back to the critical slope s between nearest neighbours as one continues to add sand. Note that the dimension of the state space for the dynamics is very large and for any given vector of initial conditions as the system is exogenously forced by adding more grains of sand from above each site, the system converges to a set S of limit states which are those that satisfy the slope condition at near neighbours. The set of

126 W. A. BROCK

limit states is large but robust as experiments on your kitchen table at home will verify.

The sandpile metaphor is a severe abstraction that is intended to abstract out and isolate the following property that is common to many dynamical systems in nature: a threshold dynamics that leads to domino effects through local interactions among neighbours.

Before getting into details about sandpile dynamics we must explain why the economist should be interested in this. As Bak and Chen (1991) point out the dynamics of these models generate power laws for the behaviour of objects such as spectra near the origin, spatial correlation on functions, distribution of sizes of activity, etc., similar to that of classical models of ferromagnetism at critical phase transition states without having to rely on some external tuning parameter such as 'temperature'. Furthermore the power law parameters are somewhat robust to changes in local details of the updating rules much like universal behaviour of critical exponents in models of magnetism as detailed, for example, in Ellis (1985, p. 173). The possibility that the sandpile abstraction might be a key abstraction to give a common explanation to the wide spread phenomenon of strong temporal–spatial persistence in nature has led to a lot of interest in these models in natural science. In view of the wide spread presence of strong temporal–spatial persistence in economic time series as manifested by the near universal presence of near unit roots we should take a close look at the sandpile class of dynamical systems.

This class generates the following testable propositions on time series.

(i) Small deviations in initial conditions grow algebraically which is much slower than the exponential rate characteristic of chaotic dynamics. This pattern of growth in small deviations in initial conditions also contrasts with the pattern predicted by a log-linear model which is asymptotically stable when the external noise is shut off. This last is the usual Vector AutoRegressive (VAR) model fitted to vectors of macroeconomic time series after detrending.

(ii) Density functions of measures of activity size follow a power law in SOC models. This is not the case for Gaussian and some other densities typically used in economics.

(iii) Temporal–spatial correlation functions decay according to a power law rather than exponentially which is the case for many models fitted in economics. The rate of decay, i.e. the 'critical exponents' (Ellis, 1985, p. 173) are expected to be invariant to local details of the specification of the dynamics. While Kadanoff *et al.* (1989) have shown that such details do matter they have also shown that the power law shape is invariant to a wide range of details of specification.

(iv) Self affinity and self similarity.

Mandelbrot (*cf.* Mirowski, 1990) has stimulated much interest in self similarity and fractals. Many economic time series such as stock returns look roughly self-similar in a statistical sense. Bak and Chen (1991) stress that their self-organized criticality models generate times series that look self-similar.

Greis and Greenside (1990) study stochastic processes that are 'self-affine' and report on recent work in this area of interest to economists. Turn now to precise models.

A theme we wish to develop is how to use ideas from statistical mechanics to model forms of irrationality and 'bounded rationality'. As we shall see the treatment of statistical mechanics as given by Ellis (1985) which stresses the tension between the forces of entropy ('irrationality' for us) and energy ('rationality' for us) in leading to tension between disorder and order is especially intriguing for economics. See Li (1990a) for an approach to balancing order against disorder that has promise in economics.

3. MODELS OF INERTIA AND IRRATIONALITY

Many scientists from other fields are appalled at the economists' modelling of rationality. They are especially rankled by the hypothesis of rational expectations (see, e.g. Palmer's discussion in Anderson *et al.*, 1988). There are several reasons why economists cling to rational models. First, there are many ways agents can be wrong but few ways they can be right. Therefore rational models tend to generate more falsifiable restrictions on data than non-rational models. Second, a sea of irrational agents is too easily exploited by rational agents that have high profit incentive to do so. Third, rational models lead naturally to notions of equilibrium that help the economist interpret data.

However, there is a class of models of 'irrationality' based upon the idea of entropy maximization subject to constraint that generate tight restrictions on data. The idea is directly from ideal gas theory in statistical mechanics (*cf.* Ellis, 1985, chapter III). That is to say the consumer is treated as acting like an ideal gas over his choices. More precisely, he chooses over his choice set using the most random probability measure defined on that choice set. Furthermore this kind of model will help us capture the idea of 'noise' trader to be developed later in this article. Let us first explain entropy maximization models in the rather different context of classical demand theory.

Consider the standard theory of individual demand, where household $h = 1, 2, \ldots, H$ solves,

$$\text{Maximize } U_h(x_h), \tag{2}$$

s.t. $x_h \in B(p, I_h) \subseteq R^k$, where $B(p, I_h)$ is the budget set at prices p, for the k-vector of goods, with income I_h.

The irrational consumer could be modelled as making the most random possible choice from: (i) $B(p, I_h)$ or (ii) $\partial B(p, I_h)$. Here ∂B denotes the boundary of set B. 'Most random' can be formalized by taking a draw from the probability measure that maximizes entropy over choice set (i) or (ii). To be specific we will impose a little rationality and use (ii). In that case the mathematical expectation of demand is given by the 'demand function'.

$$D_{hi}(p, I_h) = I_h/kp_i, i = 1, 2, \ldots, k; \quad \text{for } B(p, I_h) \equiv \{x \in R^k \mid p \cdot x \equiv I_h\}. \tag{3}$$

Note that (3) generates predictions that are easy to falsify: all income elasticities are unity, all price elasticities are unity, all cross elasticities are zero.

128 W. A. BROCK

While data are sure to overwhelmingly reject these restrictions the problem here is not too few restrictions but too many. Be that as it may, it is important to recognize that (3) contains the famous idea in Gary Becker (1962) where he argued that rationality is not needed to generate the predictions of demand theory, 'irrational' choice over the budget line generates predictions like (3). Entropy maximization over constraint sets is a natural way to generalize Becker's earlier idea of modelling 'irrationality' in a 'natural' way that generates falsifiable restrictions on data.

It is clear that one can generalize classical Arrow–Debreu–McKenzie general equilibrium theory in this manner by replacing the optimizing consumers/producers over their constraint sets by choice made by draws from the maximum entropy probability measure on the constraint set for each agent. As one sees from the demand theory one does get downward sloping average demand for a homogeneous group of consumers via the ergodic theorem under usual assumptions for validity of the ergodic theorem.

The entropy maximization framework is broader, however. Drop the subscript h for now since we shall speak of a typical consumer. We can express a continuum from the most irrational consumer to the most rational consumer in the following way. Introduce the uniform measure, $v(dx)$, i.e. the most random measure over $\partial B(p, I)$. Consider the 'Gibbs' measure

$$G(dx; b) = \exp[bU(x)]v(dx)/Z, \qquad Z \equiv \int \exp[bU(y)]v(dy). \qquad (4)$$

Given $\bar{U}$ the Gibbs measure is the most random measure, i.e. the measure that maximizes entropy over the set of probability measures on $\partial B(p, I)$ that satisfies

$$\bar{U} = \int U(x) \exp[bU(x)]v(dx)/Z = \int U(x)G(dx; b), \quad \text{where} \quad b \equiv b(\bar{U}), \qquad (5)$$

is chosen to satisfy (5).

The key point is this. There is a tight relationship between b and $\bar{U}$. As $b \to \infty$, $\bar{U} \to \max\{U \text{ s.t. } x \in B(p, I)\}$. The easy way to see this is to notice that as $b \to \infty$ all probability mass of the Gibbs measure piles up onto the maximum value of U.

We shall use the ideas sketched here in Section 3 when we turn to modelling 'noise' traders in Section 5. Before we turn to the modelling of 'noise' traders we shall first show how some of the dynamics treated in complex systems theory can be embedded in classical infinite horizon rational expectations models.

4. A CLASS OF CLOSED FORM SOLUTIONS

The class of models I present below are rather wild abstractions. Yet, someone once said, 'real progress in science is made when a new set of closed form solutions is made available'. No such claim is made for the class introduced below. Yet, the class may be useful because one can analytically treat any connection structure of production externalities in the context of a tractable infinite horizon rational expectations equilibrium model.

Much like Sargent (1987b, p. 122) consider the following discrete time optimal control problem.

$$\text{Maximize} \sum \beta^{t-1} \log(c_t), \tag{6}$$

$$\text{s.t. } c_t + x_t = A_t x_{t-1}^{\alpha}, \quad t = 1, 2, \ldots; \tag{7}$$

where $0 < \alpha < 1$, $\sum$ runs from 1 to infinity, c_t, x_t denote consumption and capital stock at date t, $0 < \beta < 1$. Unlike Sargent, $\{A_t\}$ is a deterministic sequence which can be time dependent in a complicated way. Yet, a closed form solution can still be found.

PROPOSITION 4.1. If (1) has an optimum, it is of the form

$$x_t = \alpha \beta A_t x_{t-1}^{\alpha}. \tag{8}$$

Proof. If there is an optimum then the first-order necessary conditions of optimality must hold with equality. Insert the conjecture (8) and verify that it satisfies the first-order conditions. Since the problem is a concave programming problem the first-order necessary conditions characterize optimum. ∎

Remark 4.1. The important thing to note about this simple proof is this. It is valid for any $\{A_t\}$ for any complicated time dependence. Furthermore the case where $\{A_t\}$ is a stochastic process can be handled by maximizing expected discounted utility over the set of non-anticipating stochastic processes, $\{(c_t, x_t)\}$. The important thing to do is to write out the first-order necessary conditions and insert the conjecture, rather than use dynamic programming.

Now consider a lattice economy as follows. Let n individuals of type i be located at site i in the lattice. Let N_i be the set of neighbours of site i. Introduce external effects from production activities of neighbours of i in the manner of Lucas (1988) and Romer (1986). Put $A_{it} = A_i[\{x_{jt}\}, j \in N_i]$ and consider problem (6) above for each of the n individuals at site i, where each of the n individuals faces $\{A_{it}\}$ parametrically. Since n is equal for all sites, put $n = 1$ to ease notation. By Proposition 4.1 the solution for i is given by

$$x_{it} = \alpha \beta A_{it} x_{i,t-1}^{\alpha}. \tag{9}$$

We may now examine different specifications of $A[.]$ for different lattice structures. Let us look at some examples.

4.1. *Example* 1

Let there be only one site, only one type, with external effects, $A_t = A[x_{t-1}]$. Specify $A[z]$ so that

$$\alpha \beta A[z] z^{\alpha} = rz(1-z), \quad 0 \le r \le 4. \tag{10}$$

Use (10) to rewrite (9) in 'rational expectations equilibrium' à la Lucas (1988) and Romer (1986) to obtain

$$x_t = r x_{t-1}(1 - x_{t-1}). \tag{11}$$

Dynamics (11) has been analyzed extensively in the chaos literature. The limit dynamics follows the period doubling Feigenbaum cascade as r increases to the 'Feigenbaum value' $r = 3.56994\ldots$. Notice that the externality function $A[z]$ defined by (10) increases for small z, takes a maximum then falls to zero for z increasing to 1.

Example 1 is probably too stylized to be extended to stochastic cases and calibrated to data in the manner of the Real Business Cycle (RBC) school (*cf.* King *et al.*, 1988).

However, it is not totally unreasonable to posit an externality function $A[z]$ that is first increasing in z and then decreasing in z if the whole model is interpreted as a 'reduced form' for a broader concept of capital than machines. If one thinks of 'capital' as including such 'capital stocks' as 'social overhead capital' then it is natural to think of the external effect of economic activity of your fellow producers as being positive at first because of their contribution to 'social overhead capital' as a joint product of their own activity. However, as their activity continues to increase it is natural to expect negative externalities such as congestion, resource crowding out, pollution, or the 'reduced form' effect of high cost of factors of production due to high housing costs, crime, etc., in congested areas. Silicon Valley in California is a good parable to keep in mind.

Notice that in a model with externalities it is much easier to find parameter values that may be consistent with data that may be consistent with chaotic or other 'complex' dynamics especially when we turn to Example 2.

4.2. *Example 2*

Consider now a one-dimensional lattice on the subset $\{-N, -N+1, \ldots, -1, 0, 1, \ldots, N-1, N\} \equiv L_N$. Following Crutchfield and Kaneko (1987) look at the 'logistic lattice' dynamics written below,

$$x_{i,t+1} = f(x_{it}) + \varepsilon_O g(x_{it}) + \varepsilon_L g(x_{i-1,t}) + \varepsilon_R g(x_{i+1,t}), \qquad (12)$$

where $\varepsilon \equiv (\varepsilon_O, \varepsilon_L, \varepsilon_R)$ is called the coupling kernel.

By the discussion above we know how to 'rig' up the externality functions $\{A\}$ to deliver the dynamics (12) as the rational expectations equilibrium dynamics. At this point we urge the reader to take a look at Crutchfield and Kaneko (1987) and Keeler and Farmer (1986) in order to see the rich dynamics that coupled maps on a simple lattice like (12) can generate. It will be clear, especially after reading Keeler and Farmer (1986), that it is possible to find coupled map structures that generate aggregate time series that 'look' like the high persistence listed in the facts above. With such a potentiality, it is now time to turn from physics to economics.

Just as nature abhors a vacuum, economies abhor differential marginal products. In a lattice economy capital will tend to move across sites to equate marginal value products unless there are frictions that inhibit such movement. It then must be explained what these frictions are. If the frictions are national boundaries then the argument for strong externalities as reflected in the $A[.]$ functions may be weakened. Evidence suggests that there are 'convergence clubs' where convergence of growth rates seems to occur and one possible convergence club appears to be the states in the US (see, e.g. Barro, 1989 and references).

However, convergence of marginal products (or growth rates) in the context of our model means convergence of the A_{it} to a common value A which tends to eliminate the interesting dynamics. If the $A_{it}x_{i,t-1}$ are interpreted broadly as 'after tax' quantities where the idea of 'tax' itself is interpreted broadly to include 'taxes' due to incomplete or poorly enforced property right systems, increased probability of confiscation, environments where there is a stronger incentive to 'rent seek' through the political system rather than produce economically useful products, etc., then such frictions may be strong enough to stop the cross sectional smoothing effect of marginal value product equalization.

Another problem has to do with economic incentives to 'internalize' externalities in the economies with external effects. Production externalities from nearest neighbour firms could be easily internalized by merger in some cases. Frictions to prevent such mergers must be isolated. This is especially so in the Ising type models where the dynamic does not become 'interesting', i.e. non-ergodic, unless the connection strength of the external effects is sufficiently strong as in Durlauf's (1989a, b) models. However, if the external effects are strong the incentives to internalize them by merger become strengthened also. Hence there is a tension between getting time series output from the model that has near unit root persistence but at the same time finding economically realistic frictions to prevent merger from wiping out the externalities that drive the model in the first place.

Even if merger is not a problem the calibrated magnitude of the externality needed to generate the persistence one wants may be unrealistically large relative to own profits per firm. Work needs to be done calibrating the model to data perhaps along the lines pushed by Kydland, Prescott and others of 'quantitative theory' as surveyed in King *et al.* (1988). Until that is done the fear remains that the size of the external effects needed to get the strong persistent time series in this kind of model are much too large to be consistent with reality.

4.3. *Example* 3

In this class of examples we include the case where the A_{it} are cross-sectionally stochastic with weak enough dependence so that Central Limit Theory for weakly dependent processes implies. In this case, working in logs since our equation (9) is linear in logs, we have,

$$(1/N^{1/2}) \sum \log(x_{it}) \to N[\mu(t), \sigma^2(t)], \quad N \to \infty. \tag{13}$$

Here convergence is in distribution. Note that the dynamics of $[\mu(t), \sigma^2(t)]$ can be derived for different specifications of the externality functions $\{A\}$. The issue arises whether there are plausible conditions for $[\mu(t), \sigma^2(t)]$ to possess complex dynamics or chaos even though these quantities are averages. Examples can be found that yield such dynamics as we shall see below when we discuss the work of Grinstein *et al.* (1985).

132 W. A. BROCK

The point we want to make with all the preceding examples is this. There is a class of analytically tractable rational expectations models into which one can put interesting spatially extended structures such as couple map dynamics, Ising lattice dynamics, etc. One could even turn this class of models into asset pricing models using the techniques of Brock (1982) to attempt to explain the temporal–spatial pattern of asset returns observed in reality. Indeed this may be a promising strategy to link movements in macroeconomic times series listed in the Facts above with movements in asset prices. This type of activity must, of course, be disciplined by reality in some manner, perhaps along the lines of 'quantitative theorizing' as surveyed by King *et al.* (1988). Turn now to a final class of models which we shall develop in rather more detail than any of the models discussed above.

5. NOISE TRADER MODELS

Some of the ideas mentioned above may be useful to make precise the idea of noise traders in financial modelling. Shliefer and Summers (1990, hereafter SS) and their references have treated noise traders as having biases in their expectations about fundamentals. SS use noise trader modelling to explain anomalies that create difficulties for fundamentalist efficient market modelling. For simplicity's sake consider the following pricing model of short lived assets.

Let there be three types of traders. (i) 'Liquidity traders' whose demand $\{L_t\}$ is an independently and identically distributed (IID) stochastic process with mean zero and finite variance. (ii) F fundamentalist traders whose demands are given by

$$D_f(p_t) = [E_t y_{t+1} - Rp_t]/aV_t(y_{t+1}), \tag{14}$$

where E_t, y_{t+1}, R, p_t, a and V_t denote conditional expectation, value of the asset or contract at date $t + 1$, gross return on risk free asset, price of risky asset at date t, risk aversion parameter and conditional variance. Note that the asset lives only one period for simplicity. (iii) N noise traders whose demands are given by

$$D_{ni}(p_t) = [E_t y_{t+1} + \omega_{it} - Rp_t]/aV_t(y_{t+1}). \tag{15}$$

Here $\{\omega_{it}\}$ denotes a bias process for type i trader at date t. We shall use the models discussed in the above sections for the bias process. We shall use the Ising model, since it fits so naturally with the treatment of 'irrational' consumers in Section 2 above. We shall follow Ellis (1985) to save space.

The reader should be warned before we begin that we have not been able to come up with a natural interpretation in the case of economics and finance for the Hamiltonian and the connection structure of the Ising model. Because of this failure the reader is urged to think of it only as a piece of machinery to generate analytically tractable conditional probabilities. It may well be more fruitful to generate probabilities (which have rather similar structure) by using models of probabilistic choice following Manski and McFadden (1981).

Before we treat the Ising model, however, let us point out that we are not the first to use Ising models for financial modelling. Tonis Vaga (1990) uses an Ising based model to explain bull periods of higher than average return coupled with lower than average risk. One may view that what we are doing here is to outline a program to unify Vaga's model with conventional asset pricing models.

To keep things very simple indeed, let us restrict ourselves to the case where $\{y_t\}$ is IID with mean y and variance V. We set the biases of the noise traders following the treatment of Ising models of magnetism as in Ellis (1985, chapter 5) as much as possible. To be specific work on a symmetric about the origin hypercube, Λ contained in the D-dimensional integer lattice, $\mathbb{Z}^D$, where $\mathbb{Z}$ denotes the integers. Let a density function for noise trader bias in their estimates of y, be given as follows

$$P(d\omega) = \exp[\beta G(\omega)]v(d\omega)/Z, \quad \omega\varepsilon\Omega_\Lambda \equiv \{-1, 1\}^\Lambda,$$

$$G(\omega) = \sum \sum J_{ij}\omega_i\omega_j + h \sum \omega_j, \quad Z = \int \exp[\beta G(\omega)]v(d\omega). \tag{16}$$

Here $\omega_i\varepsilon\{-1, 1\}$, $\omega\varepsilon\Omega_\Lambda$ which is the space of all functions from Λ to $\{-1, 1\}$, v is the most random (i.e. uniform) measure on Λ, $0 \le \beta$, G is the negative of the usual Hamiltonian, Z is called the partition function and the measure P is called the Gibbs measure. We urge the reader to study Ellis's characterization of the Gibbs measure as that measure which maximizes entropy over the set of measures subject to two constraints: (i) the measure must add up to unity and (ii) the mean of G must take a fixed pre-assigned value.

Note that when $\beta = 0$, P collapses to v, which is the product measure which corresponds to an IID stochastic process with values in $\{-1, 1\}$ across sites i in Λ. In Ising models of ferromagnetism β is interpreted as the inverse temperature. The model is intended to capture the tension between entropy and energy, i.e. disorder and order. As β increases from zero (temperature falls from infinity) (16) states that all probability mass clumps onto the element ω_0 called the 'ground state' that maximizes G over the symmetric hypercube Λ. For various formulations of the model there will typically be a critical inverse temperature, β_c, such that the limiting behaviour of the model is much different for $\beta > \beta_c$. Limits are taken by letting Λ expand symmetrically to fill $\mathbb{Z}^D$, $|\Lambda| \to \infty$.

Table V.3 of Ellis (1985, p. 178) for the Ising model on $\mathbb{Z}^2$ illustrates the behaviour we would like the reader to focus on. Let us explain. Define $\mathbb{U} = \{(\beta, h) \mid \beta > 0, h \ne 0; 0 < \beta < \beta_c, h = 0\}$. On this set of parameter values we have a Law of Large Numbers (LLN),

$$\lim S_\Lambda/|\Lambda| = m(\beta, h) \tag{17a}$$

exists where the limit is in the almost sure and the exponential sense. Also, we have a Central Limit Theorem (CLT),

$$[S_\Lambda - |\Lambda| m(\beta, h)]/|\Lambda|^{1/2} \to N(0, \sigma^2(\beta, h)), \tag{17b}$$

where the variance σ^2 is finite, is the infinite sum of exponentially dying spatial correlations $N(0, \sigma^2)$ is the normal distribution with mean 0 and variance σ^2, convergence is in distribution. Here $S_\Lambda = \sum \omega_i$, and the sum is over Λ.

134 W. A. BROCK

At $(\beta_c, 0)$ the behaviour of the model is delicate. It is not ergodic, there are two limit measures $P(d\omega, -)$, $P(d\omega, +)$, two limit values of m, $m(\beta, 0^-)$, $m(\beta, 0^+)$, where these denote limits in h tending to 0 from the left and from the right, respectively. The law of large numbers (17) as well as the Central Limit Theorem fails for β_c unless the external field h is non-zero.

More precisely for $\beta = \beta_c$, $h = 0$, the two different limits above can be obtained for the 'magnetization' $m(\beta, 0)$ depending on boundary conditions. The 'phase' diagram on p. 93 of Ellis (1985) shows how $m(\beta, h)$ jumps from negative to positive for fixed $\beta > \beta_c$ as h moves from negative to positive. This discontinuity is an abrupt change in behaviour that happens for large β that does not happen for small β.

With this background return to our noise traders. Aggregate demand by noise traders is given by

$$D_N(p_t) = \sum [y + \omega_i - Rp_t]/aV, \quad \text{where} \quad \sum \text{ is over } \Lambda, \quad N = |\Lambda|. \quad (18)$$

Equilibrium p is given by solving

$$FD_f(p) + D_N(p) = L_t(p), \quad (19)$$

where $L_t(p)$ is stochastic demand (here taken to be IID) by liquidity traders at date t. Now let $T = F + N + L$ where L is a scaling of the liquidity traders representing the 'number' of liquidity traders.

At first let us put $L = 0$ in order to see the basic logic of the equilibration process. Putting $f = F/[F + N]$, $N = |\Lambda|, n = N/[F + N]$, we have, from (19),

$$y - Rp + n[\sum \omega_i/|\Lambda|] = 0. \quad (20)$$

Take N to infinity, holding the fraction n of noise traders fixed we have

$$Rp = y + nm(\beta, h). \quad (21)$$

We now see that the Ising noise trader model predicts a deviation from the fundamental that is proportional to a function of three parameters. The function m is key. Let us describe its behaviour in detail for a leading case, the case of a two-dimensional integer lattice with 'Hamiltonian' $G = 0.5 \sum \sum J(i - j)\omega_i\omega_j + h(\sum \omega_i)$. Note that $J(i - j)$ is positive and translation invariant. We also get rid of the traditional minus sign on the Hamiltonian because it is a nuisance.

As in Ellis (1985, p. 91) let us describe the behaviour of the function $m(\beta, h)$ as a function of h. There are three cases, $A : \beta > \beta_c$; $B : \beta = \beta_c$; $C : \beta < \beta_c$. Plot h on the horizontal axis and m on the vertical. In all three cases m is symmetric around $h = 0$, is concave for $h > 0$, convex for $h < 0$. For Case A m is negative as h increases from -1 (as a left hand asymptote) to zero from the left through negative values, m jumps from a negative left limit to a positive right limit as h passes through 0. The function m continues to increase as h increases through positive values to saturate at the value 1. In all three cases the function m is symmetric in h about zero. For Case B, the function m is negative for $h < 0$

positive for $h > 0$, is equal to zero at h equal to 0 and is continuous through 0. The slope at zero, however, is plus infinity. For Case C, m is positive for $h > 0$, negative for $h < 0$ and has finite slope at the origin. In all three cases m is concave for $h > 0$, convex for $h < 0$.

Hence, if there is no external bias, i.e. $h = 0$, we then have $m = 0$ so all the effect of the noise traders is washed out in equilibrium. Notice that this is true even though a type of 'herd' instinct is built into the 'Hamiltonian' that drives the probability whether a noise trader at site i puts a positive 'spin' $\omega_i = 1$ or a negative 'spin' $\omega_i = -1$ on a stock.

Parenthetically we remark there is nothing special about ± 1, since units of p, y can be changed to conform without loss of the points being made by the model. Like a school of Ising fish pointing one way, $+1$, or the opposite way, -1, as in Vagas (1990) our Ising traders tend all to 'point' one way or the opposite on the stock, yet their effect washes out in equilibrium because $m = 0$. The only way to get a net effect of this type of noise trader herd is to 'force' it by putting h not equal to zero.

This is a good point at which to discuss modelling philosophy in the noise trader literature.

In our view maximum entropy models are one way of giving precision to a class of traders one would want to call 'noisy' or 'irrational'. Another class would be those traders who use 'technical' trading rules where evidence for their profitability after adjustment for risk is weak.

If one takes seriously the idea of 'noise' traders then it is a natural interpretation of the word, 'noise', that their biases away from the fundamental must be roughly independent of each other. There is no reason to expect truly 'noisy' traders to be systematically biased enough to avoid the aggregate bias from being washed out by the law of large numbers. Indeed look at the average bias

$$A(\Lambda) = \sum \omega_i / |\Lambda|. \tag{22}$$

If the group Λ of traders is truly 'noisy' one might like to represent this by postulating the most random measure on Λ. A nice way of making this precise is to choose the measure that maximizes entropy subject to the condition that it integrates to unity. However, as Ellis (1985) stresses this is just the uniform measure. Under that measure the expected value of (22) is zero.

We deliberately placed the traders on a symmetric hypercube of sites with ω_i taking values in $\{-1, 1\}$ to capture the idea of i 'bearish' ($\omega_i = 1$) or i 'bullish' ($\omega_i = +1$), and to capture the idea of no bias in their 'connection' structure. The interaction J_{ij} is positive for j in the set of 'neighbours' of i and zero otherwise in the 'magnetic' case we wish to emphasize. This is an attempt to capture the idea that if one's 'neighbours' put a bullish 'spin' on things then that might push one towards a bullish bias. Unless one is an ardent fundamentalist it is hard to be bearish when your closest friends and associates are all bullish. We are deliberately modelling the noise traders as the ones that can be influenced by 'peer pressure' not the fundamentalists which simply focus on the fundamentals.

136 W. A. BROCK

Returning to the Ising model, a nice summary of its properties on, for example, $\mathbb{Z}^2$ is in Ellis (1985, p. 178). The main point is this: for β larger than the critical β, and when the external field h is zero the model is extremely sensitive to small changes in boundary conditions and in h, i.e. our noisy Ising traders have the potential to 'freeze' into bearish, $m < 0$ or bullish, $m > 0$ 'groupthink' provided the β parameter is large enough, provided the external 'field' h is <0 for bearish and >0 for bullish. At $\beta = \beta_c$ one can get 'mixed phases' when $h = 0$ rather than 'pure' phases for cases (β, h) in $\mathbb{U}$.

The above version of the model is rich enough to show how a society of noise traders can cause equilibrium price to 'freeze' above or below the fundamental. However, there are no dynamics in this model.

The paper by GJH can be used to repair this gap. GJH study a class of probabilistic Ising cellular automata that is very suggestive of an approach to dynamics that might well be worth developing. Here is the idea. Note that for a fixed date t, if we take $N = |\Lambda|$ to infinity holding the fraction of traders of each type fixed, the equilibrium price p_t is a time stationary function $p(m(\beta, h, t))$ of the limiting 'magnetization' $m(\beta, h, t)$ of the crowd of noise traders at date t. Introduce now another time scale, $t \to t + k$, for the measure $P(d\omega, t) \to P(d\omega, t + k)$. Scale it so that when $t \to t + k$, $y_t \to y_{t+1}$. GJH study a class of dynamics $\{P(., t)\}$ where the measure moves essentially in the direction of the 'gradient' of G but is perturbed by Gaussian noise in such a way that the steady state measure is the Gibbs measure $P(d\omega)$. As modellers we are free to run the time scale k faster ($k > 1$) or slower ($k < 1$) than the time scale of evolution of the stochastic process $\{y\}$. GJH show there is an interesting class of Ising models where $M(t + k) \equiv m(\beta, h, t + k) = f(M(t))$, where f depends upon the details of the model and can even be chaotic. The point is that we can induce a 'slow' dynamics in the magnetization, M, that will cause the crowd of noise traders to induce 'long waves' of bull bias followed by bear bias around the fundamental. This might generate the pattern stressed by Vaga (1990).

There is another closely related style of modelling that might generate long bull periods of above average returns and below average risk stressed by Vaga (1990) and help explain the anomalies stressed by SS. Consider our N 'noise' traders in the above model. Let the trader at Ising site i be susceptible to trying a trend chasing strategy $\omega_i = -1$ or be a solid fundamentalist, $\omega_i = 1$ with the same Ising probability structure above. Let there be F traders who are always fundamentalist as above and let $\{y_t\}$ be IID. Let the trend chasing strategy work as follows. At date t trend chasers update their expectation on y_{t+1}, call it $y + b_{it}$, as follows. Drop subscript i because we shall assume all trend chasers use the same updating rule for simplicity.

$$b_t - b_{t-1} = \lambda(p_{t-1} - MA(q, t - 1)), \tag{23}$$

where

$$MA(q, t) \equiv [p_t + p_{t-1} + \ldots + p_{t-(q-1)}]/q. \tag{24}$$

Write (23) in difference form thus

$$\Delta b_t = (\lambda/q)[(q - 1)\Delta p_{t-1} + \ldots + (q - (q - 1))\Delta p_{t-(q-1)}] \equiv \Theta(L)(\Delta p_t), \quad (25)$$

where $\Theta(L)$ is the usual function of the lag operator as in Sargent (1987a).

Now suppose all trend chasing traders use $y + b_t$ in place of y in forming their demand functions (18) above. Assume all traders have the same risk aversion parameters and the same expectations on the conditional variance as in (18) and (19) above. Put $R = 1$ for simplicity and solve for equilibrium as in (20) above and write it in difference form to obtain

$$0 = \Delta\{f[y - p_t] + n[y + b_t - p_t] = > \Delta b_t = A\Theta(L)(\Delta p_t), \quad (26)$$

for some constant A which depends upon λ and the fraction of traders that are trend chasers. A straightforward stability analysis shows that longer moving averages, i.e. an increase in q, make the fundamental equilibrium, $p = y$, more unstable in the sense that if it is unstable at q it will be unstable at $q + 1$ but not vice versa.

This is proved by examining the largest modulus root of the associated polynomial. The point we wish to make here is this. If we take the size of the lattice to infinity as in the treatment surrounding (18) and (19) above the limiting fraction of traders forming their demands using the trend chasing strategy (23), i.e. $\omega_i = -1$, may be calculated using methods from Ising models as in Ellis (1985). Once this is done it is natural to introduce a slow moving dynamics for the 'field' parameter h in the expression for the Hamiltonian where h increases as the relative profits from following fundamentalist strategy increases and vice versa. Make h positive when profits from fundamentalist strategy are greater than the trend chasing strategy and vice versa. If $\{y_t\}$ has positive support bounded away from zero and infinity then once price gets out of the support profits to a fundamentalist strategy are obviously larger than the trend chasing strategy. The slow dynamics on h then leads to a force that checks the instability in the short run. This seems to capture the intuitive idea that many people have. An asset market tends to start to 'bubble' away from the fundamental only to be crushed by fundamental traders sooner or later. How fast this 'far from equilibrium' stabilizing force works depends upon parameters of the model. It seems possible that models of this type might be promising in helping to explain the anomalies to the efficient markets hypothesis that SS are after. Note that trend chasing traders correspond to what SS call 'positive feed back traders'.

The magnetization properties discussed above depend upon what economists might think are rather special interaction functions $\{J_{ij}\}$ and rather special Hamiltonians, $G(\omega) = \sum \sum J_{ij}\omega_i\omega_j + h(\sum \omega_i)$. Some of this speciality can be relaxed using ideas from spin glass modelling (*cf.* Anderson *et al.*, 1988; Mezard *et al.*, 1987). Here the $\{J_{ij}\}$ are chosen at random from a distribution, typically Gaussian.

Statistical properties of the model are analyzed by a combination of analytical and computer simulation methods. The behaviour of these models is extremely

138   W. A. BROCK

rich. All we can do here is urge the reader to take a look at the references above and imagine what our noise trader equilibrium asset pricing model would look like if the noise traders were modelled by spin glass techniques rather than Ising techniques.

At this point we must emphasize that all this is very speculative at best and may even be considered 'premature' by many financial scholars. However, there does appear the possibility that this kind of modelling may be a way of formalizing the notion of 'noise' traders in such a way that one could get a class of parsimoniously parameterized models which in principle could be estimated on financial data on prices, p_t, earnings, y_t, and gross returns on risk free assets, R. Furthermore it should be possible to treat more general demand functions, longer lived assets, etc., by computer simulation methods coupled with analytical methods.

My own personal preference would be to build and estimate a model of this type on a subset of financial data and evaluate it relative to standard models by use of out of sample forecast evaluation and specification testing along the lines of Brock *et al.* (1990) which uses technical trading rules to specification test a null class of models by bootstrapping technical trading statistics under the null and comparing the data values of these statistics with the null distributions. Turn now to a closely related equilibrium pricing theory, to the Ising theory presented above.

The Ising theory requires tuning the parameter β to values above the critical values in order to get any 'interesting' non-ergodic behaviour. In the ergodic case the noise traders wash out in the limit unless some external source of bias is forced into the system. It would be more natural to have a model where the criticality was endogenous rather than forced. This brings us to the self organized criticality models of Bak and Chen (1991) or the E–M systems of Li (1990a).

Consider a 'sandpile' where each site i is hit by an IID shock process with zero mean and finite variance, call it $\{n_{is}\}$. Let these processes be independent across sites. Now let trader i's 'state of mind' be given by $S_{it} = \sum n_{is}$ where $\sum$ is over $s \le t$. So each trader's state of mind is a random walk on his site. Now let us think of a 'sandpile' where sand rains down from the sky in an IID manner but the 'sand' can take a positive 'sign' which adds a grain to the stack on a site or it can take a negative 'sign' in which case a grain is subtracted off the stack at a site.

The net height at i behaves like S_{it} which is a driftless random walk with mean zero, finite varince innovations. Let now a neighbourhood structure be defined on our imaginary sandpile with a critical slope given, together with dynamical rules governing the slide of 'sand' to nearest neighbours when neighbouring slopes are greater than the critical slope. One could think of the critical slope as being the maximum deviation from one of his closest neighbours 'state of mind' that a noisy non-fundamentalist trader feels comfortable with. The 'rolling of sand' to reduce the gap between states of mind between near neighbours leads to 'domino' effects on next nearest neighbours. This leads to 'sandslides' of various lengths. The same type of simulation and scaling methods used by Bak and Chen (1991) could be used to study the distribution of 'sandslides' induced by this type of pile. Furthermore the same techniques of Kadanoff *et al.* (1989) could be used to study the universality classes of power law behaviour of sand slide statistics.

It is beyond the scope of this article to do any more than simply mention this possibility in an attempt to show that the idea of diffusion/domino/Ising type dynamics triggered by relaxation of stress that crosses a threshold is a very general idea which may lead to innovations in model building in economics. What is especially intriguing is suggestion of a way of endogenizing the key parameter, β, of the Ising model, so that criticality, β_c, is reached by a self-organizing 'meta-equilibrium' process.

Ising type models seem to be useful as a way of parsimoniously parameterizing 'coordination' problems. Durlauf (1989a, b) uses them in macroeconomics to explain the strong persistence stated in fact F1 above. He needs the non-ergodic Ising model to get the strong persistence that he wants. For this to happen the 'connection strength' parameter, β, must exceed the critical values. As Ellis (1985) stresses, one can get by with a smaller β to get criticality as one increases the dimensionality of the lattice and increases the range of J_{ij} so that there are more 'neighbours' to each site i.

We can get much the same 'action' out of our Ising financial model above without indulging in the 'ad-hocery' (to some) of introducing noise traders as follows. Let all traders be fundamentalist but let their demands be given by

$$D(p, i) = [E_t y_{t+1} - Rp - aC_t(y_{t+1}, w_{i.t+1})]aV_t(y_{t+1}) \qquad (27)$$

where C_t is conditional covariance between income, y_{t+1}, from the asset and 'own' income, $w_{i.t+1}$. Demand functions of the form (27) can be derived from a utility function of terminal wealth of the form $U = -\exp[-aW]$, provided W is normally distributed conditional on t which will be the case if $(y_{t+1}, w_{i.t+1})$ is conditionally normally distributed. One may now design a conditional covariance structure that is Ising and motivate it by citing Gertler (1988) for evidence of domino effects on 'own income' and covariance C_t through credit crunches, perhaps.

Before closing this article we stress that the local neighbourhood structure represents a major flaw of this kind of model for economics and finance which is a globally connected system in reality. Economic agents probably react more to global signals than to local signals from their neighbours, however interpreted. While we have modelled prices as a global connector we have left out many other sources of global connection such as news reports. Analytically tractable models with long-range interactions with an Ising flavour include the Curie–Weiss model and the circle model (*cf.* Ellis, 1985). However, it is not clear that any microeconomic foundation exists for any of these structures.

Perhaps an even bigger gap is the lack of any discussion of how the models might contribute to an understanding of the decomposition of economic movements into the low frequencies studied by growth theory, the higher business cycle frequencies studied by macroeconomists and the high frequency movements in asset prices studied by the field of finance.

However, despite these gaps the analytic tractibility and the intellectual beauty of the class of models discused in this article may stimulate the imagination enough to help us build better models.

140 W. A. BROCK

6. SUMMARY AND CONCLUSIONS

We have tried to show how ideas from non-linear science and complex systems theory, especially statistical mechanics models such as Ising models and 'sandpile' models, can be integrated with more familiar economic modelling to shed light on possible mechanisms that might generate the patterns of strong persistence we see in many economic time series. Since these ideas are not part of the mainstream economic literature, we have had to write this paper rather in the style of a research proposal. While it is too early to tell whether any of the ideas discussed here will lead to any advances in economic science we do hope they are suggestive of exciting research topics. Indeed, we intend to put a lot of effort into researching these topics in the future.

REFERENCES

ANDERSON, P., ARROW, K. and PINES, D. (1988). *The Economy as an Evolving Complex System.* Sante Fe Institute Studies in the Sciences of Complexity, Volume V. Addison Wesley, Redwood City, CA.

BAK, P. and CHEN, K. (1991). 'Self-Organized Criticality', *Scientific American*, January, 46–53.

BARRO, R. (1989). 'A Cross-Country Study of Growth, Savings, and Government', NBER W.P. No. 2855.

BECKER, G. (1962). 'Irrational Behaviour and Economic Theory', *Journal of Political Economy*, **70**, 1–13.

BENNETT, C. and BOURZUTSCHKY, M. (1991) 'Non-criticality of the Cellular Automaton "Life".' Submitted for publication.

BROCK, W. (1982). 'Asset Prices in A Production Economy', in J. McCall (ed.), *The Economics of Information and Uncertainty.* The University of Chicago Press, Chicago.

——, LAKONISHOK, J. and LEBARON, B. (1990). 'Simple Technical Trading Rules and the Stochastic Properties of Stock Returns', Social Systems Research Institute W.P. No. 9022. The University of Wisconsin, Madison.

CRUTCHFIELD, J. and KANEKO, K. (1987). 'Phenomonology of Spatio-Temporal Chaos', in H. Bai-lin (ed.), *Directions in Chaos.* World Scientific, Singapore.

DIEBOLD, F. and RUDEBUSCH, G. (1990). 'Have Postwar Economic Fluctuations Been Stabilized'. Department of Economics, The University of Pennsylvania.

DURLAUF, S. (1989a). 'Locally Interacting Systems, Coordination Failure, and The Behaviour of Aggregate Activity'. Department of Economics, Stanford University.

—— (1989b). 'Output Persistence, Economics Structure and the Choice of Stabilization Policy', *Brookings Papers on Economic Activity*, **2**, 69–116.

ELLIS, R. (1985). *Entropy, Large Deviations and Statistical Mechanics.* Springer-Verlag, New York.

GERTLER, M. (1988). 'Financial Structure and Aggregate Economic Activity: An Overview', *Journal of Money, Credit, and Banking*, **20**, 559–588.

GREIS, N. and GREENSIDE, H. (1990), 'Does a Power-Law Power-Spectrum Imply Self-Affinity?' Department of Economics, North Carolina State University.

GRINSTEIN, G., JAYAPRAKASH, C. and HE, Y. (1985). 'Statistical Mechanics of Probabilistic Cellular Automata', *Physical Review Letters*, **55**, 2527–2530.

HAUBRICH, J. and LO, A. (1988). 'The Sources and Nature of Long-Term Memory in The Business Cycle'. Department of Finance, The Wharton School of the University of Pennsylvania.

KADANOFF, L., NAGEL, S., WU, L. and ZHOU, S. (1989). 'Scaling and Universality in Avalanches', *Physical Review A*, **39**, 6524–6537.

KEELER, J. and FARMER, J. (1986). 'Robust Space–Time Intermittency and $1/f$ Noise', *Physica*, **23D**, 413–435.

KING, R., PLOSSER, C. and REBELO, S. (1988). 'Production, Growth, and Business Cycles: I. The Basic Neoclassical Model', *Journal of Monetary Economics*, **21**, 309–342.

LEBARON, B. (1990). 'Some Relations Between Volatility and Serial Correlations in Stock Market Returns', SSRI W.P. No. 9002. The University of Wisconsin, Madison.

LI, W. (1990a). 'Expansion–Modification Systems: A Model for Spatial $1/f$ Spectra'. Santa Fe Institute Working Paper No. 90-012. *Physical Review A*, 43 (10), 1991 (forthcoming).

—— (1990b). 'Absence of $1/f$ Spectra in Dow Jones Daily Price'. Santa Fe Institute Working Paper No. 90–009.

LORIE, J. and BREALEY, R. (eds) (1972). *Modern Developments in Investment Management*. Praeger, New York.

LUCAS, R. (1988). 'On the Mechanics of Economic Development', *Journal of Monetary Economics*, **22**, 3–42.

MANSKI, C. and MCFADDEN, D. (1981). *Structural Analysis of Discrete Data with Econometric Applications*. MIT Press, Cambridge, MA.

MEZARD, M., PARISI, G. and VIRASORA, M. (1987). *Spin Glass Theory and Beyond*. World Scientific, Singapore.

MIROWSKI, P. (1990). 'From Mandelbrot to Chaos in Economic Theory', *Southern Economic Journal*, **57**, 289–307.

NELSON, C. and PLOSSER, C. (1982). 'Trends and Random Walks in Macroeconomic Time Series', *Journal of Monetary Economics*, **10**, 139–162.

POTTER, S. (1990). 'Nonlinear Time Series and Economic Fluctuations'. PhD Thesis, Department of Economics, The University of Wisconsin.

REICHL, L. (1980). *A Modern Course in Statistical Physics*. University of Texas Press, Austin.

ROMER, P. (1986). 'Increasing Returns and Long Run Growth', *Journal of Political Economy*, **94**, 1002–1073.

SARGENT, T. (1987a). *Macroeconomic Theory*. Academic Press, New York.

—— (1987b). *Dynamic Macroeconomic Theory*. Harvard University Press, Cambridge, MA.

SHLEIFER, A. and SUMMERS, L. (1990). 'The Noise trader Approach to Finance', *The Journal of Economic Perspectives*, **4**, 19–34.

TAYLOR, S. (1986). *Modelling Financial Time Series*. Wiley, Chichester.

—— (1990). 'Rewards Available to Currency Futures Speculators: Compensation For Risk or Evidence of Inefficient Pricing?'. University of Lancaster, Lancaster.

VAGA, T. (1990). 'The Coherent Market Hypothesis', *Financial Analysts Journal*, November/December, 36–49.

[3]

The Economic Journal, 100 (Conference 1990), 33–48
Printed in Great Britain

NONLINEARITIES IN ECONOMIC DYNAMICS*

José A. Scheinkman

Nonlinear models played an important role in modelling economic dynamics during the first part of this century (cf. e.g. Kaldor (1940), Hicks (1950) and Goodwin (1951)). By the 1960s, however, the profession had largely switched to the linear approach making use of Slutzky's (1927) observation that stable low order linear stochastic difference equations could generate cyclic processes that mimicked actual business cycles.

In the context of business cycle modelling there seem to have been at least two reasons that led to the dominance of the linear stochastic difference equations approach. The first one was the fact that the nonlinear systems seemed incapable of reproducing the 'statistical' aspects of actual economic time series. At best, such models were able to produce periodic motion[1] and an examination of the spectra of economic time series showed the absence of the spikes that characterise periodic data. The emphasis on the equilibrium approach to aggregate economic behaviour (cf. Lucas (1986)) would make things even more difficult. The plethora of stability results for models of infinitely lived agents with perfect foresight (Turnpike Theorems) suggested that even the regular fluctuations that had been derived in the literature on endogenous business cycles were incompatible with a theory that had solid microeconomic foundations. Further this indicated that while nonlinearities could be present, the explanations of the fluctuations had to rest solely on the presence of exogenous shocks that working through the equilibrating mechanism would create the observed randomness. If such shocks were absent, the system would tend to a stationary state.

The second reason was the empirical success of the models based on linear stochastic difference equations. Low order autoregressive processes captured some of the features of aggregate time series. In turn these processes can in principle result from an economy with complete markets where production is subject to exogenous shocks. Though the task of confronting these equilibrium models with actual data has not yielded uncontroversial results (see the discussion and references in Section I) there was no obvious gain in the introduction of nonlinearities.[2]

* The Harry Johnson Lecture. I thank William Brock, Lars Hansen, David Hsieh, Blake LeBaron, Robert Lucas, A. R. Nobay, and Michael Woodford. I owe a special debt to Michele Boldrin who made extensive comments on a first draft and helped me clarify the example at the end of Section I. I also benefited from several discussions on the subject of nonlinear dynamics with the participants at the workshops on 'The Economy as an Evolving Complex System' at the Santa Fe Institute in 1987 and 1988.

[1] There were exceptions: Ando and Modigliani (1959) realised that endogenous cycle models could produce more complicated behaviour.

[2] A third perhaps equally compelling reason is that linear or log linear models are much easier to solve and estimate. In the analysis of certain equilibrium models where one must consider explicitly the agents' forecast of the future evolution of endogenous variables the certainty equivalence principle (Simon, 1956; Theil, 1964) that applies to the linear case greatly simplifies things.

Similar conclusions appeared to be warranted from the literature on asset prices. For the most part a random walk seemed to adequately describe stock returns over periods at least as long as a week (Fama, 1970). The equilibrium asset pricing models that followed the work of Rubinstein (1976), Lucas (1978) and others, by linking stock returns to consumption variability provided, in principle, a role for nonlinearities. However, the attempts to implement these models involved parameterisations where, in the absence of shocks, fluctuations would be absent. Reasoning similar to the one concerning macroeconomic fluctuations indicated that this was the general situation.

It is now well known that deterministic systems can generate dynamics that are extremely irregular. A simple example is given by the 'tent map' $f:[0, 1] \rightarrow [0, 1]$ such that $f(x) = 2x$ if $0 < x \leqslant 1/2$, $f(x) = 2(1-x)$ if $1/2 < x \leqslant 1$. For a given x_0, let $x_t = f(x_{t-1})$, $t = 1, 2, \ldots$. This gives us a time series $\{x_t\}_{t=0}^{\infty}$. For some particular x_0 the series x_t is quite well behaved as for example when $x_0 = 2/3$ and consequently $x_t = 2/3$ for all $t = 1, 2, \ldots$. For others (cf. Fig. 1) the x_t's seem to follow a very complicated trajectory. This is the general case. In fact, it can be shown (cf. Sakai and Tokumaru (1980)) that for almost all $x_0 \in [0, 1]$ the autocorrelation at lag k of $\{x_t\}$ will be zero for any $k \neq 0$. Thus its spectra is exactly that of white noise. Many other examples of such 'chaotic' systems can be constructed – some that imitate a stationary $AR(1)$, some involving smooth functions and in higher dimension even invertible functions.[3]

Though there are many, nonequivalent ways of defining chaos, for our

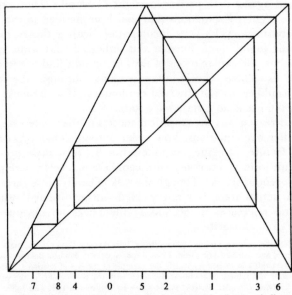

Fig. 1. Text map iterations. In this figure o indicates the initial point x_0, 1 indicates $x_1 = f(x_0)$, 2 indicates $x_2 = f(x_1)$ etc.

[3] Baumol and Benhabib (1988) provide a simple exposition of how chaos arises in one dimensional difference equations.

purposes a system $x_t = f(x_{t-1})$ where f maps a closed bounded set into itself is chaotic if it exhibits sensitive dependence to initial conditions, that is, small differences in initial conditions tend to be amplified by f. It should be obvious that the trajectories of such systems have to be quite complicated. In Section IV below I define what is meant by sensitive dependence and discuss its implications for dynamic economics.

Over the last few years a literature has developed where such complicated dynamics appears in equilibrium models where agents optimise while provided with perfect foresight (cf. Section I below). As I argue in section I, it is extremely unreasonable to believe that purely deterministic models could ever explain the behaviour of aggregate quantities or asset prices in actual economies. None the less the developments discussed in the preceding paragraphs show that nonlinearities could, in theory, explain part of the observed fluctuations in quantities or asset prices.

The tent map example also shows that linear statistical techniques may not be enough to dismiss the influence of nonlinearities. Examples such as these led to the development of measures to distinguish between data generated by a deterministic system from data generated by a 'random' system (cf. Grassberger and Procaccia (1983), Takens (1983)). Section II describes these tests as well as some applications that were made in economic time series. In Section III I expose the distribution theory developed by Brock *et al.* (1987) for statistics based on the Takens–Grassberger–Procaccia measure. Finally, Section V contains some conclusions.

I. EQUILIBRIUM MODELS THAT EXHIBIT COMPLEX DYNAMICS

Much recent work has been done showing that dynamic models with optimising agents can generate cyclic and/or chaotic trajectories. This work was done under a very strict set of rules. Agents maximise classical, i.e. concave, smooth, often time additive–objective functions subject to well defined constraints and are endowed with perfect foresight.

Benhabib and Nishimura (1979) showed that cyclical paths may arise in the context of continuous time multisector models of optimal growth with an additive, concave objective function in the presence of discounting. The well known connection between competitive equilibrium with perfect foresight and Pareto optimality can be used to reinterpret the paths that solve the Benhabib–Nishimura example as the equilibrium paths of an economy with homogeneous agents. These authors (cf. Benhabib and Nishimura (1985)) also produced an example of an infinite horizon discrete time single capital good model with optimal solutions that were two period cycles that is easy to describe. Consider an economy with a representative individual that possesses in each period an endowment of one unit of labour has a linear utility function for consumption and a discount factor δ. Leisure yields no utility. The single consumption good is produced in each period with the aid of capital (k) and labour (l) and output at time t equals $(l_t)^\beta (k_t)^\alpha$ where $l_t(k_t)$ equals the amount of labour (resp. capital) used in the production of the consumption good.

Capital depreciates totally in each period and the amount of capital available at time t equals the amount of labour used in the production of the capital good in period $t-1$. It is easy to see that the maximal utility enjoyed by the representative individual when he starts with an amount of capital k_t and produces an amount of capital k_{t+1} for the next period is $u(k_t, k_{t+1}) = (1-k_{t+1})^\beta (k_t)^\alpha$. Hence we may write the maximisation problem, using this indirect utility function as

(P) $$\text{Max} \sum_{t=0}^{\infty} \delta^t u(k_t, k_{t+1}), k_0 \text{ given.}$$

This example with $\alpha = \beta = 0.5$ was actually introduced by Weitzman (cf. Samuelson (1973)) to generate cycles with δ near 1. Weitzman's example is not however stable with respect to perturbations since if $\alpha + \beta < 1$, and δ is close to one all optimal paths converge to the unique optimal stationary state (cf. Scheinkman (1976)). Benhabib and Nishimura showed that for $\alpha + \beta < 1$, $\alpha > 0.5$ and δ small, a cycle of order two is the optimal solution for an appropriate initial k_0.

It is also not difficult to determine that a two period cycle is the most complicated behaviour one can obtain in this class of examples. Associated with a problem as (P) we have a policy function that gives the optimal capital stock at time t as a function of the capital stock at time $t-1$. In the usual Cass–Koopmans one sector model this policy function is nondecreasing and thus no cyclical behaviour can appear. One can readily verify that in the example above, the policy function is monotone and hence either there are no cycles or a cycle of period two arises.[4]

Ivar Ekeland and I (cf. Scheinkman (1984)) suggested that the following modification would generate arbitrarily long cycles for appropriate parameter values. Let
$$u(k_t, k_{t+1}) = (1-k_{t+1})^\beta (k_t - \gamma k_{t+1})^\alpha, \gamma < 1.$$

The story is just as before, except that to produce tomorrow's capital one needs one unit of labour and γ units of today's capital, in fixed proportions. Boldrin and Deneckere (1987) showed that this conjecture was in fact correct.

While these examples helped one understand the assumptions on tastes and technologies that would lead to complicated dynamics they did not provide the characterisation of the set of possible types of trajectories that could appear in these models. This question was settled by Boldrin and Montruchio (1986) that established that any (sufficiently smooth) dynamics can arise in the setting of multisector models of optimal growth with an additive, concave objective function by a suitable choice of utility function, technology and discount factor. Again, we may use the link between competitive equilibrium with perfect foresight and Pareto optimality to rephrase this result in terms of equilibria.

Other examples were derived by Benhabib and Day (1982) and Grandmont (1985) for overlapping generations economies and Woodford (1987) in the context of a model with infinitely lived consumers under borrowing constraints.

This research puts the literature on fluctuations arising from a purely

[4] Cf. Scheinkman (1984), Section 3.

deterministic system on an equal theoretical footing with the literature where such fluctuations result from exogenous shocks that constantly impact an intrinsically stable economy that otherwise would converge towards some steady state. Another entirely different matter is whether these systems are capable of fitting observed economic time series or at least of being calibrated to generate data that grossly mimics some of the statistical properties of the actual data.

Kydland and Prescott (1982) showed that a slightly modified neoclassical one good optimal growth model could, in the presence of exogenous technology shocks, generate time series that would mimic a few of the characteristics of some Post War U.S. aggregate economic time series. Further, the free parameters in the model were chosen to be somewhat consistent with microeconomic and growth observations.

There are no comparable results for the literature on deterministic fluctuations. It is extremely unlikely that macroeconomic fluctuations could ever be explained by a purely deterministic model with a manageable number of state variables. There are even theoretical reasons to support this view. The same property that makes chaotic systems look as if they were random – their sensitivity to initial conditions – makes it difficult to forecast future values of the variables that agents take as exogenous. This problem is not dissimilar to that of choosing the correct value of the costate variable in infinite horizon optimisation problems (cf. Hahn (1966)). Rational agents in such a situation would quickly understand the limitations on their ability to predict. At this point such agents may very well act as I do when facing the purely deterministic process of tossing a coin – namely, treat it as if the future values of the variables they are trying to predict are at least in part random.

None the less, nonlinearities may still be responsible for a good part of the apparent fluctuations. Much seems not to be accounted by the log-linear models of real business cycles. One difficulty pointed out by Murphy *et al.* (1989) is with explaining the observed positive correlation of output comovements across sectors. One could always assume that productivity shocks are common to all sectors, but unless that involves the cheapening of some common input or equivalently a productivity shock to a commonly used input, it seems unlikely. Murphy *et al.* argue that the data do not support the hypothesis that productivity shocks to a common input are responsible for the cycle.

All fully worked out examples in the literature on equilibrium fluctuations arising from purely deterministic systems involve single variable systems. This is due to the fact that easily checkable sufficient conditions for chaotic behaviour cover principally the single variable case. The conditions that insure chaos in multi-dimensional systems mostly involve the calculation of Liapunov exponents (cf. Section IV below) although some results by Marotto (1978) may be applicable. None the less, the mathematical intuition indicates that multi-dimensional systems can more easily give rise to chaotic dynamics than single variable ones. Nonlinear systems involving several variables are capable of getting in phase even when coupled by very weak links as in the case of coupled

38   THE ECONOMIC JOURNAL   [CONFERENCE

oscillators. Hence adding nonlinearities may improve our ability to explain the comovements.[5] Further, in the log-linear models, an important role is played by sizable and persistent technology shocks for which no good explanations exist. The introduction of nonlinearities may very well reduce the role played by these shocks.

Though some of the empirical tests described in what follows have been applied to macroeconomic time series the shortness of these series makes it hard to distinguish the presence of nonlinearities. Besides the possibility of explaining the observed comovements and diminishing the size and persistence of the exogenous shocks nonlinear models may play an important role in reconciling the existence of a cycle with the apparent unit root behaviour of aggregate time series. This is discussed in Section IV below.

Any equilibrium model has associated with it an asset pricing model. Interpreted as asset pricing models the purely deterministic models with perfect foresight have a strong prediction that is easily rejected by data. If short sales are permitted, or even if assets are held in positive net supply, the returns on all assets must be identical. This follows easily from the no-arbitrage relationships. Hence, once again, one must either assume the presence of some exogenous noise or weaken the notion of perfect foresight.

The difficulty of forecasting future values of a variable generated by chaotic systems seems to make necessary weakening the notion of perfect foresight. The following example is helpful. Consider an economy with homogeneous agents and a single type of machine. This machine outputs at time t an amount of the (non-storable) consumption good that equals x_t. The quantity x_t satisfies $x_t = f(x_{t-1})$ where f is the 'tent' map described above. The utility function of each agent is given by

$$U(c_1, c_2, \ldots, c_t, \ldots) = E \sum_{t-1}^{\infty} \delta^t (c_t)^{(1-\alpha)}/(1-\alpha); \alpha > 0.$$

The rights to the output of the machine are traded in a competitive market and its price at time t is given by p_t. Since, in equilibrium $c_t = x_t$, we must have at each time t,

$$p_t(x_t)^{-\alpha} = \delta E[(x_{t+1})^{-\alpha}(p_{t+1} + x_{t+1})/I_t)], \tag{1}$$

where I_t denotes the information used at time t by each of the homogeneous agents to predict future dividends and prices.

Of course one possible candidate for an equilibrium is the perfect foresight path. In this case agents perfectly predict as of time zero not only x_t but also p_t. Suppose however that agents are restricted to linear regressions of vector of variables on their past values. Then by looking at the single variable x_t one could not reject the hypothesis that the x_t's are distributed independently and uniformly in the interval $[0, 1]$. If the x_t's were in fact independently and identically distributed (i.i.d.) and the information that each agent uses at time t is the known distribution of x_t then a solution to (1) is given by

$$p_t = \lambda_\alpha(x_t)^\alpha \text{ where } \lambda_\alpha = [\delta/(1-\delta)] E(x_{t+1})^{1-\alpha}. \tag{2}$$

[5] This idea arose in conversations with Mike Woodford.

If $\alpha = 1$, i.e. the logarithmic utility function, then in fact the p_t given by (2) is a linear function of x_t and hence if we restrict agents to linear regressions of the observables (x_t, p_t) on their past values they could not reject the hypothesis that the dividends and prices are i.i.d. That is, if agents assumed that dividends where i.i.d., then $p_t = \lambda_1 x_t$ would be the candidate equilibrium prices and, in fact, agents could not use past prices and/or dividends to help predict future ones if they were restricted to linear regressions. One could then argue that such an economy would behave as if dividends where i.i.d. For any other value of α however, the prices given by (2) will not constitute an equilibrium even in the case where agents are restricted to linear regressions. The fact that the candidate equilibrium prices given by (2) are a nonlinear function of dividends means that one can use current dividends and prices to predict future prices linearly. In the case $\alpha = 0.5$, for instance, if the p_t's are given by (2), a regression of p_t on p_{t-1} and x_{t-1} yields an R^2 that typically exceeds 0.8 whereas that of x_t on p_{t-1} and x_{t-1} produces an R^2 that typically exceeds 0.7.[6] Hence if the market were to produce prices as if the x_t's are i.i.d., individuals using only linear regression would be able to predict future dividends and prices with some accuracy. Hence the hypothesis that the agent's information at t consists solely of the unconditional distribution of the x_t's would not be correct.

Implicit in this reasoning is a limitation on agents' ability to learn. They start with a prior that dividends are i.i.d. and that the distribution of prices is that implied by (2). They 'learn' by running linear regressions of the observables in their past values. In the logarithmic case this 'learning' would not lead them to alter their priors. This is not true for other values of α, but we have not taken the story far enough to exhibit actual equilibria.

In any case, nonlinearities may be responsible for a share of the apparent randomness in asset prices. In the next two sections we exposit some techniques that have been used to examine this question in actual economic data. In Section II we discuss the use of the correlation dimension measure. The basic idea behind the use of this measure is that in a deterministic system given by $x_{t+1} = f(x_t), x_t \in R^n$, the pairs of successive observations (x_t, x_{t+1}) lie in the graph of the function f and hence in a lower dimensional set than if the x_t's are 'random'. Section II describes these tests as well as some applications that were made to economic time series. The techniques discussed in Section II have the disadvantage that they are not accompanied by a distribution theory for the relevant statistics. Brock *et al.* (1987) produced an asymptotic theory for statistics based on the correlation dimension and this material is discussed in Section III.

II. THE CORRELATION DIMENSION

The earlier efforts in applying the ideas of chaotic dynamics in order to uncover nonlinear dependence in economic data (cf. Scheinkman (1985), Brock (1986)) consisted simply of using certain tools developed in the mathematics and

---

[6] This should not be surprising since the tent can be well approximated by a linear combination of the square root function and a linear function.

physics literature in a rather direct way. The most promising of these practices make use of the correlation dimension.

Let $\mathbf{y}_1, \mathbf{y}_2, \ldots$ be a sequence of vectors in R^p. For each $\gamma > 0$, let

$$C_m(\gamma) = \frac{2}{m(m-1)} \sum_{1 \leqslant i < j \leqslant m} \theta(\gamma - |y_i - y_j|),$$

where
$$\theta(a) = 0 \quad \text{if } a < 0$$
$$= 1 \quad \text{if } a \geqslant 0.$$

Here,
$$|y_i - y_j| = \max_k |y_i^k - y_j^k|.$$

Intuitively $C_m(\gamma)$ denotes the fraction of the first m vectors y_t's that are within γ of each other. For each γ, let

$$C(\gamma) = \lim_{m \to \infty} C_m(\gamma).$$

The quantity $C(\gamma)$ indicates the fraction of all vectors that are within γ of each other. Finally, let us define the correlation dimension of $\{y_t\}_{t=0}^{\infty}$ as

$$d = \lim_{\gamma \to 0} \frac{\log C(\gamma)}{\log \gamma}.$$

Intuition of why d is a measure of 'dimension' can be obtained by considering two examples.

Example 1: Let $\mathbf{y}_t = (x_t, x_{t+1})$ where each x_t is an independent draw of a uniform distribution in $[0, 1]$. Here as we double γ we expect to multiply by four the number of neighbours of each point. Hence $d = 2$.

Example 2: Let $\mathbf{y}_t = (x_t, \alpha x_t)$ where x_t is again an independent draw of a uniform distribution in $[0, 1]$. Here as we double γ we expect the number of neighbours to double. Hence $d = 1$.

Suppose now we are given a sequence of real numbers $x_1, x_2, \ldots$. For each N let $\mathbf{z}_t^N = (x_t, x_{t+1}, \ldots, x_{t+N-1})$, the vector of N-histories of the x's. We will write C_m^N, C^N and d^N for the quantities corresponding to C_m, C and d when $\mathbf{y}_t = \mathbf{z}_t^N$. The length of the histories, N, is called the embedding dimension. Note that

$$C_m^N(\gamma) = \frac{2}{m(m-1)} \sum_{1 \leqslant i < j \leqslant m} \prod_{k=0}^{N-1} [\theta(\gamma - |x_{i+k} - x_{j+k}|)].$$

Consider again the tent map discussed in the introduction. For a given x_0 let $x_t = f(x_{t-1})$, $t = 1, 2, \ldots$ Clearly $d^2 \leqslant 1$, since all $\mathbf{z}_t^2$'s must lie on the graph of the tent map. On the other hand, if the x_t's are independently and uniformly distributed in $[0, 1]$, as we discussed in Example 1 above, $d^2 = 2$. Hence using the correlation dimension we can distinguish between the two possibilities!

This reasoning generalises. Suppose $y_0 \in R^p$ is given and $y_t = F(y_{t-1})$, $t = 1, 2, \ldots$. Let d be the correlation dimension of $\{y_t\}_{t=0}^{\infty}$, $h: R^p \to R$ be given and $x_t = h(y_t)$. One may think of the x_t's as observation on the y_t's. Again, let

$\mathbf{z}_t^N = (x_t, x_{t+1}, \ldots, x_{t+N-1})$. Then $d^N \leqslant d$, i.e. the 'embedding dimension' does not increase indefinitely with N. Further, under some rather general conditions if $N \geqslant 2p+1$ then $d^N = d$.[7] Hence one can even find out the dimension of the unobservable time series $\{y_t\}_{t=0}^{\infty}$. On the other hand, just as in example 1 above, if the x_t's are independently and identically distributed (i.i.d.) on $[0, 1]$ and have a density then $d^N = N$.

These ideas provide a basis for distinguishing among deterministic and random systems by estimating the limit of the ratio $\log C_m^N(\gamma)/\log \gamma$ as γ becomes small for each N. Here m is the length of your data series minus the length of the longest history you are considering. The estimated $\hat{d}^N$ should stabilise as N increases if your data were generated by a deterministic system.

One can accommodate a mixture of a deterministic system contaminated by a small amount of randomness, i.e. the observed $x_t = h(y_t) + \mu_t$ where the μ_t's are i.i.d. Looking at deterministic systems were noise distributed uniformly $[-\alpha, \alpha]$ is added to a system of known dimension, many researchers (e.g. Zardecki (1982); Ben-Mizrachi *et al.* (1984); Atten and Caputto (1985)) have found that the graph of $\log [C_m^N(\gamma)]$ against $\log (\gamma)$ has the slope of the embedding dimension (i.e. N) for $\gamma \leqslant \alpha$, and has the slope of the dimension of the deterministic system above that level. Thus at a certain scale one observes behaviour as in a random system, while at a larger scale one sees the deterministic motion.

The application of these techniques to economics present several problems. First the time series in economics tend to be much shorter than it seems necessary to obtain good estimates when the dimensions of the original variable y_t is moderately large (above 2 or 3). There are a few exceptions in finance. More importantly as we argued above it is unlikely that the economic time series of interest are generated by purely deterministic systems. Further the uncertainty is likely to affect the dynamics itself as opposed to merely affecting the observable.

These comments apply specially to estimates of the dimension of the system that cannot be taken as anything but suggestive.[8] Nevertheless these techniques can be useful in detecting the presence of nonlinear dependence on data and inspired the formal statistical tests discussed in the next section.

III. DISTRIBUTION THEORY

Recall that $C_m^N(\gamma)$ is interpreted as the fraction of the first m N-histories that are within γ of each other. Let $x_1, x_2, \ldots$ be independent with a common distribution F. For each $\gamma > 0$, it is expected that, for m large

$$C_m^N(\gamma) \sim [C_m^1(\gamma)]^N. \tag{3}$$

In fact, Brock, Dechert and Scheinkman (1987) (henceforth BDS) established that $\sqrt{m}\{C_m^N(\gamma) - [C_m^1(\gamma)]^N\}$ converges to a normal law. In this section we will

[7] The interested reader may consult Takens (1983) for precise statements.

[8] See Ramsey and Yuan (1987) for a discussion of the effect of the smallness of a data set on the computation of the dimension.

present the BDS result and indicate some extensions. Let us again write $z_t = (x_t, \ldots, x_{t+N-1})$ for the vectors of N-histories of the x's. A key point in the BDS approach was the recognition that

$$C_m^N(\gamma) = \frac{2}{m(m-1)} \sum_{1 \leqslant i < j \leqslant m} \prod_{k=0}^{N-1} \theta(\gamma - |x_{i+k} - x_{j+k}|) \qquad (4)$$

is a U-Statistic in the sense of Hoeffding (1948).[9] Several results concerning Central Limit Theorems for U-Statistics exist in the literature. Modern treatments of the theory of U-Statistics can be found in Serfling (1980) and Denker and Keller (1983).

In BDS (1987) the following theorem was proved.

THEOREM

If the x_j's are i.i.d. then, $\sqrt{m}\{C_m^N(\gamma) - [C_m^1(\gamma)]^N\} \to N(0, \sigma)$.

Further in the case where the distribution F is continuous a formula to compute a consistent estimator for σ was given.

The proof of the theorem as stated here can be exposited in a straightforward manner if we forego the estimates of σ. We will do so and we will separate the argument in several steps. In what follows we will write $C(\gamma)$ for the probability that two arbitrary x_j's are within γ of each other.

Step 1 : Notice that for any pair λ_1, λ_2 and for any realisation of the histories z_1, $z_2, \ldots, z_m$ we can write,

$$\lambda_1 C_m^N(\gamma) + \lambda_2 C_m^1(\gamma) = [2/m(m-1)] \sum_{1 \leqslant i < j \leqslant m} h(z_i, z_j),$$

where

$$h(z_i, z_j) = \lambda_1 \prod_{k=0}^{N-1} \theta(\gamma - |x_{i+k} - x_{j+k}|) + \lambda_2 \theta(\gamma - |x_i - x_j|),$$

and, $z_i = (x_i, x_{i+1}, \ldots, x_{i+N-1})$. The function h is symmetric, i.e. $h(\xi_1, \xi_2) = h(\xi_2, \xi_1)$ for any pair of vectors $(\xi_1, \xi_2) \in R^{2N}$. Hence $\lambda_1 C_m^N(\gamma) + \lambda_2 C_m^1(\gamma)$ is a U-statistic and further even though two arbitrary histories z_t and z_τ are not in general independent, they will so be if $|t - \tau| > N$. Hence the theorems of Sen (1963) apply and since $Eh(z_i, z_j) = \lambda_1[C(\gamma)]^N + \lambda_2 C(\gamma)$ if $|i - j| > N$, $\sqrt{m}\{\lambda_1 C_m^N(\gamma) + \lambda_2 C_m^1(\gamma) - \lambda_1[C(\gamma)]^N - \lambda_2 C(\gamma)\}$ is asymptotically normal. In the case where F (the distribution of x_1) is continuous the formula from Sen (1963) can be used to compute the variance $\sigma(\lambda_1, \lambda_2)$ of the normal distribution.

Step 2 : Consider now the vector $[C_m^N(\gamma), C_m^1(\gamma)]$. Since a bivariate distribution is normal if (and only if) all linear combinations of its components are normal, we can use Step 1 to conclude immediately that $\sqrt{m}([C_m^N(\gamma), C_m^1(\gamma)] - \{[C(\gamma)]^N, C(\gamma)\})$ is asymptotically $N(0, \Sigma)$, for a 2×2 matrix Σ with $\Sigma_{11} = \sigma(1, 0)$, $\Sigma_{22} = \sigma(0, 1)$, $\Sigma_{12} = \Sigma_{21} = [\sigma(1, 1) - \sigma(1, 0) - \sigma(0, 1)]/2$.

---

[9] Originally U-statistics were defined for the case where $y_1, y_2, \ldots$ are i.i.d. A symmetric function $h: R^N \to R$ is a kernel for μ if $\mu = Eh(y_1, \ldots, y_N)$. Corresponding to the kernel h there is a U-statistic $U(y_1, \ldots, y_m) = \binom{m}{N}^{-1} \Sigma h(y_{i_1}, \ldots, y_{i_N})$ where the summation is over all $\binom{m}{N}$ combinations of N distinct elements $(i_1, \ldots, i_N)$ from $\{1, \ldots, m\}$.

Step 3: Finally consider $C_m^N(\gamma) - [C_m^1(\gamma)]^N = g[C_m^N(\gamma), C_m^1(\gamma)]$, where $g(u, v) = u - v^N$. Since $\sqrt{m}G(X_m)$ is asymptotically normal if $\sqrt{m}X_m \to (0, \Sigma)$ and G has non-zero gradients (this uses what is known in statistics as the delta method) we have our desired result. More precisely,[10]

$$\sqrt{m}\{C_m^N(\gamma) - [C_m^1(\gamma)]^N\} \to N(0, \sigma),$$

where

$$\sigma = [\partial g/\partial u, \partial g/\partial v]' \, \Sigma[\partial g/\partial u, \partial g/\partial v] = \{1, N[C(\gamma)]^{N-1}\}' \, \Sigma\{1, N[C(\gamma)]^{N-1}\}.$$

There are straightforward generalisations of the BDS theorem. Several forms of dependence can be treated with the use of theorems on U-statistics established by Denker and Keller (1983). These theorems allow one to deal with a strictly stationary process $x_1, x_2, \ldots$ which satisfies a mixing condition.

Since in this case the probability that two N histories are within γ of each other is no longer, in general, equal to the probability that two arbitrary points be no farther than γ, the statement of the result must change. Let F_N denote the distribution of the vectors of N histories, and

$$C^N(\gamma) = \iint \left[\prod_{k=0}^{N-1} \theta(\gamma - |x_{i+k} - x_{j+k}|) \right] dF_N(\mathbf{z}_i) dF_N(\mathbf{z}_j)$$

and

$$\mathbf{z}_l = (x_l, \ldots, x_{l+N-1}).$$

Then,

$$\sqrt{m}(C_m^N(\gamma) - [C_m^1(\gamma)]^N - \{C^N(\gamma) - [C(\gamma)]^N\}) \to N(0, \sigma).$$

The computation of the variance of the estimator under any specific alternative hypothesis to i.i.d. can also be quite complicated. Hsieh and LeBaron (1988a) restate the theorem and propose numerical methods to implement the test under these conditions.

The BDS theorem can be used to test for departures from i.i.d. in data sets where linear tests failed. As such it has power against simple nonlinear deterministic systems that 'look' random from the linear viewpoint – as the 'tent' map mentioned above – as well as related nonlinear stochastic systems. Simulations reported in BDS, Brock *et al.* (1988), and Hsieh and LeBaron (1988a, b) show that it has good power against many of the favourite nonlinear alternatives. There are of course many other tests for nonlinearities.[11] Further this test has been used to detect departures from random walk behaviour in several economic time series including stock returns (cf. Scheinkman and LeBaron (1989a), LeBaron (1988)), foreign exchange rates (Gallant *et al.* 1988; Hsieh, 1989), and some macroeconomic time series (Brock and Sayers, 1988; Scheinkman and LeBaron, 1989b).

The fact that $C_m^N(\gamma)$ is a U-statistic, and that smooth functions of asymptotically normal variables are themselves asymptotically normal, can also be used to show asymptotically normal behaviour of statistics related to several of the measures discussed earlier as the following examples show.

---

[10] Cf. Serfling (1980), chapter 3.
[11] Some popular examples are in Engle (1982), Hinich (1982) and Tsay (1986).

Example 1 : Note that $\lambda_1 C_m^N(\gamma_1) + \lambda_2 C_m^P(\gamma_2)$ is also a U-statistic for any vector of parameters $(\lambda_1, \gamma_1, N, \lambda_2, \gamma_2, P)$. For simplicity suppose again that the x_j's are independent. Just as in Steps 1 and 2 of the proof of the theorem above one shows that the vector $\sqrt{m}\{C_m^N(\gamma_1) - [C(\gamma_1)]^N, C_m^N(\gamma_2) - [C(\gamma_2)]^N\}$ is asymptotically a bivariate Normal $N(0, \Sigma)$. Let $g(z, y) = \log z - \log y$. Then $g'(x, y) \neq 0$ and hence it follows from the delta method that

$$\sqrt{m}[\log C_m^N(\gamma_1) - \log C_m^N(\gamma_2) - N\log C(\gamma_1) + N\log C(\gamma_2)] \text{ is } N(0, \sigma),$$

where $$\sigma = \{[C(\gamma_1)]^{-N}, [C(\gamma_2)]^{-N}\}' \Sigma \{[C(\gamma_1)]^{-N}, [C(\gamma_2)]^{-N}\}.$$

In this way one can in theory compute confidence intervals for measures of the slope of $\log [C^N(\gamma)]$ like the ones reported in Scheinkman and LeBaron's (1986). One difficulty lies in estimating the elements of Σ. This, in principle, can be done even in the more interesting case where the x_j's exhibit some dependence provided one is willing to assume enough mixing to apply the results from Denker and Keller. Again one must account for the fact that with dependence

$$\lim_{m \to \infty} C_m^N(\gamma) - [C_m^1(\gamma)]^N \neq 0$$

and that the dependence has also to be considered in the calculation of the asymptotic variance.

Example 2: Consider the quantity $S_m^N(\gamma) = C_m^{N+1}(\gamma)/C_m^N(\gamma)$ introduced by Scheinkman and LeBaron (1986). The expression

$$S^N(\gamma) = \lim_{m \to \infty} S_m^N(\gamma)$$

gives us the conditional probability that two points are no further than γ given that their past histories of length N are at least that close. Just as above, under independence, we can use the fact that the vector $\sqrt{m}\{C_m^{N+1}(\gamma) - [C(\gamma)]^{N+1}, C_m^N(\gamma) - [C(\gamma)]^N\}$ is asymptotically a bivariate Normal to infer that $\sqrt{m}[S_m^N(\gamma) - C(\gamma)]$ is itself asymptotically normal. Scheinkman and LeBaron (1989 *b*) contains a formula for estimating the variance of this distribution.

Frequently one is interested in finding nonlinear dependence on the residuals of particular models fitted to the data. In many macroeconomic time series, for example, low order autoregressive models are known to yield a good fit. In the analyses of foreign exchange rates, ARCH models (cf. Engle (1982)) were used by Hsieh (1989) to pre-filter the data.

In practice one can proceed as in Scheinkman and LeBaron (1989 *a, b*) to examine the distribution of the estimated residuals. First the model is estimated and a set of residuals is generated. These residuals are randomly reordered and data sets are then reconstructed using the estimated model. In each of these data sets one reestimates the model and measures the BDS statistics on the residuals. This 'bootstrap' like procedure is then used to determine the significance of the value of the statistics in the original residuals.

Another possibility is to use extensions of the BDS theorem that apply to the case where x_j's are estimated residuals. Some of these are discussed in Brock (1988) and Brock *et al.* (1988).

IV

From the viewpoint of economic dynamics there seem to be two related properties of nonlinear systems of interest. The first one is that such systems can generate the quasi-periodic or even erratic behaviour that characterises some of the economic time series. If the true system exhibits nonlinear dependence then treating the time series as if it was generated simply by a linear stochastic difference equation will lead us to have an exaggerated view of the amount of randomness affecting the system. The second is that such nonlinear systems can generate sensitive dependency to initial conditions, i.e. small initial differences can be magnified by the dynamics. Of course that is a property shared by unstable linear systems but in the nonlinear case this sensitive dependence can occur while the system remains confined to a bounded region which is a necessary requirement in some economic applications. The study of this sensitive dependence to initial conditions is at the heart of nonlinear dynamics and attempts to measure this sensitivity in data generated by dynamical systems are helped by an extremely well developed mathematical theory.

Let us start with a deterministic system $x_{t+1} = f(x_t)$ with f sufficiently smooth. If the initial state is disturbed the characteristic or Liapunov exponents measure the rate at which the initial perturbation increases (decreases). Let us write $x_t(x_0)$ for the solution that starts at x_0. Then, to a first order,

$$|x_T(x_0 + y_0) - x_T(x_0)| = |f^T(x_0 + y_0) - f^T(x_0)| \approx |Df^T(x_0) y_0|.$$

Recall that a probability measure ρ is an invariant measure for f if $\rho[f^{-1}(E)] = \rho(E)$ and that an invariant measure is called ergodic if $f^{-1}(E) = E$ implies that either $\rho(E) = 0$ or $\rho(E) = 1$.

Oseledec's theory (cf. Eckman and Ruelle (1985)) implies that under some regularity conditions if ρ is an invariant measure for f that is ergodic, for ρ-almost all x_0

$$\lambda(x_0, y_0) = \lim_{T \to \infty} [T^{-1} \log |Df^T(x_0)(y_0)|]$$

exists and equals one of possible N values $\lambda^1 \geqslant \ldots \geqslant \lambda^N$. Further for almost all y_0 this limit equals λ^1. In other words for almost all choices of x_0 and infinitesimal y_0 the change at time T, δx_T will satisfy

$$\delta x_T \approx y_0 e^{\lambda^1 T}.$$

In particular, if λ^1 is positive, small changes in initial conditions will tend to be amplified through time, i.e. the system will exhibit sensitive dependence to initial conditions. If the system lies in a bounded set such amplification cannot go on forever and it is precisely this combination of boundedness and sensitivity that characterises chaotic dynamics. The λ^i's are called the characteristic or Liapunov exponents of the map f.

These results remain true when one deals with a stochastic difference equation $x_{t+1} = f(x_t, \mu_t)$ where each t, $f(\cdot, \mu_t)$ is chosen at random independently and according to a fixed law (cf. Kifer (1986), for details). This, of course, is the case of interest for economic applications.

Eckman *et al.* (1986) construct an algorithm for computing Liapunov exponents from an experimental time series. Eckman *et al.* (1988) applied this algorithm to the CRSP value-weighted portfolio weekly returns and estimated $\lambda^1 = 0.15$/week. Since the distribution theory for this estimate is unknown, this value can at this time be taken only as suggestive.

Much attention had been paid recently to the existence of unit roots in macroeconomic time series as well as the implications of the presence of such unit roots. Quah (1987) constructs a stochastic process y_t where the conditional expectation of $y_{t+\tau}$ satisfies $E(y_{t+\tau}|y_t) = \Gamma^\tau y_t$, with $|\Gamma| \geq 1$, but none the less possesses a stationary distribution with zero mean. The conditional expectation shows in the case where $|\Gamma| > 1$ a tendency to diverge and in the case where $\Gamma = 1$ no tendency to settle down. This property is of course shared by the usual (linear) unit-root processes, but this has no implications concerning the stationarity of the process. He further argues that this distinction between unit-roots and lack of stationarity – that is missed in much of the macroeconomic literature on unit roots – may be empirically relevant by examining US aggregate output.

Let us consider a system
$$x_t = h(x_{t-1}) + w_t, \tag{5}$$

where x_t lies in a subset of R^N, w_t is i.i.d. and such that an ergodic measure ρ exists. A possible definition of 'locally explosive' conditional expectation is exactly that the largest Liapunov exponent is positive. Note that this definition involves changes in the state at time $t+\tau$ in response to a small (infinitesimal) shock w_t at time t as τ gets large and not simply changes at time $t+1$. Oseledec's theorem roughly states that the magnitude of this change is (with probability one) independent of either the state at time t, the direction of the shock or the ensuing history of w_τ's. In particular the conditional expectation of the magnitude of the change is independent of either the state at time t or the direction of the shock. If the largest Liapunov exponent is positive then the system exhibits sensitive dependence and infinitesimal deviations are amplified. From a local point of view the system behaves as a linear systems with a root outside the unit circle. Obviously, if one considers a finite shock and the support of ρ is compact then the magnitude of the change cannot exceed the diameter of the support of ρ. In spite of this sensitive dependence the process x_t is stationary.

V. CONCLUSION

The research we reviewed in this lecture is clearly in its initial stage. There is no guarantee that yet this attempt to bring nonlinearities to the centre of the study of economic dynamics will succeed. But the vast progress in the mathematics of nonlinear systems has already brought in some interesting dividends in economics. On the theoretical side it has clarified how complicated economic dynamics can be even in the most benign environment. On the empirical side it has led to the development of new tools to detect dependence. To be fair none of these developments are far enough along to bring about a change in the way economic practitioners proceed.

There are at least two directions that could prove specially useful for future work. The first one involves attempts to build explicit computable models that combine small amounts of randomness with nonlinearities and that succeed in generating data that replicate some of the aspects of economic or financial time series. The other is the development of a distribution theory for estimates of Liapunov exponents that would allow one to decide whether sensitive dependence is present on data.

University of Chicago

REFERENCES

Atten, P. and Caputto, J. C. (1985). 'Estimation expérimental de dimension d'attracteurs et d'entropie.' In *Traitement Numérique des Attracteurs Etranges* (ed. M. Cosnard and C. Mira), Conference Proceedings, Grenoble.

Ando, A. K. and Modigliani, F. (1959). 'Growth, fluctuations and stability.' *American Economic Review Papers and Proceedings*, vol. 49, pp. 501–24.

Baumol, W. and Benhabib, J. (1989). 'Chaos: significance, mechanism, and economic applications.' *Journal of Economic Perspectives*, vol. 2, pp. 77–105.

Benhabib, J. and Day, R. (1982). 'A characterization of erratic dynamics in the overlapping generations model.' *Journal of Economic Dynamics and Control*, vol. 4, pp. 35–7.

—— and Nishimura, K. (1979). 'The Hopf bifurcation and the existence and stability of closed orbits in multisector models of optimum economic growth.' *Journal of Economic Theory*, vol. 21, pp. 421–44.

—— and — (1985). 'Competitive equilibrium cycles.' *Journal of Economic Theory*, vol. 35, pp. 284–306.

Ben-Mizrachi, A., Procaccia, I. and Grassberger, P. (1984). 'Characterization of experimental (noisy) strange attractors.' *Physical Review* A, vol. 29, pp. 975–7.

Boldrin, M. and Deneckere, R. (1987). 'Simple macroeconomic models with a very complicated behaviour.' Mimeo, University of Chicago and Northwestern University.

—— and Montrucchio, L. (1986). 'On the indeterminacy of capital accumulation paths.' *Journal of Economic Theory*, vol. 40, pp. 26–39.

Brock, W. A. (1986). 'Distinguishing random and deterministic systems: an expanded version.' Department of Economics, University of Wisconsin, Madison.

—— (1988). 'Notes on nuisance parameter problems and BDS type tests for IID.' working paper, Department of Economics, University of Wisconsin, Madison.

——, Dechert, W. A. and Scheinkman, J. A. (1987). 'A test for independence based on the correlation dimension.' Department of Economics, University of Wisconsin-Madison, University of Houston, and University of Chicago.

——, ——, —— and LeBaron, B. (1988). 'A test for independence based upon the correlation dimension. Department of Economics, University of Wisconsin-Madison, University of Houston, and University of Chicago.

—— and Sayers, C. L. (1988). 'Is the business cycle characterized by deterministic chaos? *Journal of Monetary Economics*, vol. 22(2), pp. 71–90.

Denker, M. and Keller, G. (1983). 'On U-Statistics and von Mises statistics for weakly dependent processes.' *Zeitung Wahrscheinlichkeitstheorie* verw. Gebiete, 64, pp. 505–22.

Eckman, J. P. and Ruelle, D. (1985). 'Ergodic theory of chaos and strange attractors.' *Review of Modern Physics*, vol. 57, No. 3, Pt. 1, pp. 617–56.

——, Kamphorst, S. O., Ruelle, D. and Ciliberto, S. (1986). 'Lyapunov exponents for time series.' *Physical Review* A, vol. 34, pp. 4971–9.

——, ——, —— and Scheinkman, J. (1988). 'Lyapunov exponents for stock returns'. In *The Economy as an Evolving Complex System* (ed. P. W. Anderson, K. J. Arrow and D. Pines). New York: Addison-Wesley.

Engle, R. (1982). 'Autoregressive conditional heteroskedasticity with estimates of the variance of the U.K. inflations.' *Econometrica*, vol. 50, pp. 987–1007.

Fama, E. (1970). 'Efficient capital markets: review of theory and empirical work.' *Journal of Finance*, May, pp. 383–417.

Gallant, A. R., Hsieh, D. and Tauchen, G. (1988). 'On fitting a recalcitrant series: the dollar/pound exchange rate.' University of Chicago, Graduate School of Business.

Goodwin, R. M. (1951). 'The nonlinear accelerator and the persistence of business cycles.' *Econometrica*, vol. 19, pp. 1–17.

Grandmont, J. M. (1985). 'On endogenous competitive business cycles.' *Econometrica*, vol. 5 (September), pp. 995–1045.

Grassberger, P. and Procaccia, I. (1983). 'Measuring the strangeness of strange attractors.' *Physica*, vol. 9D, pp. 189-208.

Hahn, F. (1966). 'Equilibrium dynamics with heterogeneous capital goods.' *Quarterly Journal of Economics*, vol. 80, pp. 633-46.

Hicks, J. (1950). *A Contribution to the Theory of the Trade Cycle*. Oxford: Clarendon Press.

Hinich, M. (1982). 'Testing for guassianity and linearity of stationary time series.' *Journal of Time Series Analysis*, vol. 3, pp. 169-76.

Hoeffding, W. (1948). 'A class of statistics with asymptotically normal distribution.' *Annals of Mathematical Statistics*, vol. 19, pp. 293-325.

Hsieh, D. (1989). 'Testing for nonlinear dependence in foreign exchange rates.' *Journal of Business*, (July), pp. 339-68.

—— and LeBaron, B. (1988a). 'Finite sample properties of the BDS statistic I: Distribution under the null hypothesis.' Graduate School of Business and Department of Economics. The University of Chicago.

—— and —— (1988b). 'Finite sample properties of the BDS statistic II: Distribution under alternative hypotheses.' Graduate School of Business and Department of Economics, The University of Chicago.

Kaldor, N. (1940). 'A model of the trade cycle.' ECONOMIC JOURNAL, vol. 50, pp. 78-92.

Kifer, Y. (1986). 'Multiplicative ergodic theorems for random diffeomorphisms.' *Contemporary Mathematics*, vol. 50, pp. 67-78.

Kydland, F. and Prescott, E. C. (1982). 'Time to build and aggregate fluctuations.' *Econometrica*, vol. 50, pp. 1345-70.

LeBaron, B. (1988). 'Nonlinear puzzles in stock returns.' Ph.D. thesis, University of Chicago.

Lucas, R. E., Jr. (1978). 'Asset prices in an exchange economy.' *Econometrica*, vol. 46, pp. 1429-45.

Marotto, F. R. (1978). 'Snap-back repellers imply chaos in R^n.' *Journal of Mathematical Analysis and Applications*, vol. 73, pp. 199-223.

Murphy, K. M., Shleifer, A. and Vishny, R. W. (1989). 'Building blocks of market clearing business cycle models.' Mimeo NBER Annual Conference on Macroeconomics.

Ramsey, J. and Yuan, K. (1987). 'The statistical properties of dimension calculation using small data sets.' Mimeo New York University.

Quah, D. (1987). 'What do we learn from unit roots in macroeconomic time series?' NBER Working Paper Series.

Rubinstein, M. (1976). 'The valuation of uncertain income streams and the pricing of options.' *Bell Journal of Economics*, vol. 7, pp. 407-25.

Sakai, H. and Tokumaru, H. (1980). 'Autocorrelations of a certain chaos.' *IEEE Transactions Acoustic Speech Signal Process*, vol. 28, pp. 588-90.

Samuelson, P. A. (1973). 'Optimality of profit, including prices under ideal planning.' *Proceedings of the National Academy of Science (USA)*, vol. 70, pp. 2109-11.

Scheinkman, J. A. (1976). 'On optimal steady state of n-sector growth models when utility is discounted.' *Journal of Economic Theory*, vol. 12, pp. 11-30.

—— (1984). 'General equilibrium models of economic fluctuations: a survey.' Mimeo, Department of Economics, University of Chicago, (September).

—— (1985). 'Distinguishing deterministic from random systems: an examination of stock returns.' Manuscript prepared from the Conference on Nonlinear Dynamics, CEREMADE at the University of Paris IX.

—— and LeBaron, B. (1986). 'Nonlinear dynamics and stock returns unpublished, University of Chicago.

—— and —— (1989a). 'Nonlinear dynamics and stock returns *Journal of Business*, (July), pp. 311-37.

—— and —— (1989b). 'Nonlinear dynamics and GNP data.' In *Chaos, Complexity, Sunspots and Bubbles* (ed. W. Barnett, J. Geweke and K. Shell). Proceedings of the Fourth International Symposium in Economic Theory and Econometrics, Cambridge: Cambridge University Press.

Sen, P. (1963). 'On the properties of U-statistics when the observations are not independent: Part One.' *Calcutta Statistical Association Bulletin*, vol. 12, pp. 69-92.

Serfling, R. (1980). *Approximation theorems of mathematical statistics*. New York: Wiley.

Simon, H. A. (1956). 'Dynamic programming under uncertainty with a quadratic objective function.' *Econometrica*, vol. 24 (1), pp. 74-81,

Slutzky, E. (1927). 'The summation of random causes as the source of cyclic processes.' *Econometrica*, vol. 5, pp. 105-46.

Takens, F. (1983). 'Distinguishing deterministic and random systems.' In *Non Linear Dynamics and Turbulence* (ed. G. Borenblatt, G. Looss and D. Joseph). Boston: Pitman Advanced Publishing Program, pp. 315-33.

Theil, H. (1964). *Optimal Decision Rules for Government and Industry*, Amsterdam: North Holland.

Tsay, R. (1986). 'Nonlinearity tests for time series.' *Biometrika*, vol. 73, pp. 461-6.

Woodford, M. (1988). 'Expectations, finance constraints and aggregate instability.' In *Finance Constraints, Expectations and Macroeconomics* (ed. M. Kohn and S. C. Tsiang). New York: Oxford University Press.

Zardecki, A. (1982). 'Noisy Ikeda attractor.' *Physics Letters*, vol. 90A(6), pp. 274-7.

[4]

Journal of Mathematical Economics 20 (1991) 521–550. North-Holland

On lags and chaos in economic dynamic models*

Sergio Invernizzi

University of Trieste, Trieste, Italy

Alfredo Medio

University of Venice, Venice, Italy

Submitted July 1989, accepted August 1990

Abstract: This paper discusses the role of lags in dynamic economic models. Applications of discrete dynamical systems to economics are considered and the shortcomings of their (implicit) treatment of lags are criticized. An abstract, probabilistic view of lags is then provided, within which fixed delay lags are shown to be a special case. A basic equivalence is proved between: (i) a system with an indefinitely large number of agents, reacting to inputs with randomly gamma distributed, discrete lags, and (ii) a system with one single 'representative' agent reacting to inputs with a continuous, multiple exponential lag. Finally, the paper analyses a single-loop feedback system coupling a multiple exponential lag and a non-linearity of the one-hump type. The dynamic behavior of the system is studied by means of analytical and numerical methods, and the conditions for periodic and chaotic solutions are investigated.

1. Introduction

The discovery that deterministic, low-dimensional models may exhibit complex dynamic behavior[1] raised a considerable stir in the scientific community and, with an unusually short temporal lag, in the economic profession as well. Indeed, there have always been economists dissatisfied with analyses of economic fluctuations (of income, employment, prices, etc.), essentially based on exogenous random shocks. For these economists (a majority in the thirties, a minority perhaps today), the recent sensational

---

*The authors are indebted to Giancarlo Benettin, Colin Sparrow and two anonymous referees for valuable comments and criticisms on an earlier draft. Financial support from the Italian Ministry of Education (Ministero della Pubblica Istruzione, fondi 40%) is also gratefully acknowledged.
[1]By 'deterministic' we mean a model which does not include any stochastic elements. 'Low-dimensional' is used here as a loose equivalent of 'finite-dimensional', in a sense that will be made more precise later. The phrase 'complex dynamics' refers to any behavior more complex than that corresponding to quasi-periodic orbits.

results in the field of non-linear dynamics, and more specifically those broadly labelled as 'chaos', seemed to open a breech into a realm of scientific explanation hitherto considered inaccessible.

If we consider, however, the existing applications of chaotic dynamics to economic problems, we will notice that, with very few exceptions,[2] they consist of adaptations (with various amounts of value added) of the celebrated first-order, non-linear difference equation, so brilliantly studied by R. May (1976), and subsequently investigated in a large number of papers and books.[3]

As is well known, the May equation has the general form

$$x_{t+T} = f(x_t), \tag{1}$$

where $x \in R, f: R \rightarrow R$ is a smooth 'one-hump' function, and T is the length of a fixed delay, which of course can always be made equal to one by appropriately choosing the unit of measure of time. It is known that the behavior of the discrete dynamical system described by eq. (1), quite independently of the specific form of $f(\cdot)$, essentially depends on a single parameter and, over a certain interval of values of this parameter, it may display chaotic behavior in the sense defined, for example, by Devaney (1986, p. 50).

The question which immediately suggests itself is the following: How general are the (essentially mathematical) results derived from investigation of the discrete dynamical system (1), and how relevant are they to economic theory?

The original motivation of this paper was to respond to this question. In this endeavour, however, we have found some results which, we believe, may be of more general relevance and interest.

Notice, first of all, that a system described by eq. (1) may be conceived as a highly aggregate mechanism, consisting of two parts, namely a non-linear functional relationship and a lag, the latter being, in this particular case, a fixed delay. Let us then consider these two elements in turn.

The non-linearities implied by single-hump functions are of a rather common kind, and their presence has been detected in situations pertaining to practically all branches of natural and social sciences. Economists may (and do) disagree on the likelihood of such non-linearities actually affecting

---

[2]See, for example, Puu (1987) and Lorenz (1989, ch. 4, pp. 135–175).

[3]We shall limit ourselves here to quote the classic work of Collet and Eckmann (1980) and the more recent introductory book by Devaney (1986), which provide a comprehensive treatment of the matter and a rich bibliography.

the operation of real economic systems, and some of them are busy proving (or disproving) their existence in specific cases.[4] There should be consensus, we believe, that the general laws governing rational economic behavior, as postulated by the prevailing theory, do not exclude a priori, and in fact in some cases logically imply, the presence of non-monotonic functional relationships of the one-hump type.

This point can be appreciated by considering some of the applications to economics of eq. (1), including, among others, macroeconomic models [e.g., Stutzer (1980) and Day (1982)], models of rational consumption [e.g., Benhabib and Day (1981)], models of overlapping generations [e.g., Benhabib and Day (1982), Grandmont (1985)], models of optimal growth [e.g., Deneckere and Pelikan (1986)]. Recent overviews of the matter, with further instances of one-hump functions derived from economic problems can be found in Baumol and Benhabib (1988) and Lorenz (1989).

On the contrary, the role of the second element of the May model, i.e, the lag, has been rather neglected in the economists' discussions of chaotic dynamics. Comments on this point are often limited to some passim observations that most mathematical theorems utilized in this case only apply to discrete, one-dimensional systems, and that the most interesting result (the occurrence of chaotic dynamics) disappears when (supposedly) equivalent continuous time formulations of the same problems are considered.

This neglect is particularly surprising since there exists in the economic literature a lively and intellectually stimulating debate on the relative virtues and shortcomings of discrete and continuous models, which is very relevant to the point in question and to which our discussion, although differently motivated, is obviously related.[5] Indeed this paper may be thought of as an attempt to clarify some obscure aspects of this unresolved issue.

For this purpose, it will be expedient to briefly recall the main difficulties that arise when one studies an aggregate model (economic or otherwise), by means of the so-called 'period analysis', i.e., in discrete time.[6] First of all, even though economic transactions of a given type do not take place continuously and are therefore discrete, in general they will not be perfectly synchronized as period analysis implicitly assumes, but overlap in time in some stochastic manner. Only in very rare circumstances (e.g., in an agricultural, single-crop economy), could one define a 'natural period' for the economic activity under investigation. Whenever this is not possible, the

---

[4]See, for example, Brock and Sayers (1988).
[5]For an overview of this problem, see Gandolfo et al. (1981).
[6]This paragraph follows closely the discussion developed in May (1970) (a different May!). Foley (1975), and Turnovsky (1977). In order to facilitate reference to economic literature, in what follows we use the concepts of 'period' and 'fixed delay lag' as synonyms.

danger is present that the implicit assumption underlying the fixed delay hypothesis may yield misleading conclusions.

In order to circumvent this danger, Foley introduced the methodological precept that 'no sustantive prediction or explanation in a well-defined macroeconomic model should depend on the real time length of the period.' [On the other hand,] 'if the results of a period model do not depend in any important way on the period, the model can be formulated as a continuous model. The method used to accomplish this is to retain the length of the period as an explicit variable in the mathematical formulation of a period model and to make sure that it is possible to find meaningful limiting forms of the equations as the period goes to zero' [Foley (1975, pp. 310–311)].

The danger that some of the conclusions obtained by means of period analysis may be mere artifacts owing to misspecification of the model, is clearly present in virtually all the existing applications of eq. (1) to economic problems, for which no aggregate 'natural period' could be defined. Those who think that chaotic dynamics do exist in real economies (these authors are among them) are therefore under obligation to show how this particular misspecification can be avoided.

In what follows we shall discuss a procedure which, although methodologically akin to that of May (1970) and Foley (1975), and motivated by similar preoccupations, is different both conceptually and mathematically.[7]

Our approach is based on the hypothesis that, although the economic transactions under investigation do not possess in general any common 'natural period', and therefore each transaction may be characterized by a different discrete lag, for any specific class of transactions there does exist an *expected* value of the lag, with a varying degree of dispersion around it, in the usual probabilistic sense. This hypothesis does not necessarily apply to every and all circumstances, but we believe it to be sufficiently general to cover most of commonly studied cases in economics. Different though individual reaction times may be, each class of events must after all have a common psychological or technological substratum, without which modelling the behavior of these events would itself become an impossible task.

If this rather mild assumption is granted, a more general formulation of dynamic aggregate problems is possible, of which the fixed delay model is a limiting special case. Moreoever, we shall show that certain interesting dynamic features of models of the R. May type, and in particular the occurrence of chaotic dynamics, may be detected in less special cases, represented by continuous time, low-dimensional models.

The paper is divided in four parts. In the first two parts, we shall briefly discuss some basic concepts and results concerning lags, respectively from a

[7]The same line of research is pursued by one of the present authors in a forthcoming paper [see Medio (1991)].

probabilistic and from an analytic point of view. In the third part, we shall present our general model, in which lags are analysed within a feedback system approach. We shall then formulate a general continuous time model and derive some basic analytical results. In the fourth and last part we shall consider a specific formulation of the model and apply certain analytical and numerical tools to investigate its dynamic behavior and, in particular, to detect the presence of chaotic dynamics.

2. Lags: A probabilistic view

Let us consider any of the economic models discussed in section 1 and suppose that, although we accept the author's argument in any other respects, for the reason discussed above we reject the hypothesis of a single fixed delay as an unduly crude way of aggregating the economy. Then, while retaining the relevant non-linear relationship, we wish to re-model the lag structure of the economy. Instead of a single 'representative' economic agent (or unit), as implicitly postulated by those models, we consider a hypothetic economy consisting of an indefinitely large number of agents, who respond to a certain signal with given discrete lags. The lengths of the lags are different for different agents, and are distributed in a random manner over all the population. In this situation, the economy's aggregate time of reaction to the signal can be modelled by a real non-negative random variable T, the overall length of the delay. When observations on T can be repeated indefinitely, the frequency-ratio for any specific range of values will tend to the corresponding probability. The set of observations approached in the limit is the *population* of our observations. In this respect, therefore, every hypothetic economy may be characterized by the continuous, essentially positive, nonconstant random variable T, whose distribution can be estimated through the usual statistical procedures.

A continuous random variable is known if its probability distribution is known. In principle, the overall reaction time T can be distributed in a number of different ways, depending on the specific problem at hand. In the present discussion, we shall assume that the distribution of T belongs to the class of two-parameter gamma distribution. The justification for this choice is twofold. First of all, under rather mild restrictions, this particular distribution is 'optimal' in a sense that will be discussed in a moment. Secondly, as we shall see in the next section, it can be associated with a dynamical system whose analysis is relatively simple and produces interesting results.

In the attempt to estimate the true distribution of a random variable, a statistician, in order to avoid unjustified biases, should formulate his assumptions so as to maximize the uncertainty about the system, subject to the constraints deriving from his prior knowledge of the problem. A rigorously defined measure of uncertainty (i.e., lack of information) is provided by 'entropy', which, for essentially positive random variables with density, is defined as

$$H = -\int_0^\infty f(\tau) \log(f(\tau)) \, d\tau,$$

where $f(\tau)$ is the density function.

The concept of entropy was introduced after World War II in the context of Information Theory by Shannon (1948), but the idea can be traced back to Boltzmann (1910–12) and earlier. The 'principle of maximum entropy' for selecting probability distribution was put forward in the economic literature by Theil and Fiebig (1981) and can be looked at as a generalization of the famous Bernouilli–Laplace 'principle of insufficient reason'.

In the case of lags, for example, if the only constraint on the probability distribution is that the range of T is a bounded interval, then we should choose the uniform distribution.

If, on the other hand, the range of T is $(0, \infty)$ and the only constraint is that the expected value of T exists and is equal to τ, then the principle of maximum entropy requires that we choose the (one parameter) exponential distribution, with parameter $\theta = 1/\tau$. Moreover, if an additional independent constraint is assumed, e.g., if we fix the geometric mean,[8] the maximum entropy criterion requires the choice of a two-parameter gamma distribution.

We shall recall that, if we indicate by α the shape parameter and β the scale parameter, the density of a two-parameter gamma random variable can in general be written as

$$g(\alpha, \beta; t) = \begin{cases} 0 & \text{if } t \le 0, \\ \{\beta^\alpha \Gamma(\alpha)\}^{-1} t^{\alpha-1} e^{-t/\beta} & \text{if } t > 0, \end{cases} \tag{2}$$

where Γ is the gamma function and $\alpha, \beta > 0$.

From the knowledge of the pair (α, β), one can promptly derive expressions for different indicators of the probability distribution. Thus, the mean value

[8]This is in fact the case considered by Theil and Fiebig (1981). Incidentally, Theil and Fiebig's statement that geometric mean is zero for exponential distribution is incorrect: In fact it is equal to $\tau e^{-\gamma}$, where $\gamma \approx 0.577$ is the Euler–Mascheroni constant. This can be readily seen by putting $\alpha = 1$ in the expression below. For distributions over the entire real line constrained by the mean and the variance, Kampé de Fériet (1963) has proved that the normal distribution satisfies the principle of maximum entropy [see, Guiaşu (1977)].

of the distribution associated with (2) is equal to $\beta\alpha$, the variance is $\beta^2\alpha$, the skewness $2/\sqrt{\alpha}$, and finally the geometric mean is equal to $\beta\exp\{\Gamma'(\alpha)/\Gamma(\alpha)\}$.

In the present discussion, we would like to be able to ascertain how the dynamical behavior of hypothetical economies, characterized by gamma distributed reaction times with the same mean value τ, is affected by different degrees of homogeneity, or lack of it. It is therefore natural to choose, as the second parameter of the gamma distribution, the variance, which is observable and can be the object of econometric estimation.

Moreover, keeping in mind that the dimension of variance, is $(\text{time})^2$, without loss of generality, we can postulate $\text{Var}(T) = \tau^2/n$, with n integer ≥ 1. Thus, the parameter discriminating between different economies with the same expected overall reaction time, is a positive integer n.[9] Therefore, putting $\alpha = n$ and $\beta = \tau/n = 1/\theta n$, we can re-formulate the density function (2) in a manner which will prove very useful in the sequel of the argument, thus:

$$w_n(t) = \begin{cases} 0 & \text{if } t \leq 0, \\ \theta(n^n/(n-1)!)(\theta t)^{n-1}e^{-n\theta t} & \text{if } t > 0. \end{cases} \tag{3}$$

The corresponding cumulative distribution function F_n can be computed by means of inductive integration by parts which (after certain computations which will be omitted here) gives

$$F_n(t) = \begin{cases} 0 & \text{if } t \leq 0, \\ 1 - e^{-n\theta t}\sum_{j=0}^{(n-1)}(n\theta t)^j/j! & \text{if } t > 0. \end{cases} \tag{4}$$

[This formula can be easily verified by checking that $dF_n(t)/dt = w_n(t)$ and that $F_n(+\infty) = 1$.]

In terms of our model, the parameter n, which depends (inversely) on the variance of the distribution, gives us a measure of the degree of dispersion around the mean of individual agents' reaction times. Its inverse, $\theta = 1/\tau$ indicates the (expected) overall speed of adjustment.

It is now interesting to consider two extreme cases. If $n = 1$, the distribution of the lag T is a simple exponential with parameter θ, that is to say, we have

$$w_1(t) = \begin{cases} 0 & \text{if } t \leq 0, \\ \theta e^{-\theta t} & \text{if } t > 0. \end{cases}$$

Next, let us consider the opposite extreme $n \to +\infty$. In order to study this

[9]In this form, the gamma distribution is also known as Erlang distribution.

case, we observe that, under the assumptions postulated above, the distribution of the random variable T can be described by a n-fold convolution of n exponentials, each of them with expectation τ/n.

We can then write:

$$T = \frac{1}{n} \sum_{k=1}^{n} T_k,$$

where the terms T_k designate k independent random variables, each of them exponentially distributed with parameter τ.

Then Khinchine's version of the strong law of large numbers[10] can be applied, and we conclude that, as $n \to +\infty$, T converges to τ with probability 1. Here τ has the meaning of a random-but-constant variable, distributed with Dirac density exactly as its only possible value.

Since convergence with probability 1 implies convergence in distribution (or in law), taking into account that the cumulative distribution of τ is a Heaviside function centered precisely in τ, we have established in this simple way the following result:

Proposition 1. The sequence $F_n(t)$, defined in (4), is pointwise convergent to 0, if $t < \tau$ and to 1, if $t > \tau$.

We can complete the argument by proving also the following:

Proposition 2. As $t \to \tau$, $F_n(t) \to 1/2$.

Proof. Consider that, by the definition of $F_n(t)$ given in (4), we have

$$F_n(\tau) = 1 - e^{-n\theta\tau} \sum_{j=0}^{n-1} (n\theta\tau)^j / j!.$$

By Stirling's formula, $e^{-n}n^n/n! \to 0$, as $n \to +\infty$. Let $P_n = \sum_{j=0}^{n} n^j/j!$. According to a known result,[11] we have that, as $n \to +\infty$, $e^{-n}P_n \to 1/2$, so that, as $n \to +\infty$, $F_n(\tau) = e^{-n}(e^n - P_n + n^n/n!) \to 1/2$.   Q.E.D.

Let us finally consider any bounded Borel-measurable deterministic function $\phi: R \to R$, continuous at $1/\theta = \tau$. Then $\phi(T)$ converges to $\phi(\tau)$ with probability 1, and therefore, by change of variables and making use of the *bounded convergence theorem*, we obtain

[10]Cf. Billingsley (1979, Theorem 22.5).
[11]Cf. Dieudonné (1971, pp. 103–104).

$$\int_{-\infty}^{+\infty} \phi(s) w_n(s)\, \mathrm{d}s = E[\phi(T)] \rightarrow E[\phi(\tau)] = \phi(\tau), \tag{5}$$

where $E(\cdot)$ of course means expected value.

We shall make use of the result above in the next section, where we shall also consider some further analytical properties of the sequences w_n and F_n.

3. Lags: An analytic view

We shall now look at the problem discussed in the previous section from a different point of view, in which no direct probabilistic consideration is involved.

A time lag corresponding to an economy's reaction time is, in a sense, a link between an input to, and an output from that economy. Therefore, a lag can also be modelled as an input–output device. Let us consider here the simple case of an output Y, lagged on an input Z. We shall assume that Z can be represented by a function $Z = Z(t)$, which is equal to zero for all times $t < 0$ and bounded and continuous for $t > 0$, where $t = 0$ indicates the time at which the input is instantly delivered. The actual value of Z at $t = 0$ is here inessential.

Two simple cases can be most often found in the economic literature namely:

(i) *The fixed delay*: i.e., there exists a rigidly fixed lag of τ time units, so that Y is a solution to the following (trivial) functional equation:

$$Y(t) = Z(t - \tau). \tag{6}$$

(ii) *The simple exponential lag*: i.e., the reaction to the input starts immediately at $t = 0$, but the temporal evolution of the output, that is the growth of Y, is proportional to the excess of the input over the output. This leads to the following ordinary differential equation:

$$\dot{Y}(t) = \theta[Z(t) - Y(t)], \tag{7}$$

where $\theta > 0$ has dimension $(\text{time})^{-1}$ and represents the *speed of adjustment*, whereas its inverse $1/\theta = \tau$ can be considered the length of the simple exponential lag. In economic applications, the variable Z sometimes represents the desired, or equilibrium value of Y, defined in another part of the model, so that eq. (7) depicts an 'Achilles and the Tortoise' situation in which the actual magnitude *chases* the desired one, approaching it at an exponentially slowing speed, and catching up with it only in the limit for $t \rightarrow +\infty$.

Both the fixed delay and the simple exponential lag, or exponential lag of

530   *S. Invernizzi and A. Medio, Lags in economic dynamic models*

order one, correspond to rather special (and crude) formalizations of economic reaction mechanisms. More general (and satisfactory) results can be obtained modelling the response of output Y to input Z by means of successive applications of n simple exponential lags, each of length $\tau/n = 1/n\theta$, with an overall length of τ time units.

In this case, the evolution of the variable Y would be given by the solution of the nth order scalar, ordinary differential equation

$$\left(\frac{D\tau}{n} + 1\right)^n Y = Z(t), \tag{8}$$

where $D \equiv (d/dt)$ and with given suitable initial conditions $Y^{(k)}(0) = y_k$, $k = 0, 1, \ldots, (n-1)$.[12] We shall refer to this case as *the multiple exponential lag of order n*.

In the sequel, we shall show not only that the multiple lag is a very flexible tool of analysis, but also that its choice responds to a certain criterion of optimality for a large class of situations.

It is immediately evident that, putting $n = 1$ in (8), we get the simple exponential lag. We shall see that the multiple lag also 'contains' – in the limit, as $n \to \infty$ – the case (i), i.e., the fixed delay of length τ.

First of all, since the lag operator on the left-hand side of eq. (8) is linear, we can apply the general theory of linear systems [e.g., Kaplan (1962)]. The solution of any initial value problem associated with eq. (8) can be obtained in terms of *Duhamel's integral*, namely:

$$Y(t) = C_n(t) + \int_0^\infty Z(t-s) w_n(s) \, ds, \tag{9}$$

where C_n is the solution of the homogeneous equation

$$\left(\frac{D\tau}{n} + 1\right)^n C = 0, \tag{10}$$

with the given initial conditions $C^{(k)}(0) = y_k$, $k = 0, 1, \ldots, (n-1)$ and w_n is the first derivative $w_n = dF_n/dt$ of the solution F_n of the equation

$$\left(\frac{D\tau}{n} + 1\right)^n F = h(t), \tag{11}$$

---

[12]There are pretty few applications in economics of multiple exponential lags. The cases $n = 2, 3$ are considered by Allen (1967, pp. 91–93).

with null initial conditions, i.e., $F^{(k)}(0)=0$, $k=0,1,\ldots,(n-1)$, and the right-hand term $h(t)$ defined by $h(t)=0$, if $t<0$; $h(0)=1/2$; $h(t)=1$ if $t>0$ (the Heaviside function at $t=0$).

The function C_n will have the form $C_n(t)=e^{-nt}\sum_{j=0}^{n-1}a_{nj}t^j$, where the coefficients $(a_{n0}, a_{n1}, \ldots, a_{n.n-1})$ depend linearly on the initial conditions.

The function w_n is called the *weighting function* for the multiple exponential lag of order n. That is to say, if we consider a time stretch from now to an indefinitely distant past, the value of w_n corresponding to a certain instant $\bar{t}$ 'weighs' the impact of the input delivered at $\bar{t}$ on the output now.[13]

The function $w_n(t)$ can be determined by solving the initial value problem

$$\left(\frac{D\tau}{n}+1\right)^n F=h(t),$$

$$F(0)=F'(0)=F''(0)=\cdots=F^{n-1}(0)=0. \tag{12}$$

Standard theory[14] indicates that the solution of (12) has the form $F_n(t)=y_n(t)h(t)$, where y_n is the classical solution, i.e., it is a smooth function defined on R, of the problem

$$\left(\frac{D\tau}{n}+1\right)^n y=1,$$

$$y(0)=y'(0)=y''(0)=\cdots=y^{n-1}(0)=0. \tag{13}$$

Essentially the theory solves the case of a general time-variable input $Z(t)$, as soon as we are able to solve the case with a step-input, i.e., an input defined by a (positive) unit step change at $t=0$. A tedious but straightforward calculation gives the following result

Lemma 1.   The solution y_n of (13) is

$$y_n(t)=1-e^{-n\theta t}\sum_{j=0}^{n-1}(n\theta t)^j/j!, \tag{14}$$

and therefore $F_n(t)=y_n(t)h(t)$ is nothing but the cumulative distribution function of a gamma distribution with parameters $(n, \tau/n)$, exactly as defined in (4).

---

[13]In the literature the integral on the right-hand side of eq. (9) is sometimes called 'memory function', or 'delay kernel'.

[14]See, for example, Jones (1966).

532   *S. Invernizzi and A. Medio, Lags in economic dynamic models*

We have therefore established a very interesting correspondence between the probabilistic and the analytic properties of lags. The weighting function w_n of a multiple exponential lag of order n with adjustment speed θ, coincides with the density function of a two-parameter gamma distribution. From this it also follows that, in the present context, the choice of multiple exponential lags is not arbitrary, but it shares the same 'optimality' property as the associated distribution function.

This basic correspondence allows us to apply the convergence result of (5) to the Duhamel integral formula (9). If we assume that the initial values y_k are all zero, so that C_n must be identically zero, we have the following result:

Proposition 3. Let $Z: R \rightarrow R$ be an (input) bounded function, continuous at every t, except possibly at $t=0$, and such that $Z(t)=0$, for $t<0$. For any $n \geq 1$, let

$$Y_n(t) = \int_0^\infty Z(t-s)w_n(s)\,ds$$

be the output function, lagged on Z through a multiple exponential lag of order n with length τ (or, equivalently, with speed of response θ).
  On the other hand, let

$$Y(t) = Z(t-\tau)$$

be the output lagged on Z through a fixed delay lag of length τ.
  Then, for every $t \neq \tau$, we have

$$Y_n(t) \rightarrow Y(t).$$

Proof. Let $t \neq \tau$ be fixed. Since $w_n(s)=0$ for $s<0$, we have $Y_n(t) = \int_{-\infty}^{+\infty} Z(t-s)w_n\,ds$. Define $\phi(s) = Z(t-s)$. Then $Y_n(t) = \int_{-\infty}^{+\infty} \phi(s)w_n(s)\,ds \rightarrow \phi(\tau) = Z(t-\tau)$, provided ϕ is continuous at τ, i.e. provided Z is continuous at $t-\tau$. But Z, by assumption, can be discontinuous only at 0, and since $t \neq \tau$, the result is proved.   Q.E.D.

For the sake of completeness, we investigate the asymptotic behavior of the sequence $Y_n(\tau)$, which represents the output generated through a multiple exponential lag of order n, exactly at time τ. There is no a priori reason to expect that this sequence should converge to $Z(\tau-\tau)=Z(0)$, or even to expect that $Y_n(\tau)$ is convergent at all. In fact the value of Z at time 0 is not 'defined' in our model: It could be any real number without that modifying the preceding results. In order to establish some sufficient conditions ensuring convergence of $Y_n(\tau)$ (not necessarily the weakest ones), we shall prove the following result:

Proposition 4. Suppose the right limit $Z(0^+) = \lim_{t \to 0; t > 0} Z(t)$ exists. Define $Z(0) = Z(0+)$, and let the modified function Z be absolutely continuous over the interval $[0, \tau]$. Then $Y_n(\tau)$ converges to $(1/2)Z(0^+)$.

Proof. Since $Z(t) = 0$ for $t < 0$, we have $Z(\tau - s) = 0$ for $s > \tau$, so that

$$Y_n(\tau) = \int_0^\tau Z(\tau - s) w_n(s) \, ds.$$

Integration by parts yields

$$Y_n(\tau) = Z(\tau - s) F_n(s) \big|_{s=0}^{s=\tau} + \int_0^\tau Z'(\tau - s) F_n(s) \, ds$$

$$= Z(0+) F_n(\tau) + \int_0^\tau Z'(\tau - s) F_n(s) \, ds.$$

Now $F_n(s) \to 0$ for almost every s, $0 \leq s \leq \tau$ (convergence with probability 1 implies convergence in distribution), and therefore, the integral above tends to 0 by the dominated convergence theorem. Then Proposition 2 above implies the result.   Q.E.D.

The preceding analysis shows that the weights of a multiple exponential lag concentrate at τ as $n \to +\infty$ or, equivalently, its density 'tends' to a Dirac δ function concentrated at τ. To formalize this idea by means of a suitable notion of convergence, we shall state and prove the following:

Proposition 5. The sequence of the weighting functions w_n of a multiple exponential lag of order n and length τ converges to the Dirac $\delta(t - \tau)$-distribution in the weak* topology of $\mathscr{D}'(R)$.[15]

Proof. Proposition 1 shows that the sequence of continuous functions F_n converges pointwise for every t to the locally integrable Heaviside function $h(t - \tau)$, and $|F_n(t)| \leq 1$ for all t. The bounded convergence theorems implies that F_n converges to the Heaviside distribution at τ in the weak* topology

---

[15]In Appendix A, we shall recall some elementary facts concerning the space $\mathscr{D}'(R)$ of real distributions on the real line.

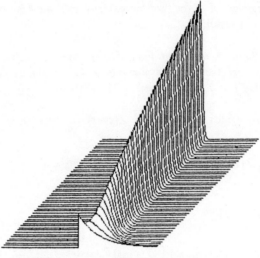

Fig. 1

$\mathscr{D}'(R)$, so that the sequence of first derivatives $w_n(t) = dF_n(t)/dt$ converges to $\delta(t - \tau)$ in the same sense.

It is also interesting to study the *rate* at which a multiple exponential lag of length τ converges to a fixed delay of τ time units. This can be done by taking the interval $[\tau - \sigma_n, \tau + \sigma_n] = [\tau(1 - 1/\sqrt{n}), \tau(1 + 1/\sqrt{n})]$ as a rough indicator of the dispersion near the time τ of the delayed effects of an input at time $t = 0$. We can see in this way that, as n increases, the convergence of the lag from the simple exponential case ($n = 1$) to the limit case, i.e. the shift of τ time units of the input ($n \to +\infty$), is *quite slow*, actually sublinear with exponent $1/2$. A further indication in this direction comes from the following estimate of the maximum value of w_n, which is attained at $t = \tau(1 - 1/n)$:

$$\theta\left(\frac{n-1}{n-3/4}\right) n[2\pi(n-1)]^{-1/2} < \max w_n < \theta n[2\pi(n-1)]^{-1/2}.$$

These inequalities are obtained by Stirling's formula, which gives, for $w_n(t)$, with $t > 0$:

$$(1 + 1/4n)^{-1} \theta(n/2\pi)^{1/2} \omega(\theta t) < w_n(t) < \theta(n/2\pi)^{1/2} \omega(\theta t),$$

where $\omega(s) = \exp[n(1 - s) + (n-1)\log(s)]$. The diagrams of w_n with $\tau = 1$ are plotted in fig. 1, for $n = 1, 2, \ldots, 100$: the sublinear growth of w_n toward the Dirac distribution is quite evident. To fix ideas, fig. 2 illustrates the cases of a sinusoidal input subjected to multiple exponential lags of degrees 1, 10, 50 and 150. The shift effect is again quite evident.

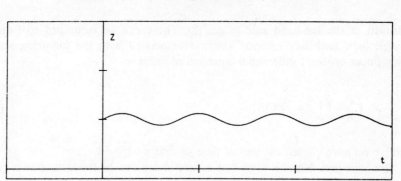

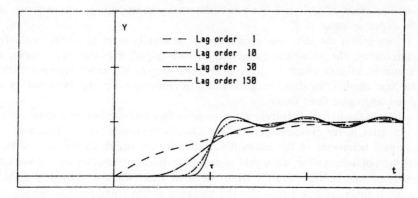

Fig. 2

We suspect therefore that in practical situations (for a finite n), the existence of the limit-effect may be perceptible only for quite large values of n. This implies that the variance of the corresponding distribution must be quite small.

4. Lags and feed-back systems

Equipped with the results of sections 2 and 3, we would now like to provide a generalized version of the problem with which we started, formulated in terms of a feed-back system combining a lag operator and a non-linearity.[16]

Let $f : R \rightarrow R$ be a non-linear function, and let L^n be the linear operator

[16]A similar approach to this problem can be found in a paper by Sparrow (1980), from the study of which we have greatly benefited. In fact, some of the results in this section and the following one can be considered as further developments of the same line of research. See also R. May's comments on this point (1983, pp. 548–549 and 555).

defined in the left-hand side of eq. (8). These can be combined to form a single loop feed-back system, which is associated with the following scalar non-linear ordinary differential equation of order n:

$$\left(\frac{D}{n}+1\right)^n Y = f(Y), \tag{15}$$

where we have chosen the unit of time so that $\tau = 1/\theta = 1$.

We have just demonstrated that a fixed delay can be thought of as a limit case of a family of multiple exponential lags, as the parameter $n \to \infty$. From the discussion of section 1, we know the case corresponds to convergence to the expected value of T.

If we accept the idea that agents do not generally react to signals with the same delay, the approach suggested in this paper, provides, we believe, a treatment of lags which is superior to (and empirically more relevant than) the one implicit in those models which directly assume the existence of a given, aggregate fixed delay.

The mathematical literature on non-invertible one-dimensional maps indicates, that, in the aforementioned limit case, for a certain class of functions f, complex behaviour of the relevant variable Y may occur. In the light of the results obtained so far, we would now like to find out whether such complex behavior can be observed far from the limit case, when n, though possibly large, is finite, and consequently the variance of the (random) overall lag T, though possibly small, is non-zero.

For this purpose let us re-write (15) in the form of a system of n first-order ODEs. We have defined the operator

$$L = \left(\frac{D}{n}+1\right),$$

which correspond to a simple exponential lag with length equal to $1/n$. Therefore, (15) is equivalent to the system

$$Lx_1 = f(x_n), \tag{16}$$

$$Lx_j = x_{j-1}, \quad j = 2, 3, \ldots, n. \tag{17}$$

We now present some general results concerning the dynamics of this system which are independent of n. On the other hand, since we are looking for complex behavior, and this is obviously excluded in the cases $n = 1, 2$, we assume from the beginning that $n \geq 3$.

We assume that the function $f: R \to R$ is continuous and satisfies

$$0 < f(s) \leqq K \quad \text{for} \quad s > 0,$$

where K is a positive constant. The solutions of all the initial value problems of (16)–(17) with positive initial conditions at $t = 0$ exist globally on $[0, \infty)$. Moreover, we assume uniqueness and continuous dependence on initial conditions of these solutions. These assumptions are satisfied, for example, if f is C^1.

We shall first of all prove that the dynamics of (16)–(17) admits an open invariant set, by means of the following:

Proposition 6.   *The open positive orthant* $\mathcal{O} = \{x \in R^n : x_j > 0, j = 1, 2, \ldots, n\}$ *is positively invariant for the flow induced by the system (16)–(17).*

Proof.   Assume, by contradiction, that a solution x of (16)–(17) with $x(0) \in \mathcal{O}$ touches the boundary of $\mathcal{O}$ at some positive time. Then there is a positive time

$$t^* = \min\{t > 0: \exists \text{ some } j, \; 1 \leqq j \leqq n, \text{ with } x_j(t) = 0\},$$

and the set of all indexes j for which $x_j(t^*) = 0$ has a maximum, say m. If $m \geqq 2$, the mth equation of (16)–(17) gives $x_{m-1}(t^*) = (1/n)\dot{x}_m(t^*) \leqq 0$. The opposite inequality $\dot{x}_m(t^*) > 0$ is not allowed because $x_m(0) > 0$ and given the definition of t^*. But $x_{m-1}(t^*)$ cannot be negative, since $x_{m-1}(0) > 0$ and again given the definition of t^*. Therefore, $x_{m-1}(t^*) = 0$. Recursively, we obtain that

$$x_m(t^*) = \cdots = x_2(t^*) = x_1(t^*) = 0.$$

The same conclusion trivially holds if $m = 1$. The first equation of (16)–(17) gives that $nf[x_n(t^*)] = \dot{x}_1(t^*) \leqq 0$. Using the sign conditions assumed on f, we get $x_n(t^*) \leqq 0$, and, since $x_n(t^*) < 0$ is not allowed [because $x_n(0) > 0$ and given the definition of t^*], we deduce that $x_n(t^*) = 0$, that is to say, $m = n$. Hence, $x_j(t^*) = 0 \, \forall j$ and this is impossible, as we have assumed uniqueness in all initial value problems with positive initial conditions, and the origin is an equilibrium.

Next, we shall prove a dissipativity property of the dynamical system (16)–(17), namely the existence of a set $\mathcal{B}$ absorbing in $\mathcal{O}$, i.e., such that the orbit of any bounded subset of $\mathcal{O}$ enters into $\mathcal{B}$ after a certain time (which can depend on the subset). We shall first need the following simple, but useful lemma:

Lemma 2.   *Let $\alpha > 0$ and $\beta \geqq 0$ be real numbers, and let u be a $C^1(R, R)$ map* *such that the inequalities* $u(s) > 0$ *and* $\dot{u}(s) + \alpha u(s) \leq \beta$ *hold for all* $s \geq s_0$; *let* $u_0 = u(s_0)$. *Then the Gronwall inequality*

$$u(s) \leq u_0 \exp[\alpha(s_0 - s)] + (\beta/\alpha)(1 - \exp[\alpha(s_0 - s)]),$$

$$\leq u_0 \exp[\alpha(s_0 - s)] + \beta/\alpha,$$

holds for all $s \geq s_0$. *Given* $\sigma > 0$, *define*

$$s^* = \max\{s_0, s_0 - (1/\alpha)\log(\sigma/u_0)\}.$$

Then, $\forall s \geq s^*$,

$$u(s) \leq \beta/\alpha + \sigma.$$

The proof can be omitted, but remark that s^* is (weakly) increasing with respect to s_0 and u_0.

We can now state the following:

Proposition 7. Any box $\mathcal{B} = \{x \in R^n : 0 < x_j < K + \varepsilon, j = 1, 2, \ldots, n\}, \varepsilon > 0$, *is absorbing for the bounded subsets of the open orthant* $\mathcal{O}$.

Proof. Let $\mathcal{B}_l$ be a bounded subset of $\mathcal{O}$; assume that

$$\|y\|_\infty = \max\{y_1, y_2, \ldots, y_n\} \leq C,$$

for any y in $\mathcal{B}_l$. Let $\varepsilon > 0$ be fixed and let x be a solution to (16)–(17), with initial conditions $x(0)$ in $\mathcal{O}$. From the first equation we deduce that $\dot{x}_1 + nx_1 \leq (nK)$ for $t \geq 0$. Let $\sigma = \varepsilon/n$. Applying Lemma 2, we find a time t_1 such that $x_1(t) \leq K + \sigma$, providing that $t \geq t_1$. That is to say,

$$t_1 = \max\{0, -(1/n)\log(\sigma/x_1(0))\}.$$

Now, $\dot{x}_2 + nx_2 \leq n(K + \sigma)$, for $t \geq t_1$, gives a time

$$t_2 = \max\{t_1, t_1 - (1/n)\log(\sigma/x_2(0))\},$$

such that $x_2(t) \leq K + 2\sigma$, provided that $t \geq t_1$. Step by step, we find n times $0 \leq t_1 \leq t_2 \leq \cdots \leq t_n$, such that $t \geq t_k$ implies

$$x_k(t) \leq K + k\sigma \leq K + n\sigma = K + \varepsilon,$$

for $k = 1, 2, \ldots, n$. Moreover, t_n is an explicitly computable function of the initial values $x_1(0), x_2(0), \ldots, x_n(0)$, which is (weakly) increasing in each of these variables. Therefore, if we compute t_n for the solution of (16)–(17) with initial values $(C, C, \ldots, C)$ at $t = 0$, we obtain that, for any solution x of (16)–(17) with initial values $x(0)$ in $\mathscr{B}, \forall j = 1, 2, \ldots, n$, we have

$$x_j(t) \leqq K + \varepsilon, \quad \text{for} \quad t \geqq t_n.$$

This, together with Proposition 6, implies the result.

The fact that bounded sets are dissipated by (16)–(17), allows us to apply a classical result on the existence of attractors.[17] We can thus state the following:

Theorem 1. *Let $\mathscr{A}$ be the ω-limit set of $\mathscr{B}$. Then $\mathscr{A}$ is a non-empty compact connected attractor, which attracts the bounded sets of the positive orthant $\mathcal{O}$: moreover, $\mathscr{A}$ is the maximal bounded attractor (for the inclusion relation), in the closure of $\mathcal{O}$.*[18]

In order to carry further our analysis, from now on we shall assume that the function f of eq. (16) has the following form:

$$f(s) = rs \, e^{-s}, \quad r > 0. \tag{18}$$

In order to investigate the properties of the attractor whose existence we just proved, we look first of all for equilibria in the closure of $\mathcal{O}$. It is easy to see that there exists exactly one such equilibrium, namely,

$$x^a = 0 \quad \text{if} \quad 0 < r \leqq 1,$$

and exactly two equilibria, namely,

$$x^a = 0 \quad \text{and} \quad x^b = (\log(r), \log(r), \ldots, \log(r)) \quad \text{if} \quad r > 1.$$

To check for their (linear) stability, we consider the vector field

$$f(x; r) = n[f(x_n) - x_1, x_1 - x_2, \ldots, x_{n-1} - x_n],$$

and its Jacobian matrix $A(x; r)$ with respect to the variables x.

---

[17]To simplify matters, we have adopted here Temam's definition of attractor [(1988, Definition 1.2)], which does not distinguish between 'attracting sets' and 'attractors'. In the literature on dynamical systems, however, the definition of the latter concept often includes the additional requirement of indecomposability.

[18]Cf. Temam (1988, Theorem 1.1).

A straightforward computation shows that the characteristic polynomial of $A(x;r)$ is

$$\det(A(x;r)-\lambda I)=(-1)^n\{(\lambda+n)^n-n^n f'(x_n)\}.$$

Taking into account that $f'(x_n)=re^{-x_n}(1-x_n)$, we obtain the eigenvalues of $A(x;r)$, thus:

$$\lambda_k(x)=\begin{cases} n\{r^{1/n}e^{-x_n/n}(1-x_n)^{1/n}e^{i2k\pi/n}-1\} & \text{if } 0\leq x_n<1, \\ -n & \text{if } x_n=1, \\ n\{r^{1/n}e^{-x_n/n}(x_n-1)^{1/n}e^{i(2k+1)\pi/n}-1\} & \text{if } x_n>1 \end{cases}$$

$(k=0,1,\ldots,n-1)$.

Therefore, at $x=x^a$, we get

$$\lambda_k(x^a)=n\{r^{1/n}e^{i2k\pi/n}-1\} \quad (k=0,1,\ldots,n-1),$$

so that $x^a=0$ is *asymptotically stable* if $0<r<1$, but it is *unstable* for $r>1$ (at $r=1, \lambda_0(x^a)=0$).

At the second equilibrium point x^b, the eigenvalues are as follows:

$$\lambda_k(x^b)=\begin{cases} n\{(1-\log(r))^{1/n}e^{i2k\pi/n}-1\} & \text{if } 1<r<e, \\ -n & \text{if } r=e, \\ n\{(\log(r)-1)^{1/n}e^{i(2k+1)\pi/n}-1\} & \text{if } r>e, \end{cases}$$

so that x^b is *asymptotically stable* for $1<r<r_H$, but it is *unstable* for $r>r_H$, where

$$r_H=\exp\{1+(\cos(\pi/n))^{-n}\}.$$

Actually r_H is the value of r for which the n-gon (in C), with center -1 and radius $(\log(r)-1)^{1/n}$, has exactly two vertices on the imaginary axis, and the remaining $n-2$ with negative real parts.

The two eigenvalues with zero real parts at $r=r_H$ are λ_0 and $\lambda_{n-1}=\bar{\lambda}_0$. Since, by assumption, $n\geq 3$, we have:

$$(d/dr)\,\text{Re}\,\lambda_0(x^b)\big|_{r=r_H}=r_H^{-1}[\cos(\pi/n)^n]\neq 0. \tag{19}$$

Consequently, a Hopf bifurcation of periodic solutions emanating from the equilibrium x^b, occurs at $r=r_H$. (For a concise description of the Hopf bifurcation, cf. Appendix B.)

The quantitative analysis of the Hopf bifurcation has been performed for $n=50$ by means of a method developed by one of the present authors [see Invernizzi (1991)], as a variation of the usual bifurcation formulae derived from the centre manifold theory [cf., Hassard et al. (1981)]. The computed value of the coefficient whose sign determines the direction of the bifurcation is $+0.0107$, so that the bifurcating periodic solutions exist for $r>r_H$, i.e., the bifurcation is supercritical. Moreover, the period of the orbits and the exponent which determines their stability are, respectively,

$$p=1.997[1+0.775\delta^2+O(\delta^4)], \quad \beta=-0.221\delta^2+O(\delta^4),$$

with $\delta^2=(r-r_H)+O(|r-r_H|^2)$, $r_H=8.197$. Thus, since $\beta<0$ for r near r_H, these solutions are asymptotically orbitally stable (with asymptotic phase).[19]

5. Chaotic dynamics

From the analysis developed in the previous section, we know that, for any value of $n\geq3$, according to the steepness of the 'hump' described by the non-linear function f (parametrized by r), the attractor $\mathscr{A}$ described in Theorem 1 contains a fixed point or a limit cycle. On the other hand, we also know that, in the limit for $n\to\infty$, the differential equation of our system converges to a fixed delay equation for which the presence of complex (chaotic) behavior has been proved, over a certain range of values of the parameter r.

We would now like to ascertain whether such complex behavior may appear for finite values of n, too. An indication that this is the case has been provided by Sparrow's analysis (1980) of a similar model. Integrating the system of ODEs numerically, Sparrow finds that, for $n=50$, when r passes a certain threshold value $21<r_c<22$, periodic solutions can no longer be visually detected, and concludes that the system must have entered a chaotic region.

In order to verify this qualitative statement, we have computed the Lyapunov Characteristic Exponents (LCEs) for the flow generated by the dynamical system (16)–(17).

LCEs play an important role in the analysis of dynamical systems, providing a rigorous method for diagnosing the presence in a system of *sensitive dependence on initial conditions* (SDIC), which is generally associated

---

[19]These results are in harmony with those obtained by Sparrow (1980), employing a special technique developed by Allwright (1977) for single loop feedback systems.

with chaotic dynamics.[20] Moreover, there exists a close link between LCEs and other measures of stochasticity, such as fractal dimension.

For a thorough discussion of the theory of LCEs, we shall make reference to the classic paper of Benettin et al. (1980), and shall briefly recall here the basic ideas and definitions.

Intuitively, we can describe LCEs of order one (i.e., LCEs of a vector) as follows. Let $\mathcal{M} \subset R^n$ be the phase space of trajectories generated by a certain dynamical system. Consider, at time $t = 0$, two nearby points in $\mathcal{M}$ and take their distance, say d_0. As time goes by, the distance between the two points will change and, if the system is described by differential equations, we may express the rate at which they diverge (converge) by the following equation:

$$d(t) = d_0 \, e^{\chi t}.$$

Suppose now that, as $t \to \infty$, χ converges to a limit. The values taken by the latter are then called LCEs of a trajectory. Clearly, if one or more of the limit values of χ is positive, we may say that the phase space trajectory has SDIC. Moreover, if the trajectory belongs to a compact attractor, we may say that the attractor has SDIC, i.e., it is chaotic.

More rigorously, for a flow ϕ generated by an autonomous system of first-order ODEs,

$$\dot{x} = f(x),$$

the first-order LCEs (or LCEs of a vector) can be defined as

$$\chi(x, w) = \lim_{t \to \infty} \frac{1}{t} \log \frac{\|D\phi_t(x)w\|}{\|w\|},$$

where $D\phi_t(x)$ is the derivative with respect to x of ϕ_t at x, w is a vector of $T_x\mathcal{M}$ (the tangent space to $\mathcal{M}$ at x), and $\|\cdot\|$ is the Euclidean norm. It has been shown that, under rather mild conditions, χ exists and is finite, ρ-almost everywhere for a suitable measure ρ [Oseledec (1968)].

Before stating the results of our computations, let us consider fig. 3, which depicts a 3-D projection of phase space trajectories of our system (for $n = 50, r = 22$), after some transients have been removed. Visual inspection suggests that trajectories are attracted to a bounded sheet-like geometrical structure embedded in R^3, which, adapting Rössler's (1976) terminology, may be dubbed 'doubly spiral chaos'.

Thus, we should expect the Hausdorff dimension of the attractor to be $2 < d < 3$, and the LCEs to have the sign pattern $(+, 0, -, \ldots, -)$. The

---

[20]Some authors [e.g., Eckmann and Ruelle (1985, p. 624)] actually *define* chaotic motions in terms of SDIC.

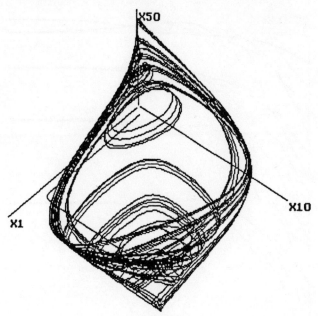

Fig. 3

interpretation is that the motion of the system is convergent toward the attractor from all directions but two. The zero Lyapunov exponent is associated with the direction of the motion along the flow. The presence of one positive exponent indicates that, on the attractor, there exists a direction along which nearby trajectories, on the average, diverge exponentially. This is tantamount to saying that the attractor $\mathscr{A}$ described in Theorem 1 has sensitive dependence on initial conditions, i.e., it is chaotic.

Our computations strongly confirm these expectations. Applying a well-known algorithm first developed by Benettin et al. (1980), we have estimated all the 50 LCEs of our system, starting from different points, presumably located on or near the attractor, and performing approximately 200,000 integration steps. The approximate values for the first three LCEs are the following (the remaining 47 exponents are all strongly negative and they are irrelevant here):

$$\chi_1 \approx 0.26, \quad \chi_2 \approx 0.00, \quad \chi_3 \approx -0.63.$$

Figs. 4 and 5 show our results and indicate a pretty sharp convergence as t increases. We also notice that the dominant LCE is neatly positive, having a value fairly large vis-à-vis those of similar strange attractors studied in the literature.

By making use of a method first suggested by Kaplan and Yorke (1979), we can derive from the calculated LCEs a measure of the Hausdorff dimension of the attractor. Suppose the LCEs are ordered in the usual way, i.e.,

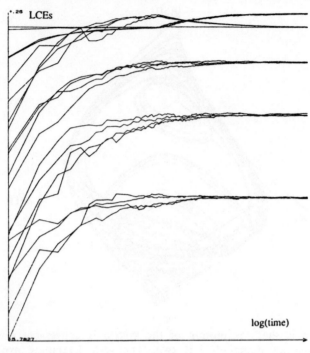

Fig. 4

$$\chi_1 > \chi_2 > \cdots > \chi_n.$$

Let j be the largest integer for which we have

$$\chi_1 + \chi_2 + \cdots + \chi_j > 0.$$

Then a measure of the fractal dimension can be written as

$$d = j + \frac{\sum_{i=1}^{j} \chi_i}{|\chi_{j+1}|}.$$

In our case, we obtain

$$d \approx 2.4,$$

which perfectly confirms the theoretical expectations.

6. Conclusion

Let us now summarize the results obtained so far.

First of all, we have proved that there is a basic equivalence between the following two representations of a lag structure:

(i) a system with an indefinitely large number of agents, each of them reacting to inputs with a *discrete* lag of length τ_i, $i = 1, 2, \ldots$, such that the (positive) quantities τ_i are randomly distributed, and the overall lag T is a

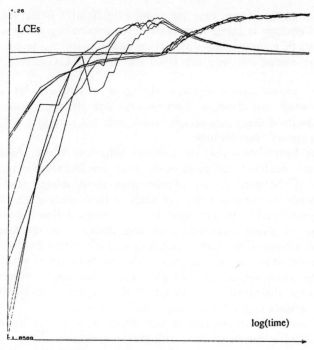

Fig. 5

random, gamma distributed variable with shape parameter *n* and expectation τ;

(ii) a system with one single 'representative' agent reacting to inputs with a continuous, multiple exponential lag of order *n*, with time-constant τ (or, equivalently, a speed of response $\theta = 1/\tau$).

The variable *n* appearing in both representations, plays a twofold role. On the one hand, it indicates the order of the multiple exponential lag; on the other hand, since *n* varies inversely with the variance of the distribution of *T*, it provides a measure of the degree of homogeneity of the economy under consideration.

Secondly, we have established that, as $n \to +\infty$, the overall lag *T* converges to its expected value τ, while the multiple exponential lag tends to a fixed delay with the same length τ. In this limit case, the system may be represented by a discrete-time, one-dimensional model like that described by eq. (1).

In applications, however, except in those special cases in which there exists a 'natural period', uniform over the system, the hypothesis of zero variance (corresponding to $n \to +\infty$) is a farfetched one, and we must take into account the fact that reaction times of different agents are spread around their mean value, according to some distribution to be estimated. We have suggested that, in the present case, the gamma distribution is 'optimal' in the sense that, if entropy is taken as a measure of uncertainty about a certain random event, then the gamma distribution contains the maximum amount of uncertainty compatible with the given restraints. [Cf. Guiaşu (1977, pp. 293–294).]

These two results taken together also give a criterion for dynamic aggregation which, we claim, is more general and rigorous than the one entailed by the fixed delay assumption, which does not take into account the differences in agents' reaction times.

Thirdly, we have shown that the complex behaviour which characterizes certain dynamic models investigated in the economic literature is not only a consequence of the non-linearity appearing in those models, but it also crucially depends on the distribution of reaction times among the individual economic agents or units. In particular, from our investigation it follows that the emergence of chaos associated with non-linearities of the 'one-hump' kind, is not restricted to the highly special case of a constant fixed delay, but can be observed whenever the variance of the lag distribution is sufficiently small. By the same token, on the other hand, one might observe that, however 'strong' the nonlinearity in question may be, a sufficiently large value of the variance could exclude any complex behavior.

Thus, the discussion on the realism and relevance of chaotic dynamics in an economic context can be pursued with greater generality.

Our discussion has been deliberately concentrated on the lag structure of the system, and little has been said with regards to its (single) non-linearity. We shall not provide any full-fledged analysis of this problem here. We surmise, however, that the approach employed in this paper could be conveniently extended to cover it. It is known that 'generically quadratic' non-linearities, with which we are concerned here, can always be character-ized by a single parameter, r. If we assume that the type of response to a signal is the same for all the agents [for example that is has the functional form described by eq. (18)], whereas r is randomly distributed over the entire economy, with a given expected value, the 'representative agent' could be characterized by two (rather than one) numbers, respectively an overall lag of response and an overall steepness of the reaction function. Both of these magnitudes would then be random variables, whose distribution would have to be estimated.

If we assumed again a gamma distribution, the parameter r appearing in the function $f(x_n)$ of eq. (18), could then be re-interpreted as the steepness coefficient pertaining to the 'representative agent', and its value would be determined as soon as n is fixed.

Appendix A

We recall that the symbol $\mathscr{D}(R)$ denotes the linear space of all infinitely differentiable 'test-functions' $R \to R$, which are identically zero on the complement of a compact set. An element of $\mathscr{D}'(R)$, i.e., a *distribution* on R, is a real linear functional S on $\mathscr{D}(R)$ such that, for every compact subset K of R, there exist constants C and N such that $|S(\phi)| \leq C \sum_{k=0}^{N} \sup |d^k \phi/dt^k|$ for all test-functions ϕ vanishing outside K. For any locally integrable function $f: R \to R$, we have a corresponding distribution F defined by

$$F(\phi) = \int_{-\infty}^{+\infty} \phi(t) f(t) \, dt.$$

One often identifies a locally integrable function and the corresponding distribution. Furthermore, there are several concepts of convergence for a sequence of distributions. In the previous section, we have used the following one: a sequence S_n in $\mathscr{D}'(R)$ is said to be *weakly** convergent (or convergent *in the weak* topology*) to an element of S of this space if and only if, for every test-function $\phi, S_n(\phi) \to S(\phi)$. When S_n and S correspond to locally integrable functions, the weak* convergence means that, for every test-function ϕ, we have

$$\int_{-\infty}^{+\infty} \phi(t) S_n(t) \, dt \to \int_{-\infty}^{+\infty} \phi(t) S(t) \, dt.$$

We recall also that the derivative dS/dt of a distribution S is simply defined by the equation $(dS/dt)(\phi) = -S(d\phi/dt)$. A particular feature of the weak* convergence is that, if $S_n \to S$ weakly*, then, for every order k, $(d^k S_n/dt^k) \to (d^k S/dt^k)$ weakly*.

If h is the Heaviside unit function at $t = 0$, then we can consider h as an element of $\mathscr{D}'(R)$. Its derivative is the Dirac δ-distribution at $t = 0$, which is defined on test-functions, requiring that $\delta(\phi) = \phi(0)$. The distribution defined by $\phi \to \phi(t_0)$ is usually denoted by $\delta(t - t_0)$, and it is the derivative of the Heaviside distribution centered at $t = t_0$, denoted by $H(t - t_0)$.

Appendix B

Following Hassard et al. (1981), we recall here the version of the Hopf bifurcation theorem which we used in section 4. Consider an autonomous ordinary differential equation on an open set $\mathscr{U} \subseteq R^n$,

$$\dot{x} = f(x; r), \tag{B.1}$$

where $x \in \mathscr{U}$ and r is a real scalar parameter varying in some open interval

$I \subseteq R$. Suppose that f is a C^5-function $\mathcal{U} \times I \to R^n$, and that for each r in I there is an isolated equilibrium point $x^* = x^*(r)$ of (B.1). Assume that the Jacobian matrix of f with respect to x, evaluated at $(x^*(r); r)$, has a pair of simple complex conjugate eigenvalues $\lambda(r)$ and $\bar{\lambda}(r)$ such that, at the critical value r_H of the parameter, we have

$$\operatorname{Re} \lambda(r_H) = 0, \quad \operatorname{Im} \lambda(r_H) \neq 0, \quad \frac{d}{dr} \operatorname{Re} \lambda(r_H) \neq 0,$$

while $\operatorname{Re} \rho(r_H) < 0$ for any other eigenvalue ρ. Then (B.1) has a family of periodic solutions. More precisely:
(i) there exist a number $\varepsilon_0 > 0$ and a C^3-function $r:]0, \varepsilon_0[\to R$, with a finite expansion

$$r(\varepsilon) = r_H + \mu_2 \varepsilon^2 + O(\varepsilon^4),$$

such that there is a periodic solution $x_\varepsilon = x_\varepsilon(t)$ of

$$\dot{x} = f(x; r(\varepsilon)). \tag{B.2}$$

The coefficient μ_2 can be computed, employing, for example, the algorithm discussed in Hassard et al. (1981) quoted above.
  If $\mu_2 \neq 0$, then
(ii) there exists a number ε_1, $0 < \varepsilon_1 \leq \varepsilon_0$, such that $r = r(\varepsilon)$ is bijective from $]0, \varepsilon_1[$ either onto $J =]r_H, r(\varepsilon_1)[$ when $\mu_2 > 0$, or onto $J =]r(\varepsilon_1), r_H[$ when $\mu_2 < 0$; therefore, the family $x_\varepsilon = x_\varepsilon(t)$ (for $0 < \varepsilon < \varepsilon_1$) of periodic solutions of (B.2) can be re-parametrized by the original parameter r as $x = x(t; r)$.
  Moreover,
(iii) the stability of $x = x(t; r)$ depends just on a single Floquet exponent $\beta = \beta(r)$, which is a C^2-function of $|r - r_H|^{1/2}$, and it has a finite expansion

$$\beta = \beta_2 \varepsilon^2 + O(\varepsilon^4)$$

with $\beta_2 = -2\mu_2 (d/dr) \operatorname{Re} \lambda(r_H)$, and $\varepsilon^2 = (r - r_H)/\mu_2 + O(r - r_H)^2$; thus, for r near r_H, $x(t; r)$ is orbitally asymptotically stable if $\beta_2 < 0$, but it is unstable when $\beta_2 > 0$. Observe that $\beta_2 \neq 0$.
  Finally,

(iv) the period $p = p(r)$ of $x(t; r)$ is a C^2-function of $|r - r_H|^{1/2}$, with a finite expansion

$$p = \frac{2\pi}{|\text{Im } \lambda(r_H)|} (1 + \tau_2 \varepsilon^2 + O(\varepsilon^4)),$$

with ε^2 is as in (iii) and τ_2 is also a computable coefficient.

References

Allen, R.G.D., 1967, Macro-economic theory (Macmillan, London and Basingstoke).
Allwright, D.J., 1977, Harmonic balance and the Hopf bifurcation, Mathematical Proceedings of Cambridge Philosophical Society 82, 453–467.
Baumol, W.J. and J. Benhabib, 1989, Chaos: Significance, mechanism, and economic applications, The Journal of Economic Perspectives 3, no. 1, 77–107.
Benettin, G., L. Galgani, A. Giorgilli and J.M. Strelcyn, 1980, Lyapunov characteristic exponents for smooth dynamical systems and for Hamiltonian systems: A method for computing all of them, Meccanica 15, 9–30.
Benhabib, J. and R.H. Day, 1981, Rational choice and erratic behavior, Review of Economic Studies 48, 459–471.
Benhabib, J. and R.H. Day, 1982, A characterization of erratic dynamics in the overlapping generations model, Journal of Economic Dynamics and Control 4, 37–55.
Billingsley, P., 1979, Probability and measure (Wiley, New York).
Boltzmann, 1910–12, Vorlesungen über Gastheorie (Leipzig).
Brock, W.A. and C.L. Sayers, 1988, Is the business cycle characterized by deterministic chaos? Journal of Monetary Economics 22, 71–90.
Collet, P. and J.P. Eckmann, 1980, Iterated maps on the interval as dynamical systems (Birchaeuser, Basel, Boston, MA).
Day, R.H., 1982, Irregular growth cycles, American Economic Review 72, 406–414.
Deneckere, R. and S. Pelikan, 1986, Competitive chaos, Journal of Economic Theory 6, 13–25.
Devaney, R.L., 1986, Introduction to chaotic dynamical systems (Benjamin/Cummings, Menlo Park, CA).
Dieudonné, J., 1971, Infinitesimal calculus (Hermann, Paris).
Eckmann, J.P. and D. Ruelle, 1985, Ergodic theory of chaos and strange attractors, Review of Modern Physics 57, 617–656.
Foley, D.K., 1975, On two specifications of asset equilibrium in macroeconomic models, Journal of Political Economy 83, 303–324.
Gandolfo, G., G. Martinengo and P.C. Padoan, 1981, Qualitative analysis and econometric estimation of continuous time dynamic models (North-Holland, Amsterdam).
Grandmont, J.M., 1985, On endogenous competitive business cycles, Econometrica 53, 995–1045.
Guiaşu, 1977, Information theory with applications (McGraw-Hill, Bristol).
Hassard, B.D., N.D. Kazarinoff and Y.-H. Wan, 1981, Theory and applications of Hopf bifurcation, London Mathematical Society Lecture Note Series 41 (Cambridge University Press, Cambridge).
Invernizzi, S., 1991, Remarks on Hopf bifurcation formulae, Rend. Ist. Mat. Univ. Trieste (forthcoming).
Jones, D.S., 1966, Generalized functions (McGraw-Hill, London).
Kampé de Fériet, J., 1963, Théorie de l'Information. Principe du Maximum de l'Entropie et ses Applications à la Statistique et à la Mécanique (Publications du Laboratoire de Calcul de la Faculté des Sciences, Université de Lille, Lille).
Kaplan, W., 1962, Operational methods for linear systems (Addison-Wesley, Reading, MA).
Kaplan, J. and J. Yorke, 1978, Chaotic behavior of multidimensional difference equations, in: H.O. Peitgen and H.O. Walther, eds., Functional differential equations and approximation of fixed points, Lecture Notes in Mathematics 730 (Springer-Verlag, New York).

550   *S. Invernizzi and A. Medio, Lags in economic dynamic models*

Lorenz, H.W., 1989, Nonlinear dynamical economics and chaotic motion (Springer-Verlag, Berlin–Heidelberg–New York).

May, J., 1970, Period analysis and continuous analysis in Patinkin's macroeconomic model, Journal of Economic Theory 2, 1–9.

May, R.M., 1976, Simple mathematical models with very complicated dynamics, Nature 261, 459–467.

May, R.M., 1983, Nonlinear problems in ecology and resource management, in: G. Ioos, R.H.G. Helleman and R. Stora, eds., Comportement Chaotique des Systèmes Déterministes/Chaotic behaviour of deterministic systems (North-Holland, Amsterdam) 514–563.

Medio, A., 1991, Discrete and continuous-time models of chaotic dynamics in economics, Structural Change and Economic Dynamics, forthcoming.

Oseledec, V.I., 1968, A multiplicative ergodic theorem. Lyapunov characteristic numbers for dynamical systems, Transactions of Moscow Mathematical Society 19, 197.

Puu, T., 1987, Complex dynamics in continuous models of the business cycle, in: D. Batten, J. Casti and B. Johansson, eds., Economic evolution and structural change (Springer-Verlag, Berlin–Heidelberg–New York).

Rössler, O.E., 1976, An equation for continuous chaos, Physics Letters 57A, 397–398.

Shannon, C.E., 1948, A mathematical theory of communication, Bell Systems Technical Journal 27, 379.

Sparrow, C., 1980, Bifurcation and chaotic behaviour in simple feedback systems, Journal of Theoretical Biology 83, 93–105.

Stutzer, M., 1980, Chaotic dynamics and bifurcation in a macro-model, Journal of Economic Dynamics and Control 2, 253–276.

Teman, R., 1988, Infinite-dimensional dynamical systems in mechanics and physics (Springer-Verlag, New York).

Theil, H. and D. Fiebig, 1981, A maximum entropy approach to the specification of distributed lags, Economics Letters 7, 339–342.

Turnovsky, S.J., 1977, On the formulation of continuous time macroeconomic models with asset accumulation, International Economic Review 18, 1–28.

[5]

Econ. Theory 2, 437–445 (1992)

Economic
Theory
© Springer-Verlag 1992

Research articles

Chaotic tatonnement*

Venkatesh Bala[1] and Mukul Majumdar[2]
[1] Department of Economics, McGill University, Montréal, Québec, H3A 2T7, CANADA
[2] Department of Economics, Cornell University, Ithaca, NY 14853, USA

Received: January 4, 1991; revised version March 26, 1991

Summary. Debreu's theorem on excess demand functions is used to demonstrate the possibilities of ergodic and topological chaos in a discrete-time tatonnement process with only two goods. The result is in sharp contrast with the well-known result of Arrow and Hurwicz on system stability in a continuous time model of price adjustment with two commodities.

I. Introduction

In their well-known paper, Arrow and Hurwicz (1958) showed (Theorem 6) that in a model with two commodities, the tatonnement process formalized in terms of a differential equation is *system stable*, i.e. for each initial price system, there is some equilibrium price vector to which the process converges. Notwithstanding the well-taken objections to the tatonnement and the auctioneer, the result has been of considerable interest given the extensive use of two commodity models to apply Walrasian equilibrium analysis. It is one of the admittedly special cases where such a price adjustment process can be introduced to illustrate how a Walrasian equilibrium can be attained. Since economic theory has a rich tradition of "period" analysis, which attempts to capture the lags involved in responses of economic agents, it is of some interest to see whether such a result carries over to a discrete time formulation as well.[1] In this context, Saari's (1985) result is particularly important: he showed that for *any* price adjustment rule which the economy follows,

---

* We would like to thank Professors Jess Benhabib, Richard Day, John Guckenheimer, Philip Holmes, Nicholas Kiefer and Tapan Mitra.

[1] See, e.g. the discussion in Baumol (1971) and the references he cites to the earlier works of Lindahl and Metzler. Also, Saari (1985, p. 1119) remarks, "It can be argued that the correct dynamical process associated with the tatonnement process is an iterative one. Just one supporting argument is that the differential dynamic requires a continuum of information. At each instant of time the information must be updated; so a continuous mechanism is far beyond the capability of any 'auctioneer'."

there exists an open set of excess demand functions (in the $C^2[0,1]$ sup norm topology) where the price adjustment rule fails to converge to an equilibrium starting from an open set of initial conditions. Furthermore, he recognized [p. 1126] that even in the simple two-commodity world, far more complex dynamic behavior can occur. In this paper we draw upon the literature on chaotic dynamical systems[2] and provide a self-contained exposition of the possibilities of *both* "topological" and "ergodic" chaos (defined in Sect. II) in a discrete time tatonnement with two commodities. Section II recalls the technical preliminaries. The main result (see Sect. III) *constructs an excess demand function for which the tatonnement process leads to "ergodic" chaos. In addition, on an open neighborhood (in the C^0 sup norm topology) containing this excess demand function, the price adjustment process yields "topological" chaos.*

Our results supplement the earlier examples of Scarf (1960) and Gale (1963), and given the relative simplicity may be of independent interest in capturing some of the complexity of disequilibrium dynamics.

Before we proceed to the technical part of the paper, some remarks are in order. A priori, it would seem to be quite trivial to demonstrate chaos in the tatonnement process, since the literature on dynamical systems yields many instances of continuous functions with chaotic properties, and the Debreu–Mantel–Sonnenschein-type theorems tells us that all such continuous maps are, roughly speaking, aggregate demand functions. However, there are some subtleties involved. First, there is an "ε-qualification" in these theorems which leads to boundary problems. Second, we are interested in "robust" chaos, i.e. chaos which in some sense persists when we perturb the economy. Now, the natural space to carry out these perturbations would be in the class of continuous functions. Since many of the results in chaos theory depend upon the smoothness of the underlying dynamical system (usually C^k maps for $k \geq 3$) even if we started out with a C^k aggregate demand function, arbitrarily small C^0 perturbations can totally destroy the smoothness, making the dynamical behavior in these perturbed systems difficult to study. Furthermore, we need to ensure that boundary restrictions hold for perturbed economies as well. These difficulties preclude a straightforward demonstration of the possibility of chaos in the tatonnement process, and necessitate a somewhat more sophisticated approach to the problem, which is our attempt in this paper.

II. Technical preliminaries

Given a map $f: X \to X$, and any $x \in X$ we define $f^0(x) \equiv x$, $f^1(x) \equiv f(x)$ and for any integer $k \geq 2$,

$$f^k(x) \equiv \overbrace{f \circ f \circ \cdots \circ f}^{k \text{ times}}(x), \quad x \in X.$$

---

[2] Chaotic systems in dynamical economies have been analyzed by Day, Benhabib, Brock, Grandmont and others. See reviews from different perspectives by Baumol–Benhabib [1989], Brock and Dechert [1990], Grandmont [1988] and Day and Pianigiani [1991].

For any integer $k \geq 1$, a point $x \in X$ is a *periodic point of prime period k* if $f^k(x) = x$, and $f^j(x) \neq x$ for all $j = 1, \ldots, k-1$. We denote the set of periodic points in X (i.e. points which have prime period k for some $k \geq 1$) by $\mathscr{P}(X)$. Its complement in X, the set of non-periodic points, is denoted $\mathscr{N}(X)$.

Consider a dynamical system described as $x_{t+1} = f(x_t)$. For characterizing the behavior of this dynamical system we recall the following [Li–Yorke (1975), Devaney (1989)]:

Theorem 2.1. *Let $X = [\alpha, \beta]$ be a non-degenerate compact interval and let $f : X \to X$ be continuous. Suppose there exist points a, b, c, d in X such that*

$$d \leq a < b < c, \quad and \quad f(a) = b, \quad f(b) = c, \quad f(c) = d. \qquad (\text{L–Y})$$

Then,

(1) *for any integer $k \geq 1$ there exists $x_k \in X$ such that x_k is a periodic point of prime period k for the function f.*
(2) *there is an uncountable set $W \subset \mathscr{N}(X)$ satisfying the following conditions:*
(2a) *If $p, q \in W$ with $p \neq q$ then*

$$\limsup_{k \to \infty} |f^k(p) - f^k(q)| > 0, \quad \liminf_{k \to \infty} |f^k(p) - f^k(q)| = 0.$$

(2b) *$p \in W$ and $q \in \mathscr{P}(X)$ implies*

$$\limsup_{k \to \infty} |f^k(p) - f^k(q)| > 0.$$

Remark. Note that (1) in the above result is actually a consequence of Sarkovskii's theorem (see Devaney [1989]).

Theorem 2.1 provides us with sufficient conditions for 'turbulent' or 'chaotic' behavior. In particular, (2a) says that there are pairs of initial positions arbitrarily near other such that the sequences of iterates move apart and return close to each other infinitely often. Furthermore, as (2b) above states, if the initial position is in the set W then the system does not approach any periodic point even asymptotically. Formally,

Definition 2.1. f is said to exhibit *topological chaos on the set X* if (1) and (2) hold.

It has been argued (Collet and Eckmann [1980], Day and Shafer [1987], Grandmont [1988]) that topological chaos can be "unobservable" since the uncountable set W in (2) may have Lebesgue measure zero. This motivates the following definition:

Definition 2.2. f is said to exhibit *ergodic chaos* on the interval $X \equiv [\alpha, \beta]$ if there exists a unique probability measure v satisfying:

(i) v is a absolutely continuous with respect to Lebesgue measure on X.
(ii) $v(f^{-1}(B)) = v(B)$ for every Borel set $B \subset X$.
(iii) for every v-integrable real valued function ϕ:

$$\lim_{T \to \infty} T^{-1} \sum_{j=1}^{T} \phi(f^j(x)) \to \int \phi \, dv.$$

for v-a.e. initial condition $x \in X$.

Furthermore, if v is the unique probability measure which satisfies (i)–(iii) above, it is called the *ergodic measure* of f.

If a function f has an ergodic measure v, then for v-a.e. initial condition $x \in X$ (and hence on a set of initial conditions having positive Lebesgue measure) the sequence of iterates $\{f^j(x)\}$ will 'fill up' the support of the measure v, and as a consequence, will have extremely complicated trajectories.

Next, we introduce the notion of a Schwarzian derivative (see Devaney [1989]). Recall that $X \equiv [\alpha, \beta]$. Let $f : X \to \mathscr{R}$ be of class C^3. The Schwarzian derivative $Sf(x)$ is given by:

$$Sf(x) \equiv f'''(x)/f'(x) - (3/2)\{f''(x)/f'(x)\}^2, \quad x \in X, \quad f'(x) \neq 0.$$

The following theorem provides sufficient conditions for ergodic chaos.

Theorem 2.2. *Let $f : X \to X$ satisfy the following conditions:*

(i) f *is of class* C^3, *and there exists* $x^* \in (\alpha, \beta)$ *such that* $f'(x^*) = 0$, $f'(x) > 0$ *for* $x < x^*$, $f'(x) < 0$ *for* $x > x^*$ *and* $f''(x^*) < 0$.
(ii) $f(x) > x$ *for all* $x \in (\alpha, x^*)$, $f(x^*) \in (x^*, \beta]$, $Sf(x) < 0$ *for all* $x \in X$ *except* $x = x^*$.
(iii) *There exists* $k \geq 2$ *such that* $y = f^k(x^*)$ *is an unstable fixed point of* f, *i.e. satisfies* $f(y) = y$, $|f'(y)| > 1$.
     Then f exhibits ergodic chaos.

A detailed discussion of Theorems 2.1 and 2.2 may be found in Grandmont [1988].[3]

III. Chaotic price tatonnement

In this section, we demonstrate that there exists an economy for which the tatonnement process yields ergodic and topological chaos. Furthermore, the process exhibits topological chaos for all economies in an open[4] neighborhood (in the sup norm topology) of the above economy. We write $I^0 \equiv (0, 1)$, and for $\varepsilon < 1/2$, $I_\varepsilon \equiv [\varepsilon, 1 - \varepsilon]$. I_ε may be regarded as the projection of the set S_ε onto its first coordinate, where S_ε is defined as:

$$S_\varepsilon \equiv \{(p, q) : p^2 + q^2 = 1, p \geq \varepsilon, q \geq \sqrt{2\varepsilon - \varepsilon^2}\}.$$

For any continuous, real-valued function ϕ on I^0, there exists a continuous function $\hat{\phi}$ on I^0, obtained via Walras' Law:

$$\hat{\phi}(p) \equiv -(1 - p^2)^{-1/2} p \phi(p), \quad p \in I^0. \tag{3.0}$$

Debreu's theorem (Debreu [1974]) implies that for any continuous function ϕ on I^0, and for any $\varepsilon \in (0, 1/2)$, there exists a two-agent, two-commodity exchange

---

[3] Some of these conditions have been reformulated.
[4] Alternatively, structural robustness of chaos may be studied in the context of finite-dimensional (i.e. parametric) variations of the dynamical system. While our approach yields stronger conclusions, parametric perturbations may be of interest in studying the robustness of ergodic chaos (See Day and Shafer [1987]).

economy with each agent having strictly convex, continuous and monotone preferences, whose excess demand functions agree with $(\phi, \hat{\phi})$ on the set I_ε.

Let $C(J)$ represent the space of continuous real-valued functions on a closed interval J, endowed with the sup norm. In what follows, for an appropriate I_ε, we identify a particular ζ in $C(I_\varepsilon)$ with the economy whose existence follows from Debreu's theorem, it being understood that $(\zeta, \hat{\zeta})$ is the pair of excess demand functions on I_ε for this economy (where $\hat{\zeta}$ is computed according to (3.0)).

In the tatonnement process, prices are raised (resp. lowered) in response to positive (resp. negative) excess demand and left unchanged at any competitive equilibrium. Thus, for the excess demand function $z(p)$, a given $\varepsilon \in (0, 0.1)$ and any initial condition $p_0 \in I_\varepsilon$:

$$
p_{t+1} = \begin{cases} p_t + \theta z(p_t), & \text{if} \quad p_t + \theta z(p_t) \in I_\varepsilon \\ 1 - \varepsilon, & \text{if} \quad p_t + \theta z(p_t) > 1 - \varepsilon \\ \varepsilon, & \text{if} \quad p_t + \theta z(p_t) < \varepsilon \end{cases} \tag{3.1}
$$

where $\theta > 0$ is a 'speed of adjustment' parameter.

For the excess demand functions we shall be dealing with, the process will always stay in the interior of I_ε so the second and third cases in (3.1) above are only provided for the sake of completeness.

Theorem 3.1. *Consider the open interval $E = (0, 0.01)$. For every $\varepsilon \in E$, there exists an economy $\zeta_\varepsilon \in C(I_\varepsilon)$ such that:*

(3.1a) *ζ_ε has a competitive equilibrium in the interior of I_ε, i.e. there is a $\tilde{p}, \varepsilon < \tilde{p} < 1 - \varepsilon$, with $\zeta_\varepsilon(\tilde{p}) = 0$, $\hat{\zeta}_\varepsilon(\tilde{p}) = 0$. In addition,*
(3.1a') *for a neighborhood $(\tilde{p} - \eta, \tilde{p} + \eta) \subset I_\varepsilon$, the excess demand function $\zeta_\varepsilon(\cdot)$ is strictly decreasing.*
(3.1b) *The tatonnement process $p_{t+1} = p_t + \theta \zeta_\varepsilon(p_t)$ exhibits* **ergodic** *chaos on I_ε.*

Furthermore, there exists an open neighborhood K (depending upon ε) of ζ_ε such that, if $\phi \in K$, then (3.1a) above holds for ϕ in place of ζ_ε, and:
(3.1c) *The tatonnement process $p_{t+1} = p_t + \theta \phi(p_t)$ exhibits* **topological** *chaos on I_ε.*

Before we embark upon proving the above, we first demonstrate the following corollary to Theorem 2.1.

Corollary 3.1. *Let $f : X \to X$ satisfy (L–Y) in Theorem 2.1 with the strict inequality $d < a$. In addition, suppose $\alpha < r(X, f) < R(X, f) < \beta$, where $R(X, f)$ and $r(X, f)$ are the maximum and minimum respectively of f on the interval $X \equiv [\alpha, \beta]$. Then, there exists an open neighborhood $N \subset C(X)$, containing f, such that $g \in N$ implies that (1) and (2) of Theorem 2.1 hold with g in place of f.*[5]

---

[5] Following a referee's suggestion, we contrast our corollary with a counter-example due to Butler and Pianigiani [1978]. They construct a map $\tau : [0, 1] \to [0, 1]$ as follows:

$$
\tau(x) = \begin{cases} 1/2 + x & \text{if} \quad 0 \leq x \leq 1/2, \\ 2 - 2x & \text{if} \quad 1/2 < x \leq 1. \end{cases}
$$

The function τ satisfies (L–Y) of Theorem 2.1 (i.e. has a period 3 orbit) with $a = 0$, $b = 1/2$, $c = 1$ and

(*Footnote continued*)

Proof. First, we show the following: Given $k \geq 1$, $\varepsilon > 0$ and $x \in X$ there exists $\delta(k, \varepsilon) > 0$ such that

$$\| g - f \| < \delta(k, \varepsilon) \Rightarrow |g^j(x) - f^j(x)| < \varepsilon, \quad j = 1, \ldots, k. \tag{3.1'}$$

The proof is by induction on k. It is clearly true for $k = 1$ with $\delta(1, \varepsilon) = \varepsilon$. Assume that it holds for $k = m$ and not for $k = m + 1$. Then, there exists an $\varepsilon > 0$ and a sequence of functions $\{g_n\}$ satisfying $\| g_n - f \| \to 0$ such that $|g_n^{m+1}(x) - f^{m+1}(x)| \geq \varepsilon$. Let $g_n^m(x) = y_n$ and $f^m(x) = y$. Then, by the induction hypothesis, $y_n \to y$. From Rudin (1981, Chapter 7) we conclude that $g_n(y_n) \to f(y)$, which yields a contradiction. Thus, we can continue the induction.

Next, choose a real number ρ satisfying $0 < \rho < \min 1/2\{(a - d), (b - a), (c - b)\}$ and $\delta > 0$ such that (and here we use (3.1') above)

$$\| g - f \| < \delta \Rightarrow |g^j(a) - f^j(a)| < \rho, \quad j = 1, 2, 3.$$

Clearly, we can choose δ to also satisfy the inequality $\delta < \min \{\beta - R(X, f), r(X, f) - \alpha\}$. Now define N to be the open set $\{g \in C(X) : \| g - f \| < \delta\}$. Then it follows that any g in N also maps X into X, since the maximum value of g is bounded above by $R(X, f) + \delta < \beta$ and the minimum of g is likewise bounded below by α. All that remains is to show that we can satisfy (L–Y) of Theorem 2.1 for any g in N. Recall that $f(a) = b$, $f(b) = c$ and $f(c) = d$. Hence, since $|g(a) - f(a)| \equiv |g(a) - b| < \rho$, we have

(i) $g(a) > b - \rho > a + \rho > a$.

Likewise, since $g(a) < b + \rho$, and $|g^2(a) - c| < \rho$, we get

(ii) $g^2(a) > c - \rho > b + \rho > g(a)$.

Finally, since $|g^3(a) - d| < \rho$, we get

(iii) $g^3(a) < d + \rho < a - \rho < a$.

If we define b' to be $g(a)$, c' to be $g^2(a)$ and d' as $g^3(a)$, then (i)–(iii) above satisfy (L–Y) for the function g with b', c' and d' replacing b, c and d. Hence, we can apply Theorem 2.1 to g to prove the result. $\square$

Proof of Theorem 3.1. We start with the logistic family of maps[6]

$$h_\mu(p) = \mu p(1 - p) \quad 3 < \mu < 4, \quad p \in (0, 1). \tag{3.2}$$

$d = 0$. Consider next the family of maps $\{\tau_\varepsilon\}_{\varepsilon > 0}$ given by

$$\tau_\varepsilon(x) = \begin{cases} 1/2 + \varepsilon & \text{if } 0 \leq x \leq \varepsilon, \\ 1/2 + x & \text{if } \varepsilon < x \leq 1/2, \\ 2 - 2x & \text{if } 1/2 < x \leq 1. \end{cases}$$

It is easily seen that $\lim_{\varepsilon \to 0} \| \tau_\varepsilon - \tau \| = 0$. It can also be shown that for all ε less than some $\varepsilon_0 > 0$, τ_ε has no periodic point of prime period 3. Thus the period-3 orbit of the map τ can be destroyed by arbitrarily small C^0 perturbations. This example is, however, somewhat special, because the requirement $d \leq a$ of condition (L–Y) can only be satisfied by τ with strict equality. Our corollary rules out these kinds of maps by requiring $d < a$.

[6] Jakobson [1981] shows the existence of an absolutely continuous invariant measure for the logistic family of maps $\{h_\mu\}$ for a set of μ-parameters having strictly positive Lebesgue measure. His result cannot be used directly since we require sharp bounds upon μ in order to apply Corollary 3.1.

Since $h'_\mu(p) = \mu(1 - 2p)$, the function h_μ has a unique critical point at $p^* = 1/2$. In addition, $h_\mu(p)$ has a fixed point at $\bar{p} = 1 - 1/\mu$, where the slope is $h'_\mu(\bar{p}) = (2 - \mu)$. Hence, for any $\mu \in (3, 4)$, $|h'_\mu(\bar{p})| > 1$.

From condition (iii) of Theorem 2.2, we require that for some $k \geq 2$, and some $\mu \in (3, 4)$:

$$h^k_\mu(p^*) - (1 - 1/\mu) = 0. \tag{3.3}$$

Let $k = 5$. Equation (3.3) can be expanded (calculated using integer arithmetic on a computer) to a 31-degree polynomial in μ. In what follows, all numerical calculations are exact, but are reported only to two decimal places.

For $\mu = 3.92$ the left hand side of (3.3) above is -0.09, while for $\mu = 3.93$ the left hand side of (3.3) is $+0.03$. Hence, by the intermediate value theorem, Eq. (3.3) has a solution in the interval $(3.92, 3.93)$. We shall refer to this solution as μ^*. Likewise, we shall denote

$$h^*(p) \equiv h_{\mu^*}(p) \equiv \mu^* p(1 - p). \tag{3.4}$$

We require a restriction on ε which ensures that the dynamical system $p_{t+1} = h^*(p_t)$ remains in the interval I_ε for every initial condition $p_0 \in I_\varepsilon$. Let $r(I_\varepsilon, h^*)$ and $R(I_\varepsilon, h^*)$ denote the minimum and maximum respectively of h^* on I_ε. It is easy to see that

$$r(I_\varepsilon, h^*) = h^*(\varepsilon) = h^*(1 - \varepsilon) = \mu^* \varepsilon(1 - \varepsilon)$$

and

$$R(I_\varepsilon, h^*) = h^*(p^*) = \mu^*(1/2)(1 - 1/2) = \mu^*/4 < 0.99.$$

Hence, we write $E = (0, 0.01)$. It can be seen that for every $\varepsilon \in E$:

$$\varepsilon < r(I_\varepsilon, h^*) \leq h^*(p) \leq R(I_\varepsilon, h^*) < 1 - \varepsilon, \quad p \in I_\varepsilon. \tag{3.5}$$

From now onwards, fix $\varepsilon \in E$. Define ζ_ε as:

$$\zeta_\varepsilon(p) = \theta^{-1}\{(\mu^* - 1)p - \mu^* p^2\}, \quad p \in I_\varepsilon. \tag{3.6}$$

We see that $p + \theta\zeta_\varepsilon(p) \equiv h^*(p) = \mu^* p(1 - p)$, $p \in I_\varepsilon$. Also note that $\zeta_\varepsilon(p)$ equals 0 at $\bar{p} = (\mu^* - 1)/\mu^*$ which lies in the interior of I_ε. Furthermore, $\zeta'_\varepsilon(p)$ evaluated at $\bar{p}$ equals $\theta^{-1}\{(1 - \mu^*)\} < 0$. Hence, (3.1a) and (3.1a') of Theorem 3.1 is proved.

It is not difficult to check that conditions (i) and (ii) of Theorem 2.2 are satisfied by h^* on I_ε. Since μ^* has been chosen to ensure that condition (iii) is satisfied, the tatonnement process:

$$p_{t+1} = h^*(p_t) \equiv p_t + \theta\zeta_\varepsilon(p_t), \quad t \geq 1, \quad p_0 \in I_\varepsilon. \tag{3.7}$$

exhibits ergodic chaos on I_ε, i.e. we have proved (3.1b) of Theorem 3.1.

All that remains to be shown is that topological chaos exists in a neighborhood of ζ_ε. To apply Corollary 3.1, we need to show the existence of points a, b, c, d such that:

$$\varepsilon < d = h^*(c) < a < b = h^*(a) < c = h^*(b) < 1 - \varepsilon. \tag{3.8}$$

Let $a = 0.18$; we will employ a perturbation argument involving Eq. (3.2) to obtain bounds on the iterates $\{h^{*k}(a)\}$ for $k = 1, 2, 3$. The perturbations also employ integer arithmetic on a computer, and only the truncations to two decimal digits are reported here.

Recall that $\mu^* \in (3.92, 3.93)$. For $e \in [0, 0.01]$, using Eq. (3.2), we get:

$$(3.92 + e)(0.18)(1 - 0.18) = 0.58 + 0.15e.$$

Thus,

$$b = h^*(a) \equiv h^*(0.18) \in (0.58, 0.58 + (0.15)(0.01)) \subset (0.58, 0.59) > 0.18.$$

Likewise, it can be shown that $c = h^*(b) \in (0.95, 0.98) > b$ and $d = h^*(c) \in (0.11, 0.17) < a$. Furthermore, since $\varepsilon < 0.01$, we have demonstrated Eq. (3.8) above. Consequently, we can apply Corollary 3.1 to the dynamical system h^*, to obtain a neighborhood N around h^*, such that all dynamical systems in N exhibit topological chaos. Now, let $\mathrm{id}_\varepsilon(\cdot)$ be the identity map on I_ε. Since $C(I_\varepsilon)$ is a topological vector space, the translate $K \equiv \theta^{-1}\{N - \mathrm{id}_\varepsilon\}$ is open in $C(I_\varepsilon)$. However, $\zeta_\varepsilon \equiv \theta^{-1}\{h^* - \mathrm{id}_\varepsilon\}$ and hence ζ_ε lies in K. If ϕ is an economy in K, then by definition, the corresponding tatonnement dynamic $\mathrm{id}_\varepsilon + \theta\phi$ lies in N and exhibits topological chaos. This proves (3.1c). $\square$

IV. Concluding remarks

It should be mentioned that our main result is of independent interest from a methodological standpoint: the proof involves an explicit numerical solution to a high order (31-degree) polynomial equation associated with a specific parametric family of maps. To ensure that the rigor expected in contemporary economic theory is not compromised, the proof employs computer algebra and integer (as opposed to floating-point) arithmetic implemented on a high end computer for complete mathematical accuracy.

We also note that by restricting ourselves to topological chaos, it is possible to prove stronger results than demonstrated above. Formally, we can define a *generalized tatonnement process* as a continuous map $M : I_\varepsilon \times \mathcal{R} \to I_\varepsilon$ satisfying:

(i) $M(p, 0) = p$ for all $p \in I_\varepsilon$.
(ii) $M(p, z)$ is non-decreasing in z, for every $p \in I_\varepsilon$.
(iii) $M(p, z) \neq p$ if $z \neq 0$ and $p \in (\varepsilon, 1 - \varepsilon)$.

It is easily seen that the process defined by (3.1) is a special case of the above. Given a generalized process M, it can be shown, using techniques similar to those employed here, that there exists a piece-wise linear, everywhere non-increasing excess demand function ϕ for which the process M yields topological chaos. Furthermore, chaos persists on an open neighborhood containing ϕ.

References

Arrow, K.J., Hurwicz, L.: On the stability of competitive equilibrium, I. Econometrica **26**, 522–552 (1958)
Baumol, W.J.: Economic dynamics, 3rd. edn. London: Macmillan Company 1971
Baumol, W.J., Benhabib, J.: Chaos: significance, mechanism and economic applications. J. Econ. Perspect. **3**, 77–105 (1989)
Benhabib, J., Day, R.H.: Erratic accumulation. Econ. Lett. **6**, 113–117 (1980)

Boldrin, M., Deneckere, R.J.: Simple macroeconomic models with very complicated dynamics. UCLA Working Paper No. 527 (1989)

Brock, W.A., Dechert, W.D.: Nonlinear dynamical systems: instability and chaos in economics. to appear in: Hildenbrand, W., Sonnenschein, H. (eds.) Handbook of mathematical economics, vol. 4. 1990

Butler, G.J., Pianigiani, G.: Periodic points and chaotic functions in the unit interval. Bull. Austr. Math. Soc. **18**, 255–265 (1978)

Collet, P., Eckmann, J.-P.: Iterated maps on the interval as dynamical systems. Boston: Birkhäuser 1980

Day, R.H.: The emergence of chaos from classical economic growth. Q. J. Econ. **98**, 201–213 (1983)

Day, R.H., Pianigiani, G.: Statistical dynamics and economics. J. Econ. Behav. Organiz. **16**, 37–84 (1991)

Day, R.H., Shafer, W.: Ergodic fluctuations in deterministic economic models. J. Econ. Behav. Organiz. **8**, 339–361 (1987)

Debreu, G.: Excess demand functions. J. Math. Econ. **1**, 15–21 (1974)

Devaney, R.L.: An introduction to chaotic dynamical systems. New York: Addison Wesley 1989

Gale, D.: A note on the global instability of competitive equilibrium. Naval. Res. Log. Q. **10**, 81–87 (1963)

Grandmont, J.-M.: Nonlinear difference equations bifurcations and chaos: an introduction. CEPREMAP Working Paper No. 8811, Paris (1988)

Grandmont, J.-M.: Periodic and apriodic behavior in discrete one dimensional dynamical systems. In: Hildenbrand, W., Mas-Colell, A. (eds.) Contributions to mathematical economics in honor of Gerard Debreu. New York: North Holland 1986

Jakobson, M.V.: Absolutely continuous invariant measures for one-parameter families of one-dimensional maps. Commun. Math. Phys. **81**, 39–88 (1981)

Li, T., Yorke, J.A.: Period three implies chaos. Am. Math. Mon. **82**, 985–992 (1975)

Lichtenberg, A.J., Lieberman, M.A.: Regular and stochastic motion. Berlin Heidelberg New York: Springer 1983

Rudin, W.: Principles of mathematical analysis, 3rd. edn. New York: McGraw-Hill 1976

Saari, D.G.: Iterative price mechanisms Econometrica **53**, 1117–1132 (1985)

Scarf, H.: Some examples of global instability of competitive equilibrium. Int. Econ. Rev. **1**, 157–172 (1960)

Wolf, A.: Quantifying chaos with Lyapunov exponents. In: Holden, A.V. (ed.) Chaos. Princeton: Princeton University Press 1986

[6]

Journal of Economic Behavior and Organization 16 (1991) 37–83. North-Holland

Statistical dynamics and economics*

Richard H. Day and Giulio Pianigiani

University of Southern California, Los Angeles, CA 90089-0253, USA

Received October 1990, final version February 1991

It is shown in this paper how complex economic dynamics can be characterized using the statistical or distributional theory of dynamical systems. The basic concepts of the latter are summarized. Then applications to supply and demand adjustments in competitive markets, aggregate business fluctuations and economic growth in the very long run are briefly reviewed.

Complex dynamic behavior involves unstable, non-periodic (chaotic) fluctuations in contrast to stationary states, periodic cycles or paths that converge to such orbits. It arises in economic processes as a generic consequence of inherent nonlinearity. This fact is by now well known. Its relevance has been explored in models of consumer behavior, business fluctuations, stock market behavior, population dynamics, growth cycles, competitive market mechanisms and optimal intertemporal equilibrium theory.[1]

Simple dynamics can readily be characterized (at least in the long run or in the limit) by stationary states or stable, periodic orbits; chaotic trajectories cannot. A similar problem arose in physics more than a century ago when it was realized that an ensemble of interacting particles could move in such a complicated way that there was no chance to represent the behavior of any of its individual components. Rather, the distribution of particles and the proportions of time given events occur might behave in a coherent way and in the long run according to stable probabilistic laws. Clausius, Boltzman and Maxwell, the founders of thermodynamics, are generally credited with originating this point of view. It was given an early systematic development by Gibbs. It is interesting to note that these early contributors used the term

---

*These notes are based on lectures given at the Workshop on Dynamical Sciences held first at the University of Southern California in May 1988 and in the succeeding year in Stockholm at the Industrial Institute for Economic and Social Research (IUI), May 1989.

[1]For representative collections see Galeotti, Geronazzo and Gori (1978), Medio (1986), Grandmont (1987), and for useful reviews, see Baumol and Benhabib (1989) and Boldrin (1988).

'chaotic' to describe the seemingly random behavior of deterministic systems.[2]

The modern mathematical theory of non-linear dynamical systems was also originated in the 19th century. Poincaré, its founder, recognized that even relatively simple ensembles, such as those of classical, celestial mechanics, could display complex behavior. Eventually, Ulam showed that a discrete time system, one represented by a single variable 'tent map', could exhibit the statistical properties of the ergodic theory of deterministic dynamical systems that had been developed after Poincaré by Birkhoff and others. The upshot of all this is that it is not complexity of structure that gives rise to complex behavior but non-linearity.

The discovery that deterministic dynamic *economic* models could generate erratic paths raised the possibility of statistical behavior in that context also. Although an immediate answer was not obvious, constructive methods that had already appeared facilitated the investigation.[3] By now it is clear that quite standard economic models not only can generate chaotic time-paths, but these time-paths, when viewed in the limit, can indeed obey certain properties of stochastic processes and the frequencies of their values can converge to stable density functions. The purpose of these notes is to survey the basic concepts involved and to introduce their application to the study of dynamic economic processes.

One must be careful in interpreting what is accomplished in any analysis based on limiting or 'long-run' arguments as is the case here. Real world economic systems do not hold still in the long run; the system generating economic data during one time frame is different from the one generating it at an earlier or later time. Nonetheless, if the relative frequencies of the values generated by a given model converge to a density function, that fact explains erratic short-run behavior, even though it would not completely explain real world behavior in the long run (because the model itself would have to change).

Exogenous changes can sometimes be conveniently treated as random perturbations to a given economic model. It is important in such a case to consider the dynamics of the deterministic part of the system on its own terms to see if at least part of the irregular nature of the generated data could be due to the intrinsic interaction of the endogenous variables. It may also be useful to think of changes in structure as the result of deterministic dynamics using multiple phase dynamical systems that possess more than one structural regime. In this case the distribution theory may be used to explain how a system's behavior can escape its domain of viability. Such an escape could be interpreted as the demise of a system or more generally as a

---

[2]On the origin of statistical mechanics, see Gibbs (1901). On the mathematical theory, see Dunford and Schwartz (1958, pp. 726–730).

[3]See below, sections 1.4–1.6.

description of how a given regime might switch to a different one governed by a different dynamic law. In this way the statistical dynamics can provide an intrinsic explanation of economic evolution. In this paper we show how these ideas arise naturally in the study of economic processes.

Section 1 contains a brief survey of some basic concepts used in the statistical theory of dynamical systems. Section 2 uses a model of competitive price adjustment to illustrate how questions of distribution theory arise in a standard economic setting. In section 3 similar results are obtained for the familiar real/monetary business cycle theory. Section 4 briefly considers economic growth in the very long run using the theory of statistical dynamics to suggest how the varied patterns of economic evolution that have occurred in the historical record could have arisen.

1. Chaos, measure and escape[4]

1.1. Dynamical systems

Consider the class of all recursive economies whose structure on a domain $X \subset \mathbb{R}$ can be represented by a continuous map $\theta : X \to \mathbb{R}$. The state of the economy in a given period t is given by a value $x_t \in X$. The succeeding state is generated by the difference equation

$$x_{t+1} = \theta(x_t; \pi) \equiv \theta(x_t), \tag{1.1}$$

where π is a vector of parameters for the function θ. Define the iterated map $\theta^n : X \to X$ by $\theta^0(x) \equiv x$ and $\theta^n(x) = \theta \circ \theta^{n-1}(x)$, $n = 1, 2, 3, \ldots$. Then the sequence $\tau(x) = \{\theta^n(x)\}_{n \geq 0}$ is called the *trajectory* from the initial condition x. The *orbit* from x is the *set* $\gamma(x) = \{\theta^n(x) | n \geq 0\}$. The asymptotic behavior of a trajectory is described by the *limit set* $\omega(x)$ of the trajectory $\tau(x)$; $\omega(x)$ is defined to be the set of all limit points of $\tau(x)$, i.e., by

$$\omega(x) := \bigcap_{n=1}^{\infty} c\ell\, \gamma(\theta^n(x)),$$

where $c\ell(S)$ means the closure of the set S. Note that $\omega(x)$ is closed and $\theta(\omega(x)) = \omega(x)$.

An *attractor* for θ is closed set $F \subset X$ such that $\omega(x) = F$ for x in a set of positive Lebesgue measure which we shall define below. Attractors represent the asymptotic behavior of solutions for a non-trivial set of initial conditions.

---

[4]In addition to the references cited in the text, the reader who wants to explore the background and details of the topics covered should consider Lasota and Mackey (1985) and, for a more advanced treatment, Dunford and Schwartz (1988, Part I, chapter VIII). A good text on measure theory is also useful, such as Halmos (1950).

A point $y \in X$ is a periodic point of period n if $\theta^n(y) = y$ and $\theta^j(y) \neq y$ for $0 < j < n$. A periodic point y and the corresponding periodic orbit $\gamma(y)$ are called *asymptotically stable* if there is a non-degenerate interval V containing y such that $\omega(x) = \gamma(y)$ for all $x \in V$. It is not unusual for a map to have many, perhaps an infinite number of periodic points. It is also possible that none of the periodic points is asymptotically stable. It is in this situation that the theory of statistical dynamics can be used to describe the asymptotic behavior of trajectories.

1.2. Invariant measure

A σ-algebra is a collection of subsets Σ of a set X:

(i)   That contains X,
(ii)   that contains the complement of any set in Σ, and
(iii) that contains the union of any countable collection of subsets in Σ.

Let $\{X_n\}_{n=1}^\infty$ be a countable collection of disjoint sets in σ-algebra Σ. A *measure* is a map with images in the non-negative real numbers and arguments in Σ such that:

(i) $\mu(\emptyset) = 0$,
(ii) $\mu(\bigcup_{n=1}^\infty X_n) = \sum_{n=1}^\infty \mu(X_n)$.

An example is the Lebesque measure on the real line, denoted $m(\cdot)$, which associates with an interval its length. Thus, if $I := [a, b]$ is an interval, then $m(I) = |b - a|$. In general if a measure μ is zero on points, it is called *continuous* or *non-atomic*.

A *probability space* is a triple (X, Σ, μ), where X is a set, Σ a σ-algebra of subsets of X and μ is a measure such that $\mu(X) = 1$. In what follows by a measure we shall always mean a probability measure.

A mapping θ from X into itself is said to be *measure preserving* and μ is said to be *invariant* under θ if

$$\mu(\theta^{-1}E) = \mu(E) \quad \text{for all} \quad E \in \Sigma.$$

As an example, consider the tent map,

$$T_M(x) := \begin{cases} 2Mx, & x \in [0, \tfrac{1}{2}) \\ 2M(1-x), & x \in [\tfrac{1}{2}, 1] \end{cases} \tag{1.2}$$

Using the definition it is easy to check that $T_1(\cdot)$ preserves Lebesgue measure, i.e., Lebesgue measure is invariant under $T_1(\cdot)$. This is not true

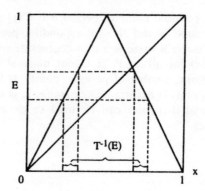

Fig. 1.1. A tent map (that preserved Lebesgue measure for $M = 1$).

when $M \neq 1$ as you can readily see. [We use $T(\cdot)$ to denote a map defined on the unit interval.] (See fig. 1.1.)

For measure preserving transformations Poincaré established a famous recurrence theorem. It is not difficult to prove and it affords a simple example of how the concept of measure can be used to determine properties of dynamical systems.

The Poincaré Recurrence Theorem. Let (X, Σ, μ) be a probability space and let μ be invariant under θ. Let E be any set of positive measure. Then almost all points of E return to E infinitely often.

Proof. For any $k \geq 0$ consider the set

$$E_k = \bigcup_{n=k}^{\infty} \theta^{-n}(E),$$

where $\theta^0(E) := E$. E_k is just the set of points that map into E after at least k periods, that is, for all $x \in E_k$ there is an $n \geq k$ such that $\theta^n(x) \in E$. It follows that $E_{k+1} = \theta^{-1}(E_k)$ and that $E_0 \supset E_1 \supset \cdots \supset E_n \ldots$ so $E^* = \bigcap_{k=0}^{\infty} E_k \subset E_0$. Of course, $E \subset E_0$. By assumption μ is invariant with respect to θ so $\mu(E_{k+1}) = \mu(E_k)$ for all k which implies that $\mu(E^*) = \mu(E_0)$. Consequently,

$$0 < \mu(E) = \mu(E \cap E_0) \leq \mu(E_0) = \mu(E^*).$$

This implies that

$$\mu(E \cap E^*) = \mu(E \cap E_0) = \mu(E) > 0.$$

Now consider an $x \in E \cap \bigcap_{k=0}^{\infty} E_k$. For such a point for all k there exists an $n \geq k$ such that $\theta^n(x) \in E$. But $x \in E$ also. Therefore, for μ-almost all $x \in E$, x 'returns' to E infinitely often. $\qquad \square$

1.3. Ergodic measure

Suppose that there exists $E \in \Sigma$ such that $\theta^{-1}(E) = E$ (and hence $\theta^{-1}(X \backslash E) = X \backslash E$) then the dynamics is split into two separate parts; in fact, if $x \in E$, then $x \in \theta^{-1}(E)$ which implies $\theta(x) \in E$ and the trajectory of x will stay in E forever. Likewise for $X \backslash E$. This motivates the concept of ergodicity.

Definition. A map θ is *ergodic* if $E \in \Sigma$ and $\theta^{-1}(E) = E$ imply that either $\mu(E) = 0$ or $\mu(E) = 1$.

Ergodicity means that you cannot split the system into non-trivial parts. As an example of an ergodic system, we mention the rational rotation on the circle with the usual Lebesgue measure. Also, the tent map introduced in eq. (1.2) is ergodic with respect to Lebesgue measure for $M = 1$.

A major result in ergodic theory due to Birkhoff and von Neuman is

The Mean Ergodic Theorem.[5] *Let* (X, Σ, μ) *be a probability space and let* θ *be measure preserving and ergodic. Let* $g(\cdot)$ *be an integrable function. Then*

$$\lim_{n \to \infty} \frac{1}{n} \sum_{i=0}^{n-1} g(\theta^i(x)) = \int_X g \, d\mu \quad \text{for almost all} \quad x \in X. \tag{1.3}$$

To understand the implications of this theorem, note that the left side of (1.3) is the average value of $g(\cdot)$ evaluated along the trajectory $\tau(x)$. The right side is the mean value or expected value of $g(\cdot)$ evaluated on the space X. Thus, it is said that 'the time average equals the space average'.

Let $E \in \Sigma$ be any set with $\mu(E) > 0$ and consider a generic trajectory. We ask how much time does this trajectory spend in E? The characteristic function of points in the trajectory given a set E is

$$\chi_E(\theta^t(x)) = \begin{cases} 1, & \theta^t(x) \in E \\ 0, & \theta^t(x) \notin E \end{cases}$$

summed over points in the trajectory we get the number of times the trajectory 'enters' the set E. According to Poincaré's Recurrence Theorem, we

[5]See Dunford and Schwartz (1958, pp. 661–684). This combines Theorem 9, p. 667, with the Corollary 10 on p. 668. See also, Lasota and Mackey (1985, pp. 57–59).

expect this to be infinite if $\mu(E) > 0$. However, the *average* time spent can be finite. Indeed, the Birkhoff ergodic theorem says that the time average,

$$\lim_{n \to \infty} \frac{1}{n} \sum_{i=0}^{n-1} \chi_E(\theta^i(x)) = \mu(E), \tag{1.4}$$

for almost x in X. To see this we let $g(x) := \chi_E(x)$. This gives the left side of (1.3). Then $\int_X g(x)\,d\mu = \int_X \chi_E(x)\,d\mu = \mu(E)$. *This implies that a typical trajectory will visit every measurable set proportionally to its measure.*

1.4. The existence of continuous measures

As a typical trajectory visits every set of positive measure, the system behaves in a 'chaotic' way if the measure μ is supported in a 'large' set. If, for a contrary example, the measure μ is concentrated on a fixed point x_0, then μ is certainly invariant and ergodic. The Birkhoff mean ergodic theorem applies, but 'almost everywhere' here means just for $x = x_0$, and a typical trajectory is stationary at x_0. The same is true for cycles of any period n except the measure is concentrated equally on the periodic points.

A result which guarantees the existence of an invariant measure supported on a 'large set' is the following theorem due to Lasota and Pianigiani (1977).

Theorem 1. Let X be a topological space and let $\theta : X \to X$ be continuous. Let θ satisfy the following 'expansivity' condition: there are two compact disjoint sets A and B such that

$$\theta(A) \cap \theta(B) \supset A \cup B. \tag{1.5}$$

Then there exists an ergodic invariant measure μ that is continuous, i.e., $\mu\{x\} = 0$ for all singletons $\{x\}$.

Remark. As $\mu\{x\} = 0$ for all $\{x\}$ it follows that the support of such a measure is an uncountable set.

We now present a set of conditions for which continuous ergodic, invariant measures exist. These are given in the well-known condition of Li and Yorke (1975).

Theorem 2. Let $\theta : X \to X$ be continuous and suppose there exists a point such that either

$$\theta^3(x) \leq x < \theta(x) < \theta^2(x) \quad or \quad \theta^3(x) \geq x > \theta(x) > \theta^2(x). \tag{1.6}$$

Then:

(i)   *There exist periodic cycles of every period;*
(ii)   *there exists an uncountable set E containing no periodic points such that for all x, y ∈ E, x ≠ y we have*

$$\limsup |\theta^n(x) - \theta^n(y)| > 0, \qquad \liminf |\theta^n(x) - \theta^n(y)| = 0;$$

(iii) *if y is a periodic point, then for all x ∈ E*

$$\limsup |\theta^n(x) - \theta^n(y)| > 0.$$

A mapping θ for which (ii) is satisfied is often called chaotic in the sense of Li–Yorke.[6]

Corollary 1.   Given the hypothesis of the Li–Yorke Theorem, there exists a continuous, invariant ergodic measure μ.

Proof. It is easily checked that the existence of a point satisfying either of the two sets of inequalities (1.6) implies the existence of two disjoint intervals I, J for which $\theta^3(I) \cap \theta^3(J) \supset I \cup J$. Theorem 1 implies, therefore, the existence of a measure μ invariant and ergodic for θ^3. The measure v defined by

$$v(A) = (\mu(A) + \mu(\theta^{-1}A) + \mu(\theta^{-2}A))/3$$

is invariant and ergodic under θ. As $\mu\{x\} = 0$ for all $\{x\}$, clearly $v\{x\} = 0$ also.   □

1.5. Absolutely continuous invariant measures for expansive maps

The previous theorems guarantee the existence of an ergodic invariant measure supported on an uncountable set. This set, however, can still be rather small in comparison to the space on which the given dynamical system is defined.

Consider the quadratic mapping $\theta x = Ax(1-x)$ defined on the interval $[0, 1]$. For a value of A near 3.83, it can be shown that $\theta^3(\frac{1}{2}) = \frac{1}{2}$. As this is a point of period 3, by the Li–Yorke Theorem there exists an uncountable set in which we have chaotic dynamics. On the other hand, the orbit of $\frac{1}{2}$ is asymptotically stable (the derivative of θ^3 in the orbit is equal to zero) and it is possible to show that it attracts m-almost all points of $[0, 1]$. Hence, we have chaos but only in a set E of Lebesgue measure zero. Suppose we work

[6]Related but weaker constructive conditions are described in Li, Misiurewicz, Pianigiani and Yorke (1982).

with a computer and begin with an initial condition; we will never be able to see the chaotic set E. The smallest round off error will drive the trajectory out of this set and make it converge rapidly toward the attracting periodic orbit. This raises the question as to how important the idea of chaos is. Does it occur almost surely under some conditions, or almost surely not?[7]

Such a paradoxical situation cannot occur if the invariant measure μ is 'more regular'. This leads to the concept of *absolute* continuity.

A measure μ is said to be *absolutely continuous* (with respect to the Lebesgue measure m) if there exists an integrable function $f(\cdot)$ such that $\mu(E) = \int_E f \, dm$ for all measurable sets E. The function f is called the *density* of μ.

Remark. If μ is absolutely continuous with respect to m, then the support of μ cannot be a set of Lebesgue measure zero; in fact, $m(\text{supp} \, \mu) = 0$ would imply $\mu(\text{supp} \, \mu) = 0$.

An early result establishing the existence of an absolutely continuous invariant measure is the well-known theorem of Lasota and Yorke (1973). It applies to the class of piecewise C^2 mappings. A mapping θ is piecewise C^2 if there exists a partition $0 = x_0 < x_1 < x_2 < \cdots < x_n = 1$ such that θ restricted to each (x_i, x_{i+1}) is a C^2 function which is extendable as a C^2 function to the closed interval $[x_i, x_{i+1}]$.

Theorem 3. Let $\theta: X \rightarrow X$ be piecewise C^2 and assume that X is an interval. If

$$|\theta'(x)| \geq \lambda > 1, \quad m\text{-almost everywhere} \tag{1.7}$$

then there exists an absolutely continuous invariant measure.

A map that satisfies (1.7) is called *expansive*. For such maps all periodic orbits are unstable.

As an example, consider the 'check' map shown in fig. 1.2,

$$\theta(x) = \begin{cases} \theta_1(x) := n(1-x), & x \in [0, 1) \\ \theta_2(x) := x - 1, & x \in [1, \infty). \end{cases} \tag{1.8}$$

Observe that $\theta(1) = 0$, $\theta(0) = n$ and $\theta(x) < x$ all $x > 1$. Consequently, all trajectories are trapped by the set $V := [0, n]$. What happens in this set determines the long-run dynamics of the process (1.1). The previous theorem

---

[7]For a discussion of this question in an economic context see Benhabib and Day (1982), and Melese and Transue (1986).

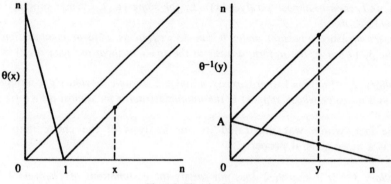

Fig. 1.2. The check map.

cannot be exploited directly because $\theta_2(\cdot)$ is not expansive. Indeed, if $n=1$, $\theta_1(\cdot)$, any point in $[0,1]$ is a neutrally stable 2-cycle.

Note that the points $\{0, 1, \ldots, n\}$ are $n+1$-cyclic. In general, for $n \geqq 2$ the iterated map $\theta^n(p)$ for θ given by (1.8) is expansive because $|d\theta^n(p)/dp| \geqq n$. This is because $\theta^n(p)$ must enter the set $[0,1]$ at least once for any p. Consequently, every cycle is unstable and by the Lasota–Yorke Theorem an absolutely continuous measure exists that is invariant for θ^n.

1.6. Measures and attractors

The theorem does not say how many measures exist or if they are ergodic. We should also like to know how measures are related to the limit sets and whether or not the latter are attractors. These questions were answered for a class of expansive, piecewise strictly monotonic C^2 functions in Li and Yorke (1978).

Theorem 4.   Let $\theta(\cdot)$ be defined on an internal $I: =[a, b] \rightarrow I$. Suppose there is a finite set of points $A: = \{y^i\}_{i=0}^{k+1}$ with $a = y^0 < y^1 < \cdots < y^k < y^{k+1} = b$ such that $\theta(\cdot)$ restricted to each (y^i, y^{i+1}) is:

(i)   Strictly monotonic,
(ii)   twice continuously differentiable,
(iii)   expansive.

Then there exists a finite collection of sets $L_1, \ldots, L_m$ and a set of absolutely continuous invariant measures $\mu_1, \ldots, \mu_m$, $m \leq k$, such that:

(1)   Each L_i, $i=1, \ldots, m$ is a finite union of closed intervals;
(2) $\mu_i(L_i) = 1$, $i=1, \ldots, m$, i.e., each μ_i is ergodic;

(3) *if $y \in I$, then m-almost surely $\omega(x) = L_i$ for some $i \in \{1, \ldots, m\}$; supp $\mu_i = L_i$, $i = 1, \ldots, m$;*

(4) *every measure invariant under θ can be written as a linear combination of the μ_i. (That is, the μ_i form a basis in the space of invariant measures.)*

Corollary 2. For $k = 1$ there exists a unique, ergodic absolutely continuous invariant measure whose support is the unique attractor for almost all $x \in I$.

The fact, which was illustrated in our analysis of the check map 1.8, reflects a more general property.

Corollary 3. If a map $\theta(\cdot)$ does not satisfy the assumptions of Theorem 4 but there exists an integer, say p, such that the map $\theta^p(\cdot)$ satisfies them, then the theorem holds.

Proof. It is easy to verify that if μ_p is an ergodic measure invariant for θ^p, then $\mu := (1/p) \sum_{i=0}^{p-1} \mu_p \theta^{-i}$ is an ergodic measure invariant for θ. $\square$

1.7. The Frobenius Perron operator

The proof of the theorem of Lasota–Yorke relies on the properties of the Frobenius Perron operator which is defined as follows. Let θ be piecewise C^2 and let f be any integrable function and define

$$Pf(x) = \frac{d}{dx} \int_{\theta^{-1}([a, x])} f \, dm. \tag{1.9}$$

The main properties of P are

(i) $P: L^1 \to L^1$ is linear (where L^1 is the space of integrable functions),
(ii) $Pf \geq 0$ if $f \geq 0$,
(iii) $\int Pf \, dm = \int f \, dm$,
(iv) $Pf = f$ if and only if the measure μ defined by $\mu(E) = \int_E f \, dm$ for all E is invariant under θ.

The explicit form of the Frobenius Perron operator is the following

$$Pf(x) = \sum_{i=0}^{n-1} |\phi_i'(x)| f(\phi_i(x)) \chi_{[\theta(y_i), \theta(y_{i+1})]}(x) \tag{1.10}$$

where $\phi_i: [\theta(y_i), \theta(y_{i+1})] \to [0, 1]$ are the inverses of θ and $\chi_A(x)$ is the characteristic function of the set A.

As a first example consider the tent map 1.2 for $M = 1$. Using the definition you can show that $f(x) \equiv 1$.

As a second example, return to the check map given in (1.8). Even though the latter is not expansive, we used the Lasota–Yorke Theorem to show that an absolutely continuous invariant probability measure exists. We can actually construct it.

To do this we obtain the inverse map $\theta^{-1}(\cdot)$ of (1.8). It is

$$\theta^{-1}(x) = \begin{cases} \phi_1(x): = 1 - (1/n)x, & x \notin R_n \\ \phi_2(x): = 1 + x, & x \in R_n \end{cases}$$

where $R_1 = [0, 1]$, $R_i = (i - 1, i]$, $i = 2, \ldots, n$. See fig. 1.2b. The set $\theta^{-1}[0, x]$ given by

$$\theta^{-1}[0, x] = \begin{cases} [1 - (1/n)x, 1 + x], & x \notin R_n \\ [1 - (1/n)x, n], & x \in R_n \end{cases}$$

is the interval in the shaded area above x. We want to solve the functional equation

$$f(x) = Pf(x) = \mathrm{d}/\mathrm{d}x \int_{\theta^{-1}[0,x]} f(u)\,\mathrm{d}u,$$

for $f(x)$. Expanding the right side of this expression we get

$$Pf(x) = \begin{cases} \mathrm{d}/\mathrm{d}x[\int_{1-(1/n)x}^{1+x} f(u)\,\mathrm{d}u] & \chi_{R_1 \cup \ldots \cup R_{n-1}}(x) \\ + \mathrm{d}/\mathrm{d}x[\int_{1-(1/n)x}^{n} f(u)\,\mathrm{d}u] & \chi_{R_n}(x) \end{cases}$$

Carrying through the differentiation and setting $f(x) = Pf(x)$ we get

$$f(x) = \begin{cases} [f(1+x) + \sum_{i=1}^{n-1}(1/n)f(1-(1/n)x)] & \chi_{R_i}(x) \\ + (1/n)f(1-(1/n)x) & \chi_{R_n}(x). \end{cases} \tag{1.11}$$

Supposing that $f(\cdot)$ is constant on each zone R_i; and let $\alpha_i := f(x)\chi_{R_i}(x)$, set $\alpha_n = \alpha$ and multiply both sides of (1.12) by n. Then

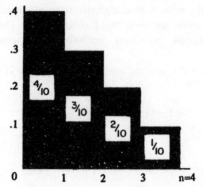

Fig. 1.3. The density for the dynamical system 1.9, $n=4$.

$$\alpha_1 = n\alpha$$

$$\alpha_2 = (n-1)\alpha$$

$$\vdots$$

$$\alpha_n = \alpha. \tag{1.12}$$

As the α_is must add up to one, we get $1 = \sum_i \alpha_i = \alpha(n+1)n/2$. So

$$\alpha = 2/n(n+1).$$

Consequently,

$$\alpha_i = 2(n+1-i)/n(n+1), \quad i=1,\ldots,n. \tag{1.13}$$

The density function that characterizes the long-run statistical behavior of trajectories is therefore the step function illustrated in fig. 1.3.

1.8. Absolutely continuous invariant measures for non-expansive maps

Consider the smooth quadratic map

$$T_A(x) = Ax(1-x), \quad x \in [0,1]. \tag{1.14}$$

As this map is not expansive, the Lasota–Yorke Theorem does not apply. However, let us consider it from the point of view of the Frobenius Perron operator. For $A=4$ we have $T_4^{-1}(0,x) = (0, \frac{1}{2} - \frac{1}{2}\sqrt{1-x}) \cup (\frac{1}{2} + \frac{1}{2}\sqrt{1-x}, 1)$, the Frobenius Perron operator is

$$Pf(x) = (1/(4\sqrt{1-x}))[f(\tfrac{1}{2} - \tfrac{1}{2}\sqrt{1-x}) + f(\tfrac{1}{2} + \tfrac{1}{2}\sqrt{1-x})].$$

We have $P(1) = 1/2\sqrt{1-x}$ so that the Lebesgue measure is not invariant. However, it is possible to prove that $P^n(1)$ converges to $f(x) = 1/\pi\sqrt{x(1-x)}$ and it is easily seen that $P(f) = f$ so that f is the density of the invariant measure.[8]

For $A < 4$ we have

$$Pf(x) = \frac{1}{4\sqrt{1-(4/A)x}}\left[f\left(\tfrac{1}{2} - \tfrac{1}{2}\sqrt{\frac{A-4x}{A}}\right) \right.$$

$$\left. + f\left(\tfrac{1}{2} + \tfrac{1}{2}\sqrt{\frac{A-4x}{A}}\right) \right] \chi_{[0, A/4]}(x).$$

The behavior of the system, as A varies, is extremely complicated and is not yet completely understood. It is known that there exists a set of the parameter values of A for which there exists an absolutely continuous invariant measure, and this set has the power of the continuum. Recently, Carleson proved that this set of parameter values has positive Lebesgue measure.

A companion to Theorem 4 for non-expansive maps was established by Misiurewicz (1981) for a class of piecewise, strictly monotonic functions which satisfy certain properties that replace the expansivity condition. This class includes the quadratic map (1.15) as a special case.

Theorem 5. Let θ be defined on an interval $I := [a, b]$ and suppose there is a finite set of points $A := \{y_i\}_{i=0}^{k+1}$ with $a = y^0 < y^1 < \cdots < y^{k+1} = b$ such that for each i, $\theta(\cdot)$ restricted to (y^i, y^{i+1}) is:

(i)   *Strictly monotonic;*
(ii) *three times differentiable;*
(iii) $|\theta'(x)|^{-\frac{1}{2}}$ *is a convex function on each set (y^i, y^{i+1}), $i = 1, \ldots, k$;*
(iv) *any cyclic point in I is unstable;*
(v)   *let θ', θ'' and θ''' have one sided derivatives at each critical point; then $\theta'(y^i) \cdot \theta''(y^i) \cdot \theta'''(y^i) \neq 0$ for all $i \in \{1, \ldots, k\}$;*
(vi) *there is a neighborhood U of A such that $\gamma(y^i) \subset A \cup (I \setminus U)$.*

[Recall that $\gamma(y^i)$ is the orbit through y^i. This means that every iterate either belongs to the set of critical points or remains a finite distance from it.] Then the results of Theorem 4 hold.

[8]See Pianigiani (1979).

1.9. The Central Limit Theorem[9]

A dynamical system that generates a chaotic trajectory is not thereby a stochastic process. Indeed, for any given value x_t, x_{t+1} is exactly determined by (1.1), and, likewise, for any given initial condition $x \in X$ the entire trajectory $\tau(x)$ is exactly determined. Nonetheless, trajectories do have certain properties like a stochastic process. From the point of view of these properties, a trajectory appears to be like the realization of a stochastic process yielding a series of independent, identically distributed random variables even though the values in a trajectory are not drawn at random and are not independent. In particular the trajectories satisfy certain standard laws of large numbers and a central limit theorem.

Consider our familiar check map (1.8). If $x_0 \in R_2$ we could say that $x_1 \in R_3, \ldots, x_{n-2} \in R_n$, $x_{n-1} \in R_1$ but we could not say for sure where x_n lies unless we knew in which of the sets $R_1 \cap \theta^{-1}(R_i)$, $i = 1, \ldots, n$ the point x_{n-1} lies. As t gets large, however, we know that

$$\Pr(x_t \in R_i) \cong \mu(R_i) = \int_{R_i} f(u)\,du = \alpha_i, \quad i = 1, \ldots, n.$$

Think now of a finite sequence $\{x_t\}_0^{N-1}$ generated by (1.1) from an initial condition $x_0 = x$ as a 'sample' of the trajectory. From the mean ergodic theorem [letting $g(y) \equiv y$] we get

$$\lim_{N \to \infty} \frac{1}{N} \sum_{n=0}^{N-1} \theta^n(x) = \int_X uf(u)\,du, \tag{1.15}$$

so the 'sample mean' $\bar{x}(N)$ converges to the mean of the distribution. Likewise, the sample variance converges to the variance of the distribution which is seen by setting $g(y) = (y - m)^2$ and using the mean ergodic theorem to get

$$\lim_{N \to \infty} \frac{1}{N} \sum_{n=b}^{N-1} [\theta^n(x) - m]^2 = \int_x (u - m)^2 f(u)\,du. \tag{1.16}$$

In addition to these laws of large numbers, a still more remarkable property holds. Consider the 'sample means' obtained by averaging values in the trajectory, then the subsequent values and so on. Denote these by

---

[9] As a useful background on laws of large numbers and central limit theorems, see Rao (1973, chapter 2). For a discussion see Day and Shafer (1987).

$$\bar{x}^p(N) = \frac{1}{N} \sum_{t=pN}^{(p+1)N-1} \theta^t(x), \quad p = 0, 1, 2, 3, \ldots, P. \tag{1.17}$$

Then we have the following central limit theorem established by Hoffauer and Keller (1982) and Ziemien (1985).

Theorem 6. Let θ satisfy the assumptions of Theorems 4 or 5. Let μ_i be the absolutely continuous invariant ergodic measure with corresponding support L_i, $i = 1, \ldots, k$. Then for almost any x the time averages *(1.17)* converge in distribution to a normal distribution as $P \to \infty$ and $N \to \infty$.

1.10. Escape: Conditional invariance

Suppose we have a transformation defined on an interval and we cut a hole in the interval. If the point falls into the hole, we say it escapes. Suppose a point is started somewhere in the interval. If an iterate of the point falls into the hole, we do not consider it any more. If we know that at the time n it has not yet fallen in the hole, what can be said of its distribution? Does it tend to a limit distribution as n goes to infinity? And if it does, which are its properties? This problem is studied extensively in Pianigiani and Yorke (1979). There is introduced the notion of conditionally invariant measure.[10]

Let $\theta: X \to \mathbb{R}$; we say that μ is *conditionally invariant* with respect to θ if there exists a constant α, $1 > \alpha > 0$ such that $\mu(\theta^{-1}S) = \alpha\mu(S)$ for all measurable S. Of course, if $\alpha = 1$ the measure μ is invariant.

Consider the family of piecewise monotonic maps defined in Theorem 5 and assume the following additional condition. Let $U = X \backslash A$ when $A = \{y^0, y^1, \ldots, y^{k+1}\}$

(i) $\theta(U) \supset \supset U$. This means that θ maps at least some points in U outside of U.
(ii) $\theta(y^i) \notin U$ so the points in A map outside U.
(iii) $\theta(y)$ is expansive.
(iv) θ is transitive on components. That is, for all $U_i = (y^i, y^{i+1})$ and for all U_j there exists an integer n which depends on (i,j) such that

$$U_i \cap \theta^n(U_j) \neq \emptyset,$$

that is, there exist trajectories that visit every set so the system is indecomposable. Piecewise monotonic maps that satisfy (i)–(iv) will be called *strongly expansive*. For such maps we have the following useful result established in Pianigiani and Yorke (1979).

[10]See also Pianigiani (1981).

Theorem 7.   Let θ be a piecewise C^2 transformation as defined in Theorem 5. If θ is strongly expansive, then there exists an absolutely continuous measure conditionally invariant with respect to the Lebesgue measure.

Define the *kickout time* function n_θ by

$$n_\theta(x) = \max \{n : \theta^i(x) \in (0, 1), \quad i = 1, \ldots, n\}.$$

It is easily seen that if μ is the conditionally invariant measure, then

$$\mu\{x : n_\theta(x) \geq k\} = \mu\theta^{-k}(0, 1) = (\mu\theta^{-1}(0, 1))^k = \alpha^k,$$

which means that the system decays in an exponential way.

Return to the tent map of eq. 1.2, and let $M > 1$. Then T_M is no longer into nor onto. Indeed, $T_M(x) > 1$ for all $x \in E := [1/2M, 1 - 1/(2M)]$. The set $\mathscr{E} = \sum_{i=0}^{\infty} T_M^{-i}(E)$ is the set of all points in $[0, 1]$ that eventually enter E and escape.

This map is strongly expansive so by the theorem the probabilities of escape in periods $k = 1, \ldots$ are just

$$\mu(E), \alpha\mu(E), \alpha^2\mu(E), \ldots.$$

Consider the Lebesgue measure $m(\cdot)$. It is easily seen that $E = [1/2M, 1 - (1/2M)]$ so $m(E) = 1 - 1/M$. Moreover,

$$T^{-1}(E) = \left[\left(\frac{1}{2M} \right)^2, \frac{1}{2M} - \left(\frac{1}{2M} \right)^2 \right].$$

As the right inverse is symmetric,

$$m(T^{-1}(E)) = \frac{1}{M}\left(1 - \frac{1}{M}\right) = \frac{1}{M} m(E)$$

so $m(\cdot)$ is conditionally invariant for T_M with $\alpha = 1/M$. Thus, the chance for escape after $k = 0, 1, \ldots$, periods given an initial condition drawn at random are the values $1 - 1/M$, $1/M(1 - 1/M)$, $(1/M)^2(1 - 1/M), \ldots, (1/M)^k(1 - 1/M)$ which sum to unity. Therefore, $\mu(\mathscr{E}) = 1$ and escape occurs almost surely.

1.11. Multiple-phase dynamics

It is often the case in economics, as in other fields, that quite different forces or relationships govern behavior in differing situations of state. Or it can be that behavior in one situation is so different from that in another that we want to distinguish it. Multiple-phase dynamical systems and switching regimes formalize these ideas.

Consider a single-valued mapping $\theta_p : x \to \theta_p(x)$, $p \in \mathscr{P} = \{0, \ldots, n\}$ called a *phase structure*. Each map $\theta_p(\cdot)$ is defined on a set $D^p \subset \mathbb{R}$ called the pth *phase domain*. A *regime* is a pair $\mathscr{R}_p := (\theta_p, D^p)$. The dynamics within any phase domain is given by the *phase equation*

$$x_{t+1} = \theta_p(x_t), \quad x_t \in D^p, \tag{1.18}$$

where it is assumed that $D^p \cap D^q = \emptyset$ all $p \neq q \in \mathscr{P}$.

Defining the map

$$\theta(x) := \theta_p(x), \quad x \in D^p \tag{1.19}$$

with domain $D := \bigcup_p D^p$ we have the usual dynamical system (θ, D) with dynamics

$$x_{t+1} = \theta(x_t), \quad x_t \in D.$$

Let $\chi_S(x)$ be the indicator function. Then another way to write (1.17) is

$$x_{t+1} = \theta(x_t) = \sum_{p = \mathscr{P}} \chi_{D_p}(x) \theta_p(x_t). \tag{1.20}$$

The collection $\{(\theta_p, D^p), p \in \mathscr{P}\}$ we shall call a *multiple phase* or *multiple regime dynamical system*. The null domain D^0 means that for all $x \in D^0$ the system is inviable and no consistent structure capable of perpetuating behavior exists. The *null phase structure* is the identity map $\theta_0(x)$. The check map again provides an example. Let $D^1 = (0, 1]$, $D^2 = (1, \infty)$ and $D^0 = \backslash(D' \cup D^2)$. Then (1.8) gives a three regime system including the null regime.

A trajectory of a system can be characterized by the sequence of regimes through which it passes. Define the regime index of a given state by $I(x) := p \chi_{D_p}(x)$. The sequence

$$I(\theta^t(x), \quad t = 0, 1, 2, 3, \ldots \tag{1.21}$$

gives the dynamics of the system as a sequence of regimes. A given trajectory can now be decomposed into a denumerable sequence of *epochs*, each one of which represents a sojourn within a given regime. Let

$$0 = s_1(x) \leqq t < s_2(x), \quad I(\theta^t(x)) = p_1,$$

$$s_2(x) \leqq t < s_3(x), \quad I(\theta^t(x)) = p_2,$$

$$s_3(x) \leqq t < s_4(x), \quad I(\theta^t(x)) = p_3,$$

$$\vdots \quad \vdots \quad \vdots \qquad \vdots \qquad \vdots \tag{1.22}$$

The quadruple

$$\{\theta^{p_i}(\cdot), D^{p_i}s_i(x), s_{i+1}(x)\}, \quad i = 1, 2, 3, \ldots \tag{1.23}$$

is ith *epoch*; the state $\theta^{s_i(x)}$ is called the *kickin state*; the period $s_i(x)$ is called the ith *kickin* time; the period $s_{i+1}(x)$ is the *kickout* time of epoch i (and the kickin time of epoch $i+1$); the *duration* of the ith epoch is $s_{i+1}(x) - s_i(x)$. The sequence of epochs associated with a given trajectory is an *epochal evolution*.

Suppose in (1.23) the sequence is finite. Then $s_{n+1}(x) = \infty$ and the trajectory is *trapped* in the phase domain D^{p_n}. The associated epochal evolution *converges* to phase D^{p_n}. This does *not* mean that the trajectory converges to a stationary, steady or periodic state, however, but only that the phase structure governing change converges. If $p_1 < p_2 < p_3 < \cdots$ the epochs form a *progression*. If $p_{i+k} = p_i$, $i = 1, 2, 3, \ldots$ the evolution is *phase cyclic*. If the sequence (1.23) is not finite and *non-periodic*, then we will call it a non-periodic (chaotic) evolution.

The piecewise maps often discussed above can all be viewed as examples of multiple phase maps with each piece representing a distinct regime. Note that a periodic sequence of regimes (phase cyclicity) does not imply that trajectories are periodic. For example, (1.8) gives a 2 cyclic phase cycle with the probability of phase one being $2/(n+1)$ and that of phase two being $(n-1)/(n+1)$. Almost all trajectories are chaotic.

2. Competitive markets

2.1. Tâtonnement

To see how the concepts of statistical dynamics arise naturally in the study of economic processes, consider the classical concept of a competitive market in which firms and households supply and demand commodities in response to prices according to their individual best interests. If supply and demand is out of balance, competition forces price adjustments until a balance is established and markets clear. A century later Walras described this process as market groping or tâtonnement, a process in which an 'auctioneer' adjusts prices in proportion to excess demand. Samuelson gave the model a specific mathematical form and provided a formal stability analysis. Most of the important mathematical economists at mid 20th century contributed to this theory but none seems to have guessed that tâtonnement could generate chaotic price sequences, a possibility that is now well understood.[11]

Let $S(p)$, $D(p)$ be supply and demand functions for a given commodity with price p. Excess demand is $e(p) = D(p) - S(p)$. Tâtonnement is then represented by the difference equation

$$p_{t+1} = 0(p_t) := \max\{0, p_t + \lambda e(p_t)\},\tag{2.1}$$

where λ is a positive constant.

A competitive equilibrium occurs at a stationary state $\tilde{p}$ such that $e(\tilde{p}) = 0$. It is asymptotically stable if

$$-2/\lambda < D'(\tilde{p}) - S'(\tilde{p}) < 0.\tag{2.2}$$

For any demand and supply function such that $D'(\tilde{p}) < S'(\tilde{p})$. This will be true if λ is small enough but untrue if λ is big enough.

2.2. Walras' graph

Walras did not actually carry the analysis of tâtonnement very far. He did, however, illustrate supply and demand functions as shown in fig. 2.1a. The corresponding excess demand function (obtained graphically) is shown in fig. 2.1b. The graphical analog of eq. (2.1) for $\lambda = 1$ is shown in fig. 2.1c. Evidently, the Li–Yorke inequality (1.6) is satisfied so Theorem 2 holds: price cycles of all orders are present and an uncountable, scrambled set of chaotic trajectories exists. Moreover, according to Theorem 1 the scrambled set has positive measure for some continuous (non-atomic) measure. No doubt Walras would be surprised at this finding.

2.3. A mathematical analog

A formula that gives a downward bending supply function like Walras' is

[11]See Saari and Simon (1978), Saari (1985), Cigno and Montrucchio (1983), and Bala and Majumdar (1990).

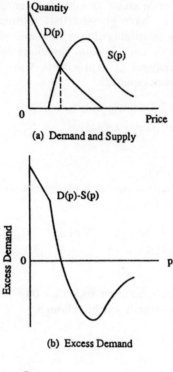

(a) Demand and Supply

(b) Excess Demand

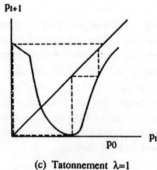

(c) Tatonnement $\lambda=1$

Fig. 2.1. Walras example.

$$S(p) = \begin{cases} 0, & 0 < p < p'', \\ B(p - p')e^{-\delta p}, & p' \leqq p. \end{cases} \qquad (2.3)$$

(Note that a downward bending Walrasian supply function is equivalent to

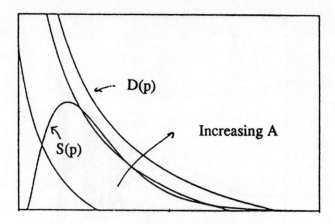

Fig. 2.2. Supply and demand.

a Marshallian backward bending supply function.) A demand function like Walras' is

$$D(p) = \begin{cases} (A/(a+p)) - b, & 0 \leqq p \leqq p^0, \\ 0, & p^0 < p, \end{cases} \qquad (2.4)$$

where $p^0 := A/b - a$. See fig. 2.2.

To illustrate the possibilities, some numerical experiments have been conducted. Parametered A, a, b, B, p' and δ have been chosen and trajectories computed for various values of λ which represents an increase in the magnitude of price adjustment. The resulting bifurcation diagram is shown in fig. 2.3. You can see that it is similar to that for the quadratic map shown above in fig. 4.

For λ less than about 0.43, prices converge asymptotically to a competitive equilibrium. Above this value asymptotically stable two period cycles emerge (the competitive equilibrium is now unstable). Above about 0.52 these become unstable and asymptotically stable four period cycles emerge. As λ is increased further, the familiar picture appears with ranges of apparently chaotic or very high period cycles interspersed with stable periodic cycles. Note the range where the asymptotically stable three period cycle occurs near 0.77. Here is an example of parameter values for which a scrambled set and a continuous measure exist according to Theorems 1 and 2. The attractor is just the three cyclic points so the measure is not an absolutely continuous one.

Fixing $\lambda = 0.4$ (where the process is convergent for the given parameter

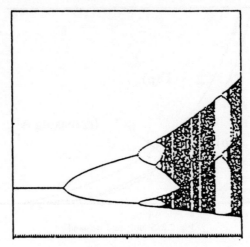

Fig. 2.3. Bifurcation diagram or $\lambda\mu$.

values) a second bifurcation diagram was computed by varying A, which has the effect of shifting demand outward as A increases. See fig. 2.2. When A is small enough there is a single, asymptotically stable stationary state which occurs at a point where supply is rising. When A is increased enough, three equilibria appear; at least two occur where supply is decreasing. As A increases still more, the equilibrium is again unique. *The intricate pattern indicates how striking changes in the qualitative behavior of prices can come about from very small changes in demand.* The bifurcation diagram of fig. 2.4 shows how the orbits shift in the range $5 \leqq A \leqq 12$.

Could the long-run attractor be the support of an absolutely continuous invariant measure for some parameter values? An affirmative answer is suggested by the histograms for two values of A given in fig. 2.5. But, of course, this is just a conjecture based on the numerical experiments. The map given by (2.1) is continuous and smooth almost everywhere. If the other conditions of Theorem 5 hold for a 'large' number of parameters (and it seems quite possible that they do), then this conjecture will be true for all those parameter values.

2.4. Pure exchange

The results obtained for the Walrasian type of market does not depend on the downward sloping curve; they also arise for upward sloping supply functions. Consider the simplest example of a pure exchange economy, one with two individuals (or two types of individuals), Mr. Alpha, say, and Ms.

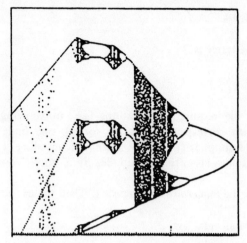

Fig. 2.4. Bifurcation diagram for the demand parameter *A*.

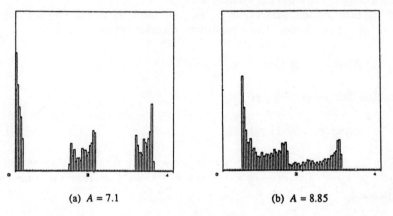

(a) *A* = 7.1   (b) *A* = 8.85

Fig. 2.5. Histograms of prices for two levels of demand (see fig. 2.4 for corresponding places in the bifurcation diagrams).

Beta. There are two goods to be chosen in amounts x and y, respectively. Suppose the utility functions of the two individuals are the same,

$$u(x, y) = Ax^\gamma y^{1-\gamma}, \tag{2.5}$$

where $\gamma \equiv \alpha$ for Mr. Alpha and $\gamma \equiv \beta$ for Ms. Beta. Let p, q be the prices of the two goods. Suppose Mr. Alpha's endowment is $(\bar{x}, 0)$ and Ms. Beta's is $(0, \bar{y})$. The income constraint for the former is

$$px + qy \leqq p\bar{x}, \tag{2.6}$$

while that for the latter is

$$px + qy \leqq q\bar{y}. \tag{2.7}$$

Carrying out the required calculations [i.e., maximizing (2.4) subject to (2.5) or (2.6) with corresponding values for γ], one finds that Mr. Alpha consumes $\alpha\bar{x}$ and supplies $(1-\alpha)\bar{x}$ of x while demanding $(1-\alpha)p\bar{x}/q$ of good y. Ms. Beta consumes $(1-\beta)\bar{y}$ and supplies $\beta\bar{y}$ of good y and demands $\beta q\bar{y}/p$ of good x.

Let good y be the *numeraire* so that $q \equiv 1$. Then the excess demand for x is

$$e(p) = (\beta\bar{y}/p) - (1-\alpha)\bar{x}. \tag{2.8}$$

That for y is its mirror image. The tâtonnement process is obtained by substituting p_t for p in (2.8) and using (2.1).

It is easy to see that $\theta(p) \to \infty$ as $p \to 0$ and that $\theta(p) \to p - \lambda(1-\alpha)\bar{x}$ as $p \to \infty$. A unique competitive equilibrium therefore exists, which is

$$\tilde{p} = (\beta/(1-\alpha)) \cdot (\bar{y}/\bar{x}). \tag{2.9}$$

The first derivative of $\theta(\cdot)$ is

$$\theta'(p) = 1 - \lambda\beta\bar{y} \cdot (1/p^2), \tag{2.10}$$

which changes from $-\infty$ to $+1$ as p increases from zero, so $\theta(\cdot)$ has a fishhook form. Substituting (2.9) into (2.10) we find that tâtonnement is *unstable* if

$$\lambda \cdot \frac{(1-\alpha)^2}{\beta} \cdot \frac{\bar{x}^2}{\bar{y}} > 2. \tag{2.11}$$

This happens for λ or $\bar{x}$ large enough or for β or $\bar{y}$ small enough. Then locally expanding cycles must occur near $\tilde{p}$.

It is possible that price becomes zero (if excess supply is great enough for some $p > \tilde{p}$). Since $\theta(0) = \infty$, the model would be globally unstable. Let p^* minimize $p + \lambda e(p)$. At such a value $1 + \lambda e'(p^*) = 0$. After a little calculation we find that $p^* = (\lambda\beta\bar{y})^{\frac{1}{2}}$. The condition for global stability is therefore $p^* + \lambda e(p^*) > 0$. Substituting for p^*, rearranging terms and combining with (2.11) we find that for any combination of parameters such that

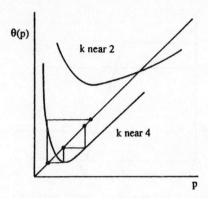

Fig. 2.6. A Li–Yorke point exists (when K is close enough to 4).

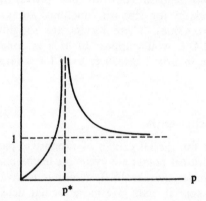

Fig. 2.7. The Schwartzian condition: $|\theta'(p)|^{-1}$ is piecewise convex.

$$2 < \lambda \frac{(1-\alpha)^2 \bar{x}^2}{\beta \bar{y}} < 4 \tag{2.12}$$

tâtonnement is globally stable but that fluctuations are perpetuated almost surely. Call the expression in the middle, K. When K is less than 2, competitive equilibrium is asymptotically stable. When K is close to 4, $\theta(p^*)$ becomes arbitrarily large. The right inverse $\theta_r^{-1}(p^*)$ is bounded so Theorems 1 and 2 are satisfied robustly, that is, for a continuum of parameter values a scrambled set exists with continuous measure. (See fig. 2.6.)

Now consider the Schwartzian condition $|\theta'(p)|^{-\frac{1}{2}}$. It is routine to show that it is piecewise convex and has the appearance shown in fig. 2.7.

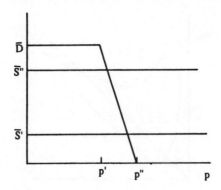

Fig. 2.8. Piecewise linear demand and supply.

Numerical calculations suggest (but do not prove) that the remaining conditions of Theorem 5 for smooth functions are satisfied for a large number of parameter values. These results are roughly similar to those obtained in section 2.4. It would appear to be a reasonable conjecture that absolutely continuous invariant measures exist for a large set of parameter values for this model.

2.5. Piecewise linear tâtonnement

We have seen that for special classes of expansive, piecewise linear maps [ones for which the critical points are cyclic (as in the check map (1.8))], the densities that characterize the absolutely continuous invariant measures can be constructed. Such special cases give more regular densities than is typical (i.e., when the critical points are non-cyclic), but they yield concrete examples of what we are trying to show. In this section we shall see how this can be done for tâtonnement.

Consider the piecewise linear demand function and constant supply function as follows:

$$D(p) = \begin{cases} \bar{D}, & p \in [0, p'], \\ \bar{D} - b(p - p'), & p \in [p', p''), \\ 0, & p \in [p'', \infty], \end{cases} \tag{2.13}$$

$$S(p) = \bar{S}, \quad p \geqq 0. \tag{2.14}$$

These may be thought of as approximations to more general non-linear functions as illustrated in fig. 2.8.

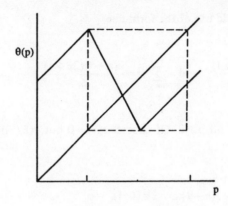

Fig. 2.9. Piecewise linear tâtonnement (all trajectories enter the trapping set).

To simplify what are at best rather tedious calculations, let $\lambda = \frac{1}{2}$, $\bar{D} = 2(n+1) = b$, $\bar{S} = 2$, $p'' - p' = 1$. Then

$$e(p) = \begin{cases} 2n, & p \in [0, p'), \\ 2n - 2(n+1)(p - p'), & p \in [p', p''), \\ -2, & p \in [p'', \infty), \end{cases}$$

and

$$\theta(p) = \begin{cases} p + n, & p \in [0, p'), \\ n + p' - n(p - p'), & p \in [p', p''), \\ p - 1, & p \in [p'', \infty). \end{cases}$$

See fig. 2.9. There is obviously a trapping set within which all trajectories are eventually confined. Let $x = p - p'$, on $[p', p'')$ and p elsewhere. Then we get the equivalent tâtonnement process

$$\phi(x) = \begin{cases} n(1 - x), & p \in [0, 1), \\ x - 1, & p \in [1, n), \end{cases}$$

which is just eq. (1.8) for the check map.

The stationary state is $\tilde{x} = n/(n+1)$. The expected value is

$$E(x) = \int x f(x)\, dx = \sum_{i=1}^{n} \int_{i-1}^{i} x \frac{2(n+1-i)}{n(n+1)}\, dx = \frac{2n-1}{6},$$

where we have made use of the formulae

$$\sum_{i=1}^{n} i = \frac{n(n+1)}{2} \quad \text{and} \quad \sum_{i=1}^{n} i^2 = \frac{n(n+1)(2n+1)}{6}. \tag{2.15}$$

Note that $E(x) > \tilde{x}$ all $n \geq 2$. Of course, $e(\tilde{x}) = 0$ but $e(E(x)) < 0$ which is seen by noting that

$$e(x) = \begin{cases} 2n - 2(n+1)x, & x \in [0, 1), \\ -2, & x \in [1, n], \end{cases}$$

so

$$e(E(x)) = \begin{cases} -1, & n = 2, \\ -2, & n \geq 3. \end{cases}$$

Nonetheless, using the density (1.14) and (2.15) we find that

$$E[e(p)] = \int_0^n e(p)f(p)\,dp = \int_0^1 [2n - 2(n+1)x]n - \sum_{i=2}^{n} 2 \int_{i-1}^{i} \alpha_i\,dx = 0.$$

On this ground we can think of the density $f(\cdot)$ as a kind of statistical price equilibrium. Unfortunately, there is a fundamental difficulty with this interpretation. If prices do not converge, then all the transactions implied by demand and supply can not take place. There must be a short side to the market. This is often gotten around either by assuming away the possibility that demand is not equal to supply or by assuming that convergence occurs and is so rapid that disequilibria can be ignored. The first approach rules out any attempt to understand how markets respond to disequilibria. The second fails to recognize that for *any* λ there exist supply and demand functions that can cause chaos, so rapid convergence can not be taken for granted.

These difficulties in the theory of competitive markets stand after two centuries and remain to be given an adequate mathematical treatment. To pursue it here would carry us beyond the scope of the present introductory lectures, but the methods illustrated here will surely be found useful in that undertaking.

3. Irregular business cycles[12]

3.1. The basic model

From the dynamics of individual markets with competitive price adjustments we turn to the dynamics of the aggregate economy with quantity
adjustments and sticky prices. We consider the Keynesian real/monetary
macro theory in essentially the form given it by Metzler, Modigliani, and
Samuelson in the 1940s, except that here we retain the full non-linearity of
the model and study its global behavior.

The model consists of monetary and real sectors. The monetary sector is
represented by the demand for money, $D^m(r, Y)$, where r is the interest rate
and Y is real national income; the supply of money, $S^m(r, Y; M)$, where M is
a money supply parameter; and a market clearing equation, $D^m(r, Y) =
S^m(r, Y; M)$. The latter implicitly defines the LM curve, $r = L(Y; M)$, which
gives the market-clearing, temporary equilibrium interest rate.

The real sector is represented by an induced consumption function
$C = C(r, Y)$, and an induced investment function, $I = I(r, Y)$. The sum of
autonomous investment, government and consumption expenditure is the
parameter 'A'. Substituting the LM function for interests in the consumption
and investment functions, we obtain respectively the consumption–income
(CY) function, $G(Y; M): = C(L(Y; M), Y)$, and the investment–income (IY)
function, $H(Y; M): = I(L(Y; M); Y)$. Assuming that current consumption and
investment demand depend on lagged income, we get the difference equation

$$Y_{t+1} = \theta(Y_t; \mu, M, A): = G(Y_t; M) + \mu H(Y_t; M) + A, \tag{3.1}$$

where $\mu \geq 0$ is a parameter measuring the 'strength' or 'intensity' of induced
investment. The model is relevant in the 'Keynesian Regime', i.e., for
$Y_t \in [0, Y^F]$ where Y^F is the highest level of income compatible with available
capacity Y^f, the supply of labor and the supply of money.

Under standard assumptions the CY curve is continuous, monotonically
increasing function with $G(0) = 0$ and the IY curve is a more-or-less bell
shaped curve which eventually falls as increasing transactions crowd the
money market and interest rates rise which in turn reduces investment
demand. Consequently, aggregate demand $\theta(Y)$ has the cocked-hat or tilted-z
profile shown in fig. 3.1a. Note that the non-linearity becomes more
pronounced when induced investment is important, i.e., when μ is 'large'.

Let $\tilde{Y}$ be the largest stationary state. (There can be one, two or three of
them.) If $\theta'(\tilde{Y}) < -1$ it is unstable and fluctuations are perpetuated. Notice
that there is a minimum Y^{min} and a local maximum Y^{max} such that

---

[12]This section summarizes results in Day and Shafer (1987) from which the diagrams are
taken, and Day and Lin (forthcoming).

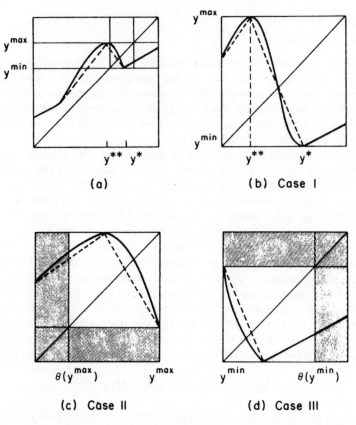

Fig. 3.1. The Keynesian model. (a) Aggregate demand; (b)–(c) Aggregate demand in the trapping set.

$Y^{\min} < \tilde{Y} < Y^{\max}$. Let $V := [Y^{\min}, Y^{\max}]$. Within this *trapping set* increases in the aggregate demand for goods, accompanied by rising labor and money demand is followed by a decline in aggregate demand for goods, labor and money and so on, so fluctuations are perpetuated. Three distinct cases can be identified which depend on the relation of the maximum 'overshoot' $\theta(Y^{\min})$ and $\theta(Y^{\max})$ to the boundary values $Y^{\min}$ and $Y^{\max}$ of V. These three cases are shown in fig. 3.1b, c and d.

3.2. A piecewise smooth example

Suppose, for example, that the demand for money $D^m(r, Y) := \lambda/(r, r') + kY$ so that the *LM* curve is $r = r' + \lambda/(M - kY)$. Suppose also that investment demand is

$$I(r, Y) := \begin{cases} 0, & 0 \leq Y \leq Y', \\ b[(Y - Y')/(\zeta Y^f)]^\beta (p/r)^\gamma, & Y \geq Y', \end{cases} \qquad (3.2)$$

where b, ζ, p, β and γ are parameters and where Y^F is full capacity and Y' a threshold above which the Kaldorian multiplier effect of increasing income on investment is positive. Let induced consumption demand be αY. Then the model (3.1) becomes a two phase dynamical system with

$$Y_{t+1} = \theta(Y) := \begin{cases} A + \alpha Y_t, \\ A + \alpha Y_t + \mu B(Y_t - Y')_t^\beta [r' + \lambda/(M - k Y_t)]^{-\gamma}, \end{cases}$$

for
$$\begin{array}{l} 0 \leq Y \leq Y', \\ Y' \leq Y \leq M/k, \end{array} \qquad (3.3)$$

where $B = b p^\gamma (\zeta Y^F)^{-\beta}$ is a constant.

In the first regime the monetary sector has no influence; in the second, the two sectors interact. Divide the interval $[Y', M/k]$ into two sub-intervals $[Y', Y^{**})$, $[Y^{**}, M/k]$ where $\theta(Y^{**})$ is the maximum GNP obtained on $[Y', M/k]$. In the first, money is in relative abundance; in the second, it is in relatively short supply and the crowding out of investment occurs as interests rates rise. If β and γ are both larger than unity then this function exhibits the piecewise smooth, 'cocked-hat' shape shown by the solid lines in fig. 3.1a.

Numerical experiments suggest that Theorem 5 is true for a large set of parameter values. In fig. 3.2a the graph of eq. (3.3) in the trapping set is shown for several values of μ. Each graph has been normalized on the interval $[0, 1]$. In fig. 3.2b the Schwartzian derivative condition is shown for one of these cases. Clearly, it is piecewise convex as required. Detailed numerical computations shown in fig. 3.3 produce a complex bifurcation picture for continuous changes in μ. An example of a computed histogram and measure are shown together with the distribution of sample means in fig. 3.3. This evidence clearly supports the conjecture that the frequency distribution of model generated data converges to an absolutely continuous, invariant measure for a large set of parameter values and that sample means converge to a normal distribution. Theorems 6 and 7 would appear to hold on the basis of this evidence.

3.3. A piecewise linear example

Stronger analytical results can be obtained for the piecewise linear version of the model. First is the demand for money, $D^m(r, Y) = L^0 - \lambda r + k Y$, where L^0 is a constant, and λ and k parameters. Given M, the supply of money, the *LM* curve can be written

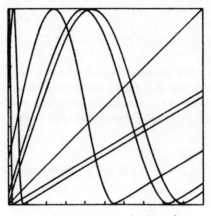

(a) The map for several values of μ.

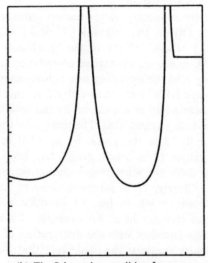

(b) The Schwarzian condition for one μ.

Fig. 3.2. The Case I map.

$$r = L^m(Y; M) := \begin{cases} 0, & 0 \leq Y \leq Y^{**}, \\ (k/\lambda)(Y - Y^{**}), & Y^{**} \leq Y \leq M/k, \end{cases} \tag{3.4}$$

where $Y^{**} = (M, L^0)/k$. Assume induced consumption is αY where α is the marginal propensity to consume and let investment demand be $I(r, Y)$: $= \max\{0, \beta(Y - Y') - \gamma r\}$, where Y' is a threshold above which the direct

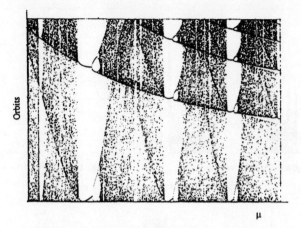

Fig. 3.3. Bifurcation diagram (orbits are normalized on [0, 1]).

effect of income on investment is positive. With these assumptions the adjustment equation for GNP is

$$Y_{t+1} = \theta(Y_t) := \begin{cases} A + \alpha Y_t, & 0 \leq Y_t \leq Y', \\ B + b Y_t, & Y' \leq Y_t < Y^{**}, \\ C - c Y_t, & Y^{**} \leq Y_t \leq Y^*, \\ A + \alpha Y_t, & Y^* \leq Y_t \leq Y^f, \end{cases} \tag{3.5}$$

where A is autonomous consumption and investment expenditure,

$$b = \alpha + \mu\beta, \quad c = \mu\sigma - \alpha, \quad \sigma = \gamma k/\lambda - \beta,$$

$$B = A - \mu\beta Y', \quad C = A + \mu\sigma Y^*,$$

and

$$Y^* = [(\gamma k/\gamma) Y^{**} - \beta Y']/\sigma, \quad Y^{**} = (M - L^0)/k.$$

If $c > 0$ then Y^{**} locally maximizes GNP and Y^* locally minimizes GNP. We therefore get the tilted-Z profile for aggregate demand that is of interest, and all of the cases shown by the dashed lines in fig. 3.1 can occur.

Now there are four distinct regimes. In the first and fourth regimes there is no interaction between monetary and real sectors. In the second there is an abundance of money and investment is stimulated by a rise in GNP. In the

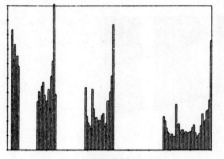

(a) Histogram of GNP values   (b) Cumulative distribution

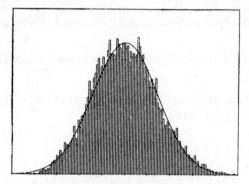

(c) Histogram of sample means and the normal curve

Fig. 3.4. Ergodic behavior for the type I (tilted-Z) map.

third investment is crowded out as the interest rate rises with increasing GNP.

If $\sigma > 0$ then for all $\mu > (1 + \alpha)/\sigma$ the parameter $c = \mu\sigma - \alpha > 1$. Hence, if there is a stationary state in the third, interest sensitive regime it is unstable and bounded oscillations are perpetuated. In this locally unstable situation the trapping sets are non-degenerate so any given map will be equivalent to one of the following maps on the unit interval:

Case 1. $Y^{\min} < Y^{**} < Y^* < Y^{\max}, \quad y = (Y - Y^{\min})/(Y^{\max} - Y^{\min}),$

$$T(y) := \begin{cases} 1 - by^{**} + by, & y \in [0, y^{**}], \\ 1 + cy^{**} - cy, & y \in [y^{**}, y^*], \\ -\alpha y^{**} + \alpha y, & y \in [y^*, 1], \end{cases} \qquad (3.6)$$

where we note that $y^{**} - y^* = 1/(c)$.

Case 2. $Y^{\min} < Y^{**} < Y^{\max} < Y^{*}$, $\quad y = [Y - \theta(Y^{\max})]/[Y^{\max} - \theta(Y^{\max})]$,

$$T(y): = \begin{cases} 1 + by^{**} + by, & y \in [0, y^{**} = 1 - 1/c], \\ 1 + cy^{**} - cy, & y \in [y^{**}, 1]. \end{cases} \qquad (3.7)$$

Case 3. $Y^{**} < Y^{\min} < Y^{*} < Y^{\max}$, $\quad y = [Y - Y^{\min}]/[\theta(Y^{\min}) - Y^{\min}]$,

$$T(y): = \begin{cases} cy^{*} - cy, & y \in [0, y^{*} = 1/c], \\ -\alpha y^{*} + \alpha y, & y \in [y^{*}, 1]. \end{cases} \qquad (3.8)$$

Theorem 5 can be used to show that almost all trajectories are chaotic for a very large set of parameter values and representable in the long run of absolutely continuous invariant ergodic measures. This means that GNP evolves erratically through regimes where the interest rate is important and where it is not.

Note that y^{*} and y^{**} are the transformed turning points Y^{*} and Y^{**} respectively. By setting $1 - y = x$ and substituting we find that Cases 2 and 3 are equivalent. Case 2 is a map with two piecewise segments and a single turning point. Using Theorems 5 and 7, the following has been obtained by Day and Shafer (1986).

Proposition 1. Let T be a Type II canonical map and let $k \geq 1$ be the minimum integer such that $T^{k-1}(0) < y^{**}$ and $T^{k}(0) \geq y^{**}$. If $b^{k}c < 1$ there exists a unique stable orbit of least period $k + 1$. Its support attracts almost every $x \in I$. If $b^{k}c > 1$ there exists a unique absolutely continuous invariant ergodic measure μ for T which attracts almost every $x \in I$, i.e., $\mathrm{supp}\,\mu$ is an attractor. Furthermore, the laws of large numbers and the central limit Theorem 7 of section 1.10 hold.

On the basis of this theorem a complete characterization of the model can be obtained for Case 2. This characterization is shown in fig. 3.5. The shaded regions give the parameter values [in terms of b and c of (3.7)] for which almost all trajectories converge to stationary or cyclic orbits. Note that this includes set $S_3, S_5, \ldots$ where odd cycles occur. Hence, chaos exists there with positive continuous measure (Theorems 1 and 2). However, the measure is not absolutely continuous. '*Most*' *trajectories converge to cycles*. The unshaded region gives the parameter combinations for which ergodic behavior representable by absolutely continuous invariant measures does exist. Here *almost all trajectories are chaotic*.

Elsewhere the dependence of the distributional properties of trajectories on policy instruments (tax rates, money supply, government expenditure) have

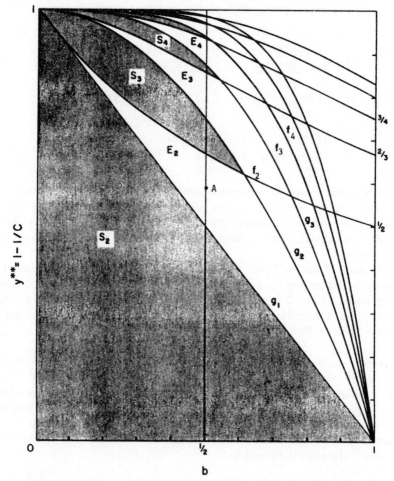

Fig. 3.5. Regions of stable and ergodic behavior (stable cycles appear in shaded regions; ergodic behavior appears in unshaded regions where Theorems 5 and 6 apply).

been conducted. There it is shown that the statistical behavior of GNP over time can change drastically with changes in the policy instruments.[13]

Note that the check map of eq. (1.8) can be used here. For very special combinations of the parameters b and c (and hence of α, β, λ, γ, k, μ) the long-run statistical behavior of trajectories will appear as a step function like that shown in fig. 1.3.

[13]See Day (1989).

4. Economic growth in the very long run[14]

4.1. A multiple phase model

As a third area of application of the concepts of statistical dynamics, consider economic growth in the very long run. On the basis of the evidence accumulated by historians, archaelogists and anthropologists the process is a complicated one involving distinct epochs with characteristics of production, exchange and socio-political organization so different as to set off the dynamics of one epoch from that of another, both in terms of structure and qualitative behavior. There are stages or phases of growth. Growth may not occur uniformly within a given stage; it may ebb and flow. The stages may be traversed in varying orders and with switching or skipping among them. Still, in the very long run a rough progression appears from relatively simple regimes with small numbers of people to successively more complex regimes with large numbers of people.

To formalize all this in the simplest possible terms, measure the size of an economic unit (band, tribe, nation, civilization) by the number of families, x. Each household supplies one adult equivalent of effort to society, either as part of the work force or as part of the managerial force; one adult equivalent of effort is utilized in household production, childrearing and leisure. If the size of a 'production unit' is G, then $G = M + L$ where M is the number of adult equivalents in the managerial force and L the number in the work force.

Planning, coordination and control of economic activity becomes increasingly difficult as population grows within a unit. Let the maximum number compatible with an effective socio-economic order be denoted by N. The term $N - G = S$ represents the social 'space' or 'slack'. If S is large the unit may increase in size without depressing productivity very much. When S is small, increases in size begins to lower productivity – at first marginaly, then absolutely. When $S \leq 0$, the group cannot function.

Suppose now that the productive activity within a group can be represented by a group production function continuous in the arguments L and S. Thus, $Y = h(L, S)$. Substituting $S = N - G$ and $L = G - M$ we get

$$Y = h(G - M, N - G) \equiv g(G). \tag{4.1}$$

In fig. 4.1a the standard power production function is illustrated. In fig. 4.1b the infrastructural management, M, has been added which has the effect of

---

[14]This section draws on the work of Day and Walter (1988).

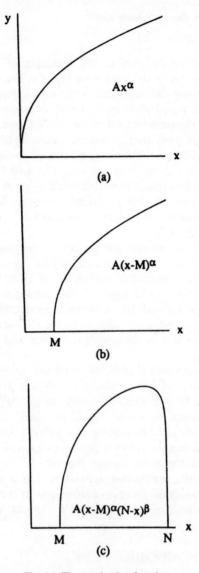

Fig. 4.1. The production function.

shifting the function to the right. In fig. 4.1c the externality term $N - G$ has been incorporated with the result that the production function in terms of labor is single-peaked.

Allowing for the splitting of units, the total population is organized into

$n_k = 2^k$ groups of average size $G = x/2^k$ in such a way as to achieve a maximum output

$$Y = f(x) := n_k g(x/n_k) = \max_n \{ng(x/n)\} \tag{4.2}$$

gives the output Y of a population x that possesses a given techno-infrastructure.

The external diseconomy that becomes increasingly important when the absorbing capacity of the environment is increasingly stressed is expressed by a function

$$p(x, \bar{x}) \begin{cases} = 1, & x = 0, \\ \in (0, 1), & 0 < x < \bar{x}, \\ = 0, & x \geq \bar{x}. \end{cases} \tag{4.3}$$

The social production function is then defined to be

$$F(x) \equiv f(x)p(x, \bar{x}). \tag{4.4}$$

It is illustrated in fig. 4.2. Whether or not it is smooth as in fig. 4.2a, or kinked as in fig. 4.2b, or non-overlapping as in fig. 4.2c, depends on the size of M.

The family function that determines the average number of surviving children per family is assumed to depend on the average level of well being in the population as a whole, $y = Y/x$. We denote it

$$b(y) = \min \{\lambda, h(y)\} \tag{4.5}$$

where

$$h(y) \begin{cases} = 0, & 0 \leq y \leq \eta, \\ > 0, & y \leq \eta. \end{cases} \tag{4.6}$$

The parameter η is called the birth threshold. The function is assumed to have the classical shape shown in fig. 4.3.

Now begin with an initial population x_0. Putting this into (4.1) we get the number of groups and into (4.4) the total output taking account of both the internal and external diseconomies of population size. This gives average welfare y which using (4.6) yields the next generation of families x_1 and so on. This process is carried out generation after generation. It is described by the difference equation

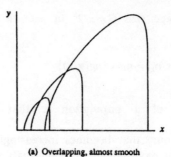

(a) Overlapping, almost smooth

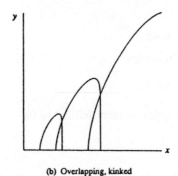

(b) Overlapping, kinked

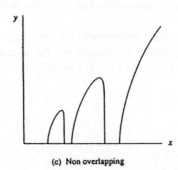

(c) Non overlapping

Fig. 4.2. The production function.

$$x_{t+1} = \theta(x_t) := \tfrac{1}{2} x_t b(F(x_t)/x_t).$$ (4.7)

Now suppose there are several quite different techno-infrastructures available which we may denote by a set of indexes $\tau := \{1, 2, 3, \ldots, j, \ldots\}$. The various components and parameters are then indexed accordingly so that a given system can be indicated by

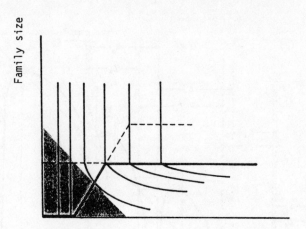

Fig. 4.3. Demographic behavior based on household preferences (the dark piecewise linear line is the demo economic line; the shaded triangular area is the 'budget set' for a given income; the vertical lines that turn into curved lines are indifference curves).

$$S^j := \{g_j(\cdot), M^j, N^j, x_j(\cdot), \bar{x}^j, h_j(\cdot), \eta^j, \lambda^j\} j \in \tau. \qquad (4.8)$$

Suppose as before that society is organized so as to maximize output for any given population (again, to simplify the analysis). Then

$$F_{i,k}(x) := \max_{j \in \tau} \{p_j(x, \bar{x}) 2^k g_j(x/2^k)\}. \qquad (4.9)$$

The index pair $I(x) = (i, k)$ gives the efficient techno-infrastructure i and the efficient number of economic units $n = 2^k$ for each population x. Using the birth function (4.5) indexed to indicate the system to which it applies, we get a difference equation for each regime

$$x_{t+1} = \theta_{i,k}(x_t) := \tfrac{1}{2} x_t b_i(F_{i,k}(x_t)/(x_t). \qquad (4.10)$$

Let $X_{i,k}$ be the set of populations for which the efficient infrastructure and number of units is the pair (i, k). Then

$$I(x) = (i, k) \quad \text{for all} \quad x \in X_{i,k}. \qquad (4.11)$$

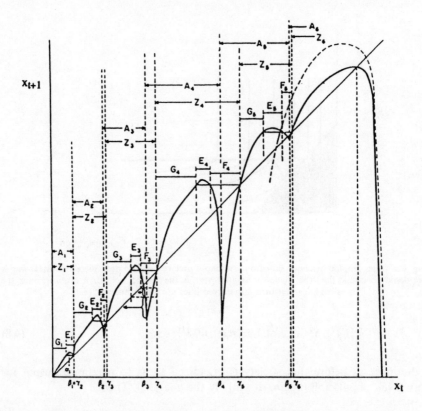

Fig. 4.4. Multiple-phase dynamics. (There are six regimes. Theorem 8 can be used to determine the probability of escape from fluctuation sets F_i. The G_i sets exhibit monotonic growth. The E_i sets are the escape sets.)

In this way we arrive at the multiple regime difference equation

$$x_{t+1} = \theta(x_t) := \theta_{I(x_t)}(x_t). \tag{4.12}$$

When population becomes too large for a given techno-infrastructure, it can divide or split to form additional more-or-less independent economic units, each with a similar techno-infrastructure, or it can switch to a new regime. The results are alternatively:

(i) the switch to a new regime allows for renewed growth and permits a further expansion of population;

(ii) a sudden decline in well being and population and a resumption of growth within the regime;

(iii) a disintegration to a larger number of smaller societies whose infrastructure requirements are smaller.

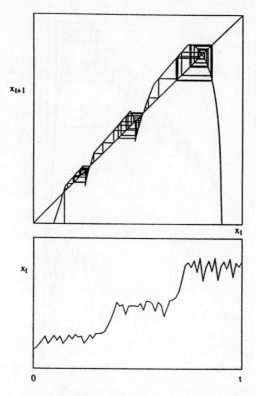

Fig. 4.5. Growth switching, collapse and reswitching.

4.2. Possible dynamics

The map $\theta(\cdot)$ defined in (4.12) has, under reasonable economic conditions, a continuous, piecewise strictly monotonic profile of the kind involved in Theorems 4 and 5 (see fig. 4.4). If the conditions of one or the other of these theorems were satisfied, then the epochal evolution would have to consist of a subset of regimes repeated endlessly in a periodic or non-periodic order or eventually become trapped in a given regime. The trajectories of the variables (GWP, per capita income, population) would show an erratic pattern when viewed in the very long run, although over a few generations or centuries, an orderly growth or Kondratiev type cycle might appear.

If the number of regimes is unbounded, then a continuing progress could occur with (perhaps vast) intervals of time when collapses, growth and reswitching took place.

To see how these sorts of possibilities can come about, various numerical experiments have been carried out, two of which are shown in figs. 4.5 and 4.6. In the first a progression occurs; in the second a collapse with phase reswitching.

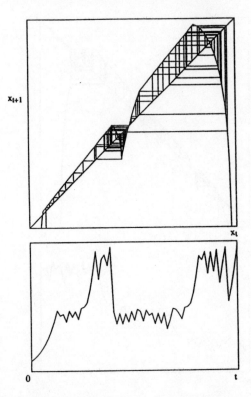

Fig. 4.6. An epochal progression (growth interspersed with chaos and phase switching).

Evolution in the sense of eventually increasing regime index and system size, can occur only if there exist regime sequences, each member of which can be escaped. It can occur with positive probability only if each such regime has a positive probability of escape. It can occur with probability one only if each such regime has a conditional probability of escape of one.

How these possibilities can arise for various underlying parameters of technology and behavior involves the application of Theorem 8 to regions where the production functions of neighboring regimes overlap. The analysis is intricate and the interested reader is referred to the detailed exposition in Day and Walter's paper referred to in footnote 6.

References

Bala, Vankatesh and Majumdar, 1990, Chaotic tatonnement (Cornell University, Ithaca, NY).
Baumol, William J. and Jess Benhabib, 1989, Chaos: Significance, mechanism and economic applications, Journal of Economic Perspective 3, 77–105.
Benhabib, Jess and Richard H. Day, 1982, A characterization of erratic dynamics in the overlapping generations models, Journal of Economic Dynamics and Control 4, 37–55.

Boldrin, Michele, 1988, Persistent oscillations and chaos in economic models: Notes for a survey, in: Phillip W. Anderson, Kenneth A. Arrow and David Pines, eds., The economy as an evolving complex system (Addison-Wesley, Redwood City, CA).

Collett, P. and J.P. Eckmann, 1980, Iterated maps on the interval as dynamical systems (Birkhäuser, Basel).

Day, Richard H., 1989, Comparative fiscal and monetary policy dynamics, in: E. Nell and W. Semmler, eds., Financial dynamics and business cycles (M.E. Sharpe, New York).

Day, Richard H., Chaos and evolution in economic growth, in: K. Velupillai, ed., Nonlinearities, disequilibrium and simulation. Essays in honor of Björn Thalberg (in preparation).

Day, Richard H. and T.Y. Lin, A Keynesian business cycle, in: E.J. Nell and W. Semmler, eds., Nicolas Kaldor and mainstream economics (Macmillan, New York) (forthcoming).

Day, Richard H. and Wayne Shafer, 1987, Ergodic fluctuations in economic models, Journal of Economic Behavior and Organization 8, 339–361.

Day, Richard H. and Jean-Luc Walter, 1989, Economic growth in the very long run: On the multiple-phase interaction of population, technology, and social infrastructure, in: W.A. Barnett, J. Geweke and K. Shell, eds., Economic complexity: Chaos, sunspots, bubbles and non-linearity (Cambridge University Press, Cambridge).

Dunford, Nelson and Jacob T. Schwartz, 1958, Linear operators. Part I: General theory (Interscience, New York).

Galeotti, M., L. Geronazzo and F. Gori, 1988, Nonlinear dynamics in economics and social sciences (Pitagora Editrice, Bologna).

Gibbs, J. Willard, 1901, Elementary principles in statistical mechanics, reprinted in 1981 (Oxbow Press, Woodbridge, CT).

Grandmont, Jean-Michele, 1985, On endogenous competitive business cycles, Econometrica 53, 995–1045.

Grandmont, Jean-Michele, ed., 1987, Nonlinear economic dynamics (Academic Press, Boston, MA).

Halmos, P., 1949, Measurable transformations, Memoirs of the American Mathematical Society 55, 1015–1034.

Hofbauer, F. and G. Keller, 1982a, Equilibrium states for piecewise monotonic transformation, Ergodic Theory and Dynamical Systems 2, 23–43.

Hofbauer, F. and G. Keller, 1982b, Ergodic properties of invariant measures for piecewise monotonic transformation, Mathematische Zeitschrift XX, 119–140.

Lasota, A. and G. Pianigiani, 1977, Invariant measures on topological spaces, Bolletino U.M.I. 14-B, no. 5, 592–603.

Lasota, Andrzej and James A. Yorke, 1973, On the existence of invariant measures for piecewise monotonic transformations, Transactions of the American Mathematical Society 186, 481–488.

Lasota, Andrzej and Michael C. Mackey, 1985, Probabilistic properties of deterministic systems (Cambridge University Press, Cambridge).

Li, Tien-Yien and James Yorke, 1978, Ergodic transformations from an interval into itself, Transactions of the American Mathematical Society 235, 183–192.

Li, Tien-Yien, Michal Misiurewicz, Giulio Pianigiani and James A. Yorke, 1982, No division implies chaos, Transactions of the American Mathematical Society 273, 191–199.

Melese and Transue, 1986, Unscrambling the concept of chaos through thick and thin, Quarterly Journal of Economics, May, 425–426.

Medio, Alfredo, ed., 1987, Advances in nonlinear economic dynamics, Journal of Economic Behavior and Organization 8, 331–541.

Misiurewicz, Michal, 1980, Absolutely continuous measures for certain maps of an interval, Publications Mathematiques 53, 17–51.

Montrucchio, Luigi and Franco Cugno, 1983, Some new techniques for modelling non-linear economic fluctuations: A brief survey, Working paper presented at the Workshop on non-linear models of fluctuating growth: Theory and empirical evidence, Siena, Italy.

Pianigiani, Giulio, 1979, Absolutely continuous invariant measures for the process $x_{n+1} = Ax_n(1-x_n)$, Bolletino, U.M.I. 16A, no. 5, 374–378.

Pianigiani, Giulio, 1981, Conditionally invariant measure and ecponential decay, Journal of Mathematical Analysis and Application 82, 75–84.

Pianigiani, Giulio and James A. Yorke, 1979, Expanding maps on sets which are almost invariant: Decay and chaos, Transactions of the American Mathematical Society 252, 351–366.

Rao, C. Radhakrishna, 1973, Linear statistical inference and its application, 2nd edition (Wiley, New York).

Saari, Donald A., 1985, Iterative price mechanisms, Econometrica 53, 1117–1131.

Saari, Donald A. and Carl Simon, 1978, Effective price mechanisms, Econometrica 46, 1097–1125.

Ziemian, K., 1985, Almost sure invariance principle for some maps of an interval, Ergodic Theory and Dynamical Systems 5, 625–640.

[7]

Econ Theory (1991) 1: 147–167

Economic
Theory
© Springer-Verlag 1991

Non-parametric estimation of deterministically chaotic systems*

Mahmoud A. El-Gamal

Division of the Humanities and Social Sciences 288-77, California Institute of Technology, Pasadena, CA 91125, USA

Received: January 25, 1990

Summary. This paper studies theoretical and econometric issues that arise in systems characterized by deterministic chaos. Such systems can arise from standard dynamic economic models and are extensively used in Monte Carlo and other simulation-based statistical procedures which use pseudo-random number generators. The virtues of studying chaotic laws of motion in the space of densities over the state space are shown. A complete characterization of deterministic stationary ergodic processes in that space of densities is suggested and proved when the invariant measure is unknown. The asymptotic properties of the kernel estimators of the stationary density and the law of motion in the density space are studied, and shown to hold for chaotic systems. Small sample behavior for the estimators is subjectively shown to be good even when optimal choices of the kernel and smoothing parameters are not exploited.

1. Introduction

Recently, there has been a surge of interest in economic circles concerning the philosophical and empirical problem of stochastic versus deterministic explanations of some economic processes. The resulting literature suggests that we may be able to see a truly deterministic process as a stochastic one if only we chose to focus on a certain side of our models.[1] In those studies, similarities were

---

* This paper was presented at the winter meetings of the Econometric Society in Atlanta, December 1989. I am grateful to Bo Honoré, Dale Mortensen, Dan Sullivan and especially to Ian Domowitz for many useful comments on early versions of this paper. The comments of participants at Northwestern, Rochester, and UCSD Econometrics Workshops, and of three anonymous referees, are gratefully acknowledged. Related discussions with William Brock, Lars Hansen and Jeffrey Wooldridge were also very useful. All remaining errors are, of course, my own.

[1] This section only speaks generically about that literature, for a more extensive survey, see [10, 11], or the more recent and comprehensive survey of [3] and the references therein.

drawn between computer algorithms for pseudo-random number generation and deterministic difference equations arising from economic models.

With the familiarity of ARMA models, there was a surprise generated by the result of Sakai and Tokumaru [22] that most trajectories of the difference equation popularly known as the tent map:

$$x_{t+1} \begin{cases} \dfrac{x_t}{a}; & x_t \in [0, a] \\[2mm] \dfrac{1 - x_t}{1 - a}; & x_t \in [a, 1] \end{cases}$$

generate the same stochastic behavior (in terms of autocorrelation coefficients) as the AR(1) process:

$$y_{t+1} = (2a - 1)y_t + \varepsilon_t$$

for i.i.d. ε_t. The resulting literature on chaotic dynamics in economics has mainly dealt with two issues:

1. Devising economic models that endogenously exhibit chaotic behavior (see [3] and the references therein).
2. Using and developing asymptotic theory for tests of correlation dimension to detect deviation of actual observed time series from the i.i.d. assumption. Heuristically, those tests were used to detect *extra-structure* in residuals from standard models (see [4, 10, 11] and the references therein).

This paper tries to tackle the problem of econometric practice with data generated from deterministically chaotic models.[2] Despite the apparent unorthodoxy of that problem, it is a very relevant one in a number of contexts:

1. Recently popularised simulation estimators cannot use real random number generators (r.n.g.'s), and hence use chaotic series arising from pseudo-r.n.g.'s.
2. Monte Carlo investigations of the small sample behavior of estimators, or the power of statistical tests uses pseudo-r.n.g.'s
3. Las Vegas simulations (the use of human subjects in economic experiments) use pseudo-r.n.g.'s.
4. Due to the observational indistinguishability of chaotic and truly stochastic time series, any observed economic time series could have been generated from a

---

[2] To the best of our knowledge, this paper is the only one to date that attacks this problem. A paper by Geweke [14] deals with a similar problem, but at closer inspection diverges in its objective. The first major difference is the definition of chaos that the two papers use. Later in this paper, we shall argue for the use of the definition of chaos as ergodicity, whereas the definition used in [14] is a form of topological chaos. The second major difference is Geweke's introduction of 'measurement errors' which allows him to estimate the law of motion by means of a maximum likelihood approach (which introduces further complications due to the excessive multimodality of the likelihood function). This of course is avoiding the problem that we address in this paper which is having to deal with deterministic systems. The latter problem strips us of a number of our familiar statistical results, and this paper salvages those results in the chaotic case.

chaotic process. More credibility is given to that claim by the economic models that endogenously generate chaotic behavior. For instance, Prescott and Stengos [20] use kernel estimation of the law of motion for certain asset prices where they suspect chaotic behavior. The theorems of section 7 of this paper justify their procedure.

In all of the above situations, we observe econometric practices whose theory is developed for truly stochastic processes. We need to justify those practices by showing that for a certain class of chaotic processes, those theoretical statistical results are still valid. This paper furnishes such a justification for the class of deterministic ergodic processes, and in the process, it offers a different angle for viewing time series models.

The next section starts by suggesting to analyze the bahavior of the deterministic dynamic process in the space of densities over the state space (referred to as the hyper-state space), introducing a stochastic element through the initial condition for the law of motion. One will show that the corresponding law of motion in the hyper-state space will be linear despite the non-linearity of the state space law of motion. Moreover, the estimation procedure will be done independently of the functional form and parameter values of the model, and hence the results should be robust to model mis-specification up to the result of chaotic behavior of the state variable. The rest of this section will be spent on generically obtaining state space dynamics.

Generically, an economic model starts with a maximizing agent solving the problem

$$\max_{(y_t)} \sum_{t=0}^{\infty} u_t(x_t, y_t)$$

$$\text{s.t. } x_{t+1} = g_t(x_t, y_t); \quad \forall t.$$

It is standard in economic literature to then simplify the model and put

$$u_t(\cdot, \cdot) = \beta^t u(\cdot, \cdot); \quad g_t(\cdot, \cdot) = g(\cdot, \cdot); \quad \forall t.$$

Under regularity conditions (e.g. [17]) we get an optimal action correspondence which admits a measurable selection

$$y_t = h(x_t)$$

This relation in turn implies the law of motion for x:

$$x_{t+1} = g(x_t, h(x_t)) = S(x_t).$$

Regardless of the method of achieving the law of motion[3], this paper starts at the stage where one would normally proceed to do some econometric estimation of the underlying parameters of the model.

For our purposes, since the economic model in question remains generic, one starts by defining the simplest possible model that is rich enough to demonstrate

---

[3] The law of motion may be achieved numerically. It is theoretically stochastic if the dynamic programming problem is stochastic, but once pseudo-r.n.g.'s are used, it becomes a deterministic system.

all the interesting aspects of our approach. The model is a non-overlapping generations economy where each individual lives for only one period and is succeeded by his son the moment he dies. The only product in that economy is mangos, and a mango seed takes one period (generation) to grow into a tree and bear one fruit, after which it dies instantly. A son inherits all the trees that his father planted, chooses the number of mangos to eat and the number of seeds to plant. If a person decides not to plant a seed, then that causes him some pain, either because of a bequest motive or because he would have to eat the seed, which is not a pleasant experience. Notice that the family line can look like an infinitely lived individual with infinite discounting of future utility, but the dynamics of the system still stem from the bequest motive. The model, thus could be written as follows:

$$\max_{L_t} u(C_t, L_t)$$

$$\text{s.t. } L_t \leqq C_t \quad \text{and} \quad C_{t+1} = g(C_t, L_t)$$

where the first constraint is that the number of seeds (units of labor) thrown cannot exceed the number of mangos eaten. The second constraint specifies the technology of growing trees, and drives the dynamics of the system. To further simplify the system, we specify the Cobb–Douglas utility function $u(C, L) = CL$ which together with the first constraint will obviously give us $C_t = L_t$; $\forall t$. We then specify the technology that drives the system and study the behavior of consumption (our state variable) in the state space as well as the density space. The discontinuities in the technology can easily be explained by a soil corrosion argument.

$$C_{t+1} = 2L_t \bmod 1$$

and, thus, our law of motion is

$$C_{t+1} = 2C_t \bmod 1.$$

This simple example will be carried throughout the paper due to its transparency so that we can see the workings of all the theoretical and statistical issues that we will have to develop. At various points, we shall demonstrate its similarities and/or differences with other equally simple laws of motion to demonstrate some otherwise obscure issues. The rest of the paper will proceed as follows: In section 2, we define the law of motion in density (hyper-state) space corresponding to our law of motion in the state space. In section 3, we define notions of equilibrium and chaos and offer a proof for the ergodic theorem of Lasota and Mackey [16] in the measure preserving case. In section 4, we discuss the importance of the measure preservation assumption for that ergodic theorem, and its unrealism in economic contexts. In section 5, we state and prove a generalization of the ergodic theorem of [16]. This gives us a full characterization of stationary ergodic (when the stationary measure is absolutely continuous, we call them chaotic) deterministic laws of motion which sets up the estimation section. In sections 6 and 7, we then extend some of the consistency and asymptotic normality results of kernel density estimators to the deterministically chaotic case. Small sample performance of those estimators is then discussed and shown to be sufficiently good.

2. Defining the corresponding law of motion in the hyper-state space

At this point, we shall take the law of motion

$$x_{t+1} = S(x_t)$$

as our starting point. Although the law of motion for the state variable x is completely deterministic, one could study the evolution of the economy over time within a probabilistic framework. For although each infinitely lived individual's behavior of x follows the law of motion S (which is assumed to be identical for all individuals), starting from an initial distribution of individuals in the state space, the evolution of that distribution could have rather interesting characteristics. Another way to look at that treatment is that it introduces a stochastic element through the randomness of the initial condition of our difference equation as suggested by Bellman [2]. We are now ready to define the induced law of motion in the density space. We start by defining a complete normalized measure space $(X, \mathcal{F}, \mu)$, i.e. $\mu(X) = 1$. A transformation $S: X \to X$ is non-singular if for all sets $B \in \mathcal{F}$ with $\mu(S(B)) = 0$, it follows that $\mu(B) = 0$. For every non singular law of motion S,

$$\exists ! P: L^1 \to L^1$$

defined by:

$$\int_A Pf(x)d\mu(x) = \int_{S^{-1}(A)} f(x)d\mu(x)$$

where P is usually (but not necessarily) restricted to D, the space of all densities defined on X, i.e. the space of nonnegative L^1 functions on X whose integral is 1. P is called the Frobenius–Perron operator corresponding to S [16]. The following properties of the operator P follow directly from the definition:

1. P is a Markov operator (hence we can restrict it to D).
2. P is linear.
3. If $S_n = S \circ S \circ \cdots \circ S$, then the corresponding F–P operator is $P_n = P^n$.

Property 3 tells us that as long as time is discrete, (or as long as there is a lower limit on the time it takes an individual to make a decision), the sampling period and the decision making period need not be identical (as long as the former is an integer multiple of the latter). Also, all limiting properties of the F–P operators corresponding to the different periods are the same.

The F–P operator gives us precisely the behavior of the evolution of the density of the initial states over time as the individual goes through the process of maximization which is summarized by the law of motion S. One (the frequentist) interpretation would be that there are many (in our example a continuum of) individuals in the economy, and as each of them changes his state variable by passing through the operator S, the overall distribution over the state space moves according to P. Another (the Bayesian) interpretation would be that we would initially put some likelihood measure over the state space and knowing the individual's behavior, we could consistently put a measure of probability on where our representative individual would be after n periods of time, or asymptotically.

The distinction between these two interpretations is important since it allows for vastly different uses of the F–P operator.

Our mango economy example simplifies things tremendously since we have $S: [0,1] \to [0,1]$ and we could specify the measure to be Lebesgue measure. Working with continuous densities, we can simplify the definition of the F–P operator since the Lebesgue and Riemann integrals will coincide, and we write:

$$Pf(x) = \frac{d}{dx} \int_{S^{-1}([0,x])} f(s) \cdot ds$$

3. The definition of equilibrium and chaos

As we abandon the state space in favor of the hyper-state space, we need to be able to define the counterparts to the most important features of the state space. The main four characteristics of the state space that we naturally discuss are initial conditions, laws of motion, equilibria, and chaos. The concept of initial condition is obviously replaced by that of initial density, and the law of motion by the Frobenius–Perron operator discussed in the previous section. In this section, we define the counterparts of equilibrium and chaos in the hyper-state space to complete the framework. Natural notions of equilibrium follow.

Definition 1 (Weak Equilibrium). *A weak equilibrium is defined by a stationary density $f*$ such that $Pf* = f*$.*

Definition 2 (Strong Equilibrium). *A strong equilibrium is defined by an asymptotically stable (with respect to $\|\cdot\|$) density $f*$ such that $\lim_{n \uparrow \infty} \|P^n f - f*\| = 0$; $\forall f \in D$.*

The most commonly used definition of chaos in state space representations is topological chaos, usually associated with a positive Liapunov exponent. It is clear that topologically chaotic behavior might only be valid for a set of initial conditions that is of measure zero. This argument is used by Day and Shafer [6], and Day and Lin [5] to motivate studying ergodic (sometimes referred to as observable) chaos. For our purposes, we rigorously define the notion [16] of ergodic chaos. We say a non-singular transformation $S: X \to X$ is chaotic if it is ergodic with the unique stationary measure being absolutely continuous. This in turn justifies working with densities on the state space instead of all probability measures.

Definition 3 (Chaos). *If $\forall A \in \mathcal{F}$ with $S^{-1}(A) = A$, it follows that $\mu(A) = 0$, or $\mu(X \backslash A) = 0$, then we say that S is ergodic. If, moreover, $\exists v \ll \mu$ with a stirctly positive Randon–Nikodym derivative $dv/d\mu$ such that $v(S^{-1}(A)) = v(A)$, $\forall A \in \mathcal{F}$, then we say that S is chaotic.*

This is clearly a natural concept of chaos since it states that the only invariant sets are trivial sets, and thus, that as time progresses, one could not trace back the initial condition. Now, we are ready to state the following theorem which describes chaotic behavior of X in the density space. We define D to be the space of all non-negative functions in L^1 with unit norms whose support is X.

Theorem 1. *Given* $S: (X, \mathscr{F}, \mu) \to (X, \mathscr{F}, \mu)$ μ *preserving* (*i.e.* $\mu(S^{-1}(A)) = \mu(A)$; $\forall A \in \mathscr{F}$), *with* $\mu(X) = 1$, S *is chaotic if and only if*

$$\lim_{n \uparrow \infty} \frac{1}{n} \sum_{k=0}^{n-1} P^k f(x) = 1; \quad a.e.$$

$\forall f \in D.$

Proof[4]. For the only if part, one starts by showing that there can be at most one stationary density for S ergodic (chaotic). Assume that f_1 and f_2 were both stationary densities of P, let $g = f_1 - f_2$, then by the linearity of P, $Pg = g$, and since $g = g^+ - g^-$ (the positive and negative parts of g), g^+ and g^- are also stationary functions for P (by proposition 3.1.3 [16]). Let $A = \{x: g^+(x) > 0\}$ and let $B = \{x: g^-(x) > 0\}$, then clearly, $A \cap B = \phi$ and $\mu(A) > 0$ and $\mu(B) > 0$, since f_1 and f_2 are densities that are different. It follows that

$$A \subset S^{-1}(A) \subset \cdots \subset S^{-n}(A)$$

and

$$B \subset S^{-1}(B) \subset \cdots \subset S^{-n}(B)$$

Letting $A* = \bigcup_{n=0}^{\infty} S^{-n}(A)$ and $B* = \bigcup_{n=0}^{\infty} S^{-n}(B)$, we have $A*$ and $B*$ being invariant sets, that are non-trivial, i.e. $S^{-1}(A*) = A*$ and $\mu(A*) \neq 1$ or 0, and the same for $B*$, but that violates the definition of ergodicity by all invariant sets being trivial, hence we have a contradiction and there could be at most one stationary density. Now, Lasota Mackey [16], Theorem 5.2.2, pp. 85–86 proves the existence of the Cesàro limit for $P^n f$ if $\exists$ a unique stationary density, and we have the obvious result (since by above, the only $f: Pf = f$ is $f = 1$, see proof of lemma 1 below):

$$\lim_{n \uparrow \infty} \frac{1}{n} \sum_{k=0}^{n-1} P^k 1 = 1$$

It follows that there exists a unique Cesàro limit for $P^n f$. Since S is measure preserving, it is readily seen that $P1 = 1$ and hence, 1 has to be the unique limit, i.e. we have shown that:

$$\frac{1}{n} \sum_{k=0}^{n-1} P^k f(x) \to 1$$

$\forall f \in D$ which concludes the proof for the only if part.

For the if part, let the Cesàro convergence to 1 be given, and assume that $f*$ is a stationary density, i.e. $P^k f* = f*, \forall k$, then $\lim_{n \uparrow \infty} \frac{1}{n} \sum_{k=0}^{n-1} P^k f* = 1$ and thus, $f* = 1$, and hence, 1 is the unique stationary density for P. Now, assume S is not ergodic; then $\exists A$ non-trivial s.t. $S^{-1}(A) = A$, and letting $B = X \backslash A$, i.e. the complement of

---

[4] This theorem is stated without proof as part of a theorem 4.4.1 and a sketch of a proof is given in Corollary 5.2.3 of Lasota and Mackey [16]. The following proof draws heavily on results in Lasota and Mackey [16] and Walters [23] and is included for completeness.

A with respect to X. we get $S^{-1}(B) = B$. Now, let us write (by the linearity of P)

$$f* = I_A f* + I_B f* = PI_A f* + PI_B f*$$

then we have $I_A f* = PI_A f*$ and $I_B f* = PI_B f*$ where $I_Y(x)$ is the indicator function which takes the value 1 if $x \in Y$, and 0 otherwise. Letting $f_1 = I_A f*/\int I_A f*$ and $f_2 = I_B f*/\int I_B f*$, it follows that f_1 and f_2 are two distinct stationary densities for P which results in a contradiction. Hence S has to be ergodic (chaotic) and the proof of Theorem 1 is finished.

To get an intuitive feeling for the origin of that result, notice that by the Birkhoff Ergodic Theorem [23], it follows that with S μ-preserving:

$$\frac{1}{n} \sum_{i=0}^{n-1} f(S^i(x)) \to f* \in D \quad \text{a.e.}$$

and if S is chaotic, $f*$ is constant almost everywhere, and hence, with a normalized measure space, and since $f* \in D$, it must be that starting from any $f \in D$, the density converges to 1 a.e. The result of the Birkhoff ergodic theorem obviously does not deal with the F–P operator but rather with its conjugate, but Lasota and Mackey ([16], thm. 5.2.2) show that the same result is true for the Cesàro limit of the F–P operator if S is chaotic. This theorem is very powerful since it states that given a maximization problem that yields a chaotic S mapping, regardless of what our priors are, or regardless of the initial distribution of the agents in the state space, we should expect the distribution of the individuals to be asymptotically uniform (with respect to the measure μ which we shall usually specify to be Lebesgue measure).

At this stage, we are ready to analyze the chaotic behavior of our mango economy. Figure 1a shows the trajectory of consumption under this law of motion (which is called the diadic transformation). The driving technology, the diadic transformation, is obviously Lebesgue measure preserving. From Fig. 2a, it is clear that the state space has only two steady state equilibria, namely 0 and 1, both of which are unstable. The trajectory of C does not seem to show any short term periodicity. As a matter of fact, one can easily show that the diadic transformation is chaotic. To show this notice that

$$S^{-1}([0,x]) = \left[0, \frac{x}{2}\right] \cup \left[\frac{1}{2}, \frac{1+x}{2}\right]$$

which gives:

$$Pf(x) = \frac{d}{dx} \sum_{i=0}^{1} \int_{i/2}^{(i+x)/2} f(s) \cdot ds = \frac{1}{2} \sum_{i=0}^{2-1} f\left(\frac{i+x}{2}\right)$$

and clearly, by a simple inductive argument:

$$P^n f(x) = \frac{1}{2^n} \sum_{i=0}^{2^n-1} f\left(\frac{i+x}{2^n}\right) \to \int_0^1 f(s) \cdot ds = 1 \quad \text{as} \quad n \uparrow \infty$$

uniformly in x, $\forall f$. Hence, the iterates of a density converge strongly to the uniform density. Strong convergence implies Cesàro convergence, and by Theorem 1, since the diadic transformation is Lebesgue measure preserving, this process is chaotic. The

Deterministically chaotic systems

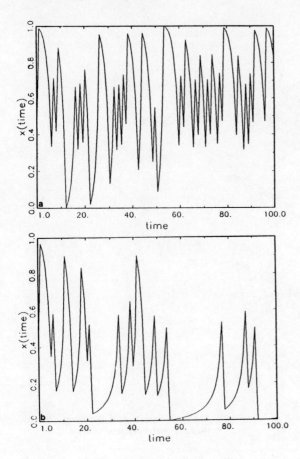

Fig. 1 a, b. Trajectory of the diadic (a) and weak repellor (b)

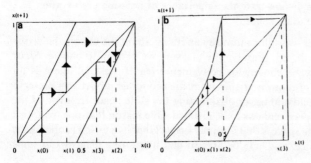

Fig. 2 a, b. Three steps of the diadic (a) and weak repellor (b)

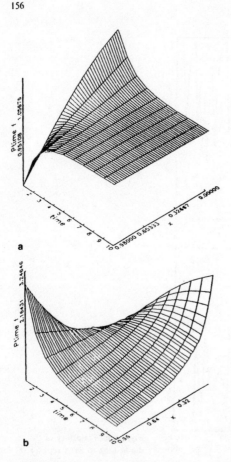

a

b

Fig. 3 a, b. Evolution of the density for the diadic (**a**) and weak repellor (**b**)

speed of convergence to the uniform density starting from any density is 2^n as is shown in the proof above. Figure 3a shows the convergence of densities for an initial density that is a randomly chosen fifth degree polynomial (using the algorithm for randomly selecting densities devised in Domowitz and El-Gamal [8]).

4. A counter example to demonstrate the importance of measure preservation and analysis in the hyper-state space

At this stage of the paper, we still cannot say anything about the chaotic behavior of transformations that do not preserve the measure we happen to choose. Since a measure will typically be chosen for convenience (e.g. Lebesgue), there is no guarantee that the law of motion arising from the economic model will preserve that measure. Also, the advantage of abandoning the state space in favor of the unfamiliar hyper-state space remains to be justified. One reason that one may wish to analyze the hyper-state space is that one may suspect that by putting probabilistic weights on the state space, one may be able to find interesting behavior in some cases where the state space exhibits a multiplicity of unstable equilibria, and hence may exhibit chaotic behavior. If one does not wish to assume that the process starts on a stable manifold (which in general is of measure zero, and may not exist in many cases) or at a steady state equilibrium, then we may be able to study the likelihood of the process being in any particular region of the state space given an initial distribution. Again, we can interpret that initial density as a probabilistic prior or as an actual distribution of agents when the process starts. The case of the diadic transformation analyzed above clearly satisfied the condition of having multiple unstable equilibria. In that case, however, the trajectory in the state space seemed to be sufficient for detecting the chaotic behavior of the variable. To see how dramatic the difference between that apparent behavior in the state space and actual behavior in the density space can be, let us change our technology in the mango economy to:

$$C_{t+1} = \begin{cases} \dfrac{L_t}{(1 - L_t)}; & L_t \in [0, \frac{1}{2}] \\ 2L_t - 1; & L_t \in (\frac{1}{2}, 1] \end{cases}$$

This example is especially tailored to yield a transformation which looks essentially similar to the diadic transformation in that the two steady states 0 and 1 are unstable. Moreover, looking at Fig. 1b, it seems that the trajectory does not have a short period. Notice, however, that the transformation here is not lebesgue measure preserving, and thus, the result of Theorem 1 does not apply. Comparing Fig. 2a and b, it is clear that the only change we introduced in Fig. 2b is the slower speed of repulsion from 0. The result of such a minor change, however, is remarkably strong, for one can show[5] that $\forall \varepsilon > 0$:

$$\lim_{n \uparrow \infty} \int_{\varepsilon}^{1} P^n f(s) \cdot d\mu(s) = 0$$

i.e. asymptotically, all the mass is on the stationary point 0. It follows that the weak repellor does not preserve any measure that is absolutely continuous with respect to Lebesgue measure. Figure 3b shows the evolution of the densities for the weak repellor from a randomly chosen fifth degree polynomial. It is clear how all the mass is quickly accumulating near the point 0. In the next section, we shall consider the case where there is a stationary measure absolutely continuous with respect to the measure that we choose.

5. Characterizing chaotic behavior when the invariant measure is unknown

Since we shall be interested in empirically analyzing the behavior of the density space, it would be useful to know when a transformation preserves a certain measure using only the density space behavior. We construct the following lemma to achieve such a result:

---

[5] This is the example referred to as the paradox of the weak repellor in Lasota and Mackey [16].

Lemma 1. *A non-singular transformation* $S:(X,\mathscr{F},\mu)\to(X,\mathscr{F},\mu)$ *with* $\mu(X)=1$ *is* μ-*preserving if and only if* 1 *is a stationary density for P, the F–P operator corresponding to S.*

Proof. For the if part of the lemma, let 1 be a stationary density, then $P1=1$ and $\forall A\in\mathscr{F}$, since by definition

$$\int_A Pf\,d\mu = \int_{S^{-1}(A)} f\,d\mu$$

we have

$$\int_A 1\,d\mu = \int_{S^{-1}(A)} 1\,d\mu$$

but that simply saus that $\mu(A)=\mu(S^{-1}(A))$, i.e. that S is μ preserving.

For the only if part, let S be measure preserving, then $\mu(A)=\mu(S^{-1}(A))$ and hence

$$\int_A 1\,d\mu = \int_{S^{-1}(A)} 1\,d\mu$$

but by the definition of the F–P operator,

$$\int_A P1\,d\mu = \int_{S^{-1}(A)} 1\,d\mu$$

Hence, since this has to hold for all sets $A\in\mathscr{F}$, $P1=1$ a.e. $[\mu]$, and since we are not considering sets of measure zero, 1 is a stationary density for P.

We consider the result of Theorem 1 above to be too restrictive since our characterization of chaotic behavior will only apply in cases where the uniform density is stationary, i.e. where the transformations preserve the chosen measure (which will usually be Lebesgue measure). We therefore construct the following theorem to generalize that result and allow ourselves to define chaos in the density space under certain circumstances where the transformation in question does not preserve our measure. The trick is to try to find a measure which that transformation preserves and then go back to analyze chaotic behavior using the result of Theorem 1.

Theorem 2. *Given the probability space* $(X,\mathscr{F},\mu)$, *let the non-singular* $S:X\to X$ *have the F–P operator P, and let* $\exists f>0$ *such that* $Pf=f$, *then S is chaotic if and only if* $\forall g\in D$, f *is the Cesàro limit of* $P^n g$; *i.e.*

$$\lim_{n\uparrow\infty}\frac{1}{n}\sum_{k=0}^{n-1}P^k g = f$$

Proof. Given $f>0$ is a stationary density for P_μ, we can define the measure v as follows

$$v(A)=\int_A f\,d\mu; \quad \forall A\in\mathscr{F}$$

Clearly, S preserves v since $P_\mu f=f$:

$$v(A)=\int_A f\,d\mu = \int_A P_\mu f\,d\mu$$

$$=\int_{S^{-1}(A)} f\,d\mu = v(S^{-1}(A)); \quad \forall A\in\mathscr{F}$$

and hence, by Theorem 1, since S preserves v, S is ergodic (chaotic) $[v]$ (i.e. all S invariant sets are of v measure 0 or 1) if and only if the uniform density with respect to v is the Cesàro limit of $P_v^n g$ for all $g \in D$.

For the if part of Theorem 2, we need to show that if f is the Cesàro limit of P_μ, then S is ergodic $[\mu]$. But notice that the uniform density $[v]$ corresponds to f $[\mu]$, since:

$$v(A) = \int_A 1 \, dv = \int_A f \, d\mu; \quad \forall A \in \mathscr{F}$$

and by the linearity of integration, and linearity of P_μ, consider any initial density $j > 0$ with respect to μ, then both measures μ and v are absolutely continuous with respect to the measure generated by integrating j with respect to μ. Hence, there exists a corresponding density g with respect to v such that:

$$\int_A \frac{1}{n} \sum_{k=0}^{n-1} P_\mu^k g \, dv = \int_A \frac{1}{n} \sum_{k=0}^{n-1} P_v^k j \, d\mu$$

and taking limits of both sides, and using the dominated convergence theorem, since

$$\lim_{n \uparrow \infty} \frac{1}{n} \sum_{k=0}^{n-1} P_v^k g = 1$$

we use the definition of the measure v and get

$$\lim_{n \uparrow \infty} \frac{1}{n} \sum_{k=0}^{n-1} P_\mu^k j = f$$

Hence, S is $[v]$ ergodic if and only if f is the Cesàro limit of $P_\mu^n j$ for all $0 < j \in D$. But remembering that we were not interested in $[v]$ ergodicity but rather in $[\mu]$ ergodicity, notice that by the definition of v:

$$v(A) = \int_A f \, d\mu$$

it follows that $f > 0$ is the Radon–Nikodyn derivative of v with respect to μ, and thus, $\mu \ll v$; and by that absolute continuity, if S is ergodic $[v]$, all invariant sets are of v measure zero and hence of μ measure zero or of v measure 1, and hence their complements are of v and μ measure zero. Hence, all invariant sets have to also be of μ measure 0 or 1, and S is ergodic (chaotic) $[\mu]$ which completes the proof of the if part of the theorem.

For the only if part, we follow the same proof strategy as that of Theorem 1. Since the ergodicity $[\mu]$ of S implies that P_μ has at most one stationary density (this claim is proved in the beginning of the proof of Theorem 1), and by f being stationary, it follows that f has to be the unique stationary density for P_μ. And by Theorem 5.2.2 pp. 85–86 in Lasota and Mackey [16], it follows that f is also the Cesàro limit for P_μ.

At this stage, we have the result that any non-singular process which is in a weak equilibrium is chaotic if and only if the stationary density defined by that weak equilibrium is also the Cesàro limit density for the corresponding F–P operator. Given a model which suggests the chaotic behavior of the state or policy variable, we could characterize the behavior of that variable in the hyper-state space. The economist does not have to even be able to solve for the closed form of the operator S, as long as he could demonstrate its chaotic behavior. The analytical demonstration of the chaotic behavior of a given law of motion is in general extremely difficult. Domowitz and El-Gamal [8] offers a numerical/statistical consistent test of the hypothesis that a known law of motion is chaotic.

6. The framework for estimation

We observe a time series $\{x, t \geq 1\}$ which is a Markov process on $(X, \mathscr{F}, \mu)$. By the chaotic assumption, and the above assumption of observing the process in equilibrium, it follows that the process x_t is strictly stationary. For simplicity, we assume that the process takes values in $\mathfrak{R}$, with σ-algebra $\mathscr{B}$ which is the σ-algebra generated by the Borel sets of $\mathfrak{R}$. The assumption that the process is univariate will be relaxed in later research, but it seems sufficient as a first step for the simplicity of exposition as well as the fact that most of the economic models generating deterministic chaos are univariate. The existing results on estimation in Markov processes that will be used in Theorems 3 and 4 below will require that one also makes the assumption that Doeblin's condition holds, i.e., that $\exists \lambda$ a finite measure on $\mathscr{B}$ with $\lambda(\mathfrak{R}) > 0$, and an integer $\nu \geq 1$ and $\varepsilon > 0$ such that $\forall \zeta \in X$,

$$Tr^{(\nu)}(\zeta, A) \leq 1 - \varepsilon \quad \forall A \in \mathscr{B}, \lambda(A) \leq \varepsilon$$

where $Tr^{(n)}$ is the n-period transition probability. It is clear that this assumption will not hold for the deterministic law of motion that we have.

For the purposes of the following discussion, let us define $f(x)$ to be the unique stationary ergodic density. Also let $j(x, x')$ be the joint density of x_t and x_{t+1} at the values x and x', and let $p(x'|x) = j(x, x')/f(x)$ be the transition density defining the Chapman–Kolmogorov type equation

$$\int_X p(x'|x) f(x) \cdot dx = f(x')$$

Notice that defining j and p as densities is an abuse of notation since for our system, $p(x'|x) = \delta_{S(x)}$ the Dirac delta function at $S(x)$. The estimators of f, j, p will be referred to as f_n, j_n, p_n respectively. The asymptotic results in the statistical literature that we shall use in the following section were proved for ergodic Markovian processes satisfying Doeblin's condition defined above and with continuous joint density j. Both of these assumptions are clearly false in this case. We shall show, however, that the most important aspects of the available asymptotic results can be salvaged in the case where S is chaotic. We shall add the assumption that S has at most a finite number of discontinuities. The trick we shall utilize is to take a sequence of truly stochastic Markov processes whose law of motion converges (in a sense to be defined below) to that of our chaotic time series $\{x_t\}_{t=1}^n$. The ergodicity of that observed time series will play a very important role in driving the results through.

Consider the sequence of stochastic processes $\{x_t^m\}$ with $x_1^m = x_1$ and transition density

$$p^m(x'|x) = \frac{m}{\sqrt{2\pi}} e^{-m^2(x' - S^m(x))^2/2}$$

S^m is taken to be a sequence of continuous functions converging to S pointwise. If x is a discontinuity point of S, then choose $x + \varepsilon/m$ and $x - \varepsilon/m$ continuity points of S (this is always possible under the assumption that S has at most a finite number of discontinuity points). In the interval $(x - \varepsilon/m, x + \varepsilon/m)$, set

$$S^m(y) = S(x - \varepsilon/m) + \frac{m(S(x + \varepsilon/m) - S(x - \varepsilon/m))}{2\varepsilon}(y - x + \varepsilon/m)$$

and set $S^m(x) = S(x)$ elsewhere. Then, as $m \uparrow \infty$, $S^m \to S$ pointwise, and $p^m \to p$ weakly. Now consider the sequence of Chapman–Kolmogorov type equations

$$\int_X p^m(x'|x) f^m(x) \cdot dx = f^m(x')$$

Since for all m, the process x_t^m is also ergodic, f^m in the above equation is uniquely defined. Now, taking limits of both sides as $m \uparrow \infty$ and by the above constructed weak convergence of p^m to p and the dominated convergence theorem, it follows that

$$\int_X p(x'|x) \lim_{m \uparrow \infty} f^m(x) \cdot dx = \lim_{m \uparrow \infty} f^m(x')$$

But by the ergodicity of the original chaotic time series generated by p, the fixed point for $\int p \cdot f = f$ is uniquely determined by the stationary ergodic density f. Hence, f^m converges pointwise of f, and trivially, $j^m(x, x') = p^m(x'|x) \cdot f^m(x)$ converges weakly to j. Notice moreover that for each m, the process $\{x_t^m\}$ is ergodic, statisfies Doeblin's condition, and p^m and j^m are continuous.

In the following section, we shall use the approximation procedure in the previous paragraph to show that slightly different asymptotic results for the estimators f_n and p_n still hold. It is obvious, then, that forecasting the probability of the system being in some set at some point in time can be performed by estimating the density at that point in time using the Chapman–Kolmogorov equations, and then integrating the density over the set of interest.

7. Asymptotic results

In the following statements, K is a symmetric, bounded kernel and h_n is the smoothing factor in the kernel estimators. We observe $(x_1, \ldots, x_{n+1})$ and estimate the densities of interest by:

1. The stationary density:

$$f_n(x) = \frac{1}{nh_n} \sum_{j=1}^{n} K\left(\frac{x - X_j}{h_n}\right)$$

2. the joint density:

$$j_n(x, x') = \frac{1}{nh_n} \sum_{j=1}^{n} K\left(\frac{x - X_j}{\sqrt{h_n}}\right) K\left(\frac{x - X_{j+1}}{\sqrt{h_n}}\right)$$

and of course,

3. the transition conditional density:

$$p_n(x'|x) = \frac{j_n(x, x')}{f_n(x)}$$

and the corresponding distribution function

$$G_n(x'|x) = \int_{-\infty}^{x'} p_n(x''|x) \cdot dx''$$

An alternative estimation approach used by Gallant and Nychka [13] and others is to use orthogonal series polynomial expansions of the densities resulting in what they called *seminonparametric* estimators. One of the necessary conditions for the consistency of most of those seminonparametric estimators, however, is that the estimated densities have to be in L^2. The reason for this restriction is that most of those series expansions (e.g. trigonometric, Hermite, and Legendre) form systems that do not form a basis for L^1, and hence, the respective estimators are not consistent for some densities in L^1.[6] For that reason, one prefers to use the kernel estimators which are themselves densities and thus form a basis for L^1.

We state the following set of assumptions varying in their strength for use in Theorems 3 and 4. Notice that they are not mutually exclusive, and though restrictive, there is still a large class of kernels and smoothing parameters that can satisfy all the conditions, and thus, achieve the warranted properties proved in the following two theorems.

1. (a) $\lim_{|x|\uparrow\infty} |x|K(x) = 0$

(b) $\int_{-\infty}^{\infty} x^2 K(x)dx < \infty$.

2. (a) $nh_n \to \infty$ as $n\uparrow\infty$.
(b) $\exists \{\alpha_n\}, \{\beta_n\}, \{\gamma_n\}$ of integers tending to ∞ such that $\beta_n\gamma_n\alpha_n^{-1} \to 0$ and $\alpha_n h_n \to 0$.
3. (a) $f(x)$ is continuous.
(b) f is absolutely continuous satisfying:

$$|f(x') - f(x)| \leqq M(x)|x - x'|$$

(c) S has at most a finite number of discontinuities.

Theorem 3. 1. *Given assumptions 1.a, 2.a & 3.a,c,* $\int_{-\infty}^{\infty} |E[f_n(x)] - f(x)|dx \to 0$.

2. *Given 1.a, 1.b, 2.a,b, 3.a,b,c,* $\sqrt{nh_n}[f_n(x) - E(f_n(x))] \to N(0, \sigma^2(x)) \, \forall x$, *where* $\sigma^2(x) = f(x)\int K^2(z)dz$.

Proof. For part 1, Basawa and Prakasa-Rao [1] prove the result under the assumptions of Doeblin's condition and the continuity of j. Hence, with the

---

[6] See Theorems 1, p. 294, 5, p. 312, and 6, p. 317 in Devroye and Györfi [7] for the respective inconsistency results for the trigonometric, Hermite, and Legendre polynomial estimators.

framework defined in the previous section, for all m,

$$\int_{-\infty}^{\infty} |E[f_n^m(x)] - f^m(x)| \cdot dx \to 0$$

Using the triangle inequality, we can write

$$\int_{-\infty}^{\infty} |E[f_n(x)] - f(x)| \cdot dx \leq \int_{-\infty}^{\infty} |E[f_n(x)] - f_n^m(x)| \cdot dx + \int_{-\infty}^{\infty} |E[f_n^m(x)] - f^m(x)| \cdot dx$$

$$+ \int_{-\infty}^{\infty} |f^m(x) - f(x)| \cdot dx$$

Fixing the initial condition $x_1^m = x_1$, the first term converges to 0 as $m \uparrow \infty$ by the weak convergence of p^m to p proven in the previous section. The second term converges to 0 as $n \uparrow \infty$ for any m by Basawa and Prakasa-Rao [1], and the third term converges to 0 as $m \uparrow \infty$ by the pointwise convergence of f^m to f proven in the previous section. Hence, the desired result follows.

For part 2 of the theorem, we start by quoting the following general Central Limit Theorem (this is a special case of Basawa and Prakasa-Rao [1], Theorem 2.5 p. 305):

Theorem
Given $\{x_n\}$ a Markov process satisfying Doeblin's condition. Let $u_n \uparrow \infty$ and let $\{L_n\}$ be a sequence of uniformly bounded functions $L: \mathfrak{R} \to \mathfrak{R}$ such that

1. $E|L_n(x_1)|^2 = O(u_n n^{-1})$. Let $v_n(x_i) = L_n(x_i) - EL_n(x_i)$:
2. $E|v_n(x_1)v_n(x_i)| = O(u_n^2 n^{-2})$ uniformly in $1 \leq i \leq n$.
3. $E|v_n(x_1)v_n(x_i)v_n(x_j)| = O(u_n^3 n^{-3})$ uniformly in $1 \leq i \leq j \leq n$.
4. $n u_n^{-1} var(L_n(x_1)) \to \sigma^2 < \infty$.

and suppose that $\exists$ sequences of integers $\{\alpha_n\}$, $\{\beta_n\}$, $\{\gamma_n\}$ tending to ∞ such that

$$\beta_n \gamma_n \alpha_n^{-1} \to 0 \cdot$$

and $\alpha_n u_n n^{-1} \to 0$, then

$$\sqrt{u_n^{-1}} \sum_{j=1}^{n} [L_n(x_j) - EL_n(x_j)] \to N(0, \sigma^2).$$

Now, following Basawa and Prakasa-Rao [1], Theorem 2.6, p. 306, let $u_n = nh_n$, and let

$$L_n(z) = K\left(\frac{x-z}{h_n}\right)$$

It is clear that for any finite m, the conditions of the theorem are satisfied and

$$\sqrt{nh_n}(f_n^m(x) - E[f_n^m(x)]) \to N(0, \sigma^2(x))$$

Let us write the L.H.S. of the expression in part 2 of Theorem 3 as

$$\sqrt{nh_n}\{(f_n(x) - f_n^{m(n)}(x)) + (f_n^{m(n)}(x) - E[f_n^{m(n)}(x)]) + (E[f_n^{m(n)}(x)] - E[f_n(x)])\}$$

Where $m(n)$ is a subsequence of n chosen for the given initial condition $x_1^m = x_1$ and such that the first and third terms of the above expression are each less than $\varepsilon/2$ after multiplication by $\sqrt{nh_n}$; this is always possible due to the pointwise convergence of f^m to f and the weak convergence of p^m to p proven in the previous section. But since the choice of ε is arbitrary, the desired result follows.

Theorem 4. *Given assumptions 1.a, 2.a, 3.a,c and defining the estimate of* $G(\cdot|\cdot)$

$$G_n(x'|x) = \int_{-\infty}^{x'} p_n(x''|x)dx''$$

we have the result: $\forall x \in X, \delta > 0, \exists A$ *with* $\mu(A) < \delta$ *such that*

$$\sup_{x' \notin A} |G_n(x'|x) - G(x'|x)| \to 0 \text{ in probability } \forall x \in X$$

Proof[7]. We start by proving the result for any finite m as in the construction of section 6. By the definition of $f_n^m, j_n^m,$ & p_n^m, we have:

$$p_n^m(x''|x) - p^m(x''|x) = \frac{1}{f_n^m(x)} [j_n^m(x, x'') - j^m(x, x'')]$$

$$+ \frac{1}{f^m(x)f_n^m(x)} [f^m(x) - f_n^m(x)] j(x, x'')$$

but by the definition of G^m

$$G_n^m(x'|x) - G^m(x'|x) = \int_{-\infty}^{x'} [p_n^m(x''|x) - p^m(x''|x)]dx''$$

and using the above equality together with the obvious fact that

$$\int_{-\infty}^{x'} j^m(x, x'')dx'' \leq \int_{-\infty}^{\infty} j^m(x, x'')dx'' = f^m(x)$$

and using the triangle inequality, and taking sup over all x', we get:

$$\sup_{x'} |G_n^m(x'|x) - G^m(x'|x)| \leq \frac{1}{f_n^m(x)} \sup_{x'} \int_{-\infty}^{x'} |j_n^m(x, x'')|dx'' + \frac{1}{f_n^m(x)} |f^m(x) - f_n^m(x)|$$

Taking plims of both sides, and using the facts that the LHS is non-negative, and that the first term on the RHS converges in probability to $0, \forall x$ by Roussas [21] lemma 3.3, and the second term converges in probability to 0 by its L^1 convergence to 0 (Theorem 3 above), the LHS converges to 0 in probability.

---

[7] This theorem with the assumptions of Doeblin's condition and the continuity of $j(\cdot, \cdot)$ and a stronger result of convergence of the sup over $x \in X$ is stated in a different form without proof in Prakasa-Rao [19], and proved in Roussas [21], the proof provided here uses results from both sources and replaces the assumption of continuity of $j(\cdot, \cdot)$ by continuity of S except at a finite number of points. Unfortunately, since we only have weak convergence of p^m to p and not uniform convergence, we cannot reproduce the result of Roussas for the chaotic case. We show that we can still get the desired type of convergence outside an arbitrarily small set.

Deterministically chaotic systems 165

Now, as in the proof of Theorem 3, fixing x, and for any $\delta > 0$ we can (by the continuity except at a finite number of points of S) choose a neighborhood A of $S(x)$ such that the measure of A is less than δ, and an m large enough such that the first and third terms on the R.H.S. of the following inequality are less than $\varepsilon/2$ each

$$\sup_{x' \notin A} |G_n^m(x'|x) - G(x'|x)| \leqq \sup_{x' \notin A} |G_n(x'|x) - G_n^m(x'|x)| + \sup_{x' \notin A} |G_n^m(x'|x) - G^m(x'|x)|$$

$$+ \sup_{x' \notin A} |G^m(x'|x) - G(x'|x)|$$

since ε is arbitrary, and the middle term has been shown to converge to 0 in probability, the desired result follows.

The results of Theorems 3 and 4 give us all the necessary ingredients for statistical inference. With the consistency and asymptotic normality of the stationary density estimate (Theorem 3), and the consistency of the transition function (Theorem 4), we can forecast the probability of the sytem being in some

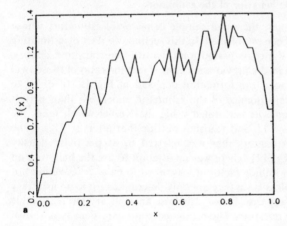

Fig. 4 a–c. Estimated stationary (a) and joint density (b) for the diadic transformation, and joint density for the tent map (c)

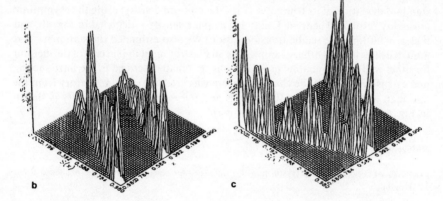

set at some point in time. Moreover, with the estimate of the transition function, we can forecast the evolution of densities starting from an initial density other than the stationary one, and hence examine the short term effects of redistribution policies.

One more issue needs to be discussed in this section before we turn to numerical performance of the proposed estimation techniques. It is customary in economics to estimate the actual law of motion in the state space S. This is heuristically equivalent to plotting x' versus x and trying to interpolate in a statistically sophisticated way for values of x at which no data was observed (which is a set of measure 1). The kernel estimators of the joint density and the marginal stationary density offered in this section are obviously sufficient for that. Indeed if one were to opt for estimating a kernel regression (sometimes also called a kernel smoother) for $S(x)$, the consistency of this estimator only requires the consistency of the densities in question, and it therefore follows trivially from the asymptotic results that we prove in this section.

8. Unoptimized small sample behavior of the estimators

It is a common practice to test the small sample behavior of estimators whose asymptotic properties have been established. In this section, we start by estimating the stationary density, and the cross-period joint density (the transition density, or the F–P operator as seen in the previous sections is just the ratio of those two) for the trajectory of the diadic transformation depicted in Fig. 1a. In order to qualitatively evaluate the performance of the estimator under less than perfect circumstances, the estimation was performed using the Kernel which takes the value 0.5 on the interval $[-1,1]$, and vanishes outside that interval. This is the grandfather of all kernel estimators that was referred to as the naive density estimator by Fix and Hodges [12]. There was no attempt to use the literature on the optimal choice of the smoothing factor, it was taken to be $n^{-0.75}$. We did not try to use those optimal choices since they are only determined up to an arbitrary factor of proportionality in any case, so we just chose an arbitrary but reasonable value for the parameters in question. The estimated stationary density is shown in Fig. 4a, and the estimate of $f(x)$ at any particular point x is within one or two standard deviation of its true value (1 for the uniform density) using the asymptotic normality result of Theorem 3, part 2. The joint density is depicted in Fig. 4b, and it clearly outlines the diadic transformation. We also estimated the stationary and joint densities for two other examples. As an illustration of the success of the method for other well known chaotic processes, the tent map described in the introduction and extensively used in the chaos literature was used. A typical trajectory from the tent map was generated for 100 periods and the estimated joint density is shown in Fig. 4c, which clearly outlines that map.

References

1. Basawa I, Prakasa-Rao B (1980) Statistical inference for stochastic processes. Academic Press, London

Deterministically chaotic systems   167

2. Bellman R (1973) Methods of non-linear analysis, vols. 1, 2. Academic Press, New York
3. Boldrin M, Woodford M (1989) Equilibrium models displaying endogenous fluctuations and chaos: a survey. Working paper #530, UCLA Department of Economics, October 1989
4. Brock W (1986) Distinguishing random and deterministic systems. J Econ Theor 40: 168–195
5. Day R, Lin T-Y (1987) Irregular fluctuations and comparative policy dynamics in Keynesian regimes. MRG Paper #8604, Uiversity of Southern California
6. Day R, Shafer W (1987) Ergodic fluctuations in deterministic economic models. MRG Paper #8631, University of Southern California
7. Devroye L, Györfi L (1985) Nonparametric density estimation, the L^1 view. Wiley & Sons, New York
8. Domowitz I, El-Gamal M (1988) A test of the Harris ergodicity of stationary dynamical economic models. RCER working paper #157, University of Rochester
9. Eckmann J, Ruelle D (1985) Ergodic theory of chaos and strange attractors. Review of modern physics 57: 617–656
10. El-Gamal M (1988a) Estimation in economic systems characterized by deterministic chaos. PhD Dissertation, Northwestern University
11. El-Gamal M (1988b) Simple methods of estimation and inference for systems characterized by deterministic chaos. RCER working paper #147, University of Rochester
12. Fix E, Hodges J (1951) Discriminatory analysis nonparametric estimation: consistency properties. Report No 4, Project No 21-49-004, USAF School of Aviation Medicine, Raudolph Field, Texas
13. Gallant A, Nychka W (1987) Seminonparametric maximum likelihood estimation. Econometrica 55: 363–390
14. Geweke J (1989) Inference and forecasting for chaotic nonlinear time series. Institute of Statistics and Decision Sciences DP #89-06, Duke University
15. Kushner H (1984) Approximation and weak convergence methods for random processes, with applications to stochastic systems theory. MIT Press, Cambridge
16. Lasota A, Mackey M (1985) Probabilistic properties of deterministic systems. Cambridge University Press, Cambridge
17. Maitra A (1968) Discounted dynamic programming on compact metric spaces. Sankhya Ser A 30: 211–221
18. Prakasa-Rao B (1977) Berry–Essen bound for density estimators of stationary Markov processes. Bull Math Stat 17: 15–21
19. Prakasa-Rao B (1983) Nonparametric functional estimation. Academic Press, Orlando
20. Prescott D, Stegnos T (1989) Do asset markets overlook exploitable nonlinearities? The case of gold. University of Guelph, Ontario
21. Roussas G (1969) Nonparametric estimation of the transition distribution function of a Markov process. Ann Math Stat 40: 1386–1400
22. Sakai H, Tokumaru H (1980) Autocorrelations of a certain chaos. IEEE Trans Acoust Sp Sig Proc 5: 588–590
23. Walters, P (1982) An introduction to ergodic theory. Springer, Berlin Heidelberg New York

[8]

Review of Economic Studies (1991) **58**, 697–716
0034-6527/91/00400697$02.00
© 1991 The Review of Economic Studies Limited

Some Theory of Statistical Inference for Nonlinear Science

WILLIAM A. BROCK
University of Wisconsin-Madison

and

EHUNG G. BAEK
Iowa State University

First version received August 1988; final version accepted December 1990 (Eds.)

This article shows how standard errors can be estimated for a measure of the number of excited degrees of freedom (the correlation dimension), and a measure of the rate of information creation (a proxy for the Kolmogorov entropy), and a measure of instability. These measures are motivated by nonlinear science and chaos theory. The main analytical method is central limit theory of U-statistics for mixing processes. The paper takes a step toward formal hypothesis testing in nonlinear science and chaos theory.

1. INTRODUCTION

Empirical nonlinear science has enjoyed a boom in economics. Examples are Brock (1986), Barnett and Chen (1988), Brock and Sayers (1988), Frank and Stengos (1988a, b; 1989), Gennotte and Marsh (1987), Hsieh (1989), Sayers (1986), Scheinkman and LeBaron (1989a, b), Ramsey and Yuan (1989, 1990).

Much of the excitement has to do with the possibility of quantifying such vague notions as "level of complexity", "degree of instability", and "number of active nonlinear degrees of freedom". At a general level nonlinear science has a rich storehouse of ideas to inspire the field of nonlinear time-series analysis, and vice versa.

Most of the work to date has relied on diagnostics such as correlation dimension, Kolmogorov entropy, and Lyapunov exponents. Expository papers in this area are Brock (1986), Frank and Stengos (1988b) for economics, and Eckmann and Ruelle (1985), Theiler (1990b) for natural science. Eckman and Ruelle (1985) is an especially detailed and comprehensive review of nonlinear science. Brock (1986) contains some applications to economics and a discussion of some pitfalls to avoid. Frank and Stengos (1988b) surveys some of the useful literature and techniques and studies empirical chaos in economics by using daily rates of return on gold.

Unfortunately no formal theory of statistical inference exists for the dimension measures and the instability measures of nonlinear science. Brock, Dechert, and Scheinkman, hereafter, BDS (1987) developed some statistical theory (discussed below) for the correlation integral of Grassberger/Procaccia/Takens (a measure of spatial non-linear correlation) and used this theory to formulate a test of the null hypothesis of independently and identically distributed (i.i.d.) for a univariate series against an unspecified alternative. This work was extended to the vector case by Baek and Brock (1988). Brock and Dechert (1988a) provided some ergodic theorems for the correlation integral and some convergence theorems for a Lyapunov exponent estimation algorithm.

The new contribution of this paper is to provide some statistical inference theory for dimension measures and Kolmogorov entropy. Central limit theorems for weakly-dependent stochastic processes and for U-statistics provide the tools needed for this paper. They are presented in Section 2. Asymptotic standard errors of dimension and Kolmogorov entropy estimates are derived as applications of the theory. Nuisance parameter problems occurring in these measures are discussed. In Section 3 we calculate the correlation dimension estimates, the Kolmogorov entropy estimates, and their standard errors by using returns on weekly stock market index studied by Scheinkman and LeBaron (1989a). Final remarks and conclusions are in Section 4.

2. THEORY OF STATISTICAL INFERENCE

Let $\{a_t\}$, $t = 1, 2, \ldots, T$ be a sample from a strictly stationary and ergodic stochastic process which we abuse notation by also denoting by $\{a_t\}$, or a deterministic chaos with unique, ergodic invariant measure as in Brock (1986). This assumption allows us to replace all limiting time-averages by corresponding phase-averages. Also the limiting value of all time-averages will be independent of initial conditions. The data, $\{a_t\}$ can be "embedded" in m-space by constructing "m-futures"

$$a_t^m = (a_t, \ldots, a_{t+m-1}), \qquad t = 1, 2, \ldots, T - m + 1.$$

The correlation integral for embedding dimension m is defined by

$$C(\varepsilon, m, T) = \sum_{1 \leq t \neq s \leq T_m}^{T_m} I(a_t^m, a_s^m; \varepsilon) / [T_m(T_m - 1)] \tag{2.1}$$

where $T_m = T - m + 1$, $I(x, y; \varepsilon) = 1$ if $\|x - y\| \leq \varepsilon$ and 0 otherwise, $\|x\|$ denotes the maximum norm, i.e. $\|x\| = \max_{0 \leq i \leq m-1} |x_i|$ on R^m. The correlation integral measures the fraction of total number of pairs (a_t^m, a_s^m) such that the distance between a_t^m and a_s^m is no more than ε. In other words, it is a measure of spatial correlation. Note that $C(\varepsilon, m, T)$ is a double average of an indicator function. Hence one expects it to converge as $T \to \infty$. Denker and Keller (1986, Theorem 1 and (3.9)) and Brock and Dechert (1988a) show that

$$C(\varepsilon, m, T) \xrightarrow{d} C(\varepsilon, m). \tag{2.2}$$

It is worthwhile to give some intuition into the measure $C(\varepsilon, m)$. Let $x \equiv (x_0, x_1, \ldots, x_{m-1})$, $y \equiv (y_0, y_1, \ldots, y_{m-1})$, and

$$F_m(x_0, x_1, \ldots, x_{m-1}) \equiv \text{Prob} \{a_t \leq x_0, a_{t+1} \leq x_1, \ldots, a_{t+m-1} \leq x_{m-1}\} \equiv \text{Prob} \{a_t^m \leq x\}.$$

Then $C(\varepsilon, m)$ is given by

$$C(\varepsilon, m) = \int_{R^m} \int_{R^m} I(x, y; \varepsilon) dF_m(x) dF_m(y). \tag{2.3}$$

For example, look at $C(\varepsilon, 1)$

$$C(\varepsilon, 1) = \int_R \int_R I(x_0, y_0; \varepsilon) dF_1(x_0) dF_1(y_0)$$

$$= \int_R [F_1(x_0 + \varepsilon) - F_1(x_0 - \varepsilon)] dF_1(x_0). \tag{2.4}$$

In case $\{a_t\}$ is i.i.d., $F_m(x) = \prod_{i=0}^{m-1} F_1(x_i)$, hence, by (2.3) we have

$$C(\varepsilon, m) = [C(\varepsilon, 1)]^m. \tag{2.5}$$

BROCK & BAEK   STATISTICAL INFERENCE   699

In general $C(\varepsilon, m)$ measures the concentration of the joint distribution of m consecutive observations, a_i^m. It describes the mean volume of a ball of radius ε. The elasticity of $C(\varepsilon, m)$ describes the mean percentage of new neighbours of the centre of a ball of radius ε that are captured as the radius of the ball increases by one percent. The measure $C(\cdot)$ is an example of a gauge function (Mayer–Kress (1987)). Its elasticity is a measure of dimension which is discussed below.

The information dimension (Eckmann and Ruelle (1985)) is estimated by measuring, for each embedding dimension m, the slope of $\log(C(\varepsilon, m, T))$ plotted against $\log(\varepsilon)$ in a zone where the slope appears constant (Ramsey and Yuan (1989, 1990), Scheinkman and LeBaron (1989a)).[1] One then looks to see if these estimated dimensions become independent of m as m increases. An alternative measure of dimension is the point elasticity $d[\log(C(\varepsilon, m, T))]/d[\log(\varepsilon)] \equiv C'(\varepsilon, m, T)\varepsilon/C(\varepsilon, m, T)$ where $C'(\varepsilon, m, T)$ is the derivative of $C(\varepsilon, m, T)$ with respect to ε. We will focus on the point elasticity here because it (cf. (2.18) below) can be written as a function of U-statistics. If $\{a_i\}$ is i.i.d. the correlation integral takes a simple form. A useful nonparametric test of the null hypothesis of i.i.d., which uses the correlation integral and which illustrates the methods to be used in this paper is in Brock, Dechert, and Scheinkman (1987).

BDS (1987) proved

Theorem 2.1.   *Let $\{a_i\}$ be IID and assume $V > 0$ in (2.7) below, then*

$$T^{1/2}[C(\varepsilon, m, T) - [C(\varepsilon, 1, T)]^m] \xrightarrow{d} N(0, V) \quad as \ T \to \infty. \tag{2.6}$$

Here "$\xrightarrow{d} N(0, V)$" means "convergence in distribution to $N(0, V)$" and $N(0, V)$ denotes the normal distribution with mean 0 and variance V where

$$V = 4[K^m + 2\sum_{i=1}^{m-1} K^{m-i} C^{2i} + (m-1)^2 C^{2m} - m^2 K C^{2m-2}], \tag{2.7}$$

$$C = EI(a_i, a_j; \varepsilon) \quad and \quad I(a_i, a_j; \varepsilon) = \begin{cases} 1 & \text{if } |a_i - a_j| \leq \varepsilon \\ 0 & \text{otherwise} \end{cases} \tag{2.8}$$

where $|x|$ is the absolute value of the real number x,

$$K = EI(a_i, a_j; \varepsilon) I(a_j, a_k; \varepsilon). \tag{2.9}$$

This theorem was used by BDS to build a nonparametric test for i.i.d. that had good size and power characteristics (especially against deterministic chaos) in comparison to some other popular tests for independence (cf. Hsieh and LeBaron (1988a, b)). The proof of Theorem 2.1 uses the theory of U-statistics. U-statistics are a type of generalized time-average. $C(\varepsilon, m, T)$ is an example. They behave enough like simple time-averages that a central limit theory exists for U-statistics that parallels the central limit theory for simple time-averages like the sample mean.

U-statistics

We will follow Sen (1972), Serfling (1980), and Denker and Keller (1983). A measurable function $h: \Omega^n \to R$ is called a kernel for $\theta = Eh$ if it is symmetric in its n arguments. Typically $\Omega = R^k$ for some positive integer k. A U-statistic for estimating θ is given by

$$U_T = \sum \{h(a_{i_1}, \ldots, a_{i_n})\}/T_n^*, \tag{2.10}$$

---

1. "Log" denotes the natural logarithm in this paper.

where $\sum$ is taken over $1 \leq t_1 < \cdots < t_n \leq T$, T_n^* is the number of n-subsets of $\{1, \ldots, T\}$, and $\{a_t\}$ is a strictly stationary stochastic process with values in Ω. U–statistics are interesting because (i) they have many of the desirable properties of the simple time-average $u_T \equiv \sum_{t=1}^{T} a_t / T$, including central limit theorems and laws of large numbers, (ii) in a certain context they are minimum variance estimators of θ in the class of all unbiased estimators of θ (Serfling (1980, p. 176)), (iii) they converge rapidly to normality (Serfling (1980, p. 193, Theorem B)), and (iv) many useful statistics can be written in U-statistic form (Serfling (1980, Chapter 5)). We will only use the case $n = 2$. So from now on n is fixed at 2. Before going on we stress that $\{a_t\}$ can be an R^k-valued stochastic process in the general theory below.

The projection method of Hoeffding is applied by Denker and Keller (1983) to obtain the decomposition

$$U_T = \theta + (2/T) \sum \{h_1(a_t) - \theta\} + R(T) \quad \text{if } n = 2 \tag{2.11}$$

where

$$h_1(a) = E\{h(a_1, a_2) | a_1 = a\} \quad \text{and} \quad \theta = Eh_1(a).$$

$\sum$ runs from 1 to T, and $R(T)$ is a remainder that goes to 0 in distribution when multiplied by $\sqrt{T}$ as $T \to \infty$. Let us denote by

$$\sigma_T^2 = E\{\sum_{t=1}^{T} g_1(a_t)\}^2 \quad \text{where } g_1(a) = h_1(a) - \theta, \tag{2.12}$$

the exact variance of the leading term in the above decomposition. Let us denote by

$$\sigma^2 = E\{g_1(a_1)^2 + 2 \sum_{1 < i} g_1(a_1) g_1(a_i)\} \tag{2.13}$$

its asymptotic variance, provided the sum coverges absolutely. In this case

$$\sigma^2 = \lim_{T \to \infty} \sigma_T^2 / T. \tag{2.14}$$

We state part of one of Denker and Keller's theorems below.

Theorem 2.2. (Denker and Keller (1983, p. 507)). *Let $\sigma^2 > 0$, then,*

$$T/(2\sigma_T)[U_T - \theta] \xrightarrow{d} N(0, 1) \quad \text{as } T \to \infty, \tag{2.15}$$

provided that the following condition is satisfied: the strictly stationary stochastic process $\{a_t\}$ is absolutely regular with coefficients β_t satisfying

$$\sum \beta_t^{\delta/(2+\delta)} < \infty \text{ for some } \delta > 0, \sigma^2 > 0, \quad \text{and} \quad \sup [E\{|h(a_{t_1}, \ldots, a_{t_n})|^{2+\delta}\}] < \infty. \tag{2.16}$$

Here the "sup" is taken over $1 \leq t_1 < \cdots < t_n < T$. "Absolutely regular" asks that

$$\beta_t = \sup E[\sup \{|P(A | G(1, s)) - P(A)| \, | \, A \in G(s + t, \infty)\}] \tag{2.17}$$

tends to zero as $t \to \infty$. Here the outside "sup" is taken over s in $\{1, 2, \ldots\}$ and the inside "sup" is taken over A in $G(s + k, \infty)$. The symbol "$G(s, v)$" denotes the sigma algebra generated by $\{a_t | s \leq t < v\}$ $(1 \leq s, v \leq \infty)$. Other mixing conditions besides (2.17) including two by Denker and Keller yield similar results. The point is that we need some type of condition on the rate of decay of dependence over time, i.e. a mixing condition, in order to get the central limit theorem for dependent processes. Condition (2.17) seems as useful as any.

In the applications to follow we use Theorem 2.2 and the delta method (Serfling (1980, p. 124)) to obtain central limit theorems for differentiable functions $H(z_1(T), \ldots, z_k(T))$ of the k-vector of U-statistics $z(T) = (z_1(T), \ldots, z_k(T))$ where each $z_i(T)$ has symmetric kernel function $h_i(a_t, a_s) = h_i(a_s, a_t)$. Here is the basic method. Let $\bar{z} = Ez(t)$. Provided $H(x)$ has non-zero derivative at $\bar{z}$ and the component U-statistics have nondegenerate asymptotic distributions then we know from the delta method (Serfling (1980, p. 124)) that $T^{1/2}(H(z(T)) - H(\bar{z}))$ has the same limit law as $T^{1/2}(DH(\bar{z}) \cdot (z(T) - \bar{z}))$ where $DH(\bar{z})$ is the derivative of H evaluated at $\bar{z}$ and "$\cdot$" denotes scalar product. Put $g(a_1, a_2) = DH(\bar{z}) \cdot (h(a_1, a_2) - \bar{z})$, $g_1(a) = E\{g(a_t, a_s)|a_t = a\}$. Then the formula (2.13) can be used to calculate the asymptotic variance of the limit distribution and Theorem 2.2 applies. With this background turn now to applications.

Applications

In the applications below we will assume $\{a_t\}$ is i.i.d. to simplify calculations of asymptotic variances from (2.13). But the methods apply to any general process to which Theorem 2.2 applies.

1. *Standard errors of dimension estimates*

The statistical properties of dimension calculations are investigated by Ramsey and Yuan (1989, 1990) and Theiler (1990a). As Ramsey and Yuan point out, the point estimate of correlation dimension is typically derived from ordinary least squares (OLS) regression over an apparent constant slope zone on a log–log plot (Ramsey and Yuan (1990, pp. 157, 160–161), Scheinkman and LeBaron (1989a)). Problems of subjectivity in the choice of the apparent constant slope zone, together with the mathematical form of the OLS estimator, lead us to focus upon the elasticity measure of dimension. We also wanted to see how well our methodology would perform on the most volatile measure of dimension. Derivatives are well known to be noisy and difficult to estimate. Another reason for concentration on this form is that we can write various estimators of the elasticity as a function of U-statistics. We calculate the slope of $[\log(c)/\log(\varepsilon)]$ of two nearby points for a point estimate of correlation dimension. Sample properties of our estimate are discussed in section 3. Using this dimension concept enables us to apply the theory of U-statistics. While Denker and Keller (1986) use U-statistics theory to derive asymptotic standard errors for a Grassberger-Procaccia type of correlation dimension estimate, our work was done independently.[2]

Let $\{a_t\}$ be an i.i.d. stochastic process with finite moments as in (2.16).[3] Then $\{a_t^m\}$ satisfies the mixing condition of Theorem 2.2. The dimension estimate, which is intended to approximate the elasticity, $d[\log(C)]/d[\log(\varepsilon)]$, that we will examine is defined as

2. After our work was completed Dee Dechert told us about Denker and Keller (1986). They choose 5 values $\varepsilon_i = 0.08 \times 2^{-i}$, $i = 0, 1, 2, 3, 4$ and write the OLS estimators of α, β in the OLS regression, $\log C(\varepsilon_i, m) = \alpha + \beta \log(\varepsilon_i) + \eta_i$, in U-statistic form. In this way they obtain an estimate of β from the vector of estimates $\{C(\varepsilon_i, m)\}$ and a standard error for β. They show the results are very good for a certain dynamical system on the plane.

3. The assumption of i.i.d. is not needed for any of the applications. It is used to simplify the variance formulae for the statistics to be treated below. If one imposes the mixing assumptions of Denker and Keller (1983, 1986) one can develop a variance formula like (2.13) which is an infinite sum of relevant covariances. One can then use a consistent estimator of this infinite sum to develop the general theory along the lines of the special case of i.i.d. developed here. For example the general theory can be used to estimate confidence intervals for estimates of objects like Kolmogorov entropy and dimension.

follows:

$$d_m(\varepsilon, \Delta\varepsilon, T) = \frac{\log C(\varepsilon + \Delta\varepsilon, m, T) - \log C(\varepsilon, m, T)}{\log(\varepsilon + \Delta\varepsilon) - \log(\varepsilon)} \qquad (2.18)$$

Since $C(\varepsilon, m, T) \xrightarrow{d} C(\varepsilon, m)$ therefore,

$$d_m(\varepsilon, \Delta\varepsilon, T) \xrightarrow{d} d_m(\varepsilon, \Delta\varepsilon) \quad \text{as } T \to \infty.^4 \qquad (2.19)$$

Note that $d_m(\varepsilon, \Delta\varepsilon, T)$ is a function of two quantities, $C(\varepsilon + \Delta\varepsilon, m, T)$ and $C(\varepsilon, m, T)$, i.e. $d_m(\varepsilon, \Delta\varepsilon, T) \equiv D(C(\varepsilon + \Delta\varepsilon, m, T), C(\varepsilon, m, T))$. By (2.11), we have

$$C(\varepsilon + \Delta\varepsilon, m, T) - \theta(\varepsilon + \Delta\varepsilon, m) = \frac{2}{T} \sum (h_1(a_i^m, \varepsilon + \Delta\varepsilon) - \theta(\varepsilon + \Delta\varepsilon, m)) + R_1, \qquad (2.20)$$

$$C(\varepsilon, m, T) - \theta(\varepsilon, m) = \frac{2}{T} \sum (h_1(a_i^m, \varepsilon) - \theta(\varepsilon, m)) + R_2 \qquad (2.21)$$

where $\theta(\varepsilon, m) = C(\varepsilon, m) = EC(\varepsilon, m, T)$. Hence, we may apply the delta method (Serfling (1980, p. 124)) to prove the following theorem. The proof is in the Appendix.

Theorem 2.3. *Assume* $\{a_i\}$ *is i.i.d. and satisfies the moment condition in* (2.16). *Suppose the differential of* $D(\cdot, \cdot)$ *is nonzero at* $(C(\varepsilon + \Delta\varepsilon, m), C(\varepsilon, m))$, *and the covariance matrix of* $(C(\varepsilon + \Delta\varepsilon, m, T), C(\varepsilon, m, T))$ *is nonsingular, and* VD_m *defined below is positive. Then*

$$T^{1/2}[D\{C(\varepsilon + \Delta\varepsilon, m, T), C(\varepsilon, m, T)\} - D\{\theta(\varepsilon + \Delta\varepsilon, m), \theta(\varepsilon, m)\}] \xrightarrow{d} N(0, VD_m) \qquad (2.22)$$

where

$$VD_m = 4\gamma^2[A^m + B^m - 2C^m + 2\sum_{j=1}^{m-1}\{A^{m-j} + B^{m-j} - 2C^{m-j}\}], \qquad (2.23)$$

$$\gamma = [\log(\varepsilon + \Delta\varepsilon) - \log(\varepsilon)]^{-1},$$

$$A = K(\varepsilon + \Delta\varepsilon)/C(\varepsilon + \Delta\varepsilon)^2,$$

$$B = K(\varepsilon)/C(\varepsilon)^2,$$

$$C = W(\varepsilon + \Delta\varepsilon, \varepsilon)/(C(\varepsilon + \Delta\varepsilon)C(\varepsilon)),$$

$C(\cdot), K(\cdot)$ *are defined in* (2.8), (2.9) *and* $W(\varepsilon + \Delta\varepsilon, \varepsilon) = EI(a_i, a_j; \varepsilon + \Delta\varepsilon)I(a_i, a_j; \varepsilon)$.

Theorem 2.3 is a basis for setting up hypothesis testing concerning dimension. For example Scheinkman and LeBaron (1989a) produced a point estimate of about 6 for the correlation dimension of stock returns. This number has been widely cited. With our methods one can now estimate a standard error for such point estimates of dimension. This was not possible before. We investigate this problem in Section 3.

2. *Standard errors of Kolmogorov entropy*

The standard error of the approximate Kolmogorov entropy $K_m(\varepsilon) \equiv \log[C(\varepsilon, m)/C(\varepsilon, m+1)]$ can be derived following the procedure of Theorem 2.3 since the sample estimator of $K_m(\varepsilon)$, $K_m(\varepsilon, T)$, is a differentiable function of two U-statistics, $C(\varepsilon, m, T)$, $C(\varepsilon, m+1, T)$.

---

4. A continuous function of random variables which converge in distribution also converges in distribution. (Serfling, (1980, p. 24, Theorem)).

The Kolmogorov entropy of a deterministic dynamical system, $y_{t+1} = f(y_t)$, $y_t \in R^k$, $f: R^k \to R^k$, is a measure of how fast a pair of states become distinguishable to a measuring apparatus with fixed precision under forward interation (Eckmann and Ruelle (1985, p. 637)). For example if $\{a_t\}$ is i.i.d., the limit of the approximate Kolmogorov entropy, $K_m(\varepsilon)$, is infinity as ε goes to zero. For finite ε, $\{a_t\}$ i.i.d. implies $K_m(\varepsilon) = -\log(C(\varepsilon, 1)) \to \infty$, $\varepsilon \to 0$. The proof of the following theorem is found in the Appendix.

Theorem 2.4. Make the same assumptions as in Theorem 2.3. If $\{a_t\}$ is an i.i.d. process,

$$T^{1/2} K_m(\varepsilon, T) \xrightarrow{d} N(-\log C(\varepsilon), VK_m), \tag{2.24}$$

$$T^{1/2}[K_m(\varepsilon, T) + \log(C(\varepsilon, 1, T))] \xrightarrow{d} N(0, VK'_m) \tag{2.25}$$

where $K_m(\varepsilon, T)$ is the sample estimate of the Kolmogorov entropy,

$$VK_m = 4[\{K(\varepsilon)/C(\varepsilon)^2\}^{m+1} - \{K(\varepsilon)/C(\varepsilon)^2\}^m] \tag{2.26}$$

and

$$VK'_m = 4[\{K(\varepsilon)/C(\varepsilon)^2\}^{m+1} - \{K(\varepsilon)/C(\varepsilon)^2\}^m + \{K(\varepsilon)/C(\varepsilon)^2 - 1\}].^5 \tag{2.27}$$

For some applications, the invariance property, i.e. the first-order asymptotics of the correlation dimension and the Kolmogorov entropy evaluated at estimated residuals are the same for true residuals, can be shown. We sketch this idea here.

First, in many applications we replace the series of observations $\{a_t\}$ by the standardized series in an attempt to scale the series so that its mean is zero and its variance is unity. But this introduces two nuisance parameters that are estimated by the sample mean and the sample standard deviation. These nuisance parameters may change the asymptotic distributions above.

A second fundamental concern is that often we are really interested in testing the estimated residuals of some parametric model such as an Autoregressive Moving Average (ARMA) model or an Autoregressive Conditional Heteroscedastic (ARCH) model for temporal dependence or instability. But then the distribution of the estimated residuals is contaminated by the estimation procedure. Some limited results are discussed below. Consider null models of the form

$$y_t = G(y_{t-1}, y_{t-2}, \ldots, y_{t-q}; b) + e_t \tag{2.28}$$

where G is $\mathscr{C}^2$ (twice-continuously differentiable), the parameter vector b is estimated $\sqrt{T}$-consistently and $\{e_t\}$ is i.i.d. with mean zero and unit variance. Then under modest regularity conditions the argument in Brock and Dechert (1988b) can be extended to show that, under (2.28), if $Eh'_1(u) = 0$, the limit law of $\sqrt{T}(C(\varepsilon, m, T) - C(\varepsilon, m))$ is the same whether $C(\varepsilon, m, T)$ is evaluated at the true $\{e_t\}$ or the estimated $\{e_t\}$. The full details are in Brock and Dechert (1988b) for the case $m = 1$ and G is a linear autoregression. We call this property "the invariance property". A similar argument can be developed to show the invariance property, under (2.28) for the limit law of

$$\sqrt{T}[F\{C(\varepsilon, 1, T), \ldots, C(\varepsilon, k, T)\} - F(C(\varepsilon, 1), \ldots, C(\varepsilon, k))] \tag{2.29}$$

---

5. We thank Pedro DeLima for help with this formula. A similar independence test based upon the Kolmogorov entropy was independently developed by Hiemstra (1990). We highly recommend this excellent study to the reader. It contains not only a study of independence tests but also applications to testing the efficient markets hypothesis.

where F is $\mathscr{C}^2$. This includes the correlation dimension estimate and the Kolmogorov entropy estimate discussed in this paper.

Remark. For the indicator kernel $h_1(u) = E[I(u, v; \varepsilon)|u] = F_e(u + \varepsilon) - F_e(u - \varepsilon)$. So $Eh'_1(u) = 0$ in this case. Here $F_e(u) \equiv \text{Prob}(e_t \leq u)$.

These results are of limited usefulness in applications. First, they do not cover all F in (2.29) when the variance of e_t must be estimated. An invariance result for the BDS (1987) statistic is in Brock (1989). Second, they apply only to the estimated residuals of null models where the true residuals are assumed i.i.d. We would like to get away with assuming weaker maintained assumptions on these residuals. Unfortunately we have not obtained any useful results under more general assumptions.

3. EMPIRICAL APPLICATION

In this section we apply the theory. Scheinkman and LeBaron (1989a) estimated the correlation dimension for 1226 weekly observations on the CRSP value-weighted U.S. stock returns index starting in the early 1960's. They arrived at roughly a dimension of 6. They then calculated another estimate of dimension due to Takens which was also close to 6. Here we provide asymptotic estimates of standard errors for the elasticity estimate of dimension for Scheinkman and LeBaron's data set.

The embedding dimension is increased from 1 to 14, and the resolution parameters $\varepsilon + \Delta\varepsilon, \varepsilon$ are adjusted from $0 \cdot 9, 0 \cdot 9^2$ to $0 \cdot 9^4, 0 \cdot 9^5$. For each embedding space and parameter value, a point estimate of the correlation dimension is reported in Table 1. Dimension estimates are between 7 and 9 in high embedding dimensions, and their standard errors are low enough to make the test statistic values significant at the 5% level under the assumption of asymptotic normality. Note that the null hypothesis of i.i.d. is rejected in favour of a lower dimensional alternative. This is consistent with the results of Scheinkman and LeBaron.

Table 2 reports the dimension estimates and their associated standard errors computed for 1226 i.i.d. observations to compare with the 1226 actual weekly stock returns. An IMSL standard normal subroutine DRNNOA was used to generate the pseudo-random numbers. Since the correlation integral loses too many comparable pairs in high embedding dimensions, we report the results for embeddings only up to 8 dimensions. We can see the correlation dimension estimate and the embedding dimension go almost together as they should. When the resolution parameter ε is too small, we lose comparable pairs very fast. Since there is downward bias in the dimension estimates the test statistics become statistically significant with i.i.d. observations in Table 2. We show how to correct this bias problem in Examples 1 and 2 later.

To estimate the speed of information creation, K_m, we also estimate the approximate Kolmogorov entropy. Tables 3 and 4 are entropy estimates and their standard errors computed from actual stock returns and standard-normal random numbers. Theoretically if the stock returns process is i.i.d. then the entropy estimate should be close to the value, $-\log(C(\varepsilon, 1, T))$. The Kolmogorov entropy estimate becomes smaller than $-\log(C(\varepsilon, 1, T))$ when actual values are used in Table 3, but this is not true when random numbers are used in Table 4. Actual data generate statistically significant test statistics, in other words, the test rejects the null hypothesis that stock returns are generated by an i.i.d. stochastic process.

6. For the case of standardized t and standard normal distributions, DIM calculations are approximately equal to m for each embedding dimension m.

BROCK & BAEK   STATISTICAL INFERENCE   705

TABLE 1

Correlation dimension estimate of weekly stock returns

	$\varepsilon+\Delta\varepsilon=0.9$	$\varepsilon=0.9^2$		$\varepsilon+\Delta\varepsilon=0.9^2$	$\varepsilon=0.9^3$	
m	DIM	ASE/$\sqrt{T}$	TEST	DIM	ASE/$\sqrt{T}$	TEST
1	0·82	0·012	−15·0	0·86	0·011	−12·7
6	4·28	0·098	−17·6	4·42	0·098	−16·1
8	5·24	0·151	−18·3	5·36	0·152	−17·4
10	5·89	0·220	−18·7	5·96	0·221	−18·3
12	6·55	0·370	−17·8	6·53	0·310	−17·6
14	7·19	0·417	−16·3	7·09	0·422	−16·4

	$\varepsilon+\Delta\varepsilon=0.9^3$	$\varepsilon=0.9^4$		$\varepsilon+\Delta\varepsilon=0.9^4$	$\varepsilon=0.9^5$	
m	DIM	ASE/$\sqrt{T}$	TEST	DIM	ASE/$\sqrt{T}$	TEST
1	0·88	0·010	−12.0	0·89	0·010	−11·0
6	4·52	0·085	−17·4	5·01	0·088	−11·3
8	5·53	0·133	−18·6	6·34	0·136	−12·2
10	6·46	0·195	−18·2	7·50	0·199	−12·6
12	7·52	0·276	−16·2	7·31	0·279	−16·8
14	8·47	2·379	−14·6	7·73	0·381	−16·5

Notes.[1] 1226 standardized weekly stock returns are used, i.e. $z_i=(r_i-\hat{r})/\hat{\sigma}$ for $i=1,2,\ldots,1226$ where

$$r=\sum r_i/T,\ \hat{\sigma}=\sum(r_i-\hat{r})^2/(T-1)\text{ and }T=1226.$$

m is the embedding dimension, DIM is the dimension estimate, and ASE is the empirical asymptotic standard error from the data

$$\text{ASE}=[4\gamma^2\{A^m+B^m-2C^m+2\sum_{j=1}^{m-1}(A^{m-j}+B^{m-j}-2C^{m-j})\}]^{1/2},$$

where

$$\gamma=[\log(\varepsilon+\Delta\varepsilon)-\log(\varepsilon)]^{-1},\quad A=K(\varepsilon+\Delta\varepsilon)/C(\varepsilon+\Delta\varepsilon)^2,\quad B=K(\varepsilon)/C(\varepsilon)^2,$$

$$C=W(\varepsilon+\Delta\varepsilon,\varepsilon)/(C(\varepsilon+\Delta\varepsilon)C(\varepsilon)),\quad W(\varepsilon+\Delta\varepsilon,\varepsilon)=EI(a_i,a_j;\varepsilon+\Delta\varepsilon)I(a_i,a_j;\varepsilon).$$

TEST is the test statistic, i.e. TEST $=\sqrt{T}(\text{DIM-}m)/\text{ASE}$.[6] We thank Craig Hiemstra for discovering the computation error of W.

Note from Table 4 that the K_m estimates are all positive even though the process is i.i.d. Eckman and Ruelle (1985, Sections 4 and 5) point out that K_m is a lower bound to the true Kolmogorov entropy and positive Kolmogorov entropy is associated with chaos. Our results caution the investigator that stochastic processes such as i.i.d. processes are also consistent with positive Kolmogorov entropy. This indeterminacy brings up a natural question: What do we learn when we reject the null hypothesis of i.i.d. with the K_m-based test statistic as in Table 3? Let us explain.

Note that $\log(C(\varepsilon,m)/C(\varepsilon,m+1))=\log(C(\varepsilon,1))^{-1}$ if and only if $C(\varepsilon,m+1)/C(\varepsilon,m)=C(\varepsilon,1)$, i.e. Prob $(X_{t+1}|X_t,X_{t-1},\ldots,X_{t-(m-1)})=$ Prob (X_{t+1}) when "X_t" is shorthand for the event $|X_t-X_s|\leq\varepsilon$. Hence failure to reject the null of i.i.d. under a K_m-based test is consistent with the m-past $(X_t,X_{t-1},\ldots,X_{t-(m-1)})$ having no predictive power for the future, X_{t+1}. We say more about this in Baek and Brock (1990) where we show that this kind of testing methodology based upon K_m leads naturally to tests of whether one series $\{Y_t\}$ helps predict another series $\{X_t\}$.

Monte Carlo experiments were done to examine the quality of normal approximation of the test statistics and small-sample bias pointed out by Ramsey and Yuan (1989). 2500 samples were replicated to generate a sampling distribution. The same experiments were

TABLE 2

Correlation dimension estimates of standard normal random numbers

	$\varepsilon + \Delta\varepsilon = 0.9$	$\varepsilon = 0.9^2$		$\varepsilon + \Delta\varepsilon = 0.9^2$	$\varepsilon = 0.9^3$	
m	DIM	ASE/$\sqrt{T}$	TEST	DIM	ASE/$\sqrt{T}$	TEST
1	0.89	0.009	-12.2	0.91	0.010	-9.0
2	1.78	0.020	-11.0	1.82	0.022	-8.2
6	5.29	0.070	-10.1	5.66	0.076	-4.5
8	7.00	0.101	-9.9	8.30	0.111	2.7

	$\varepsilon + \Delta\varepsilon = 0.9^3$	$\varepsilon = 0.9^4$		$\varepsilon + \Delta\varepsilon = 0.9^4$	$\varepsilon = 0.9^5$	
m	DIM	ASE/$\sqrt{T}$	TEST	DIM	ASE/$\sqrt{T}$	TEST
1	0.94	0.011	-5.5	0.93	0.011	-6.4
2	1.86	0.024	-5.8	1.88	0.024	-5.0
6	5.59	0.083	-4.9	4.97	0.083	-12.4
8	8.29	0.120	2.4	5.13	0.121	-23.7

Notes. IMSL subroutine DRNNOA was called to generate 1226 standard normal random numbers, and RNSET was called to set an initial seed. m is the embedding dimension, DIM is the dimension estimate, and ASE is the empirical asymptotic standard error from the data

$$\text{ASE} = [4\gamma^2\{A^m + B^m - 2C^m + 2\sum_{j=1}^{m-1}(A^{m-j} + B^{m-j} - 2C^{m-j})\}]^{1/2},$$

where

$$\gamma = [\log(\varepsilon + \Delta\varepsilon) - \log(\varepsilon)]^{-1}, \quad A = K(\varepsilon + \Delta\varepsilon)/C(\varepsilon + \Delta\varepsilon)^2, \quad B = K(\varepsilon)/C(\varepsilon)^2,$$

$$C = W(\varepsilon + \Delta\varepsilon, \varepsilon)/(C(\varepsilon + \Delta\varepsilon)C(\varepsilon)), \quad W(\varepsilon + \Delta\varepsilon, \varepsilon) = EI(a_i, a_j; \varepsilon + \Delta\varepsilon)I(a_i, a_j; \varepsilon).$$

TEST is the test statistic, i.e. TEST = $\sqrt{T}(\text{DIM}-m)/\text{ASE}$. Less than 0.01% of the total number of pairs are available to calculate the dimension estimates beyond $m = 8$.

performed with different values of the sample size and the parameter ε. But we only report the results where the sample size is 1000, and $\varepsilon + \Delta\varepsilon$, ε are 0.9, 0.9^2 for the correlation dimension and $\varepsilon = 0.9$ for the Kolmogorov entropy in Tables 5 and 6.

In Table 5, the second column shows that the correlation dimension estimate is biased downward which makes the test statistic take negative values. The average empirical asymptotic standard errors (ASE) which are computed by the 2500 empirical ASE's based on (2.23) are in the third column. The fourth column contains the true ASE's of the test statistic, $[d_m(\varepsilon. \Delta\varepsilon, T) - m]$, computed by using numerically calculated $C(\varepsilon + \Delta\varepsilon)$, $C(\varepsilon)$, $K(\varepsilon + \Delta\varepsilon)$ $K(\varepsilon)$ and $W(\varepsilon + \Delta\varepsilon, \varepsilon)$.[7] Even though C, K, and W are consistently estimated, there is a big deviation between the mean ASE and true ASE (See the proof of Theorem 2.3 in Appendix for notations.).[8] The main reason for this is that the γ parameter exaggerates the ASE in our dimension calculation method. For instance $\gamma^2 \approx 90$ when $\varepsilon + \Delta\varepsilon = 0.9$ and $\varepsilon = 0.9^2$. If there is a 1% discrepancy between the true value and the estimated value except for the factor, $4\gamma^2$, in the variance formula then we expect there will be a 360% difference in the variance. As long as the normal approximation is good, there should not be a big problem to use the empirical ASE for hypothesis testing. If the sampling distribution is well approximated by a normal distribution, $\sqrt{T} \cdot SD$ is close to the mean of the empirical ASE. By comparing the third column and the last column, we may see how good the normal approximation is. In the high embedding dimensions

7. The true ASE of the test statistic uses numerically integrated values of K, C, and W for the calculation of ASE. For details see (2) of Appendix B.
8. Table B1 in Appendix B shows that the sample estimates of K, C, and W converge to their true values consistently.

TABLE 3

Kolmogorov entropy estimates of weekly stock returns

m	$\varepsilon = 0.9$			$\varepsilon = 0.9^2$		
	ENTROPY	ASE/$\sqrt{T}$	TEST	ENTROPY	ASE/$\sqrt{T}$	TEST
1	0·592	0·031	−1·74	0·675	0·033	−1·77
6	0·405	0·038	−6·34	0·458	0·041	−6·75
8	0·360	0·042	−6·84	0·397	0·045	−7·45
10	0·306	0·046	−7·37	0·338	0·050	−7·84
12	0·269	0·051	−7·35	0·310	0·057	−7·46
13	0·254	0·054	−7·23	0·279	0·060	−7·53

m	$\varepsilon = 0.9^3$			$\varepsilon = 0.9^4$		
	ENTROPY	ASE/$\sqrt{T}$	TEST	ENTROPY	ASE/$\sqrt{T}$	TEST
1	0·761	0·034	−1·84	0·849	0·035	−1·88
2	0·723	0·035	−2·83	0·806	0·037	−2·99
6	0·510	0·043	−7·27	0·560	0·045	−7·84
8	0·427	0·048	−8·19	0·479	0·051	−8·51
10	0·371	0·055	−8·30	0·412	0·058	−8·61
12	0·333	0·062	−7·91	0·390	0·067	−7·85
13	0·316	0·066	−7.67	0·359	0·072	−7·73

Notes. 1226 standardized weekly stock returns are used, i.e. $z_i = (r_i - \hat{r})/\hat{\sigma}$ for $i = 1, 2, \ldots, 1226$ where

$$\hat{r} = \sum r_i / T, \hat{\sigma} = \sum (r_i - \hat{r})^2/(T-1) \text{ and } T = 1226.$$

m is the embedding dimension, ENTROPY is the entropy estimate, and ASE is the empirical asymptotic standard error from the data

$$\text{ASE} = [4\{(K(\varepsilon)/C(\varepsilon)^2)^{m+1} - (K(\varepsilon)/C(\varepsilon)^2)^m + K(\varepsilon)^2 - 1\}]^{1/2}.$$

TEST is the test statistic, i.e. $\text{TEST} = \sqrt{T}[\text{ENTROPY} + \log(C(\varepsilon, 1, T))]/\text{ASE}$.

TABLE 4

Kolmogorov entropy estimates of standard normal random numbers

m	$\varepsilon 0.9$			$\varepsilon = 0.9^2$		
	ENTROPY	ASE/$\sqrt{T}$	TEST	ENTROPY	ASE/$\sqrt{T}$	TEST
1	0·758	0·026	−0·05	0·852	0·027	−0·01
2	0·756	0·027	−0·12	0·850	0·028	−0·10
6	0·756	0·030	−0·11	0·840	0·032	−0·40
8	0·751	0·032	−0·25	0·892	0·034	1·17

m	$\varepsilon = 0.9^3$			$\varepsilon = 0.9^4$		
	ENTROPY	ASE/$\sqrt{T}$	TEST	ENTROPY	ASE/$\sqrt{T}$	TEST
1	0·948	0·028	−0·02	1·046	0·028	−0·06
2	0·945	0·029	−0·14	1·040	0·029	−0·24
6	0·956	0·033	0·22	1·070	0·033	0·68
8	1·154	0·035	5·88	1·150	0·036	2·86

Notes. IMSL subroutine DRNNOA was called to generate 1000 standard normal random numbers, and RNSET was called to set an initial seed. m is the embedding dimension, ENTROPY is the entropy estimate, and ASE is the empirical asymptotic standard error from the data

$$\text{ASE} = [4\{(K(\varepsilon)/C(^+)^2)^{m+1} - (K(\varepsilon)/C(\varepsilon)^2)^m + K(\varepsilon)/C(\varepsilon)^2 - 1\}]^{1/2}.$$

TEST is the test statistic, i.e. $\text{TEST} = \sqrt{T}[\text{ENTROPY} + \log(C(\varepsilon, 1, T))]/\text{ASE}$. Less than 0·01% of the total number of pairs are available to calculate the Kolmotorov Entropy estimates beyone $m = 8$.

TABLE 5

Monte Carlo simulation, correlation dimension estimates and standard errors
Number of Replications = 2500; Sample Size = 1000; $\varepsilon + \Delta\varepsilon = 0.9$, $\varepsilon = 0.9^2$

Embedding dimension	Average of Dim Est	Mean ASE	True ASE	$\sqrt{T}$ SD
1	0·885 (0·008)	0·397 (0·039)	0·526	0·246
2	1·770 (0·019)	0·822 (0·080)	1·087	0·600
3	2·655 (0·036)	1·288 (0·127)	1·696	1·131
4	3·540 (0·063)	1·797 (0·179)	2·359	1·980
5	4·425 (0·102)	2·354 (0·237)	3·077	3·235
6	5·310 (0·166)	2·961 (0·302)	3·857	5·241
7	6·198 (0·271)	3·623 (0·376)	4·702	8·561
8	7·083 (0·437)	4·344 (0·458)	5·617	13·822
9	7·978 (0·701)	5·129 (0·550)	6·609	22·161
10	8·906 (1·115)	5·983 (0·654)	7·682	35·271

Notes: IMSL subroutine DRNNOA was called to generate 1000 standard normal random numbers, and RNSET was called to set an initial seed. Average of Dimension Estimates = mean of the correlation dimension estimates of the 2500 replications. The standard error of sample mean out of the 2500 replications is reported in parenthesis for given dimension. Mean ASE = mean of the 2500 empirical ASE's,

$$\text{ASE} = [4\gamma^2\{\hat{A}^m + \hat{B}^m - 2\hat{C}^m + 2\sum_{j=1}^{m-1} (\hat{A}^{m-j} + \hat{B}^{m-j} - 2\hat{C}^{m-j})\}]^{1/2},$$

where

$$\gamma = [\log(\varepsilon + \Delta\varepsilon) - \log(\varepsilon)]^{-1}, \quad \hat{A} = K(\varepsilon + \Delta\varepsilon)/C(\varepsilon + \Delta\varepsilon)^2, \quad \hat{B} = K(\varepsilon)/C(\varepsilon)^2,$$
$$\hat{C} = W(\varepsilon + \Delta\varepsilon, \varepsilon)/(C(\varepsilon + \Delta\varepsilon)C(\varepsilon)).$$

Standard normal random numbers of size of 1000 were used to calculate $K(\varepsilon + \Delta\varepsilon)$, $K(\varepsilon)$, $C(\varepsilon + \Delta\varepsilon)$, $C(\varepsilon)$ and $W(\varepsilon + \Delta\varepsilon, \varepsilon)$ at which $\hat{A}$, $\hat{B}$ and $\hat{C}$ are evaluated. The standard error of the mean ASE is reported in parenthesis.
True ASE is obtained from the same ASE formula which is given above. But $\hat{A}$, $\hat{B}$ and $\hat{C}$ were evaluated at numerically calculated values of $K(\varepsilon + \Delta\varepsilon) = 0.2511$, $K(\varepsilon) = 0.2098$, $C(\varepsilon + \Delta\varepsilon) = 0.4755$. $C(\varepsilon) = 0.4332$. and $W(\varepsilon + \Delta\varepsilon, \varepsilon) = 0.2295$ for $\varepsilon + \Delta\varepsilon = 0.9$ and $\acute{\varepsilon} = 0.9^2$. $\sqrt{T}$ SD = $\sqrt{T}$ × standard error of $[D(\cdot) - m]$ of the 2500 replications.

9 and 10, the approximation is quite good. However, when the data is embedded in low dimensions, the test statistic has smaller dispersion than the standard normal distribution. Since previous studies such as Scheinkman and LeBaron (1989*a*) indicate the meaningful embedding dimension range is high-dimensional space, we think that our previous application to stock returns is suggestive.

It is important to realize that even though the test of i.i.d. based upon the derivative measure of dimension is capable of rejecting the null hypothesis of i.i.d. for stock returns in favour of some "lower dimensional" alternative. This does not necessarily mean chaos is present. There are many stochastic processes where close *m*-histories tend to be followed by close descendants that must be ruled out before one can claim chaos. Also, consistent with Ramsey and Yuan (1989, 1990), biases appear in the dimension estimates and the asymptotic standard errors grow dramatically with the embedding dimension. Although theory implies that these biases disappear in the limit, bootstrapping and bias reduction techniques along the lines of Efron (1982) have potential to improve performance. We suspect that bootstrapping, rather than using asymptotics will improve performance of all the statistics discussed in this paper because bootstrapping apparently helps approximate some of the higher-order terms in the Edgeworth expansion (Efron (1982), Efron and Tibshirani (1986) and references) whereas our methods capture only the first-order terms.

BROCK & BAEK   STATISTICAL INFERENCE   709

TABLE 6

Monte Carlo simulation, Kolmogorov entropy estimates and standard errors
Number of Replications = 2500; Sample Size = 1000; $\varepsilon = 0.9$

Embedding dimension	Average of Entropy	Mean ASE	True ASE	$\sqrt{T}$ SD
1	0.0006 (0.0073)	0.967 (0.029)	0.966	0.230
2	0.0011 (0.0105)	0.994 (0.031)	0.994	0.334
3	0.0013 (0.0135)	1.024 (0.034)	1.024	0.426
4	0.0012 (0.0164)	1.057 (0.037)	1.056	0.518
5	0.0019 (0.0196)	1.092 (0.041)	1.091	0.618
6	0.0019 (0.0238)	1.129 (0.044)	1.128	0.751
7	0.0025 (0.0295)	1.169 (0.049)	1.168	0.933
8	0.0031 (0.0379)	1.212 (0.053)	1.211	1.197
9	0.0053 (0.0512)	1.259 (0.059)	1.257	1.618

Notes: IMSL subroutine DRNNOA was called to generate 1000 standard normal random numbers, and RNSET was called to set an initial seed. Average of Entropy = mean of the Kolmogorov Entropy estimate $[K_m(\cdot) + \log C(\varepsilon, 1, T)]$ of the 2500 replications. The standard error of sample mean out of the 2500 replications is reported in parenthesis. Mean ASE = mean of the 2500 empirical ASE's,

$$\text{ASE} = [4\{(K(\varepsilon)/C(\varepsilon)^2)^{m+1} - (K(\varepsilon)/C(\varepsilon)^2)^m + K(\varepsilon)/C(\varepsilon)^2 - 1\}]^{1/2}.$$

Standard normal random numbers of size of 1000 were used to calculate $K(\varepsilon)$, $C(\varepsilon)$ at which ASE is evaluated. The standard error of the mean ASE is reported in parenthesis. True ASE is obtained from the same ASE formula which is given above. But it was evaluated at numerically calculated values of $K(\varepsilon) = 0.2511$, $C(\varepsilon) = 0.4755$ for $\varepsilon = 0.9$. $\sqrt{T}$ SD = $\sqrt{T} \times$ standard error of $[K_m(\cdot) + \log C(\varepsilon, 1, T)]$ of the 2500 replications.

Another technique that may improve performance of dimension-based tests is to fix a zone of epsilons of the $\log(C(\varepsilon, m))$ vs. $\log(\varepsilon)$ plot and follow Denker and Keller (1986) to estimate the slope of the $\log(C(\varepsilon, m))$ vs. $\log(\varepsilon)$ plot over this zone. Since our derivative estimate of dimension performed better than we thought (even though it performed poorly) we believe the Denker and Keller procedure may perform well.[9] Turn now to the K_m-based test which performed much better.

We analysed the reliability of the K_m-based test in a similar way in Table 6. From the second column, there is no clear evidence that the entropy estimate is biased. Also the consistent estimates of C and K bring the mean ASE based on (2.27) very close to its true value. By comparing the third and last column we can say that the normal approximation is good for high embedding dimensions. The histogram (not reported in this paper) constructed by the sampling distribution also shows evidence of good normal approximation. Extended tables and histograms are available at the reader's request. (cf. Brock and Baek (1990)).

Finally we turn to the two examples which show how our dimension test can be applied without such a serious bias problem.

Example 1.   Suppose you have two time-series $\{a_{1t}\}$ and $\{a_{2t}\}$ and you want to test whether their dimensions are the same. I.e. you want to capture, in some reasonable way, the notion of a statistically significant difference in the number of "possibly nonlinear factors" or active modes in the two series.

---

9. Note that the bad performance of our dimension based statistic is due to the "magnification" quantity $4\gamma^2$. In a comparison test of whether true dimension estimates were significantly different this quantity could be cancelled which may lead to better performance.

To do this one could, under the maintained hypothesis of stationarity and mixing as in Theorem 2.2, set up the null hypothesis that the dimension for m, ε for the two series is the same against the alternative that it is not. The asymptotic variance under the null for the difference of the two dimension estimates could be derived as in the proof of Theorem 2.3, but the variance formula will need to be modified to include a string of covariance terms.

As a special case we will construct a test of the null hypothesis that $\{a_{1t}\}$ and $\{a_{2t}\}$ are both i.i.d. and mutually independent. This test is based upon comparison of the dimension estimates. The i.i.d. null leads to asymptotic null standard normality being achieved for a test statistic with a simple asymptotic variance formula but it opens a gap between the null hypothesis of the same dimension and alternatives of different dimension. That is to say, the test developed under the i.i.d. null may reject the null because i.i.d. does not hold even though the dimensions are the same. This can happen through the change in the variance formula. At the risk of repeating, however, under a suitable weak-dependence condition, it would be possible to construct a test of the more desirable null hypothesis that the dimensions are the same which has a limiting null standard distribution but a more complicated variance formula. We have

Theorem 3.1. *Let $d^1_m(\varepsilon, \Delta\varepsilon)$ and $d^2_m(\varepsilon, \Delta\varepsilon)$ be the correlation dimension of the first series and the second series respectively. The null hypothesis that both series are i.i.d. and mutually independent with common distribution function is tested by $d^1_m(\varepsilon, \Delta\varepsilon) = d^2_m(\varepsilon, \Delta\varepsilon)$, and the alternative hypothesis is $d^1_m(\varepsilon, \Delta\varepsilon) \neq d^2_m(\varepsilon, \Delta\varepsilon)$. Then under the null hypothesis,*

$$T^{1/2}[d^1_m(\varepsilon, \Delta\varepsilon, T) - d^2_m(\varepsilon, \Delta\varepsilon, T)]/(\hat{V}D_1)^{1/2} \xrightarrow{d} N(0, 1) \tag{3.1}$$

where $d^1_m(\varepsilon, \Delta\varepsilon, T) =$ the correlation dimension estimator of the first sample, $d^2_m(\varepsilon, \Delta\varepsilon, T) =$ the correlation dimension estimator of the second sample, $\hat{V}D_1 =$ the consistent estimator of the variance, $8\gamma^2[\hat{A}^m + \hat{B}^m - 2\hat{C}^m + 2\sum_{j=1}^{m-1}\{\hat{A}^{m-j} + \hat{B}^{m-j} - 2\hat{C}^{m-j}\}]$, A, B and C are defined in (2.23).

Proof. The proof is similar to the proof of Theorem 2.3. ‖

For practical purposes we computed $\hat{V}D_1$ from the first sample because the two series have the same distribution under the null hypothesis. When we prepared a histogram of the statistic (3.1) with 2500 iterations it did not show downward bias because the bias factors in the numerator cancel and the γ factors are cancelled from the numerator and the denominator of (3.1). It also showed that the sampling distribution has thin tails relative to the standard normal distribution.

Example 2. The second application is designed to test whether the given series $\{a_t\}$ is i.i.d. or not. The i.i.d. test based on the dimension estimate is constructed in a similar way as the first example. First of all a bootstrap sample is generated from the given sample with replacement. If the series $\{a_t\}$ has a chaotic attractor which shows a low dimension estimate, the difference between the original and the bootstrap sample correlation estimates should be statistically significant since the chaotic structure is destroyed by shuffling. However if $\{a_t\}$ is i.i.d., the difference between them should not be significantly large. The formal test statistic will be the following.

Theorem 3.2. *Let $d_m(\varepsilon, \Delta\varepsilon)$ and $d_m^*(\varepsilon, \Delta\varepsilon)$ be the correlation dimension of the original and the bootstrap series respectively. The null hypothesis of i.i.d. is tested by $d_m(\varepsilon, \Delta\varepsilon) = d_m^*(\varepsilon, \Delta\varepsilon)$ against the alternative hypothesis, $d_m(\varepsilon, \Delta\varepsilon) < d_m^*(\varepsilon, \Delta\varepsilon)$ to set up a one-tail test. Then under the null hypothesis,*

$$T^{1/2}[d_m(\varepsilon, \Delta\varepsilon, T) - d_m^*(\varepsilon, \Delta\varepsilon, T)]/(\hat{V}D_2)^{1/2} \xrightarrow{d} N(0, 1) \qquad (3.2)$$

where $d_m(\varepsilon, \Delta\varepsilon, T) = $ the correlation dimension estimator of the original sample, $d_m^*(\varepsilon, \Delta\varepsilon, T) = $ the correlation dimension estimator of the bootstrap sample, $\hat{V}D_2 = $ the consistent estimator of the variance, $8\gamma^2[\hat{A}^m + \hat{B}^m - 2\hat{C}^m + 2\sum_{j=1}^{m-1}\{\hat{A}^{m-j} + \hat{B}^{m-j} - \hat{2}C^{m-j}\}]$, A, B and C are defined in (2.23).

Proof. The proof is similar to that of Theorem 2.3. ‖

We computed $\hat{V}D_1$ from the original sample because the bootstrap sample gives a close value under i.i.d. assumption. A histogram based on 2500 iterations of this experiment (available upon request) showed no clear evidence of downward bias. The same cancelling of the γ factor that occurred in (3.1) also occurred in (3.2).[10]

4. CONCLUSION AND FUTURE RESEARCH

This paper has shown that central limit theory for U-statistics under assumptions of weak dependence may be fruitfully applied to provide inference theory using objects of nonlinear science such as the correlation dimension and the approximate Kolmogorov entropy. For example we derived asymptotic standard errors for correlation dimension estimates and estimates of approximate Kolmogorov entropy. We then estimated these quantities for stock returns. Dimension estimates appear rather unstable. Kolmogorov entropy estimates were better behaved.

The performance of the dimension estimate was poor, due to a bias in the dimension estimate itself and bias in the standard error estimate. But inference was improved by use of bias reduction techniques. U-statistic theory can also be applied to provide inference theory for measures of instability (cf. Brock and Baek (1990)).

Our methods are general. For example the correlation integral can be used to build tests for nonlinear "Granger/Wiener" causality, as well as for "instability." This work is in progress and is touched upon in Brock and Baek (1990).

APPENDIX A

1. *Proof of Theorem 2.3*

Put $\varepsilon' = \varepsilon + \Delta\varepsilon$. Applying the delta method (Serfling (1980, p. 124)) to $[D\{C'(\varepsilon', m, T), C'(\varepsilon, m, T)\} - D\{\theta(\varepsilon', m), \theta(\varepsilon, m)\}]$, we have

$$dD = D_1 \frac{2}{T}\sum\{h_1(a_i^m, \varepsilon') - \theta(\varepsilon', m)\} + D_2\frac{2}{T}\sum\{h_1(a_i^m, \varepsilon) - \theta(\varepsilon, m)\}$$

$$+ o_p(T^{-1/2}), \qquad (A.1)$$

10. Since there are well-known alternative tests for i.i.d. besides dimension based tests and Kolmogorov entropy based tests, the issue of comparison arises. A serious discussion of this issue is beyond the scope of this paper. More detailed comments can be found in (4) of Appendix B.

where

$$D_1 = \frac{1}{\ln(\varepsilon') - \ln(\varepsilon)} \frac{1}{\theta(\varepsilon', m)}$$

$$D_2 = -\frac{1}{\ln(\varepsilon') - \ln(\varepsilon)} \frac{1}{\theta(\varepsilon, m)}.$$

The formula for the variance will be derived as in (2.13) after using the delta method. Put

$$g_1(a_i^m) = 2[D_1\{h_1(a_i^m, \varepsilon') - \theta(\varepsilon', m)\} + D_2\{h_1(a_i^m, \varepsilon) - \theta(\varepsilon, m)\}]. \tag{A.2}$$

By Theorem 2.2, $T^{1/2} dD \xrightarrow{d} N(0, VD_m)$ where $VD_m = E[g_1(a_i^m)^2 + 2\sum_{j=1}^{m-1} g_1(a_i^m)^2 g_1(a_{i+j}^m)]$. Under the i.i.d. assumption on the $\{a_t\}$ process, $\theta(\varepsilon', m)$ and $\theta(\varepsilon, m)$ are $C(\varepsilon')^m$ and $C(\varepsilon)^m$. Denote $[\log(\varepsilon') - \log(\varepsilon)]^{-1}$ by γ. Then D_1, D_2 equal $\gamma[C(\varepsilon')]^{-m}$, $-\gamma[C(\varepsilon)]^{-m}$. First, recalling

$$h_1(a_i^m, \varepsilon) = E[I(a_i^m, a_s^m; \varepsilon) | a_i^m]$$

$$= \prod_{i=0}^{m-1} [F(a_{i+i} + \varepsilon) - F(a_{i+i} - \varepsilon)]$$

where $F(x) \equiv \text{Prob}\{a \le x\}$, we compute

$$E[g_1(a_i^m)^2] = 4\gamma^2[(K(\varepsilon')/C(\varepsilon')^2)^m + (K(\varepsilon)/C(\varepsilon)^2)^m - 2\{Eh_1(a_i^m, \varepsilon')h_1(a_i^m, \varepsilon)/C(\varepsilon')^m C(\varepsilon)^m\}].$$

Next, compute

$$E[g_1(a_i^m)g_1(a_{i+j}^m)] = 4\gamma^2[(K(\varepsilon')/C(\varepsilon')^2)^{m-j} + (K(\varepsilon)/C(\varepsilon)^2)^{m-j}$$

$$- Eh_1(a_i^m, \varepsilon')h_1(a_{i+j}^m, \varepsilon)/(C(\varepsilon')C(\varepsilon))^m - Eh_1(a_i^m, \varepsilon)h_1(a_{i+j}^m, \varepsilon')/(C(\varepsilon')C(\varepsilon))^m].$$

Then,

$$E[g_1(a_i^m)^2] + 2\sum_{j=1}^{m-1} E[g_1(a_i^m)g_1(a_{i+j}^m)] = 4\gamma^2[(K(\varepsilon')/C(\varepsilon')^2)^m + (K(\varepsilon)/C(\varepsilon)^2)^m$$

$$+ 2\sum_{j=1}^{m-1} \{(K(\varepsilon')/C(\varepsilon')^2)^{m-j} + (K(\varepsilon)/C(\varepsilon)^2)^{m-j}\}] + R,$$

where

$$R = 4\gamma^2[-2/(C(\varepsilon')C(\varepsilon))^m][Eh_1(a_i^m, \varepsilon')h_1(a_i^m, \varepsilon) + \sum_{j=1}^{m-1} Eh_1(a_i^m, \varepsilon')h_1(a_{i+j}^m, \varepsilon)$$

$$+ \sum_{j=1}^{m-1} Eh_1(a_i^m, \varepsilon)h_1(a_{i+j}^m, \varepsilon')].$$

Moreover $Eh_1(a_i^m, \varepsilon')h_1(a_{i+j}^m, \varepsilon) = Eh_1(a_{i+j}^m, \varepsilon')h_1(a_i^m, \varepsilon)$ can be shown easily. Based on this, R can be further simplified to

$$-8\gamma^2[C(\varepsilon')C(\varepsilon)]^{-m}[Eh_1(a_i^m, \varepsilon')h_1(a_i^m, \varepsilon) + 2\sum_{j=1}^{m-1} Eh_1(a_i^m, \varepsilon')h_1(a_{i+j}^m, \varepsilon)].$$

Now let $W(\varepsilon', \varepsilon)$ be $Eh_1(a_t, \varepsilon')h_1(a_t, \varepsilon)$. Then $Eh_1(a_i^m, \varepsilon')h_1(a_{i+j}^m, \varepsilon) = [C(\varepsilon')C(\varepsilon)]^j W(\varepsilon', \varepsilon)^{m-j}$ by the i.i.d. assumption. Hence

$$VD_m = 4\gamma^2[(K(\varepsilon')/C(\varepsilon')^2)^m + (K(\varepsilon)/C(\varepsilon)^2)^m - 2\{W(\varepsilon', \varepsilon)/C(\varepsilon')C(\varepsilon)\}^m$$

$$+ 2\sum_{j=1}^{m-1} [(K(\varepsilon')/C(\varepsilon')^2)^{m-j} + (K(\varepsilon)/C(\varepsilon)^2)^{m-j} - 2\{W(\varepsilon', \varepsilon)C(\varepsilon')C(\varepsilon)\}^{m-j}]]$$

$$= 4\gamma^2[A^m + B^m - 2C^m + 2\sum_{j=1}^{m-1} \{A^{m-j} + B^{m-j} - 2C^{m-j}\}]$$

where,

$$A = K(\varepsilon')/C(\varepsilon')^2, \quad B = K(\varepsilon)/C(\varepsilon)^2 \quad \text{and} \quad C = W(\varepsilon', \varepsilon)/(C(\varepsilon')C(\varepsilon)).$$

2. *Proof of Theorem 2.4*

We show the asymptotic property for (2.24). Equation (2.21) is similarly derived. Under the null hypothesis of i.i.d., $K_m(\varepsilon)$ converges to its mean $-\log C(\varepsilon)$. Let

$$K[C(\varepsilon, m, T), C(\varepsilon, m+1, T), C(\varepsilon, 1, T)] = \log[C(\varepsilon, m, T)/C(\varepsilon, m+1, T)] + \log C(\varepsilon, 1, T), \tag{A.3}$$

and define

$$dK = K[C(\varepsilon, m, T), C(\varepsilon, m+1, T), C(\varepsilon, 1, T)] - K[\theta(\varepsilon, m), \theta(\varepsilon, m+1), \theta(\varepsilon, 1)]. \qquad (A.4)$$

By Denker–Keller's (1983, p. 507) decomposition,

$$dK = K[\theta(\varepsilon, m), \theta(\varepsilon, m+1), \theta(\varepsilon, 1)] + K_1(2/T) \sum [h_1(a_i^m, \varepsilon) - \theta(\varepsilon, m)]$$

$$+ K_2(2/T) \sum [h_1(a_i^{m+1}, \varepsilon) - \theta(\varepsilon, m+1)] + K_3(2/T) \sum [h_1(a_i, \varepsilon) - \theta(\varepsilon, 1)] + o_p(T^{-1/2}),$$

where $K_1 = [C(\varepsilon)]^{-m}$, $K_2 = -[C(\varepsilon)]^{-m-1}$, and $K_3 = [C(\varepsilon)]^{-1}$. Let

$$g_1(a_i^m) = 2[K_1\{h_1(a_i^m, \varepsilon) - \theta(\varepsilon, m)\} + K_2\{h_1(a_i^{m+1}, \varepsilon) - \theta(\varepsilon, m+1)\}$$

$$+ K_3\{h_1(a_i, \varepsilon) - \theta(\varepsilon, 1)\}].$$

By the delta method $(T)^{1/2}dK \xrightarrow{d} N(0, VK'_m)$ where $VK'_m = E[g_1(a_i^m)^2 + 2\sum_{j=1}^{m-1} g_1(a_i^m)g_1(a_{i+j}^m)]$. We can easily show that

$$E[g_1(a_i^m)^2] = 4[\{K(\varepsilon)/C(\varepsilon)^2\}^{m+1} - \{K(\varepsilon)/C(\varepsilon)^2\}^m + \{K(\varepsilon)/C(\varepsilon)^2 - 1\}]$$

and $E[g_1(a_i^m)g_1(a_{i+j}^m)] = 0$ for $j = 1, \ldots, m-1$. ‖

APPENDIX B

1. Notes on DIM for embedding dimension m

Technically $\text{DIM} = m[((dC(\varepsilon)/d\varepsilon)\varepsilon]/C(\varepsilon)$ for embedding dimension m under the null of i.i.d. distribution. The following table reports the numerical calculations of $[(dC(\varepsilon)/d\varepsilon)\varepsilon]/C(\varepsilon)$ for the t and standard normal distributions. A fat-tailed t distribution of degree of freedom 3 was chosen from Hsieh and LeBaron (1988a) since we assume the underlying structure of the Scheinkman and LeBaron data is approximated by the t distribution.

ε	$x/\sqrt{3}$ where $x \sim t(3)$	x where $x \sim N(0, 1)$
0.9	0.8849	0.8721
0.9^2	0.9052	0.8954
0.9^3	0.9221	0.9145
0.9^4	0.9362	0.9303

Therefore we use m for the approximate value of DIM under the given null hypothesis in Tables 1 and 2. It can be shown, putting $C(\varepsilon, 1) = C(\varepsilon)$, and using (2.4) that $[(dC(\varepsilon)/d\varepsilon)\varepsilon]/C(\varepsilon) \to 1$, $\varepsilon \to 0$. One can evaluate the quality of the approximation near $\varepsilon = 0$ by computing the Taylor expansion of $(dC(\varepsilon)/d\varepsilon)/(C(\varepsilon)/\varepsilon)$ from (2.4) around $\varepsilon = 0$. It is quite good as the table shows.

2. ASE of the test statistic in Table 5

$$\text{ASE} = [4\gamma^2\{A^m + B^m - 2C^m + 2\sum_{j=1}^{m-1}(A^{m-j} + B^{m-j} - 2C^{m-j})\}]^{1/2},$$

where

$$\gamma = [\log(\varepsilon + \Delta\varepsilon) - \log(\varepsilon)]^{-1}, \qquad A = K(\varepsilon + \Delta\varepsilon)/C(\varepsilon + \Delta\varepsilon)^2, \qquad B = K(\varepsilon)/C(\varepsilon)^2,$$

$$C = W(\varepsilon + \Delta\varepsilon, \varepsilon)/(C(\varepsilon + \Delta\varepsilon)C(\varepsilon)).$$

REVIEW OF ECONOMIC STUDIES

True K, C, and W (by numerical integration)

ε	$K(\varepsilon)$	$C(\varepsilon)$	$W(\varepsilon', \varepsilon)$
0·9	0·2511	0·4755	0·2295 ($\varepsilon' = 0\cdot9$, $\varepsilon = 0\cdot9^2$)
0·9^2	0·2098	0·4332	0·1912 ($\varepsilon' = 0\cdot9^2$, $\varepsilon = 0\cdot9^3$)
0·9^3	0·1743	0·3938	

Notes. Error function $E(z) = (2/\sqrt{2}\pi)\int_0^z \exp(-t^2/2)dt$ was used to calculate K, C, and W. Let $f(z)$ be the probability density function of a standard normal random variable, i.e. $f(z) = (1/\sqrt{2}\pi)\exp(-z^2/2)$. Then

$$C(\varepsilon) = (1/2)\int_{-\infty}^{\infty} [E\{(x+\varepsilon)/\sqrt{2}\} - E\{(x-\varepsilon)/\sqrt{2}\}]f(x)dx,$$

and

$$K(\varepsilon) = (1/2)\int_{-\infty}^{\infty} [E\{(x+\varepsilon)/\sqrt{2}\} - E\{(x-\varepsilon)/\sqrt{2}\}]^2 f(x)dx,$$

and

$$W(\varepsilon', \varepsilon) = (1/4)\int_{-\infty}^{\infty} [E\{(x+\varepsilon')/\sqrt{2}\} - E\{(x-\varepsilon')/\sqrt{2}\}]$$
$$\times [E\{(x+\varepsilon)/\sqrt{2}\} - E\{(x-\varepsilon)/\sqrt{2}\}]f(x)dx.$$

Mathematica was used for numerical calculations. Refer to Wolfram, S. (1988) *Mathematica*, (New York: Addison Wesley).

3. Sample estimates of K, C and W

TABLE B1

Estimates of K, C, and W (standard normal)

T	ε	K	C	W
1000	0·9	0·251 (0·0052)	0·475 (0·0037)	0·228 (0·0049)
1000	0·9^2	0·210 (0·0047)	0·433 (0·0036)	0·190 (0.0044)
1000	0·9^3	0·175 (0·0042)	0·394 (0·0035)	
500	0·9	0·252 (0·0074)	0·476 (0·0053)	0·229 (0·0070)
500	0·9^2	0·210 (0·0067)	0·434 (0·0052)	0·191 (0·0063)
500	0·9^3	0·175 (0·0060)	0·394 (0·0050)	
250	0·9	0·252 (0·0104)	0·476 (0·0076)	0·229 (0·0099)
250	0·9^2	0·211 (0·0095)	0·434 (0·0073)	0·191 (0·0088)·
250	0·9^3	0·176 (0·0085)	0·395 (0·0070)	

Notes. T is the sample size.

K, C and W are calculated by 2500 replications. The standard errors for K, C and W are reported in parentheses.

4. Tests for i.i.d.

A rather extensive discussion of the power and size properties of the closely related BDS test for i.i.d. is in Brock, Hsieh, and LeBaron (1991). A comparison (with moment generating function tests, Kendall's tau, and Blum, Kiefer, Rosenblatt's test) of the size and power properties of a vector version of the BDS test is in Baek (1988).

The Kolmogorov entropy test is treated in Hiemstra (1990). Hiemstra's general conclusion is that the Kolmogorov entropy test performs quite poorly in comparison with the optimal test especially against weak linearly dependent alternatives in conditional mean and conditional variance. In general one must expect nonparametric tests like those treated in this paper to do poorly in power properties against specific parametric alternatives when compared with tests that are designed to be optimal against specific parametric alternatives. Based upon work with the closely related BDS test we expect the Kolmogorov entropy based test to do well against highly nonlinear alternatives that are predictable in the short term using nonlinear prediction schemes such as nearest neighbours. See Brock, W., Hsieh, D. and LeBaron, B. (1990) for the general argument and Monte Carlo evidence. A serious comparison study of the tests discussed in this paper must be left to future work.

Acknowledgement. The first author thanks the Guggenheim Foundation, the Wisconsin Graduate School, the Wisconsin Alumni Research Foundation, and the National Science Foundation (Grant No. SEC-8420872) for essential financial support for this work. We thank two referees and C. Bean for very helpful comments and Taeho Lee for the numerical integrations. We also thank Craig Hiemstra for discovering the computation error of *W.* None of the above are responsible for errors or shortcomings in this paper.

REFERENCES

BAEK, E. (1988) *Three Essays on Nonlinearity in Economics* (Ph.D. thesis, Department of Economics, University of Wisconsin-Madison).
BAEK, E. and BROCK, W. A. (1988), "A Nonparametric Test for Temporal Dependence in a Vector of Time Series" (University of Wisconsin-Madison SSRI Workshop Paper 8816).
BAEK, E. and BROCK, W. A. (1990), "A General Test for Nonlinear Granger Causality" (Department of Economics, Iowa State University and Department of Economics, University of Wisconsin-Madison).
BARNETT, W. and CHEN, P. (1988), "The Aggregation-theoretic Monetary Aggregates are Chaotic and have Strange Attractors", in Barnett, W., Berndt, E. and White, H. (eds.), *Dynamic Econometric Modeling* (*Proceedings of the Third International Symposium in Economic Theory and Econometrics*) (Cambridge: Cambridge University Press), 199–245.
BROCK, W. A. (1986), "Distinguishing Random and Deterministic Systems", *Journal of Economic Theory*, 40, 168–195.
BROCK, W. A. (1989), "A Proof of Invariance of the First Order Asymptotics of the BDS Statistic on Estimated Residuals of Null Models Driven by IID", forthcoming in Brock, W., Hsieh, D. and LeBaron, B. (1991) (eds.), *A Test for Nonlinear Dynamics and Chaos* (Cambridge: MIT Press).
BROCK, W. A. and DECHERT, W. D. (1988a), "Theorems on Distinguishing Deterministic from Random Systems", in Barnett, W., Berndt, E. and White, H. (eds.), *Dynamic Econometric Modeling*, (*Proceedings of the Third International Symposium in Economic Theory and Econometrics*) (Cambridge: Cambridge University Press), 247–265.
BROCK, W. A. and DECHERT, W. D. (1988b), "A General Class of Specification Tests: The Scalar Case", *1988 Proceedings of the Business and Economic Statistics Section of the American Statistical Association*, 70–79.
BROCK, W. A., DECHERT, W. D. and SCHEINKMAN, J. (1987), "A Test for Independence Based on the Correlation Dimension" (University of Wisconsin-Madison SSRI Workshop Paper 8702).
BROCK, W. A. and SAYERS, C. (1988), "Is The Business Cycle Characterized by Deterministic Chaos?", *Journal of Monetary Economics*, 22, 71–90.
BROCK, W. A. and BAEK, E. G. (1990), "Some Theory of Statistical Inference for Nonlinear Science: Expanded Version" (Department of Economics, University of Wisconsin-Madison, and Iowa State University).
DENKER, M. and KELLER, G. (1983), "On U-Statistics and V. Mises Statistics for Weakly Dependent Processes", *Zeitschrift für Wahrscheinlichkeitstheorie und Verwandte Gebiete*, 64, 505–522.
DENKER, M. and KELLER, G. (1986), "Rigorous Statistical Procedures for Data from Dynamical Systems", *Journal of Statistical Physics*, 44, 67–93.
ECKMANN, J. and RUELLE, D. (1985), "Ergodic Theory of Chaos and Strange Attractors", *Reviews of Modern Physics*, 57, 617–656.
EFRON, B. (1982) *The Jacknife, the Bootstrap, and Other Resampling Plans* (Philadelphia, Pennsylvania: Society for Industrial and Applied Mathematics).
EFRON, B. and TIBSHIRANI, R. (1986), "Bootstrap Methods for Standard Errors, Confidence Intervals, and Other Measures of Statistical Accuracy", *Statistical Science*, 1, 54–77.
FRANK, M. and STENGOS, T. (1988a), "Some Evidence Concerning Macroeconomic Chaos", *Journal of Monetary Economics*, 22, 423–438.
FRANK, M. and STENGOS, T. (1988b), "Chaotic Dynamics in Economic Time-Series", *Journal of Economic Surveys*, 2, 103–133.
FRANK, M. and STENGOS, T. (1989), "Measuring the Strangeness of Gold and Silver Rates of Return", *Review of Economic Studies*, 56, 553–567.
GENNOTTE, G. and MARSH, T. (1987), "Variations in Economic Uncertainty and Risk Premiums on Capital Assets" (School of Business Administration, University of California, Berkeley).
HIEMSTRA, C. (1990) *Applications to Macroeconomics, Finance, and Forecasting of Recently Developed Statistical Tests and Estimates Arising from Nonlinear Dynamical Systems Theory* (Ph.D. thesis, Department of Economics, University of Maryland).

HSIEH, D. and LEBARON, B. (1988a), "Finite Sample Properties of the BDS Statistic I: Size", forthcoming in Brock, W., Hsieh, D. and LeBaron, B. (1991) (eds.), *A Test for Nonlinear Dynamics and Chaos*, (Cambridge: MIT Press).

HSIEH, D. and LEBARON, B. (1988b), "Finite Sample Properties of the BDS Statistic II: Distribution Under Alternative Hypotheses", forthcoming in Brock, W., Hsieh, D. and LeBaron, B. (1991) (eds.), *A Test for Nonlinear Dynamics and Chaos* (Cambridge: MIT Press).

HSIEH, D. (1989), "Testing for Nonlinear Dependence in Daily Foreign Exchange Rates", *Journal of Business*, **62**, 339-368.

MAYER-KRESS, G. (1987), "Application of Dimension Algorithms to Experimental Chaos", in Hao Bai-lin (ed.), *Directions in Chaos*. (Singapore: World Scientific), 122-147.

RAMSEY, J. B. and YUAN, H. (1989), "Bias and Error Bars in Dimension Calculations and Their Evaluation in some simple Models", *Physics Letters A*, **134**, 287-297.

RAMSEY, J. B. and YUAN, H. (1990), "The Statistical Properties of Dimension Calculations using Small Data Sets", *Nonlinearity*, **3**, 155-176.

SAYERS, C. (1986), "Work Stoppages: Exploring the Nonlinear Dynamics" (Department of Economics, University of Wisconsin-Madison).

SCHEINKMAN, J. and LEBARON, B. (1989a), "Nonlinear Dynamics and Stock Returns", *Journal of Business*, **62**, 311-337.

SCHEINKMAN, J. and LEBARON, B. (1989b), "Nonlinear Dynamics and GNP Date", in Barnett, W., Geweke, J. and Shell, K. (eds.), *Economic Complexity: Chaos, Sunspots, Bubbles, and Nonlinearity* (Cambridge: Cambridge University Press), 213-227.

SEN, P.K. (1972), "Limiting Behaviour of Regular Functionals of Empirical Distributions for Stationary *-mixing Process", *Zeitschrift für Wahrscheinlichkeitstheorie und Verwandte Gebiete*, **25**, 71-82.

SERFLING, R. (1980) *Approximation Theorems of Mathematical Statistics* (New York: Wiley).

THEILER, J. (1990a), "Statistical precision of dimension estimators", *Physical Review A*, **41**, 3038-3051.

THEILER, J. (1990b), "Estimating fractal dimension", forthcoming in *Journal of the Optical Society of America A*, June.

[9]

Physica D 59 (1992) 142–157
North-Holland

An algorithm for the n Lyapunov exponents
of an n-dimensional unknown dynamical system

Ramazan Gencay[a,1] and W. Davis Dechert[b]

[a]*Department of Economics, University of Windsor, 401 Sunset, Windsor, Ontario N9B 3P4, Canada*
[b]*Department of Economics, University of Houston, 4800 Calhoun, Houston, TX 77204–5882, USA*

Received 7 June 1991
Revised manuscript received 26 May 1992
Accepted 26 May 1992
Communicated by J. Guckenheimer

An algorithm for estimating Lyapunov exponents of an unknown dynamical system is designed. The algorithm estimates not only the largest but all Lyapunov exponents of the unknown system. The estimation is carried out by a multivariate feedforward network estimation technique. We focus our attention on deterministic as well as noisy system estimation. The performance of the algorithm is very satisfactory in the presence of noise as well as with limited number of observations.

1. Introduction

The Lyapunov exponents measure quantities which constitute the exponential divergence or convergence of nearby initial points in the phase space of a dynamical system. A positive Lyapunov exponent measures the average exponential divergence of two nearby trajectories whereas a negative Lyapunov exponent measures exponential convergence of two nearby trajectories. If a discrete nonlinear system is dissipative, a positive Lyapunov exponents quantifies a measure of chaos.

The popular algorithms for calculating Lyapunov exponents are designed by [1,2]. The important contribution of the algorithm presented in [1] is that it is the first attempt to calculate the Lyapunov exponents from observed time series. The major shortcomings of these algorithms are that the accuracy of the estimates

[1]R.G. gratefully acknowledges financial support under a grant from the University of Windsor Research Board.

are sensitive to the number of the observations as well as the degree of the measurement or the system noise in the observations. The nature of these shortcomings are discussed in [1].

Our purpose is to design and implement a Jacobian algorithm for calculating the Lyapunov exponents such that it would achieve the following three objectives:

(1) it calculates all n Lyapunov exponents of an n-dimensional *unknown* dynamical system from observations,

(2) it achieves greater accuracy of Lyapunov exponent estimates on a relatively short length of observations and,

(3) the accuracy of the estimates is robust to the system as well as measurement noise.

The achievement of the first objective depends on how the algorithm is constructed. We use a result of [3] which shows that the n largest Lyapunov exponents of a diffeomorphism which is topologically conjugate to the data generating process are the n Lyapunov exponents of the data generating process. The second and third

R. Gencay, W. Davis Dechert / Algorithm for Lyapunov exponents 143

objectives will depend on the choice of the estimation technique. We employ multilayer feedforward networks (MFNs) as a nonparametric[*1] estimation technique. As shown by [4], these networks can asymptotically approximate a (differentiable) function and its derivatives to any degree of accuracy. In practice, as we will show in section 5, MFNs have the capability to approximate a function and its derivatives with as few as a hundred observations. In [5], it is pointed out that other types of nonparametric estimation techniques such as projection pursuit may not provide the same level of accuracy as feedforward networks. The performance of various nonparametric estimation techniques such as local thin plate splines, radial basis functions, projection pursuit and feedforward networks are also presented in [5].

In section 2 we will briefly describe the definition of Lyapunov exponents. In section 3, we will explain the algorithm studied in this paper. Section 4 will focus on multilayer feedforward networks. In section 5, simulation results with four chaotic maps will be given.

2. Lyapunov exponents

The Lyapunov exponents for a dynamical system, $f: \mathbb{R}^n \to \mathbb{R}^n$, with the trajectory,

$$x_{t+1} = f(x_t), \quad t = 0, 1, 2, \ldots, \tag{1}$$

are measures of the average rate of divergence or convergence of a typical trajectory[*2]. For an n-dimensional system as above, there are n expo-

nents which are customarily ranked from largest to smallest:

$$\lambda_1 \geq \lambda_2 \geq \cdots \geq \lambda_n . \tag{2}$$

Associated with each exponent, $j = 1, 2, \ldots, n$, there are nested subspaces $V^j \subset \mathbb{R}^n$ of dimension $n + 1 - j$ and with the property that

$$\lambda_j = \lim_{t \to \infty} t^{-1} \ln \|(D f')_{x_0} v\| \tag{3}$$

for all $v \in V^j \backslash V^{j+1}$. It is a consequence of Oseledec's Theorem [6], that the limit in eq. (3) exists for a broad class of functions[*3]. Additional properties of Lyapunov exponents and a formal definition are given in [10, p. 256]. Notice that for $j \geq 2$ the subspaces V^j are sets of Lebesgue measure zero, and so for almost all $v \in \mathbb{R}^n$ the limit in eq. (3) equals λ_1. This is the basis for the computational algorithm of [1] which is a method for calculating the largest Lyapunov exponent.

Eq. (3) suggests a more direct approach to calculating the exponents. Since

$$(D f')_{x_0} = (D f)_{x_t} (D f)_{x_{t-1}} \cdots (D f)_{x_0} \tag{4}$$

all of the Lyapunov exponents can be calculated by evaluating the Jacobian of the function f along a trajectory, $\{x_t\}$. In [11] the QR decomposition is proposed for extracting the eigenvalues from $(D f')_{x_0}$. The QR decomposition is one of many ways to calculate eigenvalues. One advantage of the QR decomposition is that it performs successive rescaling to keep magnitudes under control. It is also well studied and extremely fast subroutines[*4] are available for this type of computation. It is the method that we use here.

An attractor is a set of points towards which the trajectories of f converge. More precisely, Λ is an attractor if there is an open $U \subset \mathbb{R}^n$ with

---

[*1]The terms *parametric* and *nonparametric* are conventionally used to distinguish those problems in which the regression is known up to a finite-dimensional parameter from those in which the regression is known to be a member of some non-finite dimensional space of functions. For example, the regression might be known to be a continuous function.

[*2]The trajectory is also written in terms of the iterates of f. With the convention that f^0 is the identity map, and $f^{t+1} = f \circ f^t$, then we also write $x_t = f^t(x_0)$. A trajectory is also called an orbit in the dynamical system literature.

[*3]See [7,8,9] for precise conditions and the proofs of the theorem.

[*4]We use the IMSL routines LQRRR and LQERR for our purposes.

$$\Lambda = \bigcap_{t\geq 0} f'(\bar{U}), \qquad (5)$$

where $\bar{U}$ is the closure of U. The attractor Λ is said to be indecomposable if there is no proper subset $A \subset \Lambda$ with $f(A) = A$. An attractor can be chaotic or ordinary (i.e., non-chaotic). There is more than one definition of chaotic attractors in the literature. In practice the presence of a positive Lyapunov exponent is taken as a signal that the attractor is chaotic.

3. The algorithm

One rarely has the advantage of observing the state of the system, x_t, let alone knowing the actual functional form, f, that generates the dynamics. The model that is widely used is the following: associated with the dynamical system in eq. (1) there is a measurement function h: $\mathbb{R}^n \to \mathbb{R}$ which generates observations,

$$y_t = h(x_t). \qquad (6)$$

It is assumed that all that is available to the researcher is the sequence $\{y_t\}$. For notational purposes let

$$y_t^m = (y_{t+m-1}, y_{t+m-2}, \ldots, y_t). \qquad (7)$$

Under general conditions, it is shown in [12] that if the set $\bar{U}$ is a compact manifold then for[5] $m \geq 2n + 1$

$$J^m(x) = y_t^m$$
$$= (h(f^{m-1}(x)), h(f^{m-2}(x)), \ldots, h(x)) \qquad (8)$$

is an embedding of $\bar{U}$ onto $J^m(\bar{U})$. Generically, for $m \geq 2n + 1$ there exists a function g: $\mathbb{R}^m \to \mathbb{R}^m$ such that

$$y_{t+1}^m = g(y_t^m), \qquad (9)$$

[5]Here $2n + 1$ is the worst-case upper limit.

where

$$y_{t+1}^m = (y_{t+m}, y_{t+m-1}, \ldots, y_{t+1}). \qquad (10)$$

But notice that

$$y_{t+1}^m = J^m(x_{t+1}) = J^m(f(x_t)). \qquad (11)$$

Hence from (9) and (11)

$$J^m(f(x_t)) = g(J^m(x_t)). \qquad (12)$$

Under the assumption that J^m is a homeomorphism, f is topologically conjugate to g. This implies that certain dynamical properties[6] of f and g are the same. From eq. (9) the mapping g (which is to be estimated) may be taken to be

$$g: \begin{pmatrix} y_{t+m-1} \\ y_{t+m-2} \\ \vdots \\ y_t \end{pmatrix} \to \begin{pmatrix} v(y_{t+m-1}, y_{t+m-2}, \ldots, y_t) \\ y_{t+m-1} \\ \vdots \\ y_{t+1} \end{pmatrix} \qquad (13)$$

and this reduces to estimating

$$y_{t+m} = v(y_{t+m-1}, y_{t+m-2}, \ldots, y_t). \qquad (14)$$

It is the unknown nature of v which requires a specification-free estimation technique such as feedforward networks. In [13] and [14], a truncated Taylor series is used to calculate the function v. In [5], the feedforward networks are used to calculate the largest Lyapunov exponent.

The derivative of g is the matrix

$$(D\,g)_{y_t^m} = \begin{pmatrix} v_m & v_{m-1} & v_{m-2} & \cdots & v_2 & v_1 \\ 1 & 0 & 0 & \cdots & 0 & 0 \\ 0 & 1 & 0 & \cdots & 0 & 0 \\ \vdots & & & & & \\ 0 & 0 & 0 & \cdots & 1 & 0 \end{pmatrix}, \qquad (15)$$

where

[6]Such as the correlation and fractal dimensions, as well as the Lyapunov exponents.

$$v_m = \frac{\partial v}{\partial y_{t+m-1}}, \ldots, v_1 = \frac{\partial v}{\partial y_t}. \qquad (16)$$

In [3] it was shown that the n largest Lyapunov exponents of g have the same values as the Lyapunov exponents of f. The statement of this theorem is the following.

Theorem 3.1. Assume that M is a manifold of dimension n, $f : M \rightarrow M$ and $h : M \rightarrow \mathbb{R}$ are (at least) C^2. Define $J^m : M \rightarrow \mathbb{R}^m$ by $J^m(x) = (h(f^{m-1}(x)), h(f^{m-2}(x)), \ldots, h(x))$. Let $\mu_1(x) \geq \mu_2(x) \geq \cdots \geq \mu_n(x)$ be the eigenvalues of $(D J^m)'_x (D J^m)_x$, and suppose that

$$\inf_{x \in M} \mu_n(x) > 0, \quad \sup_{x \in M} \mu_1(x) < \infty.$$

Let $\lambda_1^f \geq \lambda_2^f \geq \cdots \geq \lambda_n^f$ be the Lyapunov exponents of f and $\lambda_1^g \geq \lambda_2^g \geq \lambda_2^g \geq \cdots \geq \lambda_m^g$ be the Lyapunov exponents of g where $g : J^m(M) \rightarrow J^m(M)$ and $J^m(f(x)) = g(J^m(x))$ on M. Then generically $\lambda_i^f = \lambda_i^g$ for $i = 1, 2, \ldots, n$.

This is the basis of our approach: estimate the function g based on the data sequence $\{J^m(x_t)\}$, and calculate the Lyapunov exponents of g. As m increases there is a value between n and $2n + 1$ at which the n largest exponents remain constant and the remaining $m - n$ exponents diverge to $-\infty$ as the number of observations increases.

4. Multilayer feedforward networks

In this paper, we use a single layer feedforward network,

$$v_{N,m}(z; \beta, w, b) = \sum_{j=1}^{L} \beta_j k \left(\sum_{i=1}^{m} w_{ij} z_i + b_j \right), \quad (17)$$

where $z \in \mathbb{R}^m$ is the input[7], the parameters to

[7]In comparison to a thin plate spline, the complexity of a feedforward network does not increase in m. The functional form remains as a simple sum of simple univariate functions. In contrast, the number of polynomial terms grows exponentially with m in a thin plate spline.

be estimated are β, w, b, and k is a known hidden unit activation function. Here L is the number of hidden units, $\beta \in \mathbb{R}^L$ represents hidden to output unit weights, and $w \in \mathbb{R}^{L \times m}$ and $b \in \mathbb{R}^L$ represent input to hidden unit weights.

In [4] a set of conditions under which the single layer feedforward networks are dense in a Sobolev space of functions is analysed. The important part of their result of which we make use is that both a function and its derivatives can be asymptotically approximated to any arbitrary degree of accuracy with a single layer feedforward network. In [15] it is shown that feedforward networks can be used to consistently estimate both a function and its derivatives[8]. They show that the least squares estimates are consistent in Sobolev norm, provided that the number of hidden units increases with the size of the data set. This would mean that larger number of data points would require larger number of hidden units to avoid overfitting in noisy environments.

For a single layer network, the least squares criterion for a data set of length T is

$$L(\beta, w, b) = \sum_{t=0}^{T-m-1} [y_{t+m} - v_{N,m}(y_t^m; \beta, w, b)]^2 . \qquad (18)$$

This is a straightforward multivariate minimization problem. We found that conjugant gradient routines given in [16] worked very well for this problem. In our work we used the logistic function (which is a sigmoid[9] function)

$$k(x) = \frac{\beta}{1 + \exp(-wx - b)} \qquad (19)$$

as the hidden layer activation function. The position and the slope of the curve are determined

[8]A minimal property for any estimation procedure is that of consistency. A stochastic sequence $\{\hat{\theta}_T\}$ is consistent for $\{\theta_0\}$ if the probability that $\{\hat{\theta}_T\}$ exceeds any specified level of approximation error relative to $\{\theta_0\}$ tends to zero as the sample size T tends to infinity.

[9]k is a sigmoid function if $k : \mathbb{R} \rightarrow [0, \beta]$, $k(a) \rightarrow 0$ as $a \rightarrow -\infty$, $k(a) \rightarrow \beta$ as $a \rightarrow \infty$ and k is monotonic.

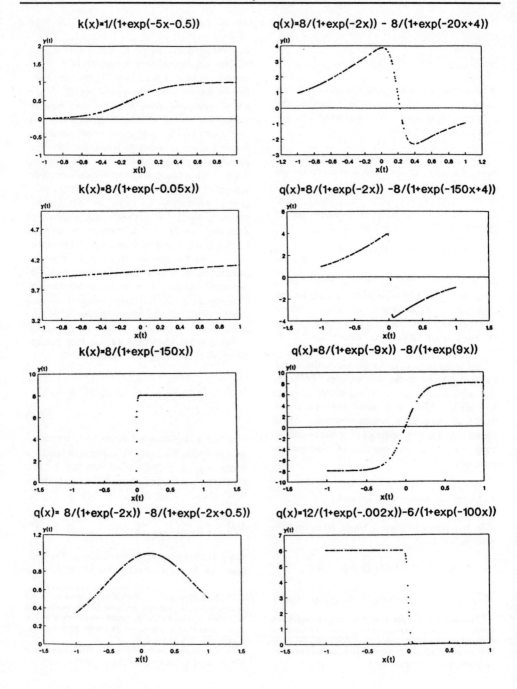

R. Gencay, W. Davis Dechert / Algorithm for Lyapunov exponents 147

by b and w and the height of the function is determined by β (see fig. 1 below). For small values of w the curve is more of a straight line whereas for large values of w the function is more like a step function. These two specifications are illustrated in figs. 2 and 3.

A combination of activation functions can result in a bell-shaped curve. This can be done by the difference of two logistic functions. Choose b of the second function to displace it from the first. Let $b_1 = 0$ and $b_2 = -c < 0$. Choose w of the two functions to be the same so that they have the same orientation. Finally, choose $\beta_2 = \beta_1$ so that the two functions have the same height,

$$q(x) = k_1(x) - k_2(x), \tag{20}$$

$$k_1(x) = \frac{\beta_1}{1 + \exp(-w_1 x)}, \tag{21}$$

and

$$k_2(x) = \frac{\beta_2}{1 + \exp(-w_2 x + c)}. \tag{22}$$

The function $q(x)$ is illustrated in fig. 4. We can obtain skewed curves, sharp spikes, or bi-modal curves by using various combinations of the parameters β, w and b. Some examples of these combinations are given in figs. 5–8. These figures clearly show the flexibility of the sigmoid functions.

5. Numerical results

In this section, we present the results on four examples.

(1) The Logistic map is the one-dimensional, discrete time, unimodal map

$$x_{t+1} = \beta x_t (1 - x_t). \tag{23}$$

For $\beta \in [0, 4]$ the state of the system maps itself onto itself in the closed interval $[0, 1]$. In the interval $\beta \in (3.5699, 4]$, the Logistic map exhibits deterministic chaos and contains the presence of periodic as well as aperiodic cycles. We set $\beta = 4$ and estimated the Logistic map with 100 observations. Four hidden units are used in a one-layer feedforward network. The results are given in figs. 9–11 along with the mean squared error of the approximations. The mean square error is calculated by

$$mse_{N,m} = \frac{1}{T - m} \sum_{t=0}^{T-m-1} (y_{t+m} - \bar{v}_{N,m,t+m})^2 \tag{24}$$

where $\bar{v}_{N,m,t+m}$ is the fit from a single hidden layer feedforward network. The mean square error of the estimate of the map and its derivative are reported in figs. 9–11 and the orders of these errors are less than 10^{-3}. The quality of this fit was achieved with only 100 observations. The value of the Lyapunov exponent from simulated data is 0.673 and the value of our estimate of the Lyapunov exponent is 0.674.

(2) The Hénon map

$$x_{t+1} = 1 - 1.4x_t^2 + y_t, \quad y_{t+1} = 0.3x_t \tag{25}$$

is a widely used example, in spite of the fact that it is not known whether or not the attractor is indecomposable. We use it in part as a benchmark to test our method against the results of others. The matrix of derivatives of the Hénon map is

$$\begin{pmatrix} -2.4x_t & 1 \\ 0.3 & 0 \end{pmatrix}. \tag{26}$$

Figs. 1–8. First column, from top to bottom: fig. 1, fig. 2, fig. 3 and fig. 4. Second column, from top to bottom: fig. 5, fig. 6, fig. 7 and fig. 8.

Figs. 1–3. In the implementation of feedforward networks the Logistic function is used as a hidden unit activation function. The figures above demonstrate this function for various parameter values.

Figs. 4–8. By the sum of two Logistic functions with different parameter values, bell-shaped curves, spikes and step functions can be obtained.

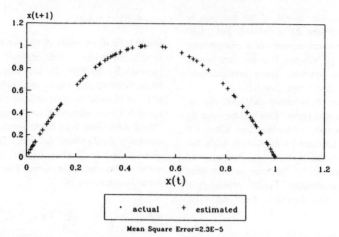

Fig. 9. The comparison of the Logistic map and its estimate by a single hidden layer feedforward network with four hidden units and 100 observations.

Since the determinant of this matrix is constant, the Lyapunov exponents for this map satisfy

$$\lambda_1 + \lambda_2 = \ln(0.3) \approx -1.2 . \tag{27}$$

We estimated the Hénon map and the first col-

umn of the matrix of partial derivatives based on 200 observations. In the estimation of this map, six hidden units are used in a single layer feedforward network. We have compared the quality of the fit with seven and eight hidden units as well, but did not observe any improvement in

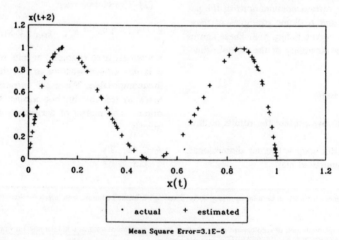

Fig. 10. The comparison of the Logistic map and its estimate by a single hidden layer feedforward network with four hidden units and 100 observations.

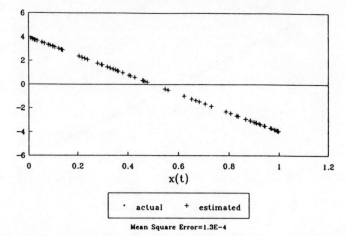

Mean Square Error=1.3E-4

Fig. 11. The comparison of the derivative of the Logistic map and its estimate by a single hidden layer feedforward network with four hidden units and 100 observations.

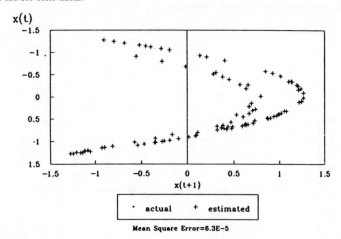

Mean Square Error=6.3E-5

Fig. 12. The comparison of the Hénon map and its estimate by a single hidden layer feedforward network with six hidden units and 200 observations.

the quality of the fit[10]. The results are given in figs. 12–14, along with the mean square error of

[10]In [15] it is pointed out that the number of activation functions should grow with the size of the data set at just the right rate to ensure good approximation without overfitting. In simulation experiments, they also reported that the quality of the fit was not very sensitive in slight variations in this proportionality.

the approximations. It can be seen that the single hidden layer feedforward network approximates the Hénon map as well as derivatives closely. For these parameter values the Lyapunov exponents of the Hénon map are 0.408 and −1.620. The calculated Lyapunov exponents are 0.405 and −1.625.

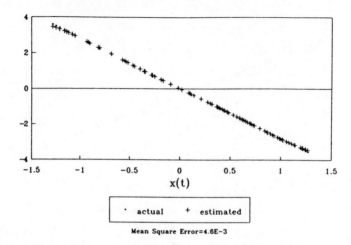

Fig. 13. The comparison of the derivative of the Hénon map with respect to $x(t)$ and its estimate by a single hidden layer feedforward network with six hidden units and 200 observations.

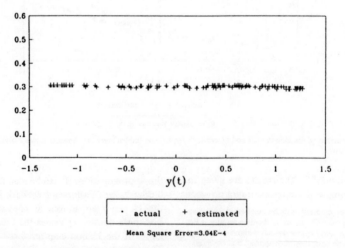

Fig. 14. The comparison of the derivative of the Hénon map with respect to $y(t)$ and its estimate by a single hidden layer feedforward network with six hidden units and 200 observations.

(3) The well-known Lorenz attractor is the three-dimensional, continuous-time system,

$$\dot{x} = a(x - y),$$

$$\dot{y} = x(b - z) - y,$$

$$\dot{z} = xy - cz, \qquad (28)$$

where a, b and c are parameters and set to $a = 16.0$, $b = 45.92$ and $c = 4.0$. For these parameter values, the Lyapunov exponents λ_1, λ_2 and λ_3 are 1.50, 0.0 and -22.5, respectively and they satisfy the rule that $\lambda_1 + \lambda_2 + \lambda_3 = -a - c - 1$ [11]. In the estimation of this map, 12 hidden units and 1000 observations are used in a single hidden layer feedforward network. In figs. 15–20 [12] the Lorenz system and its estimates with MFNs are plotted. The estimated values of the Lyapunov exponents are: 1.510, 0.7×10^{-4} and -22.57.

(4) A discrete time version of the Mackey–Glass equation,

$$x_t = x_{t-1} + \left(\frac{ax_{t-s}}{1 + (x_{t-s})^c} - bx_{t-1} \right), \qquad (29)$$

where we used $a = 0.2$, $b = 0.1$, and $c = 10.0$ and $s = 17$. The actual Mackey–Glass delay-differential equation is an infinite-dimensional dynamical system. This equation is chosen to show the performance of the feedforward network with higher dimensional systems and the resulting Lyapunov exponent estimates. The first four

[11] A differential equation has one zero exponent corresponding to perturbations along an orbit. For the Lorenz system, volumes in $\mathbf{R}^3$ contract everywhere as $\exp(-a - c - 1)t$ when $t \rightarrow \infty$. Hence $\lambda_1 + \lambda_2 + \lambda_3 = -a - c - 1$, by integrating the Lorenz system at a step size 0.02. It is reported in [13] that the Lyapunov exponents of the Lorenz system are $\lambda_1 \approx 1.50$, $\lambda_2 \approx 0.0$ and $\lambda_3 \approx -22.5$.

[12] The estimates of the Lorenz system are plotted in the following way. Let x_t, y_t, and z_t denote the components of the Lorenz system. In separate regressions each component of the system is regressed on its own three lags (e.g. x_t is regressed on x_{t-1}, x_{t-2} and x_{t-3}). The fitted values from these three regressions are obtained. In the creation of the figures, fitted values of a component are plotted against the fitted values of the other component.

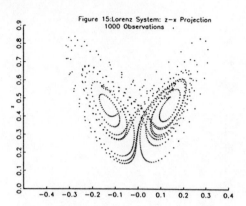

Fig. 15. The z–x projection of the Lorenz system by fourth order Runge–Kutta integration at a sampling rate of 0.02 and with 1000 observations.

largest Lyapunov exponents of the simulated data are 0.0086, 0.001, -0.0395 and -0.0505. In the estimation of this map 16 hidden units and 2000 observations are used in a single hidden layer feedforward network. The four largest estimated Lyapunov exponents of this map are 0.0091, 0.002, -0.0403 and -0.0514. The fit and its comparison to the actual simulated data are given in figs. 21–28. The mean square errors are

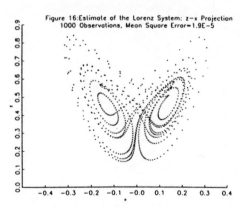

Fig. 16. The estimate of the z–x projection of the Lorenz system by a single hidden layer feedforward network with 12 hidden units and 1000 observations.

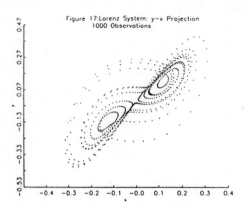

Fig. 17. The $y-x$ projection of the Lorenz system by fourth order Runge–Kutta integration at a sampling rate of 0.02 and with 1000 observations.

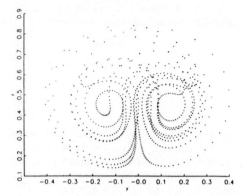

Fig. 19. The $z-y$ projection of the Lorenz system by fourth order Runge–Kutta integration at a sampling rate of 0.02 and with 1000 observations.

less than 10^{-3} and the quality of the fit is satisfactory.

5.1. Deterministic chaotic data

We chose initial conditions 0.3 for the Logistic map; $(0.1, 0.0)$ for the Hénon map; $(0.0, 1.1, 0.0)$ for the Lorenz map and 0.1 for the first 17 lags of the Mackey–Glass delay equation. These

initial conditions are then iterated forward in time. For all maps, the first 200 observations are discarded to avoid transients. The number of observations used in the estimations were: 100 observations of x_t from the Logistic map; 200 observations of x_t from the Hénon map; 1000 observations of x_t from the Lorenz map; and 2000 observations of x_t from the Mackey–Glass equation. The Lorenz map was numerically in-

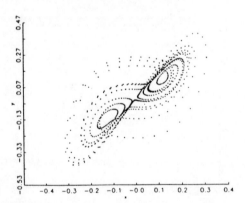

Fig. 18. The estimate of the $y-x$ projection of the Lorenz system by a single hidden layer feedforward network with 12 hidden units and 1000 observations.

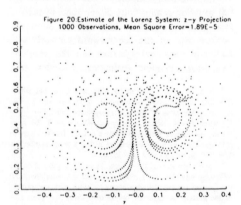

Fig. 20. The estimate of the $z-y$ projection of the Lorenz system by a single hidden layer feedforward network with 12 hidden units and 1000 observations.

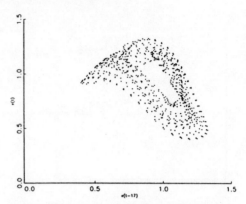

Fig. 21. A discrete variant of the Mackey–Glass delay equation with 2000 observations.

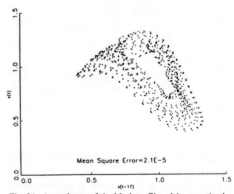

Fig. 23. A discrete variant of the Mackey–Glass delay equation with 2000 observations.

tegrated forward in time by using a fourth-order Runge–Kutta integration at a sampling rate of 0.02.

In table 1 we have summarized the estimates for the Lyapunov exponents of the Logistic and Hénon maps and the Lorenz system together with their comparisons with the algorithms of [1,13]. In table 1, *m* refers to the embedding dimension. Our estimates are denoted by DG and the estimates in [1] and [13] are denoted by

WSSV and BBA, respectively. Two points worth noting are that for embedding dimension of 2–4 the DG estimates of the first two Lyapunov exponents of the Hénon map are quite stable at approximately their true values. The spurious Lyapunov exponents at embedding dimensions 3 and 4 are quite unstable. On larger data sets, these spurious exponents converge to $-\infty$ and are more easily identified. We also capture the Lyapunov exponents of the Lorenz map quite

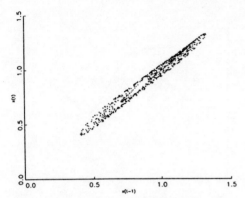

Mean Square Error = 2.1E–5

Fig. 22. An estimate of the Mackey–Glass delay equation by a single hidden layer feedforward network with 16 hidden units and 2000 observations.

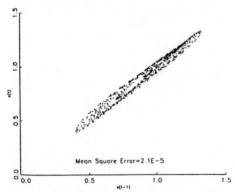

Mean Square Error = 2.1E–5

Fig. 24. An estimate of the Mackey–Glass delay equation by a single hidden layer feedforward network with 16 hidden units and 2000 observations.

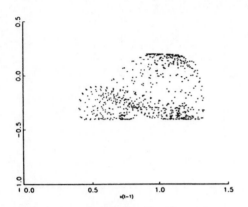

Fig. 25. Derivative of the Mackey–Glass delay equation with respect to $x(t-17)$ and with 2000 observations.

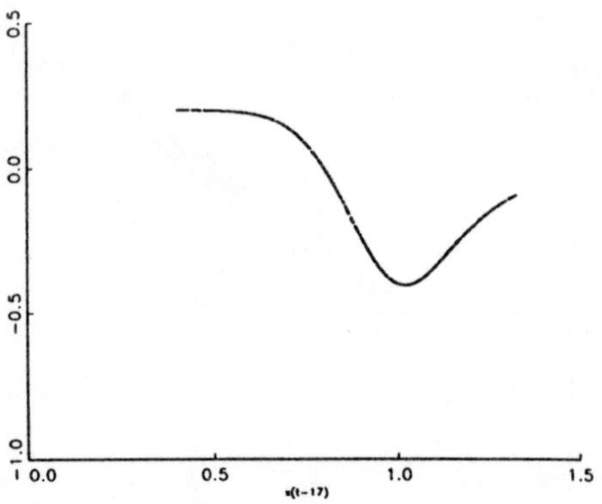

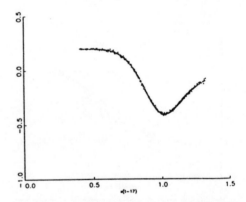

Fig. 27. Derivative of the Mackey–Glass delay equation with respect to $x(t-17)$ and with 2000 observations.

accurately with 1000 observations. For larger data sets the spurious Lyapunov exponent at $m = 4$ converges to $-\infty$. The major advantage of our algorithm is that the n Lyapunov exponents of an n-dimensional system can be calculated quite accurately with relatively small data sets. To compare the performance of our algorithm with the other algorithms, we calculated the

percentage error of the estimates by

$$pe = \left| \frac{\Sigma_{j=1}^{m} |\hat{\lambda}_j| - \Sigma_{j=1}^{m} |\lambda_j|}{\Sigma_{j=1}^{m} |\lambda_j|} \right| \times 100 . \tag{30}$$

It is worth comparing our results with the BBA algorithm results. Their method is to use a truncated Taylor series in estimating the

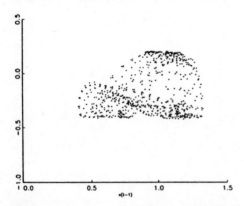

Fig. 26. Estimate of the derivative of the Mackey–Glass delay equation with respect to $x(t-17)$ by a single layer feedforward network with 16 hidden units and 2000 observations.

Fig. 28. Estimate of the derivative of the Mackey–Glass delay equation with respect to $x(t-17)$ by a single layer feedforward network with 16 hidden units and 2000 observations.

Table 1
Lyapunov exponent estimates. The BBA Algorithm estimates are obtained from [13, pp. 2790, 2799 and p. 2800]. The WSSV Algorithm estimates are obtained from [1, p.289]. The Lyapunov exponent of the Logistic map from the simulated data is 0.673.

	Logistic map	Hénon map				Lorenz system			
	DG	DG	BBA	WSSV	True	DG	BBA	WSSV	True
Number of observations	100	200	11 000	128		1000	50 000	8192	
$m = 1$	0.674								
$m = 2$	0.696	0.405	0.445	0.408					
	−5.607	−1.625	−1.609	−2.240	−1.620				
$m = 3$	0.693	0.440	0.441			1.510	1.517	2.16	1.51
	−3.623	−1.628	−0.893			0.7×10^{-4}	−0.008	0.00	0.00
	−5.785	−3.797	−1.654			−22.57	−23.09	−32.4	−22.5
$m = 4$	0.675	0.440	0.442			1.524	1.538		
	−1.902	−1.646	−0.307			0.003	−0.070		
	−2.411	−2.705	−0.804			−23.89	−22.15		
	−4.373	−2.997	−1.625			−156.9	−108.2		

dynamics[*13]. Since the Hénon map is in fact a polynomial of degree two, their methods should have a strong advantage in this case. However, they reported that when they used a quadratic polynomial in two variables, the estimated Lyapunov exponents were

$$\lambda_1 = 0.44707 , \quad \lambda_2 = -1.5096 . \quad (31)$$

These estimates were based on 11 000 observations. The percentage error of these estimates is 3.52%, compared with the percentage error of our estimates 0.0986% (which is based on only 200 observations). The percentage error of the estimated Lyapunov exponent from the WSSV algorithm is 40.2%. For the Lorenz attractor, the percentage error from our algorithm is 0.29%, the BBA algorithm's percentage error is 0.45% and the percentage error from the WSSV algorithm is 43.9%. We also calculated the Lyapunov exponents of a variant of the Mackey–Glass delay equation (29). The four largest estimated Lyapunov exponents of this map are

[*13] In [5] a Jacobian technique is used to estimate the largest Lyapunov exponent by various nonparametric estimation techniques including single hidden layer feedforward networks.

0.0091, 0.002, −0.0403 and −0.0514. The four largest Lyapunov exponents of the simulated data are 0.0086, 0.001, −0.0395 and −0.0505. The percentage error from these estimates is 3.2%.

5.2. Noisy chaotic data

An important issue is the robustness of these estimates to both measurement noise and to system noise. Table 2 summarizes a Monte Carlo simulation study with the Hénon map in the presence of two types of noise.

Table 2
Hénon map with noise. Number of observations: 200.

Type of noise	%	λ_1	λ_2
Measurement noise	0.01	0.3899	−1.7251
		(0.0573)	(0.6114)
	0.05	0.3612	−1.7961
		(0.0633)	(0.6114)
	0.10	0.3591	−2.2514
		(0.0909)	(0.5369)
System noise	0.005	0.3398	−1.8109
		(0.0879)	(0.6869)
	0.007	0.2937	−2.1902
		(0.0925)	(0.7522)

For measurement noise we use the system equation (25) along with the observation equation

$$z_t = x_t + \sigma\epsilon_t, \qquad (32)$$

where $\{\epsilon_t\}$ is an independent and identically distributed normal random variable with zero mean and standard deviation σ_ϵ. If σ_x is the standard deviation of the system data, then the signal-to-noise ratio in the data $\{z_t\}$ is

$$\frac{\sigma_x}{\sigma\sigma_\epsilon}. \qquad (33)$$

The estimated Lyapunov exponents are given in terms of the reciprocal of the signal-to-noise ratio.

For system noise we used the system model

$$x_{t+1} = f(x_t) + \sigma\epsilon_t, \quad y_{t+1} = x_t \qquad (34)$$

and again the results are reported in terms of the reciprocal of the signal-to-noise ratio. The maximum value of 0.007 for the system noise is due to the fact that for any larger value of the noise term the system gets knocked out of the basin of attraction and diverges. Each entry in table 2 is an average of 100 simulations and the numbers in parentheses are the standard deviations. The existence of noise can have two effects on the estimates of the Lyapunov exponents. First, the noise itself reduces the extent to which the deterministic relationship can be uncovered. Secondly, as pointed out in [17] the QR algorithm may deteriorate due to noise. With both types of noise, the distortion introduced to the Lyapunov exponents is rather minimal keeping in mind that the 0.007 level of system noise is the upper limit which can be imposed on the data. The estimates are also quite stable as it can be detected from the estimated standard deviations.

5.3. Detection of spurious Lyapunov exponents

Another important issue is the performance of

the algorithm in embedding dimensions higher than the dimensionality of the dynamical system under study. The Takens embedding theorem gives sufficient conditions for the minimum embedding dimension which recreates the local dynamics of the underlying attractor. However, this theorem does not tell us what would be the contribution of the embedding dimensions which are sufficiently large relative to the dimensionality of the attractor. Ideally, the algorithm should assign a zero derivative vector to a vector which does not explain the attractor. Therefore, in embedding dimensions which are large relative to the dimension of the attractor, it is expected that the Lyapunov exponents of these additional dimensions are minus infinity. With the sample size studied here, the derivative estimates of these additional dimensions are approximately 10^{-3}. With this level of accuracy the QR algorithm calculates spurious Lyapunov exponents values which are negative but far larger than minus infinity. As the sample size gets larger, the values of these spurious Lyapunov exponents get smaller negative numbers. Therefore, for a given sample size one method of detecting spurious Lyapunov exponents is to observe whether the true Lyapunov exponents are invariant in their magnitude as the embedding dimension is increased. This situation is clearly demonstrated in table 1 both in the Hénon map as well as Lorenz system Lyapunov exponents estimates.

6. Conclusion

An algorithm of estimating Lyapunov exponents of an unknown dynamical system is designed. The algorithm estimates all Lyapunov exponents of an unknown system accurately. This is due to the property that the largest Lyapunov exponents of the constructed diffeomorphism are the Lyapunov exponents of the unknown system under study. We focused our attention on deterministic as well as noisy system estimation. The performance of the algorithm is very satisfactory in the presence of noise as well as with limited number of observations. The satisfactory performance of the algorithm with limited number of observations raises the question that when this type of performance might fail. With the types of examples we studied here, the number of observations were long enough to travel the entire attractor. Therefore, we have sufficient information to calculate the Lyapunov exponents. For some dynamical systems, it might take a much larger number of data points to travel the entire attractor and 1000 observations may characterize only a portion of the attractor. In those cases, it is better to use the largest number of observations available.

References

[1] A. Wolf, B. Swift, J. Swinney and J. Vastano, Determining Lyapunov exponents from a time series, Physica D 16 (1985) 285–317.
[2] J. Kurths and H. Herzel, An Attractor in a Solar Time Series, Physica D 25 (1987), 165–172.
[3] W.D. Dechert and R. Gencay, Estimating Lyapunov exponents with multilayer feedforward network learning, Department of Economics, University of Houston (1990).
[4] K. Hornik, M. Stinchcombe and H. White, Universal approximation of an unknown mapping and its derivatives using multilayer feedforward networks, Neural Networks 3 (1990) 535–549.
[5] D. McCaffrey, S. Ellner, A.R. Gallant and D. Nychka, Estimating Lyapunov exponents with nonparametric regression, North Carolina University, Institute of Statistics Mimeo Series No: 1977R (1990).
[6] V.I. Oseledec, A multiplicative ergodic theorem. Liapunov characteristic numbers for a dynamical system, Trans. Moscow Math. Soc. 19 (1968), 197–221.
[7] M.S. Raghunathan, A proof of Oseledec's multiplicative ergodic theorem, Israel J. Math. 32 (1979) 356–362.
[8] D. Ruelle, Ergodic theory of differentiable dynamical systems, Publ. Math. IHES 50 (1979) 27–58.
[9] J.E. Cohen, J. Kesten and C.M. Newman, eds. Random matrices and their application, Contemporary Mathematics, Vol. 50 (American Mathematical Society, Providence, RI, 1986).
[10] J. Guckenheimer and P. Holmes, Nonlinear Oscillations, Dynamical Systems and Bifurcations of Vector Fields (Springer, Berlin, 1983).
[11] J.P. Eckmann and D. Ruelle, Ergodic theory of strange attractors, Rev. Mod. Phys. 57 (1985) 617–656.
[12] F. Takens, Detecting strange attractors in turbulence, in: Dynamical Systems and Turbulence (Warwick, 1980), eds. D. Rand and I. Young (Springer, Berlin, 1981) pp. 366–381.
[13] R. Brown, P. Bryant and H.D.I. Abarbanel, Computing the Lyapunov spectrum of a Dynamical system from an observed time series, Phys. Rev A 43 (1991) 2787–2806.
[14] H.D.I. Abarbanel, R. Brown and M.B. Kennel, Lyapunov Exponents in Chaotic Systems: Their Importance and Their Evaluation using Observed Data, Institute for Nonlinear Science, University of California, San Diego, 1991.
[15] A.R. Gallant and H. White, On learning the derivatives of an unknown mapping with multilayer feedforward networks, Neural Networks 5 (1992) 129–138.
[16] W.H. Press, B.P. Flannery, S.A. Teukolsky and W.T. Vetterling, Numerical Recipes, The Art of Scientific Computing (Cambridge U.P., Cambridge, 1986).
[17] S. Ellner, A.R. Gallant, D. McCaffrey and D. Nychka, Convergence rates and data requirements for Jacobian-based estimates of Lyapunov exponents from data, Phys. Lett. A 153 (1991) 357–363.

[10]

Journal of Economic Behavior and Organization 22 (1993) 209–237. North-Holland

A new test for chaos

Claire G. Gilmore*

St. Joseph's University, Philadelphia, PA 19131, USA

Received November 1990, final version received February 1992

Whether certain financial and economic time series are better described by linear stochastic models or are appropriately characterized by deterministic chaos is an issue of great current interest. Empirical research to detect the presence of chaos in such time series has been hampered by lack of an adequate test for chaotic behavior in small, noisy data sets. This paper presents a new, topological test for chaos, demonstrates its advantages over current testing methodology, and compares the results with earlier analyses based on metric tests of economic and financial series. A short-term forecasting approach for chaotic processes is also described.

1. Introduction

Recent work on nonlinear dynamics, particularly chaotic systems, in the natural sciences has provoked interest in the potential applicability of the theory of chaos to other fields. While the persistent irregularity of such variables as GNP, employment, interest rates, and exchange rates has generally been attributed to random shocks, the ability of even simple deterministic chaotic models to produce complex time paths that appear to be random has attracted attention as a possible alternative explanation. Several useful introductory discussions are now available in the literature, including Baumol and Benhabib (1989). Theoretical applications have been made in such areas as growth models [Stutzer (1980), Day (1982, 1983)], rational decisionmaking [Benhabib and Day (1981)], business cycles [Grandmont (1985), H.-W. Lorenz (1987b)], international trade [H.W. Lorenz (1987a)], and stock returns [Shaffer (1990)].

Empirical research on detection of chaotic behavior has expanded rapidly, but the results have tended to be inconclusive, due to lack of appropriate

Correspondence to: Claire G. Gilmore, St. Joseph's University, Philadelphia, PA 19131, USA.
*The author would like to thank G.B. Mindlin and X.-J. Hou for useful discussions about new topological methods, Professor James B. Ramsey for insights on nonlinear modeling, as well as the editor and anonymous referees for helpful suggestions on earlier versions of this manuscript. This work was begun at Drexel University, as part of the author's doctoral research, under the direction of Professor Thomas C. Chiang.

testing methods. Standard techniques, such as spectral analysis or the autocorrelation function, cannot distinguish whether a time series was generated by a deterministic or a stochastic mechanism [Sakai and Tokumaru (1980)]. The correlation dimension test, a metric approach developed by Grassberger and Procaccia (1983a, b), has been widely used in the natural sciences, generally in conjunction with related procedures such as the calculation of Lyapunov exponents. Application of these tests to relatively small, noisy data sets, which are common in economics and finance, is of dubious validity, and the reliability of the methodology has also come into question, even in the natural sciences, where large, fairly clean data sets are often available [Mindlin et al. (1990)]. Possible evidence of chaotic behavior has been produced by the metric approach for U.S. business cycle data [Brock and Sayers (1988)], work stoppage data [Sayers (1986, 1987)], weekly stock returns [Scheinkman and LeBaron (1986, 1989)], Treasury bill returns [Brock and Malliaris (1989)], gold and silver returns [Frank and Stengos (1989)], and several demand Divisia monetary aggregates [Barnett and Chen (1988)]. Frank and Stengos (1988) found no chaotic behavior in the Canadian counterparts of U.S. business cycle data, nor was there any indication of chaos in the GNP series for Italy, Japan, the U.K., or West Germany [Frank, Gençay and Stengos (1988)]. The Scheinkman and LeBaron (1989), Sayers (1987) and Barnett and Chen (1988) work was reexamined by Ramsey, Sayers and Rothman (1990), who applied a procedure by Ramsey and Yuan (1989, 1990) to reduce the small sample size bias in dimension calculations. They concluded that there was no evidence of chaos in any of these series, except possibly in the work stoppage data.

Recently, a promising new approach to testing for low-dimensional deterministic chaos, based on the topological properties of chaotic processes, has been developed in the physics literature [Mindlin et al. (1990), Tufillaro et al. (1990), Mindlin et al. (1991)]. This method includes a 'close returns' test for detecting chaos which is of particular interest for researchers in fields such as finance and economics, since it works well on relatively small, noisy data sets. Further, the topological approach is potentially far more useful than metric methods since it is capable of providing additional information about the underlying system generating chaotic behavior, once evidence of chaos is detected. The present study will demonstrate this new method, using a data set generated from a chaotic model, and will then adapt it to test for the presence of deterministic chaos in selected financial and economic time series data, comparing the results to those reported in earlier studies.

The metric and the topological approaches to testing for chaotic behavior will be explained and compared in section 2. In section 3 the close returns method is applied to chaotic data; a forecasting technique suggested by this test is also discussed. Results of the close returns test on economic and financial time series data are given in section 4. Conclusions are presented in section 5.

2. Metric and topological methodologies

At present there are two broad approaches to the analysis of data generated by a process exhibiting chaos: the metric and the topological. The metric approach is characterized by the study of distances between points on a strange attractor. The topological approach is characterized by the study of the organization of the strange attractor. A strange attractor is the set of points toward which a chaotic dynamical path will converge.[1]

The description of many systems is facilitated by the use of a phase space. Here the state of a system is described by a point $y = (y_1, y_2, \ldots, y_n)$, and R^n is some n-dimensional phase space. The point describing the system, $y_t = (y_{1t}, y_{2t}, \ldots, y_{nt})$, evolves with time. If the system is in a steady state, the point y_t does not move. If the system behaves cyclically, the orbit y_t is closed and periodic. If the system is governed by a set of nonlinear ordinary differential equations and the behavior is bounded but neither static nor periodic, then this deterministic nonperiodic behavior may be chaotic. The phase space trajectory which describes the behavior of the system lies on a strange attractor.

Two mechanisms are responsible for the existence of a strange attractor. These are 'stretching' and 'compressing'. The first mechanism, stretching, is responsible for 'sensitive dependence on initial conditions'. This means that two nearby points in phase space, representing slightly different initial states of the system, will evolve along divergent trajectories and exhibit dramatically different states of the system after some finite time. This mechanism is responsible for the long-term unpredictability generally attributed to systems exhibiting chaos. The second mechanism, compressing, is reponsible for the recurrent behavior exhibited by all chaotic (as opposed to stochastic) systems. If initial conditions were to be stretched apart indefinitely, the trajectories would not be confined to a bounded region of phase space. To ensure that trajectories do not run off to infinity, the flow must somehow be returned to a bounded region of phase space. The compressing mechanism is responsible for patterns which almost repeat themselves throughout a chaotic data set. This mechanism is at the heart of both the metric and the topological approaches to the analysis of chaotic data sets.

Typically, time series data for a *single* variable are available for the analysis of some process. The metric and the topological methods each depend on the recurrent nature of the time series flow to test for the existence of a strange attractor. However, they differ on how the time series data are prepared for analysis.

2.1. Metric method

In the metric approach the time series data $\{x_i\}$, where $i = (1, 2, \ldots, N)$, are

---

[1] For a discussion of strange attractors see Brock (1986).

first used to construct a series of m-tuples, $\{x_i^m\} = \{x_i, x_{i+1\tau}, x_{i+(m-1)\tau}\}$, where τ is a time-delay parameter. Each m-tuple represents a point in an m-dimensional Euclidean space. This mapping of a time series into an m-dimensional space, $\{x_i\} \rightarrow \{x_i^m\}$, is called an ($m$-dimensional) *embedding* of the data. The embedding is done for successively larger values of m. For each embedding dimension a series of calculations is carried out to estimate the recurrence properties of the trajectory. The idea is as follows. If the motion occurs on a strange attractor, then the trajectory will return to the ε-neighborhood of any point after some time. The smaller the neighborhood, the longer the time.

The correlation between points is computed by use of the correlation integral

$$C_m(\varepsilon) = \{ \# (i, j): \|x_i^m - x_j^m\| < \varepsilon \}/N_m^2, |i-j| > 1, \tag{1}$$

where x_i^m and x_j^m are the ith and jth m-tuples, respectively, N is the sample size, $N_m = N - (m-1)\tau$ is the number of m-tuples that can be produced from the sample, and ε measures the size of the sphere around each point. Theoretically, N should be infinite. The correlation integral is then used to compute metric properties such as the correlation dimension [Grassberger and Procaccia (1983a, b)]. The correlation dimension is defined as

$$D_m = \lim_{N \rightarrow \infty} \lim_{\varepsilon \rightarrow 0} \ln C_m(\varepsilon)/\ln \varepsilon. \tag{2}$$

The limit as the embedding dimension goes to infinity gives the correlation dimension of the strange attractor:

$$D = \lim_{m \rightarrow \infty} D_m. \tag{3}$$

Correlation dimension is estimated by a linear regression of $\ln C_m(\varepsilon)$ on $\ln(\varepsilon)$ over an appropriate subinterval of the range of ε. Variations of this counting procedure are used to compute other metric properties, such as the Lyapunov exponent, which measures the rate at which two nearby trajectories converge or diverge.[2] For detailed discussions of metric methods see Cvitanovic (1984). The reliability of these metric computations as a means of detecting low-dimensional chaos has been called into question, as there are a number of problems associated with its implementation:

1. The estimate of the correlation dimension converges to the dimension of the chaotic attractor as N, the number of observations, goes to infinity. With

[2] For a mathematical definition see Brock (1986).

small data sets the number of observations may be insufficient for convergence to occur;[3]

2. Noise in the time series may render dimension calculations useless [Brock (1986)];

3. Estimation of the scaling region, ε, to be used in the calculation requires the exercise of judgment and is subjective [Brock (1986)];

4. Lack of formal statistical distribution theory for the correlation dimension has made clearcut conclusions difficult, although see the recent advances by Brock and Baek (1991);

5. There is substantial bias in dimension correlations with small data sets [Ramsay and Yuan (1989, 1990)];

6. Dimension calculations provide little information on how to 'model the dynamics' of the underlying system [Gunaratne et al. (1989)]. The procedure throws away time-ordering information, so even a positive result, indicating chaos, cannot possibly lead to information about the dynamics of the process responsible for generating chaotic behavior;

7. The procedure must be implemented carefully to capture only geometric correlation in the time series and eliminate dynamic correlation [Grassberger (1990)]. Dynamic correlation contributes to the count simply because of the fact that in a smooth flow two points, x_i^m and x_{i+1}^m, which are nearby in time, will be nearby in phase space. For geometric correlation, the m-vectors x_i and x_j, where $|i-j|$ is large, can be nearby due to the recurrent nature of the flow, which the compressing mechanism causes; the counting procedure attempts to measure this proximity to capture some properties of the strange attractor. Therefore, the sum in eq. (1) must be restricted by the condition $|i-j| > fT$, where T is some characteristic period of the data, measured in terms of the sample rate, and f is some fraction of 1 (e.g., $f = 1/4$), the larger the better [Grassberger (1990)]. This is a different issue from determination of the delay parameter τ. Failure to implement this precaution has rendered many previously reported dimension calculations 'obsolete' [Grassberger (1990)].

2.2. Topological method

The topological approach analyzes the way in which the mechanisms responsible for stretching and compressing the strange attractor act on the unstable periodic orbits, intertwining them in a very specific way. Mingled with the strange attractor are periodic orbits which are unstable. Each attractor contains a large number of unstable orbits of many periodicities; they are 'dense'. For example, a time series moving in phase space around an

---

[3]There is a limited range of ε over which $C_m(\varepsilon)$ goes from 0 to 1. In this range the curve of $C_m(\varepsilon)$ is not likely to have a well-defined linear segment from which a slope could be estimated when the data set is small. See Caputo (1989).

unstable period-1 orbit will return close to its original starting point, x_i, after cycling once through phase space; for a period-2 orbit it cycles twice through phase space before returning close to x_i, and so forth for higher-period orbits.

The first stage in the topological analysis is the close returns test, which searches for the unstable periodic orbits embedded in a strange attractor. It is a qualitative method that detects whether a time series exhibits chaotic behavior by searching for evidence of the unstable periodic orbits embedded in a chaotic system's strange attractor. This test is explained below.[4] Once a positive finding of chaos is made in a time series, the topological method enables the researcher to proceed to characterize the underlying process in a quantitative way. This is possible because the topological method preserves the time ordering of the data, which the metric method does not. The mathematical description of the way these periodic orbits are linked allows one to reconstruct completely the stretching and compressing mechanisms reponsible for generating the strange attractor.[5] This process is not (yet) capable of indentifying the equation system which has generated the time series. However, it does make possible the rejection of models which are proposed as the source of an observed time series if they are incompatible with the computed reconstruction of the strange attractor for that series. The mathematical procedures involved in reconstruction of the strange attractor are beyond the scope of this paper; the reader is referred to Mindlin et al. (1990) for a detailed theoretical discussion and to Mindlin et al. (1991) for

---

[4]The close returns method, although independently developed, is similar in spirit to the recurrence plots published somewhat earlier by Eckmann, Kamphorst and Ruelle (1987). In contrast to metric tests both the recurrence plots and the close returns plots make use of time-ordering information. The recurrence plots are constructed from a d-dimensional embedding of the time series data and a coding procedure to identity near neighbors of plotted points which uses a sphere of variable radius. The close returns method uses the scalar time series (although an embedding can also be used), specifies a fixed ε value for measuring close returns, and is organized in a more easily readable horizontal form rather than the diagonal orientation of the recurrence plots. As constructed, the recurrence plots were used to measure the 'time consistency' [Eckmann, Kamphorst and Ruelle (1987)] of a dynamical system. The authors also observed the prevalence of short straight-line segments in their plots using chaotic data and correctly pointed out that these would not occur in a random data set. However, the implications of this observation were not further developed. The close returns method uses the plot initially as a means to distinguish chaotic from other types of time series behavior. If chaotic behavior is identified, the next steps in the close returns method involve a mathematical reconstruction of the strange attractor.

[5]Unlike the correlation dimension calculation, the topological method does not determine the strange attractor's dimension. Metric properties, such as correlation dimension and Lyapunov exponents, are independent of coordinate system but depend on control parameter values. That is, a small change in parameter values can produce large changes in the correlation dimension and Lyapunov exponent. The topological method aims to compute the structure of the strange attractor, for example, to distinguish the Roessler from the Lorenz attractor. This quantitative classification is independent of both coordinate system changes *and* changes in control parameter values.

the first successful application to experimental data, in which the underlying dynamic mechanism was reconstructed.[6]

The starting point for implementing the topological algorithm is the time series $\{x_i\}$ without an embedding. If one of the observations x_i occurs near a periodic orbit, then subsequent observations will evolve near that orbit for a while before being repelled away from it. If the observations evolve near the periodic orbit for a sufficiently long time, they will return to the neighborhood of x_i after some interval, T, where T indicates the length of the orbit, measured in units of the sampling rate (e.g., if the data cycles every 30 days and sampling is daily, then the length of the orbit is 30). This means that $|x_i - x_{i+T}|$ will be small. Further, x_{i+1} will be near x_{i+1+T}, x_{i+2} will be near x_{i+2+T}, and so on. Thus, it makes sense to look for a series of consecutive data elements for which $|x_i - x_{i+T}|$ is small.[7]

To detect these regions of 'close returns' in a data set a color-coded graph can be constructed. All differences $|x_i - x_{i+t}|$ are computed. If a difference is less than ε, it is coded black; if larger than ε, it is coded white. The horizontal axis of the graph indicates the observation number, i, where $i = (1, 2, \ldots, N)$, and the vertical axis is designated as t, where $t = (1, 2, \ldots, N - i)$. Close returns in the data set are indicated by horizontal line segments. For example, for a horizontal segment between i_a and i_b the beginning of the segment, observation x_{ia}, indicates where the chaotic time series begins to follow an unstable periodic orbit; the final observation in the segment is x_{ib+T}, where T is the length of the orbit in terms of the sampling rate. If the data set is chaotic, a number of horizontal line segments will be seen in this plot. However, if the data set is stochastic, a generally uniform array of black dots will appear. A periodic signal can be identified by solid black lines running horizontally across the entire graph at intervals determined by the period measured in units of the sampling time. A quasi-periodic orbit (consisting of two frequencies) produces a pattern resembling a contour map.

The determination of the appropriate size for ε for a given data set can be accomplished as follows. First, compute the maximum difference between any two observations in the set. Next, set ε at some small fraction of that difference, e.g., between 0.01 and 0.1, and construct the close returns plot. If ε is set too small, there will be an insufficient number of black points to identify a pattern that characterizes the data; as ε is reduced below the standard deviation of additive noise, the pattern degrades gracefully. If ε is too large, the pattern will be hidden. Once an appropriate range for ε is

---

[6]See, in particular, eq. (12) in Mindlin et al. (1991) and fig. 1 in Mindlin (1990).

[7]Comparing observations separated by a fixed time interval t, $(|x_i - x_{i+t}|)$, is reminiscent of the standard autocorrelation function. However, the autocorrelation is an average over the entire sample and is not designed to identify specific, highly correlated segments of data within the sample. The close returns test is specifically constructed to do this.

identified, there will be a sufficient array of points to allow determination of the type of pattern generated by the data. The level of ε can be varied within that range without altering the qualitative nature of the pattern. The exact specification of ε is *not* critical to the interpretation of the behavior of the data. Examples of these plots, together with descriptions of the data sets used in their construction, are given in section 3.

The topological method of identifying and analyzing low-dimensional chaos has several important advantages over the metric approach:

1. The topological method is applicable to relatively small data sets, such as are typical in economics and finance;

2. It is robust against noise;

3. Since the topological analysis maintains the time-ordering of the data, it is able to provide additional information about the underlying system generating chaotic behavior;

4. Falsifiability is possible, as verification can be made of the reconstruction of the strange attractor [Mindlin et al. (1991)].

The ability of the close returns test to detect low-dimensional chaos in relatively small, noisy data sets will be demonstrated in the next section. Quantitative reconstruction of a chaotic strange attractor and the method of verification are discussed in Mindlin et al. (1990, 1991).

3. Applications to simulated chaotic time series

3.1. Data

A simulated discrete time series data set generated by the Roessler model [Roessler (1976)] is used to demonstrate the close returns test. This model is a system composed of three ordinary differential equations:

$$dx/dt = -y - z,$$

$$dy/dt = x + ay, \tag{4}$$

$$dz/dt = b + z(x - c).$$

The equations of the model were integrated for 500 seconds and the results recorded at equal time intervals (0.1 second), giving a length of 5,000 for the data set. The parameter values used for the Roessler equations are: $a = 0.448$, $b = 2.0$, $c = 4.0$.

3.2. Procedure

Fig. 1 presents a plot of a 1,000 (horizontal) × 960 (vertical)-observation section of the complete graph of the 5,000-point Roessler time series. The

i

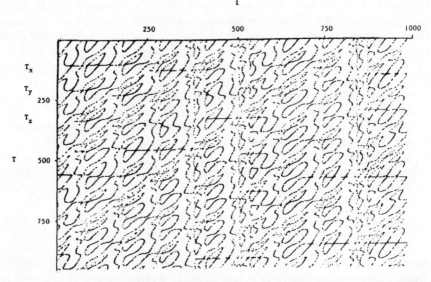

Fig. 1. Close returns plot of chaotic time series, generated from Roessler model. If difference $|x_i - x_{i+T}|$ is less than ε, the difference is coded black, otherwise white. Horizontal line segments indicate presence of unstable periodic orbits.

evidence of chaotic behavior in the data is revealed by the series of nearly horizontal line segments of close returns, which indicate the presence of unstable periodic orbits. The continuous horizontal line at the top of the graph represents $|x_i - x_{i+0}| = 0$. The pattern of the plot may be interpreted as follows. The horizontal segment in the upper left area, at T_x on the vertical axis, locates the first and second cycles of the time series trajectory around an unstable periodic orbit, probably a period-1 orbit. The first cycle consists of the i_a through i_b observations and the second of the i_{a+T} through i_{b+T} observations. The next horizontal segment below it, at T_y, identifies the third cycle of the trajectory around that unstable orbit. Traces of subsequent cycles around this orbit will gradually disappear, due to the fact that the trajectory is being 'repelled' further and further away from the unstable period orbit. Near the center of the graph, at T_z on the vertical axis, the horizontal segment likely indicates the initial cycles around an unstable period-2 or period-3 orbit. Explicit identification of each of these segments as belonging to a period-1, period-2, etc., orbit can easily be made by isolating and plotting each segment of close returns in phase space.

It should be noted that the evidence of chaotic behavior pervades the entire close returns plot of the Roessler series. Consequently, although this plot used the first 1960 (1,000 + 960) points from the 5,000-observation set, a much smaller subset would also reveal the chaotic pattern. Other chaotic

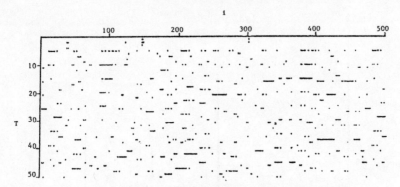

Fig. 2. Close returns plot for logistic map. The parameter $a = 3.75$.

systems will also generate a similar structure of horizontal lines in a close returns plot. For example, fig. 2 is a smaller, 500×50-observation plot from a time series produced from the logistic map, $x_{t+1} = ax_t(1 - x_t)$, with $a = 3.75$.

A useful device to summarize the occurrence of close returns in a data set is a histogram of the incidence of close returns 'hits', $H(t)$, summing at each value of t, with $H(t) = \Sigma\theta(\varepsilon - |x_i - x_{i+t}|)$, where θ is the Heaviside function. This can be done for the set of plotted observations but can also be computed across the entire data set. This is particularly convenient when the data set under study is too large to fit easily onto a single graph. Fig. 3 presents such a histogram for the full 5,000-observation Roessler set, over the first 300 values of t. For chaotic data the histogram will contain a series of sharp peaks, more or less evenly spaced.

To establish a benchmark for comparison a series of pseudorandom numbers, uniformly distributed on the interval 0 to 1, was constructed, and a $1,000 \times 960$ close returns plot was made. In contrast to the distinctive pattern produced by a chaotic time series this close returns plot, fig. 4, consists of a scattering of dots without discernible pattern where the difference $|x_i - x_{i+t}|$ is small. A histogram for a random time series will exhibit a scattering around a uniform distribution (see fig. 5).

It can be demonstrated that the close returns procedure is quite robust against noise. A subset of 2,000 points of the Roessler data set was used to illustrate this property of the close returns method. A second 2,000-observation data set of additive Gaussian noise was created and normalized to the Roessler series.[8] Increasing percentages of noise were then added to the Roessler subset. With a 15% addition of noise ($f = 0.15$) evidence of the

---

[8] A signal $S_i = R_i + f\sigma G(0, 1)$ was created, where R_i is the Roessler time series with standard deviation σ, G is a Gaussian independent and identically distributed random variable with zero mean and standard deviation $= 1$, and f is some fraction.

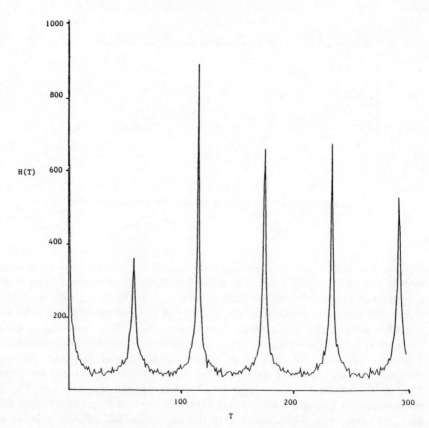

Fig. 3. Close returns histogram of Roessler chaotic series. $H(T)$ records the number of times the differential $|x_i - x_{i+T}|$ is less than the threshold ε.

unstable periodic orbits is still clearly visible (fig. 6). As the noise level is increased, the pattern becomes less distinct, and it is thoroughly obscured by a 100% addition of noise. However, even at high noise levels the chaotic signal may still be retrieved under this test by means of noise averaging. Using the chaotic data with a 200% addition of noise, each x_i value was plotted as an average of itself plus the next 9 points ($x_i = \sum_{j=0}^{9} x_{i+j}/10$). This procedure averages out some of the noise, but the chaotic behavior of the original time series is not lost, as it has a longer time scale. The differences $|x_i - x_{i+t}|$ were then replotted, and the chaotic signal reemerged (compare figs. 7a and b).

The ability of the close returns test to distinguish between a chaotic and a near unit root autoregressive process was also examined, as the dimension estimate procedure has been shown to have a poor ability to discriminate between the two [Brock and Sayers (1988)]. The near unit root process can

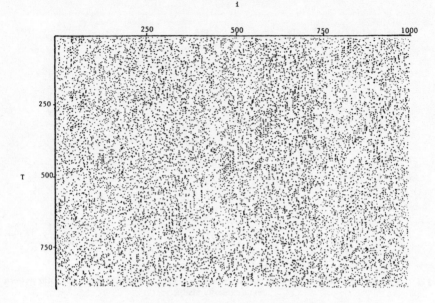

Fig. 4. Close returns plot of pseudorandom time series.

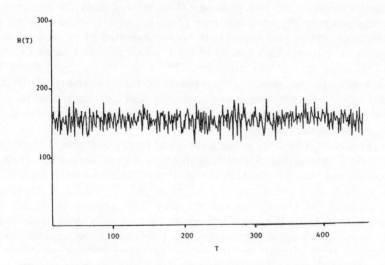

Fig. 5. Close returns histogram of a pseudo random data set. $H(T)$ records the number of times the difference $|x_i - x_{i+T}|$ is less than the threshold ε.

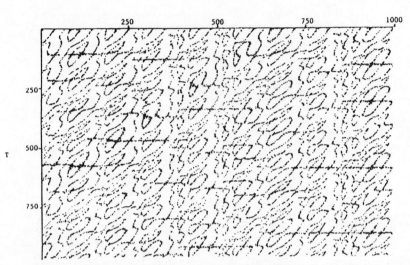

Fig. 6. Close returns plot of Roessler chaotic series with 15% addition of noise. Chaotic pattern remains easily visible.

confuse the dimension test because the number of near neighbors at any point can behave with a power law dependence on the box size, as is also the case with a chaotic process. To determine how well the close returns test can distinguish between the two processes close returns plots for a number of data sets generated by near-unit root processes were examined. In no case did the close returns plot resemble the plots generated by chaotic processes. There was a relatively high density of black points near and parallel to the x axis, indicating dynamical correlation. The results are not reproduced here but are available on request. The apparently superior ability of the close returns test to discriminate between chaotic and near-unit root processes probably arises from the fact that these plots maintain temporal correlation, while the metric test does not.

At the present time there is not a statistical theory of standard error bands for the close returns plot. Research in this area is in an early stage. It should be pointed out that the close returns plots are themselves only the first part of a multi-stage procedure whose objective is to produce a quantitative description of the chaotic strange attractor. This process yields falsifiable results; consequently, if a close returns plot erroneously indicates a chaotic time series, the chaotic explanation can ultimately be rejected in the subsequent steps. Given the results of the close returns plots for the economic and financial data tested in section 4, the quantitative steps, which are complex, are not developed here.

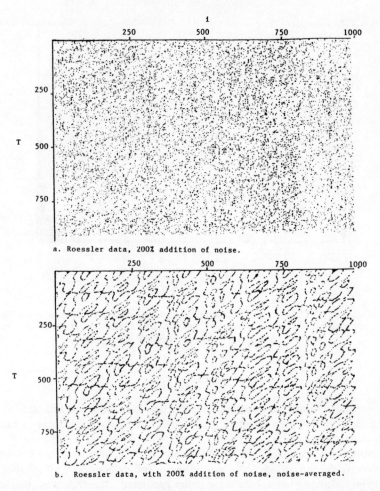

a. Roessler data, 200% addition of noise.

b. Roessler data, with 200% addition of noise, noise-averaged.

Fig. 7. In 7(a) chaotic signal is completely obscured by 200% addition of noise to Roessler series. Smoothing of data with 10-point moving average allows recovery of chaotic signal, 7(b).

3.3. Short-term forecasting

One potential benefit of the method of close returns is in applications to forecasting of financial and economic time series. There is order hidden in chaotic systems. Since chaotic systems are deterministic, they are in principle predictable, although the prediction degrades rapidly with the 'prediction horizon'. Good long-run forecasting is unlikely because of the divergence of nearby trajectories which characterizes chaos. However, the fact that nearby initial conditions evolve very similarly under a deterministic model for a short time before diverging may be used for short-term forecasting. Thus, it is potentially possible, for example, to forecast future sequences of daily

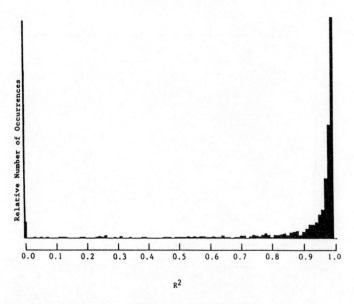

Fig. 8. Histogram of R^2 values for 2,000 short-term predictions for chaotic time series. The test segment is compared with previous segments, and the most similar previous segments are used in the prediction. Over 90% of the R^2 are in excess of 0.9.

financial data based on selected subsets of data that closely match the immediately preceding sequence, provided the underlying process is chaotic rather than random.

To apply this procedure on the 5,000-point set of data generated from the Roessler model an initial 20-point segment of x_i values was selected for which the following ten values were to be predicted. A search was then made across the entire series for closely matching sequences. All such sequences were identified and the next ten values following each set were extracted. A weighted average value was then calculated for each of the 10 x_i values to be predicted, using the corresponding values in each of the extracted sequences. The weighting procedure assigned different weights, depending on how closely the respective 20-point segments tracked the test segment. These averaged values then were used as the predicted values for the forecasting interval. This was done for 2,000 different 20-point sequences in the data set. R^2 statistics were computed for each prediction and were plotted on a histogram (fig. 8). It can be seen that the values of the R^2 statistics are very high, clustering above 0.90.

While this procedure is not valid for long-term forecasting, the short-term forecast can be updated as desired. The composition of the subsets of data used for prediction will then change as the projection path of the time series moves through different regions of the attractor.

4. Application to economic and financial data

Empirical studies, using the now-standard metric procedures of estimating correlation dimensions and Lyapunov exponents, have focused on two areas – the behavior of business cycles and of financial markets. The question of interest for business cycles is to determine whether they may be produced endogenously from the internal dynamics of the economic system. With respect to financial data the usual assumption is that in well-functioning markets changes in asset prices will be unpredictable. A chaotic explanation of asset price behavior would present significant theoretical implications.

Several economic series which have been tested for chaotic behavior using metric methods were selected for application of the topological approach. U.S. postwar macroeconomic data have been analyzed by Brock and Sayers (1988). Their series included the unemployment rate, employment, real GNP, gross private domestic investment, and industrial production. Man-days idle due to work stoppages, monthly for the period 1928 to 1981, published by the Bureau of Labor Statistics, were examined by Sayers (1986, 1987). Since financial series tend to be larger and more disaggregated than economic data, chaotic behavior, if it exists, may be easier to establish in these cases. Scheinkman and LeBaron (1989) used daily stock returns (including dividend) on the value-weighted portfolio of the Center for Research in Security Prices to construct a weekly returns series by simple compounding. Brock and Malliaris (1989) examined a Treasury bill series taken from Ibbotson and Sinquefield (1977). We have also included several series of daily exchange rates.

Brock and Sayers (1988) reported that correlation dimension estimates and calculation of Lyapunov exponents on their detrended series produced positive evidence of chaos in all cases. However, this evidence could not be accepted as conclusive since many economic time series are near unit root processes, and the ability of metric tests to distinguish between such processes and low-dimensional chaos is poor [Brock and Sayers (1988)]. Application of metric tests in such situations may give a misleading impression that the series is chaotic. Therefore, Brock and Sayers fit each series to a suitable $AR(q)$ model and ran the tests again on the residuals.[9] The rationale for the residual test is the argument that if a series is chaotic, the estimate of the correlation dimension will not be altered by the linear transformation. A unit root process, however, will yield dramatically different

[9]For a discussion of the residual test see Brock (1986); a critique of this test is in *Evolutionary Dynamics and Nonlinear Economics*, ed. Richard Day and Ping Chen, Oxford University Press, forthcoming.

results. The residual test rejected the null hypothesis of chaos for all the series. This was also not conclusive, however, since the residual test may reject the null hypothesis too often when it is true [Brock (1986)]. It proved impossible to reject the null hypothesis of linear *AR* processes for any of the macroeconomic series, but this result may have been driven by limitations in the tests applied and by the shortness of the series [Brock and Sayers (1988)]. Ramsey, Sayers and Rothman (1990) applied the Ramsey and Yuan (1989a, b) correction for small-sample-size bias in the correlation dimension estimate to work stoppage data studied by Sayers (1986, 1987). The conclusion was that there was a probability at least of a low dimension for the series, although there was no strong evidence of a strange attractor.

The results of close returns tests are presented in fig. 9a–e for the macroeconomic series. The U.S. unemployment rate data covers the period 1949:I–1982:I, producing 133 observations; employment is for 1950:I–1983:IV, for 136 observations; real gross national product and gross private domestic investment are for 1947:I–1985:I, 153 observations; and industrial production covers 1948:1–1983:12, giving 432 observations. All series are deseasonalized and are quarterly, except industrial production, which is monthly. All series were detrended as in the original research: linear detrending for all series except employment, to which a quadratic detrending was applied. The close returns plots have a triangular rather than a rectangular shape here since each of the series was small enough to fit completely onto one graph. In these and the later plots in this section an epsilon value in the range of 0.02 to 0.05 of the maximum difference $|x_i - x_{i+t}|$ was used.

In each case the plots did not produce the evidence for the presence of unstable periodic orbits which is characteristic of a strange attractor, that is, there is no pattern of horizontal lines. Thus, this test does not provide any support for the positive indications of chaos from the metric tests on the detrended data. The correlation dimension procedure was unable to distinguish between chaotic and near unit root processes, but the close returns test did so. The close returns test does support the negative findings that resulted from application of the metric tests to the residuals of linear models for each series.

Beyond showing a lack of chaotic behavior in the macroeconomic series, do the close returns plots provide any further information? This test has been developed specifically as a means to distinguish chaotic from a range of alternative types of behavior, both linear and nonlinear, deterministic and stochastic. Its ability to discriminate within this range of alternatives is a subject of further research, but some tentative comments may be made. The fluctuations of the various series around their trend, while not chaotic, are also clearly not random and are not strictly periodic. Each of the plots indicates the presence of some type of structure in the data. Areas within

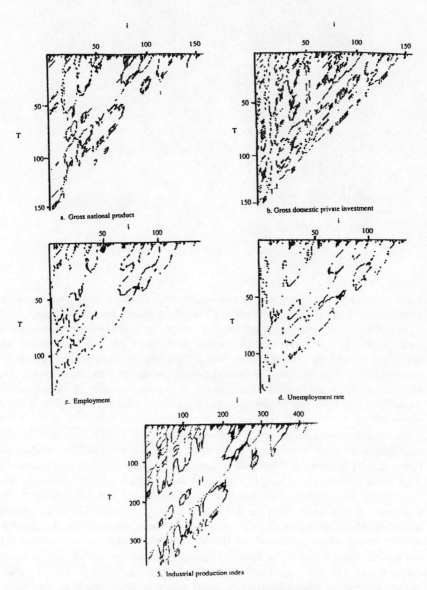

Fig. 9. Close returns plots of U.S. postwar macroeconomic series.

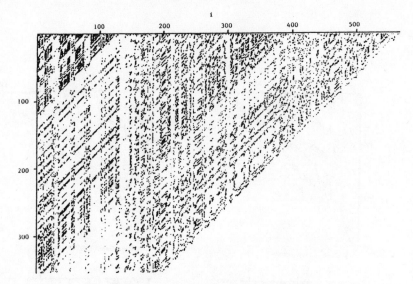

Fig. 10. Close returns plot of work stoppage data.

each plot exhibit connected curves (contour-like structure) that may be evidence of quasi-periodic behavior, of either a linear or a nonlinear origin. This possible alternative was explored by examining the Fourier spectrum of each series. For a quasi-periodic series composed of two frequencies the spectrum should be discrete with two strong peaks. If these peaks are not observed, the hypothesis of a quasi-periodic behavior can be rejected. The spectra for these series showed a pattern of a large number of strong peaks. Therefore, the null hypothesis that the data are quasi-periodic (two period) was rejected.

For the work stoppage series monthly data from 1935:1 through 1981:12, not deseasonalized, were used, producing 564 observations. The series was detrended by filtering out the low frequencies, using a fast Fourier transform. This close returns plot (fig. 10) also does not indicate chaotic behavior and thus does not sustain the tentative conclusion of Ramsey, Sayers and Rothman (1990) that there is some probability of an underlying chaotic attractor, although again there is structure evident in the series. In addition to the information contained in the close returns plot, the corresponding histogram may be able to reveal further information about the data set under study. The histogram for the work stoppage data (fig. 11) shows sharp peaks, spaced at approximately annual intervals over much of the series, revealing a strongly cyclical behavior. As indicated above, further development of the close returns procedures is needed to allow us to extract

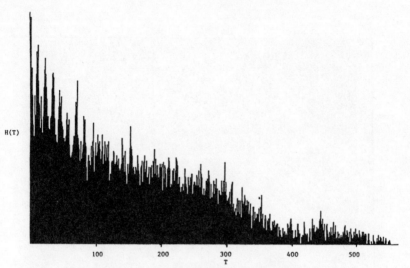

Fig. 11. Close returns histogram of work stoppage data. Note prevalence of regularly spaced sharp peaks.

additional information about the nature of the time series when it is not generated by a chaotic process.

When the topological method is applied to financial data, it again demonstrates the necessity to be cautious in drawing any conclusion, based on metric tests, that any of these series has been generated by a chaotic process. Scheinkman and LeBaron (1989) obtained dimension estimates of about six for their original stock return data and for the residuals from a fitted model. They also applied a shuffle diagnostic, which involved recreating the data series by sampling randomly with replacement from the data until a shuffled series with the same stationary distribution as the original series is obtained. If the original series is chaotic, the shuffled series should be more random, and the dimension estimate for the latter should be higher than for the original series. If the original series is stochastic, the dimension estimate should not change as a result of the shuffling. For the stock returns the shuffled series produced a higher dimension estimate than did the original series. Brock and Malliaris (1989) calculated a dimension estimate of about two for Treasury bill returns and also for the residuals from an $AR(8)$ model fit to the data. While this evidence was consistent with a chaotic solution, they also cautioned that the analysis had not been carried far enough to reach a conclusion.

Daily stock returns (including dividends) on the value-weighted CRSP portfolio were used, covering the period July 2, 1962, through December 29,

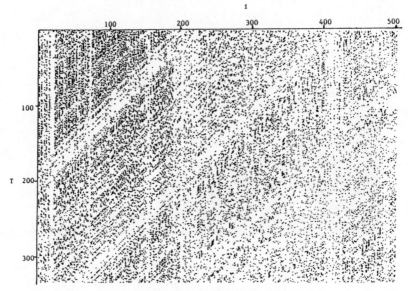

Fig. 12. Close returns plot of weekly stock returns.

1989, to obtain a weekly returns series by means of simple compounding. The weekly series contained 1,439 observations. As in the original study by Scheinkman and LeBaron (1989), the series was not detrended. The Treasury bill series contained 780 monthly observations covering the period January 1926 through December 1990. Log first differences of these returns were used in the Brock and Malliaris (1989) study for estimating a correlation dimension, and the same processing was used in the close returns test. The close returns plots for the weekly stock returns (fig. 12) and for the Treasury bill returns (fig. 13) contains no positive indication of unstable periodic orbits in the data, although some structure is again present in each case. The reservations expressed in Ramsey, Sayers and Rothman (1990) about a possible chaotic explanation for the stock data are reinforced by these close returns results.

With respect to exchange rate data, some evidence has been found by Hsieh (1989) for nonlinear structure in five daily series, although he did not test specifically for chaotic behavior. We initially carried out the correlation dimension calculations on four daily series, according to the procedure as specified in Grassberger (1990). The series were the Canadian dollar, the Deutschmark, the French franc, and the Japanese yen against the U.S. dollar, for the period 1986–1989 (935 observations in each series). The series were first made stationary by taking log first differences. Table 1 presents the

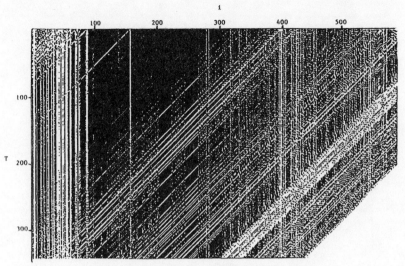

Fig. 13. Close returns plot of Treasury bill returns.

Table 1

Slopes of $\ln C_m(\varepsilon)$ vs $\ln \varepsilon$. Log-differenced exchange rates.

Exchange rate series	Embedding dimension					
	3	4	5	6	7	8
U.S.–U.K.	2.58	3.71	4.52	6.01	6.44	6.64
U.S.–Japan	3.03	3.54	4.16	5.42	6.63	6.37
U.S.–Canada	2.91	3.91	4.73	5.24	5.67	6.82
U.S.–W. Germany	2.85	3.76	4.41	5.22	5.58	6.36

results of the calculations for embedding dimensions 3 through 8.[10] Within this range of embeddings the slopes continue to increase for all four currencies. This lack of convergence suggests that the signal is stochastic rather than chaotic, but, taken alone, the evidence is not persuasive. Since it is not the purpose here to elaborate on metric methods, we will not apply further procedures of that type but will instead turn to the evidence provided by the close returns test. The plots for each series provide no support for an interpretation of chaotic behavior in exchange rates, thus confirming the tentative evidence from the correlation dimension calculations. Since all four series yielded qualitatively similar results, only the plot for the Deutschmark

[10]Given the level of precision of the data (four places) higher-dimension embeddings are not advisable. See Mitschke et al. (1988) and Lange and Moller (1989).

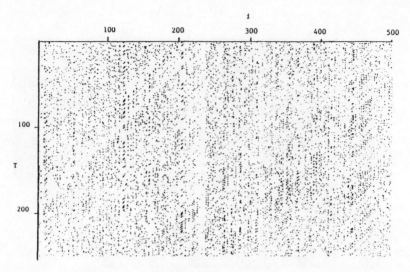

Fig. 14. Close returns plot of log first-differenced German–U.S. exchange, rate, daily January 1986–August 1989.

is shown (fig. 14). Horizonal line segments of any length are virtually nonexistent.

Given the very different results produced by the metric and the topological tests, how do we assess their relative reliability?

First, as pointed out above, Grassberger (1990) has recently clarified the necessity of calculating the dimension estimates so as to reflect only the geometrical correlation and not the dynamic correlation in the time series data. If a correction for this problem is not incorporated into the procedure it will distort the results, possibly creating spurious evidence of low dimension. Consequently, many of the earlier dimension estimates that have been reported in the literature must be viewed skeptically. Ruelle (1990) has emphasized another precaution that should be observed in calculating the correlation dimensions. One should measure the slope of $\log_{10}C_m(\varepsilon)$ versus $\log_{10}(\varepsilon)$ over at least one decade of ε in order to produce a reliable result. If this is done, the dimension estimate will saturate out at a limit of $2\log_{10}N$. Because of this 'one should not believe dimension estimates that are not well below $2\log_{10}N$' [Ruelle (1990)]. Ruelle reviewed several studies, including the Scheinkman and LeBaron (1989) analysis of stock returns (where $N \approx 10^3$ and correlation dimensions of approximately 6 were estimated), and stated that 'the "proof" that one has low-dimensional dynamics is therefore inconclusive, and the suspicion is that the time series evolutions under discussion do not correspond to low-dimensional dynamics.'

Second, the relatively small size of the economic and financial data sets examined above, several of which have fewer than 200 observations, is a serious obstacle for application of metric methods. Consequently, great care should be exercised in interpretation of the results, a point made in several of the studies reviewed. In the theoretical construction the correlation dimension estimate converges to its correct values as N, the sample size, approaches infinity. Wolf et al. (1985) estimated the minimal appropriate number of observations needed to permit estimation of an attractor's dimension at $N = a^D$, where D is the attractor dimension and a is on the order of 10. Thus, the size required increases with the attractor dimension and can quickly outstrip the data set size that may be available.

The close returns test, on the other hand, does not present such large sample size requirements. The pattern of repeated cycling of the time series trajectory around the attractor's unstable periodic orbits will emerge more clearly with a large data set, but as demonstrated in secton 3, small data sets can also produce a clear chaotic signal. Nevertheless, in analyzing very limited data sets it is possible that ambiguous results could be produced by the close returns test. This could occur, for example, if an unpredictable external influence (such as a policy shift or political event) were to disturb a chaotic system, altering the values of the variables or of the parameters of the model. Following such a disturbance the dynamical path of the data would either return to the old attractor or relax to a new one. The larger the data set available, the more likely would be the detection of chaotic behavior under such circumstances.

Unlike the relatively clean data and stationary processes that are common in the natural sciences, economic and financial data may contain considerable measurement noise and are typically nonstationary. Noise and nonstationarity are problems that can affect both the metric and the topological tests. These problems are more severe in metric tests than in close returns tests. Dimension estimates degrade rapidly with additive noise [Brock (1986)]. However, we have seen in fig. 7 that noise averaging can allow the close returns test to retrieve a chaotic signal. Nonstationarity presents a different set of problems. The Grassberger–Procaccia box counting cannot be applied to nonstationarity data [Grassberger (1990)]. The reason is that in that algorithm all nearest neighbors of any particular point are counted, no matter how distant in the time series. If the series is nonstationary, these nearest neighbors will drift away, affecting the average count. This problem is much less severe in the close returns test, in which temporal ordering of the data is maintained. This comes about because the close returns test typically searches over relatively nearby points in the time series and can produce evidence of the tracking of nearby segments even if a trend obscures that evidence for widely separated segments.

To handle noise and nonstationarity several different procedures were explored, including Fourier transforms and centered moving averages, as a

Table 2

Detrending methods.

Series	Detrending method			
	Polynomial detrending	Log first differencing	Moving average	Low frequency filtering
Unemployment rate	x	x		x
Employment	x	x		x
Real GNP	x	x		x
GPDI	x	x		x
Industrial production	x	x	x	x
Work stoppages		x	x	x
Stock returns				x
Treasury bill returns		x	x	x
Exchange rates		x	x	x

means to check whether the close returns results reported above would be altered.[11] In particular there was concern that the common practice of taking logarithmic first differences, used on several of the series, would distort the results, since that process emphasizes the noise component relative to any signal that may be present in the data, possibly obscuring the latter. In the first procedure the data were transformed using either a Fourier transform or a fast Fourier transform. The low and high frequency terms were removed, reducing the drift and noise, respectively. The inverse transform then gave a processed data set which was detrended and had reduced noise. In the second procedure moving averages were computed using a small number of neighbors and a much larger number of neighbors. The former moving average smoothed out some of the noise and the latter estimated trend. The difference between these two averages was a signal with reduced noise and trend. The appropriate widths of the moving averages can be determined by inspecting the Fourier transform spectrum. In general these procedures produce essentially indistinguishable data sets. Close returns tests were then run on these filtered series. Table 2 lists the procedures applied to each series to produce stationarity. In each case the resulting plots did not differ qualitatively from the results reported above. The evidence produced by the close returns test, therefore, appears to be fairly robust with respect to the problems of stationarity and noise when applied to economic and financial data.

[11]An anonymous referee pointed out a potential problem in detrending data with a low-frequency filter and then looking for evidence of chaotic behavior. In theory, removing the lowest frequencies will eliminate some evidence of chaos (the very high period orbits). In practice, however, this does not appear to be a problem. This detrending technique has been applied to empirical data and chaos was successfully detected [see Mindlin et al. (1991)]. This author also tested the procedure by adding a trend to simulated chaotic data. A low-frequency filter was then applied and the chaotic pattern emerged strongly in the close returns plot of the filtered data.

It should be pointed out that while the results of the topological tests conflict with the positive evidence found in some cases by the metric methods, our findings do not exclude the presence of other forms of nonlinear behavior in these data. The metric approach has given rise to new ways to test for the adequacy of linear models. In particular the BDS family of statistics is a test for general dependence which has power against both linear and nonlinear alternatives [Brock, Dechert and Scheinkman (1987)]. Using the BDS statistics and additional techniques, evidence of nonlinear behavior has been found in U.S. employment, unemployment, and industrial production series [Brock and Sayers (1988)], although not for similar Canadian series [Frank and Stengos (1988)], in Japanese GNP [Frank, Gençay and Stengos (1988)], in work stoppage data [Sayers (1986, 1987)], in stock returns [LeBaron (1988), Brock (1988), Scheinkman and LeBaron (1989)], as well as in exchange rates [Hsieh (1989)]. Analysis of these series using the close returns test is not incompatible with a nonlinear, but nonchaotic, generating mechanism.

5. Conclusions

Metric tests have become a standard procedure to test for chaotic behavior in time series data. While these methods may produce credible results for very extensive, stationary, clean data sets, they are not well adapted to the types of data generally encountered in the study of economic and financial phenomena. Some modifications have been introduced to increase the reliability of these methods, but it may be more useful in the long run to apply the newer techniques associated with a topological approach to chaos, which are currently in early stages of development. This approach provides a robust qualitative way to detect chaos, as illustrated in this paper. It also creates a means to quantitatively describe chaotic behavior when it is found to exist in a time series. The capacity to provide a quantitative description of the underlying chaotic process is beyond the ability of metric methods.

Using the close returns test, we examined a number of economic and financial series that had been analyzed for low-dimensional deterministic chaos using the metric approach. The limitations of the latter method, particularly when applied to small, noisy data sets, produced inconclusive results. It was shown that the close returns test is capable of detecting chaotic behavior in relatively small data sets, even with fairly high noise levels. The results using this more powerful method indicate that claims to find chaotic behavor in economic and financial data need to be viewed skeptically. Some type of (nonchaotic) nonlinear model may underlie some of the processes reviewed here, and reliance on linear models with stochastic disturbances may well be inappropriate to describe the behavior. Further development of techniques to identify and analyze nonlinear behavior is warranted. However, the case for a generating mechanism of low-dimensional deterministic chaos in economic and financial time series remains to be made.

References

Barnett, W. and P. Chen, 1988, The aggregation-theoretic monetary aggregates are chaotic and have strange attractors: An econometric application of mathematical chaos, in: W. Barnett, E. Berndt and H. White, eds., Dynamic econometric modeling (Proceedings of the Third International Symposium on Economic Theory and Econometrics) (Cambridge University Press, Cambridge) ch. 11.

Baumol, W.J. and J. Benhabib, 1989, Chaos: significance, mechanism, and economic applications, Journal of Economic Perspectives 3, 77–105.

Benhabib, J. and R.H. Day, 1981, Rational choice and erratic behavior, Review of Economic Studies 48, 459–472.

Brock, W.A., 1986, Distinguishing random and deterministic systems: Abridged version, Journal of Economic Theory 40, 168–195.

Brock, W.A., 1988, Nonlinearity and complex dynamics in economics and finance, in: P. Anderson, K. Arrow and D. Pines, eds., The economy as an evolving complex system, SFI studies in the sciences of complexity (Addison-Wesley, Reading, MA).

Brock, W.A. and E.G. Baek, 1991, Some theory of statistical inference for nonlinear science, Review of Economic Studies 58, 697–716.

Brock, W.A. and W.D. Dechert, 1988, Theorems on distinguishing deterministic from random systems, in: W. Barnett, E. Berndt and H. White, eds., Dynamic econometric modeling, Proceedings of the Third International Symposium on Economic Theory and Econometrics (Cambridge University Press, Cambridge).

Brock, W.A., W.D. Dechert and J.A. Scheinkman, 1987, A test for independence based on the correlation dimension (Department of Economics, University of Wisconsin, Madison).

Brock, W.A. and A.G. Malliaris, 1989, Differential equations, stability and chaos in dynamic economics (Elsevier, Amsterdam).

Brock, W.A. and C.L. Sayers, 1988, Is the business cycle characterized by deterministic chaos?, Journal of Monetary Economics 22, 71–90.

Caputo, J.G., 1989, Practical remarks on the estimation of dimension and entropy from experimental data, in: N.B. Abraham et al., eds., Measures of complexity and chaos (Plenum Press, New York).

Cvitanovic, Predrag, 1984, Universality in chaos, (Adam Helger, Bristol, U.K.).

Day, R., 1982, Irregular growth cycles, American Economic Review 72, 406–414.

Day, R., 1983, The emergence of chaos from classical economic growth, Quarterly Journal of Economics 54, 201–213.

Day, R. and P. Chen, eds., Evolutionary dynamics and nonlinear economics (Oxford University Press, Oxford) forthcoming.

Eckman, J.-P., S.O. Kamphorst and D. Ruelle, 1987, Recurrence plots of dynamical systems, Europhysics Letters 4, 973–977.

Frank, M.Z., R. Gençay and T. Stengos, 1988, International chaos?, European Economic Review 32, 1569–1584.

Frank, M.Z. and T. Stengos, 1988, Some evidence concerning macroeconomic chaos, Journal of Monetary Economics 22, 423–438.

Frank, M.Z. and T. Stengos, 1989, Measuring the strangeness of gold and silver rates of return, Review of Economic Studies 56, 553–567.

Grandmont, J.M., 1985, On endogenous competitive business cycles, Econometrica 53, 995–1045.

Grassberger, P., 1990, An optimized box-assisted algorithm for fractal dimensions, Physics Letters A 148, 63–68.

Grassberger, P. and I. Procaccia, 1983a, Measuring the strangeness of strange attractors, Physica 90, 189–208.

Grassberger, P. and I. Procaccia, 1983b, Characterization of strange attractors, Physical Review Letters 50, 346–349.

Gunaratne, G.H., P.S. Linsay, M.J. Vinson, 1989, Chaos beyond onset: A comparison of theory and experiment, Physics Review Letters A 63, 1–4.

Hinich, M. and D. Patterson, 1985, Evidence of nonlinearity in daily stock returns, Journal of Business and Economic Statistics 3, 69–77.

Hsieh, D., 1989, Testing for nonlinear dependence in daily foreign exchange rates, Journal of Business 62, 339–368.

Ibbotson, R. and R. Sinquefield, 1977, Stocks, bonds, bills and inflation: The past (1926–1976) and the future (1977–2000) (Financial Analysts Research Foundation, University of Virginia, Charlottesville, VA).

Lange, W. and M. Moller, 1989, Systematic errors in estimating dimensions from experimental data, in: N. Abraham, ed., Measures of complexity and chaos (Proceedings of a NATO Advanced Research Workshop on Quantitative Measures of Dynamical Complexity in Nonlinear Systems, Bryn Mawr College, Bryn Mawr, PA, June 22–24, 1989) (Plenum Press, New York) 137–146.

LeBaron, B., 1988, Stock return nonlinearities: Comparing tests and finding structure, Mimeo. (Department of Economics, University of Wisconsin–Madison).

Lorenz, E.N., 1963, Deterministic nonperiodic flow, Journal of the Atmospheric Sciences 20, 120–141.

Lorenz, H.-W., 1987a, International trade and the possible occurrence of chaos, Economics Letters 23, 135–138.

Lorenz, H.-W., 1987b, Strange attractors in a multisector business cycle model, Journal of Economic Behavior and Organization 8, 397–411.

Mindlin, G.B., et al., 1990, Classification of strange attractors by integers, Physical Review Letters 64, 2350–2353.

Mindlin, G.B., et al., 1991, Topological analysis of chaotic time series data from the Belousov–Zhabotinskii reaction, Journal of Nonlinear Science 1, 147–173.

Mitschke, F., et al., 1988, On systematic errors in characterizaing chaos, Optical bistability IV. W. Firth et al., eds., Editions physique, Paris, p. C2–397 [reprinted from Journal of Physics Colloquia 49, suppl. 6: C2–397 (1988)].

Ramsey, J.B. and H.J. Yuan, 1989, Bias and error bars in dimension calculations and their evaluation in some simple models, Physics Letters A 134, 287–297.

Ramsey, J.B. and H.J. Yuan, 1990, The statistical properties of dimension calculations using small data sets, Nonlinearity 3, 155–175.

Ramsey, J.B., C.L. Sayers and P. Rothman, 1990, The statistical properties of dimensions calculations using small data sets: Some economic applications, International Economic Review 31, 991–1020.

Roessler, O.E., 1976, An equation for continuous chaos, Physics Letters A 57, 397–398.

Ruelle, D., 1990, Deterministic chaos: The science and the fiction, Proceedings of the Royal Society of London A427, 241–248.

Sakai, H. and H. Tokumaru, 1980, Autocorrelations of a certain chaos, IEEE Transctions on Acoustics, Speech and Signal Processing, V.I.ASSP-28, 588–590.

Sayers, C.L., 1986, Work stoppages: Exploring the nonlinear dynamics (Department of Economics, University of North Carolina, Chapel Hill).

Sayers, C.L., 1987, Diagnostic tests for nonlinearity in time series data: An application to the work stoppage series (Department of Economics, University of North Carolina, Chapel Hill).

Sayers, C.L., 1989, Chaos and the business cycle, in: Saul Kramer, ed., The ubiquity of chaos (American Association for the Advancement of Science, Washington, D.C.)

Scheinkman, J.A. and B. LeBaron, 1987, Nonlinear dynamics and GNP data (Department of Economics, University of Chicago, Chicago, IL).

Scheinkman, J.A. and B. LeBaron, 1989, Nonlinear dynamics and stock returns, Journal of Business 62, 311–337.

Shaffer, S., 1990, Structural shifts and the volatility of chaotic markets, Journal of Economic Behavior and Organization 15, 201–214.

Solari, H.G., et al., 1988, Relative rotation rates for driven dynamical systems, Physical Review
    A 37, 8.
Stutzer, M., 1980, Chaotic dynamics and bifurcations in a macro model, Journal of Economic
    Dynamics and Control 2, 353–376.
Tufillaro, Nicholas B., 1990, Chaotic themes from strings, Unpublished Ph.D. thesis (Department
    of Physics, Bryn Mawr).
Tufillaro, Nicholas B., et al., 1990, Relative rotation rates: Fingerprints for strange attractors,
    Physical Review A 41, 5717–5720.
Wolf, A., A. Brandstater and J. Swift, 1985, Comment on recent calculations of fractional
    dimension of attractors (University of Texas at Austin, TX) preprint.

[11]

J. R. Statist. Soc. A (1990)
153, *Part* 3

Chance or Chaos?

By M. S. BARTLETT†

Exmouth, UK

[*Read before* The Royal Statistical Society *on Wednesday, March 14th, 1990,
the President*, Professor P. G. Moore, *in the Chair*]

SUMMARY

In my survey of mathematical statistics in 1940 the concept of *chance* was assigned a central role. Some remarks are now made on the comparatively new concept of *chaos* (which can arise in non-linear systems even when 'deterministic'), first of all in relation to two papers in epidemiology by Schaffer (1985) and Olsen *et al.* (1988), and then more generally on the recognition and properties of chaos and its relation with chance.

Keywords: CHANCE; CHAOS; DETERMINISM; EPIDEMICS; NON-LINEARITY; PROBABILITY; SEASONAL VARIATION; STOCHASTICITY

1. INTRODUCTORY COMMENTS

About 50 years ago I presented a paper to the Royal Statistical Society (Bartlett, 1940) which surveyed the current situation at that time in mathematical statistics. A crucial role was assigned to probability theory, though this was to some extent challenged by A. L. Bowley and M. G. Kendall among the discussants (who in view of the world situation in 1940 made their contributions in writing); moreover, I emphasized that my interpretation of probability was to be closely associated with the concept of chance. To quote (p. 8):

'In practice we find that it is often possible to ascribe probability numbers to certain events, at least with as much justification as we can ascribe mass or temperature to physical systems. Events may be said to be governed in part by the operation of the "laws of chance".'

Since then, the post-war era has seen some obviously important developments that have affected the way in which statisticians model and analyse their observed data. One, with which I have been much involved, was the development of stochastic process theory to assist in the formulation of stochastic models in connection not only with the statistical analysis of time series but also with other applications of 'applied probability'. Another is the development of the modern computer, which has now become such an essential tool for the statistician. However, the computer has even more recently played a vital role in the development of what can be called (if it does not sound too contradictory) the *theory of chaos*, i.e. the theory which investigates

'. . . the ability of even simple equations to generate motion so complex, so sensitive to measurement, that it appears random. Appropriately, it's called *chaos*.'

† *Address for correspondence:* Overcliff, 4 Trefusis Terrace, Exmouth, EX8 2AX, Devon, UK.

          0035-9238/90/153321 $2.00

(See Stewart (1989), p. 16.) May (1987), p. 31 (see also Stewart (1989), p. 269), has remarked, concerning its historical development:

'Given that simple equations, which arise naturally in many contexts, generate such surprising dynamics, it is interesting to ask why it took so long for chaos to move to centre stage the way it has over the past ten years or so. I think the answer is partly that widespread appreciation of the significance of chaos had to wait until it was found by people looking at systems simple enough for generalities to be perceived, in contexts with practical applications in mind, and in a time when computers made numerical studies easy.'

It is evident that statisticians concerned in any way with model building and the use of models for statistical applications have the responsibility of studying and trying to understand *chaos*, in various fields of application. I am not so presumptuous to think (in my 80th year) that I am the person to try to pronounce in any authoritative way on this unfamiliar theoretical discipline, but what I can do, with the help of some rather fragmentary comments, is to illustrate its relevance, raise some questions and at least indicate its interest and importance to statisticians, whatever their particular field.

Let me stress again that I am not attempting here any general exposition of this fascinating topic, which has relevance to all the sciences from physics to biology, including meteorology and economics. Those of you not already familiar with it should refer to the writings of some of those who have been most active in its development; see, for example, the 1987 Royal Society discussion on *Dynamical Chaos* (Berry *et al.*, 1987), which includes the paper by May already quoted, the book on *Non-linear Dynamics and Chaos* by Thompson and Stewart (1986), or the somewhat more popular books by Gleick (1987) and Stewart (1989).

2. CHAOS AND EPIDEMIOLOGY

Some of my more specific comments will relate to the field of epidemiology, as this subject is one with which I have been involved, although 30 years or more ago now (e.g. Bartlett (1949, 1956, 1957, 1960)). My own work then emphasized the relevance of stochastic models, e.g. in ecology and epidemiology, including in particular studying the properties of a stochastic version of what I shall still call for convenience the Hamer–Soper model (see Hamer (1906), Soper (1929) and Bailey (1957)) for recurrent measles epidemics, though Dietz and Schenzle (1985) have drawn attention to independent early work by En'ko (1889) and Martini (1921).

In contrast, let me quote from a comparatively recent paper by Schaffer (1985), where in his introduction he remarked:

'. . . it is interesting to consider the possible consequences to ecology and epidemiology were it the case that nonlinear methods applied, and further, if these methods revealed evidence for chaos.

'The obvious consequence is that fluctuations previously believed random would turn out to have a deterministic basis. This would send the theorists back to their equations.

'At the same time, the dynamical reference point i.e. the baseline dynamics assumed for the deterministic part of the motion, would change. In the specific case of childhood epidemics, the emphasis on cyclic pattern of infection e.g. biennial outbreaks in measles, three year cycles in pertussis, etc. (e.g. Anderson *et al.*, 1984) would prove misplaced. In ecology, the equilibrium view of the world (e.g. Lewontin, 1969) central to two decades of theorizing would go forever out of the window. In particular, it would no longer make sense to think of such systems in terms of a balance between intrinsic forces, forever searching out some mythical attracting point, and environmental vagaries perturbing the system away from it. Similar thinking pervades population genetics (e.g. Wright, 1968–1978), most notably in the theory of adaptive topographies.'

This quoted passage envisages the possibility of a dramatic switch in theoretical thinking. How far does Schaffer justify this view? His paper included a detailed investigation of the 'dynamics' of the so-called SEIR epidemiological model, where susceptibles (*S*), infected, but not yet infective (*E*), infective (*I*) and recovered (and immune) individuals (*R*) are governed by the deterministic model (in continuous time):

$$\begin{aligned} dS(t)/dt &= m\{1 - S(t)\} - b\ I(t)\ S(t), \\ dE(t)/dt &= b\ I(t)\ S(t) - (m + a)\ E(t), \\ dI(t)/dt &= a\ E(t) - (m + g)\ I(t). \end{aligned} \right\} \tag{1}$$

(Equations (1) are Schaffer's equations (8), with an obvious misprint correction to his first equation.) The total population $S + E + I + R$ is assumed constant, with births balancing deaths at rate *m*. Equations (1) are similar to the deterministic form of the stochastic model that I proposed (Bartlett, 1949), with the inclusion of a constant births or deaths term *m* and the extra class of latent infecteds *E*. The weakly damped deterministic oscillations which were a feature of the original model are not drastically affected by the slight extensions in model (1), as noted by Schaffer (1985), p. 237.

An important further extension of model (1), however, is to allow the infectivity coefficient *b* to have a periodic component to represent seasonal effects, as suggested by Soper (1929); see also, for example, Bartlett (1956) and Dietz (1976). The two conclusions reached by Schaffer (1985) were (p. 249):

'The first, maintenance of otherwise damped oscillations by noise appears incapable of reproducing essential features of the data. The second, cycles and chaos sustained by seasonal variation in contact rates gives qualitative and quantitative agreement between model and observation.'

My comments on these conclusions, which in the field of epidemiology appear to support Schaffer's general contentions, are as follows.

(a) It is not clear what sort of 'noise' Schaffer introduced. My own model was precisely formulated as a natural stochastic version of the deterministic model (in population studies deterministic models can be criticized for their treatment of *integers* like $I(t)$ and $E(t)$, which may at times be small, as *continuous* variables). Other sources of noise may exist as well, such as random variation of parameters (random environments) or spatial heterogeneity.

(b) The seasonal variation in infectivity adopted by Schaffer is rather larger in magnitude than that originally proposed by Soper and myself (in Schaffer's equation (10) for *b*, b_1 and b_0 should be interchanged).

(c) Nevertheless it would seem that the interaction between seasonality and the natural periodicity of the non-linear model is a significant factor which led to Schaffer's epidemiological conclusions. For small populations, where the intrinsic stochasticity becomes relatively more important, and, for diseases like measles to actual pockets of extinction of the infection, I have emphasized (e.g. Bartlett (1956, 1957)) important combined effects of stochasticity and extinction on the observed epidemic pattern.

In view of my comment (c) I was particularly interested to read also the more recent paper by Olsen *et al.* (1988), for in this paper some of my above criticisms have been met. A Monte Carlo 'simulation' of model (1) for the diseases measles, chicken-pox, rubella and mumps was reported, in which the possible transitions were assigned proportionate probabilities for a timescale that is sufficiently small for the sum of the probabilities not to exceed unity. (This presumably approximates to my own stochastic model if the timescale is sufficiently fine.) To circumvent the possibility of extinction of the infectives an additional immigration term for infectives was also introduced.

Large (fictitious) populations of 1 million and 5 million were investigated, the first value being chosen to correspond to the size of Copenhagen (Denmark). Olsen *et al.* claimed broad agreement with observation and with Schaffer's earlier conclusion of the 'chaotic' nature of the SEIR model, except for chicken-pox, where the yearly period is dominant. For smaller populations, however, Olsen *et al.* noted also the relevance of spatial heterogeneity, and the degree of linkage between communities.

To recapitulate, these (and other) researchers have demonstrated the potential relevance of chaotic fluctuations in SEIR models for large populations, due apparently to the interaction of the non-linear dynamics with the periodic seasonal factor. This is consistent with the extensive phenomenological demonstrations of the existence of chaos in many scientific disciplines. We must be careful, however, to balance any tendency there might now be to discern chaos everywhere with the responsibility of assessing its role in conjunction with other possibly relevant factors in any system under study. In the field of epidemiology, other relevant factors are those which I have previously emphasized of stochasticity, spatial heterogeneity and possible extinction of infection, especially for smaller populations. There is an obvious problem in the amount of relevant detail that should be inserted in a model, and age structure is another factor that has by now received attention (e.g. by Anderson and May (1983)). It would still seem important to determine all the main factors that are most essential for relating any successful model with its observed biological counterpart (in the case of chicken-pox, see also, for example, my remarks in Bartlett (1960), section 7.4).

3. STRUCTURES OF CHAOS IN CONTINUOUS AND DISCRETE TIME

The occurrence of chaotic behaviour in non-linear deterministic systems has raised the formidable problem of recognizing and categorizing it; for example, the conventional spectral analysis of time series data may be inadequate (see Schaffer (1985)).

Methods to date centre on the study of paths in 'phase space', i.e. in the multidimensional space of the variables of the system. For example, a simple pendulum has a two-dimensional phase space in its displacement $x(t)$ and its velocity $\dot{x}(t)$. After initial transients have damped out, this phase space path depicts what is known as the attractor, and ultimate chaotic behaviour corresponds to what is termed a *strange attractor*, as distinct from an equilibrium point or a limit cycle.

Some general theoretical results are available. Thus it is known (e.g. Thompson and Stewart (1986)) that, for continuous time systems, chaotic final behaviour requires at least three-dimensional phase space. An important example is the non-linear pendulum with a periodical forcing term (cf. the epidemiological model of Section 2). Notice that this does have a three- (not two-) dimensional phase space, because the periodic forcing term varies with the time t, which necessitates a third phase space variable t. The study of such a system can be reduced to a two-dimensional plot by choosing the values $x(t)$ and $\dot{x}(t)$ at the periods $T, 2T, \ldots$ of the forcing term—this is an example of what is termed a Poincaré section, after the great French mathematician (Poincaré, 1899) whose topological studies of such orbits at the end of the last century have only been appreciated fully in recent years. Statisticians are more likely to have heard of his treatise on probability (Poincaré, 1896).

The difficulty of studying the behaviour of actual systems in multidimensional phase space is sometimes complicated further by the unobservability of all the relevant variables. A theorem of Takens (1981) (see Stewart (1989), p. 185) states that this problem can be bypassed by studying the multivariate time series $x(t)$, $x(t+h)$, $x(t+2h)$, . . ., where $x(t)$ is any one of the original variables of the system (and h is to some extent arbitrary). The path traced out by this concocted multivariate time series provides a topological approximation to the shape of the attractor.

This seems to provide a powerful technique for studying and detecting chaotic behaviour, but I imagine that much more investigation is needed to check the efficacy of the technique, especially when other sources of random behaviour may be present.

Note also that discrete-time systems can exhibit chaos even in one dimension. Thus the iterative equation

$$x_{n+1} = F(x_n) \tag{2}$$

that has sometimes been used as a model in ecology (e.g. Moran (1950)) can for quite simple functions $F(\cdot)$ exhibit complicated and sometimes chaotic behaviour, as stressed by May (1976, 1987). A well-known and remarkable example (e.g. May (1976) and Stewart (1989)) is the discrete-time 'logistic' iterative model

$$x_{n+1} = kx_n(1 - x_n), \tag{3}$$

where x_n can represent population size for generation n (x being scaled to have maximum value unity) and k is a parameter between zero and 4. For $1 < k < 3$, x_n tends to a stable non-zero value $(k-1)/k$; for $k > 3$, x_n becomes periodic for a further interval of k-values. Around $k = 3.58$, however, chaos ensues (except for occasional 'windows' of particular k-values generating more regular periodic behaviour).

4. A CURIOUS EXAMPLE

These non-linear discrete-time systems might seem to promise easier classification and detection than continuous time systems, but there are curious features that need to be noted. Consider, for example, the simple autoregressive time series (linear stochastic model)

$$X_{n+1} = \rho X_n + Y_{n+1}, \tag{4}$$

where Y_{n+1} is independent of X_n and $\{Y_n\}$ is an independent series of values from some distribution. The correlogram is $\rho_n = \rho^n$, and the equivalent spectral density

$$f(\omega) = (1 - \rho^2)/\pi(1 + \rho^2 - 2\rho \cos \omega), \qquad 0 < \omega < \pi.$$

If Y_n is normal (Gaussian), so is X_n. When X_n has become stationary, and, say, $E\{Y\} = 0$, there are no further properties to discuss. The series reversed in time has identical statistical properties.

Consider next the stochastic model (4), with the same correlogram and spectrum, except that the random variable Y_n is not normal, but takes a few discrete values. The simplest case is two values, say $Y = 0$ or $\frac{1}{2}$, each with probability $\frac{1}{2}$. To be a little more interesting, I shall take $Y = 0$, $\frac{1}{3}$ or $\frac{2}{3}$, each with probability $\frac{1}{3}$. As n increases

$$X_n = Y_n + \rho Y_{n-1} + \rho^2 Y_{n-2} + \dots. \tag{5}$$

The case $Y = 0$ or $\frac{1}{2}$ will lead now to a uniform distribution for X, if $\rho = \frac{1}{2}$, as can be seen by our thinking of X, as expressed by series (5), as a random value between zero and unity written as a series on the binary scale. Similarly the case $Y = 0$, $\frac{1}{3}$ or $\frac{2}{3}$ will lead to a uniform distribution for X, if $\rho = \frac{1}{3}$, as can be seen by expressing X on the 'triadic' scale. In the first case $E\{Y\} = \frac{1}{4}$ instead of zero, and in the second case $E\{Y\} = \frac{1}{3}$.

Thus, when X has become stationary, choose the initial value X at random between zero and unity; in the second case, say ξ when expressed on the triadic scale. For example, from the first vertical column of Table 33 (p. II) of Fisher and Yates's (1938) *Statistical Tables*, with (0, 1, 2) taken as 0, (3, 4, 5) taken as 1 and (6, 7, 8) taken as 2 (with 9 ignored), the first 10 numbers gave X_0 to sufficient accuracy as

$$\xi = 0.1212022110 \dots$$

or 0.621 to three decimal places in ordinary decimal notation. The next number in the column gave 2, and this was taken to provide $Y = \frac{2}{3}$, so that on the triadic scale

$$X_1 = 0.1 \times \xi + 0.2 = 0.21212022110 \dots,$$

and so on. The 50 values $X_1, \dots, X_{50}$ obtained in this way are given (to three decimal places) in Table 1 and are also shown in Fig. 1.

You may wonder what relation all this has to deterministic, let alone chaotic deterministic, behaviour. I think that it was Murray Rosenblatt who first mentioned this kind of example to me many years ago (see also Degn (1982)). If we consider the series *reversed in time*, it becomes transformed into a non-linear chaotic deterministic series.

The case illustrated in Table 1 and Fig. 1 may be reversed in time to read

$$x_n = 3x_{n+1} - [3x_{n+1}], \tag{6}$$

where $[3x_{n+1}]$ denotes the 'integral part' of $3x_{n+1}$ on the triadic scale, or equivalently on the decimal scale. Clearly a plot of x_n, or even of the pair (x_{n+1}, x_n), would not automatically from its topology distinguish between the linear stochastic series (4) and the non-linear deterministic series (6), because, apart from the direction of time, they are identical. Plotting the pair (x_{n+1}, x_n) gives the regression relation between x_{n+1} and x_n; for Y Gaussian this would be contained in a bivariate Gaussian distribution, but for $Y = 0$, $\frac{1}{3}$ or $\frac{2}{3}$ consists of three parallel straight lines with slope $\frac{1}{3}$ (two lines for the $Y = 0$ or $\frac{1}{2}$ case), with of course the same average regression line as in the Gaussian case.

TABLE 1

Realization of linear stochastic model (4) (with $\rho = \frac{1}{3}$)

n	3Y	X	n	3Y	X	n	3Y	X	n	3Y	X	n	3Y	X
1	2	0.874	11	1	0.391	21	1	0.500	31	0	0.061	41	0	0.278
2	0	0.291	12	2	0.797	22	0	0.167	32	1	0.354	42	1	0.426
3	0	0.097	13	2	0.932	23	1	0.389	33	0	0.118	43	1	0.475
4	0	0.032	14	1	0.644	24	2	0.796	34	2	0.706	44	2	0.825
5	2	0.677	15	0	0.215	25	0	0.265	35	1	0.569	45	1	0.608
6	2	0.892	16	0	0.072	26	2	0.755	36	1	0.523	46	1	0.536
7	1	0.631	17	1	0.357	27	2	0.918	37	1	0.508	47	0	0.179
8	1	0.544	18	1	0.452	28	1	0.640	38	1	0.503	48	2	0.726
9	1	0.525	19	1	0.484	29	1	0.546	39	1	0.501	49	2	0.909
10	0	0.172	20	1	0.495	30	0	0.182	40	2	0.833	50	0	0.303

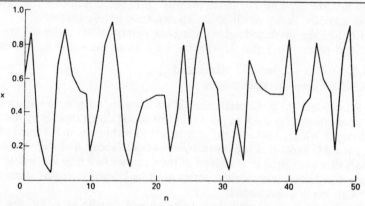

Fig. 1. Realization of stochastic model (4), with $\rho = \frac{1}{3}$ and $3Y = 0$, 1 or 2 (deterministic series (6) when reversed in time)

Three incidental remarks are as follows:

(a) if the structure of series (6) is disliked as too artificial, the 'integral part' term may be filtered off automatically by wrapping $3x_{n+1}$ round a circle (see Stewart (1989), pp. 112–113);

(b) from Fig. 1 it will be seen that (in contrast with the Gaussian case) the time direction is discernible from the shape of the fluctuations;

(c) the simple type of equation (6) will only be available for such special cases as $Y = 0$ or $\frac{1}{2}$ with $\rho = \frac{1}{2}$, or $Y = 0$, $\frac{1}{3}$ or $\frac{2}{3}$ with $\rho = \frac{1}{3}$, etc., these cases leading moreover to the uniform distribution for X, but some more arbitrary values of ρ could perhaps still be handled, though with more difficulty and with the aid of a computer.

A more relevant point is that the prediction problem, if confined to correlational properties and linear prediction, would be the same for equations (4) and (6), but a deterministic series, e.g. equation (6), should be predictable exactly, i.e. for a deterministic series (proceeding forward in time) x_{n+k} should be predictable precisely from x_n. However, not only must the equation for the system be precisely known,

TABLE 2
Prediction from the (reversed) deterministic series (6)†

n	(a)	(b)	n	(a)	(b)	n	(a)
49	0.909	0.909	44	0.825	0.887	39	0.484
48	0.726	0.727	43	0.475	(0.661)	38	0.451
47	0.179	0.181	42	0.425	(0.983)	37	0.352
46	0.536	0.543	41	0.276		36	(0.055)
45	0.608	0.629	40	0.828		35	

†(a) $x_{50} = 0.302915$; (b) $x_{50} = 0.303$.

but also the initial value x_n must be precisely known. The ultimate limitations to this last condition become obvious for series (6) when it is noted that as k increases the value of x_n as a triadic series needs to be known to k triadic places.

To illustrate this, the predicted values using the deterministic series (6) are given (to three decimal places) in Table 2, working back from the value x_{50}, when

(a) $x_{50} = 0.302915$ to six decimal places and
(b) $x_{50} = 0.303$ to three decimal places.

As anticipated, column (a) gives predicted values agreeing with x_n to within one in the third decimal place as far back as $n = 42$, but breaking down rapidly by $n = 38$–36 (about 12–14 steps), whereas column (b) only agrees to within one in the third decimal place back to $n = 48$, and breaking down by $n = 44$–42 (about 6–8 steps). This is a very elementary demonstration of the effect of the accuracy to which the 'initial' value of a univariate non-linear deterministic series must be known to ensure accuracy of the prediction so many steps ahead.

The accuracy to which x is recorded might be associated with an additional 'error term' ϵ; it then has some link with a general theoretical approach by Zeeman (1988) to a classification of the stability of dynamical systems, even chaotic ones, by introducing in the theory what he refers to as 'ϵ-diffusion'.

5. IMPLICATIONS FOR THE CONCEPTS OF PROBABILITY AND CHANCE

To return to the concepts of probability and chance which I mentioned in Section 1, we have seen that the 'strange' behaviour of chaotic systems has to be added to the possible forms of random behaviour with which some of us have been more familiar. The example in Section 4 has perhaps emphasized the need for care in discriminating between them. Extreme cases of non-linear chaotic behaviour which appear completely random are indeed already familiar in the pseudorandom sequences used in computers in place of random numbers. This links with the view expressed by Stewart (1989), pp. 299–300:

'Our most cherished examples of chance—dice, roulette, cointossing—seem closer to chaos than to the whims of outside events. So, in this revised sense, dice are good metaphor for chance after all. It's just that we've refined our concept of randomness. Indeed, the deterministic but possibly chaotic stripes of phase space may be the true source of probability.'

Such notions of probability are also illustrated by Galton's *quincunx* (see Chirikov (1987), p. 145), the apparatus made for Galton by Tisley and Spiller in 1873 to generate the normal distribution (see Stigler (1986)).

We must clearly be careful here not to become overawed by the new language. After all, 'stochastic' behaviour includes not only the behaviour of systems influenced throughout time by noise, but that of systems referred to in the above quotation which are merely sensitively dependent on *unknown initial conditions*. It is the fact that these conditions cannot in so many cases be known in practice (in the case of quantum mechanics this is believed to be inevitable because of the uncertainty principle) that the ideas of probability and chance are still relevant even when the system under study is regarded in principle as deterministic. Laplace's famous dictum on the complete predictability of deterministic systems becomes null and void; for chaotic systems the only kind of predictability must (e.g. in meteorology) be formulated as 'robust prediction', when found to be possible, for an appropriate set of neighbouring initial conditions.

It would, however, be a pity if the recognition today of the ubiquitous occurrence of chaos in deterministic non-linear systems is not followed in due course by a much more comprehensive classification and study of the possible structures and how best to handle them. The 'complete chaos' with which we are already familiar as 'complete randomness' is not the only kind that may appear; the strange attractors that have been already recognized need to be studied further not only in themselves but (as I remarked in Section 2 for the epidemiological models) when mixed with other very relevant stochastic effects that occur in the real world.

REFERENCES

Anderson, R. M., Grenfell, B. T. and May, R. M. (1984) Oscillatory fluctuations in the incidence of infectious disease and the impact of vaccination: time series analysis. *J. Hyg. Camb.*, **93**, 587–608.

Anderson, R. M. and May, R. M. (1983) Vaccination against rubella and measles: quantitative investigation of different policies. *J. Hyg. Camb.*, **90**, 259–325.

Bailey, N. T. J. (1957) *The Mathematical Theory of Epidemics*, p. 8. London: Griffin.

Bartlett, M. S. (1940) The present position of mathematical statistics. *J. R. Statist. Soc.*, **103**, 1–29.

—— (1949) Some evolutionary stochastic processes. *J. R. Statist. Soc. B*, **11**, 211–229.

—— (1956) Deterministic and stochastic models for recurrent epidemics. *Proc. 3rd Berkeley Symp. Mathematics, Statistics and Probability*, vol. 4, pp. 81–109. Berkeley: University of California Press.

—— (1957) Measles periodicity and community size. *J. R. Statist. Soc. A*, **120**, 48–60.

—— (1960) *Stochastic Population Models in Ecology and Epidemiology*. London: Methuen.

Berry, M. V., Percival, I. C. and Weiss, N. O. (eds) (1987) Discussion on Dynamical chaos. *Proc. R. Soc. A*, **413**, 1–199.

Chirikov, B. V. (1987) Particle confinement and adiabatic invariance. *Proc. R. Soc. A*, **413**, 145–146.

Degn, H. (1982) Discrete chaos is reversed random walk. *Phys. Rev. A*, **26**, 711–712.

Dietz, K. (1976) The incidence of infectious diseases under the influence of seasonal fluctuations. *Lect. Notes Biomath.*, **11**, 1–15.

Dietz, K. and Schenzle, D. (1985) Mathematical models for infectious disease statistics. In *A Celebration of Statistics*, pp. 167–204. New York: Springer.

En'ko, P. D. (1889) The epidemic course of some infectious diseases (in Russian) *Vrac'*, **10**, 1008–1010, 1039–1042, 1061–1063.

Fisher, R. A. and Yates, F. (1938) *Statistical Tables for Biological, Agricultural and Medical Research*. Edinburgh: Oliver and Boyd.

Gleick, J. (1987) *Chaos: Making a New Science*. New York: Viking.

Hamer, W. H. (1906) Epidemic disease in England. *Lancet*, i, 733–739.

Lewontin, R. C. (1969) The meaning of stability. *Brookhvn Symp. Biol.*, **22**, 13–24.

Martini, E. (1921) *Berechnungen und Beobachtungen zur Epidemiologie und Bekämpfung der Malaria.* Hamburg: Gente.

May, R. M. (1976) Simple mathematical models with very complicated dynamics. *Nature*, **261**, 459–467.

—— (1987) Chaos and the dynamics of biological populations. *Proc. R. Soc.* A, **413**, 27–44.

Moran, P. A. P. (1950) Some remarks on animal population dynamics. *Biometrics*, **6**, 250–258.

Olsen, L. F., Truty, G. L. and Schaffer, W. M. (1988) Oscillations and chaos in epidemics: a nonlinear dynamic study of six childhood diseases in Copenhagen, Denmark. *Theor. Popln. Biol.*, **33**, 344–370.

Poincaré, H. (1896) *Calcul des Probabilités.* Paris: Gauthier-Villars.

—— (1899) *Les Méthodes Nouvelles de la Mécanique Celeste*, vols 1–3. Paris: Gauthier-Villars.

Schaffer, W. M. (1985) Can nonlinear dynamics elucidate mechanisms in ecology and epidemiology? *IMA J. Math. Appl. Med. Biol.*, **2**, 221–252.

Soper, H. E. (1929) Interpretation of periodicity in disease prevalence. *J. R. Statist. Soc.*, **92**, 34–73.

Stewart, I. (1989) *Does God Play Dice? The Mathematics of Chaos.* Oxford: Basil Blackwell.

Stigler, S. M. (1986) *The History of Statistics*, p. 277. Cambridge: Harvard University Press.

Takens, F. (1981) Detecting strange attractors in turbulence. In *Dynamical Systems and Turbulence*, (eds D. A. Rand and L. S. Young), pp. 366–381. New York: Springer.

Thompson, J. M. T. and Stewart, H. B. (1986) *Nonlinear Dynamics and Chaos.* New York: Wiley.

Wright, S. (1968–78) *Evolution and the Genetics of Populations*, vols 1–4. Chicago: University of Chicago Press.

Zeeman, C. (1988) Stability of dynamical systems. *Nonlinearity*, **1**, 115–155.

Part II
Models

[12]

Journal of Economic Behavior and Organization 8 (1987) 497–511. North-Holland

ON RATIONAL DYNAMIC STRATEGIES IN INFINITE HORIZON MODELS WHERE AGENTS DISCOUNT THE FUTURE

Rose-Anne DANA*

Université de Paris VI, 75230 Paris, France

Luigi MONTRUCCHIO*

Politecnico di Torino, 10129 Torino, Italy

Received August 1986, final version received April 1987

In this paper we show that the equilibrium dynamics, arising in three models of rational choice over an infinite horizon, are described by choice functions belonging to huge classes of maps including chaotic ones. The results are obtained by studying the relationship between the primal functions of the models and the corresponding choice functions. The three models are: the economic growth model with discounting, a duopoly game with alternate moves, a duopoly with simultaneous moves.

1. Introduction

It has already been recognized for some time that rationality of the economic agents does not preclude erratic behavior. For early results in this direction see Benhabib and Day (1981, 1982) and Grandmont (1985). In this paper we show that the equilibrium dynamics infinite horizon models of rational choice are described by maps belonging to huge classes including ones that produce chaotic movements. These kinds of results are obtained by studying the relationship between the utility or return functions of the model and the corresponding dynamic choice functions that satisfy Bellman's principle of optimality.

We shall investigate here three distinct models. In each of them time is discrete, the environment is deterministic and stationary. The objective function of each agent is represented by a discounted sum of one-period utilities with a discount factor $0 < \delta < 1$.

*The second author was partially supported by the 'Ministero Italiano della Pubblica Istruzione'. We are grateful to an anonymous referee for comments that have greatly improved this paper. Any remaining errors are our own.

498 *R.-A. Dana and L. Montrucchio, Rational dynamic strategies*

The first model is a general model of intertemporal optimal planning faced by a single infinitely lived agent. Although a large variety of problems in economic dynamics can be studied using particular specifications of this model, here we shall think of it as the 'reduced form' of the optimal-consumption economic growth model. See McKenzie (1986). It will be shown that the optimal vector sequences $(x_0, x_1, x_2, \ldots)$ can be represented by a dynamical system $x_{t+1} = \tau_\delta(x_t)$, in which the choice or policy function $\tau_\delta(x)$ is a map which selects optimally the subsequent state as a function of the current state.

The second model under investigation will be a duopoly game with the assumption that the two agents move alternately and that the choice of each agent depends only on the last choice of his opponent. See Cyert and DeGroot (1970) and Maskin and Tirole (1983, 1985). We shall be concerned with choice or reaction functions $r_{1\delta}(y)$, $r_{2\delta}(x)$ that are perfect equilibria. The map $r_{1\delta}(y)$ is the dynamic strategy of agent 1 as a function of the last move of agent 2; and, ceteris paribus, the same for $r_{2\delta}$.

In the third model we shall analyse the same duopoly game but with simultaneous moves of the two agents. We shall look for dynamic equilibria of the type $r_{1\delta}(x, y)$, $r_{2\delta}(x, y)$ where the dynamic strategies of the agents depend on the state at the previous period. See Friedman (1977).

After analyzing the three examples we provide two examples of chaotic dynamics generated by equilibrium dynamic strategies.

2. McKenzie's model of optimal growth

2.1. The model

A rather general model of optimal-consumption economic growth with discounting can be described as follows, with assumptions (A.1)–(A.2) below. Let

$$W_\delta(k_0) = \max \sum_{t=0}^{t=\infty} V(k_t, k_{t+1}) \delta^t,$$

subject to $k_{t+1} \in T(k_t)$, $t = 0, 1, 2, \ldots, k_0$ given in K and with discount factor $\delta \in (0, 1)$.

(A.1) The set of feasible capital stocks $K_+ \subset R^n$ is convex, compact with non-empty interior. The technology set is represented by a set-valued correspondence T from K into K with non-empty compact convex images and a closed convex graph.

(A.2) The return function $V: K \times K \to R$ is continuous and concave and $V(k, \cdot)$ is strictly concave for every fixed $k \in K$.

It is well known that, under (A.1)–(A.2), there exists a unique optimal path

$(k_0, k_1, k_2, \ldots)$ from any initial condition k_0 in K [see McKenzie (1986) and references quoted therein]. Moreover it follows from Bellman's Principle that the optimal paths can be generated by a policy function τ_δ, called the optimal strategy, from K into K, i.e., $k_1 = \tau_\delta(k_0)$, $k_2 = \tau_\delta(\tau_\delta(k_0)) \equiv \tau_\delta^2(k_0)$, $k_3 = \tau_\delta^3(k_0)$ and so on. In the next paragraph we shall recall how the policy function τ_δ is obtained. For more details on Bellman's Principle in Dynamic Programming the reader is referred, besides Bellman (1957), to Blackwell (1965) and Denardo (1967).

2.2. Properties of the value and policy functions

Let $C^0(X)$ be the space of all real valued continuous functions on X endowed with the sup-norm topology. Let P_δ be the operator from $C^0(K)$ into itself defined as follows:

$$(P_\delta f)(k) = \max\{V(k, k') + \delta f(k'), k' \in T(k)\}.$$

It is well known [see Denardo (1967)] that P_δ is a contraction of modulus δ that maps concave functions into concave functions. The value function W_δ is its unique fixed point. It satisfies 'Bellman's equation':

$$W_\delta(k) = \max\{V(k, k') + \delta W_\delta(k'), k' \in T(k)\}, \tag{1}$$

and is therefore concave and continuous.

Once W_δ is known, the policy function τ_δ can be obtained as follows:

$$\tau_\delta(k) = \operatorname{argmax}\{V(k, k') + \delta W(k'), k' \in T(k)\}, \tag{2}$$

that is a continuous map from K into K.

We have the following proposition:

Proposition 2.1 (a) *The map* $(\delta, V) \to W_\delta$ *is continuous from* $(0, 1) \times C^0(K \times K)$ *into* $C^0(K)$. (b) *The map* $(\delta, V) \to \tau_\delta$ *is continuous from* $(0, 1) \times C^0(K \times K)$ *into* $C^0(K, K)$. *Here* $C^0(K, K)$ *is the space of continuous maps from* K *into itself endowed with the uniform topology.*

Proof Let f be fixed in $C^0(K)$. The map $(\delta, V, k, k') \to V(k, k') + \delta f(k')$, from $(0, 1) \times C^0(K \times K) \times K \times K$ into R, is continuous. By Berge's Maximum Theorem [see Hildenbrand (1974)] the map $(\delta, V, k) \to \max\{V(k, k') + \delta f(k'), k' \in T(K)\}$, from $(0, 1) \times C^0(K \times K) \times K$ into R is continuous. K being compact, the map $(\delta, V) \to P_\delta f$ is continuous from $(0, 1) \times C^0(K \times K)$ into $C^0(K)$. As W_δ is the uniform limit of the sequence: f, $P_\delta(f)$, $P_\delta(P_\delta(f)) \equiv P_\delta^2(f)$,

$P_\delta^3(f), \ldots$, the map $(\delta, V) \to W_\delta$ is continuous. This proves (a). The proof of (b) follows from (a) and the following lemma.

Lemma 2.2.   Let $V: K \times K \to R$ be continuous, and $V(k, \cdot)$ be strictly concave for every fixed $k \in K$. Let $\theta(k) = \text{argmax}\{V(k, y), y \in T(k)\}$. Then the map $V \to \theta$ from $C^0(K \times K)$ into $C^0(K, K)$ is continuous.

The proof of Lemma 2.2 is similar to the proof of 2.1(a). The map from $C^0(K \times K) \times K \times K$ into R, $(V, k, y) \to V(k, y)$, is continuous. By the Maximum Theorem the map from $C^0(K \times K) \times K$ in K, $(V, k) \to \text{argmax}\{V(k, y), y \in T(k)\}$ is continuous. K being compact the map from $C^0(K \times K)$ into $C^0(K, K)$ is continuous.

The next proposition shows that the optimal policy τ_δ is the solution to a one-period optimization problem. Similar characterization will be given in the paper (see Propositions 3.1 and 4.1) and will turn out to be the main tool used there.

Proposition 2.3.   A map $0: K \to K$ is the policy function τ_δ of the previous optimal growth model, under (A.1) and (A.2) and for a fixed value of δ in (0.1), iff the following two conditions are satisfied:

(i) There exists a real concave function $W(k, k')$ such that

$$\max\{W(k, k'), k' \in T(k)\} = W(k, \theta(k)).$$

(ii) The function $W(k, k') - \delta W(k', \theta(k'))$ satisfies (A.2).

Under these circumstances the return function is given by

$$V(k, k') = W(k, k') - \delta W(k', \theta(k')).$$

The proof of that proposition can be found in Boldrin and Montrucchio (1986).

Our knowledge about policy functions τ_δ is very poor. Well known results of 'Turnpike' guarantee the global convergence of the optimal paths to a stationary path for δ close to 1, under general assumptions on V and T. For V strongly concave and of class C^2, see Scheinkman (1976). A simple proof in the one-dimensional case can be found in Deneckere and Pelikan (1986). More general results related to the curvature of V are given in McKenzie (1986). All these results imply in turn very simple policy functions whenever δ is far enough from zero.

The next proposition shows that the class of the policy functions is very wide whenever δ is close to zero.

R.-A. Dana and L. Montrucchio, Rational dynamic strategies 501

Proposition 2.4. *Let* $\theta: K \to K$ *be of class* C^2 *and* $\theta(k) \in T(k)$ *hold for all* $k \in K$. *There exists a* $\delta^* = \delta^*(\theta) > 0$ *such that for any fixed* $0 < \delta \leq \delta^*$ *a return function* $V(k, k')$, *satisfying* $(A.1)–(A.2)$, *exists so that* θ *is its policy function when the discount factor equals* δ. *Moreover one has the estimate*

$$\delta^*(\theta) \geq [\mu k_2 + 2k_1^2 - 2k_1(k_1^2 + \mu k_2)^{\frac{1}{2}}]/\mu^2 k_2^2,$$

where $k_1 = \max_k \|D\theta(k)\|$, $k_2 = \max_k \|D^2\theta(k)\|$, μ *is diameter of* K.

Proposition 2.4 was already stated in Boldrin and Montrucchio (1986) but in the appendix we provide a simpler proof of that for the case where $T(k) \equiv K$. The method of our proofs, which make use of the characterization previously given in Proposition 2.3, are constructive ones. By such techniques it is not difficult to construct very simple two-sector, non-joint-production economies satisfying all the neo-classical assumptions and that exhibit chaotic dynamic behaviors for appropriate values of the discount factor [for further details and developments see Boldrin and Montrucchio (1986), Deneckere and Pelikan (1986) and Boldrin (1987)].

3. Maskin–Tirole's model of duopoly game

This section is concerned with the infinite horizon duopoly game described by Maskin and Tirole (1983, 1985). It can be seen as a generalization of the Cyert and DeGroot (1970) model which is a quantity setting model with finite horizon.

Time is discrete and the horizon is infinite. Periods are indexed by t $(t = 0, 1, 2, \ldots)$. Assuming a stationary environment, the two agents are fully described by a quadruple (X, Y, U^1, U^2), where X and Y are their strategy sets and $U^1(x, y)$, $U^2(x, y)$ their instantaneous profits that depend on the actions (x, y) of both agents (choice of a quantity, a price, etc.). We shall suppose that X and Y are compact and convex subsets of Euclidean spaces, that U^1 and U^2 are continuous mappings from $X \times Y$ to R, and that $U^1(\cdot, y)$ (resp. $U^1(x, \cdot)$) is strictly concave for each y (resp. for each x).

Agents are assumed to discount future utilities with the same interest rate (this assumption is not essential, it is made for sake of simplicity). Thus their intertemporal return can be written as $\tilde{U}^i = \sum_{t=1}^{\infty} U^i(x_t, y_t)\delta^{t-1}$, $i = 1, 2$, where $0 < \delta < 1$ is their discount factor. The two agents move sequentially. In odd numbered periods $(t = 1, 3, \ldots)$ agent 1 chooses an action to which he is committed for two periods. That is, $x_{2k+2} = x_{2k+1}$ for all $k \geq 0$. Similarly agent 2 moves in even numbered periods $(t = 0, 2, \ldots)$, i.e., $y_{2k+1} = y_{2k}$.

Let us consider dynamic strategies which depend only on the previous physical state of the world. Whenever agent 1 expects his opponent to use such a strategy $r_2(x)$, he solves the following problem:

$$W_\delta^1(y;r_2) = \max\{U^1(x_1,y) + \delta U^1(x_1,r_2(x_1)) + \cdots$$

$$+ \delta^{2n}U^1(x_{2n+1},r_2(x_{2n-1})) + \delta^{2n+1}U^1(x_{2n+1},r_2(x_{2n+1})) + \cdots\},$$

$$(3)$$

where the maximization is made over the sequences $(x_1,x_3,x_5,\ldots)$. $W_\delta^1(y;r_2)$ is the maximal discounted profit that agent 1 can obtain when he is about to move, the other is committed to the action 'y' and henceforth agent 2 will play according r_2. $W_\delta^2(x;r_1)$ is defined similarly.

By Bellman's Principle, (3) can be rewritten as

$$W_\delta^1(y;r_2) = \max_{x\in X}\{U^1(x,y) + \delta U^1(x,r_2(x)) + \delta^2 W_\delta^1(r_2(x);r_2)\}. \tag{4}$$

It follows that $W_\delta^1(y;r_2)$ is a fixed point of the operator $P(\delta,r_2)$ acting from $C^0(Y)$ into itself, defined by

$$(P(\delta,r_2)f)(y) = \max_{x\in X}\{U^1(x,y) + \delta U^1(x,r_2(x)) + \delta^2 f(r_2(x))\}. \tag{5}$$

The operator $P(\delta,r_2)$ turns out to be a contraction of modulus δ^2 and therefore $W_\delta^1(y;r_2)$ exists and is unique. This statement is proved in the appendix. The same argument holds for the value function $W_\delta^2(x;r_1)$ of player 2, given the reaction function $r_1(y)$ of player 1. Note however that, contrary to the classical programming case, $W_\delta^1(y;r_2)$ is not generally concave and thus there may exist several functions $r_{1\delta}^*$ that are 'best-response' to r_2.

We shall say that a pair of reaction functions $(r_{1\delta},r_{2\delta})$ forms a Markov Perfect Equilibrium (MPE) if $r_{2\delta}$ belongs to the set of agent 2's optimal policies given that henceforth agent 1 will move according to $r_{1\delta}$ and the analogous condition holds for agent 2. Thus a pair $(r_{1\delta},r_{2\delta})$ is a MPE iff

$$r_{1\delta}(y) \in \operatorname*{argmax}_{x\in X}\{U^1(x,y) + \delta U^1(x,r_{2\delta}(x)) + \delta^2 W_\delta^1(r_{2\delta}(x);r_{2\delta})\},$$

$$(6)$$

$$r_{2\delta}(x) \in \operatorname*{argmax}_{y\in Y}\{U^2(x,y) + \delta U^2(r_{1\delta}(y),y) + \delta^2 W_\delta^2(r_{1\delta}(y);r_{1\delta})\}.$$

We have the following characterization of MPE which is similar to that of Proposition 2.3.

Proposition 3.1. The pair (r_1,r_2) is a MPE of a Maskin and Tirole's model for a fixed value of δ in $(0,1)$ iff the following conditions are satisfied:

(i) *There exist two real continuous functions $G^1(x,y)$, $G^2(x,y)$ defined on $X \times Y$ such that*

$$\max\{G^1(x, y), x \in X\} = G^1(r_1(y), y),$$

$$\max\{G^2(x, y), y \in Y\} = G^2(x, r_2(x)).$$

(ii) *Setting* $W^1(y) = G^1(r_1(y), y)$ *and* $W^2(x) = G^2(x, r_2(x))$, *the two return functions* U^1, U^2 *defined as follows:*

$$U^1(x, y) = G^1(x, y) - [\delta/(1 + \delta)]G^1(x, r_2(x)) - [\delta^2/(1 + \delta)]W^1(r_2(x)),$$

$$U^2(x, y) = G^2(x, y) - [\delta/(1 + \delta)]G^2(r_1(y), y) - [\delta^2/(1 + \delta)]W^2(r_1(y)),$$

satisfy the hypothesis of the model, i.e., the former is concave in x and the latter is concave in y.

Proof. (Necessity). Let (r_1, r_2) be a MPE. Let $W^1_\delta(y; r_2)$ be the value function of player 1 associated to r_2. Define G^1 by

$$G^1(x, y) = U^1(x, y) + \delta U^1(x, r_2(x)) + \delta^2 W^1_\delta(r_2(x); r_2),$$

then

$$\max\{G^1(x, y), x \in X\} = G^1(r_1(y), y).$$

It can easily be checked that U^1, W^1, G^1 are related by the formula

$$G^1(x, y) - [\delta/(1 + \delta)]G^1(x, r_2(x)) - [\delta^2/(1 + \delta)]W^1(r_2(x)) = U^1(x, y),$$

and similarly for player 2.
(Sufficiency). Let G^i, $i = 1, 2$, be given. Define W^i and U^i as in (ii). Then

$$U^1(x, y) + \delta U^1(x, r_2(x)) + \delta^2 W(r_2(x)) = G^1(x, y), \qquad \text{and}$$

$$\max\{G^1(x, y), x \in X\} = W^1(y) = G^1(r_1(y), y).$$

W^1 is indeed the value function of one who expects two to use r_2 since W^1 is the unique function that satisfies

$$W^1(y) = \max\{U^1(x, y) + \delta U^1(x, r_2(x)) + \delta^2 W^1(r_2(x)), x \in X\}.$$

Therefore (r_1, r_2) is an MPE of the model with instantaneous payoffs U^1, U^2.

Remark. By an obvious adaptation of condition (ii), Proposition 3.1 can be restated for the case in which the two agents discount the future with two different discount factors δ_1 and δ_2.

We have not been able to give a general theorem on the existence of MPE for the model described above. The proof of the following theorem [which can be found in Dana and Montrucchio (1986)] is a trivial application of Proposition 3.1. It states that any pair of maps can be viewed as a MPE of some duopoly games and for any fixed discount factor δ, if it is small enough.

Proposition 3.2. Let $r_1 : T \to X$, $r_2 : X \to Y$ be any pair of continuous functions. Let δ be fixed in $(0, 1)$. There exist continuous payoffs U_1, U_2 such that (r_1, r_2) is a MPE for the associated Maskin–Tirole duopoly game when the discount factor equals δ. Moreover, if r_1 and r_2 are continuously twice differentiable, $U_1(\cdot, y)$ and $U_2(x, \cdot)$ can be chosen strictly concave for δ small enough.

The method behind the proof of this proposition makes use of the characterization of MPE given in Proposition 3.1. Take any pair of maps (r_1, r_2) and set

$$G^1(x, y) = -(1/2)\|x - r_1(y)\|^2 + L^1(y),$$

$$G^2(x, y) = -(1/2)\|y - r_2(x)\|^2 + L^2(x),$$

with two unspecified continuous functions L_1, L_2.

The functions G^1 and G^2 satisfy conditions (i) of Proposition 3.1 and $W^1(y) \equiv L^1(y)$, $W^2(x) \equiv L^2(x)$. Therefore the return functions U^1 and U^2, defined as in conditions (ii) of Proposition 3.1, exhibit the reaction maps (r_1, r_2) as a MPE. In general $U^1(\cdot, y)$ and $U^2(x, \cdot)$ are not concave but, whether r_1, r_2 are chosen of C^2 class, U^1 and U^2 are surely concave for δ small enough.

Contrary to the model with one decision-maker discussed in Section 2, no 'Turnpike' property seems to be true and small discount factors are no longer necessary. The next proposition is a precise statement of that.

Proposition 3.3. Let (r_1, r_2) be continuously twice differentiable and let us assume that there exist two C^2 functions: $L^1 : Y \to R$ and $L^2 : X \to R$ such that $L^1(r_2(x))$ and $L^2(r_1(y))$ are strongly convex (that means $h'D^2L^1(r_2(x))h \geq \alpha\|h\|^2$, $h'D^2L^2(r_1(y))h \geq \beta\|h\|^2$ hold for all x in X, y in Y and h in R^n and for some positive numbers α and β). Under these assumptions the statement of Proposition 3.2 holds for any fixed δ in $(0, 1)$.

Proof.   Take the functions

$$G^1(x, y) = -(1/2)\|x - r_1(y)\|^2 + m_1 L^1(y),$$

$$G^2(x, y) = -(1/2)\|y - r_2(x)\|^2 + m_2 L^2(x),$$

m_1, m_2 are positive parameters, L^1 and L^2 are the functions described in the statement of the proposition. $U^1(x, y)$ turns out to be equal to

$$U^1(x, y) = -(1/2)(1 - \mu)\|x\|^2 + (\mu/2)\|r_1(r_2(x))\|^2$$

$$- \mu \langle x, r_1(r_2(x)) \rangle - m_1 \delta L^1(r_2(x))$$

+ linear terms + a function depending on y alone. Here

$$\mu = \delta/(1 + \delta).$$

Being $L^1(r_2(x))$ strongly convex and the other terms with bounded second derivatives, $U^2(x, y)$ will be strongly concave in x for m_1 large enough. The same procedure is valid for $U^2(x, y)$ and this completes the proof.

By Propositions 3.2 and 3.3 we can construct a plethora of reaction functions exhibiting a chaotic behavior. Note that Proposition 3.3 holds for all the pairs (r_1, r_2) of maps that are invertible and of class C^2 (take $L^1(y) = (\alpha/2)\|r_2^{-1}(y)\|^2$ and $L^2(x) = (\beta/2)\|r_1^{-1}(x)\|^2$). But also several non-invertible maps can satisfy the assumptions of Proposition 3.3. For example, in Dana and Montrucchio (1986), we constructed duopoly games with a MPE formed by the choice functions: $r_1(x) = y$ and $r_2(x) = 4x(1 - x)$, x and y in $[0, 1]$ and for any fixed δ. It is easily seen that the sequences of moves of each agent are $y_{2k} = r_2^{(k)}(y_0)$, $x_{2k+1} = r_2^{(k)}(y_0)$ and y_0 is the first move of 2. Therefore, the moves of both agents are the iterates of the chaotic map r_2.

4. Reaction function equilibria

Friedman (1977) developed models of infinite horizon duopoly games with simultaneous moves and a markovian assumption on dynamical strategies. He called them 'Reaction Function Equilibria' (RFE). Similar methods to those used in section 3 may be applied. Let $W^1_{\delta r_2}(x, y)$ be the maximal value of the discounted sum of profits one may get given that in the last period the strategic variables were x and y and that player 2 will use the markovian continuous strategy $r_2: X \times Y \to Y$. Then $W^1_{\delta r_2}$ is the fixed point of the operator on $C^0(X \times Y)$,

$$(P_\delta f)(x, y) = \max_{x_1 \in X} \{U^1(x_1, r_2(x, y)) + \delta f(x_1, r_2(x, y))\},$$

and it satisfies

$$W^1_{\delta r_2}(x, y) = \max_{x_1 \in X} \{U^1(x_1, r_2(x, y)) + \delta W^1_{\delta r_2}(x_1, r_2(x, y))\}.$$

$W^2_{\delta r_1}$ is defined symmetrically.

As in the alternate case there does not exist in general a unique best-reply to a given expectation r_2. A pair $(r_{1\delta}, r_{2\delta})$ with $r_{1\delta}: X \times Y \to X$ and $r_{2\delta}: X \times Y \to Y$, is a RFE iff

$$r_{1\delta}(x, y) \in \text{argmax} \{U_1(x_1, r_{2\delta}(x, y)) + \delta W^1_{\delta r_{2\delta}}(x_1, r_{2\delta}(x, y))\},$$

$$r_{2\delta}(x, y) \in \text{argmax} \{U_2(r_{1\delta}(x, y), y_1) + \delta W^2_{r_{1\delta}}(r_{1\delta}(x, y), y_1)\}. \tag{7}$$

Contrary to the alternate case, a trivial solution always exists for any δ: $r_{1\delta}(x, y) \equiv x_0$, $r_{2\delta}(x, y) \equiv y_0$, where (x_0, y_0) is a Cournot–Nash solution of the one-shot game. This can easily be verified by setting $W^1(x, y) = U^1(x_0, y_0)/(1 - \delta)$ and $W^2(x, y) = U^2(x_0, y_0)/(1 - \delta)$ in (7).

It can also be shown [see for example Cyert and De Groot (1970)] that if agents have a finite horizon the only sequences of reaction functions that can be optimal against each other are functions equal in each period to a Nash equilibrium of the one-shot game.

The question we want to answer: does there exist models with non-trivial RFE? We first characterize RFE in a way similar to Proposition 3.1.

Proposition 4.1. The pair (r_1, r_2) is a continuous RFE for a fixed value $\delta \in (0, 1)$ iff the following two conditions are satisfied:

(i) There exist two real continuous functions G^1 defined on $X \times Y$ such that

$$\max_{x_1} G^1(x_1, r_2(x, y)) = G^1(r_1(x, y), r_2(x, y)) \equiv W^1(x, y),$$

$$\max_{y_1} G^2(r_1(x, y), y_1) = G^2(r_1(x, y), r_2(x, y)) \equiv W^2(x, y).$$

(ii) $U^1(x, y) = G^1(x, y) - \delta G^1(r_1(x, y), r_2(x, y))$ is concave in x, $U^2(x, y) = G^2(x, y) - \delta G^2(r_1(x, y), r_2(x, y))$ is concave in y.

Proof. The proof is similar to that of Proposition 3.1. Let (r_1, r_2) be a continuous RFE. Let $W^1_{\delta r_2}$ be the value function associated to r_2. Set $G^1(x, y) = U^1(x, y) + W^1_{\delta r_2}(x, y)$.

The (i) holds by taking $W^1(x, y) \equiv W^1_{\delta r_2}(x, y)$. In fact,

$$\max_{x_1} G^1(x_1, r_2(x, y)) = \max_{x_1} \{U^1(x_1, r_2(x, y)) + W^1(x_1, r_2(x, y))\}$$

$$= W^1(x, y) = G^1(r_1(x, y), r_2(x, y)).$$

Condition (ii) holds because

$$U^1(x, y) = G^1(x, y) - \delta W^1(x, y) = G^1(x, y) - \delta G^1(r_1(x, y), r_2(x, y)).$$

Conversely, suppose that G^i exist satisfying (i) and (ii). Let U^i be defined by (ii). Then, from (ii), it follows that

$$G^1(x, y) = U^1(x, y) + \delta G^1(r_1(x, y), r_2(x, y)) = U^1(x, y) + \delta W^1(x, y).$$

Thus $W^1(x, y)$ is the value function associated to r_2 since it solves the equation

$$W^1(x, y) = \max_{x_1} G^1(x_1, r_2(x, y))$$

$$= \max_{x_1} \{U^1(x_1, r_2(x, y)) + \delta W^1(x_1, r_2(x, y))\}$$

$$= G^1(r_1(x, y), r_2(x, y)).$$

Using Proposition 4.1 we can get examples of games with non-trivial RFE.

Proposition 4.2. Let r_1 and r_2 be two C^2 functions such that there exists a C^2 diffeomorphism m from Y into X such that $r_1(x, y) = m(r_2(x, y))$. Then there exists a δ^* such that for every $\delta \in (0, \delta^*)$, there exists U^1 and U^2 such that (r_1, r_2) is the RFE of the corresponding Friedman's model for the value δ.

Proof. Let $G^1(x, y)$ be a C^2 concave function in x such that $\max\{G^1(x, y), x \in X\} = G^1(m(y), y)$. (Take, for example, $G^1(x, y) = -(1/2)\|x\|^2 + \langle x, m(y) \rangle$). Then $G^1(mr_2(x, y), r_2(x, y)) = G^1(r_1(x, y), r_2(x, y))$ so that (i) of Proposition 4.1 is satisfied. Define $U^1(x, y)$ by $U^1(x, y) = G^1(x, y) - \delta G^1(r_1(x, y), r_2(x, y))$, then for δ small enough U^1 is strictly concave in x. Since $r_2(x, y) = m^{-1}(r_1(x, y))$, an analogous argument can be used for finding the payoff U^2.

Proposition 4.3. Suppose that there exist functions $s_1: X \to R$ and $s_2: Y \to R$ such that $s_2(r_2(x, y))$ is strictly convex in x and $s_1(r_1(x, y))$ is strictly convex in y. For any δ functions U^1 and U^2 exist such that (r_1, r_2) is an RFE for that value δ.

508   R.-A. Dana and L. Montrucchio, Rational dynamic strategies

Proof. Take $G^1(x, y) = s_2(y)$. We have $\max\{G^1(x_1, r_2(x, y)); x_1 \in X\} =$ $\max s_2(r_2(x, y)) \equiv s_2(r_2(x, y))$ and condition (i) of Proposition 4.1 is trivially fulfilled.

Set $U^1(x, y) = s_2(y) - \delta s_2(r_2(x, y))$. U^1 turns out to be strictly concave in x for every fixed y and thus the condition (ii) of Proposition 4.1 holds. U^2 is defined analogously as $U^2(x, y) = s_1(x) - \delta s_1(r_1(x, y))$.

5. Chaotic optimal sequences

Proposition 4.3 can be applied to the case in which $r_1(x, y) \equiv r_1(y)$ and $r_2(x, y) \equiv r_2(x)$. Here is an example of a RFE with chaotic trajectories generated by the 'tent' map.

Put $X = Y = [0, 1]$, $r_1(y) = y$, $r_2(x) = 2x$ if $x \in [0, 1/2]$ and $r_2(x) = 2(1 - x)$ if $x \in [1/2, 1]$. The function $r_2(x)$ is the 'tent' map. It leaves invariant the Lebesgue measure, it is mixing and has topological entropy equal to $2 \lg 2$ [see Dana and Montrucchio (1986) and references quoted therein].

According to Proposition 4.3, we set $s_1(x) = x^2$ and $s_2(y) = -(y)^{1/2}$. The return functions are $U^1(x, y) = -(y)^{1/2} + \delta(r_2(x))^{1/2}$ and $U^2 = x^2 - \delta y^2$.

From Proposition 4.3 it follows that (r_1, r_2) is a RFE when the discount factor equals δ. The dynamics is generated by the first-order difference system $x_t = y_{t-1}$, $y_t = r_2(x_{t-1})$. The trajectory starting at (x_0, y_0) can be written out

$$x_{2k+1} = r_2^{(k)}(y_0), \quad x_{2k} = r_2^{(k)}(x_0), \quad y_t = x_{t+1} \quad \text{for} \quad k = 0, 1, 2, \ldots,$$

and where $r_2^{(k)}(x) = r_2(r_2^{(k-1)}(x))$ and $r^{(0)}(x) \equiv x$.

It is easily seen that these sequences are chaotic as being generated by the map $r_2(x)$.

We conclude this paper by giving an example of a game with quadratic payoffs and that displays the Henon's attractor as a RFE. Let

$$r_1(x, y) = (1/2)[1 + (1 + b)x + (b - 1)y - a(x + y)^2], \quad \text{and}$$

$$r_2(x, y) = (1/2)[1 + (1 - b)x - (1 + b)y - a(x + y)^2],$$

x, y in R and a and b positive. Proposition 4.3 holds by taking $s_1(x) = -x$ and $s_2(y) = -y$. This leads to the quadratic functions $U^1(x, y) = -y + \delta r_2(x, y)$, $U^2(x, y) = -x + \delta r_1(x, y)$.

By the linear changing of variables $X = x + y$, $Y = x - y$, the first-order difference system $x_{t+1} = r_1(x_t, y_t)$, $y_{t+1} = r_2(x_t, y_t)$ becomes $X_{t+1} = 1 + Y_t - aX_t^2$ and $Y_{t+1} = bX_t$.

It is a well-known two-dimensional dynamical system pointed out by

R.-A. Dana and L. Montrucchio, Rational dynamic strategies 509

Henon (1976). For example, for $a = 1.4$ and $b = 0.3$ there is a 'strange attractor' which appears to be the product of a one-dimensional manifold by a Cantor set.

Appendix

Proposition. The operator $P(\delta, r_2)$ defined in (5) is a contraction of modulus δ^2.

Proof. Fix two functions $f_1, f_2 \in C^0(Y)$ and a point y in Y. Let us write $P(\delta, r_2)f_1 = g_1$ and $P(\delta, r_2)f_2 = g_2$, for short. By compactness and continuity of the functions, a point x_1 in X will exist such that

$$g_1(y) = U^1(x_1, y) + \delta U^1(x_1, r_2(x_1)) + \delta^2 f_1(r_2(x_1)), \qquad \text{and}$$

$$g_2(y) \geq U^1(x_1, y) + \delta U^1(x_1, r_2(x_1)) + \delta^2 f_2(r_2(x_1)).$$

Subtracting, we have

$$g_1(y) - g_2(y) \leq \delta^2(f_1(r_2(x_1)) - f_2(r_2(x_1)))$$

$$\leq \delta^2 |f_1(r_2(x_1)) - f_2(r_2(x_1))|$$

$$\leq \delta^2 \|f_1 - f_2\|.$$

Interchanging g_1 with g_2, we have

$$|g_1(y) - g_2(y)| \leq \delta^2 \|f_1 - f_2\|.$$

This holds for every y and thus

$$\|g_1 - g_2\| \leq \delta^2 \|f_1 - f_2\|$$

and the proposition is proven.

Proof of Proposition 2.4.

Let $\theta: K \to K$ be given. Consider the family of functions: $W(k, k') = -(1/2)\|k' - \theta(k)\|^2 - (m/2)\|k\|^2 + \langle a, k \rangle$, m is a positive parameter and a is a vector in R^n.

Here $\langle x, y \rangle$ denotes the scalar product and $\|x\| = (\langle x, x \rangle)^{1/2}$. The functions $W(k, k')$ satisfy (i) of Proposition 2.3 and

$$\max\{W(k, k'), k' \in K\} = W(k, \theta(k)) = -(m/2)\|k\|^2 + \langle a, k \rangle.$$

It will be sufficient to impose that condition (ii) holds.
In other words the function

$$V(k, k') = W(k, k') - W(k', \theta(k')) = -(1/2)\|k' - \theta(k)\|^2 - (m/2)\|k\|^2$$

$$+ (m\delta/2)\|k'\|^2 + \langle a, k \rangle - \langle a, k' \rangle$$

has to be strictly concave on $K \times K$.

Since $\theta \in C^2$, we can compute the second derivative of $V(k, k')$. Tedious but straightforward computations lead to the following quadratic form associated to the Hessian matrix $D^2 V(k, k')$:

$$(h, s)' D^2 V(k, k')(h, s) = -m\|h\|^2 - (1 - m\delta)\|s\|^2 - \|D\theta(k)h\|^2$$

$$+ \langle k' - \theta(k), D^2\theta(k)h^2 \rangle + 2\langle s, D\theta(k)h \rangle$$

$$\leq -(1 - m\delta)\|s\|^2 + 2k_1\|s\|\|h\| + (\mu k_2 - m)\|h\|^2.$$

Here h, s are vectors in R^n.
By setting $t = \|s\|/\|h\|$, we can write

$$(h, s)' D^2 V(k, k')(h, s) \leq \|h\|^2 [-(1 - m\delta)t^2 + 2k_1 t + (\mu k_2 - m)].$$

We deduce that $V(k, k')$ is strictly concave on $K \times K$ if $-(1 - m\delta)t^2 + 2k_1 t + (\mu k_2 - m) \leq 0$ for all $t \geq 0$. This is true iff $\delta \leq (1/m) - k_1^2/[m(m - \mu k_2)]$ and $m \geq \mu k_2$.

By simple algebraic arguments, it is not difficult to prove that the greatest value of δ, which is consistent with the last inequalities, is given by $\delta^* = [\mu k_2 + 2k_1^2 - 2k_1(k_2^2 + \mu k_2)^{1/2}]/\mu^2 k_2^2$ and this concludes the proof.

References

Bellman, R., 1957, Dynamic programming (Princeton University Press, Princeton, NJ).

Benhabib, J. and R.H. Day, 1981, Rational choice and erratic behaviour, Review of Economic Studies 48, 459–471.

Benhabib, J. and R.H. Day, 1982, A characterization of erratic dynamics in the overlapping generations model, Journal of Economic Dynamics and Control 4, 37–55.

Blackwell, D., 1965, Discounted dynamic programming, Annals of Mathematical Statistics 36, 226–235.

Boldrin, M., 1987, Paths of optimal accumulation in two-sector models, Mimeo. (University of Chicago, Chicago, IL).

Boldrin, M. and L. Montrucchio, 1986, On the indeterminacy of capital accumulation paths, Journal of Economic Theory 40, 26–39.

Cyert, R.M. and M.H. DeGroot, 1970, Multiperiod decision models with alternating choice as a solution to the duopoly problem, Quarterly Journal of Economics 84, 410–429.

Dana, R.A. and L. Montrucchio, 1986, Dynamic complexity in duopoly games, Journal of Economic Theory 40, 40–56.

Denardo, E., 1967, Contraction mappings in the theory underlying dynamic programming, SIAM Review 9, 165-177.

Deneckere, R. and S. Pelikan, 1986, Competitive chaos, Journal of Economic Theory 40, 13-25.

Friedman, J.W., 1977, Oligopoly and the theory of games (North-Holland, Amsterdam).

Grandmont, J.M., 1985, On endogenous competitive business cycles, Econometrica 53, 995–1045.

Henon, M., 1976, A two-dimensional mapping with a strange attractor, Communications in Mathematical Physics 50, 69–77.

Hildenbrand, W., 1974, Core and equilibria of a large economy (Princeton University Press, Princeton, NJ).

McKenzie, L.W., 1986, Optimal economic growth, turnpike theorems and comparative dynamics, in: K.J. Arrow and M.D. Intriligator, eds., Handbook of Mathematical Economics, Vol. III (North-Holland, Amsterdam).

Maskin, E. and J. Tirole, 1983, A theory of dynamic oligopoly competition with large fixed costs (C.E.R.A.S., Paris).

Maskin, E. and J. Tirole, 1985, A theory of dynamic oligopoly II: Price competition, Working Paper 373 (MIT, Cambridge, MA).

Montrucchio, L., 1986, Optimal decisions over time and strange attractors: An analysis by the Bellman Principle, Mathematical Modelling 7, 341–352.

Scheinkman, J.A., 1976, On optimal steady states of *n*-sector growth models when utility is discounted, Journal of Economic Theory 12, 11–30.

[13]

Journal of Economic Behavior and Organization 12 (1989) 1–28. North-Holland

DETERMINISTIC CHAOS IN AN EXPERIMENTAL ECONOMIC SYSTEM*

John D. STERMAN

Massachusetts Institute of Technology, Sloan School of Management, Cambridge, MA 02139, USA

Final version received July 1988

An experiment with a simulated macroeconomic system demonstrates that the decision-making processes of agents can produce deterministic chaos. Subjects managed capital investment in a simple multiplier–accelerator economy. Performance, however, was systematically suboptimal. A model of the subjects' decision rule is proposed and related to prior studies of dynamic decision making. Econometric estimates show the model is an excellent representation of the actual decisions. The estimated rules are then simulated to evaluate the stability of the subjects' decision processes. While the majority of the estimated rules are stable, approximately 40% yield a variety of dynamics including limit cycles, period multiples, and chaos. Analysis of the parameter space reveals a complex bifurcation structure. Implications for models of human systems and experimental studies of economic dynamics are explored.

1. Introduction: coupling nonlinear dynamics and experimental economics

Recent work in the physical sciences has shown deterministic chaos to be a common mode of behavior in dynamic systems, thus stimulating the search for chaos and other highly nonlinear phenomena in human systems. Indeed, there has been a near explosion of models and empirical studies which seek to show the relevance of nonlinear dynamics and chaos in social and economic settings. Several journals have devoted special issues to chaos and models of nonlinear, disequilibrium dynamics in human systems.[1] This robust literature can be divided roughly into (1) theoretical models of nonlinear dynamics, and (2) empirical studies which seek evidence of chaos in economic data.

Theoretical studies include the work of Day (1982), Dana and Malgrange (1984), Grandmont (1985), Rasmussen and Mosekilde (1988), Stutzer (1980),

---

*The contributions and comments of Richard Day, Christian Kampmann, Edward Lorenz, Ilya Prigogine, James Ramsey, Rebecca Waring, and particularly Erik Mosekilde are gratefully acknowledged. The usual exemption applies.

[1]Journal of Economic Theory 40(1), 1986; Journal of Economic Behavior and Organization 8(3), September 1987; System Dynamics Review 4, 1988; European Journal of Operational Research 35, 1988. See also Goodwin, Kruger and Vercelli (1984) and Prigogine and Sanglier (1987).

and many others (see note 1). A survey of these studies suggests the following generalizations. First, many standard models, both micro- and macro-economic, when modified to include realistic nonlinearities, can be shown to contain regimes of chaos and other nonlinear phenomena such as mode-locking, period multiples, and quasiperiodicity. Benhabib and Day's (1981) studies of such simple models lead them to 'expect the possibility of erratic [chaotic] behavior for a wide variety of dynamic economic models involving rational decision-making with feedback.' Subsequent work has borne out this conjecture – the possibility of chaos does not seem to depend on particular behavioral assumptions but on more fundamental properties. However, most models of nonlinear dynamics have been purely theoretical, and have not involved econometric estimation of the parameters. The few exceptions have found the estimated parameters lie well outside the chaotic regime, e.g. Candela and Gardini (1986) and Dana and Malgrange (1984). As Day and Shafer (1985, p. 293) note,

> 'Whether or not we can construct empirical models that offer convincing explanation of *real world* macro activity [in terms of deterministic chaos] is an open question: most economists would probably agree that we are as yet quite far from a definitive answer to it. What we know now ... is that among the empirical phenomena that we can hope to explain ... are stochasticlike fluctuations in economic data. Moreover, we need not expect that exotic assumptions or bizzare model structures will be required' (emphasis in original).

The relative simplicity and theoretical focus of the models is entirely appropriate to the early exploration of new concepts and analytical tools. However, the theoretical work to date leaves unanswered questions about the relevance of these models. Can chaos arise from the behavior of actual agents? Do the chaotic regimes in the models lie in the realistic region of parameter space, or are they mathematical curiosities unrealized in actual economic systems?

The empirical literature has sought to answer these questions by searching for evidence of chaos in economic data. This literature is notable for the clever adaptation of techniques originally applied in physical settings, such as the Takens (1985) method for recovering low-dimensional attractors from a single time series, the Wolf, Swift, Swinney, and Vastano (1985) technique for estimation of Lyapunov exponents from experimental time series, and the Grassberger–Procaccia (1983) correlation dimension. The results are tantalizingly suggestive but inconclusive. Brock (1986) demonstrates a method to test the hypothesis of chaos in economic data against explicit alternative hypotheses, but finds 'that there is not enough information available in U.S. real GNP, real gross private domestic investment, and Wolfer's sunspot series ... to reject the null hypothesis that ... [these series were] generated by an AR(2) process.' Chen (1988) and Barnett and Chen (1988), however, find evidence of low dimensional strange attractors in some but not all measures of U.S. monetary aggregates. Their conclusions are tempered, however, by uncertainties such as the sensitivity of the methods used to the number of data points, the number of points per orbit, the (unknown) magnitude and statistical character of process noise, and the (unknown) magnitude and character of measurement error [Ramsey and Yuan (1987)]. Brock (1986, p. 192) concludes 'It is *not* enough when you are working with short data sets to report low dimension and positive Lyapunov exponents to make the case for deterministic chaos in your data' (emphasis in original). Ramsey, Sayers, and Rothman (1988) have identified significant biases in calculations of correlation dimension caused by small sample size and conclude 'that while there is abundant evidence for the presence of nonlinear stochastic processes, there is virtually no evidence at the moment for the presence of simple chaotic attractors of the type that have been discovered in the physical sciences.'

The prevalence of chaos in the models but low power of aggregate statistical tests motivates a complementary approach based on laboratory experiments with simulated economic systems. The pioneering work of Smith (1982, 1986), Plott (1986), and others has demonstrated that many economic theories can be successfully tested in the laboratory. This paper applies these techniques to the investigation of chaos in economic systems. I report the results of an experiment with a simulated macroeconomic system, specifically a multiplier–accelerator model. In the experiment, subjects play the role of managers of the capital-producing sector of an economy. Each time period they must make a capital investment decision. The task of the agents is to manage a complex dynamic system in disequilibrium, a system with time lags, multiple feedbacks, and nonlinearities. I show that the behavior of the subjects is systematically suboptimal, suggesting the use of a common heuristic for decision making. A model of the subjects' decision rule is proposed. The model is well grounded in the literature of economics, psychology, and behavioral decision theory. Econometric estimation shows the decision rule explains the agents' behavior well. Next the estimated decision rules are simulated, and it is shown that approximately 40% of the agents produce unstable behavior, including chaos. The parameter space of the system is mapped and shown to contain a complex bifurcation structure. Thus experimental evidence is adduced that the actual decision processes of agents in a common economic context can produce chaos. Limitations of the method, implications, and suggestions for future research are discussed.

2. The model

The experiment is based on a simple model of the capital investment accelerator and is fully described in Sterman (1989). The model creates a two-sector economy with a capital producing and goods producing sector. The focus is the capital investment accelerator. Goodwin (1951, p. 4) notes that the traditional acceleration principle assumes

> ... that actual, realized capital stock is maintained at the desired relation with output. We know in reality that it is seldom so, there being now too much and now too little capital stock. For this there are two good reasons. The rate of investment is limited by the capacity of the investment goods industry. ... At the other extreme there is an even more inescapable and effective limit. Machines, once made, cannot be unmade, so that negative investment is limited to attrition from wear. ... Therefore capital stock cannot be increased fast enough in the upswing, nor decreased fast enough in the downswing, so that at one time we have shortages and rationing of orders and at the other excess capacity with idle plants and machines.

A single factor of production (capital plant and equipment) is considered. The model includes, however, an explicit representation of the capital acquisition delay (construction lag) and the capacity of the investment goods sector. As a result, orders for and acquisition of capital are not necessarily equal, and at any moment there will typically be a supply line of capital under construction. For simplicity, the demand for capital of the goods-producing sector is exogenous, and there is no representation of the consumption multiplier.

The model allows for variable utilization of the capital stock. Thus production P is the lesser of desired production P^* or production capacity C. Capacity is proportional to the capital stock, with capital/output ratio κ:

$$P_t = \min(P_t^*, C_t), \tag{1}$$

$$C_t = K_t/\kappa. \tag{2}$$

The capital stock of the capital sector is augmented by acquisitions A and diminished by depreciation D. The average lifetime of capital is given by τ:

$$K_{t+1} = K_t + (A_t - D_t) \tag{3}$$

$$D_t = K_t/\tau. \tag{4}$$

The acquisition of capital by both the capital and goods sectors (A and AG) depends on the supply line of unfilled orders each has accumulated (the backlogs B and BG) and the fraction of the backlog delivered that period ϕ (the suffix 'G' denotes a variable of the goods-producing sector):

$$A_t = B_t \cdot \phi_t, \tag{5}$$

$$AG_t = BG_t \cdot \phi_t, \tag{6}$$

$$\phi_t = P_t / P_t^*, \tag{7}$$

$$P_t^* = B_t + BG_t. \tag{8}$$

Each period both the capital and goods sectors acquire the full supply line of unfilled orders unless the capital sector is unable to produce the required amount. If capacity is insufficient so that $P^* > C$, $\phi < 1$ and shipments to each sector fall in proportion to the shortfall. Note that the formulation for ϕ implies that $A + AG = P$ at all times, ensuring that output is conserved. The explicit representation of the construction supply line and the constraint on production mean that the lag in acquiring capital may be variable. It is easily shown that the average capital acquisition lag $\Lambda = 1/\phi$. Normally, $\phi = 1$ and $\Lambda = 1$ period. If capacity is inadequate, however, ϕ falls and Λ lengthens as the backlogs of unfilled orders grow relative to output.[2]

The supply lines of unfilled orders for each sector B and BG are augmented by orders for capital placed by each sector and emptied when those orders are delivered:

$$B_{t+1} = B_t + (O_t - A_t), \tag{9}$$

$$BG_{t+1} = BG_t + (OG_t - AG_t). \tag{10}$$

Orders placed by the goods sector are an exogenous input to which the subjects of the experiment must respond by ordering an appropriate amount of capital for their own use:

$$OG_t = \text{exogenous}, \tag{11}$$

$$O_t = \text{determined by subject}. \tag{12}$$

Eqs. (1)–(12) thus define a third-order nonlinear difference equation system. The system has the interesting property that the nonlinear capacity utilization function of eq. (1) divides the system into two distinct regimes, $\phi = 1$ and $\phi < 1$. Furthermore, the equilibrium point $P^* = C$ lies exactly at the boundary. Considering each region in turn reveals interesting properties of the open loop system. When $P^* = P < C$, $\phi = 1$, and the system is linear:

[2]Conservation of output requires $P = A + AG$. But $A + AG = B \cdot \phi + BG \cdot \phi = \phi(B + BG) = (P/P^*)(B + BG) = P$. By Little's law, the average residence time of items in a backlog is the ratio of the backlog to the outflow, here given by $\Lambda = (B + BG)/(A + AG)$. By eqs. (4)–(5), $(B + BG)/(A + AG) = (B + BG)/(B \cdot \phi + BG \cdot \phi) = 1/\phi$.

$$
\begin{bmatrix} K_{t+1} \\ B_{t+1} \\ BG_{t+1} \end{bmatrix} = \begin{bmatrix} 1-1/\tau & 1 & 0 \\ 0 & 0 & 0 \\ 0 & 0 & 0 \end{bmatrix} \begin{bmatrix} K_t \\ B_t \\ BG_t \end{bmatrix} + \begin{bmatrix} 0 & 0 \\ 1 & 0 \\ 0 & 1 \end{bmatrix} \begin{bmatrix} O_t \\ OG_t \end{bmatrix}.
\tag{13}
$$

Excess capacity implies each sector receives the quantity ordered after one period. Note that the system in this regime is always stable. The capital stock is controllable via orders O (it depreciates with lifetime τ towards an equilibrium of $\tau \cdot O$). BG is not controllable – when there is excess capacity, the goods-producing and capital-producing sectors are decoupled.

When capacity is inadequate, however, $P^* > P = C$, $\phi < 1$, and the system is nonlinear. Linearizing the system around the operating point $(\overline{K}, \overline{B}, \overline{BG})$ and defining $\overline{P^*} = \overline{B} + \overline{BG}$ and $\overline{\phi} = (\overline{K}/\kappa)/\overline{P^*}$ yields

$$
\begin{bmatrix} K_{t+1} \\ B_{t+1} \\ BG_{t+1} \end{bmatrix} = \begin{bmatrix} 1 - \dfrac{1}{\tau} + \dfrac{\overline{B}}{\kappa \overline{P^*}} & \overline{\phi}\dfrac{\overline{BG}}{\overline{P^*}} & -\overline{\phi}\dfrac{\overline{B}}{\overline{P^*}} \\[2mm] -\dfrac{\overline{B}}{\kappa \overline{P^*}} & 1 - \overline{\phi}\dfrac{\overline{BG}}{\overline{P^*}} & \overline{\phi}\dfrac{\overline{B}}{\overline{P^*}} \\[2mm] -\dfrac{\overline{BG}}{\kappa \overline{P^*}} & \overline{\phi}\dfrac{\overline{BG}}{\overline{P^*}} & 1 - \overline{\phi}\dfrac{\overline{B}}{\overline{P^*}} \end{bmatrix} \begin{bmatrix} K_t \\ B_t \\ BG_t \end{bmatrix}
$$

$$
+ \begin{bmatrix} 0 & 0 \\ 1 & 0 \\ 0 & 1 \end{bmatrix} \begin{bmatrix} O_t \\ OG_t \end{bmatrix}.
\tag{14}
$$

When capacity is inadequate the goods and capital sectors are highly coupled. The eigenvalues of the open loop system for $\phi < 1$ are readily found to be

$$
\lambda = \begin{cases} 1 \\[2mm] 1 - \dfrac{1}{\tau} + \dfrac{\overline{B}}{\kappa \overline{P^*}}. \\[3mm] 1 - \overline{\phi}. \end{cases}
\tag{15}
$$

All three eigenvalues are real, indicating that the open loop system is not oscillatory. Note also that the system always has an eigenvalue of unity, indicating neutral stability and the importance of the higher order terms excluded from the linearization. The role of nonlinearity is also highlighted by the other eigenvalues, both of which are functions of the operating point around which the system is linearized. While $1 - \overline{\phi} \leqq 1$ for all $\overline{\phi}$, the term $1 - (1/\tau) + (\overline{B}/\kappa \overline{P^*})$ may easily exceed unity, in which case the open loop system is unstable.

Thus the simplicity of the system belies considerable complexity of the dynamics. Of course, the closed loop properties of the system will depend on the decision rule for orders O. Nevertheless, the sharp differences between the two regimes and strong effects of the nonlinearities suggest effective management of the system will be difficult.

3. Experimental protocol

The methodological foundations of experimental economics are discussed in the seminal work of Smith (1982) and Plott (1986). The experimental protocol used here is described in Sterman and Meadows (1985) and Sterman (1987, 1989). A continuous time version of the model is developed and analyzed in Sterman (1985). For the experiment it has been converted to discrete time. Simulation and formal analysis confirm that the conversion to discrete time does not alter the essential dynamics of the system [Rasmussen, Mosekilde and Sterman (1985), Sterman (1988a)]. The experiment is implemented on IBM PC-type microcomputers. A 'game board' is displayed on the screen and provides the subjects with perfect information. Color graphics and animation highlight the flows of orders, production, and shipments to increase the transparency of the structure (fig. 1).[3] No overt time pressure was imposed. The parameters ($\kappa = 1$ and $\tau = 10$) were chosen to minimize the computational burden imposed on the subjects, while remaining close to the original values.

The subject population ($N = 49$) consisted of MIT undergraduate, master's and doctoral students in management and engineering, many with extensive exposure to economics and control theory; scientists and economists from various institutions in the U.S., Europe and the Soviet Union; and business executives experienced in capital investment decisions including several corporate presidents and CEOs.

Subjects are responsible for only one decision – how much capital to order. The goal of the subjects in making these decisions is to minimize total costs. The cost function or score S is defined as the average absolute deviation between desired production P^* and production capacity C over the T periods of experiment:

$$S = \left(\frac{1}{T} \right) \sum_{t=1}^{T} |P_t^* - C_t|. \tag{16}$$

---

[3]Disks suitable for IBM PC's and compatibles, or for the Apple Macintosh, are available from the author.

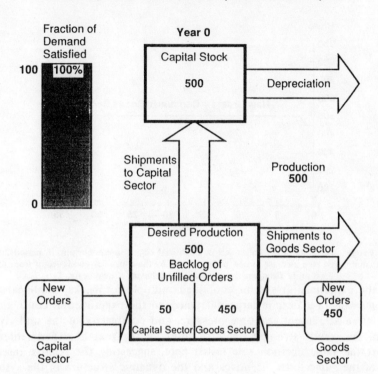

Fig. 1. Computer screen showing experimental economy, initial configuration. The subject is about to enter new orders for the capital sector.

The cost function indicates how well subjects balance demand and supply. Subjects are penalized equally for both excess demand and excess supply. Absolute value rather than quadratic or asymmetric costs provide an incentive to reach equilibrium while minimizing the complexity of the subjects' decision-making task. A caveat: monetary rewards were not used, in violation of Smith's (1982) protocol for experimental microeconomics. While many economists argue that significant performance-based rewards are necessary to establish external validity, a number of experiments in preference reversal [Grether and Plott (1979), Slovic and Lichtenstein (1983)] suggest performance is not materially affected by reward levels. Similar experiments have found weak or even negative effects of incentives on performance, though further study is needed [Hogarth and Reder (1987)]. Other experiments in dynamic decision making suggest the results are robust with respect to significant variations in the experimental environment. Sterman (1988b) describes an experiment with a simulated production-distribution system in which financial rewards were used. Like the model

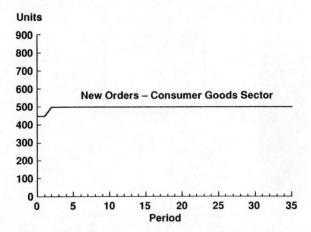

Fig. 2. Exogenous orders of the goods sector. Each trial begins in equilibrium. In period 2 there is an unannounced step increase in new orders placed by the consumer goods sector from 450 to 500 units. Compare against subjects' behavior shown in fig. 3.

here, the experimental system contained multiple feedbacks, nonlinearities, and time lags. Yet despite large differences in the experimental cover story, information set, incentives, time pressure, and complexity of the underlying system, the results strongly reinforce those of the present experiment and support the same decision rule tested here, suggesting the relative insensitivity of the subjects to incentives and the dynamic structure of the system. Other studies of dynamic decision making which generally support the results here include Brehmer (1987) and MacKinnon and Wearing (1985).

4. Results

The trials reported below were run for 36 periods. All were initialized in equilibrium with orders of 450 units each period from the goods sector and capital stock of 500 units. Depreciation is therefore 50 units per period, requiring the capital sector to order 50 units each period to compensate. By eq. (8) desired production then equals $450 + 50$, exactly equal to capacity, and yielding an initial cost of zero. Orders for capital from the goods sector OG, the only exogenous input to the system, remain constant at 450 for the first two periods. In the third period OG rises from 450 to 500, and remains at 500 thereafter (fig. 2). The step input is not announced to the subjects in advance.

Several trials representative of the sample are plotted in fig. 3; table 1 summarizes the sample. Trial 16 is typical. The subject reacts aggressively to the increase in demand by ordering 150 units in period 2. The increase in orders further boosts desired production, leading the subject to order still more. Because capacity is inadequate to meet the higher level of demand,

10   *J.D. Sterman, Deterministic chaos in an experimental economic system*

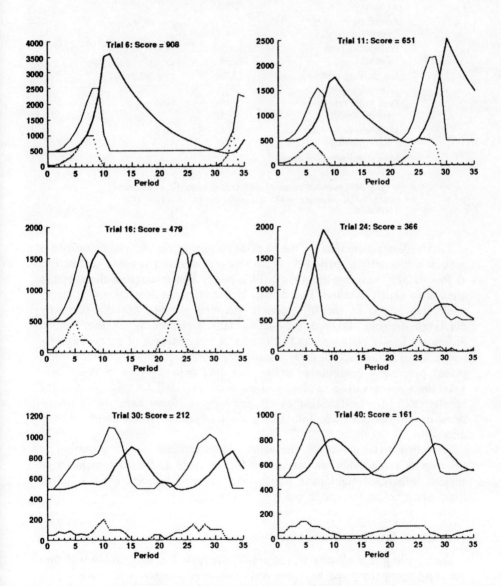

Fig. 3. Typical experimental results. N.B.: vertical scales differ.

Table 1
Summary of experimental results.[a]

	Experiment	Optimal
Costs	432	19
(units)	(382)	
Periodicity	45	no cycle
(periods)	(11)	
1st capacity peak	3,935	630
(units)	(1,346)	
2nd capacity peak	1,139	no 2nd peak
(units)	(671)	
Peak order rate	518	260
(units/period)	(501)	
Minimum order rate	4	0
(units/period)	(11)	
Minimum fraction of demand	14	62
satisfied (ϕ) (%)	(13)	

[a]Std. dev. in parentheses; $N = 48$; trial 1 excluded as an outlier (score 8,229; capacity peak $> 27,000$; maximum order rate of 6,000 units).

unfilled orders accumulate in the backlog, boosting desired production to a peak of 1,590 units in period 6. The fraction of demand satisfied ϕ drops to as low as 52%, slowing the growth of capacity and frustrating the subject's attempt to satisfy demand. Faced with high and rising demand, the subject's orders reach 500 in the fifth period. Between periods 7 and 8 capacity overtakes demand. Desired production falls precipitously as the unfilled orders are finally produced and delivered. A huge margin of excess capacity opens up. The subject slashes orders after period 5, but too late. Orders placed previously continue to arrive, boosting capacity to a peak of over 1,600 units. Orders drop to zero, and capacity then declines through discards for the next 12 periods. Significantly, the subject allows capacity to under-shoot its equilibrium value, initiating a second cycle of similar amplitude and duration.

The other trials are much the same. While specifics vary the pattern of behavior is remarkably similar. As shown in table 1, the vast majority of subjects generated significant oscillations. Only 4 subjects (8%) achieved equilibrium before the end of the trial.

5. Proposed decision rule and estimation results

The qualitative similarity of the results suggests the subjects, though not behaving optimally, used heuristics with common features. The decision rule proposed here was used in the original simulation model upon which the experiment is based [Sterman (1985)] and is a variant of rules long used in models of corporate and economic systems [Samuelson (1939), Metzler (1941), Holt et al. (1960), Forrester (1961), Low (1980)]. The rule determines orders for capital O as a function of information locally available to an individual firm. Such information includes the current desired rate of production P^*, current production capacity C, the rate of capital discards D, the supply line SL of orders for capacity which the firm has placed but not yet received, and the capital acquisition lag Λ:

$$O_t = f(P_t^*, C_t, D_t, SL_t, \Lambda_t). \tag{17}$$

Specifically, capital orders O are given by replacement of discards modified by an adjustment for the adequacy of the capital stock AC and an adjustment for the adequacy of the supply line ASL. Accounting for the nonnegativity constraint on gross investment and allowing for an additive disturbance ε yields:

$$O_t = \max(0, D_t + AC_t + ASL_t + \varepsilon_t). \tag{18}$$

Each of the three terms represents a separate motivation for investment. To maintain the existing capital stock at its current value, the firm must order enough to replace discards. The firm is assumed to adjust orders above or below discards in response to two additional pressures. The adjustment for capital AC represents the response to discrepancies between the desired and actual capital stock. The adjustment for supply line ASL represents the response to the quantity of capital in the supply line, that is, capital which has been ordered but not yet received.

The adjustment for capital is assumed to be proportional to the gap between desired capital stock K^* and the actual stock. Desired capital is determined from the desired rate of production P^* and the capital/output ratio κ:

$$AC_t = \alpha_K(K_t^* - K_t), \tag{19}$$

$$K_t^* = \kappa \cdot P_t^*. \tag{20}$$

The adjustment for capital creates a straightforward negative feedback loop.

When desired production exceeds capacity orders for capital will rise above discards until the gap is closed. An excess of capital similarly causes orders to fall below replacement until the capital stock falls to meet the desired level. Note, however, that due to the capital acquisition lag this negative loop contains a significant phase lag element, introducing the possibility of oscillatory behavior. The aggressiveness of the firm's response is determined by the adjustment parameter α_K.

The adjustment for the supply line is formulated analogously. Orders are adjusted in proportion to the discrepancy between the desired supply line SL^* and the actual supply line:

$$ASL_t = \alpha_{SL}(SL_t^* - SL_t). \tag{21}$$

In general the supply line of unfilled orders may include several stages of the capital acquisition process such as orders in planning, orders in the backlog of the supplier, and orders under construction. In the experiment these are aggregated into the backlog of unfilled orders B, thus $SL = B$. The desired supply line is given by

$$SL_t^* = D_t \cdot A_t. \tag{22}$$

To ensure an appropriate rate of capital acquisition a firm must maintain a supply line proportional to the capital acquisition delay. If the acquisition delay rises, firms must plan for and order new capital farther ahead, increasing the desired supply line. The desired supply line is based on the capital discard rate – a quantity readily anticipated and subject to little uncertainty. To illustrate the logic of the supply line adjustment, imagine an increase in desired capital. Orders will rise due to the gap betwen desired and actual capital stock. The supply line will fill. If orders in the supply line were ignored ($\alpha_{SL} = 0$), the firm would place orders through the capital stock adjustment, promptly forget that these units had been ordered, and order them again. The supply line adjustment creates a second negative feedback loop which reduces orders for new capacity if the firm finds itself over-committed to projects in the construction pipeline, and boosts orders if there are too few. It also compensates for changes in the construction delay, helping ensure the firm receives the capital it requires to meet desired production. α_{SL} reflects the firm's or subject's sensitivity to the supply line.

The decision rule in eqs. (18)–(22) is intendedly quite simple. Orders are determined on the basis of information locally available to the firm itself. Information an individual firm is unlikely or unable to have, such as the value of the equilibrium capital stock or the cost minimizing solution to the nonlinear optimal control problem, is not used. The firm's forecasting process is rather simple: capacity is built to meet current demand. The rule includes appropriate nonlinearity to ensure robust results: orders remain nonnegative even if there is a large surplus of capital. The rule also expresses the corrections to the order rate as linear functions of the discrepancies between desired and actual quantities. Undoubtedly the ordering rules of firms are more complex, and other work such as Senge (1980) considers various subtleties. One can think of the linear part of the rule as the first term of the Taylor series expansion of the more complex underlying investment rule. A large literature in psychology documents the ability of linear decision rules to provide excellent models of decision-making, even when interactions are known to exist [Dawes (1982), Camerer (1981)].

It is useful to interpret the rule in terms of the cognitive processes of the agents. The ordering rule can be interpreted as an example of the anchoring and adjustment heuristic [Tversky and Kahnemen (1974)]. In anchoring and adjustment, a subject attempting to determine an unknown quantity first anchors on a known reference point and then adjusts for the effects of other cues which may be less salient or whose effects are obscure. For example, a firm may estimate next years sales by anchoring on current sales and adjusting for factors such as macroeconomic expectations, anticipated competitor pricing, etc. Studies have shown anchoring and adjustment to be a widespread heuristic. Indeed, anchoring is so common that many people use it inappropriately. Numerous studies have documented situations in which the adjustments are insufficient or in which judgments are inadvertently anchored to meaningless cues [Hogarth (1987)]. In the experimental context, the capital discard rate forms an easily anticipated and interpreted point of departure for the determination of orders. Replacement of discards will keep the capital stock of the firm constant at its current level (assuming the capital acquisition delay remains constant). Adjustments are then made in response to the adequacy of the capital stock and supply line. No assumption is made that these adjustments are in any way optimal or that firms actually calculate the order rate as given in the equations. Rather, pressures arising from the factory floor, from the backlog of unfilled orders, from disgruntled customers, and from commitments to projects in the construction pipeline cause the firm to adjust its investment rate above or below the level that would maintain the status quo. For agents in the experiment the interpretation is parallel: replacing discards to maintain the status quo is a natural anchor. Adjustments based on the adequacy of the capital stock and supply line are then made. Again, there is no presumption that subjects explicitly calculate the adjustments using the formulae in the equations [see, e.g., Einhorn, Kleinmuntz, and Kleinmuntz (1979)].

The adjustment parameters α_K and α_{SL} reflect the firm's or subject's response to disequilibrium: large values indicate an aggressive effort to bring capacity and the supply line in line with their desired levels; small values indicate a higher tolerance for, or negligence of, discrepancies between desired and actual stocks. For both the real firm and the subjects, the hypothesis that decisions are made via a heuristic such as the proposed rule is motivated by the observation that the complexity of determining the optimal rate of investment overwhelms the abilities of the managers and the time available to make decisions [Simon (1982)].

To test the rule only the two adjustment parameters α_K and α_{SL} need be estimated. All other data required to determine orders are presented directly to the subjects. Maximum likelihood estimates of the parameters for each trial were found by grid search of the parameter space, subject to the constraints α_K, $\alpha_{SL} \geqq 0$. Assuming the errors ε are Gaussian white noise then the maximum likelihood estimates of such nonlinear functions are given by the parameters which minimize the sum of squared errors. Such estimates are consistent and asymptotically efficient, and the usual measures of significance such as the t-test are asymptotically valid [Judge et al. (1980)].

Estimates for 49 trials together with t-statistics are given in table 2. The model's ability to explain the ordering decisions of the subjects is excellent. R^2 varies between 33% and 99 +%, with an overall R^2 for the pooled sample of 85%.[4] All but two of the estimates of α_K are highly significant. The supply line adjustment parameter is significant in 22 trials, and not significantly different from zero in 27. Of course, zero is a legitimate value for α_{SL}, and the estimate of α_{SL} for 23 subjects is zero. The estimates of α_{SL} range from 0 to 4.4 while the mean 95% confidence band for the zero estimates is 0.17, less than 4% of the range of α_{SL}, indicating that the 23 zero estimates of α_{SL} are quite tight.

6. Simulation of the estimated decision rules

The estimation results indicate that the model is a good representation of the subjects' decision-making. Sterman (1989) analyzes the estimated parameters and identifies several 'misperceptions of feedback' which are responsible for the subjects' poor performance. One of these is the tendency for subjects to give insufficient attention to the supply line, as indicated by the large number of small estimates for α_{SL}. By ignoring the supply line subjects continue ordering even after the construction pipeline contains sufficient units to correct any stock discrepancy. Such overordering is a major source of instability in the closed loop system. The present concern, however, is the

---

[4]Note that the function $O = f(\cdot)$ does not contain an estimated regression constant. Thus the correspondence of the estimated and actual capital orders, not just their variation around mean values, provides an important measure of the model's explanatory power. Since the residuals e need not satisfy $\sum e_t = 0$, the conventional R^2 is not appropriate. The alternative $R^2 = 1 - \sum e_t^2 / \sum O_t^2$ is used [Judge et al. (1980)]. This R^2 can be interpreted as the fraction of the variation in capital orders around zero explained by the model.

Table 2
Estimated parameters and mode of behavior of simulated decision rules.

Trial	Score	α_S	Std. error[a]		α_{SL}	Std. error[a]		R^2	Mode
1	8,229	0.88	(0.04)	a	0.24	(0.03)	a	0.90	C
2	1,980	0.56	(0.10)	a	0.26	(0.13)	c	0.39	P1
3	1,335	1.00	(0.004)	a	0.00	(0.003)		0.99+	C
4	1,283	2.21	(0.06)	a	1.51	(0.06)	a	0.86	C
5	965	1.35	(0.01)	a	0.59	(0.01)	a	0.99	P1
6	908	0.38	(0.09)	a	0.00	(0.10)		0.48	P1
7	890	1.28	(0.02)	a	0.72	(0.02)	a	0.97	C
8	786	0.21	(0.02)	a	0.16	(0.05)	a	0.74	S
9	741	1.66	(0.05)	a	1.83	(0.07)	a	0.76	C
10	715	0.74	(0.04)	a	0.60	(0.05)	a	0.81	C
11	651	0.69	(0.02)	a	0.33	(0.03)	a	0.94	C
12	638	0.46	(0.08)	a	0.33	(0.11)	a	0.33	P5
13	634	3.73	(0.08)	a	4.44	(0.10)	a	0.63	P1
14	554	0.45	(0.04)	a	0.00	(0.06)		0.87	P1
15	482	0.32	(0.05)	a	0.20	(0.10)	b	0.57	S
16	479	2.49	(0.04)	a	2.90	(0.05)	a	0.91	C
17	467	0.87	(0.05)	a	1.38	(0.09)	a	0.57	S
18	459	0.62	(0.04)	a	0.43	(0.05)	a	0.86	P1
19	459	0.13	(0.02)	a	0.00	(0.08)		0.77	S
20	400	0.14	(0.04)	a	0.00	(0.14)		0.37	S
21	399	0.23	(0.02)	a	0.28	(0.06)	a	0.83	S
22	384	0.55	(0.04)	a	0.00	(0.05)		0.90	C
23	373	0.17	(0.03)	a	0.40	(0.13)	a	0.50	S
24	366	0.56	(0.06)	a	0.11	(0.08)		0.76	C
25	311	0.16	(0.02)	a	0.00	(0.08)		0.80	S
26	267	0.16	(0.02)	a	0.00	(0.09)		0.78	S
27	265	0.14	(0.02)	a	0.00	(0.08)		0.88	S
28	241	0.19	(0.03)	a	0.00	(0.10)		0.73	S
29	229	0.33	(0.04)	a	0.00	(0.09)		0.82	P1
30	212	0.22	(0.02)	a	0.15	(0.08)	c	0.85	S
31	212	0.04	(0.03)		0.29	(0.17)		0.74	S
32	207	0.16	(0.02)	a	0.00	(0.10)		0.80	S
33	196	0.09	(0.02)	a	0.00	(0.14)		0.79	S
34	194	0.29	(0.06)	a	0.25	(0.13)	c	0.45	S
35	189	0.09	(0.02)	a	0.00	(0.11)		0.90	S
36	183	0.42	(0.04)	a	0.00	(0.06)		0.92	C
37	164	0.14	(0.04)	a	0.00	(0.13)		0.74	S
38	164	0.22	(0.02)	a	0.00	(0.06)		0.94	S
39	161	0.02	(0.02)		0.00	(0.19)		0.87	S
40	161	0.19	(0.02)	a	0.02	(0.07)		0.93	S
41	156	0.24	(0.04)	a	0.00	(0.11)		0.82	S
42	135	0.32	(0.04)	a	0.69	(0.14)	a	0.74	S
43	120	0.16	(0.02)	a	0.00	(0.09)		0.93	S
44	118	0.15	(0.03)	a	0.00	(0.12)		0.90	S
45	108	0.44	(0.03)	a	0.40	(0.07)	a	0.94	S
46	105	0.08	(0.02)	a	0.00	(0.13)		0.96	S
47	100	0.16	(0.03)	a	0.00	(0.11)		0.91	S
48	90	0.60	(0.02)	a	0.85	(0.05)	a	0.96	S
49	77	0.11	(0.03)	a	0.19	(0.17)		0.90	S
Mean:	591	0.55			0.40			Pooled R^2: 0.85	

[a] t statistic for test of H_0: $\alpha = 0$ significant at a: 0.01; b: 0.05; c: 0.10 level. Mode: S = Stable, Pn = Period n, C = Chaotic.

relationship between the estimated parameters and the regimes of behavior in the model. Even though the subjects to not behave optimally in disequilibrium, one might expect that their decision rules would ultimately return the system to a low cost equilibrium. Simulation of the estimated rules shows this is not the case.

The rightmost column of table 2 indicates the mode of behavior produced by simulation of the decision rule with the estimated parameters. The parameters estimated for 30 subjects (61%) are stable. Most of these produce overdamped behavior of the capital stock in response to the step input. Seven parameter sets produce limit cycles of period 1 and one produces period 5. The parameters which characterize 11 subjects (22%) produce chaos. Inspection of table 2 shows that the subjects whose parameters are stable performed best in the task while those whose parameters produce periodic behavior or chaos generally had the highest costs. 1-way ANOVA confirmed the relationship: the costs achieved by the subjects strongly depend on the mode produced by simulation of the estimated decision rule ($p < 0.01$ when the modes were coded as stable, periodic, or chaotic).

Fig. 4 shows time domain and phase portraits for simulations of several sets of estimated parameters. In all cases the orbits are roughly egg-shaped, with clockwise flow. To explicate the dynamics, consider fig. 4a, showing the period 1 limit cycle produced by the parameters of subject 18 (0.62, 0.43; $R^2 = 0.86$). In equilibrium desired production must equal capacity; the locus of such points is given by the 45° line. Below the line there is excess capacity and the system is linear and stable; above it there is insufficient capacity and the system is highly nonlinear and unstable. Given the steady input of orders from the goods sector of 500 units, the equilibrium point for the system as a whole lies at (555.55, 555.55). At $t = 1$ capacity is insufficient. Shipments lag new orders, so the backlogs of the goods sector and capital sector grow. Rising desired production induces additional orders from the capital sector, causing rapid growth of desired production. Capacity, held down by the inability of the capital sector itself to fill all orders and the consequent rationing of output, lags behind. As capital stock grows, however, new orders placed by the capital sector slow, and the backlog is shipped at an increasing pace. Desired production peaks at $t = 6$. Capacity now grows rapidly as the capital sector is increasingly able to fill orders. Between $t = 7$ and $t = 8$ capacity overtakes desired production, which falls rapidly since capacity is now large enough to deliver the entire supply line in one period. As desired production plummets, capacity reaches its peak and capital sector orders fall to zero ($t = 9$). Desired production is then sustained only by the exogenous demand of the goods sector (500 units/period). Depreciation causes capital stock to decline slowly, until at $t = 15$ capital stock has fallen to a level low enough to cause the capital sector to place new orders. However, these new orders cause desired production to rise, and by the next period capacity is once again insufficient to satisfy demand, initiating the

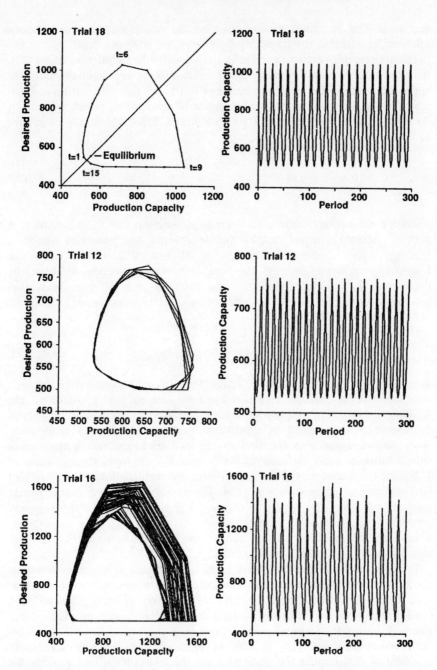

Fig. 4. Simulation of estimated decision rules. Note similarity to the experimental results (fig. 3.).

next cycle. The dynamics are the same for the period multiples and chaotic solutions, except that the trajectory does not close after one orbit.

The trajectories of chaotic systems are sensitive to initial conditions. The routes of nearby points through phase space diverge exponentially until the initial difference in the positions balloons out to fill the entire attractor. The time average rate of exponential divergence of neighboring points is given by the largest Lyapunov exponent L_+ [Wolf et al. (1985)] which may be defined as

$$L_+ = \lim_{t \to \infty} \frac{1}{t} \log_2 |x|, \tag{23}$$

where the separation vector x connects neighboring points in phase space. A positive exponent means nearby points diverge and indicates chaos; a negative exponent denotes convergence of nearby points. Because the Lyapunov exponents describe the long-term average behavior of nearby trajectories, any finite segment of the behavior may diverge from that average, including temporary reversals of sign. Nevertheless, a rough estimate of L_+ is given by the slope of

$$\hat{L}_+(t)t = \log_2 |x| \tag{24}$$

over long intervals. To calculate $\hat{L}_+(t)t$ for each of the estimated decision rules, production capacity was perturbed by one part in a trillion in the 10,000th period. The separation vector $|x|$ was measured in the two-dimensional space defined by production capacity and desired production. Since desired capacity is the sum of the two backlogs, this output space reflects all three state variables in the system. Fig. 5 shows the evolution of $\hat{L}_+(t)t$ for the parameters of subject 16 after the perturbation. The phase plot for these parameters is shown in fig. 4. The average slope of $\hat{L}_+(t)t$ is clearly positive, indicating the system is chaotic. The magnitude of the Lyapunov exponent is approximately 0.1 bits/period. The values of $\hat{L}_+$ for the subjects whose decision rules are chaotic range from about 0.01 to 0.1 bits/period, with an average of about 0.04 bits/period.

The magnitudes of the exponents determine the rate at which information about the state of the system, and hence the ability to predict its trajectory, is lost. The large measurement errors in economic systems [Morgenstern (1963)] dictate severe limits on predictability in chaotic systems. Thus if the states of the model economy were known with the not unrealistic measurement error of about 12% (3 bits of precision), the average Lyapunov exponent of 0.04 implies the uncertainty in the trajectory would grow to fill the entire attractor after only about 75 periods, corresponding in the

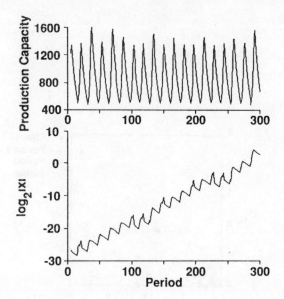

Fig. 5. Evolution of $\log_2|x|$, the distance between two neighboring trajectories, for simulation with parameters of subject 16 (2.49, 2.90) after perturbation of capacity by factor of 10^{-12} in period 10,000. The largest Lyapunov exponent, given approximately by the average slope, is positive, indicating that the two trajectories diverge exponentially and the system is chaotic.

experimental system to roughly 5 orbits. Additional precision buys little in additional predictability: cutting measurement error by a factor of two would delay the complete loss of predictability by less than 2 orbits. Of course these calculations assume no external noise, perfect specification of the model, and perfect estimates of the parameters, and thus represent an upper bound on the prediction horizon.

7. Mapping the parameter space

Additional effects of chaos on predictability arise due to uncertainty in the estimated parameters. Fig. 6 locates the modes of behavior of the estimated decision rules in parameter space. The estimated parameters are clustered in the region $0 \leq \alpha_K \leq 1$, $0 \leq \alpha_{SL} \leq 1$, with the few outside this region falling approximately along the line $\alpha_{SL} = \alpha_K$. Consistent with intuition, the stable decision rules are confined to the region where α_K is small and α_{SL} is large, while the chaotic decision rules generally involved aggressive stock adjustment and weak supply line adjustment. More aggressive attempts to correct the discrepancy between the desired and actual capital stock are destabiliz-

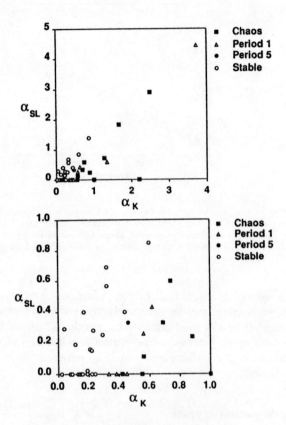

Fig. 6. Modes of behavior produced by simulation of the estimated parameters. Lower graph magnifies area bounded by $0 \leqq \alpha_K \leqq 1$, $0 \leqq \alpha_{SL} \leqq 1$.

ing: by ordering more aggressively the subject induces a larger increase in total demand, thus exacerbating disequilibrium and encouraging still larger orders in future periods. Conversely, more aggressive response to the supply line is stabilizing by constraining orders as the supply line fills. More formally, α_K determines the gain of the oscillatory negative feedback loop while α_{SL} controls the first-order, stabilizing supply line loop. To test this hypothesis the estimated parameters were regressed on the log of the cost function S. Costs provide a rough measure of instability since high costs indicate large excursions from equilibrium (standard errors in parentheses, trial 1 deleted as an outlier):

$$\ln(S) = 5.3 + 1.7\alpha_K - 1.1\alpha_{SL}, \qquad R^2 = 0.43, \quad F = 16.8 \quad (N = 48) \qquad (25)$$
$$(0.13)\,(0.33) \quad (0.30)$$

The results are highly significant and confirm the overall relationship between the parameters and stability. But is the parameter space as smooth as these results suggest?

Fig. 7 maps the parameter space for $0 \leq \alpha_K \leq 1$ and $0 \leq \alpha_{SL} \leq 1$ in steps of 0.005, representing over 40,000 simulations.[5] This region includes 86% of the estimated parameter sets, clearly showing that the fluctuating steady state solutions, including the chaotic solutions, lie in the managerially meaningful region of parameter space. The resulting bifurcation structure is surprisingly structured. First, the boundary for the bifurcation from fixed point to cyclic attractors appears to be a straight line, with stable solutions satisfying

$$\alpha_{SL} > 2.29\alpha_K - 0.706, \qquad R^2 = 0.99946 \quad (N = 42) \qquad (26)$$
$$(0.0085) \quad (0.0046)$$

Rasmussen, Mosekilde, and Sterman (1985) show that the transition from local stability to instability at the equilibrium point involves a Hopf bifurcation. In the region where capacity is inadequate ($\phi < 1$) the linearized closed-loop system is oscillatory, but for small values of α_K or large values of α_{SL}, the eigenvalues lie inside the unit circle, producing damped behavior and a stable fixed-point attractor. As the parameters become less stable (larger α_K or smaller α_{SL}) the eigenvalues cross the unit circle and the system produces expanding oscillations. These fluctuations are ultimately bounded by the nonlinearities, particularly the nonnegativity constraint on orders and the flexible utilization of capacity in eq. (1).

Inside the region of fluctuating steady state solutions, several features are apparent. Note first the striations of periodic behavior which cut across the

[5]Each simulation was 10,000 periods long. The first 8,000 were discarded in assessing the steady state mode of behavior. 10 digit accuracy was used. A simulation was assumed to be chaotic if the trajectory did not close after 100 orbits.

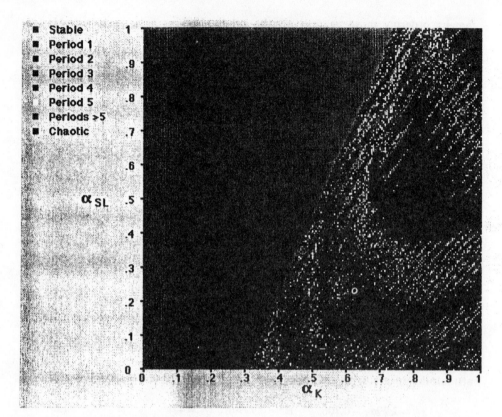

Fig. 7. Map of parameter space for $0 \leqq \alpha_K \leqq 1$ and $0 \leqq \alpha_{SL} \leqq 1$. Simulations were performed in steps of 0.005, representing $201^2 = 40,401$ simulations.

space at a somewhat shallower angle than the stability/instability boundary. The bands are thicker near the transition to stability and thinner away from it. Second, note the several large regions in which the periodic solutions are very sparse.

Fig. 8 magnifies the region $0.55 \leqq \alpha_K \leqq 0.65$, $0.50 \leqq \alpha_{SL} \leqq 0.60$ by a factor of ten in each direction. Both the chaotic regions and the bands of periodic behavior are now seen to contain irregularly distributed islands of other periodicities. Further magnification (not shown) reveals still more such islands. Such irregularity is characteristic of the fractal boundaries common in the bifurcation maps of many systems.

Simple though the model is, it is capable of generating a wide array of complex behaviors. The complexity of the parameter space shows that even small errors in estimates of the parameters may have large qualitative effects on the mode of behavior produced by the system. Indeed, the simulations

24   *J.D. Sterman, Deterministic chaos in an experimental economic system*

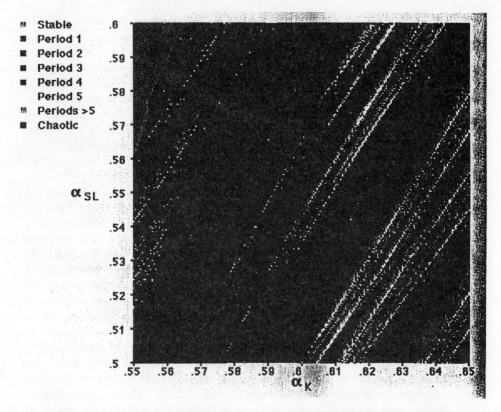

Fig. 8. Map of the region $0.55 \leq \alpha_K \leq 0.65$, $0.50 \leq \alpha_{SL} \leq 0.60$ in increments of 0.0005. Magnifies fig. 7 by a linear factor of 10 in each direction. Note the islands of higher periodicities irregularly distributed within the bands of periodic behavior.

here do not exhaust the possibilities. All the simulations described here involved no external forcing (goods sector orders for capital were constant). Larsen, Mosekilde, and Sterman (1988) have shown that sinusoidal forcing in goods sector orders (mimicking the effects of the business cycle or other cyclical modes in the economy) causes mode-locking, quasi-periodic solutions, and a devil's staircase to emerge.

8. Discussion

It is common in the social sciences to assume that decision-making behavior and thus the dynamics of human systems are, if not optimal, then at least stable. These results show that formal rules which characterize actual managerial decision making can produce an extraordinary range of disequilibrium dynamics, including chaos.

Such complexity suggests strong lessons for modelers of economic and social dynamics. The experiment shows that the regimes of fluctuating steady-state behavior, including chaos, lie squarely in the middle of the realistic region of parameter space. In consequence modelers can ignore nonlinear dynamics only at their peril. Models of economic and social dynamics should portray the processes by which disequilibrium conditions are created and dissipated. They should not assume that the economy is in or near equilibrium at all times nor that adjustment processes are stable. Models should be formulated so that they are robust in extreme conditions, since it is the nonlinearities necessarily introduced by robust formulations that crucially determine the modes of the system [see Day (1984)].

At the same time a number of questions regarding the generalization of the results to the real world and the practical significance of chaos must be asked. Chaos is a steady-state phenomenon which manifests over very long time frames, but many policy-oriented models are concerned with transient dynamics and nearly all with time horizons much shorter than those used in the analysis of chaotic dynamics. For example the simulations here were run for 10,000 periods or more. Over such extended time horizons the parameters of the system cannot be considered static but will themselves evolve with learning, evolutionary pressures, and exogenous changes in the environment. There is evidence [Sterman (1989), Bakken (1988)] that subjects begin to learn within just a few cycles, modifying the parameters of their ordering function. It appears that in the present experiment learning slowly moves the subjects away from the chaotic region towards the region of stability. However, the existence of chaos may itself hamper learning. Even though deterministic cause-effect relations exist in chaotic systems, it is impossible to predict the effects of small changes in initial conditions or parameters. Does such 'randomness' slow the discovery of cause and effect by agents in the economy and thus hinder learning or evolution towards efficiency? Indeed, does learning alter the parameters of decision rules so that systems evolve towards or away from the chaotic regime? Some argue that chaos may be adaptive. In a world whose 'fitness space' contains many local optima, a decision rule that produces chaos, by constantly exploring new pathways, may help a system evolve faster than a stable incremental decision making strategy [Prigogine and Sanglier (1987), Allen (1988)].

Chaos places an upper bound on prediction, but is that bound a binding constraint in social systems? Real social systems are bombarded by broadband noise, and it is well known that such random shocks severely degrade predictability. Does the magnitude of stochastic shocks swamp the uncertainty in trajectories caused by chaos? How does the existence of chaotic regimes in a model influence its response to policies, and the predictability of that response? Particularly troubling here is the potential for fractal basin boundaries in both initial condition and parameter space. Policy interventions often imply changes in the parameters of a decision rule or model. How can policy analysis be conducted if the 'policy space' contains fractal basin boundaries? In such systems parameter changes on the margin may produce unpredictable qualitative changes in behavior, as illustrated by the fractal distribution of modes shown in figs. 7–8. Therefore learning and experience may not transfer to circumstances which differ only slightly. Learning often involves a hill-climbing procedure of incremental movement towards a profit-maximizing peak in parameter space. How well can agents negotiate that space when the landscape not only has many local optima but is fractal as well? The development of principles for policy design in such systems is a major area for future research. The practical significance of chaos and other nonlinear phenomena in policy-oriented models of social and economic behavior remains clouded while these questions are unanswered. Some of these questions may be resolved by further application of the experimental techniques demonstrated here.

9. Conclusions

The discovery of nonlinear phenomena such as deterministic chaos in the physical world naturally motivates the search for similar behavior in the world of human behavior. Yet the social scientist faces difficulties in that search which do not plague the physicist, at least not to the same degree. Aggregate data sufficient for strong empirical tests simply do not exist for many of the most important social systems. Social systems are not easily isolated from the environment. The huge temporal and spatial scales of these systems, vast number of actors, costs and ethical concerns make controlled experiments on the systems themselves difficult at best. Finally, the laws of human behavior are not as stable as the laws of physics. Electrons do not learn, innovate, collude, or redesign the circuits in which they flow.

Laboratory experiments appear to provide a fruitful alternative. Since experiments on actual firms and national economies are infeasible, simulation models of these systems must be used to explore the decision making heuristics of the agents. Such experiments create 'microworlds' in which the subjects face physical and institutional structures, information, and incentives which mimic (albeit in a simplified fashion) those of the real world. It appears to be possible to quantify the decision making heuristics used by agents in such experiments and explain their performance well. Simulation then provides insight into the dynamic properties of the experimental systems.

These results demonstrate that chaos can be produced by the decision making processes of real people. The experiment presented subjects with a straightforward task in a common and important economic setting. The subjects' behavior is modeled with a high degree of accuracy by a simple decision rule consistent with empirical knowledge developed in psychology and long used in economic models. Simulation of the rule produces chaos for a significant minority of subjects. Chaos may well be a common mode of behavior in social and economic systems, despite the lack of sufficient information to detect it in aggregate data.

References

Allen, P., 1988, Dynamic models of evolving systems, System Dynamics Review 4, 109–130.
Bakken, B., 1988, Learning system structure by exploring computer games, presented at the 1988 International System Dynamics Conference, San Diego, CA, July.
Barnett, W. and P. Chen, 1988, The aggregation theoretic monetary aggregates are chaotic and have strange attractors: an econometric application of mathematical chaos, in: Barnett, Berndt and White, eds., Dynamic econometric modeling (Cambridge University Press, Cambridge).
Benhabib, J. and R. Day, 1981, Rational choice and erratic behavior, Review of Economic Studies 48, 459–471.
Brehmer, B., 1987, Systems design and the psychology of complex systems, in: Rasmussen, J. and P. Zunde, eds., Empirical foundations of information and software science III (Plenum, New York).
Brock, W., 1986, Distinguishing random and deterministic systems: Abridged version, Journal of Economic Theory 40, 168–195.
Camerer, C., 1981, General conditions for the success of bootstrapping models, Organizational Behavior and Human Performance 27, 411–422.
Candela, G. and A. Gardini, 1986, Estimation of a non-linear discrete-time macro model, Journal of Economic Dynamics and Control 10, 249–254.
Chen, P., 1988, Empirical and theoretical evidence of economic chaos, System Dynamics Review 4, 81–108.
Dana, R. and P. Malgrange, 1984, The dynamics of a discrete version of a growth cycle model, in: Ancot, J., ed., Analysing the structure of econometric models (Martinus Nijhoff, The Hague).
Dawes, R., 1982, The robust beauty of improper linear models in decision making, in: Kahneman, Slovic and Tversky, eds., Judgment under uncertainty: Heuristics and biases (Cambridge University Press, Cambridge).
Day, R., 1982, Irregular growth cycles, American Economic Review 72, 406–414.
Day, R., 1984, Disequilibrium economic dynamics: A post-Schumpeterian contribution, Journal of Economic Behavior and Organization 5, 57–76.
Day, R. and W. Shafer, 1985, Keynesian chaos, Journal of Macroeconomics 7, 277–295.
Einhorn, H., D. Kleinmuntz and B. Kleinmuntz, 1979, Linear regression and process-tracing models of judgment, Psychological Review 69, 465–485.
Forrester, J., 1961, Industrial dynamics (MIT, Cambridge, MA).
Goodwin, R., 1951, The nonlinear accelerator and the persistence of business cycles, Econometrica 19, 1–17.
Goodwin, R., M. Kruger and A. Vercelli, 1984, Nonlinear models of fluctuating growth (Springer-Verlag, Berlin).
Grandmont, J.-M., 1985, On endogenous competitive business cycles, Econometrica 53, 995–1046.
Grassberger, P. and I. Procaccia, 1983, Measuring the strangeness of strange attractors, Physica 9D, 189–208.
Grether, D. and C. Plott, 1979, Economic theory of choice and the preference reversal phenomenon, American Economic Review 69, 623–638.
Hogarth R., 1987, Judgment and choice, 2nd ed. (John Wiley, Chichester).
Hogarth, R. and M. Reder, 1987, Rational choice: The contrast between economics and psychology (University of Chicago Press, Chicago, IL).
Holt, C., F. Modigliani, J. Muth and H. Simon, 1960, Planning production, inventories and work force (Prentice-Hall, Englewood Cliffs, NJ).

Judge et al., 1980, The theory and practice of econometrics (Wiley, New York).

Larsen, E., E. Mosekilde and J. Sterman, 1988, Entrainment between the economic long wave and other macroeconomic cycles, presented at the IIASA Conference on Instabilities in Long-Term Economic Growth, Novosibirsk, USSR.

Low, G., 1980, The multiplier–accelerator model of business cycles interpreted from a system dynamics perspective, in: J. Randers, ed., Elements of the system dynamics method (MIT Press, Cambridge, MA).

MacKinnon, A. and A. Wearing, 1985, Systems analysis and dynamic decision making, Acta Psychologica 58, 159–172.

Metzler, L., 1941, The nature and stability of inventory cycles, Review of Economic Statistics 23, 113–129.

Morgenstern, O., 1963, On the accuracy of economic observations, 2nd ed. (Princeton University Press, Princeton, NJ).

Plott, C.R., 1986, Laboratory experiments in economics: The implications of posted price institutions, Science 232 (9 May), 732–738.

Prigogine, I. and M. Sanglier, 1987, Laws of nature and human conduct (Task Force of Research Information and Study on Science, Brussels).

Ramsey, J. and H.-J. Yuan, 1987, Bias and error bars in dimension calculations and their evaluation in some simple models (New York University, New York).

Ramsey, J., C. Sayers and P. Rothman, 1988, The statistical properties of dimension calculations using small data sets: Some economic applications, RR88-10 (Department of Economics, New York University, New York).

Rasmussen, S. and E. Mosekilde, 1988, Bifurcations and chaos in a generic management model, European Journal of Operational Research 35, 80–88.

Rasmussen, W., E. Mosekilde and J. Sterman, 1985, Bifurcations and chaotic behavior in a simple model of the economic long wave, System Dynamics Review 1, 92–110.

Samuelson, P.A., 1939, Interactions between the multiplier analysis and the principle of acceleration, The Review of Economic Statistics 21, 75–78.

Senge, P., 1980, A system dynamics approach to investment function formulation and testing, Socio-Economic Planning Sciences 14, 269–280.

Simon, H.A., 1982, Models of bounded rationality (The MIT Press, Cambridge, MA).

Slović, P. and S. Lichtenstein, 1983, Preference reversals: A broader perspective, American Economic Review 73, 596–605.

Smith, V.L., 1982, Microeconomic systems as an experimental science, American Economic Review 72, 923–955.

Smith, V.L., 1986, Experimental methods in the political economy of exchange, Science 234, 167–173.

Sterman, J.D., 1985, A behavioral model of the economic long wave, Journal of Economic Behavior and Organization 6, 17–53.

Sterman, J.D., 1987, Testing behavioral simulation models by direct experiment, Management Science 33, 1572–1592.

Sterman, J.D., 1989, Misperceptions of feedback in dynamic decision making, Organizational Behavior and Human Decision Processes, forthcoming.

Sterman, J.D., 1988a, Deterministic chaos in models of human behavior: Methodological issues and experimental results, System Dynamics Review 4, 148–178.

Sterman, 1988b, Modeling managerial behavior: Misperceptions of feedback in a dynamic decision making experiment, Management Science, 35, no. 3, 321–339.

Sterman, J.D. and D.L. Meadows, 1985, STRATEGEM-2: A microcomputer simulation game of the Kondratiev cycle, Simulation and Games 16, 174–202.

Stutzer, M., 1980, Chaotic dynamics and bifurcation in a macro model, Journal of Economic Dynamics and Control 2, 353–376.

Takens, F., 1985, Distinguishing deterministic and random systems, in: G. Borenblatt, G. Iooss and D. Joseph, eds., Nonlinear dynamics and turbulence (Pitman, Boston, MA).

Tversky, A. and D. Kahneman, 1974, Judgement under uncertainty: Heuristics and biases, Science 185, 1124–1131.

Wolf, A., J. Swift, H. Swinney and J. Vastano, 1985, Determining Lyapunov exponents from a time series, Physica 16D, 285–317.

[14]

Market Instability and Nonlinear Dynamics

Jean-Paul Chavas and Matthew T. Holt

The potential role of nonlinear dynamics in generating market instability is investigated using a simple market equilibrium model of the U.S. dairy industry. The supply function reflects the nonlinear dynamics of the dairy herd, as estimated by Chavas and Klemme. It is shown that, in the absence of any uncertainty, an inelastic demand contributes to market instability and chaos.

Key words: chaos, dairy market, market equilibrium, nonlinear dynamics, price analysis.

Government has intervened for decades in many domestic agricultural markets. The persistence of farm programs continues to generate debate among agricultural economists concerned with the motivations of government intercession (Pope and Hallam). In welfare economics, it is well known that perfectly competitive markets can lead to Pareto optimal resource allocations. This result has sometimes been used to argue that government intervention is in general inefficient and generates a social welfare loss. Alternatively, government involvement could be interpreted as a response to market failure. A frequently cited source of market failure is the so-called "instability" of agricultural markets (Schultz; Cochrane). Agricultural price and income fluctuations have motivated considerable research on the economics of market instability and stabilization policy (Schultz; Cochrane; Newbery and Stiglitz; Gardner).

It is well known that a dynamic market model can generate short-term adjustments which dampen out as the market moves toward its steady-state equilibrium. Thus, a fairly common view is that market instability is created by unpredictable supply or demand shocks as the market continuously adjusts toward its (shifting) long-run equilibrium (Cochrane; Schultz). Schultz (p. 131) attributed the main source of agricultural market instability to shocks from the industrial sector. Cochrane argued that farm income instability also was due to factors internal to agriculture, such as weather. He emphasized that agricultural price gyrations were generated, in part, by a highly inelastic demand for food (p. 42). He stressed the income consequences of a low price elasticity of demand: a fall (rise) in farm prices greatly reduces (increases) farm cash receipts.

The view that market instability is created by unpredictable shocks has stimulated much research on the economics of uncertainty. For example, Newbery and Stiglitz, Innes and Rausser, and others have investigated the inefficiency of market instability under risk and risk aversion. An important limitation of such analysis is the assumed existence of a steady-state equilibrium. Although Newbery and Stiglitz (p. 306–08) briefly allude to how such an equilibrium might be reached, they do not make explicit the nature of the adjustment process.

The above observations raise at least two important questions. First, is it possible for the market to not be in a long-run steady-state equilibrium while remaining bounded? Second, could market instability be endogenous to the market itself? As we argue below, the answers to these questions are related to one another. Here, we focus on the possibility that long-run market instability can be generated without external shocks (for example, without exogenous uncertainty). It is now known that long-run instability can be generated endogenously by "chaotic systems"—systems associated with deterministic nonlinear dynamics (May; Baumol and Benhabib; Chavas and Holt). Deterministic chaos also implies trajectories that are bounded but never reach a steady-state. Such trajectories are aper-

Jean-Paul Chavas and Matthew T. Holt are, respectively, professor and assistant professor of agricultural economics, University of Wisconsin, Madison. This research was funded by a Hatch grant from the College of Agricultural and Life Sciences, University of Wisconsin.

Review coordinated by Steven Buccola.

Amer. J. Agr. Econ. 75 (February 1993): 113–120
Copyright 1993 American Agricultural Economics Association

iodic, following cycles with different periods which never repeat. Deterministic chaos implies both long-run instability and long-run unpredictability (Hao). Chavas and Holt noted that most empirical investigations of agricultural markets have been conducted using linear models; such models cannot under any circumstances exhibit chaotic patterns. Consequently, little is known about the role of nonlinear dynamics in agricultural markets. Economic conditions (if any) under which an agricultural market is likely to be chaotic are not understood. Moreover, if a steady-state equilibrium does not exist, what might be the nature of long-run market dynamics? The investigation of these issues should provide new insights into the economics of market instability.

The objective of the present paper is to investigate the dynamics of a relatively simple but nonlinear market equilibrium model. The model consists of a simple supply-demand structure of the U.S. dairy sector. The supply function relies on dairy cow population dynamics as specified and estimated by Chavas and Klemme. The demand function exhibits constant price elasticity. Milk price is determined by equating supply and demand. Such a simple model specification is hardly novel in empirical analysis. What is novel to price and market analysis is the nature of the complicated dynamics that can be generated by such a simple model structure.

Instability and Chaos

Economists often believe that investigation of market instability issues requires including random variables which reflect uncertainty. Here, we investigate an alternative possibility: market instability can also be generated endogenously by chaos associated with nonlinear dynamics. Chaos refers to occurrence of "unpredictability" in completely deterministic dynamic systems (Lorenz; Li and Yorke; May; Hao; Baumol and Benhabib). The concept is at odds with the traditional view that accurate predictions are always possible from a deterministic model. The potential for chaos implies that apparently random fluctuations (for example in price or production) need not necessarily be associated with a stochastic process (Brock). Moreover, although chaos may imply unpredictability, it should not be associated with disorder. Rather, it is more appropriate to consider chaos as a kind of dynamic order without periodicity.

Chaos simply cannot exist in linear dynamic systems. It is a phenomenon that can appear only in nonlinear dynamic systems (Hao). As a result, the arguments presented below cannot be developed with linear models. Chaos implies small perturbations in the initial point give rise to divergent time paths. Such divergence, called "sensitivity to initial conditions," implies that accurate long-run predictions from chaotic systems are virtually impossible (Lorenz).[1]

Note, however, that divergence of neighboring paths does not preclude the convergence of dynamic paths to a bounded set of points. This bounded set of points to which various paths converge is called a chaotic attractor. Under chaos, any initial condition gives totally aperiodic (although bounded) trajectories. The dynamic path follows an infinite number of different cycles, each with a different period that never repeats (May). The result is that a chaotic, deterministic system may generate trajectories which appear completely random to the naked eye. This, in turn, can make difficult the distinction between chaos and random processes (Brock; Brock and Sayers).

How can one tell whether a particular dynamic path is chaotic? One method for detecting chaos is the use of measures called Lyapunov exponents (Benettin, Galgani, and Strelcyn). Lyapunov exponents are generalizations of characteristic roots along general forward trajectories. To see this, consider some nonlinear dynamic system $z_t = g(z_{t-1})$ and its linearized approximation $z_t = B_t + A_t z_{t-1}$ around a point. The characteristic roots of A_t determine the local stability of the nonlinear system: the system is locally stable (unstable) if the modulus of the dominant root of A_t is less than (greater than) one (Luenberger). Lyapunov exponents are generalized measures and the roots of A_t are averaged over a global trajectory. If z_t is a scalar (implying A_t also is a scalar), there is only one Lyapunov exponent, defined as

$$\lambda = \lim_{T \to \infty} \left[\sum_{t=1}^{T} \ln(|A_t|) \right] \bigg/ T.$$

From the above discussion, $\lambda > 0$ corresponds to chaotic trajectories ($|A_t| > 1$ identifying local divergence) while $\lambda < 0$ corresponds to nonchaotic trajectories ($|A_t| < 1$ identifying local

---

[1] Sensitivity to initial conditions implies, among aother things, that the concept of long-run elasticity (or long-run multiplier) essentially has no meaning.

stability). In the general case of n state variables, there exist n Lyapunov exponents, $\lambda_1 \geq \lambda_2 \geq \ldots \geq \lambda_n$. Lyapunov exponents measure the average exponential rates of divergence (if positive) or convergence (if negative) of nearby orbits. For ergodic systems, the set of Lyapunov exponents provides a global characterization of the attractor of a dynamic system. Of special interest is the value of the largest Lyapunov exponent, λ_1. A dynamic system exhibits a steady state (chaos) whenever λ_1 is negative (positive). And a system exhibiting a limit cycle implies that $\lambda_1 = 0$ (Hao). Thus a long-run equilibrium exists when all Lyapunov exponents are negative. And any system containing at least one positive Lyapunov exponent is chaotic, the magnitude of the exponent measuring the time scale on which the system dynamics become unpredictable (Benettin Galgani, and Strelcyn; Wolf et al.).

Lyapunov exponents are also related to other global properties of attractors. For example, Kaplan and Yorke suggest the dimension of a chaotic attractor be measured as

$$(1) \qquad D = j + \sum_{i=1}^{j} \lambda_i / |\lambda_{j+1}|$$

where j is the smallest integer for which $\lambda_1 + \lambda_2 + \cdots + \lambda_j > 0$ and for which $\lambda_1 + \lambda_2 + \cdots + \lambda_{j+1} < 0$.

Thus, in any nonlinear dynamic system, the largest Lyapunov exponent sheds light on the characteristics of the system's dynamic behavior. Shimada and Nagashima, and Wolf et al., proposed a numerical method to estimate the Lyapunov exponents associated with a given dynamic system. Their method provides a way of investigating the existence of chaos or limit cycles in nonlinear dynamics.

The possibility of finding chaos in the dynamics of agricultural markets suggests an important point: uncertainty (as generated by exogenous stochastic shocks) is no longer a necessary condition for market instability. In particular, with nonlinear dynamic systems, it is possible to generate unpredictable but bounded price gyrations without introducing random variables. Consequently, instability in agricultural markets could be entirely endogenous to these markets. This does not mean external shocks do not exist: they do exist, and they do influence market participants. The above observations simply imply that, under chaos, external shocks no longer are

required to be the focal point in the analysis of market instability.

Is there any indication that agricultural markets are chaotic? Chavas and Holt presented evidence that the hog market may be characterized by chaotic patterns. However, their analysis was not based on a structural model of the hog market. Research on the possible role of nonlinear dynamics in agricultural markets has been insufficient to generate conclusive results. We need to refine our understanding of the nature of dynamics in agricultural markets. Such research could provide additional evidence on the existence (or nonexistence) of chaos in agricultural markets. It may also yield new insights into factors influencing market instability.

A Simple Market Model of the U.S. Dairy Sector

This section provides an investigation into the potential role of nonlinear dynamics in the U.S. milk market. The focal point of the analysis is a relatively simple market equilibrium model based on supply and demand functions estimated in previous research. The dynamics of milk market equilibrium are closely associated with dairy cow population dynamics, as modeled by Chavas and Klemme. We begin, therefore, with a brief review of Chavas and Klemme's supply framework.

Population Dynamics

Consider an animal population classified into age categories x_{it}, $i = 0, \ldots, n$, where x_{0t} denotes number of offspring at time t and x_{it} represents the number of animals of age i at time t, n being the oldest age category. Reproduction rate γ_i is the number of offspring born per animal of age i during each period. Thus total offspring at time t is

$$x_{0t} = \sum_{i=1}^{n} \gamma_i x_{it}.$$

Similarly, the survival (or retention) rate of animals of age i at time t is

$$k_{it} = x_{i+1,t+1}/x_{it}$$

that is, the proportion of animals of age i remaining in the population after one period, $i = 0, \ldots, n$. Assuming birth and survival rates are

116 February 1993

Amer. J. Agr. Econ.

independent of population size, population dynamics can be characterized by the linear homogeneous difference equation

$$
(2) \quad
\begin{bmatrix}
x_{1,t+1} \\
x_{2,t+1} \\
x_{3,t+1} \\
\cdot \\
x_{n-1,t+1} \\
x_{n,t+1}
\end{bmatrix}
=
\begin{bmatrix}
k_{0t}\gamma_1 & k_{0t}\gamma_2 & \cdots & k_{0t}\gamma_{n-1} & k_{0t}\gamma_n \\
k_{1t} & 0 & \cdots & 0 & 0 \\
0 & k_{2t} & \cdots & 0 & 0 \\
\cdot & \cdot & \cdots & \cdot & \cdot \\
0 & 0 & \cdots & 0 & 0 \\
0 & 0 & \cdots & k_{n-1,t} & 0
\end{bmatrix}
\begin{bmatrix}
x_{1t} \\
x_{2t} \\
x_{3t} \\
\cdot \\
x_{n-1,t} \\
x_{nt}
\end{bmatrix}
$$

Consider the case where reproduction rate is identical for all adults, i.e. $\gamma_i = 0$ for $i < m$; $\gamma_i = \gamma$ for $i \geq m$, m being the earliest reproductive age. The adult population then is given by

$$
(3) \quad y_t = \sum_{i=m}^{n} x_{it}
$$

and the number of offspring at time t is $x_{0t} = \gamma y_t$. Here we are interested in determining the number of young animals of age $m - 1$, $x_{m-1,t}$, that is, the number of animals that reach reproductive age next period. We have

$$
(4) \quad x_{m-1,t} = \left[\prod_{j=1}^{m-1} k_{m-1-j,t-j} \right] \gamma y_{t-m+1}.
$$

where $[\prod_{j=1}^{m-1} k_{m-1-j,t-j}]$ denotes the proportion of animals born at time $t - m + 1$ which remains in the population at time t. From (3) and (4), the dynamics of the adult population y_t are characterized by

$$
(5) \quad y_t = \sum_{i=m}^{n} x_{it} = \sum_{i=m}^{n} \gamma \left[\prod_{j=1}^{i-m+1} k_{i-j,t-j} \right] x_{m-1,t+m-1-i}.
$$

where $[\prod_{j=1}^{i-m+1} k_{i-j,t-j}]$ measures the proportion of animals of age $m - 1$ at time $t + m - 1 - i$ still in the population at age i, $i = m, \ldots, n$.

Equations (4) and (5) are linear homogeneous difference equations that characterize animal population dynamics. They involve the retention rates k [or alternatively the culling rates $(1 - k)$] for each cohort. In other words, taking reproduction rates γ as given, population dynamics are determined exclusively by retention rate parameters k.

In the context of a dairy model, retention rates are expected to be a function of milk price at the time of culling decisions: $k(p_t, i, j, \cdot)$, where p_t is milk price at time t and "$\cdot$" denotes other factors influencing production decisions. Because retention rate k is bounded between zero and one, it cannot be represented globally as a linear function of its arguments $(p_t, i, j, \cdot)$. The nonlinear specification $k = 1/\{1 + \exp[f(p_t, i, j, \cdot)]\}$ used by Chavas and Klemme has the appealing feature that the bounds $0 \leq k \leq 1$ are satisfied globally. Chavas and Klemme assumed a parametric form of $f(p_t, i, j, \cdot)$ and estimated (4) and (5) with annual data on the U.S. dairy herd, where $m = 3$, $n = 11$, $y_t = $ number of dairy cows, and $x_{2t} = $ number of two-year-old heifers in year t. Estimates of (4) and (5) provide a complete specification of dairy cow population dynamics. The Chavas-Klemme results show the cow number elasticity with respect to milk price is positive. However, it is highly inelastic in the short run, becomes elastic in the intermediate-run (6 years), and is quite large in the long run (20–30 years).

Milk Supply

Milk supply (S_t) equals the number of dairy cows (y_t) times average production per cow (q_t). We assume production per cow takes the form

$$
q_t = A\, p_t^{\alpha},
$$

where α is elasticity of milk yield with respect to milk price.[2] Previous research has found this elasticity to be positive but small—for example, Chavas and Klemme estimated it to be 0.11.

Milk Demand

Consumer demand for dairy products in the U.S. has consistently been found to be price inelastic. Huang estimated a retail price elasticity of -0.26

---

[2] We ignore the effects of technical progress that would tend to increase production per cow over time. Thus we focus on a stationary situation for investigating the nature of long-run market equilibrium.

for fluid milk, -0.33 for cheese, and -0.17 for butter, generating a retail demand elasticity for all dairy products of -0.31 (Haidacher, Blaylock, and Myers). George and King argued that the farm-level elasticity of derived demand can be obtained as the product of retail demand and farm-retail price transmission elasticities. The price transmission elasticity of dairy products has been found to be positive but less than one (Kinnucan and Forker; Wohlgenant and Haidacher). For example, Wohlgenant and Haidacher reported a farm-retail price transmission elasticity of 0.47 for dairy products. This result suggests the farm-level price elasticity of derived demand for dairy products could be as low as -0.10. At the other extreme, and using a more sophisticated approach, Wohlgenant and Haidacher estimated the price elasticity of farm-level derived demand for U.S. dairy products to be -0.61. Overall, reported estimates of farm-level demand for dairy products are always inelastic, with estimated elasticities ranging typically from -0.1 to -0.6.

In subsequent simulations, we assume farm level derived demand for milk can be characterized by constant elasticity model

$$Q_t = B\, p_t^{\beta}$$

where β is the (constant) price elasticity of demand.

Market Dynamics

With the above specifications, market equilibrium in the dairy market occurs at the intersection of supply and demand: $y_t q_t = Q_t$. After appropriate substitutions, this can be written as $y_t A\, p_t^{\alpha} = B\, p_t^{\beta}$, or

$$(6) \qquad y_t = (B/A)\, p_t^{E}$$

where y_t is given by (4) and (5) and where $E = \beta - \alpha$, the price elasticity of farm-level demand net of the effect of milk price on production per cow. Based on previous research, we expect elasticity E to range from -0.2 to -0.7 in the U.S. dairy market. Presently, we assume α takes a value of 0.1, implying $\beta = E + 0.1$. The result is that any parametric change in E can be interpreted as a change in the elasticity β of derived demand.

Equations (4), (5), and (6) constitute a relatively simple system of supply-demand equations characterizing market equilibrium in the U.S. dairy sector. Using Chavas and Klemme's

estimates of (4) and (5), we have all the information necessary to investigate the dynamics of the U.S. dairy market. Specifically, solving the market-clearing equation (6) for p_t, and substituting the result into (4) and (5), the dynamics of the dairy market can be expressed as a first-order nonlinear difference equation $\mathbf{z}_t = g(z_{t-1})$, where $\mathbf{z}_t = (y_t, y_{t-1}, \ldots, y_{t-8}; x_{m-1,t}, x_{m-1,t-1}, \ldots, x_{m-1,t-8})$, is an (18×1) vector of state variables. No analytical results currently exist on the dynamics of a nonlinear dynamic system involving so many state variables (Hao). As a result, we focus our attention on numerical simulations obtained from the above dairy model.

We first calculated Lyapunov exponents for selected values of E. Results are reported in table 1.[3] In addition, we simulated the model numerically for 500 periods using 1968 values as initial conditions. The trajectories generated for cow numbers (y_t) and heifer numbers (x_{2t}) are reported in figure 1 for selected values of E ranging between -1.5 and -0.3.

Table 1 illustrates the interaction between the elasticity of demand and market dynamics. Note that the largest Lyapunov exponent (λ_1) tends to increase as demand becomes more inelastic.[4] Recall that λ_1 can be interpreted as a measure of the rate of divergence (if positive) or convergence (if negative) of neighboring forward trajectories. The largest Lyapunov exponent is negative for $E = -1.3$ or -1.5, indicating the existence of a steady-state equilibrium when demand is sufficiently elastic. Estimates of λ_1 are nonnegative when the derived demand is inelastic ($|\beta| < 1$, which corresponds to $|E| < 1.1$), and positive when demand becomes very inelastic. Based on our model specification, it follows that a steady-state equilibrium does not exist under an inelastic demand. When E equals -1.1, -0.9, or -0.7, the largest Lyapunov exponent is zero, corresponding to the existence of limit cycles (figure 1). And for $E = -0.5$, the λ_1 estimate becomes positive. These results can be interpreted as indicating the existence of chaos in the dairy market under a very inelastic demand.

It follows from table 1 that elastic demand contributes to the existence of a steady-state equilibrium. As demand becomes more elastic, the speed of convergence of the market to its

---

[3] With 18 state variables, there are 18 Lyapunov exponents. Only the three largest Lyapunov exponents are reported in table 1.

[4] One should be cautious not to infer from table 1 that λ_1 is a monotonic function of E. As shown by May, parameter values that generate limit cycles $(\lambda_1 = 0)$ can sometimes be found within the range of parameter values generating chaos $(\lambda_1 > 0)$.

118 *February 1993* *Amer. J. Agr. Econ.*

Table 1. Estimates of The Three Largest Lyapunov Exponents (λ_i)[a]

Value of E[b]	λ_1	λ_2	λ_3	Dimension of the attractor[c]
−1.50	−0.0671	−0.0676	−0.2749	—
−1.30	−0.0310	−0.0310	−0.2628	—
−1.10	0.0000	−0.0931	−0.4027	—
−0.90	0.0000	−0.2477	−0.2477	—
−0.70	0.0000	−0.0537	−0.2338	—
−0.50	0.0606	−0.0277	−0.2362	2.14

[a] The Lyapunov exponents were estimated using the algorithm proposed by Shimada and Nagashima and Wolf et al. using 5,000 years of forward simulation of the model.
[b] The Shimada-Nagashima-Wolf et al. algorithm created overflow problems for $E = -0.3$. As a result, the Lyapunov exponents could not be estimated for $E = -0.3$.
[c] The estimate of the dimension of the chaotic is given by equation (1).

long-run equilibrium is increased. Alternatively, for values of E in the inelastic region, a steady-state equilibrium does not exist and the dynamic model exhibits either limit cycles (with moderately inelastic demand) or chaotic patterns (with very inelastic demand). Thus inelastic demand is identified as playing a major role in generating market instability.

We indicated above that previous estimates suggest the farm-level demand for milk is inelastic. To the extent our model provides a reasonable representation of the U.S. dairy market, the implication is that, if allowed to function in isolation, the U.S. milk market would not exhibit a steady-state equilibrium.

Trajectories associated with the above simu-

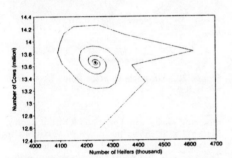

Figure 1a. Impacts of the price elasticity of demand: $E = -1.5$

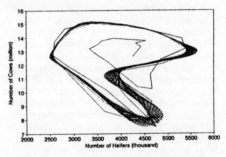

Figure 1c. Impacts of the price elasticity of demand: $E = -0.7$

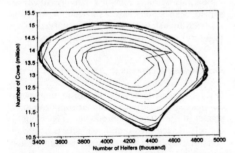

Figure 1b. Impacts of the price elasticity of demand: $E = -1.1$

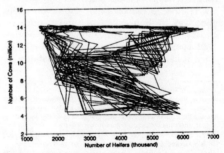

Figure 1d. Impacts of the price elasticity of demand: $E = -0.3$

lations further highlight the potential role of nonlinear dynamics in the U.S. dairy market (figure 1). In particular, figure 1 suggests market dynamics become more complex as demand becomes increasingly inelastic. The range of long term variations in herd size increases as |E| decreases: the range is from 10.5 to 15 million cows for E = −1.1; from 8 to 15 million cows for E = −0.7; and from 4 to 14 million cows for E = −0.3 (see figure 1). Figure 1 also shows the nature of the limit cycles associated with E = −1.1 or E = −0.7. Those cycles involve short-term cycles (with a period of about 14 years) embedded within a longer term cycle (with a period that can reach several hundred years).[5] Finally, figure 1 shows the chaotic dynamics of the milk market when E = −0.3. Note that the chaotic case (where E = −0.3 or β = −0.2) is quite consistent with several previous estimates of milk demand (Haidacher, Blaylock, and Myers). The complicated patterns and the range of variations in the state variables illustrate that market instability can be substantial.

Results in figure 1 assume a competitive milk market in absence of government programs. Given an inelastic demand, it seems plausible to question whether government interventions could affect market instability or, conversely, market dynamics. To address this issue, we investigate next the effect of a price support or price floor on dairy market dynamics. We consider the simple case where a support price (*SP*) is set and where "excess production" is withdrawn from the market and destroyed whenever market price falls below floor price. Figure 2 reports dynamic market trajectories for different values of *SP* given that E = −0.3.[6] Recall that E = −0.3 generates chaotic patterns in absence of a support price. Figure 2 shows that a price floor does indeed affect the nature of market dynamics. The market remains chaotic when support price is low relative to market price. However, chaos gives way to limit cycles as support price increases.[7] In other words, although the support price does not generate a steady-state equilibrium, it can reduce market unpredictability by

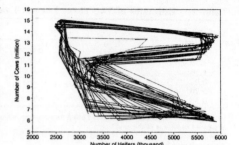

Figure 2a.   Impacts of price floor: *E* = −0.3; *SP* = 0.8

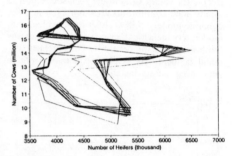

Figure 2b.   Impacts of price floor: *E* = −0.3; *SP* = 0.9

replacing chaos with (predictable) limit cycles. Figure 2 also shows the range of variations in the state variables decreases as support price rises. This suggests that market instability diminishes as the minimum price increases. It shows the effects of market interventions (such as government pricing policy) on dynamic resource allocation may be more complex than previously assumed. Such results indicate a need for additional research focusing on the welfare analysis of agricultural policy in a dynamic environment.

Concluding Remarks

We have investigated the nature of market dynamics using a simple nonlinear supply-demand model of the U.S. dairy industry. The model is entirely deterministic and neglects possible effects of exogenous shocks (such as from weather or technical change). In this context, we presented empirical evidence that an inelastic demand is a key source of market instability. Sim-

---

[5] In other words, it takes about 14 years to complete one revolution around the "circles" shown in figure 1. However, the state variables do not come back to the same position after one revolution because these short-term cycles are imbedded in a longer cycle that slightly alters the points visited each revolution.

[6] Price *p*, was normalized to 1 in year 1968. Thus support price *SP* is measured as a percentage of the 1968 milk price. For example, *SP* = 0.8 in figure 2 implies the support price is set at 80% of the 1968 milk price.

[7] The market dynamics become unbounded when support price is set at 0.95 or above.

120   *February 1993*

Amer. J. Agr. Econ.

ulation results suggest that a steady-state equilibrium does not exist in the U.S. dairy market under an inelastic demand. For moderately inelastic demand, and in the absence of government programs, the U.S. dairy market exhibits limit cycles. And under highly inelastic demand, the market becomes "unstable" as its dynamics take the form of deterministic chaos. This implies that the market path, while remaining bounded, becomes unpredictable in the long run, even in the absence of exogenous shocks.

The linkage between market instability and inelastic food demand was presented by Cochrane over 30 years ago. Of interest here is the possibility that market instability is entirely endogenous to the market itself. Our findings thus reinforce Cochrane's argument that the highly inelastic nature of food demand may be crucial in explaining why the agricultural sector is different from the rest of the economy.

Our results help identify sources of agricultural market instability and suggest new directions in government policy evaluation. For example, the conclusion that support prices help remove a chaotic market's long-term unpredictability points to the value of analyzing stabilization policy in a dynamic setting. Unfortunately, little is known about the efficiency and welfare implications of chaotic markets. Nor is the role of expectation formulation in chaotic markets well understood. It would be helpful to explore the possibility of chaos in a multi-market framework and to improve the empirical distinction between chaotic and stochastic processes.

[Received August 1991; final revision received April 1992.]

References

Baumol, J. W., and J. Benhabib. "Chaos: Significance, Mechanism, and Economic Applications." *J. Econ. Perspect.* 3,1(1989):77–106.

Benettin, G., L. Galgani, and J.-M. Strelcyn. "Kolmogorov Entropy and Numerical Experiments." *Physical Review A* 14,6 (1976):2338–45.

Brock, W. A. "Distinguishing Random and Deterministic Systems: Abridged Version." *J. Econ. Theory* 40,1(1986):168–95.

Brock, W. A., and C. L. Sayers. "Is the Business Cycle Characterized by Deterministic Chaos?" *J. Monetary Econ* 22(1988):71–90.

Chavas, J. P., and R. Klemme. "Aggregate Milk Supply Response and Investment Behavior on U.S. Dairy Farms." *Amer. J. Agri. Econ.* 68(1986):55–66.

Chavas, J. P., and M. T. Holt. "On Nonlinear Dynamics: The Case of the Pork Cycle." *Amer. J. Agr. Econ.* 73(1991):819–828.

Cochrane, W. W. *Farm Prices: Myth and Reality*. Minneapolis: University of Minnesota Press, 1958.

Gardner, B. L. *The Economics of Agricultural Policies* Macmillan, New York:Macmillan, 1987.

George, P. S., and G. A. King. *Consumer Demand for Food Commodities in the United States with Projections for 1980*. Giannini Foundation Monograph N. 26, University of California, Berkeley, 1971.

Haidacher, R. C., J. R. Blaylock, and L. H. Myers. *Consumer Demand for Dairy Products* USDA, ERS, Agricultural Economic Report N. 586, March 1988.

Hao, B.-L. *Chaos*. Singapore: World Scientific Publ. Co., 1984.

Huang, K. S. *U.S. Demand for Food: A Complete System of Price and Income Effects* USDA, ERS, Technical Bulletin N.1714, December 1985.

Innes, R. D., and G. C. Rausser. "Incomplete Markets and Government Agricultural Policy." *Amer. J. Agr. Econ.* 71(1989):915–31.

Kaplan, J., and J. Yorke. "Chaotic Behavior of Multidimensional Difference Equations." In *Functional Differential Equations and Approximation of Fixed Points*, ed. H. O. Peitgen and H. O. Walther. Berlin: Springer Verlag, 1979.

Kinnucan, H. W., and O. D. Forker. "Asymmetry in Farm-Retail Price Transmission for Major Dairy Products." *Amer. J. Agri. Econ.* 69(1987):285–92.

Li, T. Y., and J. A. Yorke. "Period Three Implies Chaos." *Amer Math Monthly* 82(1975):985–92.

Lorenz, E. N. "Deterministic Non-Periodic Flow." *J. Atmospher. Sci.* 20,130(1963):130–41.

Luenberger, David G. *Introduction to Dynamic Systems: Theory, Models and Applications*. New York: John Wiley and Sons,1979.

May, R. M. "Simple Mathematical Models with Complicated Dynamics." *Nature* 261(1976):459–67.

Newbery, D. M. G., and J. E. Stiglitz, *The Theory of Commodity Price Stabilization: A Study in the Economics of Risk*. Oxford: Clarendon Press,1981.

Pope, R. D., and A. Hallam. "A Confusion of Agricultural Economists? A Professional Interest Survey and Essay." *Amer. J. Agr. Econ.* 68(1986):572–94.

Schultz, T. W. *Agriculture in an Unstable Economy*. New York: McGraw-Hill,1945.

Shimada, I., and T. Nagashima. "A Numerical Approach to Ergodic Problem of Dissipative Dynamical Systems." *Progress of Theoretical Physics* 61(1979):1605–15.

Wolf, A., J. B. Swift, H. L. Swinney, and J. A. Vastano. "Determining Lyapunov Exponents from a Time Series." *Physica* 16D(1985):285–317.

Wohlgenant, M. K., and R. C. Haidacher. *Retail to Farm Linkage for a Complete Demand System of Food Commodities* USDA, ERS, Technical Bulletin N. 1775, December 1989.

Young, D. L. "Risk Preferences of Agricultural Producers: Their Use in Extension and Research." *Amer. J. Agr. Econ.* 61(1979):1063–70.

[15]

Economics Letters 36 (1991) 127–132
North-Holland

Adaptive learning and roads to chaos

The case of the cobweb

Cars H. Hommes *

Rijksuniversiteit Groningen, NL-9700 AV Groningen, Netherlands

Received 15 October 1990
Accepted 6 December 1990

We investigate the dynamics of the cobweb model with adaptive expectations, a linear demand curve, and a nonlinear, S-shaped, increasing supply curve. Both stable periodic and chaotic price behaviour can occur. We investigate, how the dynamics of the model depend on the parameters. Both infinitely many period doubling and period halving bifurcations can occur, when the demand curve is shifted upwards. The same result holds with respect to the expectations weight factor.

1. Introduction

In economics there is a growing interest in the use of non-linear deterministic models. The main reason is that a non-linear deterministic model may exhibit both stable periodic and chaotic behaviour, and hence may provide an endogenous explanation of the periodicity and irregularity observed in economic time series. [For a survey on non-linear economic models exhibiting chaos, see e.g. Lorenz (1989).]

In this paper, we investigate the dynamics of one of the simplest nonlinear economic models: the cobweb model with adaptive expectations. The demand curve is linearly decreasing, while the supply curve is non-linear, S-shaped and increasing. The dynamics of the expected prices in the model is described by a one-dimensional nonlinear difference equation $x_{n+1} = f(x_n)$. Chiarella (1988) approximated this model by the well known logistic map $x_{n+1} = \mu x_n(1 - x_n)$. Unfortunately, since the map f is either increasing or has two critical points, the quadratic map (which has one critical point) is not a good approximation of the map f. In another related paper, Finkenstädt and Kuhbier (1990) present numerical evidence of the occurrence of chaos, in the case of linear supply and a non-linear, decreasing demand curve.

In particular, we investigate how the dynamics of the model depend on the height of the demand curve and the expectations weight factor. In this paper we present numerical results, and explain the validity of these results by means of theoretical results. The proofs of these theoretical results will be presented in a forthcoming long paper [Hommes (1991)].

* The paper was written during a visit to the Institute for Physical Science and Technology, University of Maryland, College Park. Financial support from the Netherlands Organization of Scientific Research (NWO) is gratefully acknowledged. I would like to thank Helena E. Nusse for several discussions and for helpful comments.

2. The cobweb model with adaptive expectations

The well known cobweb model is one of the simplest economic models. The model described the price behaviour in a single market. We write p_t for the price, $\hat{p}_t$ for the expected price, q_t^d for the demand for goods and q_t^s for the supply for goods, all at time t. The *cobweb model* is given by the following three equations:

$$q_t^d = D(p_t), \tag{1}$$

$$q_t^s = S(\hat{p}_t), \tag{2}$$

$$q_t^d = q_t^s. \tag{3}$$

In the traditional version of the cobweb model, the expected price equals the previous actual price, that is $\hat{p}_t = p_{t-1}$. It is well known that if in the traditional cobweb model both the supply and demand curves are monotonic, then basically three types of price dynamics occur: Convergence to an equilibrium price, convergence to period two price oscillations or unbounded, exploding price oscillations. Recently, it was shown by Artstein (1983) and Jensen and Urban (1984) that chaotic price behaviour can occur if at least one of the supply and demand curves is non-monotonic, see also Lichtenberg and Ujihara (1989).

Nerlove (1958) introduced adaptive price expectations into the cobweb model, in the case of linear supply and demand curves. Adaptive expectations is described by the following equation

$$\hat{p}_t = \hat{p}_{t-1} + w(p_{t-1} - \hat{p}_{t-1}), \quad 0 \leq w \leq 1. \tag{4}$$

The parameter w is called the *expectations weight factor*, and for $w = 1$ the model reduces to the traditional cobweb model. In the case of linear supply and demand curves, the introduction of adaptive expectations in the cobweb model has a stabilizing effect on the price dynamics, see Nerlove (1958). However, the equilibrium price may still be unstable.

The question we address is: '*What can be said about the price behaviour in the case of non-linear, monotonic supply and demand curves?*'

For simplicity we assume that the demand curve is linearly decreasing, and is given by

$$D(p_t) = a - bp_t, \quad b > 0. \tag{5}$$

Concerning the supply, we start off with the following two Economic Considerations:

(*EC1*) If prices are low then supply increases slowly, because of start-up costs and fixed production costs.

(*EC2*) If prices are high then supply increases slowly, because of supply and capacity constraints.

Based on these considerations we choose a non-linear, increasing supply curve.

The simplest smooth curve satisfying (EC1) and (EC2) is an S-shaped curve S with the property that S has a unique inflection point $\bar{p}$, such that (1) the slope S' of S is maximal in $\bar{p}$, (2) S' is increasing for $p < \bar{p}$ and (3) S' is decreasing for $p > \bar{p}$. We change coordinates and choose the inflection point of the supply curve to be the new origin. Note that with respect to this new origin both 'prices' and 'quantities' can be negative. As an example of an S-shaped supply curve satisfying the above assumptions we choose

$$S_\lambda(x) = \arctan(\lambda x), \quad \lambda > 0. \tag{6}$$

Observe that the parameter λ tunes the 'steepness' of the S-shape.

Equations (1) through (5) yield a difference equation $x_{t+1} = f(x_t)$ describing the expected price dynamics, with f given by

$$f_{a,b,w,\lambda}(x) = -wS_\lambda(x)/b + (1-w)x + aw/b. \tag{7}$$

We would like to point out that the price dynamics and the quantity dynamics are equivalent to the dynamics of the expected prices.

The map $f_{a,b,w,\lambda}$ has a unique fixed point, which is the equilibrium price corresponding to the intersection point of the supply and demand curves. An important question is: 'What can be said about the global dynamics of the model, when the equilibrium price is unstable?'

3. Roads to chaos

In this section we investigate how the dynamics of the model depends on the height of the demand curve (parameter a) and the expectations weight factor w. Figure 1 shows a bifurcation diagram with respect to the parameter a, with the other parameters fixed at $b = 0.25$, $w = 0.3$ and $\lambda = 4.8$. In fact a

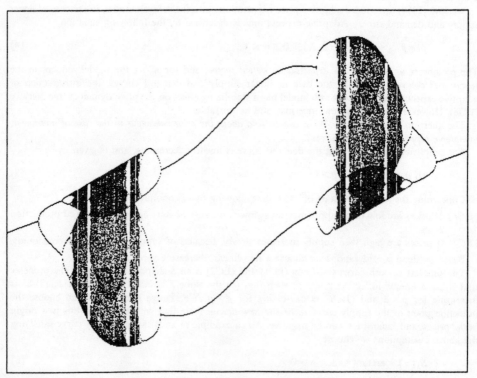

Fig. 1. Shifting the demand curve upwards, stable periodic and chaotic price behaviour may interchange several times.

bifurcation diagram of a one-dimensional model shows an attractor of the model as a (multi-valued) function of one parameter.

Figure 1 suggests the following bifurcation scenario. If a is small then there exists a stable equilibrium. If a is increased, then the equilibrium becomes unstable and period doubling bifurcations occur. After infinitely many period doubling bifurcations the price behaviour becomes chaotic, as a is increased. Next, after infinitely many period halving bifurcations the price behaviour becomes more regular again. A stable period 2 orbit occurs for an interval of a-values, containing $a = 0$. When a is further increased, once more, after infinitely many period doubling bifurcations chaotic behaviour arises. Finally, after infinitely many period halving bifurcations, we have a stable equilibrium again, when a is sufficiently large.

Concerning the dynamics of the model, for the particular supply curve in (6), the results in Hommes (1991) imply the following (we write f for $f_{a,b,w,\lambda}$).

Given $b > 0$ and $0 < w < 1$, if λ is sufficiently large, then there exist $a_1 < a_2 < 0 < a_3 < a_4$ such that:

(1) f has a globally stable fixed point, if $a < a_1$.
(2) f has a period 3 orbit, for $a = a_2$.
(3) f has an unstable fixed point, a stable period 2 orbit, and no other periodic points, for $a = 0$.
(4) f has a period 3 orbit, for $a = a_3$.
(5) f has a globally stable fixed point, fi $a > a_4$.

From a well known result by Li and Yorke (1975) it follows that in the cases (2) and (4) the map $f_{a,b,w,\lambda}$ is topological chaotic, that is: (i) there exist infinitely many periodic points with different period, and (ii) there exists an uncountable set of aperiodic points, for which there is sensitive dependence on initial conditions. Concerning the bifurcations scenario with respect to the parameter a, properties (1)–(5) imply the following:

(a) Infinitely many period doubling bifurcations occur in the parameter intervals (a_1, a_2) and $(0, a_3)$.
(b) Infinitely many period halving bifurcations occur in the parameter intervals $(a_2, 0)$ and (a_3, a_4).

Nusse and Yorke [1988] present a nice example $x_{n+1} = \mu F(x_n)$ (where F is a one-hump map with negative Schwarzian derivative and μ is a parameter) for which they showed that both infinitely many period doubling and period halving bifurcations do occur as μ is increased.

Recall that increasing the parameter a is just shifting the demand curve vertically upwards. Hence our theoretical results imply that, if the demand curve is shifted vertically upwards, then both infinitely many period doubling and period halving bifurcations occur and periodic and chaotic behaviour interchange several times.

A bifurcation diagram with respect to the expectations weight factor w, with the other parameters fixed at $a = 0.8$, $b = 0.25$ and $\lambda = 4$, is shown in figure 2. The diagram suggests that a stable equilibrium occurs for w close to 0. After infinitely many period doubling bifurcations the price dynamics becomes chaotic, as w is increased. Next, after infinitely many period halving bifurcations, the price behaviour becomes more regular again, until a stable period 2 cycle occurs, for w close to 1.

The results in [H] imply the following. Given $b > 0$, if λ is sufficiently large and for a suitable choice of the parameter a we have:

(1) f has a globally stable fixed point for w close to 0.
(2) f has a period 3 orbit for intermediate values of w.
(3) f has a stable period 2 orbit for w close to 1.

This result implies that both infinitely many period doubling and period halving bifurcations occur as w is increased from 0 to 1.

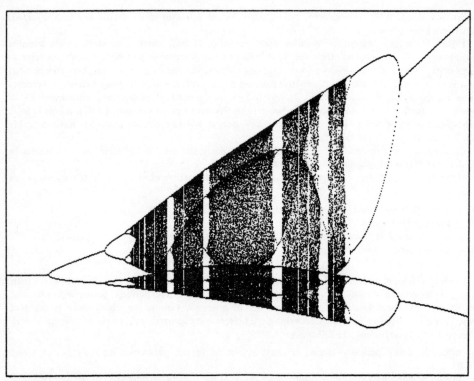

Fig. 2. For w close to 0 a stable equilibrium occurs, while for w close to 1 stable period 2 oscillations with large amplitude occur; for intermediate values of w chaotic price oscillations with moderate amplitude arise.

In the case of linear supply and demand curves, the introduction of adaptive expectations into the cobweb model has a stabilizing effect on the price dynamics, see Nerlove (1958). We present a corresponding result, in the case of non-linear, monotonic supply and/or demand curves. Recall that $w = 1$ corresponds to the traditional cobweb model. As w is decreased from 1 to 0, then the amplitude of the price oscillations becomes smaller, see fig. 2. In the case of non-linear, monotonic supply and/or demand curves the introduction of adaptive expectations into the cobweb model dampens the amplitude of the price cycles. Meanwhile a price cycle may become unstable and chaotic price oscillations may arise. Hence, from a quantitative point of view adaptive expectations have a stabilizing effect, but from a qualitative point of view adaptive expectations may have a destabilizing effect upon the price behaviour.

4. Discussion

Expectations and learning behaviour play an important role in economics. One of the fundamental differences between the physical and the social sciences is that in a physical system the laws of the system are often fixed, while in a social system individuals learn from he past and influence the laws of the system. It has been argued, that, because of this fundamental difference, deterministic chaos, which plays an important role in the physical sciences nowadays, is of less interest to the economic and social sciences.

In the traditional cobweb model, there is no learning behaviour: the suppliers believe that today's price will also hold tomorrow. Recently, Holmes and Manning (1988) showed that in a cobweb model with nonlinear, monotonic supply and demand, when the suppliers learn by arithmetic mean, that is, if they employ the mean of all past prices as their expectation of tomorrow's price, then prices always converge to a stable equilibrium. Holmes and Manning conclude that if agents use their memories, then chaos can not occur; only when agents are forgetful, chaos may occur. Stated according to their aphorism: '*Those who do not learn from history are condemned to never repeat it*', see Holmes and Manning (1988, p. 7).

Our results show that the conclusions of Holmes and Manning are not true in general. Whether or not chaotic behaviour is possible when agents learn from the past, depends on both the model and the type of learning behaviour. We have seen that in a cobweb model with adaptive learning and non-linear, monotonic supply and demand, chaotic price behaviour is possible, even in the long run. It is well known that adaptive price expectations means that the expected price is a weighted average, with geometrically declining weights, of all past observed prices. Hence, adaptive learning seems to be much more realistic than learning by arithmetic mean, since adaptive learning puts higher weights to the most recent prices. Unlike the aphorism of Holmes and Manning, one might say: *Even those who learn from the past, may never repeat it*.

In Hommes (1991) we will analyse the dynamics of the model, for a general class of S-shaped supply curves, in more detail. Moreover, we will present a geometric explanation of the occurrence of chaotic price behaviour in the cobweb model with adaptive expectations, for a large class of non-linear, monotonic supply and demand curves.

References

Artstein, Z., 1983, Irregular cobweb dynamics, Economics Letters 11, 15–17.

Chiarella, C., 1988, The cobweb model. Its instability and the onset of chaos, Economic Modelling, 377–384.

Finkenstädt, B. and P. Kuhbier, 1990, Chaotic dynamics in agricultural markets, Paper Freie Universität Berlin, presented at the OR 90 conference in Vienna.

Hommes, C.H., 1991, Adaptive expectations and nonlinear cobweb models: Stable cycles, chaos and bifurcations. In preparation.

Holmes, J.M. and R. Manning, 1988, Memory and market stability. The case of the cobweb, Economics Letters 28, 1–7.

Jensen, R.V. and R. Urban, 1984, Chaotic price behaviour in a nonlinear cobweb model, Economics Letters 15, 235–240.

Li, T.Y. and J.A. Yorke, 1975, Period three implies chaos, American Mathematical Monthly 82, 985–992.

Lichtenberg, A.J. and A. Ujihara, 1989, Application of non-linear mapping theory to commodity price fluctuations, Journal of Economic Dynamics and Control 13, 225–246.

Lorenz, H.-W., 1989, Non-linear dynamical economics and chaotic motion (Springer-Verlag, Berlin).

Nerlove, M., 1958, Adaptive expectations and cobweb phenomena, Quarterly Journal of Economics 72, 227–240.

Nusse, H.E. and J.A. Yorke, 1988, Period halving for $x_{n+1} = mF(x_n)$ where F has negative Schwarzian derivative, Physics Letters 127A, 328–334.

[16]

Journal of Economic Dynamics and Control 14 (1990) 1–19. North-Holland

RESOLUTION OF CHAOS WITH APPLICATION TO A
MODIFIED SAMUELSON MODEL

H.E. NUSSE and C.H. HOMMES*

Rijksuniversiteit Groningen, NL-9700 AV Groningen, The Netherlands

Received August 1987, final version received July 1989

Recently, several discrete nonlinear growth models with complicated dynamical behavior have been introduced in the literature. A great deal of these papers are numerically oriented and claim to establish chaotic dynamics (showing the existence of a periodic three-cycle) without elaborating very much on the mathematical aspects of the involved maps. We will see that for a suitable class of discrete processes there is order in the erratic dynamics. In fact, the dynamics of these simple processes will be dominated by ultimately periodic behavior, and we will show that this behavior is persistent under small smooth perturbations.

To illustrate bifurcation phenomena, we will consider a modified Samuelson model [a nonlinear multiplier–accelerator model introduced by Gabisch (1984)]. We will show that period-doubling bifurcation as well as period-halving bifurcation can occur as a parameter value is increased. For this model Gabisch showed that for a certain range of parameter values there is chaos in the dynamics in the sense of Li and Yorke. We will not only present results concerning the regularity in the complicated dynamics, but also we will show that the range of parameter values k, for which there is chaos in the sense of Li and Yorke, is small. Finally, the chaos will disappear when the accelerator is increased.

Furthermore, we will give an example (a modified Cobweb model) in which such period-doubling bifurcations do not occur. In particular, for these kinds of models, as soon as the equilibrium is unstable, there exist infinitely many periodic points with different period and there exist also aperiodic points.

1. Introduction

Recently, several discrete nonlinear models have been discussed in the economic literature: a discrete version of the Haavelmo model by Stutzer (1980), a model concerning rational choice by Benhabib and Day (1981), a discrete version of Goodwin's growth model by Pohjola (1981), a (neo)classical growth model by Day (1982, 1983), a modified Cobweb model by Cugno and Montrucchio (1984), a modified version of Samuelson's model by Gabisch (1984), competitive business cycles by Grandmont (1985, 1986), and several models in the monograph *Business Cycle Theory* by Gabisch and Lorenz (1987).

*We are grateful to the referees for the comments improving the paper.

0165-1889/90/$3.50©1990, Elsevier Science Publishers B.V. (North-Holland)

A number of these discrete models can be represented by a nonlinear difference equation $x_{t+1} = f(x_t)$, with f some continuous function from an interval into itself. The mapping f occurring in these difference equations often has the following properties: $f(0) = 0$, f assumes its maximum value at c for some positive real number c, f is increasing for all x with x smaller than c, f is decreasing for all x with x larger than c. Such a point c is called a critical point. Moreover, the map f will contain one or more parameters which tune the steepness of the 'hump' in the graph of f; these parameters will have some economic significance.

In the celebrated paper 'Period Three Implies Chaos' Li and Yorke (1975) studied iteration of continuous maps from an interval into itself. A special case of their main result is the following: Assume that a continuous map f has a periodic point with period three; then (1) f has a periodic point with smallest period k for each positive integer k, and (2) there exists an uncountable set in the interval consisting of aperiodic points. The dynamical behavior of a map with infinitely many periodic points with different periods may be extremely complex. In fact, considering the dynamical behavior of physical, biological, and economic systems which can be modeled using such functions, Li and Yorke used the word chaos describing such behavior. Mostly, in the analysis of the models mentioned above, one verifies the existence of a periodic point with period three; thereafter one concludes that there is chaos (in the sense of Li and Yorke).

As an example we will consider the nonlinear multiplier–accelerator model as introduced by Gabisch (1984) and a modified Cobweb model described by Cugno and Montrucchio (1984). The Gabisch model is a modification of the Samuelson model which suggests a general occurrence of chaotic dynamics, and it is given by a nonlinear difference equation $x_{t+1} = G(x_t)$, where G is a map having the properties as the maps f above. We will call G the Gabisch map. Gabisch obtained that for a certain range of parameter values there is chaos in the sense of Li and Yorke. Moreover he argues that, within this chaotic range of parameter values, the solutions are highly sensitive to a variation of the parameters or initial values, so that long-term predictions are useless; see also Day (1982), Stutzer (1980), and Pohjola (1981).

It is the purpose of this paper to present results which might be rather surprising compared with the results mentioned above. We will formulate some results concerning the regularity (i.e., periodic behavior) in the complicated dynamics and the persistence of this regularity under small smooth perturbations of the system. In particular, G has at most one stable periodic orbit and, whenever G has an attracting periodic orbit P, then we have: (1) the orbits of almost all initial values will converge to P, and the orbit of the critical point will converge to P; (2) if the orbit of the initial value x will converge to P, then the orbit of every initial value y will converge to P too with y sufficiently close to x; (3) a sufficiently small variation of the parameter values does not change the qualitative behavior of the system. Secondly, if the parameter value α is close to one, then the range of parameter values k for which there is chaos (in the sense of Li and Yorke) is small. In particular, if $k > (\alpha + 1)/2$ then there is no chaos at all, because of the existence of an equilibrium, being globally stable. This means that if the multiplier α is near one then, by increasing the accelerator k slightly, chaos will disappear.

The paper is organized as follows. In section 2 we will recall the modified Samuelson model as introduced by Gabisch (1984), we will present a few bifurcation diagrams (by varying one of the parameters), and we will formulate some properties for this model. Furthermore, we will consider the regularity in the complicated dynamics of the Gabisch map, and we will show that the regularity is persistent under small smooth perturbations of the system. Definitions (including two definitions of chaos) and some notations are given in section 3; hence readers not familiar with the notations in section 2 are advised to consult section 3. In section 4 we will describe the pitch-fork bifurcations which can occur in one-dimensional one-parameter families of maps, and we will describe two bifurcations occurring in the Gabisch map: a period-doubling and a period-halving bifurcation. In section 5 we will recall a modified Cobweb model and show that the transition from a system with a stable fixed point to a chaotic system by increasing a parameter does not imply that there is a sequence of parameter values for which period-doubling bifurcations will occur. Section 6 deals with the regularity in the complicated dynamics of one-dimensional maps. Finally, we will make some concluding remarks.

2. A modified Samuelson model

Gabisch (1984) introduced the following modified Samuelson model:

$$Y_t = C_t + I_t.$$

$$I_t = k[Y_t - Y_{t-1}], \quad k > 1,$$

$$C_t = c[Y_{t-1}]^\alpha, \quad \alpha \geq 1, \quad 0 < c < 1,$$

with Y = national product, C = consumption, and I = investment. The Gabisch model is ad hoc, but a possible way to justify the modification of the Samuelson model is in considering the following question: 'What happens if (due to statistical, observational, or expectational influences) the actual realization of a standard behavioral assumption slightly diverges from the theoretical ideal?' In that case it is important to consider a small neighborhood of, e.g., the parameter $\alpha = 1$. The first equation determines the national product.

According to the second equation the investment depends on changes in Y with k being the accelerator. In order to avoid confusion, we would like to mention that the investment function in the original Samuelson model is different from the one in Gabisch's model: Samuelson assumed $I_t = k(C_t - C_{t-1})$. The consumption function is contained in the third equation. By substitution one obtains:

$$Y_{t+1} = Y_t \{ k - c[Y_t]^{\alpha-1} \} / (k-1).$$

Therefore we consider the three-parameter family of maps $G(x; \alpha, k, c)$ from the real line into itself defined by

$$G(x; \alpha, k, c) = x(k - cx^{\alpha-1})/(k-1).$$

We will call the map G the Gabisch map. Note that the point zero is an unstable fixed point of the map G. Clearly, the point $x^* = [1/c]^{1/(\alpha-1)}$ is a fixed point of G, and the derivative of G at this point [which equals $(k - \alpha)/(k - 1)$] is -1 if and only if $k = (\alpha + 1)/2$. Gabisch concluded that if $k = [1 + \alpha^{\alpha/(1-\alpha)} - \alpha^{1/(1-\alpha)}]^{-1}$, then there exists a periodic orbit with period three; hence there is chaos in the sense of Li and Yorke (1975).

We will address the following questions:

(1) Will bifurcations occur by varying the parameters?
(2) Is there regularity in the complicated dynamical behavior of G?
(3) Will the qualitative dynamical behavior of the map G persist under small perturbations?

The first question can be answered affirmatively, and we will analyze the type of bifurcations for two choices of the parameter values (see section 4 for the details).

We choose the parameter values: $\alpha_0 = 1.1$, $k_0 = 1.05$, $c_0 = 0.8$. We have that the point $x_0 = (1.25)^{10}$ is a fixed point of G with eigenvalue -1.

I. We vary the parameter α and we let the values k_0 and c_0 constant. In fig. 1 we have given the bifurcation diagrams for G_α with (a) $1.095 \le \alpha \le 1.138$ and (b) $1.118 \le \alpha \le 1.138$. Note that for α close to one, chaos disappears.

II. Now we vary k and keep α_0 and c_0 constant. The bifurcation diagrams for G_k with (a) $1.0364 \le k \le 1.053$ and (b) $1.0364 \le k \le 1.042$ are presented in fig. 2. It is not difficult to show that for all $k \ge 1.05$ the map G_k has a globally attracting fixed point w.r.t. the open interval $(0, (k/c)^{1/(\alpha-1)})$. Using this fact and the bifurcation diagram, it follows that chaos (even in the sense of Li and Yorke) only occurs for a small range of parameter values k. Consequently, there is resolution of chaos when the accelerator is increased.

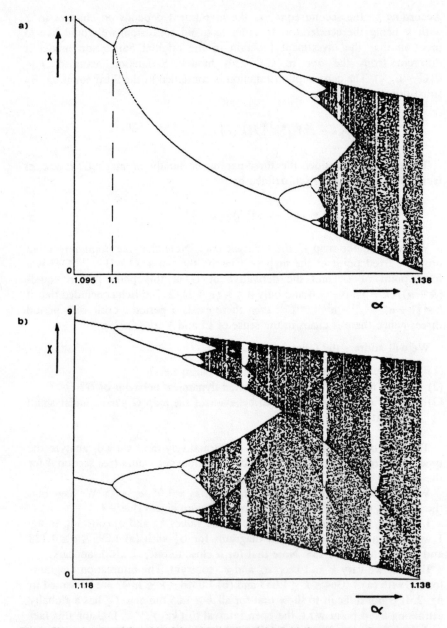

Fig. 1. Plots of a part of the orbit of the critical point of the Gabisch map versus the parameter α. For each α the first 200 points of the orbit have been neglected, thereafter the next 200 points were plotted. $k = 1.05$, $c = 0.8$. (a) $1.095 \leq \alpha \leq 1.138$, $0 \leq x \leq 11$; (b) $1.118 \leq \alpha \leq 1.138$, $0 \leq x \leq 9$.

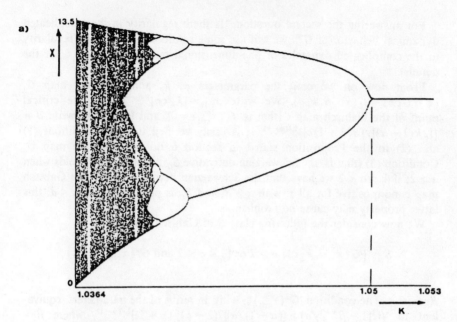

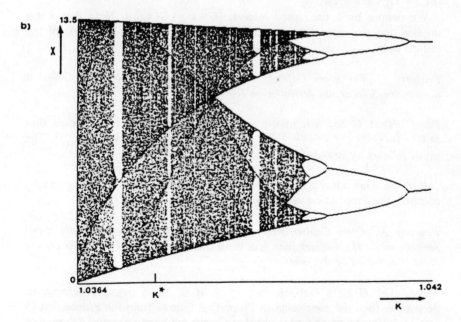

Fig. 2. Plots of a part of the orbit of the critical point of the Gabisch map versus the parameter k.
$\alpha = 1.1$, $c = 0.8$. (a) $1.0364 \leq k \leq 1.053$, $0 \leq x \leq 13.5$; (b) $1.0364 \leq k \leq 1.042$, $0 \leq x \leq 13.5$.

For answering the second question, 'Is there regularity in the complicated dynamical behavior of G?', we will use some results concerning the regularity in the complicated dynamics of one-dimensional maps (see section 6 for the details).

From now on we omit the parameters α, k, and c in the map G, i.e., $G(x) = G(x; \alpha, k, c)$. We write $x_{crit} = [k/c\alpha]^{1/(\alpha-1)}$ for the critical point of the Gabisch map G[that is, $G'(x_{crit}) = 0$], and further we write $d = \{[2k(2-\alpha)]/[\alpha(\alpha+1)c]\}^{1/(\alpha-1)}$. It is easily verified that the conditions (1) and (2) in the Proposition stated in section 6 do hold for the map G. Condition (3) (that is, the Schwarzian derivative S_G is nonpositive) holds when $\alpha \geq 2$; if $1 < \alpha < 2$ we have that the Schwarzian derivative S_G of the Gabisch map is nonpositive for all x with $x \geq d$, and S_G is positive for all $x < d$; this latter property may cause no problem.

We now consider the following class S of Gabisch maps:

$$S = \left\{ G(x; \alpha, k, c): \alpha \geq 2 \text{ or } \left(1 < \alpha < 2 \text{ and } G^2(x_{crit}) \geq d\right)\right\}.$$

Remark. The condition '$G^2(x_{crit}) \geq d$' is, in terms of the parameters, equivalent to '$\beta^2[1 - \beta^{\alpha-1}/\alpha] \geq [(\alpha-1)/\alpha][2(2-\alpha)/(\alpha+1)]^{1/(\alpha-1)}$, where $\beta = [k(\alpha-1)]/[\alpha(k-1)]$'.

We denote by I the closed interval $[G^2(x_{crit}), G(x_{crit})]$. Note that $k < \alpha$ implies that the map G has a fixed point x^* on the right-hand side of the critical point x_{crit}, and in particular $G^2(x_{crit}) < x^* = G(x^*) < G(x_{crit})$.

Property 1. *For every Gabisch map G in the class S, we have G has a nonpositive Schwarzian derivative on I.*

Proof. That G has a nonpositive Schwarzian derivative on I means that $D_S G(x) = G'''(x)/G'(x) - \frac{3}{2}[G''(x)/G'(x)]^2 \leq 0$ for all x in $I/\{x_{crit}\}$. The proof follows by straightforward computation. ∎

For the Gabisch maps in the class S we obtain the following result; compare the Proposition in section 6:

Property 2. *Every Gabisch map in S has at most one asymptotically stable periodic orbit. If a Gabisch map in S has a stable periodic orbit, then the critical point is attracted by this orbit.*

Proof. Let G be a Gabisch map in S. If G has a negative Schwarzian derivative, then the conclusion in Property 2 follows from the Proposition in section 6. From now on we assume that G does not have a negative Schwarzian derivative.

Obviously, for each x with $0 < x < d$ there exists a positive integer N so that $G^n(x)$ is in I for every $n \geq N$. From this fact, Property 1, and the Proposition in section 6 the result follows. ∎

Concerning the regularity in the complicated dynamics for the Gabisch map we have the following result:

Property 3. Let G be a Gabisch map in class S. If the orbit of the critical point of G converges to an asymptotically stable periodic orbit with period p, then almost every point (in the sense of Lebesgue measure) is asymptotically periodic with period p.

Proof. If the parameter values α, k, and c are given such that the map G has a negative Schwarzian derivative, then the result follows from Theorem GMSN (section 6). From now on we assume that the Schwarzian derivative is not negative everywhere. Applying Properties 1 and 2 above and Theorem B in Nusse (1987), we obtain that almost every point in I is asymptotically periodic with period p, where p is the period of the asymptotically stable periodic orbit. Clearly, for each nonnegative real number x there exists a nonnegative integer N so that $G^n(x)$ is in I for every $n \geq N$. The conclusion is that almost every point is asymptotically periodic with period p. ∎

Remark. The proofs of the results concerning the regularity in the complicated dynamics in the Gabisch maps when $1 < \alpha < 2$ are based on the assumption that $G^2(x_{\text{crit}}) \geq d$. This assumption implies that G has a nonpositive Schwarzian derivative on the interval $[G^2(x_{\text{crit}}), G(x_{\text{crit}})]$. For the parameter values $\alpha = 1.1$ and $c = 0.8$ we have that $G^2(x_{\text{crit}}) \geq d$ if and only if $k \geq k^*$, where $k^* \approx 1.0376$.

Now we will consider the third question, 'Will the qualitative dynamical behavior of the map G persist under small perturbations?' In particular, we will deal with the question 'Does the asymptotically periodic behavior in the complicated dynamics of the Gabisch map persist under small perturbations?' If we allow continuous perturbations of the map G, where G denotes the Gabisch map $G(x; \alpha, k, c)$, then the answer is negative by using the arguments given in Nusse (1986).

In order to answer the question concerning smooth perturbations we define a neighborhood of G in the class of C^2 functions. From now on, for each G in S, we write J_G for a bounded open interval containing $[0, (k/c)^{1/(\alpha - 1)}]$.

For each G in S and for every $\varepsilon > 0$, we define the set $U_\varepsilon(G)$ of C^2 maps by

$$U_\varepsilon(G) = \left\{ f\colon J_G \to J_G\colon \sum_{k=0}^{2} \sup\left[|G^{(k)}(x) - f^{(k)}(x)|\colon x \text{ in } J_G \right] < \varepsilon \right\},$$

where $G^{(k)}$, respectively $f^{(k)}$, means the kth derivative of G, respectively f.

The property that small smooth perturbations of G do not change the qualitative behavior of the dynamics follows from the following result.

Property 4. *Let G be a Gabisch map in S. Assume that the map G has an asymptotically stable periodic orbit P with period p.*

There exists a positive real number $\varepsilon > 0$ such that for each f in $U_\varepsilon(G)$ we have:

(1) *The orbit of almost each point converges to the asymptotically stable periodic orbit of f with period p.*

(2) *The number of periodic points for f with period n is equal to the number of periodic points for G with period n, for each positive integer n.*

Proof. Let G be as in the Theorem. Apply the Properties 2 and 3 above, Theorem B in Nusse (1987), and Theorems B, C, and E in Nusse (1988). ∎

Remark. (1) We would like to point out that a variation in one of the parameters appearing in the Gabisch map is a smooth perturbation. (2) The above properties hold for general one-dimensional maps [see Nusse (1988) for details].

3. Chaotic systems

Let f be a differentiable map from an interval into itself. For any positive integer N we write f^N for the Nth iterate of the map f (the Nth iterate f^N is obtained by N times composing the map f with itself). For each point x in the interval, the *orbit* (or *trajectory*) of x is the set $\{f^n(x): n$ nonnegative integer$\}$.

We denote by x^* a fixed point of the map f, i.e., $f(x^*) = x^*$. The fixed point x^* is called *asymptotically stable* if there exists a neighborhood U of x^* such that $\lim_{n \to \infty} f^n(x) = x^*$ for all x in U; and x^* is called *unstable* if it is not an asymptotically stable fixed point. Obviously, if $|f'(x^*)| < 1$, then x^* is asymptotically stable, and if $|f'(x^*)| > 1$, then x^* is unstable.

A point x is called a *periodic point* for f with period p if $f^p(x) = x$ for some positive integer p; the orbit of a periodic point is called a *periodic orbit*. The *period of a periodic orbit* is the number of points in that orbit. A point x is called an *asymptotically stable periodic point* with period p if x is an asymptotically stable fixed point of f^p.

A point x is called an *asymptotically periodic point* for f if, for some positive integer m, $\lim_{n \to \infty} f^{nm}(x)$ exists. A point x is called an *aperiodic point* for f if (1) x is not an asymptotically periodic point for f and (2) the orbit of x is bounded. A point x is called a *critical point* for f if $f'(x) = 0$.

The map f is called a *chaotic map* if there exists a periodic point with period different from a power of two. This definition evolved from the original definition due to Li and Yorke (1975). If the map f is chaotic, then there exists infinitely many periodic points with different period, and there is an uncountable set of aperiodic points [see Li and Yorke (1975)]. The following result due to Li et al. (1982a, b) holds: 'The map f is chaotic if and only if there exists a positive integer N so that the map f^N has a periodic orbit with odd period ≥ 3.'

We recall two definitions of chaos and assume that the orbits under f are bounded. The first definition only depends on the periodic and aperiodic points and it is as follows. The system $x_{t+1} = f(x_t)$ is called a *chaotic dynamical system* if the map f is chaotic. This kind of chaos is nowadays called the Li-Yorke chaos. The second definition depends on the notion of 'sensitive dependence on initial values'. We will say that the system $x_{t+1} = f(x_t)$ is called a *chaotic dynamical system* if it has sensitive dependence on initial values, where sensitive dependence on initial values means that we can find with probability p (where $0 < p \leq 1$) a point x so that for each open neighborhood U of x there is a point y in U such that the trajectories of x and y will not be close to each other forever [see Guckenheimer (1979)]. Note that the size of such a neighborhood U may be arbitrarily small.

Remark. Assuming the map f is a chaotic map, then the system $x_{t+1} = f(x_t)$ does not necessarily have sensitive dependence on initial values.

4. Bifurcations

First we will reformulate some known results from bifurcation theory. Our sources are Allwright (1978), Iooss (1979), Whitley (1983), and Guckenheimer and Holmes (1983). We write $D_r g$ for the partial first derivative of the map g w.r.t. the rth variable; we write $D_{rs} g$ for the partial second derivative of the map g w.r.t. the rth and sth variable; and we write $D_{rst} g$ for the partial third derivative of the map g w.r.t. the rth, sth, and tth variable.

Theorem (Flip-bifurcation). Let $F: \mathbf{R} \times \mathbf{R} \to \mathbf{R}$ be a one-parameter family of C^3 maps such that $F(\cdot; \mu_0)$ has a fixed point x_0 with eigenvalue -1, i.e., $F(x_0; \mu_0) = x_0$ and $D_1 F(x_0; \mu_0) = -1$. Assume that F satisfies the following conditions:

(i) $\quad D_2 F(x_0; \mu_0) D_{11} F(x_0; \mu_0) + 2 D_{12} F(x_0; \mu_0) \neq 0,$

(ii) $\quad 2 D_{111} F(x_0; \mu_0) + 3[D_{11} F(x_0; \mu_0)]^2 \neq 0.$

Then there is a smooth curve of fixed points of F passing through $(x_0; \mu_0)$, and the stability of the fixed points changes at $(x_0; \mu_0)$. There is also a smooth curve passing through $(x_0; \mu_0)$ which has a quadratic tangency with the line $\mathbf{R} \times \{\mu_0\}$ at this point, so that this curve is the union of the periodic points of F with smallest period two.

For clarity we will consider the four possible cases concerning the conditions (i) and (ii) of the Theorem separately. Let F be a map as in the Theorem. We write:

$$A = D_2 F(x_0; \mu_0) D_{11} F(x_0; \mu_0) + 2 D_{12} F(x_0; \mu_0),$$

$$B = 2 D_{111} F(x_0; \mu_0) + 3 [D_{11} F(x_0; \mu_0)]^2,$$

F_μ for the map defined by $F_\mu(x) = F(x; \mu)$.

Case 1: $A > 0$, $B > 0$
There exist real numbers $\varepsilon > 0$ and $\delta > 0$ so that (a) if $\mu_0 - \delta < \mu < \mu_0$, then F_μ has one unstable fixed point and one stable two-cycle in the interval $(x_0 - \varepsilon, x_0 + \varepsilon)$, and (b) if $\mu_0 < \mu < \mu_0 + \delta$, then F_μ has one stable fixed point in the interval $(x_0 - \varepsilon, x_0 + \varepsilon)$.

Case 2: $A > 0$, $B < 0$
There exist real numbers $\varepsilon > 0$ and $\delta > 0$ so that (a) if $\mu_0 - \delta < \mu < \mu_0$, then F_μ has one stable fixed point and one unstable two-cycle in the interval $(x_0 - \varepsilon, x_0 + \varepsilon)$, and (b) if $\mu_0 < \mu < \mu_0 + \delta$, then F_μ has one unstable fixed point in the interval $(x_0 - \varepsilon, x_0 + \varepsilon)$.

Case 3: $A < 0$, $B > 0$
There exist real numbers $\varepsilon > 0$ and $\delta > 0$ so that (a) if $\mu_0 - \delta < \mu < \mu_0$, then F_μ has one stable fixed point in the interval $(x_0 - \varepsilon, x_0 + \varepsilon)$, and (b) if $\mu_0 < \mu < \mu_0 + \delta$, then F_μ has one unstable fixed point and one stable two-cycle in the interval $(x_0 - \varepsilon, x_0 + \varepsilon)$.

Case 4: $A < 0$, $B < 0$
There exist real numbers $\varepsilon > 0$ and $\delta > 0$ so that (a) if $\mu_0 - \delta < \mu < \mu_0$, then F_μ has one unstable fixed point in the interval $(x_0 - \varepsilon, x_0 + \varepsilon)$, and (b) if $\mu_0 < \mu < \mu_0 + \delta$, then F_μ has one stable fixed point and one unstable two-cycle in the interval $(x_0 - \varepsilon, x_0 + \varepsilon)$.

Now we will apply these bifurcation results to the Gabisch map. Recall from section 2 the three-parameter family of maps $G(x; \alpha, k, c)$ from the real line into itself defined by

$$G(x; \alpha, k, c) = x(k - cx^{\alpha-1})/(k - 1).$$

We addressed in section 2 the question: 'Will bifurcations occur by varying the parameters?' We will analyze the type of bifurcations for two choices of the parameter values.

We choose the parameter values: $\alpha_0 = 1.1$, $k_0 = 1.05$, $c_0 = 0.8$. The point $x_0 = (1.25)^{10}$ is a fixed point of G with eigenvalue -1, that is, $G(x_0; \alpha_0, k_0, c_0) = x_0$ and $D_1 g(x_0; \alpha_0, k_0, c_0) = -1$. First we vary the parameter α and we let the values k_0 and c_0 constant. We obtain:

$$D_2 G(x_0; \alpha_0, k_0, c_0) D_{11} G(x_0; \alpha_0, k_0, c_0)$$

$$+ 2 D_{12} G(x_0; \alpha_0, k_0, c_0) = -40,$$

$$2 D_{111} G(x_0; \alpha_0, k_0, c_0) + 3[D_{11} G(x_0; \alpha_0, k_0, c_0)]^2 = 18.48 \, (0.8)^{20}.$$

From case 3 above it follows that there exist real numbers $\varepsilon > 0$ and $\delta > 0$ such that (a) if $1.1 - \delta < \alpha < 1.1$, then G_α has one stable fixed point in $(x_0 - \varepsilon, x_0 + \varepsilon)$, and (b) if $1.1 < \alpha < 1.1 + \delta$, then G_α has one unstable fixed point and one stable two-cycle in $(x_0 - \varepsilon, x_0 + \varepsilon)$. In other words, there is a period doubling bifurcation at $\alpha_0 = 1.1$ when varying the parameter α (see also fig. 1).

Varying k and keeping α_0 and c_0 constant gives:

$$D_3 G(x_0; \alpha_0, k_0, c_0) D_{11} G(x_0; \alpha_0, k_0, c_0)$$

$$+ 2 D_{13} G(x_0; \alpha_0, k_0, c_0) = 80,$$

$$2 D_{111} G(x_0; \alpha_0, k_0, c_0) + 3[D_{11} G(x_0; \alpha_0, k_0, c_0)]^2 = 18.48 \, (0.8)^{20}.$$

Now it follows from case 1 above that there exist numbers $\varepsilon > 0$ and $\delta > 0$ such that (a) if $1.05 - \delta < k < 1.05$, then G_k has one unstable fixed point and one stable two-cycle in $(x_0 - \varepsilon, x_0 + \varepsilon)$, and (b) if $1.05 < k < 1.05 + \delta$, then G_k has one stable fixed point in $(x_0 - \varepsilon, x_0 + \varepsilon)$. In other words, there is a period-halving bifurcation at $k_0 = 1.05$ when varying the parameter k (see also fig. 2).

5. A modified Cobweb model

By increasing a parameter value in the modified Samuelson model we have seen two bifurcation phenomena, namely period-doubling bifurcation and period-halving bifurcation when increasing a parameter. Now we will show that periodic points with period 2^k for some positive integer k, will not always arise through period-doubling bifurcation. In order to do so, we will consider a modified Cobweb model.

The simplest version of a Cobweb model is $q_t = f(p_{t-1})$, $p_t = F(q_t)$, with q_t the quantity at time t, p_t the price at time t, f the supply function, and F the Marshallian demand function. This model can be reduced to the difference equation $q_{t+1} = f \circ F(q_t)$.

Cugno and Montrucchio (1984) considered a modified version of this model. Modifying the supply function f by taking into account an upper bound for the variation rate of q, say $\rho > 0$, one obtains

$$q_{t+1} = \min\{(1 + \rho)q_t, f \circ F(q_t)\}.$$

As a special case Cugno and Montrucchio defined

$$f(p_{t-1}) = -a + bp_{t-1}, \qquad F(q_t) = c - dq_t,$$

with the parameters a, b, c, and d all positive, and they obtained

$$q_{t+1} = \min\{(1 + \rho)q_t, bc - a - dbq_t\}$$

We quote from Cugno and Montrucchio: 'By the Cobweb theorem we know that the equilibrium point, $\bar{q} = (bc - a)/(1 + bd)$, is stable when at the margin the supply is less sensitive to changes in p_{t-1} than the demand to changes in p_t, i.e., when $bd < 1$. At $bd = 1$ we have the first bifurcation and we get rising of two-period solutions. As bd increases beyond 1 orbits of period 2^n arise.'

Let a, b, c, d, and ρ be positive numbers so that $bc > a$. We consider the map $M: [0, (bc - a)/bd] \rightarrow [0, (bc - a)/bd]$ defined by

$$M(x) = \min\{(1 + \rho)x, bc - a - bdx\}.$$

The map M is piecewise linear; in particular, M is monotone increasing on $[0, (bc - a)/(bd + 1 + \rho)]$ and M is decreasing on $[(bc - a)/(bd + 1 + \rho), (bc - a)/bd]$. Hence, the point $c^* = (bc - a)/(bd + 1 + \rho)$ is a turning point (critical point) for the map M. Since $M(0) = 0 = M((bc - a)/bd)$, $q_t \geq 0$ for each integer $t \geq 0$, and $q_{t+1} = M(q_t)$ it is sufficient to study the map M.

As it can be seen in the following property, the magnitude of the factor bd is crucial.

Property 5. For the map M the following hold:
(1) *If $bd < 1$, then M has an asymptotically stable fixed point and this fixed point attracts all the points x with $M(x) > 0$.*
(2) *If $bd = 1$, then for all x in $[c^*, M(c^*)]$ different from $(bc - a)/(bd + 1)$, x is a periodic point with smallest period two.*
(3) *If $1 < bd \leq (1 + \rho)/\rho$, then both the 'Li–Yorke' chaos and the 'sensitive dependence on inital values' chaos occur.*

Proof. (1) Assume that $bd < 1$. It is easily verified that the point $x^* = (bc - a)/(bd + 1)$ is an asymptotically stable fixed point of M $[M'(x^*) = -bd]$ and that x^* attracts all the points x with $M(x) > 0$.

(2) Assume that $bd = 1$. For each x in the interval $[c^*, M(c^*)] = [(bc - a)/(2 + \rho), (1 + \rho)(bc - a)/(2 + \rho)]$ we have $M^2(x) = M(M(x)) = M(bc - a - x) = bc - a - (bc - a - x) = x$ and $M(x) \neq x$ for $x \neq (bc - a)/(bd + 1)$. So x is a periodic point with smallest period two if x is different from $(bc - a)/(bd + 1)$.

(3) Assume that $1 < bd \leq (1 + \rho)/\rho$. Then $M'(x) = 1 + \rho > 1$, respectively $M'(x) = -bd < -1$, for $0 < x < (bc - a)/(bd + 1 + \rho)$, respectively $(bc - a)/(bd + 1 + \rho) < x < (bc - a)/bd$. Hence, the map M is piecewise expanding. This implies that the map M is chaotic in the sense of Li and Yorke [see, e.g., Byers (1981) for this kind of piecewise linear expanding maps]. From arguments in Guckenheimer (1979) it follows that there is sensitive dependence on initial conditions. ∎

We would like to point out that if $bd > (1 + \rho)/\rho$, then almost all trajectories will escape from the interval $(0, (bc - a)/bd)$ and the trajectories are not bounded. On the other hand, if we consider the bounded trajectories, we have 'Li–Yorke' chaos when $bd > (1 + \rho)/\rho$. Consequently, if $bd > 1$, then the map M has infinitely many periodic points with different periods and there exists an uncountable set of aperiodic ponts. Using the Sharkovsky Theorem it follows that the periodic points with period 2^n, $n \geq 1$, do not arise through period-doubling. Cf. Cugno and Montrucchio (1984).

Remark. Cugno and Montrucchio concluded: 'If $(2 + \rho)/(1 + \rho) \leq bd < (1 + \rho)/\rho$, then the time paths of q_t and p_t are chaotic and the solutions are meaningful from the economic point of view. It follows from Property 5 that this conclusion can be improved to $1 < bd \leq (1 + \rho)/\rho$.

6. Regularity in complicated dynamics

For a nonlinear difference equation $x_{t+1} = f(x_t)$ one can ask the following question: 'Let any fixed initial value x be given. What is the probability that the orbit of x under f will converge to an asymptotically stable periodic orbit?' In this section we will give sufficient conditions such that the orbit of almost every initial value will converge to an asymptotically stable periodic orbit.

Singer (1978) introduced the Schwarzian derivative for real-valued mappings; see also Allwright (1978). For any mapping f the Schwarzian derivative $D_S f$ of f at a point x with $f'(x) \neq 0$ is defined by

$$D_S f(x) = f'''(x)/f'(x) - \tfrac{3}{2}[f''(x)/f'(x)]^2.$$

Singer showed that the class of maps with negative Schwarzian derivative is closed under composition. Consequently, any iterate of a map with negative Schwarzian derivative has a negative Schwarzian derivative, i.e., $D_S f(x) < 0$ implies $D_S f''(x) < 0$ for all x with $(f'')'(x) \neq 0$, for each positive integer n.

Let J denote a closed interval with zero as the left end point, i.e., $J = [0, b]$ for some $b > 0$, or $J = [0, \infty)$. The following Proposition is slightly more general than a result due to Singer (1978) [see Nusse (1987)].

Proposition.   *Let f be a smooth map with a continuous third derivative, which maps the interval J into itself, such that:*
(1) *f has one critical point c, f is strictly increasing on $[0, c]$, and f is strictly decreasing on $\{x \text{ in } J: x \geq c\}$, that is, $f'(x) > 0$ if $x < c$ and $f'(x) < 0$ if $x > c$.*
(2) *The left point of J is a repelling fixed point of f, that is, $f(0) = 0$ and $f'(0) > 1$.*
(3) *f has a nonpositive Schwarzian derivative, that is, $D_S f(x) \leq 0$ for all x in $J \setminus \{c\}$.*
Then (i) f has at most one asymptotically stable periodic orbit, and (ii) if f has an asymptotically stable periodic orbit P, then P attracts the critical point c.

We would like to emphasize that the asymptotically stable periodic orbit is contained in the interval $[f^2(c), f(c)]$.

If a continuous map f has a period-three orbit, then we know from the result due to Li and Yorke (1975) that f has periodic points with smallest period k, for each positive integer k. If such a map f satisfies the conditions mentioned above, then the Proposition says that at most one of these infinitely many periodic points is attracting.

If one removes the condition (2), then it may happen that the map f has many fixed points [see Nusse (1987)]. Even in the case when f has a negative Schwarzian derivative it may occur that f has an asymptotically stable periodic orbit and an asymptotically stable fixed point in $[0, f^2(c))$ [see, e.g., Collet and Eckmann (1980)].

If one removes the condition (3), then many asymptotically stable periodic orbits can co-exist [see Nusse (1983)]. For illustration, see fig. 3. In this case two asymptotically stable periodic orbits co-exist, namely one orbit with period three and one orbit with period five. Consequently, the fact that an analytical map has one critical point does not imply that f has at most one asymptotically stable periodic orbit [cf. Pohjola (1981)].

Studying chaotic maps (e.g., maps for which there exists at least one periodic orbit with odd period ≥ 3), we know that there are many irregular orbits. The question arises: 'What is the probability that a randomly chosen point is an aperiodic point?'

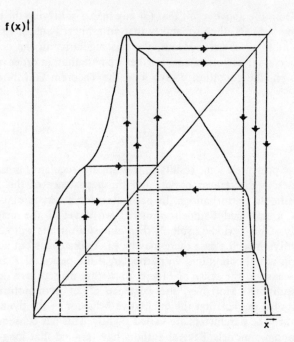

Fig. 3. Graph of an analytical map with one critical point and the coexistence of two asymptotically stable periodic orbits, namely a period-three cycle and a period-five cycle.

Now, we will present a reformulated result due to Guckenheimer (1979), Misiurewicz (1981), and van Strien (1981); see also Nusse (1987) and Collet and Eckmann (1980).

Theorem GMSN. Let f be a smooth map from the compact interval $J = [0, b]$ into itself with the following properties:
(1) *f has one critical point c, f is increasing on $[0, c]$, and f is decreasing on $[c, b]$.*
(2) *$f(0) = 0$ and $f'(0) \geq 1$.*
(3) *f has a negative Schwarzian derivative.*
(4) *f has an asymptotically stable periodic orbit P.*
    Then the set of points, whose orbits will not be attracted to the asymptotically stable periodic orbit P, has Lebesgue measure zero. Consequently, almost every point is asymptotically periodic with period p, where p is the number of elements of P. In particular, the orbit of the critical point of the map will converge to the orbit P.

It follows from the above result that for any map f satisfying the conditions of the Theorem GMSN, the probability that an arbitrarily chosen point is an aperiodic point for f is zero. Hence, there is regularity in the complicated dynamics of a class of chaotic maps. Further we note that, in order to have the same conclusion, the condition $f'(0) \geq 1$ in the Theorem GMSN cannot be omitted.

7. Discussion

(1) We have presented some results concerning the regularity in the complicated dynamics in discrete processes, and the persistence of this regularity under small smooth perturbations. In particular, for a certain class of maps appearing in a modified Samuelson model we have: if the map has an asymptotically stable periodic orbit P, then almost all orbits will converge to P. Consequently, in such a case there may be Li–Yorke chaos but no sensitive dependence on initial conditions. In particular, if the period of P is odd ≥ 3, then there is chaos in the sense of Li and Yorke but no sensitive dependence on initial conditions. Moreover, the existence of an asymptotically stable periodic orbit also implies that the qualitative behavior of the dynamics does not change when the parameters are varied slightly. This has consequences for nonlinear economic models. Several authors have argued that long-term predictions in nonlinear economic models are useless, because of the solutions are highly sensitive to a small variation of the parameters or the initial values [see, e.g., Gabisch (1984), Day (1982), Pohjola (1981), and Stutzer (1980)]. Our results seem to be contradictory with these observations: If one can determine the parameters and the initial value sufficiently accurately, and if one can show that the system has an asymptotically stable periodic orbit, then long-term prediction is possible. From theoretical point of view our results are quite satisfactory. However, from practical point of view it is a little unsatisfactory, since one should realize that the asymptotically stable periodic orbit might have a high period. Moreover, the range of parameter values, for which a stable periodic orbit with such a high period exists, may be small.

(2) The Gabisch model is an ad hoc modification which suggests a general occurrence of chaotic dynamics. A closer examination uncovers that this may be true only for a small range of the parameter without much justification of the magnitudes. On the other hand, there exist parameter values for which the Gabisch map does not have an asymptotically stable periodic orbit. Only for these parameter values it might occur that the system associated with the Gabisch map has sensitive dependence on initial values. We would like to emphasize that the absence of an asymptotically stable periodic orbit for the Gabisch map does not necessarily imply that the associated dynamical system has sensitive dependence on initial values.

(3) In section 6 we raised the question 'What is the probability that a randomly chosen initial point is aperiodic?'. We already have seen that if the parameter value is chosen in such a way that there exists an asymptotically stable periodic orbit, then this probability is zero. But what is the probability that, for a randomly chosen parameter value, there exists an asymptotically stable periodic orbit?

Note that in the modified Cobweb model there is no stable periodic orbit when $bd > 1$. However, for systems like the Gabisch model, this question is a very difficult one, and exact answers are not known.

In practice it is very difficult to observe asymptotically stable periodic orbits with high periods. Therefore, it is almost impossible to determine from figs. 1 and 2 whether or not there is a stable periodic orbit for a given parameter α and k.

Related to these matters we would like to mention the discussion between F. Melese & W. Transue and R.H. Day (The Quarterly Journal of Economics 1986, pp. 419–426, and 1987, p. 171) in which they discuss the notions of thick chaos and thin chaos. In fact, Melese and Transue consider the set of parameter values for which the orbit of the critical point does not converge to an asymptotically stable periodic orbit; for such parameter values they introduce the notion of thick chaos. It has been argued that the probability that thick chaos occurs is positive. We would like to point out that Melese and Transue claim, among other things, that the set of parameter values for which there is thin chaos (i.e., there exists an asymptotically stable periodic orbit) is dense in the parameter space. Unfortunately, up to now it is not yet proved, although it is widely believed to be true.

References

Allwright, D.J., 1978, Hypergraphic functions and bifurcations in recurrence relations, SIAM Journal of Applied Mathematics 34, 687–691.

Benhabib, J. and R.H. Day, 1981, Rational choice and erratic behaviour, Review of Economic Studies XLVIII, 459–471.

Byers, B., 1981, Periodic points and chaos for expanding maps of the interval, Bulletin of the Australian Mathematical Society 24, 79–83.

Collet, P. and J.-P. Eckmann, 1980, Iterated maps on the interval as dynamical systems (Birkhäuser, Boston, MA).

Cugno. F. and L. Montrucchio, 1984, Some new techniques for modelling nonlinear economic fluctuations: A brief survey, in: R.M. Goodwin, M. Krüger, and A Vercelli, eds., Nonlinear models of fluctuating growth, Lecture notes in economics and mathematical systems 228 (Springer Verlag, Berlin) 146–165.

Day, R.H., 1982, Irregular growth cycles, American Economic Review 72, 406–414.

Day, R.H., 1983, The emergence of chaos from classical economic growth, Quarterly Journal of Economics 98, 201–213.

Gabisch, G., 1984, Nonlinear models of business cycle theory, in: G. Hammer and D. Pallaschke, eds., Selected topics in operation research and mathematical economics, Lecture notes in economics and mathematical systems 226 (Springer Verlag, Berlin) 205–222.

Gabisch, G. and H.-W. Lorenz, 1987, Business cycle theory, Lecture notes in economics and mathematical systems 283 (Springer Verlag, Berlin).

Grandmont, J.M., 1985, On endogenous competitive business cycles, Econometrica 53, 995–1045.
Grandmont, J.M., 1986, Stabilizing competitive business cycles, Journal of Economic Theory 40, 57–76.
Guckenheimer, J., 1979, Sensitive dependence to initial conditions for one dimensional maps, Communications of Mathematical Physics 70, 133–160.
Guckenheimer, J. and P. Holmes, 1983, Nonlinear oscillations, dynamical systems and bifurcation of vector fields, Applied mathematical sciences 42 (Springer Verlag, Berlin).
Iooss, G., 1979, Bifurcations of maps and applications, Mathematical studies 36 (North-Holland, Amsterdam).
Li, T.-Y. and J.A. Yorke, 1975, Period three implies chaos, American Mathematical Monthly 82, 985–992.
Li, T.-Y., M. Misiurewicz, G. Pianigiani, and J.A. Yorke, 1982a, No division implies chaos, Transactions of the American Mathematical Society 273, 191–199.
Li, T.-Y., M. Misiurewicz, G. Pianigiani, and J.A. Yorke, 1982b, Odd chaos, Physics Letters 87A, 271–273.
Misiurewicz, M., 1981, Absolutely continuous measures for certain mappings of an interval , IHES Publications Mathmatiques 53, 17–51.
Nusse, H.E., 1983, Chaos, yet no chance to get lost: Order and structure in the chaotic dynamical behaviour of one dimensional noninvertible axiom A mappings arising in discrete biological models, Thesis (Rijksuniversiteit Utrecht).
Nusse, H.E., 1986, Persistence of order and structure in chaos, Physica 20D, 374–386.
Nusse, H.E., 1987, Asymptotically periodic behaviour in the dynamics of chaotic mappings, SIAM Journal of Applied Mathematics 47, 498–515.
Nusse, H.E., 1988, Qualitative analysis of the dynamics and stability properties for axiom A maps, Journal of Mathematical Analysis and Applications 136, 74–106.
Pohjola, M.T., 1981, Stable, cyclic and chaotic growth: The dynamics of a discrete time version of Goodwin's growth cycle model, Zeitschrift für Nationalökonomie 41, 27–38.
Singer, D., 1978, Stable orbits and bifurcations of maps of the interval, SIAM Journal of Applied Mathematics 35, 260–267.
Strien, S.J. van, 1981, On the bifurcations creating horseshoes, in: D. Rand and L.-S. Young, eds., Dynamical systems and turbulence, Lecture notes in mathematics 898 (Springer Verlag, Berlin) 316–351.
Stutzer, M.J., 1980, Chaotic dynamics and bifurcation in a macro model, Journal of Economic Dynamics and Control 2, 353–376.
Whitley, D., 1983, Discrete dynamical systems in dimensions one and two, Bulletin of London Mathematical Society 15, 177–217.

[17]

Nonlinearities and Chaotic Effects in Options Prices

Robert Savit

I. INTRODUCTION

Recently, a good deal of evidence has been accumulated which suggests that prices in certain markets and over certain time horizons may be correlated in subtle ways that elude even common statistical tests. Although there are exceptions, such correlations may be induced by an underlying nonlinear process, and in particular, one that is chaotic, or nearly chaotic. Such nonlinear processes are expected to occur, generically, in self-regulating systems. Indeed, studies in a wide range of fields have indicated the important role that such processes play in systems as diverse as the human heart, the heating of water in a teapot, animal populations, and the availability of production parts in manufacturing. Insofar as the financial and commodities markets are self-regulating systems with intricate feedback and feedforward loops, one may expect to find effects of these nonlinearities in the prices generated by those markets.[1]

In one important development, Brock, Dechert, and Scheinkman[2] have developed a new statistical test (the BDS statistic), based on the idea of the correlation dimension, a notion developed in the physical sciences in the study of nonlinear dynamical systems. The BDS statistic, and related methods of analysis[3] are explicitly constructed to be sensitive to the kinds of higher dimensional correlations that are typically induced by nonlinear processes, and against which many common statistical tests have little power. Using the BDS statistic, various detrended macroeconomic data sets[4] as well as more market specific data[5] including the price movements of certain fixed income instruments[6] have been shown to have a significant nonrandom structure, common statistical tests to the contrary, notwithstanding. Specifically, the BDS test is a test against the null hypothesis that a sequence of numbers is IID. The failure of detrended economic and financial data to pass this test, despite their consistency with other more common tests of randomness, strongly suggests that such data may be produced by processes in which there are underlying dynamics with at least a partially deterministic character. Understanding the nature of the subtle deterministic correlations in this kind of data is cer-

I am grateful to the Center for the Studies of Futures Markets at Columbia University for partial support for this work. I also thank Mark Powers for his encouragement, David Hirschfeld for comments on the manuscript, and Matthew Green for help with the numerical simulations.

[1]For a pedagogical review of nonlinear dynamics and chaos, and its applicability to finance see R. Savit (1988a).
[2]See W. Brock., W. Dechert, and J. Scheinkman (1986); W. Brock and W. Dechert (1987).
[3]R. Savit and M. Green (1989).
[4]W. Brock and C. Sayers (1985); W. Brock (1988), and references therein.
[5]J. Scheinkman and B. LeBaron (1986); D. Hsieh (1987).
[6]R. Savit (1988b).

Robert Savit is a Professor of Physics at the University of Michigan

The Journal of Futures Markets, Vol. 9, No. 6, 507–518 (1989)
© 1989 by John Wiley & Sons, Inc.   CCC 0270-7314/89/060507-12$04.00

tainly of great importance, both for honing investment strategies and for gaining a more basic understanding of economic dynamics. Equally important, however, is understanding the effects of these correlations on derivative market instruments such as options. This work is a first step in that direction.

The standard options price formula, the Black-Scholes result, or one of its close cousins, is based on two assumptions: (1) the options price is determined by the arbitrage condition that there be no riskless profitable arbitrage opportunities, and (2) the price of the underlying asset follows a random walk in the logarithm of the price as a function of time. In the limit of continuous trading, this random walk just means that the logarithm of the price of the underlying security is driven by a diffusive process. This article examines the effect on options prices of altering the standard random walk assumption to consider the possibility that the underlying instrument's price time series is only apparently random, and is actually driven by a noisy nonlinear process. In the specific case considered, the nonlinear process is chaotic but, as shall be explained, most conclusions apply also to other nonchaotic nonlinear price sequences.

The calculations will show that a noisy chaotic sequence, which generates a price path that looks completely random, and which in any case has only short term higher dimensional correlations, alters the value of the usual expression for a call option in a risk-neutral economy for all times to expiration. This result has far reaching implications for the construction of hedging strategies in the presence of nonlinear price movements, as will be discussed in section IV. It should be emphasized that the price path generated by this noisy chaotic map is indistinguishable from any random path when subjected to standard statistical tests. Nonetheless, when folded into the options calculation, its subtle short term correlations can significantly alter the evaluation of the correct, arbitrage free options price. The model presented herein is not necessarily intended to be a realistic model of price movements in financial markets. Rather, it is a simple model introduced to show the effects that nonlinear dynamics in the trading of the underlying asset can have, in general, on options calculations.

The rest of this article is organized as follows: In section II we describe the general strategy of the calculation and introduces the tent map, a very simple chaotic map which will be used as a model of a nonlinear process. In section III the specific calculation will be described and the results presented. Section IV consists of a summary, comments about the implications of this work and suggestions for future study.

II. THE OPTIONS FORMULA AND THE TENT MAP

Consider a risk-neutral economy in which an underlying asset moves according to a random walk. The standard options pricing formula, either in its continuum, Black-Scholes manifestation, or in a discrete time version, calculates the value of, say, a call option by computing the expectation value of the price of the underlying asset at expiration, and subtracting from that the striking price.[7] (This article, for simplicity, always considers European options. Most of the qualitative conclusions are expected to be valid for American options, also.) It is convenient to cast the calculations in terms of a discrete

---

[7]For clarity, the effects of nonlinearities are discussed in the context of a risk-neutral economy. In other environments the interpretation of the option price is somewhat different, but still involves a sum, the argument of which is still related to the expected price movements of the underlying assets. As will become clear, therefore, similar nonlinear effects may be expected in these other environments also. Furthermore, for convenience, the calculations will be carried out in the context of a discrete binomial version of the options pricing formula. But, the distinction between the continuum Black-Scholes result and its various discrete time versions is unimportant here, and so these differences will be ignored in our discussions.

binary pricing model. That is, it is assumed that at each time step in a discrete process, the value of the underlying asset can move up by a factor of u or down by a factor of d. Then, the value of a call option which can be exercised (and expires) at time T is given by

$$C(T) = r^{-T} \sum_{n=0}^{T} P(n) \text{Max}[u^n d^{T-n}S - K; 0] \tag{1}$$

where S is the initial stock price, K is the striking price, r is the "riskless" interest rate, and $P(n)$ is the probability that at expiration the price will have suffered exactly n upward movements.

Since the underlying asset is assumed to execute a random multiplicative walk in price space, $P(n)$ is just given by the binomial coefficient,

$$P(n) = \frac{T!}{n!(T-n)!} q^n (1-q)^{T-n}. \tag{2}$$

Here q is the probability that the asset price rises by a factor of u at any given time, and according to the assumption of risk-neutrality has the value $q = (r - d)/(u - d)$.

With these assumptions it is quite easy to do the sum in (1), and one thus arrives at the standard result. Another way of describing this calculation is to say that (1) represents a sum over all possible paths in price space starting at the price S. According to the random walk assumption, each distinct path is weighted equally in the sum. Operationally, one can imagine that a given price path is generated in the following way: Divide the interval (0,1) into two segments $(0, 1 - q)$ and $(1 - q, 1)$. Generate random numbers uniformly distributed on the interval (0,1). If a given random number is less than $1 - q$, then the price falls by a factor of d, at that time step, otherwise the price rises by a factor of u.

Consider, now, an investor who wishes to price options on some asset. He observes the price movements of the asset for some period of time and computes the autocorrelation functions of the price movements and the probability distribution of asset prices. He finds that the autocorrelation functions are zero and that the price distribution is, over long times, lognormal. Moreover, he observes that the probability of up and down price movements satisfies the condition for risk-neutrality. On the basis of this information he concludes that the asset price is executing a random multiplicative walk in price space, and he calculates the value of a call option using expressions (1) and (2).

Although this investor's conclusions concerning the price behavior of the underlying asset seem reasonable, it is possible that the price movements of the underlying asset are not at all random, while still having the same values for the autocorrelation functions and unconditional price distribution as prices generated by simple random walk dynamics. Such a situation may occur if the asset price is driven by a nonlinear chaotic process (either with or without noise). In that case, the subsequent price movements of the underlying asset would not be that expected by the investor, and the correct evaluation of the right hand side of (1) could be different. This in turn would render the investor's pricing of the option unreliable, and a new options price would have to be derived.

An example of a chaotic process which will give the same autocorrelation functions[8] and price distributions as the random walk is the tent map. The tent map is a nonlinear map which expresses the $(m+1)^{st}$ value of an iterate, y, in terms of the mth value:

[8]H. Sakai and H. Tokumaru (1980).

$$y(m + 1) = f[y(m)] = \begin{cases} 2y(m) & \text{if } 0 < y(m) < \dfrac{1}{2} \\ 2 - 2y(m) & \text{if } \dfrac{1}{2} < y(m) < 1 \end{cases} \qquad (3)$$

The tent map is shown in Figure 1. Note that all the y's are between 0 and 1.

The tent map is a very simple example of a chaotic map and has the following important properties:

(1) For almost all initial values, $y(0)$, the iterates $y(m)$ are uniformly distributed on the interval $(0,1)$ as m gets large.

(2) The autocorrelation functions

$$\sum_{j=1}^{L} \left[<y(j)y(j + b)> - \frac{1}{4} \right] \qquad (4)$$

go to zero as L gets large for any b not equal to zero.

(3) Suppose there is some small uncertainty, δ, in the value of $y(0)$. This uncertainty gets magnified exponentially fast. That is, consider two sequences $y(m)$ and $z(m)$. If $y(0)$ and $z(0)$ are identical then for all m $y(m) = z(m)$, exactly. But if $z(0) = y(0) + \delta$ then, generically, $|y(m) - z(m)|$ will be of order $\exp(\gamma m)$, where, for the tent map, $\gamma = \ln 2$. (Subject, of course to the condition that z and y are always between 0 and 1.) That is, even if there is some small uncertainty in the value of y, that small uncertainty quickly becomes magnified, until the subsequent y's are completely unpredictable. This exponential growth of uncertainty is typical of chaotic systems. The quantity γ is called the Lyapunov exponent.

Using the tent map, a price sequence with the same autocorrelation functions and unconditional distributions as the random walk can be produced in the following way:

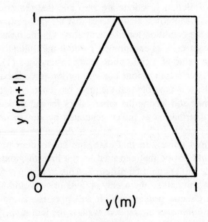

Figure 1
The Tent Map Described in Eq. (3).

Let the sequence of up and down price movements be determined by the sequence of the values of the iterates $y(m)$ generated by expression (3), rather than by a random number. If $y(m)$ is less than $q - 1$, then the asset price moves down at time m by a factor of d, otherwise it moves up by a factor of u. It is clear, from properties 1 and 2 above, that any particular realization of the price path would look completely random. On the other hand, if one happened to know with arbitrary accuracy the value $y(0)$, it is also clear that the value of the underlying asset could be predicted with certainty at any time, and so one would (trivially) be able to derive the correct arbitrage free value of the options price.[9]

Of course, in the real world, one cannot predict with absolute certainty the price movements for all time. Even if the endogenous dynamics of some market were completely understood, that market is continually subject to exogenous influences as new information affecting the market becomes known. To model this more reasonable situation, suppose that each $y(m)$ is determined by the tent map (3), only to within some uncertainty. Specifically, we consider the sequence of iterates given by

$$y(m + 1) = f[y(m)] + \delta\zeta(m) \qquad (5)$$

where $\zeta(m)$ is a random number uniformly distributed between 0 and 1. δ is then a parameter that controls the size of the noise in this stochastic chaotic map, and is a measure of the degree to which new information affects the price dynamics of the system. If, for example, $\delta = 0.1$, then we can say that the iterates are determined by the tent map to within about a 10% accuracy[10] at each time step. From property 3 above, it is clear that these errors will accumulate very quickly, and after a few iterates the sequence $y(m)$ will bear no resemblance to that which would have been generated by the noiseless case with the same starting value, $y(0)$. In fact, given only the value of $y(0)$ the price movements will be essentially unpredictable after only a few time steps. These noisy iterates again satisfy the same unconditional distributional properties and autocorrelation functions as a sequence of random numbers uniformly distributed on $(0,1)$. Thus, if the noisy $y(m)$'s are used to generate the price paths of the underlying asset, and hence the $P(n)$'s in (1), one might suppose that for all but very short times-to-expiration, T, the evaluation of the right-hand side of (1) using (5) to determine the price movements, would be indistinguishable from the standard Black-Scholes or binomial price result. As will be shown in the next section, this is not the case.

III. RESULTS

To see the effect of noisy chaotic trajectories on the options price, computer simulations were performed using the following strategy: Values of S, K, r, q, u, d, and δ were chosen with q chosen to satisfy the conditions for a risk-neutral economy. Then an initial value $y(0)$ was chosen and a sequence of values $y(m)$ for $m = 1$ to T was generated using (5) with a good random number generator for the $\zeta(m)$'s. This sequence of $y(m)$'s was used

[9]Observation of the price movement at time m contains information about the value of $y(m)$ but in a discrete process does not determine it, even in the absence of noise. In the limit that the price movements take on continuous values, however, it is possible to relate the size of the price movement to the value of $y(m)$, and so, in the absence of noise, determine the y's directly from the price movements. Of course, such a determination requires an analysis that goes beyond the study of ordinary autocorrelation functions.

[10]Adding noise to the tent map as in (5), will sometimes produce an iterate that is greater than one or less than zero. It is assumed, therefore, that there are periodic boundary conditions on the tent map, so that if $y(m + 1)$ is greater than one it is reset according to $y(m + 1) \rightarrow y(m + 1) - 1$ and if $y(m)$ is less than one it is reset according to $y(m + 1) \rightarrow y(m + 1) + 1$. The iterates are then always between zero and one. A little thought will reveal that this procedure still results in y's that uniformly distributed on the interval $(0,1)$.

to determine a path in price space by associating a price increase at time *m* if $y(m)$ was greater than $1 - q$, and a price drop otherwise. Using the same initial $y(0)$, another sequence was generated in the same way, and associated with another path. In our calculations, 2000 paths were generated and used to determine $P(n)$ (which in the risk-neutral economy is the distribution of prices of the underlying asset at time T).

Figure 2, shows the right-hand-side of (1) as a function of time to expiration for various values of δ. Look first at Figure 2(a) in which results are presented for δ = 0.1. Notice that the two sample options results computed with different values of $y(0)$ differ significantly from each other and from the standard binomial pricing model result which is plotted on the same graph. Notice, in particular, that significant differences are apparent for times to expiration which greatly exceed the time scale over which the underlying asset price can be said to be reasonably predictable. With δ = 0.1 this time of predictability is only of the order of 5 to 10 time steps, or less. The errors on the individual option price curves is about 2%. It is clear that these examples differ from the

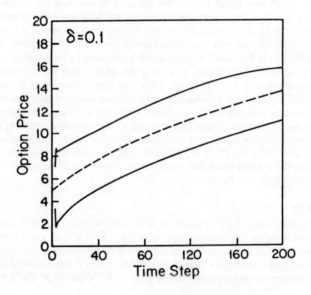

Figure 2a

The value of the right-hand-side of (1) as a function of time to expiration, assuming that the price movements of the underlying asset are driven by a noisy (chaotic) tent map, as described in the text. In each graph two examples of the evaluation for different starting values, $y(0)$, of the tent map iterate are shown. Also shown for comparison is the Black-Scholes result (dashed line). All graphs are computed with the values $S = 100$, $K = 95$, $u = 1.02$, $d = 0.98$, $r = 1.0$, and $q = 0.5$. (a) δ = 0.1, (b) δ = 0.25, and (c) δ = 1.0.

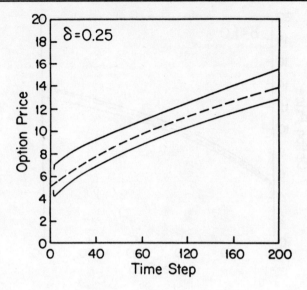

Figure 2b

standard binomial pricing model result by much more than that. Figures 2(b) and 2(c) present the same kind of plots for the same values of the parameters S, K, r, u, d, and q, and for $\delta = 0.25$ and $\delta = 1.0$, respectively. In Figure 2(b) one again sees significant differences between expression (1) evaluated under the assumption of a noisy chaotic map, and those evaluated under the standard random walk assumption with the same distributional properties. In this case, however, the differences, although significant, are smaller than in Figure 2(a). Finally, in Figure 2(c), all the cases seem to be quite similar. In fact, this is what one expects, since when $\delta = 1.0$ it is easy to see that the sequence of iterates, $y(m)$, are just a set of random numbers uniformly distributed on $(0,1)$.

Although the results in Figure 2 convincingly illustrate that a noisy chaotic price sequence can alter the evaluation of (1) when compared to a similarly distributed random walk, it is useful to make these results somewhat more quantitative. Table I lists the average fractional deviation as a function of time to expiration between the noisy chaotic evaluation of (1) for various values of δ and the purely random (Black-Scholes) result. Specifically, this table lists values of

$$\Psi(T) = \frac{\left[\frac{1}{N}\sum_i (C_i(T) - C_R(T)^2\right]^{1/2}}{C_R(T)} \tag{6}$$

where $C_R(T)$ is the standard random (Black-Scholes) options price and $C_i(T)$ is the noisy chaotic value of (1) computed for some starting value, $y_i(0)$ of the tent map. The sum

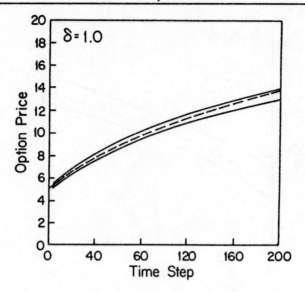

Figure 2c

over i is a sum over N (in Table I, $N = 100$) noisy chaotic evaluations computed with the same values of the options parameters and the same value of δ, but with different (randomly chosen) initial values, $y_i(0)$, of the tent map iterates.

It is apparent that there is a persistent difference between the random and chaotic cases for all times to expiration. For example, if $\delta = 0.25$, there is about a 8% difference between a typical noisy tent map evaluation of (1) and the Black-Scholes result even for very long times. For shorter times the typical difference is, of course, much greater. Notice also that the difference between the chaotic and random results decreases as the noise increases, as one expects. In the case $\delta = 1.0$, the values of Ψ are consistent with the values obtained by computing Ψ between different Monte-Carlo generated samples of the standard binomial pricing formula with the same statistics. That is, for $\delta = 1.0$ the $C_i(T)$'s are indistinguishable from the Black-Scholes result given the statistical accuracy of the Monte-Carlo calculations, as expected.

IV. DISCUSSION

Perhaps the most startling result of the calculation is the observation that the evaluation of (1) based on the assumption of a noisy chaotic process for the underlying asset differs from the usual random walk-based options price for all times to expiration. To better appreciate why this is so unexpected, recall the following facts:

(1) The chaotic tent map used in this model produces, even in the absence of noise, time series which are (linearly) indistinguishable from the corresponding random series

Table I

T	ψ $\delta = 0.1$	$\delta = 0.25$	$\delta = 1.0$
1	.34	.24	.01
2	.41	.26	.01
3	.42	.25	.02
4	.40	.24	.02
5	.38	.22	.02
6	.36	.21	.02
7	.35	.20	.02
8	.34	.20	.02
9	.33	.19	.02
10	.31	.19	.02
25	.22	.15	.02
50	.18	.11	.03
75	.15	.10	.03
100	.13	.10	.04
125	.12	.09	.04
150	.11	.07	.04
175	.11	.07	.04
200	.11	.07	.04

Fractional difference between the Binomial Pricing Model and the right-hand-side of eq. (1) when evaluated using the tent map for various strengths of the noise, as a function of time.

of price movements, in the sense that (a) the unconditional distributions of the price movements are the same and (b) their autocorrelation functions are the same.

(2) In the presence of noise, knowledge of the initial value of the map is quickly lost (the map has a positive Lyapunov exponent), and so, *given only the value* $y(0)$ the paths that contribute to the evaluation of (1) are, after a very short time, no more predictable than a random series.

On the basis of these facts, an apparently reasonable expectation would have been that the chaotic and random evaluations of (1) differ significantly only for a very short initial period.

In fact, it is not difficult to understand the persistence of this difference. Recall that the usual binomial (or Black-Scholes) option formula has a strong dependence on the initial stock price, S. (If the striking price, K, is less than S, then this dependence is nearly linear for a broad range of values of the parameters in the options formula.) If one looks at the paths in price space generated by the noisy chaotic process, one sees that with a given $y(0)$, the paths are relatively similar for the first few time steps, and after that look like a collection of random walks. (The initial time over which the paths appear to be similar is determined by a combination of δ and the value of the Lyapunov exponent, which for the tent map is $\ln 2$.) Thus, the distribution of prices, S', a few time steps into the future is less random than that which would result from a random walk (with the same starting asset price, S and the same values of u, d, r, and q), and so we have some predictive power for the price of the underlying asset over this time scale. In general, the expectation value (and certainly the distribution) of S' will not be the same as the initial starting price, S. Therefore, (1) evaluated for a noisy chaotic process will resemble the random walk options price but with a different effective starting price which will be close to the expectation value of S', the price at the time at which the set of noisy chaotic paths begins to appear random. Thus, if the underlying asset undergoes price movements generated by a noisy chaotic process, the value of (1) will differ for all times from that associated with an underlying asset whose price path is generated by a random process, even though all initial parameters defining the option are the same and all the unconditional distributions and autocorrelations of the price movements are the same.[11] This heuristic explanation of these results is also consistent with the observation that as δ approaches 1, the nonlinear chaotic evaluation of (1) approaches the Black-Scholes result. The point is that for larger δ, the set of paths in price space appear random sooner so that S', the distribution of prices of the underlying asset at the time at which the set of price paths begins to look random, becomes closer to the original starting price, S.

A few more comments should be made concerning this result:

(1) The fundamental origin of the discrepancy between the binomial pricing evaluation of (1), and the tent map evaluation can be traced to the fact that processes with different conditional distributions may have the same unconditional distributions. The tent map has the same unconditional distributions as a sequence of random numbers uniformly distributed on the unit interval, but has different conditional distributions. In a random process the $(n + 1)^{st}$ number is, by definition, unrelated to the nth number. In the noisy tent map this is not the case. Because $y(0)$ is the same for a given evaluation of (1) with the noisy tent map, the evaluation of (1) depends on the conditional distributions for this stochastic nonlinear process. The unexpected result of this paper is that this dependence persists for all times-to-expiration, T.

(2) This article does not intend to suggest that the noisy tent map is a realistic model of the price movements of some asset. Rather, it is a simple example of a chaotic map which illustrates the expected effects of nonlinearities on options calculations. Qualitatively, the behavior found can be expected in most situations in which an underlying asset's price contains some deterministic nonlinear component. It is not necessary that the nonlinearities be chaotic. In fact, in the presence of nonchaotic nonlinear price movements, it is expected that the evaluation of (1) will differ even more strongly from the standard Black-Scholes result than in the chaotic case discussed here. The reason is that, generally, nonchaotic behavior has a greater degree of predictability than chaotic behavior.

Although the noisy tent map is not necessarily a realistic model for asset price movements, it does contain ingredients which are likely to be a part of a more complete description of financial markets. Since the financial markets are complex self-regulating systems, they have their own internal dynamics which affect the behavior of price movements in a constant external environment. It is of course possible that such dynamics leads to a simple equilibrium (or fixed point) distribution of prices in the absence of new external information. This fixed point behavior is the simplest kind of behavior a complex system can manifest. But it is not the only possible behavior, nor (as studies of self-regulating systems in the physical sciences reveal) is it the most common. Fortified by the empirical studies cited in references 2–5, one can be encouraged to consider behaviors for financial markets other than fixed point behavior. In that case, the use of a noisy nonlinear iterative map to describe price movements is appropriate: The deterministic aspect of the map models the internal market dynamics and the stochastic noise models the influence on the market of new, exogenous information.

---

[11] The early time behavior of the noisy chaotic price paths depends on $y(0)$. For some values of $y(0)$, the options price computed using (3) will be fairly close to the standard random walk result. However, these are special cases, and as shown in Table I, generally the noisy chaotic and random evaluations of (1) are significantly different.

(3) Notice that even though the *set* of noisy chaotic paths appears random only after some initial time period, any one of the paths will still appear to be random for *all* times when analyzed according to tests based on autocorrelation functions and unconditional price distributions. Since one can ever observe only one price history, one might (mistakenly) believe that the process producing that sequence is random even if it is not. Under such as assumption, one's expectation of the value of the right-hand-side of (1) would be wrong for all T. To properly distinguish between randomness and chaos, one must have recourse to methods of analysis based on ideas from the study of nonlinear systems.

(4) Two important effects, of considerable significance for investment strategies, follow from the observation that a single price history which appears random may, in fact, be driven by a noisy nonlinear process. First, there may be unrecognized short term price predictability, and second, as shown in this paper, there may be systematic mispricing of the associated options *over all time scales*. Chaotic price movements are predictable only over short times. Nonetheless, using options may allow one to gain a long time advantage from this short term information.

These observations indicate the need for further examination of the problem of options pricing in the presence of a nonlinear process for asset price movements. This work has shown that the evaluation of the usual expression for an option based on a reasonable expectation that price movements are random may be quite inaccurate if the real price process is nonlinear, even though all unconditional distributions and autocorrelation functions are the same. On the other hand, a derivation of the arbitrage-free options price for chaotic price movements requires a study of the construction and evolution of a properly hedged portfolio in a nonlinear market. It is important to stress that the evaluation of (1) for a noisy chaotic process may not be the same as the correct arbitrage-free options price in a nonlinear market. Work on this problem is in progress.

Contrary to naive expectations, a noisy nonlinear process for the price movements of an asset may affect the calculation of the price of an option written on that asset for all times-to-expiration. The origin of this effect is the fact that in the presence of nonlinear effects, the expectations of future price movements are dependent on conditional distributions of the underlying process. Thus, an option computed for a nonlinear process may differ from that computed for the random process with the same unconditional distributions.

Given a knowledge of the underlying nonlinear process, the correct arbitrage-free options price requires the construction of a hedged portfolio. But on the basis of the work in this article, such an options price may differ from the Black-Scholes expression for all times to expiration. In this context, knowledge of conditional price distributions is tantamount to the ability to make short term predictions in the asset price. Such knowledge may result in improvements in the calculation of long-term options prices.

Many financial sequences have been shown to have significant nonlinear components. Using the techniques of nonlinear analysis, it is possible in those cases to better understand short term price movements. Such an analysis may improve short term price predictability and, with the use of options, may allow one to realize long term improvement in investment strategies.

Bibliography

Brock, W., Dechert, W., and Scheinkman, J. (1986): "A Test for Independence Based on the Correlation Dimension," unpublished.

Brock, W., and Dechert, W. (1987): "Theorems on Distinguishing Deterministic from Random Systems," University of Wisconsin preprint, unpublished.

Brock, W., and Sayers, C. (1985): "Is the Business Cycle Characterized by Deterministic Chaos?" University of Wisconsin preprint.

Brock, W. (1988): "Nonlinearity and Complex Dynamics in Economics and Finance," in *The Economy as an Evolving Complex System*, D. Pines, Ed., New York: Addison-Wesley.

Hsieh, D. (1987): "Testing for Nonlinear Dependence in Foreign Exchange Rates: 1974–1983," University of Chicago preprint.

Sakai, H., and Tokumaru, H. (1980): IEEE Trans. Acoust. Speech Signal Process. V. I. ASSP-28, 588.

Savit, R., and Green, M. (1989): "Time Series and Dependent Variables," University of Michigan preprint.

Savit, R. (1988a): "When Random is Not Random: An Introduction to Chaos in Market Prices," *The Journal of Futures Markets*, 8: 271–291.

Savit, R. (1988b): "Notes on the Price Behavior of Fixed Income Instruments," unpublished.

Scheinkman, J., and LeBaron, B. (1986): "Nonlinear Dynamics and Stock Returns," University of Chicago preprint.

[18]

Scand. J. of Economics 91 (1), 161–167, 1989

Does an Unstable Keynesian Unemployment Equilibrium in a non-Walrasian Dynamic Macroeconomic Model Imply Chaos?

*Cars H. Hommes and Helena E. Nusse**

University of Groningen, The Netherlands

I. Introduction

Simonovits (1982) introduced a non-Walrasian dynamic macromodel which is based on the disequilibrium model with inventory dynamics due to Honkapohja and Ito (1980). This model describes transactions on two markets (one market for labor and one market for goods) and contains five parameters. Obviously, there is an equilibrium which is the so-called Keynesian unemployment equilibrium point. For suitable choices of the parameters, this equilibrium point is locally stable and, according to Simonovits (1982), the Keynesian unemployment equilibrium point is also globally stable, i.e., the trajectories of all initial values converge to the equilibrium point.

For many parameter values the equilibrium point is unstable; this is in fact the case when the product of the two eigenvalues at the equilibrium point is greater than 1. Simonovits' (1982) conjecture says: "If the Keynesian unemployment equilibrium point is unstable, then there is chaos".

First, we recall some definitions of chaos. We restrict our attention to systems whose trajectories are bounded. A first definition is the following. A system is chaotic if there exist infinitely many periodic points with different period and if there is an uncountable set of aperiodic points. This kind of chaos is nowadays called Li-Yorke chaos; see Li and Yorke (1975) and Diamond (1976). Before turning to a second definition, we need the notion of "sensitive dependence on initial values". A system may be said to have sensitive dependence on initial values if we can find, with probability p (where $0 < p \leq 1$), a point x such that for every open neighborhood U of x there is a point y in U such that the trajectories of x and y will not be close

---

*Research partially supported by the Dutch VFO project *Wiskundige metoden en hun toepassing naar aanleiding van economische problemen*. We thank G. F. Pikkemaat for valuable discussions.

162   *C. H. Hommes and H. E. Nusse*

to each other forever. Note that the size of the neighborhood U may be arbitrarily small. We may now give the second definition. A system is chaotic if it has sensitive dependence on initial values; see Ruelle (1979) and Guckenheimer (1979).

II. Simonovits' Model

For clarity, we recall the model as presented by Simonovits (1982). We consider two markets, one for goods and one for labor. We write $L^D(t)$ (resp. $L^S(t)$) for the demand for (resp. supply of) the number of units of labor at time t, with integer $t \geq 0$, and we write $L(t)$ for the minimum of these two values. Similarly, we write $Y^D(t)$ (resp. $Y^S(t)$) for the demand for (resp. supply of) the number of units of goods at time t, and we write $Y(t)$ for the minimum of these two values. Note that $L(t)$ and $Y(t)$ represent the actual transactions on the markets at time t.

The inventory $I(t)$ at time t is given by the difference between the supply and the transactions of the goods at time t, i.e., $I(t) = Y^S(t) - Y(t)$. Note that $I(t) \geq 0$ for every integer $t \geq 0$.

Simonovits made the following assumptions:

A-1. The supply of labor is constant: $L^S(t) = d$ for some $d > 0$.

A-2. Labor is the only input for production, and the production function is linearly homogeneous. Hence, the aggregate supply of goods equals the inventory at time $t-1$ plus production: $Y^S(t) = I(t-1) + \delta L(t)$ for some $\delta > 0$.

A-3. The demand for goods is a linear function of labor: $Y^D(t) = a + bL(t)$ for some $a > 0$, $b \geq 0$; and the production is profitable: $\delta > b$.

A-4. The optimal level of inventory $I_{opt}(t)$ at time t is proportional to the expected demand $E[Y^D(t)]$ for goods at time t: $I_{opt}(t) = \beta E[Y^D(t)]$ for some $\beta \geq 0$.

A-5. The firms have naive expectations of the demand for goods: $E[Y^D(t)] = a + bL(t-1)$.

A-6. Production minus demand, both taken at full employment, is positive: $(\delta - b)d - a > 0$.

Under the above assumptions, Simonovits' model is given by:

$$L(t+1) = \begin{cases} 0 & \text{if } I(t) \geq (\beta + 1)[a + bL(t)] = I_1(t) \\ [(\beta+1)\{a + bL(t)\} - I(t)]/\delta & \text{if } I_2(t) \leq I(t) \leq I_1(t) \\ d & \text{if } I(t) \leq I_1(t) - \delta d = I_2(t) \end{cases}$$

Does unstable equilibrium imply chaos? 163

$$I(t+1) = \begin{cases} I(t)-a & \text{if } L(t+1)=0 \\ \langle[b(\beta+1)\{(\delta-b)L(t)-a\}+bI(t)+a\beta\delta]/\delta\rangle_+ & \text{if } 0 < L(t+1) < d \\ I(t)+(\delta-b)d-a & \text{if } L(t+1)=d \end{cases}$$

where $\langle x\rangle_+$ denotes the maximum value of $\{0, x\}$.

Simonovits conjectured that for $b(\beta+1)/\delta > 1$, there is chaos in the dynamics of the above system.

III. The Simonovits Model with Specified Parameter Values

We now present a specified Simonovits model in which the equilibrium is unstable; this system would exhibit chaos if the conjecture were true. We choose: $a=8$, $b=9$, $d=10$, $\beta=0.3$, and $\delta=10$. These values satisfy the condition in Simonovits' conjecture, because $b(\beta+1)/\delta = 1.17 > 1$.

Proposition. *The set of periodic points of the specified Simonovits system consists of one attracting periodic orbit with period 28, one repelling periodic orbit with period 28, and the unstable equilibrium. Furthermore, the stable periodic orbit will attract the trajectories of almost all initial values.*

Corollary. The specified Simonovits model does not exhibit chaos in the dynamics.

The point (8,24) is the Keynesian unemployment equilibrium of the specified Simonovits system. The equilibrium is unstable; see Section IV for details. The initial part of the orbit of (8,23.5), which consists of 20,000 points, is shown in Figure 1. The figure shows not only that the orbit of (8,23.5) converges to an attracting periodic orbit with period 28, but also that it converges very rapidly.

Remark: The specified model is structurally stable w.r.t. the parameters; the qualitative behavior in the dynamics of this model will not change when the parameter values are varied slightly.

IV. The Analysis

We consider the discrete dynamic system that is associated with Simonovits' model. We write L_t for $L(t)$ and I_t for $I(t)$, and $(L_{t+1}, I_{t+1}) = F(L_t, I_t)$, where F maps the set W (in the nonnegative quadrant of the plane) consisting of points (x, y) with $0 \le x \le 10$ and $y \ge 0$ into itself. The action of the map F may be described in a geometric way.

We write S_T for the points (x, y) with $y = 11.7x + 10.4$; S_B for (x, y) with $y = 11.7x - 89.6$; S_L for $(0, y)$; and S_R for $(10, y)$.

Let V be the region in W bounded by the four lines S_T, S_B, S_L, and S_R, let Z be the region in W above V, and let U be the region in W below V; see Figure 2.

164   *C. H. Hommes and H. E. Nusse*

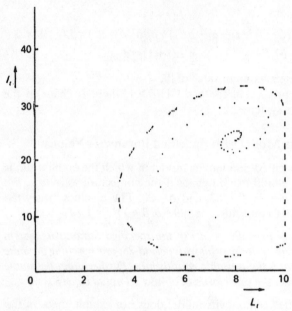

Fig. 1.

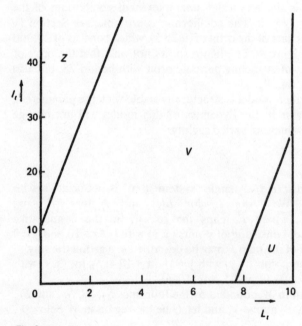

Fig. 2.

Does unstable equilibrium imply chaos?   165

The map F is defined as follows: $F(L_t, I_t) = (0, I_t - 8)$ for (L_t, I_t) in Z;

$F(L_t, I_t) = (10, I_t + 2)$ for (L_t, I_t) in U; and for (L_t, I_t) in V

$F(L_t, I_t) = (1.17L_t, -0.1I_t + 1.04, \langle 1.17L_t + 0.9I_t - 6.96 \rangle_+)$.

The map F is piecewise linear and continuous. The eigenvalues of the derivative of F in the equilibrium point $(8,24)$ are $1.035 \pm i\sqrt{0.3142849}$. Consequently, the equilibrium is unstable.

Now we consider the line segment S_P, where S_P consists of the points (x,y) with $x = 10$ and $27.4 \leq y < 29.4$. Straightforward computation shows that for every initial point (x_0, y_0) in W, there is a smallest positive integer N so that the Nth iterate (x_N, y_N) is in S_P. Therefore, it is sufficient to consider only those orbits which start in S_P.

In order to analyze the specified Simonovits model, we consider the return map g on S_P which is defined as follows. Let $(10, I_0)$ be in S_P. Then $g(10, I_0) = (10, I_m)$, where $(10, I_m)$ is the image of $(10, I_0)$ under the mth iterate of F such that $(10, I_m)$ is in S_P, and $(10, I_k)$ is not in S_P for each integer k with $0 < k < m$. The map g is in fact a one-dimensional map from the interval $[27.4, 29.4)$ into itself; see Figure 3. We would like to emphasize that if $(10, I_0')$ is in S_P, $g(10, I_0') = (10, I_n')$, and $I_0 \neq I_0'$, then n and m might be different. In particular, if $27.4 \leq I_0 < I^*$ then $m = 29$ and if

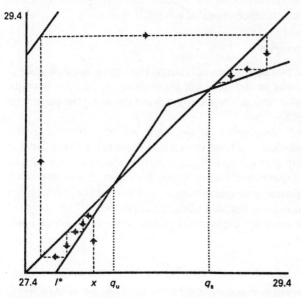

Fig. 3.

166 C. H. Hommes and H. E. Nusse

$I^* \le I_0 < 29.4$ then $m = 28$, where I^* is the solution of $F^{28}(10, I^*) = (10, 27.4)$ and this is a point of discontinuity of the return map g.

Let J denote the interval $[27.4, 29.4)$. Write q_s (resp. q_u) for the stable (resp. unstable) fixed point of g in J. Obviously, if $x = q_u$, then the n'th iterate of x under g is equal to q_u for every integer $n \ge 0$.

We now show that if x is in J and x is different from q_u, then the n'th iterate of x under g is going to q_s as n goes to infinity. This is clearly true if $x = q_s$, because the n'th iterate of x under g equals q_s for each n. From now on we assume that x is not a fixed point of g.

Case 1. $q_u < x < q_s$. In this case the sequence $\{g^n(x)\}$ is strictly increasing and bounded, and it converges to q_s as n goes to infinity.

Case 2. $q_s < x < 29.4$. The sequence $\{g^n(x)\}$ is strictly decreasing and bounded, and it converges to q_s as n goes to infinity.

Case 3. $27.4 \le x < q_u$. There exists a positive integer N such that the N'th iterate of x under g is in the interval $(q_s, 29.4)$, because if $27.4 \le x < I^*$, then $q_s < g(x) < 29.4$ and, if $I^* \le x < q_u$, then there is a positive integer K such that the sequence $\{g^n(x)\}$ is strictly decreasing for $0 \le n \le K$ and $27.4 \le g^K(x) < I^*$. Therefore the sequence $\{g^n(x)\}$ converges to q_s as n goes to infinity. This completes the proof of the proposition.

Note that the sequence $F^k(10, q_s)$ with $1 \le k \le 28$ is the stable periodic orbit of the specified Simonovits model.

Conclusion: In the dynamics of the system, there is neither Li-Yorke chaos nor sensitive dependence on initial values.

V. Concluding Remarks

Independently of the two definitions of chaos given above, the dynamics of the specified Simonovits model does not show chaos. In fact the dynamic behavior is very regular, and this regularity will persist when the parameter values are varied slightly.

For one specified Simonovits model with an unstable Keynesian unemployment equilibrium, we have shown that there is no chaos. Several other very interesting phenomena might occur, e.g. coexistence of two stable cycles and coexistence of three chaotic attractors. Some important questions are: (i) How many simple attractors can coexist? (ii) What is the number of chaotic attractors that can occur simultaneously? (iii) Does the existence of a simple attractor imply that there is no sensitive dependence on initial values?

References

Diamond, P.: Chaotic behaviour of systems of difference equations. *International Journal Systems Science* 7, 953–6, 1976.

Does unstable equilibrium imply chaos? 167

Guckenheimer, J.: Sensitive dependence to initial conditions for one dimensional maps. *Communications of Mathematical Physics 70*, 133-60, 1979.

Honkapohja, S. & Ito, T.: Inventory dynamics in a simple disequilibrium macroeconomic model. *Scandinavian Journal of Economics 82*, 184-98, 1980.

Li, T.-Y. & Yorke, J. A.: Period three implies chaos. *American Mathematical Monthly 82*, 985-92, 1975.

Ruelle, D.: Sensitive dependence on initial condition and turbulent behavior of dynamic systems. In O. Gurel and O. E. Rössler (eds.), *Bifurcation Theory and Applications in Scientific Disciplines*, 408-16, New York Academy of Sciences, New York, 1979.

Simonovits, A.: Buffer stocks and naive expectations in a non-Walrasian dynamic macro-model: stability, cyclicity and chaos. *Scandinavian Journal of Economics 84*, 571-81, 1982.

First version submitted April 1987;
final version received November 1987.

Part III
Evidence

[19]

CHAOTIC DYNAMICS IN ECONOMIC TIME-SERIES

Murray Frank

University of British Columbia, Canada
and
Thanasis Stengos

University of Guelph, Canada

Abstract. There has recently been considerable interest in chaotic dynamics in a variety of disciplines. This paper introduces and then surveys some of the associated literature and techniques. Applications to economic theory are discussed but the primary focus is on empirical applicability. In addition to surveying the literature we also provide an example of the use of these techniques in economics. We conclude by highlighting the importance of the techniques for empirical work as well as considering their context in econometric methodology.

Keywords. Chaos; nonlinear dynamics; correlation dimension; nonparametric; martingale hypothesis.

1. Introduction

According to Einstein, 'God does not play dice with the universe'. This strong stance reflects a view that ultimately all systems are deterministic. One may model a system as if it were the outcome of a random process but that is merely a simplification for purposes of modelling. This perspective is a minority perspective, but has been held by some extremely influential scientists. Recent advances have altered our understanding of the philosophical debate between a stochastic and a deterministic perspective. In this article we will consider some of these advances as they apply to economics. Our emphasis will be strongly oriented towards those aspects of the advances which have direct empirical applications.

It has been known for quite some time that nonlinear difference equations and systems of differential equations can generate exceedingly complex time paths. If one were to observe such a time-series, unaware of the generating mechanism, it would be natural to suppose that it was the outcome of a random process. This observation raises the question concerning the actual mechanisms which generate observed, apparently stochastic, time-series. If such series could be shown to have been deterministically generated than a much more complete understanding of the process will have been attained. We prefer to avoid the philosophical issues connected with whether observations are 'truly' random or 'truly' deterministic. Instead we ask whether a useful deepening of our comprehension of observed time-series is available. As recently as the influential review by May (1976) chaotic

0950-0804/88/02 0103–31 $02.50/0

JOURNAL OF ECONOMIC SURVEYS Vol. 2, No. 2

dynamics were regarded more as a curious theoretical possibility than as a practical concern for empirical research. Things have changed. Examples of apparently chaotic empirical phenomena include: nonlinear electrical circuits, some chemical reactions and hydrodynamic turbulence (Swinney, 1983); solar pulsations (Kurths and Herzel, 1987); measles epidemics (Schaffer and Kot, 1985); acoustic turbulence (Lauterborn and Holzfuss, 1986); dripping faucets (Cruchfield *et al.*, 1986); cardiac cells reaction to electrical impulses (Glass *et al.*, 1983); long-term climatic change (Nicolis, 1986). This listing is itself far from complete. Chaos has proved to provide a fruitful approach to organizing one's thoughts concerning many observed phenomena. Interest by economists is quite natural.

Before evaluating a fix, consider at least a simple example of the problem. The following *ad hoc* example provides a useful illustration of the problem. It is constructed for its simplicity, not for its realism.

$$x_{t+1} = ax_t(1 - x_t) \tag{1}$$

$$P_{t+1} = P_t + x_t - 0.5 \tag{2}$$

To make matters concrete let $a = 4$, $x_1 = 0.3$ and $P_1 = 100$. If you have ready access to a computer, simulate this system until you have a reasonable number of observations, say 1000 iterations. Imagine that this series P_t was presented to you as an asset price time-series. Following Samuelson (1965), Fama (1970) and countless textbooks, you want to determine whether the market for this asset is efficient. No patterns in the data are apparent to the eye. Except by accident, extraneous possible explanatory variables will not work since they truly had nothing to do with the generation of $\{P_t\}$.

To test the applicability of Samuelson's statement that 'properly anticipated prices fluctuate randomly', the following test is quite natural and quite common:

$$\Delta P_t = \psi_0 + \psi_1 \cdot \Delta P_{t-1} + U_t \tag{3}$$

where $\Delta P_t = P_t - P_{t-1}$. The idea is that past price changes should not help in predicting future price changes. In this example, of course, the price changes are completely predictable since you know how the data has been generated. Given the state at date t you can predict the state at date $t + 1$ with as much precision as you care to (say, double precision on your PC). To test the efficient markets hypothesis one tests whether $\psi_0 = \psi_1 = 0$. For those without ready access to a computer, Table 1 reports the outcome of such a test.

Neither White's (1980) general test for heteroskedasticity of an unknown form (W) nor Godfrey's (1978) test for AR(1) errors (G) find any problems. Following Engle (1982) it is now common to test financial data for ARCH (Autoregressive Conditional Heteroskedastic) errors. The test is performed as nR^2 from a regression of the squared residuals from (3) on their lagged values and a constant[1]. The finding of ARCH errors is quite common in financial data and does not directly contravene the efficient markets hypothesis, see Engle and Bollerslev (1986). The market is efficient by these standard tests. You can make a lot of money in an 'efficient market' like this one.

Table 1. Estimation using generated data. Dependent variable: ΔP_t.

Independent variable	Coefficient estimates	Standard errors
constant	-0.0139	0.0135
ΔP_{t-1}	0.0135	0.0317

S.S.R. = 127.86; $R^2 = 0.0002$; $\log L = 390.75$

Observations = 998

Test Statistics
(1) AR(1) $G = 1.281$
(2) Heteroskedasticity $W = 0.516$
(3) ARCH(1) $A = 8.932$

The critical value at 95% level of confidence of a (chi square) distribution with one degree of freedom is 3.84.

This simple example is intended merely to indicate that chaos has the potential to cause problems for empirically oriented economists. Not only theorists with their 'heads in the clouds' may be affected by these observations. The example is just about as simple a nonlinear system as one can imagine and already it illustrates the issue. How much more complex might real world chaos be? (About another five dimensions actually, but that is getting a bit ahead of ourselves.)

Section 2 considers some basic mathematical concepts useful in characterizing chaos. Section 3 reviews theoretical economic models that generate chaotic trajectories. Section 4 reviews empirical studies of chaos in economics. Section 5 provides an illustrative example of empirical chaos testing. Some conclusions are drawn in Section 6.

For those who become interested in delving more deeply into the issues we raise in this survey, the following references may be particularly useful. Brock (1986) is a relatively technical paper on empirical chaos in economics. Eckmann and Ruelle (1985) deal with empirical chaos from a mathematical physics point of view. Eckmann (1981) reviews geometric aspects of dynamical systems theory. Devaney (1986) is a particularly accessible introduction to the mathematics of nonlinear dynamical systems. Nicolis (1986) surveys dissipative dynamical systems. Guckenheimer and Holmes (1986) is very much the standard reference work in this literature. The literature on nonlinear dynamics is large, technical, and is growing rapidly in many disciplines, including economics.

2. Mathematics

Many of the issues are well illustrated by the classic example known as the logistic map:

$$x_t = ax_{t-1}(1 - x_{t-1}) \equiv f(x_{t-1}). \tag{4}$$

This equation was the focus of May (1976) and it has been termed 'the simplest nonlinear difference equation'. In equation (4) the value of a is crucial for the

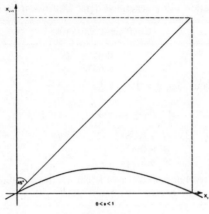

Figure 1.

nature of the system's dynamics. The value of *a* is sometimes termed the 'knob setting'.

The first thing to notice is that (4) has two fixed points, $x_t = 0$ and $x_t = 1 - 1/a$. Multiplicity of fixed points is part of what gives nonlinear equations some of their remarkable properties. The fixed points are only a small part of the nature of this system.

First suppose that we set $0 < a < 1$. This situation is depicted in Figure 1. If the system starts outside the unit interval $[0, 1]$ it is sent to negative infinity. So only points starting in $[0, 1]$ will be of interest. These starting points all end up tending to zero. If the equation is modelling population growth, for example, then asymptotically this population dies out.

Figure 2 depicts the same equation but with $1 < a < 3$. To carry out the graphical analysis start at a point such as x^*. From x^* proceed vertically to the function being depicted, $f(x^*)$. From $f(x^*)$ proceed horizontally to the $45°$ line. Along the $45°$ line $x_t = x_{t+1}$ so we can use the $45°$ line to depict another iteration of the equation. From the $45°$ line proceed vertically again to the function, this gives $f(f(x^*))$ which we denote by $f^2(x^*)$. Proceeding in this manner we obtain a qualitative depiction of the system's dynamics.

In the present case the fixed point at $x_t = 0$ is 'repelling' since any deviation from zero causes the system to move further away. The fixed point at $x_t = 1 - 1/a$ is 'attracting'. This is because there is a neighbourhood of points near $1 - 1/a$ all of which are asymptotically tending towards $1 - 1/a$. The dynamics in this case are quite simple and well understood.

When *a* becomes larger than 3, the fixed point at $1 - 1/a$ also becomes unstable. As *a* is gradually increased beyond 3 a quite remarkable transition takes place. At $a = 3.2$ the system has a period 2 cycle between $x_t \cong 0.8$ and $x_t \cong 0.5$. This cycle is stable. Increase *a* a little bit more and this 2-cycle becomes unstable. Slightly higher values of *a* result in a 4-cycle. That cycle in turn becomes unstable

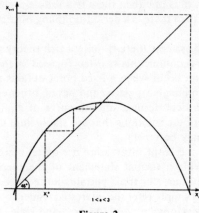

Figure 2.

and is replaced by an 8-cycle, 16-cycle, 32-cycle, ... and so on. This sequence of period doublings eventually accumulates into a 2^{∞}-cycle at $a \cong 3.57$. Feigenbaum (1978) discovered a universal feature in this path to chaos. As 'a' increases, the range of values of 'a' for which a particular cycle is stable decreases as the periodicity of the cycle increases. This causes there to be a rapid accumulation of cycles of ever longer periodicity. Feigenbaum showed that the interval over which a cycle remains stable shrinks at a geometric rate $\sim 4.66920160910\ldots$.

In what sense is this 'universal'? It turns out that the long-term behaviour of the trajectories depends only on the shape of the function at its peak. The logistic map, a sine wave and a circle for example, all have quadratic type behaviour at the maximum. Feigenbaum's ideas have turned up in empirical applications, see the survey by Swinney (1985).

For (4) with $3.57 < a < 4$ there is an infinite number of cycles with differing periodicity as well as an infinite number of fixed points. The actual time path of the system depends crucially on precisely where it starts. This type of behaviour is called 'chaos'. For further analysis of the fascinating behaviour of (1) see May (1976) and Devaney (1986).

The sequence of period doublings is one route to chaos. It is not the only route. Getting to chaos typically involves some form of bifurcation. Bifurcations are a major focus of catastrophe theory. They have also played an important role in theoretical papers on chaos. Bifurcation means splitting in two. In dynamics it refers to abrupt qualitative changes in a system's behaviour which occur as some parameter is changed. At points of bifurcation the nature of a system is altered discontinuously.

As parameter 'a' in equation (4) is increased from 3 to 4, bifurcations occur. This sequence is known as the period-doubling bifurcation, the flip bifurcation or sometimes as the subharmonic bifurcation. In one-dimensional systems bifurcations take place when the eigenvalue at a periodic point is either plus or minus one. If the eigenvalue is plus one then there is a saddle-node bifurcation. If the eigenvalue is minus one then there is a period-doubling bifurcation (see Devaney, 1986).

In higher dimensional systems there is quite a rich theory of possible bifurcations. Most attention by economic theorists has focused on the Hopf bifurcation. The Hopf bifurcation can occur when a fixed point obtains a pair of imaginary eigenvalues with nonzero imaginary parts, and has no other eigenvalues with real parts. Beyond such a critical point a smooth curve of equilibria emerge. This curve may consist of periodic solutions that are stable limit cycles. Alternatively the periodic solutions may be repelling.

The ideas underlying the Hopf bifurcation are quite interesting but relatively technical. Even to provide a formal statement of the theorem would require substantial set-up costs. Since this topic pertains more to economic theory than to empirical work we will simply refer the interested reader to Abraham and Shaw (1982) for a geometric development, and to Chow and Hale (1982) for a rigorous development of bifurcation theory.

At this point it is convenient to take a definitional digression. Thus far the terms random and deterministic have been used without being defined. In a formal sense equation (4) is an example of a semi-deterministic process rather than a deterministic process. Following Arnold (1973): 'a process is said to be deterministic if its entire future course and its entire past are uniquely determined by its state at the present instant of time. The set of all possible states of a process is called its phase space.' A semi-deterministic process has its future determined by its present. The past may or may not be determined by the present.

Consider x^* in Figure 2. We illustrated the graphical procedure by which its future may be determined. But where did x_t^* come from? Looking up to the 45° line we then check horizontally to see what generated x_t^*. But do we look to the left or to the right? There are two possible pasts for x_t^* one iteration ago. Looking further back in time only compounds the trouble. If we were not careful enough to have recorded how we got to x_t^* then we cannot use our knowledge of the law of motion (equation (4)) and its current position to predict the past. This is the sense in which equation (4) is only semi-deterministic. If our interest is in equation (4) then the historian has a much harder task than does the forecaster. (Of course, if the historian makes a mistake it is not on display in quite the same way that the forecaster's accuracy is displayed.) We suggest that the reader give a moment's thought to changing the direction of the time subscript in equation (4). Replace x_{t-1} by x_{t+1} whenever it appears, including on the axes of Figures 1 and 2. Is this what we mean by a random process? For further depth concerning the notions of randomness and complexity the reader might look at Grassberger (1986), Jensen (1987), Kaspar and Schuster (1987), and their references.

In 1975 Li and Yorke published an article entitled 'Period three implies chaos'. That article attracted a great deal of attention since it demonstrated under fairly minimal assumptions that the existence of chaos could be ensured. Roughly speaking, Li and Yorke consider a continuous mapping F from an interval to itself. If that mapping has a periodic point of period 3, then the map also has periodic points of all other periods. In this theorem a map of period 3 means that for $a < b < c$ in the interval, $F(a) = b$, $F(b) = c$ and $F(c) = a$. This remarkable result caused considerable excitement since it obtains very strong results from quite minimal assumptions. Benhabib and Day (1980, 1981) were among the first to make use of this theorem in economic theory models, see Section 3.

The Li and Yorke theorem among other things indicated that there are patterns and order even in quite irregular appearing systems. However, they lost some of the dramatic impact when the much earlier and more general result due to Sarkovskii (1964) was rediscovered. Among other things, this bit of history shows the effect of publishing in a relatively obscure journal.

To state Sarkovskii's theorem we must first take the natural numbers and reorder them as follows:

$$3 > 5 > 7 > \cdots > 2(3) > 2(5) > 2(7) > \cdots > 2^2(3) > 2^2(5) > 2^2(7) > \cdots$$
$$> 2^3(3) > 2^3(5) > 2^3(7) > \cdots > 2^3 > 2^2 > 2 > 1.$$

In words, Sarkovskii's ordering first lists all odd numbers except one, then it lists 2 times the odds, 2^2 times the odds, 2^3 times the odds and so on. This uses up all of the natural numbers except the powers of 2. The powers of 2 get listed last in decreasing order. (Don't ask how Sarkovskii thought of such an ordering in the first place.)

SARKOVSKII'S THEOREM. *Suppose F is a continuous mapping from the real numbers to the real numbers. Suppose that F has a periodic point with prime period k. If $k > m$ in Sarkovskii's ordering, then F also has a periodic point of period m.*

REMARK. A point x is a periodic point of period n if $F^n(x) = x$. The smallest positive n for which $F^n(x) = x$ is termed the prime period of x. The theorem by Sarkovskii is proved in a number of places including Collet and Eckmann (1980), Devaney (1986), Steffan (1977).

Notice that in the Sarkovskii ordering 3 is the largest number. Accordingly, the Li–Yorke theorem is a part of this more general result. For an economic theorist it is probably the two ends of the Sarkovskii ordering which are of the most use. Prove that a model has a point of period 3 and you know that all the other periodic points are present. Prove that there is no point of period 2 and then you needn't worry about the possibility of higher order periodicities in the model. Grandmont (1985) applies the Sarkovskii theorem to an overlapping generations model to prove the existence of chaos.

While the Sarkovskii theorem is quite remarkable in the case of one-dimensional systems, it is actually quite limited in the following sense. It does *not* generalize to systems with more dimensions. In particular, there are counter examples to the ordering in two-dimensional systems. Eventually someone may work out an appropriate generalization, but the ordering will not be the same. Being limited to one-dimensional systems, it is a quite limited result for economic applications.

Since our main interest is with respect to empirical applications we now focus on the mathematical necessities for such work.

2.1. *Dimension*

Dimension is perhaps the most basic attribute of any object. It is the first level of question that one might like to have answered. So basic is this issue that it is frequently overlooked since the answer is so obvious. Matters are not always so simple.

The most traditional concept of dimension is the cardinality of the set of basis vectors for the space in which the object is to be found. An object in R^n is said to be n-dimensional. A rectangle is a two-dimensional object. An object that is sufficiently 'thin' in some direction becomes of an effectively lower dimension than its ambient space. Thus a plane in R^3 is only two-dimensional and a line is one-dimensional. The traditional idea is that an object is n-dimensional if the smallest number of parameters needed to describe the points in the object is n.

This traditional approach ran into difficulties in the early part of the present century. Cantor discovered a one-to-one correspondence between the points on a line and the points on a plane. Peano discovered a continuous mapping from an interval on the whole of a square. The question then arises as to whether there is a meaningful distinction between Euclidean n-space and Euclidean m-space. Earlier intuitions were given precision in work summarized by Hurewicz and Wallman (1948), a classic. A surprising outcome was the development of the Hausdorff dimension. The surprising feature of the Hausdorff dimension is that it is not always integer-valued. The current understanding of the Hausdorff dimension is synthesized and extended by Falconer (1985). For a variety of different notions of dimension see Farmer *et al.* (1983).

Until fairly recently this branch of mathematics appeared esoteric and far removed from any practical scientific concerns. This began to change when Mandelbrot (1967) asked the seemingly innocuous question: 'How long is the coast of Britain?' One's first inclination might be to look up the answer in an encylopedia. Mandelbrot looked up the lengths of many national borders in a number of encyclopedias. A joint border between two nations is routinely reported as longer in the encyclopedia of the smaller country. The length of a natural national border depends upon ε, the length of your measuring rod. Smaller nations typically use shorter rods that are more sensitive to the detailed twists and turns. Credit the smaller country with greater precision.

Recognizing that the smaller country measure is still incomplete, how is one to proceed in search of the 'true' length of the border? Perhaps one might take the limit as the length of the measuring rod shrinks to zero. Conceptually this is like using an infinitely twistable length of string. Trouble arises. The limit does not converge. On this basis the British coast is infinitely long! The problem is that every time ε is reduced a whole new set of twists and turns must be taken into account. There is an unending set of smaller and smaller bends in the coastline.

One needs an alternative approach to organizing one's thoughts about this problem.

Try a number of different small values for ε. Then the coastal length scales in proportion to a power of ε. The rate at which one needs more rods to measure the coast or border as the rod length shrinks is determinate. Call this number D. For different coasts and for different national borders different values for D are obtained. In general, D is not an integer. D matches the previously esoteric mathematical notion of the Hausdorff dimension. Mandelbrot has coined the term 'fractal' to refer to objects with fractional dimension. Fractals are now known to be common in nature (see *Physica D* 7, 1983 and Mandelbrot (1982) for examples).

Subsequent to Mandelbrot (1967) a variety of distinct definitions of dimension were proposed. The only definition to attract much attention in economics is the 'correlation dimension' first proposed by Grassberger and Procaccia (1983a) and Takens (1983). The various notions of dimension all give the same integer to nice simple objects. Fractal objects get slightly different numbers from different definitions, see Farmer *et al.* (1983) and Eckmann and Ruelle (1985). Before formally defining the correlation dimension we first describe the sorts of objects that we wish to characterize, 'strange attractors'.

2.2. *Strange attractors*

First consider an ordinary attractor. The analysis concerns the long-term behaviour of a system. The system could be modelled either as difference equations or as differential equations. The system exists in an n-dimensional phase space, R^n. After a period of time the system may settle into some smaller area within R^n. That smaller area is an attractor. Characterization of the attractor sometimes permits relatively simple structures to be found despite there being an extremely large number of degrees of freedom. For example, a system may have Avogadro's number of degrees of freedom (6.02×10^{23}) and yet settle onto a low finite dimensional set in phase space. The existence of such structures is necessary if there is to be much hope of characterization of complex systems (see Grassberger, 1986).

An 'attractor' then is a subset S of the phase space towards which almost all nearby starting points are eventually attracted. To put it another way, almost every trajectory that begins in a prescribed (possibly quite small) neighbourhood of S is attracted to S eventually.

A familiar economic example of an ordinary attractor is the Cournot tatonnement to the Cournot equilibrium. Consider the textbook Cournot duopoly with intersecting linear reaction functions. This model is frequently explained as a series of (less than fully rational) actions and reactions that converge to the well-known Cournot equilibrium. In this case the attractor is the equilibrium point. Disturb the Cournot equilibrium just a little and the system heads back towards the Cournot equilibrium. This is an example of a zero-dimensional attractor. Many attractors consist of more than just a single point.

To define a strange or chaotic attractor we can no longer avoid some definitional precision. The literature contains a number of different definitions of chaos. A strange attractor will be an attractor which satisfies a definition of chaos. Consider the following definition due to Devaney (1986).

DEFINITION. Let V be a set. $f: V \to V$ is said to be chaotic on V if:
1. f has sensitive dependence on initial conditions,
2. f is topologically transitive,
3. periodic points are dense in V.

This 'reduces' the need to define one term into the need to explain three conditions. Progress. Take these conditions in reverse order.

3. Periodic points are dense in V. It has already been explained that a periodic point is a point that gets repeated when the function gets iterated. $x' = f^n(x')$, so when point x' gets iterated n-times by the function f then the system returns to point x'. Density has to do with a subset that in some sense fills up the original set. To be more precise, suppose that $u \in S$ and $u < v$. If so then there is a point $p \in Q$ such that $u < p < v$ where Q is a subset of S. If this is true then Q is said to be dense in S. This condition imposes some regularity on the turmoil.

2. f is topologically transitive. This means that any pair of small neighbourhoods are eventually joined together by iterating the map. This condition prevents the attractor from being separated into disjoint sets. The entire attractor remains 'in touch' eventually. If there is a single trajectory that is dense in V then that will be enough to ensure that condition 2 is satisfied.

1. f has sensitive dependence on initial conditions. This condition is the hallmark of chaos. Start any two trajectories near to each other but not quite at the same place. The trajectories do not move in tandem, they separate. In general, they separate exponentially rapidly. After a few periods one could not use knowledge of the position of the one trajectory to usefully predict the location of the other trajectory.

A variety of nice examples of such behaviour have been used to illustrate this idea.

> 'Imagine a game of billiards, somewhat idealized so that the balls move across the table and collide with a negligible loss of energy. With a single shot the billiard player sends the balls into a protracted sequence of collisions. The player naturally wants to know the effects of the shot. For how long could a player with perfect control over his or her stroke predict the cue ball's trajectory? If the player ignored an effect even as miniscule as the gravitational attraction of an electron at the edge of the galaxy, the prediction would become wrong after one minute!' Crutchfield *et al.* (1986).

In the literature on weather forecasting this is sometimes called the 'butterfly effect'. An overlooked butterfly behaviour in New York could seriously disrupt the next day's weather forecast in Boston.

There are a number of ways one might translate condition 1 into notation. For example: Let Ω be a space with metric[2] d and let $f: \Omega \to \Omega$ be a continuous mapping defined on Ω. A discrete dynamical system (Ω, f) is said to have sensitive dependence on initial conditions if there is a $\delta > 0$ such that for all $\omega \in \Omega$ and all $\varepsilon > 0$ there is another $\omega' \in \Omega$ and a $'k$ such that $d(\delta, \delta') < \varepsilon$ but $d(f^k(\omega), f^k(\omega')) \geqslant \delta$. So distinct points that start within ε after k-iterations are farther than δ apart.

The three components in Devaney's definition of chaos give chaos a topological characterization. Others define chaos in measure theoretic fashion. Some definitions have touched off debate, for example Melese and Transue (1986, 1987), Day (1986) and Day and Kim (1987). Such debates may be of mathematical interest but they are of quite limited economic significance. One can define chaos so that it is of measure zero in some sense. By the same token one might define a measure over prices and then claim that supply = demand is a measure zero event. Whether supply = demand is a useful construct is an essentially economic question, not a mathematical question. It is an empirical question whether chaos will provide a useful approach to organizing our understanding of economic phenomena. Of course some definitions are more useful than others.

Since conditions 2 and 3 in the definition of chaos are not empirically verifiable we will follow Eckmann and Ruelle (1985) in identifying chaos with sensitive dependence on initial conditions. This condition can be verified by checking whether there is a positive Lyapunov exponent. The Lyapunov exponents will be discussed below.

2.3. Correlation dimension

Start by assuming that the system of interest lies on an attractor in a phase space. Of course the attractor may be quite complex, for example it could be fractal. The true system that underlies the observations is

$$X_{t+1} = F(X_t). \tag{5}$$

Here X_t is a vector with n entries where n could be extremely large and will normally include many variables which we know nothing about. The function F transforms the system from one moment to the next [3]. Since the researcher knows neither X_t nor F, characterizing the system is a little challenging. One does get to observe a time-series of scalars $x_t, t = 1, 2, \ldots T$. The observables are generated according to

$$x_t = h(X_t). \tag{6}$$

We refer to the function h as the observer function. The time-series is assumed to have been generated by a trajectory that is dense on the attractor. To obtain evidence about the original system we need some way in which to go back from the observable to the underlying system. This is done through the creation of 'M-histories' as $x_t^M = (x_t, x_{t+1}, \ldots, x_{t+M-1})$. This converts the series of scalars into a slightly shorter series of vectors with overlapping entries.

To motivate the creation of the M-histories consider the tent map. The tent map is a very simple chaotic equation with a single peak in the unit interval, much the same as the logistic map described above. However, the peak of the tent map is not smooth as the peak of the logistic map. One can define the tent map as $x_{t+1} = f(x_t)$ where $f(x) = 2x$, $x_t \in [0, \frac{1}{2}]$; $f(x) = 2(1 - x)$ for $x_t \in [\frac{1}{2}, 1]$. Use it to generate a long time-series. That time-series will appear to be uniformly distributed on $[0, 1]$. If it completely fills the unit interval then the object under consideration must be at least one-dimensional. Next consider (x_t, x_{t+1}) or '2-histories'. If the observations evenly filled the unit square then the object would be seen to be at least two-dimensional. Of course for the tent map the unit square will not be filled. The observations will line up along the tent itself. For more complex objects it will be necessary to consider successively higher dimensional cubes. For a completely random series there will be essentially no limit to the length of the M-history that you can consider, the M-cube will continue to be evenly filled up.

A more formal result is due to Takens (1981). If the true system that generated the time-series is n-dimensional, and provided $M \geqslant 2n + 1$, then generically the M-histories recreate the dynamics of the underlying system. There is a diffeomorphism between the M-histories and the true data generating process. Broomhead and King (1986) discuss some practical limitations on the applicability of Takens' (1981) extremely useful theorem.

Having created the M-histories, the next step is to calculate the correlation integral, $C^M(\varepsilon)$.

$$C^M(\varepsilon) = \{\text{the number of pairs } (i \neq j) \text{ with distance } \| x_i^M - x_j^M \| \leqslant \varepsilon\}/T^2. \quad (7)$$

Strictly speaking one would like $T \to \infty$. In practice, data restricts the length of T. Limitations on data length cause certain further practical problems.

To move from the correlation integral to the correlation dimension one proceeds much as did Mandelbrot (1967). One looks to see how the correlation integral scales as ε shrinks. As shown by Grassberger and Procaccia (1983a) $C^M(\varepsilon) \sim \varepsilon^D$ so that D becomes the notion of dimension. Changing ε changes the number of neighbouring points that get included in the correlation integral. For a completely random series, new neighbours get included from each of the M degrees of freedom. If not all the degrees of freedom are being exploited by the system then proportionately fewer new neighbours get included when you increase ε. For example, consider a two-dimensional object embedded in 3-space. Increase ε a little and new neighbours are gained in only two of the three available directions. More formally,

$$D^M = \lim_{\varepsilon \to 0} \{\ln C^M(\varepsilon)/\ln \varepsilon\}. \quad (8)$$

As a practical matter one investigates the estimated values of D^M as M is increased. If as M increases so does D^M then the system is regarded as being high dimensional or stochastic. If however D^M settles down, or saturates at some level D, then D is the estimated dimension of the system. The higher is an estimated value of D the more complicated is the system that is being investigated. If the system that is under investigation is fractal then the estimated value D will not be an integer[4].

2.4. *Lyapunov exponents*

The next concept is that of the Lyapunov exponent. This concept is fundamental. Frequently the presence of at least one positive Lyapunov exponent is taken to be the definition of chaos. The Lyapunov exponents measure the average stability properties of the system on the attractor. For a fixed-point attractor, the Lyapunov numbers[5] are the absolute values of the eigenvalues of the Jacobian matrix evaluated at the fixed point. So the Lyapunov exponents are generalizations of the familiar notion of the eigenvalues.

There are as many Lyapunov exponents as there are degrees of freedom for a system. For a system with two degrees of freedom the time path can either separate or join points in two directions. If separate points are always moved closer together, then the Lyapunov exponents must all be negative and the system converges. If at least one of the Lyapunov exponents is positive, then it will have the effect of separating nearby points. The negative Lyapunov exponents contract the system, the positive Lyapunov exponents stretch the system. The interaction of stretching and contracting is what yields the highly folded or wrinkled structures typical of chaos.

On a strange attractor, nearby points give rise to paths which separate at an exponential rate. Accordingly, the actual time path of any such system will be highly sensitive to the precise starting location. Any imprecision gets magnified. Even if one knows the true equations of motion for such a system, one cannot necessarily predict the distant future of a deterministic system. Slight errors or uncertainty about the current state of the system makes the exercise of predicting the future time path extremely difficult. For example, suppose you would like to reproduce our simulation exercise from the introduction. If your computer has a slightly different degree of precision than does ours, then your simulated data may differ subtantially from ours. However, the econometric implications will be robust to such differences.

To get more of a sense of this sensitivity consider Table 2. This table presents simulations of equation (1) starting at $X_1 = 0.3$, 0.30000001, 0.30001, 0.31. Let us take as a definition that the first observation in which the first digit after the decimal point would differ from the $X_1 = 0.3$ series (if rounded) is the divergence point. For $X_1 = 0.31$ the divergence point occurs at the fifth iteration. For $X_1 = 0.30001$ divergence occurs at period 15 while for $X_1 = 0.30000001$ divergence does not happen until period 26. After the divergence the various series move quite differently from each other. In an economic model an iteration might correspond to some unit of clock time such as a year or a minute; or else it might correspond to an individual trade.

There are several different approaches to formally explaining the Lyapunov exponents. The following seems to us to have the most familiar structure. Consider the following dynamical system

$$\frac{dX}{dt} = F(X). \tag{9}$$

In (9) let X be a vector with N components and let F have components $f_1, ..., f_N$, so (9) is an Nth order dynamical system. Think of X as the state of the economy and (9) gives the evolution of the economy over time. Consider a particular trajectory $X^*(t)$ that satisfies (9), and an arbitrarily small but positive initial displacement from the start of $X^*(t)$, call it $D(0)$.

Table 2.

$X_1 = 0.3$	$X_1 = 0.30000001$	$X_1 = 0.30001$	$X_1 = 0.31$
0.30000000000000	0.30000000100000	0.30001000000000	0.31000000000000
0.84000001907349	0.84000001600000	0.84001599960000	0.85560000000000
0.53759994312012	0.53759995648000	0.53755648006405	0.49419456000000
0.99434497560546	0.99434497309081	0.99435804322079	0.99986518746563
0.02249218037456	0.02249219031939	0.02244050041163	0.00053917743982
0.08794512878622	0.08794516677611	0.08774769741162	0.00215554691003
0.32084313243598	0.32084325766734	0.32019215604233	0.00860360211021
0.87161126721860	0.87161144670699	0.87067655700517	0.03411832056375
0.44762026430475	0.44761973070535	0.45039556034717	0.13181704306264
0.98902545315398	0.98902522955448	0.99015759826691	0.45776524088344
0.04341642467017	0.04341729943675	0.03898211544484	0.99286490048947
0.16612575495610	0.16612895018546	0.14985004048114	0.02833675946204
0.55411195398546	0.55412048838295	0.50958002339577	0.11013515010091
0.98828758574350	0.98828389094876	0.99963289260695	0.39202159525264
0.04630093443514	0.04631536735975	0.00146789050086	0.95336265643286
0.17662863162228	0.17668101642432	0.00586294319336	0.17784920700857
0.58172383245409	0.58185933943835	0.02331427636190	0.58487546629997
0.97328486083607	0.97319619418687	0.09108288351849	0.97118462088145
0.10400576201354	0.10434144722826	0.33114716739378	0.11194021217920
0.37275425392611	0.37381723847429	0.88595488368342	0.39763840430591
0.93523408042439	0.93631164277499	0.40415531104368	0.95808841490784
0.24223518094854	0.23852860151597	0.96325518239547	0.16062001650890
0.73433228316509	0.72653083109922	0.14157854393498	0.53928490722232
0.78035351489326	0.79473513024599	0.48613623932891	0.99382678425813
0.68560762674798	0.65252481199552	0.99923118456022	0.02454042859708
0.86219923557193	0.90694472690293	0.00307289745040	0.09575278384540
0.47524685500444	0.33758395698361	0.01225381900664	0.34633675292503
0.99754912725131	0.89448411588359	0.04841465170557	0.90555042599351
0.00977946388582	0.37752912926217	0.18428269282319	0.34211540790593
0.03873530388771	0.94000354328287	0.60129032779608	0.90028982231716
0.14893952048174	0.22558752759407	0.95896107797985	0.35907223259720
0.50702615888163	0.69879117995225	0.15741891559831	0.92055745749945
0.99980253236548	0.84192826709277	0.53055280244063	0.29252569976641
0.00078971456421	0.53234024065174	0.99626610505209	0.82781765897032
0.00315636366048	0.99581643533835	0.01487981190570	0.57014232986887
0.01258560411568	0.01666424979349	0.05863361241339	0.98032021424226
0.04970882673890	0.06554621028924	0.22078284763497	0.07716996716106
0.18895143713258	0.24499961842385	0.68815112730066	0.28485905331768
0.61299516615245	0.73989922158406	0.85839661318196	0.81485749224254
0.94892836970472	0.76979345393344	0.48620747063880	0.60345903831495

Substitution of $X(t) = X^*(t) + D(t)$ into (9) and expansion in D gives

$$\frac{dD}{dt} = \frac{(\partial F)}{(\partial X)}\bigg|_{X = X^*} + O(D^2).$$ (10)

In (10) the term $(\partial F)/(\partial X)|_{X = X^*}$ is an $N \times N$ Jacobian matrix with time-dependent elements, while $O(D^2)$ collects the terms that are second-order small. Dropping the terms that are second-order small, we get a set of linear homogeneous equations. The solution to that system will take the form

$$D(t) = M(t)D(0).$$ (11)

Now $M(t)$ will also be an $N \times N$ matrix. Under fairly general conditions, for a given $D(0)$ the following limit exists

$$\lambda_i = \lim_{t \to \infty} t^{-1} \ln |D_i(t)| \qquad i = 1, 2, ..., N.$$ (12)

The existence conditions were originally due to Oseledec (1968) after whom the existence theorem is now named. In (12) the λ_i are the Lyapunov exponents for the trajectory $X^*(t)$ and the disturbance $D(0)$. Notice that there are as many Lyapunov exponents as there are degrees of freedom. However, the Lyapunov exponents do not match up with the axes of the state space.

What we have done is to fix a trajectory $X^*(t)$ and consider another trajectory which starts at almost the same place. For example, these might be the $X_1 = 0.3$ and $X_1 = 0.30000001$ trajectories as in Table 2. If one experiments with various displacements, it is found that apart from statistical fluctuations, the λ_i are independent of the choice of $D(0)$, provided the displacement remains on the attractor. Accordingly, the Lyapunov exponents are *not* local properties. They reflect the overall behaviour of the attractor. Pick any initial position on an attractor, all nearby trajectories separate (as long as some $\lambda_i > 0$) at an exponential rate. The bigger the largest Lyapunov exponent, the more rapid the separation.

The remarkable constancy of the Lyapunov exponents on a given attractor becomes intuitive when one recalls the nature of an attractor. By definition, the various trajectories go almost everywhere on the attractor. Accordingly, the λ_i can be understood as the average rate of separation over the entire strange attractor.

For the estimation of the Lyapunov exponents there is an algorithm developed by Wolf *et al.* (1985). Brock and Dechert (1987) elaborate on its properties. Given the complexity of the algorithm, the interested reader is referred to the original articles.

2.5 *Kolmogorov entropy*

A chaotic system produces information as time passes. The sense in which this information is produced is that as time passes two distinct but empirically indistinguishable starting points produce trajectories which are distinguishable.

The mean rate at which they become distinguishable is the mean rate of information creation, or the Kolmogorov entropy, K. The Lyapunov exponents quantify the stretching and contracting in various directions, the Kolmogorov entropy measures an aggregate of the stretching. For a regular time path $K = 0$, for a chaotic time path $0 < K < \infty$ and for a random system $K = \infty$.

The relationship between K and the Lyapunov exponents is important. Under certain technical conditions (see Eckmann and Ruelle, 1985) we get Pesin's identity:

$$K = \sum_i \text{positive } \lambda_i \tag{13}$$

Under more general but weaker conditions, K is a lower bound on the sum of the positive Lyapunov exponents. For a formal treatment of K, see Eckmann and Ruelle (1985).

From our perspective interest in the Kolmogorov entropy is due to an approximation due to Grassberger and Procaccia (1983b) (see also Caputo and Atten, 1987). The approximation is denoted K_2 and $K_2 \leqslant K$. Grassberger and Procaccia (1983b) proposed K_2 using the Euclidean norm. To define K_2:

$$K_2 = \lim_{\varepsilon \to 0} \lim_{M \to \infty} \lim_{N \to \infty} \ln \left[\frac{C^M(\varepsilon)}{C^{M+1}(\varepsilon)} \right] \tag{14}$$

The empirical attraction of K_2 is that it can be calculated quite readily using the same basic information as one obtained in calculating the correlation dimension. This makes its implementation easier than calculation of the Lyapunov exponents. If one is mainly interested in establishing or rejecting the presence of chaos, the greater ease with which K_2 is calculated is a strong recommendation. In general, K_2 does tend to underestimate the sum of the positive Lyapunov exponents.

Scheinkman and LeBaron (1986) have emphasized another attractive aspect of K_2 when one carries out the calculations using the supremum norm. In the process of calculating K_2 one gets $S^M = C^M(\varepsilon)/C^{M-1}(\varepsilon)$. The interpretation of S^M is that it gives the conditional probability that two points will be close together, given that their past histories have been close together. Given a fixed ε if the X_t's are independent then S^M will be independent of M. If however, past values of X_t help to predict future values, then S^M will tend to rise with M. So the behaviour of S^M as M rises measures departures from independence. For more about the Kolmogorov entropy, see Cohen and Procaccia (1985) and Petersen (1983). For some other related entropies see Eckmann and Procaccia (1986) and Pawelzik and Schuster (1987).

2.6. *Brock's residual test*

Brock (1986) has argued that the above procedure, i.e. correlation dimension estimates, Lyapunov exponents and/or K_2 estimates, is incomplete in providing evidence for chaos, especially for economic time-series. Many economic time-series are generated by near unit root processes (see Nelson and Plosser, 1982). Near unit root processes can generate low-dimension estimates which in turn give the misleading impression that the data generating process is chaotic. A unit root process generating $\{X_t\}$ will result in the variance of the innovation in $\{X_t\}$ being near zero. Consequently, successive draws from this process will be close together and for a wide range of ε one would pick up pseudo-structure between the M-histories in the data. Only for ε very small will one be able to avoid the problem.

Brock (1986) has proposed the following test as a way of avoiding the unit root trap. His test is based on a striking property of chaotic equations — invariance to linear transformations. If one carries out a linear transformation of chaotic data, then both the original and the transformed data should have the same correlation dimension and the same Lyapunov exponents. This invariance property forms the basis for Brock's Residual Test:

Let $\{X_t; t = 1, 2, \ldots\}$ be an infinite deterministic chaotic time-series. Then fit a linear model to the data with a finite number of lags, i.e.

$$X_t + \psi_1 X_{t-1} + \cdots + \psi_N X_{t-N} = U_t, t = N + 1, N + 2, \ldots .$$

U_t is the residual at time t and $\psi_i, i = 1, \ldots N,$ are the estimated coefficients. Then the correlation dimension estimates and the largest Lyapunov exponent of $\{X_t\}$ and $\{U_t\}$ are the same.

This test introduces some tightness into a fairly loose domain. If the calculated dimension and Lyapunov exponents are substantially altered, then the hypothesis of a deterministic law is suspect. Certainly, the above test is able to distinguish between low-dimensional processes which in fact are unit root processes and real chaotic processes. If a low-dimension estimate of the original series is not confirmed by the residual series, then the original series may well not be chaotic. This test is further discussed by Brock and Sayers (1986).

2.7. *Shuffle diagnostic*

Scheinkman and LeBaron (1986) proposed the following procedure as a way of detecting the presence of nonlinear structure in the data. Suppose the original series has been 'whitened' by, say, fitting to it an AR-process. If the whitened series does not possess any nonlinear structure and comes from an i.i.d. (independence identically distributed) data generating process, then shuffling of the series by sampling with replacement would create a new series with a dimension estimate similar to the original series. If, however, the series still possesses nonlinear structure, the shuffling process would destroy it. In other words, the shuffled series would become like an i.i.d. series even though the original whitened series was not. In that case the correlation dimension estimate of the shuffled series would be much higher than the dimension estimate of the original whitened series.

One could repeat the above shuffling process to obtain a number of shuffled series. If the original unshuffled series was i.i.d., then its dimension estimate would be similar to the average estimate from the shuffled series. One would expect that individual estimates from the shuffled series would be as likely to be above as to be below the original estimate of the unshuffled series. On the contrary, if the proportion of shuffled estimates above the original series is, say, more than 95%, then that would be evidence that the unshuffled series was not i.i.d. In this context, repeated shuffling allows one to make inferences about the presence of structure in the data, and to make confidence-interval type statements. The above procedure was used in Frank and Stengos (1987b).

An alternative approach to addressing the question of statistical inference has recently been proposed by Brock *et al.* (1987). They developed a family of test statistics based on the correlation integral. The statistical foundation of their approach is nonparametric and is closely related to the literature on U-statistics, see Serfling (1980). The test statistics in question test the null hypothesis of an i.i.d. process against general nonlinear dependent alternatives. They are based on the standardized difference between the correlation integral and the one implied by the null for each M and ε. For a full discussion of their proposed test statistics and some Monte Carlo evidence about its performance in small samples, see Brock *et al.* (1987) and Brock (1987).

3. Chaos in economic theory

Aspects of the mathematics of chaos have been being invoked by economic theorists and by game theorists for almost a decade. Virtually any dynamic model is potentially chaotic under some circumstances. There is very little in standard economic theory to rule out chaos. Take almost any model with an intertemporal linkage. Replace the equation which describes that link by a known chaotic equation. The resulting example now exhibits chaos. Some applications involve little more than such a procedure. Early papers carrying out this procedure were valuable in alerting economists to the potential of chaos in familiar environments. In the long run, more interesting are economic models whose fundamentals induce (or preclude) chaos. The applications to the overlapping generations model seem the most developed. But even there the gulf between theory and interesting, potentially refutable implications is large. The value of these theoretical models seems mainly to be in terms of highlighting the possibility of chaos. Such general results as are available seem a bit discouraging, see the discussion of Boldrin and Montrucchio (1986) below.

3.1. *Microeconomic chaos*

There are relatively few models of chaos in microeconomic contexts. Benhabib and Day (1981) considered a consumer problem in which erratic choices by consumers are derived in a stationary environment. This requires some sort of intertemporal linkage through wealth effects, labour–leisure effects, habit persistence or something similar. Ostensibly, cyclical choices need not contradict the usual choice axioms when such linkages are present. The Benhabib and Day

(1981) paper is based on a slightly extended version of the Li and Yorke (1975) theorem.

In game theoretic economic models there has been considerable concern about multiplicity of equilibria. Even when the equilibrium is unique in a dynamic game, the equilibrium need not possess any simple regularity. Dana and Montrucchio (1986) analyse the complexity of time paths generated by the Maskin and Tirole (1986) model of dynamic oligopoly. For small discount factors, essentially anything is possible as a trajectory for the market prices and outputs. There is, however, an interesting relationship between the classical Cournot tatonnement and the equilibria of the model that Dana and Montrucchio analyse.

An earlier application of chaos in game theory was by Rand (1978). In that paper, a very sophisticated mathematical technique (symbolic dynamics) was employed to analyse an economically questionable model. The duopolists are myopic and never learn, despite their anticipations never being correct. Rand (1978) is an interesting example of an approach to modelling dynamics that has not yet enjoyed wide application in the economics literature. The mathematical approach taken by Rand is of interest.

Saari (1985) and Saari and Williams (1986) are concerned about the local stability of informationally decentralized systems. The interest here is on the informational requirements for convergence. In this context, interest is more about ruling out chaos rather than developing its properties. Saari (1984) has also looked at chaos as the outcome of voting mechanisms.

To date nobody has considered business firms as expressions of nonlinear dynamics. However, we believe that it is just a matter of time until someone models firms as dissipative structures, see Nicolis (1986). The reason is that many of the properties of such structures seem suggestive of firms and of the elusive concept of 'corporate culture'. For such structures historical accidents can have long-term significance. Accumulation of economic information may play a role akin to increasing entropy. Both cause time to move in one direction only.

3.2. *Macroeconomic chaos*

Most of the theoretical chaos models are aggregative in nature. These papers may be subdivided into (i) overlapping generations models (OLG), (ii) growth models, (iii) other aggregative models. In this section, we limit attention to models pertaining to chaos. In particular, we do not deal with the many models of catastrophe theory following Thom (1975) and Zeeman (1977).

3.2.1. *Overlapping generations models.* Gale (1973) is the first example of a perfect foresight business cycle in an overlapping generations endowment economy. He appears to regard this possibility as little more than 'an amusing example'. His example has quadratic utility and a cycle of period 2 as it oscillates between generations above and below the golden rule. His model had a limit cycle, but no chaos.

The first OLG models with chaos were due to Benhabib and Day (1980, 1982). In their 1980 paper Benhabib and Day apply the Li–Yorke theorem to a modified version of the Diamond (1965) version of the OLG model with capital. In the modification, rich generations care more for current consumption, while members of poorer generations care more about the future. Their 1982 paper shows that the erratic trajectory of a chaotic OLG economy is Pareto-efficient. This has proved to be true of many models with endogenous chaos.

Grandmont (1985) gives a very thorough analysis of a chaos due to the inter-action of a wealth effect and an intertemporal substitution effect, all mediated by the movements in real interest rates. Grandmont shows how monetary policy can effectively stabilize these fluctuations. Such stabilization is unrelated to the 'sur-prises' popular in the New Classical tradition. Anyone interested in chaos can learn much from Grandmont (1985). Yet there are difficulties. The analysis is based on the flip bifurcation (see Guckenheimer and Holmes (1986)), which is sensitive to shortening of the period length. Further discomfort arises from Grandmont's assumption that increases in interest rates are negatively related to savings. Grandmont (1986) and Grandmont and Laroque (1986) extend the analysis of the framework of Grandmont (1985). Grandmont (1986) is concerned with the effects of various government policies, while Grandmont and Laroque (1986) demonstrate the importance of the expectation formation mechanism for the stability of the economy. This is true even in the perfect foresight context that they consider.

Farmer (1986) and Reichlin (1986) both consider production economies and both make use of the Hopf bifurcation which is often thought to be more robust than the flip bifurcation, again see Guckenheimer and Holmes (1986). In Farmer (1986) the chaos depends upon the government's debt policy. One may think of Farmer (1986) as showing that a government can cause chaos. Reichlin (1986) has chaos in situations with limited substitution between capital and labour. There is a tension between savings out of wages and an intertemporal substitution due to factor price changes. It is these opposing effects which generate chaos in Reichlin (1986). In Farmer (1986) it is shown that the government can cause chaos, while in Reichlin (1986) it is shown that fiscal policy can cure chaos. The OLG model appears to be a particularly tractable context in which to consider issues of chaos. But even here to date the literature seems to consist mainly of examples and possibilities.

3.2.2. *Growth models.*

Both descriptive and optimal growth models have long been a favourite context for economists investigating intertemporal issues, see Burmeister (1980). In this setting chaos is closely related to the general issue of the global stability of an economy. We consider optimal growth models after first considering descriptive growth models.

Day (1982, 1983) attracted considerable attention by alerting economists to the possibility of chaos in two quite familiar contexts, a classical growth model and a Solow growth model. In both papers, the examples of chaos were based on variants of the logistic map that we discussed in Section 2. In both papers he draws attention to the applicability of the Li–Yorke theorem.

Chaos has also been analysed in the context of a multiplier–accelerator type of model by Dana and Malgrange (1984). They use numerical simulations along with applying the Hopf bifurcation idea. Stutzer (1980) analysed chaos in the context of a growth model due to Haavelmo (1956).

Several researchers have considered the cyclical properties of optimal growth models. Benhabib and Nishimura (1979) employ the Hopf bifurcation in their study of how the properties of an optimal growth model are affected by the discount rate. Benhabib and Nishimura (1985) offer sufficient conditions for periodic cycles in a two-sector neoclassical model. The importance of capital intensity assumptions and adjustment costs are discussed. Neither of these papers by Benhabib and Nishimura go the full way to chaos, although the 1985 paper discusses the difficulty of constructing chaotic examples when there is an infinite horizon concave utility function being maximized. These difficulties were overcome by Deneckere and Pelikan (1986). Along with an example of chaos, they also discuss some necessary and sufficient economic conditions for chaos. The notion of chaos used by Deneckere and Pelikan is the Lyapunov exponent definition, and hence is closer to the definition used in empirical research than the Li–Yorke definition. It also avoids the debate about whether with probability 1 chaos does not occur.[6]

Boldrin and Montrucchio (1986) provide a constructive proof of a destructive result. For any continuous twice differentiable map, they show how to construct an optimal growth model for which that map is an optimal policy function. Accordingly, if one wishes for empirical predictions, added structure is needed beyond what has been standard in the optimal growth literature. They also show that in this context, to generate chaos, the discount factor must be low. This result apparently contradicts a conjecture of Dechert (1984).

3.2.3. Other aggregative models. Two macroeconomic chaos papers do not fit in the previous categories. Day and Shafer (1985) analyse a Keynesian fix-price model. Van der Ploeg (1986) analyses a bond pricing model due to Begg (1984). Both Day and Shafer (1985) and Van der Ploeg (1986) are recent examples of papers drawing attention to the applicability of the Li–Yorke theorem in an economic context.

4. Empirical chaos in economics

To date, the applications of empirical chaos testing have been either in the context of macroeconomics or else in finance. Since longer and more disaggregated data are available in finance, it is perhaps not surprising that it is there that the results appear most promising.

Brock and Sayers (1986) carried out extensive tests of various American macroeconomic time-series. Their results are not supportive of low-order deterministic chaos. However, some evidence of nonlinearity was found for the investment and unemployment data. The evidence of nonlinearity in unemployment complements the findings of Neftci (1984). Neftci used quite a different methodology. Sayers (1986) found evidence of nonlinearity in some American workstoppage data. In contrast to the American data, Frank and Stengos (1987b) find no evidence of significant nonlinearity in Canadian macroeconomic time-series. Even the Canadian unemployment data rejects the chaos hypothesis.

Barnett and Chen (1986) considered some American monetary aggregates. On some log linear detrended monetary aggregates, they found evidence of low correlation dimension. Their dimension estimate is between 1.3 and 1.5, implying that the relevant state space is at least two-dimensional.

Scheinkman and LeBaron (1986) examined data on American stock prices. On a weekly index of stocks a dimension of about 6 was found. Reshuffling the data raised the dimensionality. Their results are consistent with chaos. Frank and Stengos (1987a) examined rates of return on gold and silver. Daily, weekly and biweekly series were considered. The results were quite consistent with the results of Scheinkman and LeBaron (1986). The estimated dimensionality was between 6 and 7, while the Kolmogorov entropy estimates were around 0.2. Shuffling raised the dimension estimates substantially.

These methods do seem to be able to find evidence of structures not picked up by more familiar econometric procedures, at least in some settings. Barnett and Choi (1987) discuss the relationship between chaos and more traditional approaches to data analysis. Brock *et al.* (1987) have developed a statistical test for independence based on the correlation dimension. Brock (1987) has used this test to provide evidence of nonlinearity for a number of macroeconomic time-series. He has also used this test as part of a more general questioning of the relationship between economic theories and empirical procedures of the ARCH class.

In sum, the chaotic testing procedures have proved to be helpful directly in contexts where long time-series of high quality data are available. This literature also seems to be developing in the direction of providing some useful nonparametric time-series techniques. The empirical issues being raised are potentially quite important.

5. Looking for chaos in economic time-series: an empirical example[7]

In the introduction we presented an example of an artificial time-series of asset prices, that according to the standard parametric econometric tests would be consistent with the efficient market hypothesis. By construction, the artificial series was generated by a known deterministic process. The market for that asset would not be efficient in the usual sense, since knowledge of the data generating process (DGP) by agents would allow them to make infinite profits.

In the following example we will consider an actual time-series for daily gold rates of return. The equation under examination is

$$r_t = \beta_0 + \beta_1 r_{t-1} + u_t \tag{15}$$

In (15) we have $r_t = (P_t - P_{t-1})/P_{t-1}$, where P_t is the price of the gold asset at date t. According to the martingale hypothesis $\beta_0 = \beta_1 = 0$. In other words, one should expect the above regression model to fit the data badly in terms of a low R^2, if the market is efficient. Table 3 reports the results of the estimation of (15). We also examined the error structure of (15) and tested for the possible presence of a general ARCH (p) process. We found that an ARCH (12) process fits the data best. As expected, the results in Table 3 appear supportive of the martingale hypothesis. The finding of ARCH effects is also fairly common in financial time-series, see Engle and Bollerslev (1986).

The picture changes dramatically when we apply the techniques described above to the same data. Specifically, we will estimate the dimension of the series, obtain an estimate of the Kolmogorov entropy measure and conclude by assessing the implications of these results for econometric methodology.

Table 3. AR(1) results for gold.

r_t	β_0	β_1	R^2	$A(6)$	$A(12)$
Gold	0.0004	−0.0606	0.0003	35.72	88.43
(S.E.)	(0.3199)	(0.0866)			

The columns beneath $A(6)$ and $A(12)$ give the results of ARCH tests for an ARCH(6) and an ARCH(12) process. These were computed as nR^2 from regressing the squared residuals of the AR(1) regressions given above on their own 6 lags or 12 lags respectively. And n is the number of observations. The critical values of χ^2 with 6 and 12 degrees of freedom at the 5 per cent level are 12.59 and 21.03 respectively.

5.1. *Correlation dimension estimates*

We have already indicated that a certain amount of judgement is required to measure the correlation dimension. One must choose reasonable values for ε and M. For the gold data, the relevant range for ε-values was between $(0.9)^{20}$ and $(0.9)^{33}$.

For each embedding dimension one plots $\ln C^M(\varepsilon)$ against $\ln \varepsilon$. Over the relevant range of values of ε, one calculates the slopes by ordinary least squares. Figure 3 depicts the plots and Table 4 reports the results of these calculations for $M = 5, 10, 15, 20, 25$. At $M = 25$ the series has a correlation dimension estimate of 6.3. Column R of Table 4 reports the results for estimates from a computer-generated normally distributed random number series of length 3000 observations with the same mean and variance as the gold series. The computer-generated random numbers are higher dimensional than the actual rates of return series.

We next carried out Brock's (1986) Residual Test. If a series is deterministic chaos, then the residuals from a linear or smooth nonlinear transformation of the data should yield the same correlation dimension as the original series. To

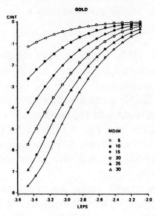

Figure 3.

Table 4. Correlation dimensions for daily data.

M	G	R	ARCHG	SHG
5	1.11	3.15	1.25	2.85
10	2.45	5.42	2.23	5.12
15	3.83	8.91	4.51	7.01
20	5.41	11.52	5.82	9.51
25	6.31	13.48	6.65	11.27

M = embedding dimension
G = daily gold series
R = computer-generated (pseudo-)random numbers
ARCHG = residuals from ARCH(12) of the gold series
SHG = reshuffled ARCHG series

CINT = log $C^M(\varepsilon)$
LEPS = log ε
MDIM = embedding dimension

implement this test, we took the residuals from the ARCH(12) specifications and calculated their correlation dimensions. As reported in Table 4, at $M = 25$ the correlation dimension estimate again turns out to be between 6 and 7. The daily series appears to pass Brock's Residual Test.

We then proceed to apply Scheinkman and LeBaron's (1986) 'shuffle diagnostic'. Recall that one recreates the data series by sampling randomly with replacement from the data until one obtains a shuffled series of the same length as the original. The shuffled series should be considerably more random than the original one if the latter is chaotic. If the original series is stochastic, then the shuffling will leave the correlation dimension unchanged, since there was no structure present to be destroyed by the shuffling process. To carry out the shuffle diagnostic we resampled from the ARCH residuals using a uniform pseudo-random number generator. If the ARCH procedure picked up the relevant structure then the reshuffled series will have the same correlation dimension.

Table 5. Correlation dimension (*D*) estimates at *M* = 25. For each series we report the unshuffled dimension estimate as well as the maximum and minimum values obtained from 30 reshufflings of the data.

	Daily data		
Series name	Unshuffled *D*	Maximum shuffled *D*	Minimum shuffled *D*
G	6.31	11.44	9.23
ARCHG	6.65	12.01	9.45

G = gold series
ARCHG = residuals from the ARCH(12) gold series for the daily data.

Table 4 reports estimates for a typical reshuffled series. The dimension estimates are raised substantially.

Next we attempt to generate an empirical distribution for the shuffle diagnostic, in order to carry out inferences based on confidence intervals. Under the null hypothesis of an independence identically distributed process (i.i.d.), a series which is repeatedly reshuffled should result in some of the reshuffled series estimates below and some above the dimension estimate of the original series. If, on the other hand, most of the reshuffled estimates lie above (say 95% of the time), then this is evidence against the null hypothesis. We performed repeated shuffling of the original series as well as for the ARCH residuals. At *M* = 25 we performed 30 replications of each shuffle. The range of estimates thereby obtained is reported in Table 5. At *M* = 25 the original estimates are below all the estimates from the shuffled series.

5.2. *Kolmogorov entropy estimates*

As previously indicated, we calculate the Grassberger and Procaccia (1983b) approximation to the Kolmogorov entropy, denoted K_2. Recall that K_2 measures how strange a time-series is. If a time-series is completely random, then $K_2 = \infty$. Entropy measures the rate at which indistinguishable paths become distinguishable when the system is observed with only some finite level of accuracy. The lower the value of K_2, the more predictable the system is in principle. Our estimate of $K_2 = 0.15 \pm 0.07$. At an embedding dimension of roughly 25, this is similar to a tent map system with dimensionality anywhere from 3 to 6, but lower than a ten-dimensional tent map.

5.3. *Implications for econometric methodology*

The above empirical example illustrates the far-reaching significance that these techniques can have on our understanding of empirical phenomena. Using familiar econometric techniques which concentrate on linear or smooth nonlinear model formulations, we were led to conclude that the martingale hypothesis was validated by the data. In other words, standard parametric econometric techniques were not able to detect any structure in the data. In contrast the correlation dimension and Kolmogorov entropy estimates suggest that there is structure in the data not captured by the usual parametric techniques. In general, this is illustrative of the difference between parametric and nonparametric inference methods. If the true DGP is well approximated by a parametric formulation, then obviously test statistics that look into directions that resemble the DGP (data generating process) formulation will have a lot of power. In that instance, parametric inference is superior. However, in the absence of any clear idea about the DGP formulation and in the case that the latter is fairly complicated, nonparametric techniques may be able to capture characteristics of the data that otherwise would have been totally missed by their parametric counterparts. In our example, the correlation dimension estimates as well as the entropy measure estimate suggest the presence of structure in the data (even if it is fairly complicated).

Recently a number of studies have applied these concepts in economics. Brock and Sayers (1986) and Frank and Stengos (1987b) apply these concepts to the US and Canadian macro-series respectively. In each case the evidence does not appear supportive of chaos. The former study found evidence of nonlinear structure in US employment and unemployment series, the US post war industrial production series and US pig iron production between 1877 and 1937. Sayers (1986) found nonlinearities present in a series of US workstoppage data. Barnett and Chen (1986) report evidence of low dimensionality in some monetary aggregates. Scheinkman and LeBaron (1986) found evidence of chaos for American stocks using CRSP data. Frank and Stengos (1987a) find evidence consistent with chaos in the daily prices of gold and silver on the London market.

6. Conclusion

At times particular branches of mathematics have sparked interest amongst economists. Game theory, catastrophe theory and the theory of fuzzy sets come to mind. In each case, there was some initial excitement due to the potential for constructing theoretical models. In each case, initial excitement dissipated as the new theory turned out not to be a miracle cure. Interest revived in game theory a couple of decades later, and it may yet do so for the other examples. Is chaos likely to follow the same pattern? To some extent the answer is inevitably yes. Initial enthusiasm inevitably grows more temperate as the work gets more difficult. However, we would suggest that chaos is not quite of the same ilk as these others. The reason is that chaos also provides empirical tools. If these empirical tools prove fruitful in unearthing otherwise unsuspected structure in real data, then chaos may be expected to take a permanent place in the box of tools that economists employ.

If this perspective is accepted, then the next question is how likely are chaotic structures to be found in economic time-series? In markets where a great deal of high quality data is available, we believe that the prospects are quite promising. Notable cases are financial markets and foreign exchange markets. Prospects for finding chaotic structures in aggregated time-series appear to be more limited. However, the same basic research programme seems likely to provide a useful check of the functional form assumptions that are so commonly employed in time-series econometrics. In this sense empirical chaos seems likely to find a role in the growing use of nonparametric techniques by econometricians.

If we are correct, chaos may be expected to find a permanent place in economics. It will deepen our understanding of the functioning of some markets. As the research progresses, its range of applicability will probably grow. Chaos asks the economist to deepen the level at which he or she tries to understand economic phenomena. The ultimate hope would be for a complete endogenizing of the error term in economic and econometric models. Chaos will make us less sanguine about tacking Gaussian noise onto our models. The noise term itself requires explanation. This may not constitute a revolution, but we believe that it can prove useful and quite fundamental. At the least, the issues involved are worth some serious thought.

Notes

1. Here n is the number of observations in the auxiliary regression.
2. A metric is a measurement of distance.
3. Our discussion is in discrete time for convenience. For continuous time formulations see Guckenheimer and Holmes (1986).
4. Grebogi *et al.* (1984) have shown that whether an object is fractal is distinct from the question of whether it is chaotic. Their use of terminology is a little different from ours. They use the term 'strange' for what is a dynamic concept, whereas 'fractal' is a geometric concept.
5. Some researchers refer to Lyapunov numbers while others refer to Lyapunov exponents. The Lyapunov exponents are the logarithms of the Lyapunov numbers.
6. This definitional dispute, discussed in Section 3, essentially concerns the best way to define chaos. However, it has often been cast in terms suggesting considerably greater significance than it actually possesses.
7. This section draws heavily on Frank and Stengos (1987a).

References

Abraham, R. and Shaw, C. (1982) *Dynamics: The Geometry of Behavior. Part One: Periodic Behavior. Part Two: Chaotic Behavior*. Aerial Press: Santa Cruz.

Arnold, V. I. (1973) *Ordinary Differential Equations*. Cambridge, Mass: The MIT Press.

Barnett, W. and Chen, P. (1986) The aggregation-theoretic monetary aggregates are chaotic and have strange attractions. In W. Barnett, E. Berndt and H. White (eds) *Dynamic Econometric Modelling*. Cambridge: Cambridge University Press.

Barnett, W. and Choi, S. (1987) A comparison between the conventional econometric approach to structural inference and the nonparametric chaotic attractor approach. In W. Barnett, J. Geweke and K. Shell (eds) *Economic Complexity: Chaos, Sunspots, Bubbles and Nonlinearity*. Cambridge: Cambridge, University Press.

Begg, D. (1984) Rational expectations and bond pricing. *Economic Journal (Supplement)* 94, 45–58.

Benhabib, J. and Day, R. (1980) Erratic accumulation. *Economics Letters* 6, 113–18.
——(1981) Rational choice and erratic behaviour. *Review of Economic Studies* 48, 459–71.
——(1982) A characterization of erratic dynamics in the overlapping generations model. *Journal of Economic Dynamics and Control* 4, 37–55.
Benhabib, J. and Nishimura, K. (1979) The Hopf bifurcation and the existence and stability of closed orbits in multisector models of optimal economic growth. *Journal of Economic Theory* 21, 421–44.
——(1985) Competitive equilibrium cycles. *Journal of Economic Theory* 35, 284–306.
Boldrin, M. and Montrucchio, L. (1986) On the indeterminacy of capital accumulation paths. *Journal of Economic Theory* 40, 26–39.
Brock, W. (1986) Distinguishing random and deterministic systems: abridged version. *Journal of Economic Theory* 40, 168–195.
——(1987) Nonlinearity in finance and economics. Department of Economics, The University of Wisconsin – Madison. Mimeo.
Brock, W. and Dechert, W. D. (1987) Theorems on distinguishing deterministic and random systems. SSRI Working Paper No. 8701, Economics, University of Wisconsin – Madison.
Brock, W., Dechert, W. D. and Scheinkman, J. (1987) A test for independence based on the correlation dimension. SSRI Working Paper No. 8702, Economics, University of Wisconsin – Madison.
Brock, W. and Sayers, C. (1986) Is the business cycle characterized by deterministic chaos?. SSRI Working Paper No. 8617, Economics, University of Wisconsin – Madison.
Broomhead, D. S. and King, G. P. (1986) Extracting qualitative dynamics from experimental data. *Physica D* 20, 217–36.
Burmeister, E. (1980) *Capital Theory and Dynamics*. Cambridge: Cambridge University Press.
Caputo, J. G. and Atten, P. (1987) Metric entropy: an experimental means for characterizing and quantifying chaos. *Physical Review A* 35, 1311, 1316.
Chow, S. N. and Hale, J. D. (1982) *Methods of Bifurcation Theory*. New York: Springer-Verlag.
Cohen, A. and Procaccia, I. (1985) Computing the Kolmagorov entropy from time signals of dissipative and conservative dynamical systems. *Physical Review A* 31, 1872–82.
Collet, P. and Eckmann, J. (1980) *Iterated Maps on the Interval As Dynamical Systems*. Boston: Birkhauser.
Crutchfield, J. P., Farmer, J. D., Packard, N. H. and Shaw, R. S. (1986) Chaos. *Scientific American* 255, 46–57.
Dana, R. A. and Malgrange, P. (1984) The dynamics of a discrete version of a growth cycle model. In J. P. Ancot (ed.) *Analyzing the Structure of Econometric Models*. Amsterdam: Wighoff.
Dana, R. A. and Montrucchio, L. (1986) Dynamic complexity in duopoly games. *Journal of Economic Theory* 40, 40–56.
Day, R. (1982) Irregular growth cycles. *American Economic Review* 72, 406–14.
——(1983) The emergence of chaos from classical economic growth. *Quarterly Journal of Economics* 98, 201–13.
——(1986) Unscrambling the concept of chaos through thick and thin: reply. *Quarterly Journal of Economics* 101, 425–6.
Day, R. and Kim, K-H. (1987) A note on non-periodic demoeconomic fluctuations with positive measure. *Economics Letters* 23, 251–6.
Day, R. and Shafer, W. (1985) Keynesian chaos. *Journal of Macroeconomics* 7, 277–95.
Dechert, D. W. (1984) Does optimal growth preclude chaos? A theorem on monotonicity. *Zeitschrift fur Nationalökonomie* 44, 57–61.

Deneckere, R. and Pelikan, S. (1986) Competitive chaos. *Journal of Economic Theory* 40, 13–25.

Devaney, R. L. (1986) *An Introduction to Chaotic Dynamical Systems.* Menlo Park: Benjamin/Cummings.

Diamond, P. A. (1965) National debt in a neoclassical growth model. *American Economic Review* 55, 1126–50.

Eckmann, J. P. (1981) Roads to turbulence in dissipative dynamical systems. *Reviews of Modern Physics* 53, 643.

Eckmann, J. P. and Procaccia, I. (1986) Fluctuations of dynamical scaling indices in nonlinear systems. *Physical Review A* 34, 659–61.

Eckmann, J. P. and Ruelle D. (1985) Ergodic theory of chaos and strange attractors, *Reviews of Modern Physics* 57, 617–56.

Engle, R. F. (1982) Autoregressive conditional heteroskedasticity with estimates of the variance of U.K. inflation. *Econometrica* 50, 987–1008.

Engle, R. F. and Bollerslev, T. (1986) Modelling the persistence of conditional variances. Discussion Paper 86-9, University of California, San Diego.

Falconer, K. J. (1985) *The Geometry of Fractal Sets.* Cambridge: Cambridge University Press.

Fama, E. (1970) Efficient capital markets: a review of theory and empirical work. *Journal of Finance* 25, 383–417.

Farmer, D. J., Ott, E. and Yorke, J. (1983) The dimension of chaotic attractors. *Physica OD* 7, 153–180.

Farmer, R. (1986) Deficits and cycles. *Journal of Economic Theory* 40, 77–88.

Feigenbaum, M. J. (1978) Quantitative universality for a class of nonlinear transformations. *Journal of Statistical Physics* 19, 25–52.

Frank, M. Z. and Stengos, T. (1987a) Measuring the strangeness of gold and silver rates of return. Mimeo, Economics, University of Guelph.

——(1987b) Some evidence concerning macroeconomic chaos. Discussion Paper No. 1987–2, Economics, University of Guelph.

Gale, D. (1973) Pure exchange equilibrium of dynamic economic models. *Journal of Economic Theory* 6, 12–36.

Glass, L., Guevara, M. R. and Shrier, A. (1983) Bifurcation and chaos in a periodically stimulated cardiac oscillator. *Physica D* 7, 89.

Godfrey, L. G. (1978) Testing for higher order serial correlation in regression equations when the regressors include lagged dependent variables. *Econometrica* 46, 1303–10.

Grandmont, J. M. (1985) On endogenous competitive business cycles. *Econometrica* 50, 1345–70.

——(1986) Stabilizing competitive business cycles. *Journal of Economic Theory*, 40, 57–76.

Grandmont, J. M. and Laroque, G. (1986) Stability of cycles and expectations. *Journal of Economic Theory* 40, 138–51.

Grassberger, P. (1986) Toward a quantitative theory of self-generated complexity. *International Journal of Theoretical Physics* 25, 907–38.

Grassberger, P. and Procaccia, I. (1983a) Measuring the strangeness of strange attractors. *Physica D* 9, 189–208.

——(1983b) Estimation of the Kolmogorov entropy from a chaotic signal. *Physical Review A* 28, 2591–3.

Grebogi, C., Ott, E., Pelikan, S. and Yorke, J. (1984) Strange attractors that are not chaotic. *Physica D* 9, 189–208.

Guckenheimer, J. and Holmes, P. (1986) *Nonlinear Oscillations, Dynamical Systems and Bifurcations of Vector Fields* (second printing). New York: Springer-Verlag.

Haavelmo, T. (1956) *A Study in the Theory of Economic Evolution.* Amsterdam: North-Holland.

Hurewicz, W. and Wallman, H. (1948) *Dimension Theory* (revised edn). Princeton: Princeton University Press.

Jensen, R. V. (1987) Classical chaos. *American Scientist* 75, 168–81.

Kaspar, F. and Schuster, H. G. (1987) Easily calculable measure of complexity of spatiotemporal patterns. *Physical Review A* 36, 842–8.

Kurths, J. and Herzel, H. (1987) An attractor in a solar time series. *Physica D* 25, 165–72.

Lauterborn, W. and Holzfuss, J. (1986) Evidence for a low dimensional strange attractor in acoustic turbulence. *Physics Letters A* 115, 369–72.

Li, T-Y. and Yorke, J. A. (1975) Period three implies chaos. *American Mathematical Monthly* (Dec), 985–92.

Mandelbrot, B. B. (1967) How long is the coast of Britain? Statistical self-similarity and fractional dimension. *Science* 156, 636–8.

——(1982) *The Fractal Geometry of Nature*. New York: W. H. Freeman.

Maskin, E. and Tirole, J. (1986) A theory of dynamic oligopoly, Parts I–III. Harvard Institute of Economic Research, Discussion Paper No. 1270.

May, R. (1976) Simple mathematical models with very complicated dynamics. *Nature* 261, 459–67.

Melese, F. and Transue, W. (1986) Unscrambling chaos through thick and thin. *Quarterly Journal of Economics* 101, 422–4.

——(1987) Unscrambling chaos through thick and thin: an explanation. *Quarterly Journal of Economics* 102, 171.

Neftci, S. (1984) Are economic time series asymmetric over the business cycle? *Journal of Political Economy* 92, 307–28.

Nelson, C. R. and Plosser, C. I. (1982) Trends and random walks in macroeconomic time-series: some evidence and implications. *Journal of Monetary Economics* 10, 139–62.

Nicolis, G. (1986) Dissipative systems. *Reports on Progress in Physics* 49, 873–949.

Oseledec, V. (1968) A multiplicative ergodic theorem: Lyapunov characteristic numbers for dynamical systems. *Transactions Moscow Mathematical Society* 19, 197–231.

Pawelzik, K. and Schuster, H. G. (1987) Generalized dimensions and entropies from a measured time series. *Physical Review A* 35, 481–4.

Petersen, K. (1983) *Ergodic Theory*. Cambridge: Cambridge University Press.

Rand, D. (1978) Exotic phenomena in games and duopoly models. *Journal of Mathematical Economics* 5, 173–84.

Reichlin, P. (1986) Equilibrium cycles in an overlapping generations economy with production. *Journal of Economic Theory* 40, 89–102.

Saari, D. G. (1984) The ultimate of chaos resulting from weighted voting systems. *Advances in Applied Mathematics* 5, 286–308.

——(1985) Iterative price mechanisms. *Econometrica* 53, 1117–32.

Saari, D. G. and Williams, S. R. (1986) On the local convergence of economic mechanisms. *Journal of Economic Theory* 40, 152–67.

Samuelson, P. A. (1965) Proof that properly anticipated prices fluctuate randomly. *Industrial Management Review* 6, 41–9.

Sarkovskii, A. N. (1964) Coexistence of cycles of a continuous map of a line into itself. *Ukrainian Mathematical Zeitung* 16, 61–71.

Sayers, C. (1986) Workstoppages: exploring the nonlinear dynamics. Mimeo, Economics, University of Wisconsin – Madison.

Schaffer, W. M. and Kot, M. (1985) Nearly one dimensional dynamics in an epidemic. *Journal of Theoretical Biology* 112, 403–27.

Scheinkman, J. and LeBaron, B. (1986) Nonlinear dynamics and stock returns. Mimeo, University of Chicago.

Serfling, R. J. (1980) *Approximation Theorems of Mathematical Statistics*. New York: John Wiley.

Steffan, P. (1977) A theorem of Sarkovskii on the existence of periodic points of continuous endomorphisms of the real line. *Communications of Mathematical Physics* 54, 237–48.

Stutzer, M. T. (1980) Chaotic dynamics and bifurcation in a macro-model. *Journal of Economic Dynamics and Control* 2, 253–76.

Swinney, H. (1983) Observations of order and chaos in nonlinear systems. *Physica D* 7, 3–15.

——(1985) Observations of complex dynamics and chaos. In E. G. D. Cohen (ed.) *Fundamental Problems in Statistical Mechanics VI*. New York: Elsevier Science Publishers.

Takens, F. (1981) Detecting strange attractors in turbulence. In D. Rand and L. Young (eds) *Dynamical Systems and Turbulence, Warwick, 1980*. Berlin: Springer-Verlag.

——(1983) Invariants related to dimension and entropy. *Proceedings of the Thirteenth Coloquio Brasileino de Matematica*.

Thom, R. (1975) *Structural Stability and Morphogenesis*. Reading, MA; W. A. Benjamin.

Van der Ploeg, F. (1986) Rational expectations, risk and chaos in financial markets. *Economic Journal (Supplement)* 96, 151–62.

White, H. (1980) A heteroskedasticity-consistent covariance matrix estimator and a direct test for heteroskedasticity. *Econometrica* 48, 817–83.

Wolf, A., Swift, J., Swinney, H. and Vastano, J. (1985) Determining Lyapunov exponents from a time series. *Physica D* 16, 285–317.

Zeeman, E. C. (1977) *Catastrophe Theory: Selected Papers 1972–1977*. Reading, MA: Addison-Wesley.

THE JOURNAL OF FINANCE • VOL. XLVI, NO. 5 • DECEMBER 1991

Chaos and Nonlinear Dynamics:
Application to Financial Markets

DAVID A. HSIEH[*]

ABSTRACT

After the stock market crash of October 19, 1987, interest in nonlinear dynamics, especially deterministic chaotic dynamics, has increased in both the financial press and the academic literature. This has come about because the frequency of large moves in stock markets is greater than would be expected under a normal distribution. There are a number of possible explanations. A popular one is that the stock market is governed by chaotic dynamics. What exactly is chaos and how is it related to nonlinear dynamics? How does one detect chaos? Is there chaos in financial markets? Are there other explanations of the movements of financial prices other than chaos? The purpose of this paper is to explore these issues.

CHAOS HAS CAPTURED THE fancy of many macroeconomists and financial economists. The attractiveness of chaotic dynamics is its ability to generate large movements which appear to be random, with greater frequency than linear models. As a result, there has been an explosion of papers searching for chaotic behavior in macroeconomic and financial time series. The purpose of this paper is to discuss some of the methodological issues in detecting chaotic and nonlinear behavior.

Section I provides a description of the key features of deterministic chaotic systems via a number of examples. Section II shows how deterministic chaos can, in principle, be detected using the method of correlation dimension proposed by Grassberger and Procaccia (1983). Section III deals with some limitations of this method. The Grassberger/Procaccia method requires a substantial number of data points, which is difficult to obtain in standard economic and financial time series. It also lacks a statistical theory for hypothesis testing. A different but related method has been proposed by Brock, Dechert, and Scheinkman (1987). Under the null hypothesis of independence and identical distribution (IID), the Brock, Dechert, and Scheinkman statistic has been shown to have good finite sample properties and good power against departures from IID. Some Monte Carlo evidence is

---

[*] Associate Professor, Fuqua School of Business, Duke University, Durham, NC 27706. The author is grateful to comments from workshop participants at Emory University, the Federal Reserve Bank of Atlanta, University of California at Berkeley, Harvard Business School, and The University of Michigan. The paper has also benefitted greatly from the comments of an anonymous referee.

provided. When applied to stock returns, this statistic rejects the null hypothesis of IID very strongly. The remainder of the paper investigates some of the causes of the rejection of IID: Section IV checks for nonstationarity; Section V, nonlinear conditional mean changes; and Section VI, conditional heteroskedasticity. Some concluding remarks are offered in Section VII.

I. What Is Chaos?

Chaos is a nonlinear deterministic process which "looks" random. There is a very good description of chaos and its origins in the popular book by James Gleick (1987), entitled *Chaos: Making a New Science*. Also, Baumol and Benhabib (1989) gives a good survey of economic models which produce chaotic behavior. Brock (1986) provides the exact mathematical definitions and formulations.

Chaos is interesting for several reasons. In the business cycle literature, there are two ways to generate output fluctuations. In the Box-Jenkins times-series models, the economy has a stable equilibrium, but is constantly being perturbed by external shocks (e.g., wars, weather). The dynamic behavior of the economy comes about as a result of these external shocks. In the chaotic growth models, the economy follows nonlinear dynamics, which are self-generating and never die down. The fact that economic fluctuations can be internally generated has a certain intuitive appeal.

It so happens that chaotic dynamics is necessarily nonlinear, which gives it a second appeal. It is well known that linear models can only generate four types of behavior: oscillatory and stable, oscillatory and explosive, nonoscillatory and stable, and nonoscillatory and explosive. On the other hand, nonlinear models can generate much richer types of behavior. For example, the system can have sudden bursts of volatility and occasional large movements. This has caught the attention of the financial press. Stock market analysts are always looking for explanations of large movements in asset prices, such as the October 19, 1987 stock market crash.

To get some ideas about the behavior of chaotic processes, we can consider several examples.

A. Tent Map

The simplest chaotic process is the tent map. Pick a number x_0 between 0 and 1. Then generate the sequence of numbers x_t using the following rule:

$$x_t = 2x_{t-1}, \quad \text{if } x_{t-1} < 0.5,$$
$$x_t = 2(1 - x_{t-1}), \quad \text{if } x_{t-1} \geq 0.5. \tag{1}$$

The tent map is so named because the graph of x_t versus x_{t-1} is shaped like a "tent", as shown in Figure 1. Note that x_t is a *nonlinear* function of x_{t-1}.

Intuitively, the tent map takes the interval [0, 1], stretches it to twice the length, and folds it in half, as illustrated in Figure 2. Repeated application of

Chaos and Nonlinear Dynamics   1841

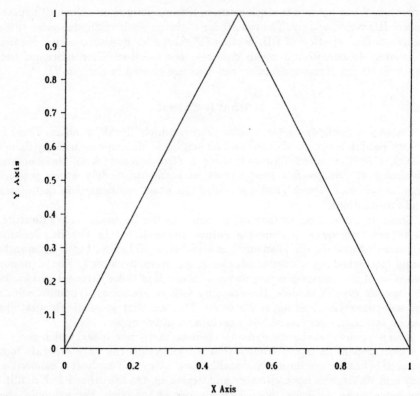

X Axis

Figure 1. The tent map. The tent map is the graph of the function $y = 2x$ if $x < 0.5$ and $y = 2(1 - x)$ if $x \geq 0.5$, where x is the horizontal axis and y is the vertical axis.

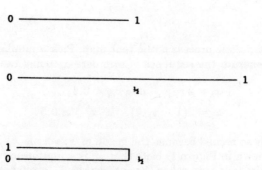

Figure 2. Stretch and fold action of the tent map. The tent map takes the unit interval [0,1], stretches it twice as long, and folds it back onto itself.

stretching and folding pulls apart points close to each other. This type of stretching and folding is characteristic of chaotic maps. It makes prediction difficult, thus creating the illusion of randomness.

There are four important properties of the tent map. One, $\{x_t\}$ fills up the unit interval [0, 1] uniformly as $t \to \infty$. Technically, this means that the fraction of points in $\{x_t\}$ falling into an interval [a, b] is (b − a) for any $0 < a < b < 1$. Two, any small error in measuring the initial x_0 will be compounded in forecasts of x_t exponentially fast. Three, x_t appears stochastic even though it is a deterministic process, in the sense that the empirical autocovariance function $\rho_{xx}(k) = E[x_t x_{t-k}] = \lim_{T \to \infty} \sum_{t=0}^{\infty} x_t x_{t-k} / T = 0$, which is the same as that of white noise. Four, x_t can have a series of small increases, and then it suddenly declines ("crashes?") sharply.

B. Pseudo Random Number Generators

A more "random" chaotic system can be obtained using the ideas of the tent map. Here is an example of a pseudo random number generator, which is very frequently used in computer programs. Take a number A (say 7^5) and a large prime number P (say $2^{32} - 1$). Pick any integer z_0, called a "seed," between 0 and P. Generate new seeds using the following rule:

$$z_t = Az_{t-1} \,(\text{mod } P), \tag{2}$$

where the notation "x (mod y)" means "the remainder of x when divided by y." Generate the sequence:

$$x_t = z_t / P. \tag{3}$$

Then x_t is "uniformly distributed" on the interval [0, 1], in the same way as is the tent map.

It turns out that this method creates pseudo random numbers which are much more "random-looking" than the tent map. This pseudo random number generator can be related to the tent map as follows. First, we modify the "tent" pattern in Figure 1 to the "diadic map" in Figure 3. This changes the "stretch and fold" action of the tent map to "stretch, cut, and stack," as illustrated in Figure 4. Second, we increase the number of teeth from two to 7^5. By this time, the graph of this map appears to "fill up" the space in the unit square, and is the reason why it appears to be much more random.

C. Logistic Map

Other chaotic maps are frequently mentioned. The logistic map is slightly more complex than the tent map. Again, select x_0 between 0 and 1, and generate the sequence of x_t according to:

$$x_t = Ax_{t-1}(1 - x_{t-1}), \tag{4}$$

where A is between 0 and 4. For small values of A, the system is stable and well behaved. But as the value of A approaches 4, the system becomes

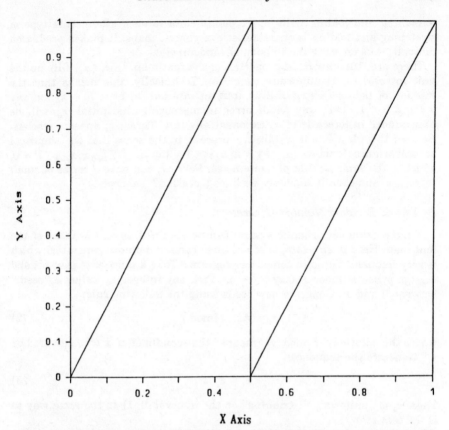

Figure 3. The diadic map. The diadic map is the graph of the function $y = 2x$ if $x < 0.5$, and $y = 2(x - 0.5)$ if $x \geq 0.5$, where x is the horizontal axis and y is the vertical axis.

chaotic. The logistic map adds a fifth property to chaotic behavior, that the dynamics of a system depends on a parameter (A in this case). For some values of the parameter, the dynamics may be simple, while for other values, the dynamics may be chaotic.

D. Hénon Map

Both the tent map and the logistic map are univariate chaotic systems. The Hénon (1976) map is a bivariate chaotic system, described by a pair of difference equations:

$$x_t = y_{t-1} + 1 - Ax_{t-1}^2, \quad A = 1.4$$
$$y_t = Bx_{t-1}, \quad B = 0.3. \tag{5}$$

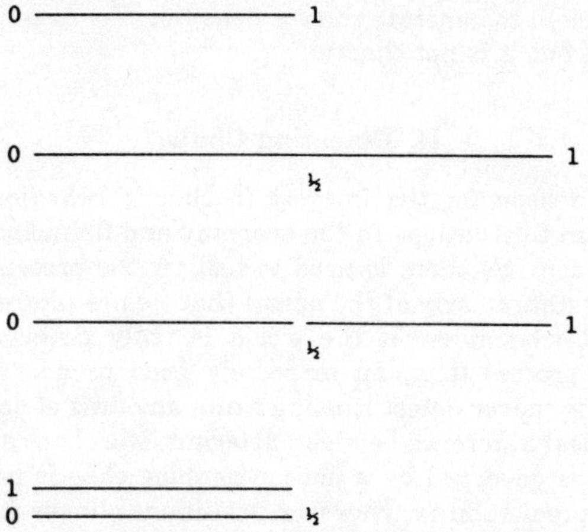

1844 *The Journal of Finance*

0 ——————————— 1

0 ————————————————— 1
½

0 ——————————— ———————— 1
½

1 ——————————
0 ——————————— ½

Figure 4. Stretch, cut, and stack action of the diadice map. The diadic map takes the unit interval [0,1], stretches it twice as long, cuts it in the middle, and stacks one piece on top of the other.

E. Lorenz Map

The Lorenz (1963) map is a trivariate chaotic system. Notice that it is a system of differential equations, rather than difference equations.

$$\dot{x} = a(y - x), \qquad a = 10,$$
$$\dot{y} = -y - xz - bx, \quad b = 28,$$
$$\dot{z} = xy - cz, \qquad c = 8/3. \tag{6}$$

F. Mackey-Glass Equation

The above chaotic maps generate "low dimensional" chaos, which means that the nonlinear structure is easily detected, as we shall show later. There are, however, "high dimensional" chaotic systems which are much harder to detect, such as that in Mackey and Glass (1977). The Mackey-Glass equation is a delayed differential equation, given by:

$$\dot{x}(t) = \frac{ax(t - c)}{1 + x(t - c)^{10}} - bx(t) \quad a = 0.2, b = 0.1, c = 100. \tag{7}$$

G. General Chaotic Maps

There are many more examples of chaotic maps. In general, chaotic maps are obtained by a deterministic rule:

$$x_t = f(x_{t-1}, x_{t-2} \dots). \tag{8}$$

Here, x_t can either be a scalar or a vector. In order to generate chaotic behavior, $f()$ must be a nonlinear function. Note, however, that nonlinearity

Chaos and Nonlinear Dynamics   1845

alone is not sufficient to generate chaotic behavior. For example, $f(x) = x^3$ is a nonlinear map, but it is not chaotic.

II. Detecting Chaos

An important reason for the interest in chaotic behavior is that it can potentially explain fluctuations in the economy and financial markets which appear to be random. So there is need to test for the presence of chaos. We should, however, state clearly at the outset that we are interested only in low complexity chaotic behavior. If the world is truly governed by a highly complex chaotic process (e.g., an extremely good pseudo random number generator), we may never detect it using finite amounts of data. In this case, there is no practical difference between deterministic chaos and randomness. But if the world is governed by a not-too-complex chaotic process, it should have short-term predictability. However, traditional linear forecasting methods would not work; nonlinear models must be used.

How then can one test for low complexity chaos? Suppose we have a string of data, $x_1, x_2, \cdots, x_t, \cdots, x_T$. One method is to observe that chaotic maps do not "fill up" enough space in high dimension. To make this concrete, consider two sets of data: a_t is generated by the tent map, and b_t is a random variable which is uniform on the interval $[0, 1]$. If we plot a_t in one dimension, it is uniform over $[0, 1]$, and so it fills up as much space as does b_t. However, consider the 2-vectors (a_{t-1}, a_t) and (b_{t-1}, b_t). If we plot them in two dimensions, the data from the tent map will fall on the tent, while the data from the uniform random variable will fall uniformly in the unit square $[0, 1] \times [0, 1]$. In other words, data from the tent map leave large "holes" in two dimensional space, while the random data do not.

When the chaotic process becomes more complex, we need to look at the data in higher dimensions. A chaotic process can fill up the first n dimensions, but leave large "holes" in the $(n + 1)$st dimension. Clearly it is not practical to do this type of graphical exercise in higher dimensions. Grassberger and Procaccia (1983) therefore developed the notion of correlation dimension. This is done in four steps.

Step 1: Remove autocorrelation, if present. Autocorrelation can affect some tests for chaos, so that we must remove it from the data. This is typically done by filtering the raw data using an autoregression, where the lag length is selected based on either the Akaike (1974) or Schwarz (1978) information criterion.

Step 2: From n-histories of the filtered data. These are denoted as follows:

$$1\text{-history: } x_t^1 = x_t.$$
$$2\text{-history: } x_t^2 = (x_{t-1}, x_t).$$
$$\vdots$$
$$n\text{-history: } x_t^n = (x_{t-n+1}, \cdots, x_t). \tag{9}$$

An n-history is a point in n-dimensional space; n is called the "imbedding dimension."

Step 3: Calculate the correlation integral:

$$C_n(\epsilon) = \lim_{T \to \infty} \# \left\{ (t, s), 0 < t, s, < T : \| x_t^n - x_s^n \| < \epsilon \right\} / T^2, \quad (10)$$

where $\| \quad \|$ is the sup- or max- norm. In words, the correlation integral, $C_n(\epsilon)$, is defined as the fraction of pairs, (x_s^n, x_t^n), which are "close" to each other, in the sense that:

$$\max_{i=0,\cdots,n-1} \left\{ | x_{s-i} - x_{t-i} | \right\} < \epsilon.$$

Step 4: Calculate the slope of the graph of $\log C_n(\epsilon)$ versus $\log \epsilon$ for small values of ϵ. More precisely, we want to calculate the following quantity:

$$v_n = \lim_{\epsilon \to 0} \log C_n(\epsilon) / \log \epsilon. \quad (11)$$

If v_n does not increase with n, the data are consistent with chaotic behavior. In fact, the Grassberger-Procaccia correlation dimension is defined as:

$$v = \lim_{n \to \infty} v_n. \quad (12)$$

The meaning of the correlation dimension becomes clear when we consider the tent map. Since the tent map is uniformly distributed on the interval [0, 1], $C_1(\epsilon)$ doubles if ϵ doubles. Thus, for small values of ϵ,

$$v_1 = \log C_1(\epsilon) / \log \epsilon = 1. \quad (13)$$

But the 2-histories do not fill up the unit square $[0, 1] \times [0, 1]$. In fact, all the points fall on the tent. For small values of ϵ, $C_2(\epsilon)$ doubles if ϵ doubles, and so

$$v_2 = \log C_2(\epsilon) / \log \epsilon = 1. \quad (14)$$

This continues to be true for any n, i.e.,

$$v_n = \log C_n(\epsilon) / \log \epsilon = 1. \quad (15)$$

So, for the tent map, the correlation dimension, v, is 1.

Next, apply this to data generated from the random variable uniformly distributed on the interval [0, 1]. Again, we would find that $C_1(\epsilon)$ doubles if ϵ doubles, so

$$v_1 = \log C_1(\epsilon) / \log \epsilon = 1. \quad (16)$$

However, since the 2-histories will uniformly fill up the unit square $[0, 1] \times [0, 1]$, $C_2(\epsilon)$ quadruples if ϵ doubles, and so

$$v_2 = \log C_2(\epsilon) / \log \epsilon = 2. \quad (17)$$

In fact,

$$v_n = \log C_n(\epsilon) / \log \epsilon = n. \quad (18)$$

For the random process, the correlation dimension, v, is ∞.

## Chaos and Nonlinear Dynamics					1847

Using this method, Grassberger and Procaccia (1983) determine the correlation dimensions for the following chaotic systems: the logistic map, 1.00 ± 0.02, the Hénon map, 1.22 ± 0.01, the Lorenz map, 2.05 ± 0.01, and the Mackey-Glass equation, 7.50 ± 0.15. This shows that the chaotic maps do not fill up enough space at a sufficiently high imbedding dimension, which is a generic property of chaotic processes.[1]

It is important to remember that the correlation dimension is a measure of how much space is "filled up" by a string of data. That is why correlation dimensions need not be whole integers. We also need to point out that the correlation dimension is in no way related to the number of "independent factors" driving a system. To appreciate this point, note that the Mackey-Glass is a univariate process which has a correlation dimension around 7.

In principle, the four-step procedure to estimate correlation dimension sounds straightforward, and has been applied by scientists in many problems. In practice, however, a number of issues surface when dealing with economic and financial data. We shall discuss them in the context of the stock market.

III. What Do We Find in the Stock Market?

Scheinkman and LeBaron (1989) used the Grassberger-Procaccia plots and calculated the correlation dimension of weekly stock returns. They found that the slope of $\log C_n(\epsilon)$ versus $\log \epsilon$ appears to be around 6, even for dimensions as high as 25. They, however, noted that this is not sufficient evidence of chaos in stock returns, because there are a number of problems with this graphical procedure.

First, Scheinkman and LeBaron (1989) pointed out that some nonlinear stochastic model, such as Engle's (1982) autoregressive conditional heteroskedasticity (ARCH) model, exhibit "dependence" similar to that of chaotic maps. Using data from the ARCH model, they showed that the slopes of the graphs of $\log_n C(\epsilon)$ versus $\log \epsilon$ increase at a rate slower than n.

Second, there is no way to verify that a process has an infinite correlation dimension using a finite amount of data. Scientists typically use 100,000 or more data points to detect low dimensional chaotic system. Financial economists have substantially fewer points. The largest data sets generally have 2,000 observations. If we use the imbedding dimension of 10, we have only 200 nonoverlapping 10-histories. It is very hard to say whether 200 10-histories "fill up" a 10-dimensional space.

Third, we have to worry about biases in small data sets. Ramsey and Yuan (1989) show that the slope of the graph of $\log C_n(\epsilon)$ versus $\log \epsilon$ is biased downward in small data sets (even with as many as 2,000 observations). This biases the results in favor of finding chaos, even if there is none.

Fourth, the graphical procedure is not a statistical test. Ideally, we want a way to quantify the accuracy of the correlation dimension. This is not readily

[1] See the discussion in Brock (1986) and the proof in Takens (1980).

available for the correlation dimension plots, so we adopt a different method proposed by Brock, Dechert, and Scheinkman (1987).[2]

Before proceeding further, we digress here to deal with the naive view that there is no data limitation in finance since data are available at the tick by tick frequency. But this is merely an illusion. Tick by tick data capture bid-ask bounces and other dependencies which are caused by the micromarket structure, such as the sequential execution of limit orders on the books of the specialist as the market moves through those limit prices. These "artificial" dependencies will be picked up by any good test of nonlinear dynamics. The financial economist must increase the sampling interval in order to average out these "artificial" dependencies. Now, in order to obtain more observations, the researcher must look at longer histories, which runs into an entirely different problem. As one extends a data-set further and further back in time, nonstationarity (e.g., an unpredictable regime change) becomes increasingly more likely. As we shall see below, tests of nonlinear dynamics will detect nonstationarity. Thus, the requirements of long sampling intervals (to avoid micromarket structure dependencies) and short histories (to avoid nonstationarity) impose severe data limitations in finance. We now return from this digression to the Brock, Dechert, and Scheinkman (1987) statistic.

A. Statistical Test: The BDS Statistic

To deal with the problems of using the Grassberger-Procaccia plots, Brock, Dechert, and Scheinkman (1987) devised a statistical test. If $\{x_t: t = 1, \cdots, T\}$ is a random sample of independent and identically distributed (IID) observations, then:

$$C_n(\epsilon) = C_1(\epsilon)^n. \tag{19}$$

One can estimate $C_1(\epsilon)$ and $C_n(\epsilon)$ by the usual sample versions $C_{1,T}(\epsilon)$ and $C_{n,T}(\epsilon)$, and show that:

$$W_{n,T}(\epsilon) = \sqrt{T}\left[C_{n,T}(\epsilon) - C_{1,T}(\epsilon)^n\right]/\sigma_{n,T}(\epsilon) \tag{20}$$

has a limiting standard normal distribution. Here, $\sigma_{n,T}(\epsilon)$ is an estimate of the asymptotic standard error of $[C_{n,T}(\epsilon) - C_{1,T}(\epsilon)^n]$. We shall refer to $W_{n,T}(\epsilon)$ as the BDS statistic.

Note that the statement $C_n(\epsilon) = C_1(\epsilon)^n$ does not imply IID. Dechert (1988) has several counter examples.

Since the BDS statistic is a relatively new procedure, it is useful to study its finite sample distribution using Monte Carlo simulations. Some of them

---

[2] Denker and Keller (1986) and Brock and Baek (1991) provide ways to do this.

were reported in Hsieh and LeBaron (1988). The first set of results measure how well the asymptotic distribution approximates the finite sample distribution of the BDS statistic. We generate 1,000 IID observations (using a good pseudo random number generator), apply the BDS test, and repeat this 2,000 times. If we use a 5% significance level, we should reject 5% of the replications. Table I shows that the asymptotic distribution of the BDS test at dimension two is a reasonable approximation for IID data from four distributions (standard normal, Student t with 3 degrees of freedom, chi-square with 4 degrees of freedom, and Cauchy), when ϵ is set between one half to two standard deviations of the data. These distributions were selected for the following reasons: the standard normal is the base case; the Student t and the Cauchy have very fat tails; and the chi-square is strongly skewed. We also added two unusual distributions: the uniform and the bimodal, for which the asymptotic distribution of the BDS does not seem to fit the finite sample distribution. Fortunately, very little financial data look like these two distributions. Similar results are obtained for dimension five in Table II. We conclude that the BDS test avoids the biases of the correlation dimension estimates.

In the second set of simulations, we measure the ability of the BDS statistic to detect departures from IID. Given that there are uncountable ways to generate non-IID data, we select models which are interesting alternatives, and report the results in Table III.

The first two models represent time-series data with linear dependence. The AR1 is the first order autoregressive model, given by:

$$x_t = \rho x_{t-1} + u_t. \tag{21}$$

The MA1 is the first order moving average model, given by:

$$x_t = \theta u_{t-1} + u_t. \tag{22}$$

In the simulations, u_t is IID standard normal, $\rho = 0.5$, and $\theta = 0.5$. The point we wish to make here is that the BDS test can detect linear dependence easily. To employ BDS as a test for nonlinearity (whether chaotic or stochastic), we must remove any linear dependence in the data.[3]

The next two models represent data which violate the assumptions of strict stationarity and ergodicity. In the "2-mean" model, the data are independent and normally distributed, where the first 500 observations have mean -1 and variance 1, and the second 500 observations have mean $+1$ and variance

---

[3] It is not surprising to find that the BDS test has low power against the AR1 when ρ is small, say less than 0.2. If one is concerned about detecting linear dependence, it is best to use a test optimized for that alternative, such as the Durbin-Watson test, along with the BDS test. Since we are interested primarily in nonlinear dependence, we will just use a linear filter to remove any serial correlation.

Table I

Simulated Size of the BDS Statistic for Dimension 2

This table provides the percentage of BDS statistics (at dimension 2, ϵ equaling 0.25, 0.5, 1, 1.5, and 2 times the standard deviation of the data) rejecting the IID null hypothesis when it is true. The Monte Carlo simulation uses 2000 replications, each having 1000 observations, for six distributions: the standard normal, the Student t with 3 degrees of freedom, the chi-square with 4 degrees of freedom, the Cauchy, the uniform, and the bimodal distribution. $N(0, 1)$ denotes the percentage for a standard normal distribution.

	ϵ/σ					
	0.25	0.50	1.00	1.50	2.00	$N(0, 1)$
Standard normal						
% < −2.33	4.65	1.40	1.05	0.90	0.80	1.00
% < −1.96	8.95	3.25	2.90	2.45	2.65	2.50
% > 1.96	6.30	3.70	2.25	2.40	2.50	2.50
% > 2.33	3.60	1.55	0.90	0.70	0.90	1.00
$t(3)$						
% < −2.33	1.25	0.65	0.85	0.50	0.40	1.00
% < −1.96	3.25	2.50	2.20	2.05	1.20	2.50
% > 1.96	4.15	3.10	2.80	3.20	3.55	2.50
% > 2.33	1.90	1.50	1.10	1.45	1.80	1.00
$\chi^2(4)$						
% < −2.33	1.65	0.90	1.10	1.20	1.10	1.00
% < −1.96	5.00	3.05	3.00	3.35	2.45	2.50
% > 1.96	5.05	3.80	3.85	3.90	3.70	2.50
% > 2.33	3.25	2.10	1.90	1.65	2.15	1.00
Cauchy						
% < −2.33	0.40	0.35	0.45	0.70	0.75	1.00
% < −1.96	1.70	0.80	1.00	1.15	0.90	2.50
% > 1.96	4.30	4.75	4.75	4.55	4.90	2.50
% > 2.33	2.30	2.85	3.30	3.35	3.55	1.00
Uniform						
% < −2.33	44.95	21.75	1.45	1.40	1.40	1.00
% < −1.96	46.05	26.60	3.60	3.00	3.15	2.50
% > 1.96	42.45	24.30	5.05	2.85	2.85	2.50
% > 2.33	41.40	21.80	3.10	1.30	1.25	1.00
Bimodal						
% < −2.33	2.30	2.55	52.70	1.40	1.10	1.00
% < −1.96	5.45	5.00	54.70	3.85	3.10	2.50
% > 1.96	6.45	5.75	29.20	3.85	3.05	2.50
% > 2.33	3.45	3.05	28.10	2.05	1.40	1.00

Note: Approximate standard error is 1.12 for these probabilities.

1. In the "2-variance" model, the data are also independent and normally distributed, where the first 500 observations have mean 0 and variance 1, and the second 500 observations have mean 0 and variance 2. These models are examples of "structural changes" or "regime changes." Table III shows that BDS also has no trouble in detecting them.

Table II
Simulated Size of the BDS Statistic for Dimension 5

This table provides the percentage of BDS statistics (at dimension 5, ϵ equaling 0.25, 0.5, 1, 1.5, and 2 times the standard deviation of the data) rejecting the IID null hypothesis when it is true. The Monte Carlo simulation uses 2000 replications, each having 1000 observations, for six distributions: the standard normal, the Student t with 3 degrees of freedom, the chi-square with 4 degrees of freedom, the Cauchy, the uniform, and the bimodal distribution. $N(0, 1)$ denotes the percentage for a standard normal distribution.

| | | \(\epsilon/\sigma\) | | | | |
		0.25	0.50	1.00	1.50	2.00	$N(0, 1)$
Standard normal							
% <	−2.33	29.85	3.60	0.55	0.80	0.75	1.00
% <	−1.96	32.75	7.40	2.35	2.35	2.55	2.50
% >	1.96	29.65	8.15	2.90	2.40	2.50	2.50
% >	2.33	26.95	5.30	1.40	1.10	1.30	1.00
$t(3)$							
% <	−2.33	6.05	0.70	0.70	0.85	0.60	1.00
% <	−1.96	9.55	2.25	2.30	2.55	2.50	2.50
% >	1.96	11.00	4.20	3.10	3.50	3.55	2.50
% >	2.33	7.55	2.25	1.95	1.70	1.60	1.00
$\chi^2(4)$							
% <	−2.33	16.15	0.95	0.85	0.85	1.00	1.00
% <	−1.96	20.65	3.45	2.30	2.25	2.30	2.50
% >	1.96	19.20	5.30	3.45	3.30	3.00	2.50
% >	2.33	15.40	2.95	1.75	1.25	1.50	1.00
Cauchy							
% <	−2.33	0.70	0.55	0.90	0.85	1.20	1.00
% <	−1.96	2.00	1.70	1.90	1.45	1.40	2.50
% >	1.96	3.50	3.80	4.40	4.75	4.50	2.50
% >	2.33	1.35	1.90	3.10	3.30	3.00	1.00
Uniform							
% <	−2.33	49.20	35.50	4.05	1.50	1.30	1.00
% <	−1.96	49.60	37.40	7.55	3.00	2.95	2.50
% >	1.96	48.05	38.50	6.85	3.75	3.40	2.50
% >	2.33	47.90	36.85	4.30	1.55	1.25	1.00
Bimodal							
% <	−2.33	15.45	7.25	46.00	2.50	1.45	1.00
% <	−1.96	20.00	10.80	47.20	5.70	3.30	2.50
% >	1.96	17.85	10.25	41.05	5.30	2.70	2.50
% >	2.33	13.65	6.85	39.95	2.80	1.40	1.00

Note: Approximate standard error is 1.12 for these probabilities.

We consider two nonlinear time-series models which have no autocorrelation but non-zero conditional means. Robinson (1977) proposed the nonlinear moving average (NMA) model:

$$x_t = u_t + \alpha u_{t-1} u_{t-2}, \qquad (23)$$

The Journal of Finance

Table III

Simulated Power of the BDS Statistic

This table provides the percentage of BDS statistics (at dimensions 2 through 5, ϵ equaling 0.5, 1, 1.5, and 2 times the standard deviation of the data) rejecting the IID null hypothesis when it is false. The Monte Carlo simulation uses 2000 replications, each having 1000 observations, for 11 non-IID alternatives: the first order autoregression (AR1), the first order moving average (MA1), the '2-mean' model (the first 500 observations have mean −1 and variance 1, the second 500 observations have mean 1 and variance 1), the '2-variance' model (the first 500 observations have mean 0 and variance 1, the second 500 observations have mean 0 and variance 2), the nonlinear moving average (NMA), the threshold autoregression (TAR), the autoregressive conditional heteroskedasticity (ARCH) model, the generalized autoregressive conditional heteroskedasticity (GARCH) model, the exponential generalized autoregressive conditional heteroskedasticity (EGARCH) model, the Mackey-Glass data filtered by an autoregression of order 3, and the "Sine" model.

		ϵ/σ			
	m	0.50	1.00	1.50	2.00
AR1	2	100.00	100.00	100.00	100.00
	3	100.00	100.00	100.00	100.00
	4	100.00	100.00	100.00	100.00
	5	100.00	100.00	100.00	100.00
MA1	2	100.00	100.00	100.00	100.00
	3	100.00	100.00	100.00	100.00
	4	99.95	100.00	100.00	100.00
	5	99.95	100.00	100.00	100.00
2-mean	2	100.00	100.00	100.00	100.00
	3	100.00	100.00	100.00	100.00
	4	100.00	100.00	100.00	100.00
	5	100.00	100.00	100.00	100.00
2-variance	2	98.75	98.30	98.10	92.65
	3	99.00	100.00	99.95	99.80
	4	100.00	100.00	99.95	100.00
	5	100.00	100.00	99.95	100.00
NMA	2	99.95	100.00	100.00	100.00
	3	100.00	100.00	100.00	100.00
	4	100.00	100.00	100.00	100.00
	5	100.00	100.00	100.00	100.00
TAR	2	99.95	99.40	91.20	62.85
	3	99.90	98.80	89.20	61.75
	4	99.30	96.95	84.25	56.65
	5	97.30	94.50	78.00	49.10
ARCH	2	100.00	100.00	100.00	100.00
	3	100.00	100.00	100.00	100.00
	4	100.00	100.00	100.00	100.00
	5	100.00	100.00	100.00	100.00
GARCH	2	74.60	78.05	81.80	82.10
	3	88.10	91.80	93.85	94.35
	4	92.25	95.65	96.95	97.30
	5	93.50	97.05	97.75	98.25

Table III—*Continued*

	m	ϵ/σ			
		0.50	1.00	1.50	2.00
EGARCH	2	22.50	21.20	20.90	20.15
	3	32.05	31.10	30.15	28.65
	4	38.50	36.40	34.30	33.20
	5	43.10	39.85	37.70	36.65
Mackey-	2	100.00	100.00	100.00	100.00
Glass	3	100.00	100.00	100.00	100.00
	4	100.00	100.00	100.00	100.00
	5	100.00	100.00	100.00	100.00
Sine	2	100.00	100.00	100.00	100.00
	3	100.00	100.00	100.00	100.00
	4	100.00	100.00	100.00	100.00
	5	100.00	100.00	100.00	100.00

where u_t is IID standard normal.[4] In the simulations, $\alpha = 0.5$. The other nonlinear time-series model is the threshold autoregressive (TAR) model in Tong and Lim (1980):

$$x_t = \alpha x_{t-1} + u_t, \quad \text{if } x_{t-1} < 1,$$
$$x_t = \beta x_{t-1} + u_t, \quad \text{if } x_{t-1} \geq 1, \tag{24}$$

where u_t is IID standard normal. In the simulations, $\alpha = -0.4$ and $\beta = 0.5$. Table III shows that BDS can detect the nonlinearity in both the NMA and the TAR.

Next, we examine nonlinear time-series models, with no autocorrelation and zero conditional means, that exhibit conditional heteroskedasticity. As discussed earlier, Engle (1982) presented the autoregressive conditional heteroskedasticity (ARCH) model:

$$x_t = \sigma_t u_t,$$
$$\sigma_t^2 = \phi_0 + \phi x_{t-1}^2. \tag{25}$$

In our simulations, $\phi_0 = 1$ and $\phi_1 = 0.5$. Bollerslev (1986) turned ARCH into Generalized ARCH (GARCH) by making σ_t a function of its own past:

$$\sigma_t^2 = \phi_0 + \phi x_{t-1}^2 + \psi \sigma_{t-1}^2. \tag{26}$$

In our simulations, $\phi_0 = 1$ and $\phi = 0.1$, and $\psi = 0.8$. Nelson (1991) changed GARCH into exponential GARCH (EGARCH) by using $\log \sigma_t^2$ instead of σ_t^2.

$$\log \sigma_t^2 = \phi_0 + \phi | x_{t-1}/\sigma_{t-1} | + \psi \log \sigma_{t-1}^2 + \gamma x_{t-1}/\sigma_{t-1}. \tag{27}$$

---

[4] The nonlinear moving average is very similar to the bilinear model in Granger and Andersen (1978).

In our simulations, $\phi_0 = 1$ and $\phi = .1$, $\psi = .8$, and $\gamma = 0.1$. Unlike simple ARCH and GARCH, EGARCH is able to capture asymmetric response of the variance to the direction of x_t, e.g., a higher variance when x_t is negative, and a lower variance when x_t is positive, a phenomenon noted by Black (1976). We refer to all three as "ARCH-type" models. These models have enjoyed a great deal of attention in the econometric literature, particularly in applications to financial time series.[5] Table III shows that BDS can easily detect the simple ARCH and GARCH models, but has trouble detecting EGARCH.

For a chaotic (i.e., nonlinear deterministic) process, we use the Mackey-Glass equation. The results for the tent map, logistic map, and Hénon maps are similar, and available upon request. The Mackey-Glass is chosen, because it has the highest correlation dimension (7.5) among this group of chaotic processes, making it the most difficult to detect. In addition, its correlation dimension is similar to that of weekly stock returns as measured by Scheinkman and LeBaron (1989). To remove any evidence of linear dependence, we filter the data using an autoregression with three lags. Table III shows that BDS has no trouble in picking up the nonlinear dependence in the (filtered) Mackey-Glass data. (We will discuss the "sine" model later.)

The third set of simulation addresses the issue of "nuisance" parameters. We have already pointed out that we must remove any linear dependence from our data before applying the BDS test for nonlinearity. The question is: will linear filtering change either the asymptotic or the finite sample distribution of the test statistic? Brock (1987) proves that the asymptotic distribution of the BDS test is not altered by using residuals instead of raw data in linear models. In fact, Brock's theorem can be extended to residuals of some nonlinear models (such as the nonlinear moving average), but not to ARCH models. This is confirmed by the simulations in Table IV. The results show that the asymptotic distribution still approximates the finite sample distribution with the same degree of accuracy even when replacing raw data with residuals of the AR1, the MA1, and the NMA. The results also show that the BDS test may reject too infrequently in the case of standardized residuals from GARCH and EGARCH models.

B. Application to Stock Returns

We now apply the BDS test of IID to stock market returns. Our data are weekly stock returns provided by Peter Rossi using the data from the Center for Research in Securities Prices (CRSP) at the University of Chicago, beginning in 1963 and ending in 1987. These data have been carefully constructed to include dividends as well as capital gains, and they have also been made into different portfolios. We examine a value-weighted index (VW) and an equally weighted index (EW).[6] In addition, we use ten value-

---

[5] See the survey article by Bollerslev et al. (1990).

[6] We also examined the value and equally weighted indices in excess of a Treasury bill return. The results did not differ from the raw indices, and so were not reported.

Table IV
Simulated Size of the BDS Statistics for Residuals

This table provides the percentage of BDS statistics (at dimensions 2, ϵ equaling 0.5, 1.0, 1.5, and 2 times the standard deviation of the data) rejecting the IID null hypothesis when applied to residuals. The Monte Carlo simulation uses 2000 replications, each having 1000 observations, for data generated by 5 non-IID models: the first order autoregression (AR1), the first order moving average (MA1), the nonlinear moving average (NMA), the generalized autoregressive conditional heteroskedasticity (GARCH) model, and the exponential generalized autoregressive conditional heteroskedasticity (EGARCH) model. $N(0, 1)$ denotes the percentage for a standard normal distribution.

	ϵ/σ				
	0.50	1.00	1.50	2.00	$N(0, 1)$
AR1 residuals ($\rho = 0.5$)					
% < −2.33	1.20	1.10	1.15	1.20	1.00
% < −1.96	3.25	2.90	2.60	2.65	2.50
% > 1.96	4.50	3.25	3.25	3.70	2.50
% > 2.33	1.90	1.65	1.20	1.50	1.00
MA1 residuals ($\theta = 0.5$)					
% < −2.33	1.30	1.00	1.25	1.20	1.00
% < −1.96	3.10	2.65	2.60	3.05	2.50
% > 1.96	4.40	3.20	3.30	3.75	2.50
% > 2.33	1.90	1.70	1.30	1.50	1.00
NMA residuals ($\alpha = 0.05$)					
% < −2.33	1.60	1.10	1.25	1.00	1.00
% < −1.96	3.75	2.70	2.90	3.00	2.50
% > 1.96	4.40	3.25	3.50	3.75	2.50
% > 2.33	2.05	1.70	1.65	1.95	1.00
GARCH standardized residuals ($\phi = 0.1$, $\psi = 0.8$)					
% < −2.33	0.40	0.30	0.20	0.25	1.00
% < −1.96	1.55	0.95	0.80	0.95	2.50
% > 1.96	1.80	1.15	0.80	0.45	2.50
% > 2.33	0.90	0.20	0.10	0.05	1.00
EGARCH standardized residuals ($\phi = 0.1$, $\psi = 0.8$)					
% < −2.33	0.20	0.00	0.00	0.05	1.00
% < −1.96	0.80	0.40	0.25	0.40	2.50
% > 1.96	3.35	2.50	1.85	1.95	2.50
% > 2.33	1.75	0.90	0.85	0.55	1.00

weighted decile portfolios in which firms are ranked by size every quarter. Results are reported for the first (smallest), fifth, and tenth (largest) decile portfolios, called DEC1, DEC5, and DEC10.[7] All data were first filtered by an autoregression whose lag length was determined by the Akaike (1974) information criterion.[8]

---

[7] The results are the same using equally weighted decile portfolios.

[8] The Schwarz (1978) information criterion was also used. The lags identified by the Akaike (Schwarz) information criterion are: VW 1 (1), EW 2 (1), DEC1 7 (1), DEC5 2 (1), DEC10 1 (0). Since there are large numbers of degress of freedom in our data, we used the longer lags identified by the Akaike information criterion.

Table V contains some descriptive statistics of these filtered series. The filtering procedure removes any nonzero mean from the data. (The means in the raw data are small to begin with.) The main point to note in this table is that all series are leptokurtic—with the coefficients of kurtosis much larger than 3—a fact which is well known.

Table VI gives the results of the BDS tests. They strongly reject the hypothesis that stock returns are IID. This is true for the market as a whole, as well as the decile portfolios.

What are the implications of the finding that stock returns are not IID? First, it does not contradict market efficiency. Market efficiency implies that forecast errors of returns are not predictable. The fact that returns themselves are not IID (and therefore *potentially* predictable) says nothing about the predictability of forecast errors.

Second, when returns are not IID, it is difficult to interpret unconditional density estimation. A number of studies have fit leptokurtic distributions to stock returns. For example, Blattberg and Gonedes (1974) found that the Student t distribution provides a better fit to stock returns than the symmetric stable paretian distribution of Mandelbrot (1963). Since both the stable paretian and the Student t are leptokurtic, the probability of observing large returns (in absolute values) is much higher than that from the normal distribution. One may therefore be tempted to "explain" crashes, such as that on October 19, 1987, as small but nonzero probability events.[9] The fact that returns are not IID,[10] however, makes this explanation for stock market crashes less plausible, because unconditional distributions will always have fatter tails than conditional distributions when the data have some type of conditional dependence.

Third, the rejection of IID does not provide direct evidence of chaos in the stock market. Our simulations in Table III show that BDS has good power to detect at least four types of non-IID behavior: linear dependence, nonstationarity, chaos, and nonlinear stochastic processes. We can rule out linear dependence, since there is little of it in the raw returns, and since we have removed whatever correlation there is by filtering the return series. We therefore concentrate on the remaining three causes.

The rejection of IID is consistent with the view that stock returns are nonstationary. Over a long time period, it is difficult to make a case that the behavior of stock returns remains unchanged. Changes in economic fundamentals, e.g., wars, can shift the mean return (represented by the "2-mean" model). Changes in the operating procedure of the Federal Reserve, e.g.,

---

[9] Table 1 in Fama and Roll (1968) shows that the probability of observing an outcome in excess of 6 standardized units is 5.36% for the Cauchy distribution, compared to almost 0% for the normal distribution. In fact, the probability of an outcome in excess of 20 standardized units is 1.59% for the Cauchy distribution!

[10] Note that the Cauchy distribution is a member of the stable paretian family. The simulations in Table I show that the asymptotic distribution of the BDS statistic can still approximate the finite distribution well, even though the Cauchy distribution has no moments.

Table V
Selective Statistics for Filtered Stock Returns

This table presents the mean, standard deviation, skewness, kurtosis, maximum, minimum, and the number of observations for 11 stock returns: the weekly value weighted portfolio (VW), the weekly equally weighted portfolio (EW), the weekly smallest decile portfolio (DEC1), the weekly fifth decile portfolio (DEC5), the weekly largest decile portfolio (DEC10), the weekly S&P500 index (SPW), the daily S&P500 index (SPD), and the 15-minute S&P500 indices for the first, second, third, and fourth quarter of 1988 (SPM1, SPM2, SPM3, and SPM4, respectively).

	Mean	Std Dev	Skewness	Kurtosis	Maximum	Minimum	No. of Observations
VW	0.0000	0.0202	−0.292	6.69	0.0875	−0.1538	1303
EW	0.0000	0.0221	0.049	9.01	0.1459	−1.1680	1302
DEC1	0.0000	0.0257	0.697	10.32	0.1797	−0.1704	1297
DEC5	0.0000	0.0239	0.001	7.13	0.1360	−0.1618	1302
DEC10	0.0000	0.0202	−0.240	6.09	0.0800	−0.1452	1303
SPW	0.0000	0.0203	−0.309	6.47	0.1243	−0.1321	1402
SPD	0.0000	0.0113	−4.275	88.99	0.0709	−0.2279	2017
SPM1	0.0000	0.00218	0.402	23.15	0.0258	−0.0158	1706
SPM2	0.0000	0.00170	−0.709	23.74	0.0150	−0.0195	1706
SPM3	0.0000	0.00138	0.139	13.60	0.0137	−0.0110	1706
SPM4	0.0000	0.00123	−0.501	11.20	0.0064	−0.0103	1707

switching from an interest rate to a money supply target during 1979–1982, can shift the volatility of financial markets (represented by the "2-variance" model).

The rejection of IID is also consistent with the view that returns are generated by nonlinear stochastic systems, e.g., NMA, TAR, and ARCH-type models. While there are few models in economics and finance which lead to nonlinear stochastic systems of these specific types, this observation does not imply that nonlinear stochastic models are not useful. The nonlinear moving average model can be regarded as a second order approximation of the Volterra representation, which all stationary (linear or nonlinear) time series possess. The threshold autoregressive process can result from an endogenous regime switching model.[11] The ARCH-type model can be thought of as approximating conditional variance changes.[12]

Finally the rejection of IID is also consistent with the presence of low complexity chaotic behavior in stock returns. Regardless of whether determinism is aesthetically appealing or not, there are many ways to generate economic models with chaotic dynamics, summarized by Baumol and Benhabib (1989). If a system is both chaotic and stochastic, we shall classify it (arbitrarily) as a stochastic system. What remains for us to do is to try to eliminate two of the three explanations for non-IID behavior of stock returns.

---

[11] See Hsieh (1990).
[12] See Nelson (1990) for a discussion.

The Journal of Finance

Table VI

BDS Statistics for Filtered Stock Returns

This table presents the BDS statistics (at dimensions 2 through 5 and ϵ equaling 0.5, 1, 1.5, and 2 standard deviations of the data) for 11 stock returns: the weekly value-weighted portfolio (VW), the weekly equally weighted portfolio (EW), the weekly smallest decile portfolio (DEC1), the weekly fifth decile portfolio (DEC5), the weekly largest decile portfolio (DEC10), the weekly S&P500 index (SPW), the daily S&P500 index (SPD), and the 15-minute S&P500 indices for the first, second, third, and fourth quarter of 1988 (SPM1, SPM2, SPM3, and SPM4 respectively).

| | m | ϵ/σ | | | |
		0.50	1.00	1.50	2.00
VW	2	8.73	7.33	7.13	8.05
	3	13.32	10.31	9.21	9.53
	4	17.26	12.14	10.34	10.13
	5	22.32	14.25	11.49	10.71
EW	2	9.48	9.03	8.42	8.37
	3	14.15	11.95	10.52	9.69
	4	17.44	13.57	11.52	10.22
	5	21.88	15.43	12.55	10.84
DEC1	2	10.84	11.21	11.26	11.29
	3	13.68	13.53	12.56	11.44
	4	15.84	15.02	13.24	11.41
	5	18.72	16.45	13.82	11.49
DEC5	2	9.19	8.92	8.24	8.02
	3	13.13	11.78	10.43	9.78
	4	15.98	13.39	11.29	10.11
	5	19.38	15.14	12.24	10.75
DEC10	2	8.69	7.37	7.29	8:40
	3	13.06	10.12	9.18	9.62
	4	17.00	12.09	10.42	10.38
	5	21.87	14.23	11.61	11.02
SPW	2	8.78	9.04	8.92	8.67
	3	11.33	10.69	10.19	9.78
	4	14.53	12.74	11.57	10.73
	5	18.24	14.59	12.71	11.49
SPD	2	2.16	4.21	6.97	9.14
	3	2.28	4.86	8.15	10.37
	4	2.60	5.39	8.98	11.29
	5	2.93	5.96	9.69	12.04
SPM1	2	7.56	6.56	5.86	4.86
	3	10.75	8.51	7.46	6.59
	4	14.14	10.71	8.90	7.79
	5	17.25	11.69	9.21	7.99
SPM2	2	8.74	7.56	5.96	3.96
	3	11.81	9.22	7.17	4.75
	4	14.82	10.11	7.30	4.82
	5	18.00	11.12	7.69	5.07
SPM3	2	9.23	6.47	4.21	2.16
	3	12.10	8.04	5.50	3.28
	4	15.22	9.01	5.88	3.71
	5	18.46	10.09	6.68	4.40

Table VI—*Continued*

| | m | \multicolumn{4}{c}{ϵ/σ} |
		0.50	1.00	1.50	2.00
SPM4	2	10.10	8.57	5.57	3.09
	3	14.30	11.91	8.34	5.47
	4	18.67	14.38	9.66	6.27
	5	23.49	16.19	10.45	6.74

IV. Is Nonstationarity Responsible for the Rejection of IID?

For financial economists, nonstationarity is synonymous with structural change. There may be many reasons for structural changes: technological and financial innovations, policy changes, etc. It would be difficult to argue that the structure of the economic and financial system has remained constant from 1963 to 1987. We must allow for the possibility that structural changes caused BDS to reject IID during this period.

In order to check this explanation, we look at the returns of the Standard & Poors 500 stock index (without dividends) for the following time periods: weekly returns from 1962 to 1989 (SPW), daily returns from 1983 to 1989 (SPD), and 15-minute returns during 1988 divided into 4 approximately equal subsamples (SPM1, SPM2, SPM3, SPM4).[13] Implicitly, we are assuming that structural changes occur infrequently. By going to higher and higher frequency data in shorter and shorter time periods, we should remove the effects of structural changes. But we stop well short of using tick by tick data to avoid picking up micromarket structure dependencies discussed in Section III.

Table VI indicates that the weekly S&P returns is not IID, the same as the value-weighted index over the same period. What is more interesting, however, is that the daily returns in 1982–1989 and the 15-minute returns in 1988 are also not IID.[14] This makes it unlikely that infrequent structural changes are causing the rejection of IID in weekly returns. It is, of course, possible that structural changes happen so frequently that they cause BDS to reject IID in the 15-minute returns over the course of 3 months. If this is the true, then econometric work on economic and financial data is virtually impossible.

---

[13] These are logarithmic differences of price changes. They are filtered by an autoregression whose lags are chosen by the Akaike (Schwarz) criterion to be: weekly returns, 6 (0), daily returns, 5(0), and 15-minute returns, 4 (1). Since we have a large number of degrees of freedom, we use the longer lag lengths.

[14] It is possible that the 15-minute return is capturing some nonlinear dynamics from the micromarket structure. This will have to be studied in the future. We checked that day-of-the-week and time-of-day effects are not responsible for the rejection of IID in the daily and 15-minute data.

V. Is Chaotic Dynamics Responsible for the Rejection of IID?

The rejection of IID is certainly consistent with the hypothesis that the stock market is governed by low complexity chaotic dynamics. The issue we raise here is—is there any direct evidence of chaotic behavior? In this section, we take two approaches to answer this question.

The first approach examines the unconditional third order moments of stock returns, following the method in Hsieh (1989). The motivation is as follows. If x_t is a chaotic process, it can be written as:

$$x_t = f(x_{t-1}, \dots). \tag{28}$$

This is a special case of a more general category of nonlinear processes:

$$x_t = f(x_{t-1}, \dots) + \epsilon_t, \tag{29}$$

where ϵ_t satisfies the condition that $E[\epsilon_t \mid x_{t-1}, \dots] = 0$. For both models, we can consider $f()$ as the mean of x_t conditional on its own past. Since $f()$ is nonlinear, these models are "nonlinear-in-mean" (as opposed to "nonlinear-in-variance," which will be discussed later).

We can test for the null hypothesis that $f() = 0$ against the alternative that $f() \neq 0$. Under the null, the unconditional third order moments, $E[x_t x_{t-i} x_{t-j}] = 0$, for $i, j > 0$. Hsieh (1989) proposes the following test:

a) Define $\rho(i, j) = E[x_t x_{t-i} x_{t-j}]/\sigma^3$, where $\sigma^2 = V[x_t]$. Estimate $\rho(i, j)$ with the appropriate sample moments: $r(i, j) = [\sum x_t x_{t-i} x_{t-j} / T] / [\sum x_t^2 / T]^{1.5}$.

b) $\sqrt{[r(i, j) - \rho(i, j)]}$ has a limiting distribution $N(0, V(i, j))$, where $V(i, j)$ can be estimated by the method of moments:

$$\left[\sum \{ x_t x_{t-i} x_{t-j} / T - r(i, j) \}^2 \right] / \left[\sum x_t^2 / T \right]^3.$$

While Hsieh (1989) tests $\rho(i, j) = 0$ individually using a t-statistic, we test the composite null hypothesis that $\rho(i, j) = 0$ for $0 < i \leq j \leq m$, for a given m, making use of the fact that the asymptotic covariance between $r(i, j)$ and $r(i', j')$ can be estimated using the obvious sample cross-moments:

$$\left[\sum \{ x_t x_{t-1} x_{t-j} / T - r(i, j) \} \{ x_t x_{t-i'} x_{t-j'} / T - r(i', j') \} \right] / \left[\sum x_t^2 / T \right]^3.$$

The composite test can be conducted using the usual χ^2 statistic.[15]

This test statistic is designed so that it will not reject models which are "nonlinear-in-variance":

$$x_t = g(x_{t-1}, \dots) \epsilon_t, \tag{30}$$

---

[15] The proof of this statement follows easily from Hsieh (1989), which can be viewed as a modification of Tsay (1986). We should note that the third order moment test can fail to detect a chaotic process whose odd product moments are zero. This can happen if the function $f()$ is antisymmetric. This is not true for any of the chaotic examples in this paper.

where $g(\ )$ is a nonlinear function. Since x_t and ϵ_t take on both positive and negative values, we cannot take logarithms of both sides and transform this model to one being nonlinear-in-mean. However, the third order moment test should detect hybrid models, those which are "nonlinear-in-mean" as well as "nonlinear-in-variance":

$$x_t = f(x_{t-1}, \ldots) + g(x_{t-1}, \ldots)\epsilon_t. \tag{31}$$

(The GARCH-in-mean model, where the conditional variance appears in the conditional mean, is such an example.)

As in the case of the BDS test, we perform simulations to evaluate the finite sample distribution of the third order moment test as well as its ability to detect nonlinearity-in-mean. The results are reported in Table VII.

The first 4 models use IID data generated by the standard normal, Student t with 3 degrees of freedom, Cauchy, and the chi-square with 4 degrees of freedom. They show that the asymptotic distribution of the third order moment test approximates the finite sample distribution for 1000 observations tolerably well for IID data generated by the standard normal and the $\chi^2(4)$, but rather poorly for the $t(3)$ and the Cauchy. The latter two distributions do not have fourth or higher moments, which are assumed to exist in the derivation of the asymptotic distribution of the third order moment test statistic. Thus care must be used when applying the third order moment test to very fat tailed data.[16]

The next 5 models have non-IID data, but do not have nonlinearity-in-mean. There is a slight tendency for the test to reject too infrequently. This is more so for the AR1, MA1, and MA1, and 2-mean, and less so for the 2-variance and EGARCH.

The next 4 models (NMA, TAR, filtered Mackey-Glass, and GARCH-in-mean), generate non-IID data which have nonlinearity-in-mean and nonzero third order moments. The third order moment test can detect the first 3 models nearly 100% of the time, but the power against the GARCH-in-mean model is low, probably because the high order moments of the GARCH-in-mean model do not exist.[17]

The last simulation uses the "sine" model which is nonlinear-in-mean but has zero third order moments:

$$x_t = \sin[x_{t-1}] + \epsilon_t, \tag{32}$$

where ϵ_t is IID standard normal. The simulation shows that the third order moment test, as expected, cannot pick up the nonlinearity in this model. The reason is quite simple. If the conditional means are zero, then the third order moments are zero. However, the converse is not true: if the third order

---

[16] The failure of existence of fourth moments can also affect the distribution of the Tsay (1986) nonlinearity test and the Hinich and Patterson (1985) nonlinearity test. It is difficult to test whether fourth moments exist in a finite data set. This points to one of the advantages of the BDS test, whose limiting distribution does not require the existence of any moments.

[17] We also reject 100% of the replications using the tent map, the Hénon map, and the logistic map (when $A = 4$).

Table VII

Simulated Size and Power of the Third Order Moment Test

This table presents the percentage of the third order moment test (using 5 lags). The Monte Carlo uses 2000 replications, each having 1000 observations, for data generated by: (a) nine models for which the conditional mean is zero or linear: the standard normal, the Student t with 3 degrees of freedom, the chi-square with 4 degrees of freedom, the Cauchy distribution, the first order moving average (MA1), the first order autoregression (AR1), the '2-mean' model (the first 500 observations have mean −1 and variance 1, the second 500 observations have mean 1 and variance 1), the '2-variance' model (the first 500 observations have mean 0 and variance 1, the second 500 observations have mean 0 and variance 2), and the exponential generalized autoregressive conditional heteroskedasticity (EGARCH) model; and (b) five models for which the conditional mean is nonlinear: the threshold autoregression (TAR), the nonlinear moving average (NMA), the Mackey-Glass filtered by a third order autoregression, the generalized autoregressive conditional heteroskedasticity in mean model, and the "Sine" model. The "true size" denotes the percentage of rejections under the null hypothesis.

Test Statistic	Model					True Size
$\chi^2(15)$	$N(0, 1)$	$t(3)$	$\chi^2(4)$	Cauchy		
% > 22.31	9.05	6.75	12.05	18.25		10.00
% > 25.00	3.70	2.85	6.15	12.70		5.00
% > 27.49	1.70	1.15	3.05	9.60		2.50
% > 30.58	0.65	0.25	1.15	8.00		1.00
% > 32.80	0.35	0.05	0.70	7.25		0.50

	Model					True Size
$\chi^2(15)$	MA1	AR1	2-mean	2-var	EGARCH	
% > 22.31	5.60	5.40	4.90	7.95	8.55	10.00
% > 25.00	3.10	2.60	2.65	3.15	3.30	5.00
% > 27.49	1.45	1.95	1.60	1.25	1.55	2.50
% > 30.58	0.45	0.70	0.90	0.30	0.60	1.00
% > 32.80	0.15	0.40	0.55	0.20	0.40	0.50

	Model					True Size
$\chi^2(15)$	TAR	NMA	Mackey-Glass	GARCH-M	Sine	
% > 22.31	100.00	100.00	100.00	74.00	7.20	10.00
% > 25.00	100.00	100.00	100.00	61.85	4.00	5.00
% > 27.49	100.00	100.00	100.00	49.65	2.20	2.50
% > 30.58	100.00	99.85	100.00	36.35	0.80	1.00
% > 32.80	100.00	99.75	100.00	28.45	0.35	0.50

moments are zero, it does not imply that the conditional means are zero. This was first pointed out by Pemberton and Tong (1981). Note, however, that BDS has no trouble in detecting this type of nonlinearity. (See the results in Table III.)

We now apply the third order moment test to stock returns. Table VIII shows that there is no evidence to reject the null hypothesis that stock

Table VIII

Third Order Moments Test Statistics for Filtered Stock Returns

This table presents the third order moment test statistics (using 5 lags) for 11 stock returns: the weekly value-weighted portfolio (VW), the weekly equally weighted portfolio (EW), the weekly smallest decile portfolio (DEC1), the weekly fifth decile portfolio (DEC5), the weekly largest decile portfolio (DEC10), the weekly S&P500 index (SPW), the daily S&P500 index (SPD), and the 15-minute S&P500 indices for the first, second, third, and fourth quarter of 1988 (SPM1, SPM2, SPM3, and SPM4, respectively). These statistics are asymptotically $\chi^2(15)$, whose critical values (tail probabilities) are: 22.31 (10%), 25.00 (5%), 27.49 (2.5%), 30.58 (1%), and 32.80 (0.5%).

Stock Returns	Third Order Moment Statistic
VW	14.25
EW	15.43
DEC1	16.45
DEC5	15.14
DEC10	14.23
SPW	14.59
SPD	15.58
SPM1	12.05
SPM2	20.16
SPM3	10.21
SPM4	11.35

returns have zero third order moments. What does this mean? Had we rejected the null hypothesis of zero third order moments, we would have found evidence consistent with nonlinearity-in-mean (possibly chaotic dynamics). The failure to reject the null, however, does not allow us to rule out the presence of chaotic dynamics. We therefore turn to a second approach using nonparametric regressions to capture the conditional mean directly.

Suppose returns are generated by the following model:

$$x_t = f(x_{t-1}, \ldots) + \epsilon_t, \tag{33}$$

where $f()$ is nonlinear and ϵ_t is IID. This includes chaotic models as special cases, if we set $\epsilon_t = 0$. When $f()$ is a smooth function, Stone (1977) showed that a large class of nonparametric regressions can be used to fit $f()$ consistently as the sample size increases. There are many ways to implement nonparametric regression; for example, kernel estimation, series expansion, neural network, and nearest neighbor. We select Cleveland's (1979) method of locally weighted regression (LWR), which is a generalization of nearest neighbor. LWR has been used to test for nonlinearity-in-mean by Diebold and Nason (1990) in weekly exchange rate changes, and LeBaron (1988) in weekly stock returns.

Diebold and Nason (1990) gave a very good description of locally weighted regression. Briefly, the idea is this. Suppose the data are generated according to:

$$x_{t+1} = f(x_t). \tag{34}$$

We have observed x_t, x_{t-1}, $\cdots$, and would like to forecast x_{t+1}. The BDS statistic indicates that, whenever x_{t-1} was close to x_{s-1}, x_t was also close to x_s. We can look at the history of returns, find those instances when x_s was close to x_t, run a nonparametric regression of x_{s+1} on x_s to estimate the function $f(\,)$, and use $\hat{f}(x_t)$ to predict x_{t+1}, where $\hat{f}(\,)$ denotes the nonparametric estimate of $f(\,)$. The extension to the case where $f(\,)$ contains more than one lag of x_t is straightforward. Locally weighted regressions uses the k nearest neighbors of x_t, and a scheme which gives more weight to closer observations and less weight to farther observations. There are a number of parameters to be selected: (a) The number of nearest neighbors to use: We try 10% of all observations, up to 90%, increasing in steps of 10%. (b) The number of lags of x_t to include as arguments of the unknown function $f(\,)$: We use lags 1 through 5. (c) The weighting scheme: We use the "tricubic" scheme proposed by Cleveland and Devlin (1988).[18] (d) A period for out-of-sample forecasting: for the weekly returns (VW, EW, DEC1, DEC5, DEC10, SPW), we arbitrarily start the forecast at the 1001st observation and continued through the end. For the daily returns (SPD) we begin the forecast at the 1601st observation. For the 15-minute returns (SPM1, SPM2, SPM3, SPM4), we begin the forecast at the 1401st observation. This way, each series has at least 1000 observations for the locally weighted regression, and at least 300 observations for out-of-sample forecasting.

If stock returns are governed by low complexity chaos, we should be able to use locally weighted regression to forecast returns much better than simple methods, such as the random walk (RW) model of prices. In addition, our forecasts should improve as the forecast horizon becomes shorter and shorter. Neither implication is born out by the data. Table IX measures forecastability in terms of root mean squared errors. In most cases, the random walk model achieves the lowest root mean squared error. In a few instances, e.g., VW, EW, DEC1, and SPM4, the locally weighted regression has smaller forecast errors than the random walk, but the reduction in root mean squared error is less than 5%.[19] This can, however, happen by chance, given the wide range of parameter values in choosing the locally weighted regression.

One possible explanation of the inability of LWR to outperform random walk forecasts is that LWR is unable to capture conditional mean changes. We therefore perform a simulation using "2-mean," "2-variance," NMA, TAR, Sine, EGARCH, and Mackey-Glass. We generate 500 observations of each series, and begin out-of-sample forecasting at the 451st observations. The tricubic weighting function is used. Since the simulations are computationally intensive, we use only one choice of k—50 nearest neighbors (about 10% of the entire sample). We compare the root mean squared error of the LWR forecasts with that of the "random walk" forecast for 2000 replications. Table X shows that LWR beats the random walk 100% of the time in the

---

[18] We have experimented briefly with nearest neighbor, which is a rectangular weighting scheme. The results are similar to those using the tricubic weighting function.

[19] These results are consistent with the findings in LeBaron (1988).

Chaos and Nonlinear Dynamics 1865

Mackey-Glass equation, and 95% of the time for the "Sine" model, which was not detectable by the third order moment test. In addition, LWR outperforms random walk in the TAR model, even though the function f( ) is not smooth. This indicates that LWR has the ability to pick up conditional mean changes.

While we did not experiment with alternative methods of nonparametric regressions, other authors have had no more success. White (1988) found that forecasts of IBM stock returns using neural network did not outperform the random walk model. Prescott and Stengos (1988) found that forecasts of kernel estimators on gold and silver also could not outperform the random walk model.

The preponderance of the failure to outperform the random walk model in asset markets forces us to conclude that there is no strong evidence that the movements in stock market are primarily due to conditional mean changes, when conditioning on past returns.[20] In particular, there is no evidence of low complexity chaotic behavior in stock returns.[21]

VI. Is Conditional Heteroskedasticity Responsible for the Rejection of IID?

Next we proceed to consider whether stock returns are nonlinear-in-variance:

$$x_t = g(x_{t-1}, \ldots)\epsilon_t, \tag{35}$$

where $E[\epsilon_t \mid x_{t-1}, \ldots] = 0$ and $V[\epsilon_t \mid x_{t-1}, \ldots] = 1$ (without loss of generality). This is a general model of conditional heteroskedasticity, which includes ARCH-type models as special cases.

There is now growing evidence that stock market volatility is not only time-varying (e.g., French, Schwert, and Stambaugh (1987)) but is predictable (e.g., Schwert and Seguin (1990)). A number of papers have used ARCH-type models to describe conditional heteroskedasticity (e.g., Bollerslev (1987) and Nelson (1991)). We pose two questions in this section: (a) What is the evidence of conditional heteroskedasticity? (b) Does the conditional heteroskedasticity captured by ARCH-type models account for all the nonlinearity in stock returns?

To answer the first question, observe that if we take the absolute values of equation (35), we obtain:

$$|x_t| = |g(x_{t-1}, \ldots)| \ |\epsilon_t|. \tag{36}$$

If $g( )$ is differentiable, a Taylor series expansion would yield the result that $|x_t|$ depends on $|x_{t-i}|$. Thus correlation of $|x_t|$ with $|x_{t-i}|$ is evidence of

---

[20] These results could change if we increase the information set to include variables other than past returns. For example, Gallant, Rossi, and Tauchen (1990) use returns and volume in a bivariate system.
[21] Even if we had found evidence of chaotic behavior, estimating the unknown parameters of a chaotic map is next to impossible. See Geweke (1989) for a discussion.

The Journal of Finance

Table IX
Root Mean Squared Forecast Errors

The table presents the root mean squared forecast errors using the locally weighted regression with tricubic weights, using lags 1 through 5, and the number of nearest neighbors equaling the fraction (f), 0.1, 0.2, 0.3, 0.4, 0.5, 0.6, 0.7, 0.8, and 0.9 of the data. The root mean squared forecast errors of the random walk model (RW) are in parentheses. The smallest root mean squared forecast error for each series is underlined. All errors have been multiplied by 100. (See Table VIII for definitions of abbreviations.)

f	Lags				
	1	2	3	4	5
VW: (Random walk 0.05436081)					
0.10	0.05198337	0.05204231	0.05208826	0.05204822	0.05204699
0.20	0.05758597	0.05765421	0.05769833	0.05766710	0.05766342
0.30	0.05970985	0.05977849	0.05981333	0.05977608	0.05978498
0.40	0.06074411	0.06080367	0.06083238	0.06078065	0.06080701
0.50	0.06104386	0.06109431	0.06111920	0.06105552	0.06109534
0.60	0.06100911	0.06105054	0.06107035	0.06100228	0.06104746
0.70	0.06082516	0.06085788	0.06087175	0.06080501	0.06085057
0.80	0.06054519	0.06056918	0.06057733	0.06051347	0.06055829
0.90	0.06016496	0.06018105	0.06018456	0.06012428	0.06016784
EW: (Random walk 0.05320546)					
0.10	0.05317910	0.05313575	0.05297957	0.05310239	0.05310214
0.20	0.05399810	0.05394319	0.05383378	0.05387236	0.05386917
0.30	0.05475939	0.05469907	0.05462234	0.05461992	0.05461392
0.40	0.05531716	0.05526434	0.05521420	0.05518580	0.05517885
0.50	0.05571191	0.05566488	0.05563107	0.05558950	0.05558233
0.60	0.05600711	0.05596782	0.05594459	0.05589973	0.05589285
0.70	0.05620623	0.05617554	0.05616085	0.05611508	0.05610873
0.80	0.05630840	0.05628667	0.05627885	0.05623417	0.05622840
0.90	0.05630185	0.05628798	0.05628544	0.05624305	0.05623784
DEC1: (Random walk 0.06055333)					
0.10	0.05806902	0.05796735	0.05793429	0.05793747	0.05788714
0.20	0.05914330	0.05904963	0.05901102	0.05901133	0.05900607
0.30	0.05967503	0.05957489	0.05954111	0.05953993	0.05953798
0.40	0.06018445	0.06009454	0.06008802	0.06008652	0.06008414
0.50	0.06061733	0.06053545	0.06054605	0.06054455	0.06054260
0.60	0.06090465	0.06083168	0.06085730	0.06085586	0.06085410
0.70	0.06111063	0.06103978	0.06107295	0.06107149	0.06106924
0.80	0.06125867	0.06118942	0.06122721	0.06122567	0.06122274
0.90	0.06137222	0.06130418	0.06134270	0.06134127	0.06133782
DEC5: (Random walk 0.05593892)					
0.10	0.05895377	0.05907995	0.05910458	0.05904954	0.05902467
0.20	0.05939389	0.05950339	0.05953901	0.05959645	0.05960005
0.30	0.05960399	0.05969049	0.05972788	0.05980120	0.05980946
0.40	0.05971944	0.05979293	0.05982902	0.05988964	0.05989699
0.50	0.05984676	0.05991038	0.05994459	0.05998930	0.05999401
0.60	0.05986240	0.05992130	0.05995344	0.05998826	0.05999137
0.70	0.05981183	0.05986855	0.05989852	0.05992758	0.05992973
0.80	0.05969451	0.05974899	0.05977675	0.05980114	0.05980247
0.90	0.05953412	0.05958599	0.05961180	0.05963290	0.05963368

Chaos and Nonlinear Dynamics   1867

Table IX—*Continued*

f	Lags				
	1	2	3	4	5
DEC10: (Random walk 0.05488350)					
0.10	0.05305787	0.05313033	0.05313959	0.05324359	0.05315436
0.20	0.05668828	0.05675475	0.05677510	0.05680402	0.05677795
0.30	0.05872669	0.05879617	0.05882264	0.05881426	0.05881659
0.40	0.05963001	0.05969522	0.05971931	0.05969445	0.05971353
0.50	0.06005248	0.06010943	0.06012974	0.06009160	0.06012147
0.60	0.06018747	0.06023472	0.06025017	0.06020321	0.06024141
0.70	0.06013509	0.06017344	0.06018397	0.06013311	0.06017672
0.80	0.05997842	0.06000830	0.06001420	0.05996200	0.06000904
0.90	0.05975363	0.05977644	0.05977930	0.05972548	0.05977443
SPW: (Random walk 0.05083948)					
0.10	0.05955174	0.05957110	0.05956666	0.05956406	0.05955766
0.20	0.05623793	0.05623091	0.05621985	0.05621961	0.05621936
0.30	0.05506007	0.05505484	0.05504434	0.05504418	0.05504591
0.40	0.05432155	0.05431458	0.05430424	0.05430363	0.05430552
0.50	0.05375797	0.05374680	0.05373616	0.05373535	0.05373691
0.60	0.05335459	0.05334193	0.05333248	0.05333188	0.05333303
0.70	0.05306897	0.05305650	0.05304932	0.05304907	0.05304987
0.80	0.05284070	0.05282971	0.05282462	0.05282451	0.05282518
0.90	0.05259664	0.05258771	0.05258438	0.05258441	0.05258503
SPD: (Random walk 0.00658354)					
0.10	0.00721163	0.00721740	0.00721715	0.00721743	0.00721916
0.20	0.00719038	0.00719276	0.00719432	0.00719232	0.00719306
0.30	0.00721627	0.00721747	0.00721892	0.00721708	0.00721742
0.40	0.00722019	0.00722111	0.00722225	0.00722079	0.00722102
0.50	0.00722375	0.00722433	0.00722536	0.00722404	0.00722417
0.60	0.00722701	0.00722731	0.00722822	0.00722706	0.00722712
0.70	0.00722815	0.00722836	0.00722908	0.00722816	0.00722821
0.80	0.00722651	0.00722674	0.00722722	0.00722661	0.00722666
0.90	0.00721953	0.00721972	0.00721988	0.00721968	0.00721972
SPM1: (Random walk 0.00029380)					
0.10	0.00029994	0.00030069	0.00030052	0.00030053	0.00030053
0.20	0.00029738	0.00029791	0.00029779	0.00029780	0.00029781
0.30	0.00029629	0.00029667	0.00029658	0.00029660	0.00029656
0.40	0.00029540	0.00029573	0.00029565	0.00029567	0.00029562
0.50	0.00029451	0.00029487	0.00029478	0.00029480	0.00029476
0.60	0.00029395	0.00029432	0.00029423	0.00029425	0.00029421
0.70	0.00029344	0.00029380	0.00029371	0.00029372	0.00029368
0.80	0.00029279	0.00029313	0.00029305	0.00029306	0.00029301
0.90	0.00029224	0.00029255	0.00029247	0.00029248	0.00029244
SPM2: (Random walk 0.00025644)					
0.10	0.00025903	0.00025900	0.00025898	0.00025899	0.00025906
0.20	0.00025804	0.00025805	0.00025799	0.00025799	0.00025807
0.30	0.00025800	0.00025803	0.00025796	0.00025797	0.00025805
0.40	0.00025804	0.00025807	0.00025800	0.00025801	0.00025809
0.50	0.00025803	0.00025807	0.00025799	0.00025799	0.00025808
0.60	0.00025798	0.00025802	0.00025794	0.00025794	0.00025803
0.70	0.00025788	0.00025792	0.00025784	0.00025784	0.00025793
0.80	0.00025786	0.00025789	0.00025783	0.00025782	0.00025792
0.90	0.00025797	0.00025800	0.00025794	0.00025794	0.00025805

Table IX—*Continued*

f	Lags				
	1	2	3	4	5
SPM: (Random walk 0.00009105)					
0.10	0.00009783	0.00009788	0.00009752	0.00009738	0.00009736
0.20	0.00009543	0.00009549	0.00009507	0.00009493	0.00009486
0.30	0.00009409	0.00009414	0.00009379	0.00009365	0.00009356
0.40	0.00009314	0.00009319	0.00009289	0.00009277	0.00009267
0.50	0.00009268	0.00009273	0.00009246	0.00009234	0.00009224
0.60	0.00009245	0.00009249	0.00009224	0.00009213	0.00009202
0.70	0.00009225	0.00009229	0.00009205	0.00009195	0.00009183
0.80	0.00009202	0.00009206	0.00009183	0.00009173	0.00009161
0.90	0.00009166	0.00009170	0.00009147	0.00009137	0.00009125
SPM4: (Random walk 0.00007927)					
0.10	0.00008360	0.00008355	0.00008367	0.00008365	0.00008365
0.20	0.00008165	0.00008164	0.00008171	0.00008169	0.00008169
0.30	0.00008064	0.00008063	0.00008068	0.00008066	0.00008066
0.40	0.00008023	0.00008024	0.00008027	0.00008026	0.00008026
0.50	0.00008004	0.00008007	0.00008009	0.00008008	0.00008008
0.60	0.00007993	0.00007996	0.00007998	0.00007996	0.00007996
0.70	0.00007985	0.00007989	0.00007991	0.00007990	0.00007989
0.80	0.00007980	0.00007985	0.00007986	0.00007985	0.00007984
0.90	0.00007974	0.00007980	0.00007981	0.00007980	0.00007979

Table X

Forecasting Simulated Data

This table reports the percentage when the root mean squared forecast errors of the locally weighted regression is smaller than that of the random walk model. The locally weighted regression forecasts for observation 451 through 500 were generated using 5 lags, 50 nearest neighbors, and the tricubic weighting function. The Monte Carlo simulations use 2000 replications, each having 500 observations, for data generated by seven models: the '2-mean' model (the first 500 observations have mean −1 and variance 1, the second 500 observations have mean 1 and variance 1), the '2-variance' model (the first 500 observations have mean 0 and variance 1, the second 500 observations have mean 0 and variance 2), the nonlinear moving average (NMA), the threshold autoregression (TAR), the "Sine" model, the exponential generalized autoregressive conditional heteroskedasticity (EGARCH) model, and the Mackey-Glass filtered by a third order autoregression.

Model	Percentage
2-mean	96.80
2-variance	9.25
NMA	47.00
TAR	75.60
Sine	95.40
EGARCH	12.15
Mackey-Glass	100.00

Table XI

Testing for Conditional Heteroskedasticity

This table presents the autocorrelation coefficients of the absolute values of the data for 11 stock returns: the weekly value-weighted portfolio (VW), the weekly equally weighted portfolio (EW), the weekly smallest decile portfolio (DEC1), the weekly fifth decile portfolio (DEC5), the weekly largest decile portfolio (DEC10), the weekly S&P500 index (SPW), the daily S&P500 index (SPD), and the 15-minute S&P500 indices for the first, second, third, and fourth quarter of 1988 (SPM1, SPM2, SPM3, and SPM4, respectively).

	Lag					
	1	2	3	4	5	6
VW	0.242*	0.214*	0.144*	0.142*	0.133*	0.195*
EW	0.276*	0.232*	0.137*	0.112*	0.116*	0.148*
D1	0.339*	0.193*	0.140*	0.108*	0.103*	0.082*
D5	0.254*	0.224*	0.131*	0.126*	0.132*	0.152*
D10	0.244*	0.204*	0.157*	0.154*	0.138*	0.209*
SPW	0.245*	0.167*	0.168*	0.165*	0.123*	0.179*
SPD	0.228*	0.202*	0.226*	0.136*	0.217*	0.168*
SPM1	0.178*	0.149*	0.205*	0.127*	0.126*	0.042
SPM2	0.127*	0.114*	0.068*	0.094*	0.060	0.017
SPM3	0.126*	0.092*	0.070*	0.061	0.025	0.006
SPM4	0.148*	0.174*	0.092*	0.086*	0.066*	0.060

*Statistically significant at the 1% level (two-tailed test).

conditional heteroskedasticity (particularly when x_t is not correlated with x_{t-1}).[22] Table XI presents the autocorrelations of the absolute valued data. There is strong evidence of conditional heteroskedasticity in weekly and daily returns, and somewhat weaker evidence in 15-minute returns.[23]

ARCH-type models have been used to capture conditional heteroskedasticity in stock returns, and the typical diagnostic tests (e.g., autocorrelation of absolute values and squares of standardized residuals) show that they do. We are, however, interested in a deeper issue: does ARCH-type models capture all the nonlinear dependence in stock returns? To answer this question, we fit an EGARCH model to the data:

$$x_t \sim N(0, \sigma_t^2),$$

$$\log \sigma_t^2 = \phi_0 + \phi \,|\, x_{t-1}/\sigma_{t-1} \,| + \psi \log \sigma_{t-1}^2 + \gamma x_{t-1}/\sigma_{t-1}. \qquad (37)$$

EGARCH is chosen over the simpler ARCH or GARCH model for two reasons: (a) unlike the simple ARCH or GARCH model, EGARCH does not impose any restrictions on the signs of the parameters to guarantee that estimated variances are positive, thus avoiding numerical problems associated with constrained optimization, and (b) EGARCH can accommodate

[22] The same argument shows that x_t^2 would be correlated with x_{t-i}^2 under conditional heteroskedasticity. See Engle (1982) and McLeod and Li (1983).

[23] We point out here that the evidence is consistent with conditional heteroskedasticity. But it does not rule out even higher order dependence (e.g., conditional skewness, conditional kurtosis).

conditional skewness discussed in Black (1976) which is not allowed in the less flexible ARCH and GARCH models. We use the Berndt, Hall, Hall, and Hausman (1974) procedure with analytic first derivatives to estimate this model.

If the EGARCH model is correctly specified, the standardized residuals:

$$z_t = x_t / \hat{\sigma}_t, \tag{38}$$

should be IID in large samples. Here, $\hat{\sigma}_t$ is the fitted value of the standard deviation from the variance equation. Thus BDS can be used as on the standardized residuals to test if EGARCH captures all nonlinear dependence in stock returns.

Table XII shows that the BDS statistics on the standardized residuals are much smaller than those of the raw data. Only a few statistics are significant, if we use the asymptotic distribution. The trouble is that the asymptotic distribution of the BDS statistic cannot be used when dealing with ARCH, GARCH, and EGARCH standardized residuals, a point made in Table V. Therefore, we use the simulated critical values of the BDS statistic. The 2.5% and 97.5% critical values are given in Table XIII. Based on these critical values, the only series to pass the BDS diagnostic is the smallest decile portfolio, DEC1. All the other series contain several BDS statistics which are outside the 5% critical range. In particular, the daily S&P returns have the worst fit, failing the BDS diagnostic every time. There is sufficient evidence here to indicate that the EGARCH model cannot completely account for all nonlinearity in stock returns.

One problem with ARCH-type models is that the variance equation does not contain an innovation. To obtain a more general model, we add a stochastic term in the variance equation, leading to the following specification for stock returns:

$$x_t = \sigma_t z_t, \tag{39}$$

where z_t is an IID random variable, and σ_t evolves according to:

$$\log \sigma_t = \beta_0 + \Sigma_i \beta_i \log \sigma_{t-i} + v_t, \tag{40}$$

where v_t is IID, independent of z_t.

It is appropriate here to contrast this model with the mixture models in the earlier stock market literature. Blattberg and Gonedes (1974) pointed out that the symmetric stable distribution is obtained from a normal distribution whose variance is drawn from a strictly positive stable distribution, that the Student t is obtained from a normal distribution whose variance is drawn from an inverted gamma distribution, and that Clark's (1973) model is a normal distribution whose variance is drawn from a log normal distribution. Thus, all three mixture models can be written in the form: $x_t = \sigma_t z_t$, where z_t, is IID standard normal, and σ_t is another IID random variable. In these cases, x_t exhibits neither conditional heteroskedasticity or nonlinear dependence. Our more general specification allows for nonlinear dependence in the form of conditional heteroskedasticity.

Chaos and Nonlinear Dynamics   1871

To test the variance specification, we construct daily standard deviations of returns from April 21, 1982 to September 30, 1989, using the 15-minute data, after removing the serial correlation. Figure 5 is a plot of the natural logarithms of the daily standard deviations. Note that, while the volatility on October 19 and 20, 1987, were considered to be "huge" at the time, they did not show up as "outliers" in the logarithms. In fact, the volatility leading up to those days had been on the rise. This is consistent with the diagnostics on the least squares residuals. Using the Schwarz criterion, we determine the lag length to be 5.[24] The least squares fit is

$$\log \sigma_t = -0.8577 + 0.2385 \log \sigma_{t-1} + 0.1298 \log \sigma_{t-2}$$
$$\quad\quad (0.1064)\quad (0.0229)\quad\quad\quad (0.0236)$$

$$+\ 0.1129 \log \sigma_{t-3} + 0.1515 \log \sigma_{t-4} + 0.1386 \log \sigma_{t-5}$$
$$\quad (0.0236)\quad\quad\quad (0.0236)\quad\quad\quad (0.0229)$$

$$R^2 = 0.4127. \tag{41}$$

The parentheses contain the standard errors of the estimated coefficients. Clearly, there is mean reversion in volatility. But the sum of the coefficients of this autoregressive process is 0.7713, which contains much less persistence than that of the GARCH model in Bollerslev (1987) and the EGARCH model in Nelson (1991).

We ran the BDS test on the residuals to test for the appropriateness of the linear model. Panel A in Table XIV shows that the BDS statistics are very small, giving no evidence of nonlinearity. Furthermore, it is interesting to note that the coefficient of kurtosis of the residuals is 3.49, not much higher than 3. There does not appear to be extreme points.

In the last step we check whether this model of conditional heteroskedasticity can capture the nonlinear dependence in stock returns. We standardize daily returns with the fitted values $\hat{\sigma}_t$ from the variance equation: $z_t = x_t / \hat{\sigma}_t$. (Note that x_t here is the raw data, not the linearly filtered data.) We then remove linear dependence in z_t (possibly due to asynchronous trading) using a first order autoregression. This lag length was identified by both the Akaike and the Schwarz criterion. Panel B in Table XIV contains the final diagnostics of this model. It shows that the BDS statistics are substantially lower than those in Table XII (for SPD). If we use the asymptotic distribution of the BDS test, we do not reject the model.[25] This lead us to conclude that the more flexible variance specification provides a much better description of the nonlinear dependence in daily stock returns. In addition, note that the kurtosis of 88.99 for SPD in Table V has been reduced to 8.816 in Panel B of Table XIV, implying that most but not all of the leptokurtosis of daily stock returns is due to variance changes.

---

[24] The Akaike criterion led to very long lags.

[25] Hsieh (1991) shows that the asymptotic distribution applies to the BDS statistic on the residuals of the generalized heteroskedasticity model in equations (39) and (40). Even if we apply a more stringent rejection criterion by using the critical values in Table XIII, we could reject only 1 BDS statistic, at dimension 2, when $\epsilon / \sigma = 2$.

Table XII

BDS Statistics for EGARCH Standardized Residuals

This table presents the BDS statistics (at dimensions 2 through 5 and ϵ equaling 0.5, 1, 1.5, and 2 standard deviations of the data) for EGARCH standardized residuals of 11 stock returns: the weekly value-weighted portfolio (VW), the weekly equally weighted portfolio (EW), the weekly smallest decile portfolio (DEC1), the weekly fifth decile portfolio (DEC5), the weekly largest decile portfolio (DEC10), the weekly S&P500 index (SPW), the daily S&P500 index (SPD), and the 15-minute S&P500 indices for the first, second, third, and fourth quarter of 1988 (SPM1, SPM2, SPM3, and SPM4, respectively).

			ϵ/σ		
	m	0.50	1.00	1.50	2.00
VW	2	0.49	−1.47	−2.16*	−2.03*
	3	0.92	−0.96	−2.08*	−2.11*
	4	1.16	−1.18	−2.38*	−2.44*
	5	0.88	−1.02	−2.41*	−2.45*
EW	2	0.14	−0.58	−1.20	−1.23
	3	1.30	−0.09	−1.05	−1.40*
	4	1.50	−0.34	−1.42*	−1.75*
	5	2.20	−0.34	−1.52*	−1.80*
DEC1	2	0.83	1.01	1.11	1.16
	3	0.78	0.83	0.69	0.42
	4	0.17	0.60	0.35	−0.06
	5	−0.25	0.43	0.09	−0.35
DEC5	2	0.29	−0.43	−0.94	−1.04
	3	0.67	−0.31	−1.00	−1.37*
	4	0.75	−0.64	−1.56*	−2.00*
	5	0.88	−0.71	−1.74*	−2.13*
DEC10	2	0.08	−1.23	−1.82*	−1.64*
	3	0.46	−1.07	−1.88*	−1.84*
	4	0.68	−1.26*	−2.16*	−2.09*
	5	0.44	−1.14*	−2.19*	−2.14*
SPW	2	−0.26	−0.46	−0.82	−0.83
	3	−0.37	−0.89	−1.59*	−1.69*
	4	0.18	−0.76	−1.50*	−1.75*
	5	1.22	−0.39	−1.27*	−1.64*
SPD	2	−3.46*	−3.44*	−2.88*	−1.78*
	3	−4.44*	−4.39*	−3.95*	−2.74*
	4	−4.36*	−4.48*	−4.11*	−2.84*
	5	−4.05*	−4.30*	−4.06*	−2.77*
SPM1	2	0.42	−0.99	−1.31	−0.98
	3	1.72	0.11	−0.54	−0.58
	4	3.16*	1.50	0.68	0.23
	5	4.04*	1.97	0.95	0.26
SPM2	2	2.08	0.95	0.02	−0.21
	3	3.10*	1.13	−0.11	−0.63
	4	3.82*	1.32	−0.35	−0.92
	5	4.90*	1.84	0.03	−0.60

Chaos and Nonlinear Dynamics   1873

Table XII—*Continued*

	m	0.50	1.00	1.50	2.00
		ε/σ			
SPM3	2	5.41*	2.36*	0.32	−0.58
	3	7.32*	3.59*	1.26	0.10
	4	9.34*	4.36*	1.66	0.47
	5	11.56*	5.34*	2.51*	1.19
SPM4	2	−0.32	−0.99	−1.59*	−2.12*
	3	1.36	0.54	−0.06	−0.64
	4	2.65*	1.59	0.78	−0.09
	5	3.68*	2.20	1.22	0.10

*Significant at the 5% (two-tailed) test.

Table XIII

Simulated BDS Critical Values for EGARCH Standardized Residuals

This table presents the simulated 2.5% and 97.5% critical values of the BDS statistic (at dimensions 2 through 5 and ε equaling 0.25, 0.5, 1, 1.5, and 2 standard deviations of the data) when applied to EGARCH standardized residuals. The Monte Carlo simulation uses 2000 replications, each with 1000 observations. $N(0, 1)$ denotes the critical values of a standard normal distribution.

n	0.25	0.50	1.00	1.50	2.00	$N(0, 1)$
2.5% crtical values						
2	−2.21	−1.61	−1.52	−1.47	−1.49	−1.96
3	−2.86	−1.65	−1.29	−1.29	−1.29	−1.96
4	−4.46	−1.63	−1.17	−1.13	−1.12	−1.96
5	−7.77	−1.94	−1.11	−1.00	−0.99	−1.96
97.5% critical values						
2	2.88	2.11	1.96	1.85	1.88	1.96
3	3.56	2.34	2.14	2.01	2.00	1.96
4	5.42	2.49	2.25	2.17	2.14	1.96
5	9.34	2.90	2.40	2.28	2.22	1.96

This model gives rise to some interesting possibilities. The mean reversion in volatility implies that one can forecast future volatility based on past volatility. In addition, the standardized data (after dividing by expected volatility) are IID, so we can obtain a nonparametric estimate of their density, which can then be used to make probability statements that are useful in, say, setting margin requirements for stocks.

VIII. Concluding Remarks

We have found strong evidence to reject the hypothesis that stock returns are IID. The cause does not appear to be either regime changes or chaotic

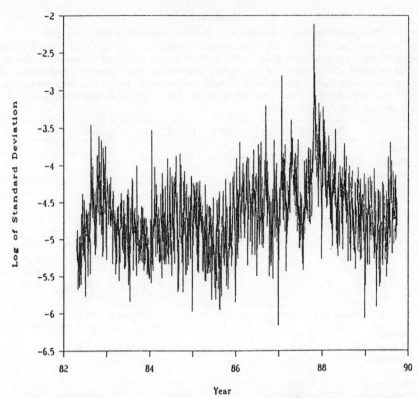

Figure 5. Logarithm of daily standard deviations of the S&P500 index. This plots the natural logarithm of the daily standard deviations of the S&P500 index, computed from fifteen minute returns during each trading day.

dynamics. Rather, the cause appears to be conditional heteroskedasticity (e.g., predictable variance changes). While we find that ARCH-type models do not fully capture the nonlinearity in stock returns, a more flexible model of conditional heteroskedasticity can. These findings have many interesting implications. One, if we want to fit conditional density functions on stock returns, we must account for their nonlinear dependence. Two, if we are interested to model the nonlinearity in stock returns, we should direct our efforts at conditional heteroskedasticity rather than conditional mean changes (which include chaotic dynamics). Three, if the flexible conditional heteroskedasticity model holds up under future analysis, it can provide conditional volatility forecasts. Those, together with a nonparametric estimate of the density of the standardized residuals, can deliver a conditional probability distribution which would be useful in many applications. Lastly, it would be interesting to see if this model can capture nonlinearity found in other

Chaos and Nonlinear Dynamics   1875

Table XIV

Diagnostics for a Generalized Heteroskedasticity Model

This table presents diagnostics for a generalized heteroskedasticity model for daily S&P500 returns. Panel A contains the diagnostics for residuals from a fifth order autoregression for the natural logarithm of daily standard deviations of the S&P500 index, computed from 15-minute returns during each trading day. Panel B contains the diagnostics from a first order autoregression for the daily S&P500 returns standardized by the fitted values of standard deviations based on the regression in Panel A.

Panel A: Residuals from: $\log \sigma_t = \beta_0 + \sum_{i=1}^{5} \beta_i \log \sigma_{t-i} + v_t$

Mean	0.0000				
Std dev	0.3666				
Skewness	0.214				
Kurtosis	3.49				
Maximum	1.481				
Minimum	−1.309				

BDS test:

m	ϵ/σ			
	0.50	1.00	1.50	2.00
2	−0.21	0.03	0.18	0.39
3	−0.02	0.09	0.14	0.28
4	0.16	0.16	0.30	0.33
5	0.29	0.31	0.40	0.37

Panel B: Residuals from: $z_t = \alpha_0 + \alpha_1 z_{t-1} + e_t$, where $z_t = x_t/\hat{\sigma}_t$

Mean	0.0000				
Std dev	1.0268				
Skewness	−0.213				
Kurtosis	8.816				
Maximum	6.410				
Minimum	−9.349				

BDS test:

m	ϵ/σ			
	0.50	1.00	1.50	2.00
2	−0.20	0.30	0.94	1.94
3	−1.25	−0.59	0.14	1.19
4	−1.42	−0.66	0.06	1.14
5	−1.18	−0.57	0.12	1.28

financial data such as exchange rates and interest rates. This is left for future research.

REFERENCES

Akaike, H., 1974, A new look at the statistical model identification, *IEEE Transactions on Automatic Control* 19, 716–723.

Baumol, W. and J. Benhabib, 1989, Chaos: significance, mechanism, and economic applications, *Journal of Economic Perspectives* 3, 77–105.

Berndt, E. K., B. H. Hall, R. E. Hall, and J. A. Hausman, 1974, Estimation and inference in nonlinear structural models, *Annals of Economic and Social Measurement* 4, 653–665.

Black, F., 1976. Studies of stock market volatility changes, *Proceedings of the American Statistical Association, Business and Economic Statistics Section* 177-181.

Blattberg, R. C. and N. Gonedes, 1974, A comparison of the stable paretian and student distribution as statistical model for prices, *Journal of Business* 47, 244-280.

Bollerslev, T., 1986, Generalized autoregressive conditional heteroskedasticity, *Journal of Econometrics* 31, 307-327.

——, 1987, A conditional heteroskedastic time series model for speculative prices and rates of return, *Review of Economics and Statistics* 69, 542-547.

——, R. Chow, and K. Kroner, 1990, ARCH modeling in finance: a selective review of the theory and empirical evidence, with suggestions for future research, working paper, Northwestern University, Georgia Tech, and University of Arizona.

Brock, W., 1986, Distinguishing random and deterministic systems: abridged version, *Journal of Economic Theory* 40, 168-195.

——, 1987, Notes on nuisance parameter problems in BDS type tests for IID, working paper, University of Wisconsin at Madison.

—— and E. Baek, 1991, Some theory of statistical inference for nonlinear science, *Review of Economic Studies*, Forthcoming.

——, W. Dechert, and J. Scheinkman, 1987, A test for independence based on the correlation dimension, Working Paper, University of Wisconsin at Madison, University of Houston, and University of Chicago.

—— and C. Sayers, 1988, Is the business cycle characterized by deterministic chaos? *Journal of Monetary Economics* 22, 71-90.

Clark, P. K., 1973, A subordinate stochastic process model with finite variance for speculative prices, *Econometrica* 41, 135-155.

Cleveland, W. S., 1979, Robust locally weighted regression and smoothing scatterplots, *Journal of the American Statistical Association*. 74, 829-836.

Cleveland, W. S. and S. J. Devlin, 1988, Locally weighted regression: an approach to regression analysis by local fitting, *Journal of the American Statistical Association* 83, 596-610.

Dechert, W., 1988, A characterization of independence for a gaussian process in terms of the correlation dimension, SSRI working paper 8812, University of Wisconsin at Madison.

Denker, G. and G. Keller, 1986, Rigorous statistical procedures for data from dynamical systems, *Journal of Statistical Physics* 44, 67-93.

Diebold, F. X. and J. A. Nason, 1990, Nonparametric exchange rate prediction? *Journal of International Economics* 28, 315-332.

Engle, R., 1982, Autoregressive conditional heteroscedasticity with estimates of the variance of U. K. inflations, *Econometrica* 50, 987-1007.

Fama, E. and R. Roll, 1968, Some properties of symmetric stable distributions, *Journal of American Statistical Association* 63, 817-837.

French, K., G. W. Schwert, and R. Stambaugh, 1987, Expected stock returns and volatility, *Journal of Financial Economics* 19, 3-29.

Gallant, R., P. Rossi, and G. Tauchen, 1990, Stock prices and volume, Working paper, North Carolina State University, University of Chicago, and Duke University.

Geweke, J., 1989, Inference and forecasting for chaotic nonlinear time series, Working paper, Duke University.

Gleick, J., 1987, *Chaos: Making a New Science* (Viking Press, New York, NY).

Granger, C. and A. Andersen, 1978, *An Introduction to Bilinear Time Series Models* (Vandenhoeck & Ruprecht, Göttingen).

Grassberger, P. and I. Procaccia, 1983, Measuring the strangeness of strange attractors, *Physica* 9D, 189-208.

Hénon, M., 1976, A two-dimensional mapping with a strange attractor, *Communications in Mathematical Physics* 50, 69-77.

Hinich, M. and D. Patterson, 1985, Evidence of nonlinearity in stock returns, *Journal of Business and Economic Statistics* 3, 69-77.

Hsieh, D., 1989, Testing for nonlinearity in daily foreign exchange rate changes, *Journal of Business* 62, 339-368.

Chaos and Nonlinear Dynamics   1877

——, 1990, A nonlinear stochastic rational expectations model of exchange rates, Working paper, Duke University.

——, 1991, Implications of nonlinear dynamics for financial risk management, Working paper, Duke University.

——, and B. LeBaron, 1988, Finite sample properties of the BDS statistic, Working paper, University of Chicago and University of Wisconsin at Madison.

LeBaron, B., 1988, The changing structure of stock returns, Working paper, University of Wisconsin.

Lorenz, N., 1963, Deterministic nonperiodic flow, *Journal of the Atmospheric Sciences* 20, 130-141.

Mackey, M, and L. Glass, 1977, Oscillation and chaos in physiological control systems, *Science* 50, 287-289.

Mandelbrot, B., 1963, The variation of certain speculative prices, *Journal of Business* 36, 394-419.

McLeod, A. J. and W. K. Li, 1983, Diagnostic checking ARM time series models using squared-residual autocorrelations, *Journal of Time Series Analysis* 4, 269-273.

Nelson, D., 1990, ARCH models as diffusion approximations, *Journal of Econometrics* 45, 7-38.

——, 1991, Conditional heteroskedasticity in asset returns: a new approach, *Econometrica* 59, 347-370.

Pemberton, J. and H. Tong, 1981, A note on the distribution of non-linear autoregressive stochastic models, *Journal of Time Series Analysis* 2, 49-52.

Prescott, D. M. and T. Stengos, 1988, Do asset markets overlook exploitable nonlinearities? The case of gold, Working paper, University of Guelph.

Priestley, M., 1980, State-dependent models: A general approach to non-linear time series analysis, *Journal of Time Series Analysis* 1, 47-71.

Ramsey, J. and H. Yuan, 1989, Bias and error bias in dimension calculation and their evaluation in some simple models, *Physical Letters A* 134, 287-297.

Robinson, P., 1977, The estimation of a non-linear moving average model, *Stochastic Processes and Their Applications* 5, 81-90.

Scheinkman, J. and B. LeBaron, 1989, Nonlinear dynamics and stock returns, *Journal of Business* 62, 311-337.

Schwarz, G., 1978, Estimating the dimension of a model, *Annals of Statistics* 6, 461-464.

Schwert, G. W. and P. J. Seguin, 1990, Heteroskedasticity in stock returns, *Journal of Finance* 45, 1129-1155.

Stone, C. J., 1977, Consistent nonparametric regressions, *Annals of Statistics* 5, 595-620.

Takens, F., 1980, Detecting strange attractors in turbulence, in D. Rand and L. Young, eds.: *Dynamical Systems and Turbulence* (Springer-Verlag, Berlin).

Tong, H. and K. Lim, 1980, Threshold autoregression, limit cycles, and cyclical data, *Journal of the Royal Statistical Society* Series B, 42, 245-292.

Tsay, R., 1986, Nonlinearity tests for time series, *Biometrika* 73, 461-466.

White, H., 1988, Economic prediction using neural networks: The case of IBM daily stock returns, Working paper, University of California, San Diego.

[21]

Journal of Business & Economic Statistics, July 1992, Vol. 10, No. 3

On Determining the Dimension of Real-Time Stock-Price Data

E. Scott Mayfield
Department of Economics, Boston College, Chestnut Hill, MA   02167

Bruce Mizrach
Department of Finance, The Wharton School, Philadelphia, PA   19104

We estimate the dimension of high-frequency stock-price data using the correlation integral of Grassberger and Procaccia. The data, even after filtering, appear to be of low dimension. To control for dependence in higher moments, we use a new technique known as the method of delays in our reconstruction. Delaying the data leads dimension estimates similar to random processes. We conclude that the data are either of low dimension with high entropy or nonlinear but of high dimension.

KEY WORDS: Correlation integral; Entropy; Method of time delays; Nonlinear dynamics.

The study of nonlinear dynamics has generated conceptual breakthroughs in areas as diverse as fluid dynamics, cardiology, and biology. Seemingly random phenomena have been modeled successfully as low-dimensional nonlinear maps. Several authors (Barnett and Chen 1988; Brock 1986; Brock and Sayers 1988; Frank and Stengos 1988, 1989, Scheinkman and LeBaron 1989) have applied nonlinear analysis to economic and financial data.

This article is an attempt to uncover evidence of complex dynamics in U.S. equity markets. We determine the dimension and entropy of real-time stock-price data using the correlation integral of Grassberger and Procaccia (1983a). Our data track the intradaily movements in the Standard and Poor's (S&P) 500 cash index, sampled at 20-second intervals, approximately 20,000 observations in all. No previous analysis of economic or financial data has used sample sizes approaching those used in the physical sciences, typically 15,000 to 40,000 observations. This allows us to compute dimension estimates with a much higher level of statistical reliability. As Ramsey and Yuan (1990) noted, dimension estimates can be significantly biased in samples under 5,000 observations.

The work of Takens (1980, 1983) underlies the empirical analysis of nonlinear systems. Takens showed that one can determine the dimension of a dynamical system from a univariate time series. Proper reconstruction of the dynamical system is critical though and requires eliminating temporal dependence from the data; failure to do so often results in dimension estimates that are biased downward. Brock (1986) noted that dimension estimates should be invariant to smooth transformations of the data and advocated reconstruction using the residuals from a linear time series model. Subse-

quently, economists have adopted the Brock residual test as the standard diagnostic.

We argue that filtering techniques can be misleading. Our concern is that the Brock residual test has little power against the alternative of dependence in higher moments, a property often found in financial data. We show that a smooth nonlinear data-generating mechanism for stock returns will generate temporal dependence in *all* of the data's moments. Under these circumstances, no finite set of filters is adequate to remove temporal dependence. Even after autoregressive moving average (ARMA) and generalized autoregressive conditional heteroscedasticity (GARCH) filtering, dimension estimates will still be biased.

This article proposes that the economics literature follow the physical sciences in using the method of time delays. Rather than trying to filter out the dependence in the time series, one uses lags of the data at which the series has become approximately independent. Choosing this lag is a crucial free parameter. If we choose too short a delay, we fail to eliminate temporal dependence. Alternatively, if the delay is too long, it is difficult to detect underlying low-dimensional structure. With sensitive dependence, any noise on the system will cause the attractor's structure to be obliterated after a limited number of iterations. Data sampled at a daily frequency stand little chance of uncovering the dynamic properties of a chaotic attractor operating at an hourly frequency.

There is an optimal frequency, in a statistical sense, at which to reconstruct the system's dynamics. This occurs at some fraction of the mean orbital time at which the data are nearly independent. In our analysis, a minimum of mutual information occurs at a sampling interval of approximately five minutes.

368   Journal of Business & Economic Statistics, July 1992

After filtering with both ARMA and GARCH models, we find very strong evidence of low dimension. From the shift in the correlation integral, we also find a very high degree of entropy. By the methods currently employed in the economics literature, one could construe this as very strong evidence for chaotic dynamics.

When we reconstruct using the method of time delays, however, we find very different results. Our dimension estimates resemble those of random processes. We conclude that the data are either not of low dimension or that entropy renders the market nearly random after only five minutes.

The organization of the article is as follows: Section 1 describes the properties of the data we are looking for, dimension and entropy. Section 2 describes the correlation integral and how to construct estimates of dimension and entropy. Section 3.1 details the standard practice in the economics literature of filtering with ARMA and GARCH models. The bulk of our contribution is in the empirical analysis of Section 3.2, where we compute estimates of dimension and entropy using filtered data. Section 4 argues why filtering is likely to be inadequate. Section 5 repeats the dimension calculations using the method of delays and comes to very different conclusions. Section 6 includes a summary of our results.

1. MATHEMATICAL CHAOS

In this article, we study discrete dynamical systems of the form

$$x_{t+1} = F(x_t), \tag{1}$$

where $F : R^n \rightarrow R^n$. Much of the empirical work in nonlinear dynamics is concerned with uncovering the dimension of the attracting set of (1). An attractor is a compact set, Λ, such that there is a neighborhood of Λ such that for almost every initial condition the limit set of iterates of (1) as $t \rightarrow \infty$ is Λ. As a practical matter, we focus attention on finding systems of low dimension; these are the only systems that can be reliably distinguished from random ones.

1.1 Reconstructing Complex Dynamics

In our application, x_t might be thought of as *the market*. We receive only a scalar signal of its "heartbeat" in the form of a univariate time series of the S&P 500 index of stocks,

$$p_t = h(x_t), \tag{2}$$

where $h : R^n \rightarrow R$ is an observer function of the market. What hope, if any, might we have of recovering the market dynamics from p_t? Takens (1980, 1983) showed that much of the system's dynamics is preserved as long as F and h are at least C^2 functions. Define an m-dimensional vector constructed from our univariate time series,

series,

$$p_t^m = (p_t, \ldots p_{t+m-1})$$
$$= (h(x_t), \ldots, h(F^{m-1}(x_t))) \equiv J_m, \tag{3}$$

where F^{m-1} is the composition of F with itself $m - 1$ times. For example, $F^2(x_t) = F(F(x_t))$. We can now state the following result.

Proposition 1.1 (Takens 1980). For smooth pairs (h, F), the map $J_m : R^n \rightarrow R^m$ will be an embedding for $m \geq 2n + 1$.

Takens' theorem is really quite remarkable and has motivated nearly all of the empirical research on chaos. As Brock (1986) noted, the theorem implies that the dynamical behavior of the m vectors of stock-price data will resemble the unobservable dynamical behavior of the market process. Most important for our purposes is that the embedding preserves both the dimension and entropy of the dynamical system.

In summary, the Takens embedding theorem allows the degree of complexity of an underlying system to be recovered from a scalar time series that is smoothly related to the state variables of the system. In practice, however, proper reconstruction of the attractor is crucial; it is extremely important to remove the temporal dependence of nearby points on the reconstructed attractor. In implementing the Grassberger and Procaccia (GP) algorithm, the choice of time delay in the m vectors is crucial in properly constructing the embedding. If the data are sampled at very fine or coarse intervals, the dynamics can remain hidden from the analyst. We develop the GP procedure in Section 2 and discuss in greater detail various experimental considerations in Section 3.

1.2 Lyapunov Exponents and Entropy

A distinguishing property of chaotic processes is that of sensitive dependence; points that are initially close together tend to spread apart eventually. This property may lead the analyst to mistake a chaotic system for a random one. Combined with measurement limitations of the current state, sensitive dependence places an upper bound on the ability to forecast chaotic processes, even if the model F is known with perfect certainty.

To formalize the notion of sensitive dependence, we use the concept of the Lyapunov exponent. Let $D_x F^N$ be the $n \times n$ Jacobian matrix evaluated at $x \in R^n$, and let $(D_x F^N)^*$ be the transpose of $D_x F^N$.

Definition 1.1 (Guckenheimer and Holmes 1985). Consider subspaces $V_1^{(1)} \supset V_1^{(2)} \supset \cdots \supset V_1^{(n)}$ in the tangent space at $F^N(x)$ and numbers $\mu_1 \geq \mu_2 \geq \cdots \geq \mu_n$ with the properties that (a) $D_x F(V^{(j)i}) = V_{i+1}^{(j)}$, (b) dimension $(V_1^{(j)}) = n + 1 - j$, and (c) $\lim_{N \rightarrow \infty}(1/N) \times \ln\sqrt{(D_x F^N)^*(D_x F^N) \cdot v} = \mu_j$ for all $v \in V_0^{(j)} - V_0^{(j+1)}$. The μ_j are then called the *Lyapunov exponents*.

As is standard in dynamic models, the largest exponent is crucial. If the map F is chaotic, at least one of the exponents must be positive. We treat the existence of a positive Lyapunov exponent as the definition of a chaotic system.

The Lyapunov exponents tell us about the average rate of expansion or contraction along the entire trajectory. In a chaotic system, points are being separated continually from one another in at least one dimension. Small discrepancies in the initial state become magnified and eventually become distinct trajectories.

In the empirical work that follows, we will not estimate the exponents directly. Rather, we will estimate the system's entropy. Pesin (1977) showed that the metric entropy equals the sum of the positive Lyapunov exponents. If we find evidence of low dimension and positive entropy, this will be strong evidence for the existence of chaotic dynamics.

2 THE CORRELATION INTEGRAL

This section details the workhorse of the empirical literature on nonlinear dynamics, the correlation integral. The first part is devoted to dimension estimation and the second part to entropy.

2.1 Correlation Dimension

Consider vector m histories of the S&P 500 index,

$$p_j^m = (p_j, \ldots, p_{j+m-1}). \qquad (4)$$

The correlation integral measures the number of m vectors within an ε neighborhood of one another (Grassberger and Procaccia 1983a, 1984). In our notation, the correlation integral is defined as

$$\tilde{C}_m(\varepsilon) = \lim_{N \to \infty} \frac{1}{N^2} \times \#\{(j, k) | \|p_j^m - p_k^m\| < \varepsilon\},$$

$$m = 2, 3, \ldots, \qquad (5)$$

where $\|\cdot\|$ is some norm, N is the number of m histories, m is the embedding dimension, and $\#$ denotes the cardinality of the set. As $\varepsilon \to 0$, $\tilde{C}_m(\varepsilon) \sim \varepsilon^\nu$, where ν, the correlation exponent, is a lower-bound estimate of the Hausdorff dimension. Thus, for small ε,

$$\ln_2 \tilde{C}_m(\varepsilon) = \ln_2 k + \nu \ln_2 \varepsilon, \qquad (6)$$

where k is a constant. In practice, (6) is calculated over a range of ε's. Brock (1986) showed that the correlation exponent is independent of any two norms and independent of m for $m \geq 2n + 1$.

2.2 Kolmogorov Entropy

Direct numerical computation of Lyapunov exponents has proven to be quite difficult in experimental systems. The most popular algorithm has been the one proposed by Wolf, Swift, Swinney, and Vastano (1985). Eckmann, Kamphurst, Ruelle, and Scheinkman (1988) and Barnett and Chen (1988) applied this algorithm to stock-market data and monetary indexes, respectively. Recently, McCaffrey, Ellner, Gallant, and Nychka (1991)

proposed a new approach that works directly with the Jacobian matrix using nonparametric regression.

Estimates of Lyapunov exponents, however, have proven to be quite sensitive to embedding dimension and initial conditions, so we motivate an alternative procedure that can be implemented using the correlation integral. Grassberger and Procaccia (1983b, 1984) showed that the vertical change in the position of the invariant portion of the correlation integral (i.e., where the slope is unchanging) is a lower-bound estimate of Kolmogorov entropy. Specifically, they defined

$$K_{2,d}(\varepsilon) = \frac{1}{\tau} \ln \frac{C_d(\varepsilon)}{C_{d+1}(\varepsilon)}, \qquad (7)$$

where $C_d(\varepsilon)$ is the value of the correlation integral for embedding dimension d and delay time between observations τ. They showed that

$$\lim_{\substack{d \to \infty \\ \varepsilon \to 0}} K_{2,d}(\varepsilon) \sim K_2, \qquad (8)$$

where K_2 is order-2 Renyi entropy, which is a lower-bound estimate of Kolmogorov entropy. As embedding dimension increases, the average vertical distance between the integrals is the GP lower-bound estimate of Kolmogorov entropy.

3. DIMENSION AND ENTROPY ESTIMATES USING FILTERED DATA

In this section, we use the correlation integral to estimate both the dimension and entropy of our real-time stock-price data. In seeking to replicate previous work in the economics literature, we first look at transformations of the data that rely only on filtering. In Section 5, we repeat our calculations using the method of delays.

3.1 Filtering

Brock and Sayers (1988) studied the effect of temporal dependence on dimension estimates. They reported low-dimension estimates for a number of quarterly economic time series, but they believed these estimates to be spurious because of near unit roots. In phase space, data that are highly correlated will lie nearly along a line. Thus the reconstructed attractor will be stretched along a ray, leading the data analyst to underestimate the true dimension. Grassberger and Procaccia (1983a) noted the same phenomena in continuous time processes sampled at very close intervals.

Addressing this problem, Brock (1986) proposed using the residuals from a linear time series model to estimate dimension. Under the chaotic null, the residuals will preserve the dimension of the attracting set.

Proposition 3.1 (Brock [1986] Residual Test Theorem). Consider the model (1), (3) with F possessing a chaotic attractor. The residuals from a finite dimen-

370 Journal of Business & Economic Statistics, July 1992

sional autoregressive (AR) process fit to p, will have the same dimension as p_t.

After filtering the data with various ARMA models, Brock and Sayers [1988] rejected the hypothesis that the true data-generating process is of low dimension. All subsequent work in the economics literature has followed Brock's procedure of whitening the data with filters.

Scheinkman and LeBaron (1989) proposed another diagnostic tool, shuffling the data. By randomizing the original series, one creates a series without temporal structure. For an iid process, randomizing will not effect the dimension, since the shuffled series will also be iid. For data generated by a low-dimensional chaotic attractor, however, the loss of structure will cause the data to become more space filling. Thus dimension calculations based on the shuffled data are a useful benchmark against which to compare actual dimension estimates.

Few studies have passed the shuffle diagnostic after ARMA filtering. Frank and Stengos (1989) and Scheinkman and LeBaron (1989) reported dimension estimates, in the range of 6 to 7 after filtering, that pass the shuffle diagnostic. If filtering has not removed all of the temporal dependence, however, these results may still be biased. Only if the dimension estimates are robust to a delay time reconstruction can we be confident that filtering has removed all of the temporal dependence.

3.2 Data

We analyze the S&P 500 stock index, sampled at approximately 20-second intervals, as a measure of real-time market-wide price fluctuations. The S&P 500 index is a weighted average of stock prices, providing a smooth aggregator of the underlying market dynamics. The principal problem in using an index is the possibility of introducing noise into the system through aggregation bias. The quality of the index can be crucial for estimates of dimension and entropy. Barnett and Chen (1988) found evidence for chaotic dynamics in five Divisia but only one simple-sum monetary aggregate. Since the S&P 500 is a widely traded asset and can be replicated with positions in the underlying stocks, arbitrage possibilities are likely to keep the noise level low.

The data are from January 1987 and were obtained from the Chicago Mercantile Exchange, which monitors the S&P 500 for the trading of index futures. There are 19,027 observations in this trading month, comparable to the sample sizes of experimental data used in the physical sciences.

Previous studies employing relatively low-frequency economic data, such as those of Brock and Sayers (1988) and Frank and Stengos (1988), have only been able to analyze data sets of 200 observations because they are limited to post-World War II quarterly observations. In a previous analysis of the S&P 500, Scheinkman and LaBaron (1989) examined a daily data set of approximately 5,000 observations. The actual dimension calculations, however, are computed for weekly return series of one-fifth that size. Frank and Stengos (1989) looked at a precious-metal series at a daily frequency but have only 12 years of data. In contrast, our real-time data set provides a virtually limitless number of time series observations reflecting market conditions.

We log-difference the original data to create a series of real-time returns. In Table 1, we show descriptive statistics for the original and log-differenced series. References to the S&P 500 are to this transformed series. There are significant departures from normality in the third and fourth cumulants. Although excess kurtosis is a common feature of high-frequency asset returns, the skewness seems to be a unique aspect of the real-time data.

Following Brock (1986), we filter the log-differenced series with linear ARMA models. On the basis of the Akaike information criterion, an ARMA $(12, 0, 0)$ model is used to filter the data. Since the stock exchange does not trade continuously, dummy variables for the first and last hours of the day are also included to account for nontrading effects.

Our next concern is dependence in the second moments, particularly because of the excess kurtosis. The squared residuals from the ARMA model are tested, and evidence of Engle's (1982) autoregressive conditional heteroscedasticity is detected. A GARCH $(1, 1)$ model is then fit by maximum likelihood, and the data are filtered again. Since we are taking a smooth transformation of the data, the Brock residual theorem applies to this series as well. Under the GARCH null, the data will be a random process after filtering. If we denote the conditional mean as $\bar{p}_t$ and the conditional variance as $\bar{\sigma}_t$, the standardized residuals,

$$v_t = \frac{(p_t - \bar{p}_t)}{\sqrt{\bar{\sigma}_t}}, \tag{9}$$

are distributed $N(0, 1)$.

After prewhitening the data, we have three time series: (1) SP500, the log difference of the original S&P 500 cash index; (2) ARMA, the residuals from passing SP500 through an ARMA $(12, 0, 0)$ filter; and (3) GARCH, the standardized ARMA residuals.

Table 1. Descriptive Statistics: S&P 500 Index

Statistic	Levels	Log-differences
Mean	263.35	.65257E-05
Standard deviation	8.8518	.13975E-03
Skewness	-.34592	-3.0980
Kurtosis	-.82171	192.47
Minimum	242.22	-.57800E-02
Maximum	280.96	.25684E-02

Table 2. Correlation Exponent Estimates

Embedding	S&P500 (1)	S&P500 (2)	ARMA (1)	ARMA (2)	GARCH (1)	GARCH (2)	DELAY 16 (1)	DELAY 16 (2)
2	1.39	1.42	1.70	1.76	1.76	1.71	1.41	1.42
3	2.33	2.49	2.39	2.55	2.45	2.48	2.40	2.49
4	2.95	3.32	2.94	3.40	3.02	3.32	3.29	3.29
5	3.37	4.16	3.38	4.16	3.51	4.02	3.98	4.15
6	3.53	4.91	3.60	4.93	3.88	4.78	4.74	4.89
7	3.53	5.67	3.63	5.82	3.95	5.72	5.43	5.64
8	3.45	6.34	3.53	6.67	3.98	6.38	6.30	6.32
9	3.37	7.25	3.44	7.38	3.88	7.15	6.91	7.25
10	3.21	7.78	3.26	8.40	3.81	8.10	7.69	7.74
15	2.83	10.77	2.85	10.89	3.17	11.44	10.33	9.90
20	2.59	12.30	2.60	12.73	3.12	14.09	11.80	12.46

NOTE: Columns (1) report estimates for original series and columns (2) report estimates for the shuffled series.

3.3 Dimension Estimates

We calculate estimates of the correlation exponent over the range of embedding dimensions $M = 2, 3, \ldots, 10, 15, 20$. Theoretically, dimension estimates are made as $\varepsilon \rightarrow 0$. In practice, estimates are made over a range of values. The smallest value of ε is determined by the precision of the raw data; the original S&P 500 cash index is reported in dollars and cents. Consequently, the smallest nonzero change in the index that can be recorded is .01. This determines the smallest nonzero distance between any two m vectors. For the SP500 time series, the lower bound of the meaningful portion of the correlation integral is $\ln_2 \bar\varepsilon = -14.7$. We set an upper bound for ε such that 50% of the calculated norms are eliminated. This rule for estimating the correlation dimension roughly coincides with estimating the slope of the steepest segment of the correlation integral as identified by the nonparametric procedure developed by Mayfield and Mizrach (1991).

Results are reported in Table 2. Columns (1) report estimates for the ordered time series, and columns (2) report estimates for the shuffled series. Using a uniform pseudorandom number generator, each shuffled series is constructed by random draws without replacement from the associated original series. For the three series SP500, ARMA, and GARCH, comparison of adjacent embedding spaces indicates that marginal increases in embedding beyond 6 and 8 fail to reveal additional structure in the attractor. By comparing dimension estimates for the original series to those for the corresponding shuffled series, it is clear that there is low-dimensional structure present in the data.

In summary, across all three times series, dimension estimates become invariant to embedding and plateau at about 3.5 to 4.0. These estimates are in striking contrast to those based on the shuffled series. For each of the shuffled series, estimates continue to increase with embedding. It is clear that, by shuffling the data, the resulting series are much more space-filling than the original ones. In Figures 1, 2, and 3, we compare dimension estimates of the ordered series with those of

the shuffled series. All three series pass the shuffle diagnostic.

In addition, by comparing the largest estimated dimension for each series (SP500: 3.53, ARMA: 3.63, GARCH: 3.98) it is clear that the low-dimension estimates reported in Table 2 are not due to the effects of a near unit-root process or GARCH process. In addition, these estimates are well below the estimates of 6 to 7 found by Scheinkman and LaBaron (1989) using daily closes.

3.4 Entropy Calculations

The results in Section 3.3 indicate that a low-dimensional process for stock-market prices exists. Furthermore, our evidence indicates that the nonlinearities are beyond GARCH. These estimates do not, by themselves, however, indicate that the underlying attractor is chaotic; the attractor must also be shown to have positive entropy.

Under the premise that the reconstruction is correct, we calculate a lower-bound estimate of its entropy based on the procedure described by Grassberger and Pro-

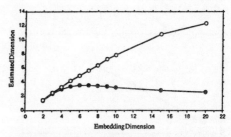

Figure 1. Dimension Estimates SP500: Ordered Versus Shuffled Data. This figure graphs the estimated GP correlation dimension for a range of embedding dimensions. The dark points (•) represent estimates for the ordered data and plateau around 3.5 as the embedding dimension rises. The dimension estimates for the shuffled data, as represented by the light points (○), continue to rise with embedding dimension.

372   Journal of Business & Economic Statistics, July 1992

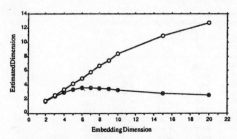

Figure 2. Dimension Estimates After ARMA Filtering: Ordered Versus Shuffled Data. The estimated correlation dimensions are graphed against their associated embedding dimensions. Using the ordered data, the estimates approach 3.5, while the estimates based on shuffled data continue to increase with embedding: •, ordered data; ○, shuffled data.

Table 3. Entropy Calculations

Embedding dimension	Δ intercept	K_2 (bits/min.)
3	−1.884	5.652
4	−1.688	5.064
5	−1.256	3.768
6	−.687	2.061
7	−.319	.957
8	−.177	.531
9	−.118	.354
10	−.095	.285
15	−.486	.291
20	−.579	.348

caccia (1983b, 1984) and described in Section 2.2. Table 3 displays the vertical change in the correlation integral and the implied entropy estimate per one minute for the series. For small ε, the entropy estimate is proportional to the negative of the change in the intercept term as the embedding dimension increases. Figure 4 shows a graph of K_2 versus embedding dimension.

Based on these calculations, the K_2 lower-bound estimate of Kolmogorov entropy is approximately one-third of a bit of information per minute. Since we reconstruct the attractor from the difference in the S&P 500 cash index, which is reported in dollars and cents, our accuracy of the current state of the system is only 1 part in 50. Thus we have no more than six bits of information on the current state of the system. Given an observation on the current state of the system and knowledge of the true underlying system, an investor would have no knowledge of the system's state after 15 to 18 minutes. We define this duration as the implied forecast horizon and use it to support our choice of delay time in Section 4.

On finding positive entropy, a researcher might conclude that the stock-return series is chaotic; however, if filtering has not removed temporal dependence in the data, this conclusion will be incorrect. In Section 5 of the article, we address the issue of time delays. If the reconstruction is correct, dimension calculations will be robust to delays within the region of sensitive dependence implied by our entropy calculations. In fact, we show that our dimension estimates are not invariant to delay time.

4. HIGHER ORDER TEMPORAL DEPENDENCE

In this section, we motivate why the data may still be temporally dependent after filtering. Assume for expository purposes that F in (1) is a scalar analytic function. Consider a series expansion of F around 0.

$$F(x_t) = \sum_{j=0}^{\infty} c_j x_t^j. \tag{10}$$

Suppose that one fits an AR(1) model to the data-generating mechanism (10). Define the residuals

$$\xi_{t+1} = x_{t+1} - \hat{\beta} x_t. \tag{11}$$

White (1980) showed that $\hat{\beta}$ will not coincide with the c_j's of the power series expansion if one estimates β

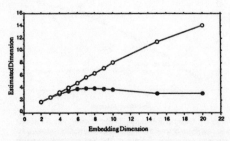

Figure 3. Dimension Estimates of Standardized GARCH Residuals: Ordered Versus Shuffled Data. After applying the GARCH filter, estimated correlation exponents peak at slightly less than 4, while the estimates using shuffled data continue to be space filling: •, ordered data; ○, shuffled data.

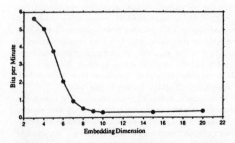

Figure 4. K_2 Lower Bound Entropy Estimate (bits per minute). This figure plots the vertical shift in the invariant segment of the correlation integral against the corresponding embedding dimension. For large embeddings, this is a lower-bound estimate of Kolmogorov entropy. At an embedding dimension of 10, the values plateau at approximately one-third of a bit of information per minute.

using ordinary least squares. More important for our purposes is that the residuals will be uncorrelated with lagged x's, but *not* independent; that is, $E[\xi_{t+1}|x_t] = 0$, but $E[\xi_{t+1}|x_t^2] \neq 0$. This result will obtain for any filter of degree k. Define the kth order residuals,

$$\xi_{t+1}^k = x_{t+1} - \sum_{j=0}^k \hat{\beta}_j x_t^j. \tag{12}$$

These residuals will still be correlated with the $k + 1$th power of x, $E[\xi_{t+1}^k|x_t^{k+1}] \neq 0$.

The data seem to show precisely this type of high-order dependence. Although GARCH filtering may account for the excess kurtosis, it is not equipped to remove the skewness. Only by delaying the data can we be sure that some higher order dependence does not remain.

5. THE METHOD OF TIME DELAYS

Takens's theorem allows us, in principle, to choose m histories with any delay time τ in reconstructing the attractor:

$$p_j^m = (p_j, p_{j+\tau}, p_{j+2\tau}, \ldots, p_{j+(m-1)\tau}). \tag{13}$$

In applied work, however, the quality of the reconstruction depends critically on the choice of τ. Empirically, it is desirable to reconstruct with data that are widely dispersed on the attractor. Filtered data, however, are no more likely to satisfy this criteria than the unfiltered data. In short, ARMA and GARCH filtering will rule out only very specific types of temporal dependence.

To ensure a wide dispersion of points on the attractor, the delay time τ is chosen so as to minimize the information on p_t contained in $p_{t-\tau}$. Holzfuss and Mayer-Kress (1986) noted that, in highly periodic data, the first zero-crossing of the autocorrelation function corresponds to the first minimum of mutual information function. In the log-differenced data, the first zero-crossing point of the autocorrelation function occurs at the 16th lag.

Using a delay of 16 observations between coordinates, we recalculate our dimension estimates. This delay corresponds to 5.33 minutes, which is well within our implied forecast horizon of 15 to 18 minutes. The fourth column of Table 2 reports these estimates as DELAY16. With this reconstruction, our dimension estimates are no longer invariant to embedding. In addition, by comparing the estimates to those from the corresponding shuffled series, as in Table 2, it is clear that the data are as space-filling as a stochastic process. With a conservative delay, the apparent structure of the system is removed.

The dramatic rise in dimension estimates is evidence of dependence in higher moments. It is not possible, however, to uniquely identify the source. With data sampled at such high frequency, nontraded stocks might be the cause. If a security does not trade within a given interval, then its most recent value is used in the calculation of the index. Thus nontraded securities could be a source of spurious dependence.

Two empirical observations lead us to the conclusion that nontraded securities are not the fundamental cause of the biased dimension estimates. First, the filters include opening and closing dummies for the first and last hours of the day. This should remove some nontrading effects, yet dimension estimates remain essentially unchanged using the filtered data. Second, based on the Wood transactions data, we compute a rough gauge on how often the stocks in the S&P500 trade. During January 1987, the lowest volume New York Stock Exchange stock in our sample is Brown and Sharpe (B&S). From a random selection of days, we estimate B&S has 35 quotes and trades per day, on average. At the other extreme, Ford Motor Company is a representative high-volume stock, with an average of 1,320 trades and quotes per day. For Ford, information arrives every 19.1 seconds, while for B&S it takes 722.9 seconds. With no delay, at an embedding dimension of 10, each m vector spans approximately 199.8 seconds (3.33 minutes). By interpolating between the rate at which Ford and B&S trade, we estimate that new information arrives on at least 371 of the S&P 500 stocks ($\approx 75\%$) within the time spanned by a given m vector.

Given that large stocks trade more frequently, over 75% of the S&P's market value is updated in this time interval. As embedding increases from 3 to 10 (or even 20), however, the dimension estimates remain very low, even though most stocks in the index have traded. Consequently, we do not believe that the dramatic change in dimension estimates using the method of delays is due to nontrading effects.

These results demonstrate that, with real-time data, filtering may not remove temporal dependence. Since filtering techniques remove only very specific types of nonlinear dependence, there is great potential for incorrectly detecting low dimension in real-time data. For this reason, we argue that the method of time delays is the appropriate reconstruction technique.

6. CONCLUSION

To gain deeper insight into the determination of stock-market prices, we apply nonlinear analysis to real-time data on the S&P 500 cash index. The use of high-frequency data enables us to examine the precise evolution of the market. Using the correlation integral, we find evidence of a low-dimensional attractor with positive entropy. These calculations are robust to ARMA and GARCH filtering but are not robust to changes in delay time.

The analysis of real-time data requires special considerations. Filtering is unable to remove temporal dependence in the stock-market data. In this instance, the choice of delay time is crucial for the proper reconstruction of the attractor; a delay long enough to elim-

374   Journal of Business & Economic Statistics, July 1992

inate the possible stretching of the attractor must be chosen. We choose a conservative delay of five minutes. With this delay time, the apparent structure of the system is removed.

Our inference concerning these results is, unfortunately, only heuristic. As Barnett and Hinich (1991) noted, no formal asymptotic theory for estimates of the correlation dimension and Kolgomorov entropy exists under the null hypothesis of chaos. Until such a theory is devised, we can only buttress evidence for nonlinear structure using existing statistical tools. Barnett and Hinich, for example, used the bispectrum.

We conclude that either the underlying system is of very high dimension or, if the true system is, in fact, of low dimension, its entropy is so high that it cannot be predicted beyond five minutes. From the standpoint of financial-market participants, these conclusions are essentially equivalent. Accepting the first conclusion, that there is a chaotic attractor, does not make the data in any sense more predictable. For very near-term forecasts, accurate prediction of the system's future state is possible; however, entropy causes these forecasts to deteriorate quickly. Our findings indicate that stock prices, even accounting for the nonlinearities, cannot be predicted over horizons of significant length.

ACKNOWLEDGMENTS

We thank Lisa Calise for her research assistance. The IBM Cambridge Research Facility generously provided time on their vector processor. Ken Kroner supplied the GARCH program used in Section 3. William Brock made helpful comments on an earlier draft that was presented at the International Symposium on Evolutionary Dynamics and Nonlinear Economics in Austin, Texas, April 1989. We also thank two anonymous referees and an associate editor for their comments. We retain responsibility for any remaining errors.

[Received August 1990. Revised February 1992.]

REFERENCES

Barnett, W. A., and Chen, P. (1988), "The Aggregation-Theoretic Monetary Aggregates Are Chaotic And Have Strange Attractors: An Econometric Application of Mathematical Chaos," in *Dynamic Econometric Modeling*, eds. W. Barnett, E. Berndt, and H. White, Cambridge, U.K.: Cambridge University Press, pp. 199–246.

Barnett, W. A., and Hinich, M. J. (1991), "Empirical Chaotic Dynamics in Economics," working paper, Washington University and University of Texas at Austin, Dept. of Economics, submitted to *Annals of Operations Research*.

Brock, W. A. (1986), "Distinguished Random and Deterministic Systems: An Expanded Version," *Journal of Economic Theory*, 90, 168–195.

Brock, W. A., and Sayers, C. (1988), "Is The Business Cycle Characterized by Deterministic Chaos?" *Journal of Monetary Economics*, 22, 71–90.

Eckmann, J. P., Kamphurst, S. O., Ruelle, D., and Scheinkman, J. (1988), "Lyapunov Exponents for Stock Returns," in *The Economy as an Evolving Complex System*, SFI Studies in the Sciences of Complexity, Reading, MA: Addison-Wesley, pp. 301–304.

Engle, R. (1982), "Autoregressive Conditional Heteroscedasticity With Estimates of the Variance of U.K. Inflation," *Econometrica*, 50, 987–1008.

Frank, M., and Stengos, T. (1988), "Some Evidence Concerning Macroeconomic Chaos," *Journal of Monetary Economics*, 22, 423–438.

―― (1989), "Measuring the Strangeness of Gold and Silver Rates of Return," *Review of Economic Studies*, 56, 553–568.

Grassberger, P., and Procaccia, I. (1983a), "Measuring the Strangeness of Strange Attractors," *Physica*, 9D, 189–208.

―― (1983b), "Estimation of the Kolmogorov Entropy From a Chaotic Signal," *Physical Review A*, 28, 2591–2593.

―― (1984), "Dimensions and Entropies of Strange Attractors From a Fluctuating Dynamics Approach," *Physica*, 13 D, 34–54.

Guckenheimer, J., and Holmes, P. (1985), *Nonlinear Oscillations, Dynamical Systems, and Bifurcations of Vector Fields*, New York: Springer-Verlag.

Holzfuss, J., and Mayer-Kress, G. (1986), "An Approach to Error-Estimation in the Application of Dimension Algorithms," in *Dimensions and Entropies in Chaotic Systems*, ed. G. Mayer Kress, New York: Springer-Verlag, pp. 114–22.

Mayfield, E. S., and Mizrach, B. (1991), "Nonparametric Estimation of the Correlation Exponent," *Physical Review A*, 88, 5298–5301.

McCaffrey, D. F., Ellner, S., Gallant, A. R., and Nychka, D. (1991), "Estimating the Lyapunov Exponent of a Chaotic System With Nonparametric Regression," Working Paper 1977R, North Carolina State University, Institute of Statistics, submitted to *Journal of the American Statistical Association*.

Pesin, J. B. (1977), "Characteristic Liapunov Exponents and Smooth Ergodic Theory," *Russian Mathematical Survey*, 32, 55–114.

Ramsey, J. B., and Yuan, H. J. (1990), "Statistical Properties of Dimension Calculations Using Small Data Sets," *Nonlinearity*, 3, 155–176.

Scheinkman, J. A., and LeBaron, B. (1989), "Nonlinear Dynamics and Stock Returns," *Journal of Business*, 62, 311–337.

Takens, F. (1980), "Detecting Strange Attractors in Turbulence," in *Dynamical Systems and Turbulence* (Lecture Notes in Mathematics 898), eds. D. Rand and L. Young, Berlin: Springer-Verlag, pp. 366–382.

―― (1983), "Distinguishing Deterministic and Random Systems," in *Nonlinear Dynamics and Turbulence*, eds. G. Borenblatt, G. Iooss, and D. Joseph, Boston: Pittman, pp. 315–333.

White, H. (1980), "Using Least Squares to Approximate Unknown Regression Functions," *International Economic Review*, 21, 149–170.

Wolf, A., Swift, J., Swinney, H., and Vastano, J. (1985), "Determining Lyapunov Exponents From a Time Series," *Physica*, 16 D, 285–317.

[22]

JOURNAL OF FINANCIAL AND QUANTITATIVE ANALYSIS   VOL. 28, NO. 1, MARCH 1993

Implications of Nonlinear Dynamics for Financial Risk Management

David A. Hsieh*

Abstract

This paper demonstrates that when log price changes are not IID, their conditional density may be more accurate than their unconditional density for describing short-term behavior. Using the BDS test of independence and identical distribution, daily log price changes in four currency futures contracts are found to be not IID. While there appear to be no predictable conditional mean changes, conditional variances are predictable, and can be described by an autoregressive volatility model that seems to capture all the departures from independence and identical distribution. Based on this model, daily log price changes are decomposed into a predictable part, which is described parametrically by the autoregressive volatility model, and an unpredictable part, which can be modeled by an empirical density, either parametrically or nonparametrically. This two-step seminonparametric method yields a conditional density for daily log price changes, which has a number of uses in financial risk management.

I. Introduction

A number of recent papers in the economics and finance literature have found strong evidence of nonlinear dynamics in short-term movements of asset returns.[1] The next logical question is: What is the relevance of this finding? In the presence of any dynamics (whether linear or nonlinear), conditional densities can provide a better description of short-term asset price movements than can unconditional densities. This may be important for financial risk management, especially when highly leveraged instruments, such as futures contracts, are involved. For example, hedge ratios and the amount of capital needed to cover possible losses during the time a futures position is held depend critically on the probability distribution of changes in futures prices.

---

*Fuqua School of Business, Duke University, Durham, NC 27706. The author acknowledges the help of Cathy McCrae and Richard McDonald of the Chicago Mercantile Exchange in providing the data used in the analysis. He is grateful for comments from Francis Diebold and JFQA Referee Wayne Ferson, as well as participants at the November 1991 Conference on Volatility at the Amsterdam Institute of Finance and the April 1992 Conference on Global Risk Management of Interest Rate and Exchange Rate Risk at the Berkeley Program in Finance.

[1]See LeBaron (1988), Scheinkman and LeBaron (1989), and Hsieh (1991) for stock returns, and Hsieh (1989) for exchange rates.

Traditional methods of estimating a probability density use a smoothed histogram of past price changes. This corresponds to the unconditional density. A conditional density can provide a more accurate assessment of price changes, since it uses more information. If the dynamics of asset prices were linear in nature, their conditional densities could be obtained in a straightforward manner. The empirical finding that the dynamics of asset prices are nonlinear, however, complicates substantially the estimation of their conditional densities. This paper illustrates how the conditional density can be estimated in a computationally efficient manner, and then it is applied to foreign currency futures.

The outline of the paper is as follows. Section II discusses the difference between conditional and unconditional densities. If price changes are independent and identically distributed (IID), then the two densities are the same. It is, therefore, important to test for independence and identical distribution. Section III introduces the Brock, Dechert, and Scheinkman (1987) test for independence and identical distribution, which is applied to four currency futures contracts traded on the Chicago Mercantile Exchange. It finds that price changes are not IID. In particular, there is strong evidence of conditional heteroskedasticity. Section IV describes a simple two-step seminonparametric method for approximating the conditional densities. Step one extracts the predictable parts of price changes parametrically. For the futures data, the conditional mean is approximately zero, but the conditional variance can be modeled by an autoregressive process. Step two describes the remaining unpredictable movements of price changes nonparametrically. Applications to futures trading are then provided in Section V. The section shows how to determine the capital needed to cover a given probability of losses over the next trading day. Using the estimated conditional density, the capital requirement changes with the conditional variance of futures price changes, while that based on the unconditional density is constant over time. Section V also shows how to use simulation to determine the capital needed to cover a given probability of cumulative losses over a longer horizon. The section finds that the unconditional density can give time-varying capital requirements, which may be more accurate than those from the unconditional density. Concluding remarks are offered in Section VI.

II.   Conditional and Unconditional Densities

This section describes the difference between conditional and unconditional densities. To facilitate discussion, let P_t be the price of an asset at time t. Define $x_t = \text{Log}(P_t/P_{t-1})$ as its continuously compounded rate of change. The unconditional density of x_t is obtained by fitting a density to the histogram of x_t, using either parametric or nonparametric methods. The conditional density of x_t, given its own past values, is obtained by postulating and estimating a complete probability model for the law of motion of x_t over time.[2] Usually the unconditional density is much simpler to estimate, particularly in the case of the parametric method,

---

[2]This is more restrictive than the general notion, which allows conditioning on other information. The univariate approach in this paper is much simpler computationally than the multivariate approach. When conditioning on other information, such as trading volume, these additional variables will need to be modeled.

which explains its popularity in finance.[3] There are situations, however, when the conditional density gives a more accurate probability model of the short-term behavior of x_t.

To highlight the differences between conditional and unconditional densities, consider the following example. Let x_t be a first order autoregressive process,

$$x_t = \alpha + \beta x_{t-1} + u_t,$$

where u_t is IID, normal, with mean 0 and variance σ_u^2, and $|\beta| < 1$. The conditional distribution of x_t is normal, with mean $\alpha/(1-\beta)$ and variance $\sigma_u^2/(1-\beta^2)$, while the distribution of x_t conditional on x_{t-1} is normal, with mean $(\alpha + \beta x_{t-1})$ and variance σ_u^2. The conditional and unconditional distributions are the same whenever $\beta = 0$, i.e., x_t is IID. They are different whenever $\beta \neq 0$, i.e., x_t is not IID.

The two distributions are related as follows. Suppose only x_{t-2} is observed. Then, the conditional distribution of x_t given x_{t-2} is normal, with mean $(\alpha(1 + \beta) + \beta^2 x_{t-2})$ and variance $\sigma_u^2(1 + \beta^2)$. By repeated substitution, it can be shown that the conditional distribution of x_t, given x_{t-k}, converges to the unconditional distribution as $k \rightarrow \infty$. In other words, the unconditional distribution describes the long-run behavior of x_t, while the conditional distribution describes its short-run behavior. In the first order autoregression, the conditional variance is always smaller than the unconditional variance. In general, however, the conditional variance can be larger or smaller than the unconditional variance.[4]

III. Test of Independence and Identical Distribution

The Brock, Dechert, and Scheinkman (1987) (BDS) test for independence and identical distribution is used. This test is chosen because it can detect many types of departures from independence and identical distribution, such as nonstationarity, nonlinearity, and deterministic chaos. Any of these departures from the IID case imply that the conditional distribution is different from the unconditional distribution. Furthermore, the BDS test can serve as a general model specification test, especially in the presence of nonlinear dynamics.[5]

The BDS test has been discussed in detail elsewhere.[6] Only a brief review is provided here. Let $\{x_t, t = 1,\ldots,T\}$ be a time series, and denote $x_t^m = (x_t, x_{t-1},\ldots,x_{t-m+1})$ a point in the m-dimensional Euclidean space. De-

---

[3]Parametric unconditional densities have been estimated by Fama (1965) and Blattberg and Gonedes (1974) for stock returns, and Westerfield (1977), Rogalski and Vinso (1978), and Boothe and Glassman (1987) for exchange rates.

[4]Suppose x_t is given by the following process,

$$x_t = \sigma_t u_t,$$
$$\text{Log } \sigma_t = \alpha + \beta \text{ Log } \sigma_{t-1} + v_t,$$

where u_t is IID, normal, with mean 0 and variance 1, and v_t is IID, normal, with mean 0 and variance σ_v^2. Furthermore, u_t and v_s are independent for all t and s, and $|\beta| < 1$. It is easy to verify that the conditional and unconditional distribution of x_t is different, and that the conditional variance of x_t can be either larger or smaller than the unconditional variance.

[5]See Brock, Hsieh, and LeBaron (1991) for a discussion of this point.

[6]See Scheinkman and LeBaron (1989) and Hsieh (1989).

fine the correlation integral $C_m(\delta)$ to be the fraction of pairs of points, x_t^m and x_s^m, which are within a distance δ of each other,

$$C_m(\delta) \;\; = \;\; \text{plim}_{T\to\infty}\# \left\{ (t,s), \;\; 0 < t < T, \right.$$

$$\left. 0 < s < T : \max_{i=0,\dots,m-1} |x_{t-i} - x_{s-i}| < \delta \right\} /T^2.$$

For the purposes here, the maximum norm will be used, although the standard Euclidean norm is perfectly acceptable. If $\{x_t\}$ were IID, then $C_m(\delta) = (C_1(\delta))^m$. Brock, Dechert, and Scheinkman (1987) construct a statistic for testing the null hypothesis that $C_m(\delta) = (C_1(\delta))^m$.[7] They show that the test statistic is asymptotically a standard normal distribution. Brock, Hsieh, and LeBaron (1991) and Hsieh and LeBaron (1988) report extensive simulations and show that the asymptotic distribution is a good approximation of the finite sample distribution, when there are more than 500 observations. They recommend using δ between one-half to two times the standard deviation of the raw data. Also, the accuracy of the asymptotic distribution deteriorates for high imbedding dimensions, particularly when m is 10 or above.

    The data consist of daily settlement prices for four currency futures contracts traded on the Chicago Mercantile Exchange (CME): the British pound (BP), Deutsche mark (DM), Japanese yen (JY), and Swiss franc (SF), from February 22, 1985, to March 9, 1990, totaling 1275 observations per contract. The starting date corresponds to the time when daily price limits were removed. Currency futures expire four times per year. In order to obtain a continuous time series, the contracts were rolled over to the next expiration cycle one week prior to expiration.

    It is appropriate to discuss why currency futures prices were chosen for analysis instead of forward exchange rates, even though the forward exchange market is many times the size of the currency futures markets. The reason is that financial risk management is generally concerned with the market value of a futures or forward contract over its entire life. Unfortunately, daily forward exchange rates are typically given in fixed maturities of one month, three months, ... etc., which do not provide sufficient information. For this reason, currency futures are turned to, because futures exchanges provide information on daily movements of the futures price throughout the life of a futures contract. Cornell and Reinganum (1981) find that there is practically no difference between forwards and futures in the foreign exchange market. Therefore, futures prices can be used to construct a probability model, which can be applied to forward contracts as well.

    Table 1 provides a statistical description of log price changes. The means are not statistically different from zero. The annualized standard deviations are 12.96 percent, 12.47 percent, 11.26 percent, and 13.82 percent, respectively, for the BP, DM, JY, and SF, assuming that each calendar year consists of 253 trading days. All four series have strong departures from normality, as the coefficients of skewness and kurtosis are statistically different from those of a normal distribution. The BDS statistics for testing independence and identical distribution are provided in

---

[7]Note that IID implies that $C_m(\delta) = (C_1(\delta))^m$, but the converse is not true. Dechert (1988) gives some pathological examples of non-IID data for which $C_m(\delta) = (C_1(\delta))^m$.

Table 1, for imbedding dimensions (m) 2 through 5, and distances (δ) 0.5, 1.0, 1.5, and 2.0 times the standard deviation of the raw data. If the 1-percent marginal significance level is used, independence and identical distribution will be rejected in all 16 statistics for the BP and the JY, 11 of the 16 for the DM, and four of the 16 for the SF. Even though the BDS statistics for each of the currency futures are not independent, they show strong evidence of departure of independence and identical distribution for at least three currency futures. This is consistent with similar findings in the spot currency markets, as in Hsieh (1989).

TABLE 1

Statistical Description of Daily Log Price Changes
February 22, 1985–March 9, 1990 (1275 observations)

		BP	DM	JY	SF
Mean		0.00045	0.00043	0.00032	0.00037
Median		0.00036	0.00000	0.00000	0.00016
Std. Dev.		0.00815	0.00784	0.00708	0.00869
Skewness		0.36	0.28	0.34	0.18
Kurtosis		6.25	5.32	7.81	4.94
Maximum		0.04553	0.04832	0.05333	0.04967
Minimum		−0.02899	−0.03264	−0.04133	−0.03692
BDS Statistics					
m	δ				
2	0.5	2.39*	1.68	4.15*	1.01
3	0.5	2.76*	2.23	4.95*	1.08
4	0.5	3.58*	3.16*	6.39*	1.77
5	0.5	4.40*	3.91*	7.88*	2.57
2	1.0	3.34*	1.48	4.06*	0.46
3	1.0	4.00*	2.10	4.49*	0.85
4	1.0	4.86*	3.11*	5.69*	1.59
5	1.0	5.73*	3.85*	6.52*	2.40
2	1.5	3.96*	1.99	3.68*	0.81
3	1.5	4.84*	2.97*	4.29*	1.62
4	1.5	5.75*	3.95*	5.61*	2.57
5	1.5	6.54*	4.69*	6.32*	3.38*
2	2.0	3.88*	2.51*	3.16*	1.35
3	2.0	4.86*	3.79*	3.84*	2.37
4	2.0	5.77*	4.75*	5.14*	3.30*
5	2.0	6.54*	5.53*	5.73*	4.02*

*Significant at the 1-percent level using a two-tailed test.

m is the imbedding dimension.

δ is the distance between points, measured in terms of number of standard deviations of the raw data.

The critical values (marginal significance level) of the statistics for a two-tailed test are: 1.645 (10%), 1.960 (5%), 2.326 (2%), and 2.576 (1%).

As the BDS test is sensitive to any departure from independence and identical distribution, it is useful to know the cause of the rejection. Table 2 provides some information. It shows that the autocorrelation coefficients of log price changes are not statistically different from zero, either individually or jointly (using the

46   Journal of Financial and Quantitative Analysis

Box-Pierce statistic for the first 15 lags).[8] On the other hand, the autocorrelation coefficients of the absolute values of log price changes are much larger. More than half of them are statistically different from zero, and the joint test using the Box-Pierce statistic rejects the hypothesis that the first 15 lags are zero. This evidence is consistent with the hypothesis that the rejection of independence and identical distribution is not due to linear, but rather nonlinear, dependence in exchange rates.[9]

The rejection of independence and identical distribution implies that the conditional density differs from the unconditional density in describing short-term dynamics of futures prices. Furthermore, the presence of nonlinear dependence implies that linear (e.g., Box-Jenkins) methods cannot be used to model the conditional density. This motivates the goal in the rest of this paper, namely, to obtain a useable form of the conditional density that takes into account the nonlinear dependence, and to provide some interesting applications.

IV. A Two-Step Method for Estimating Conditional Densities

In theory, the conditional density can be estimated nonparametrically, for example, using kernels, splines, neural networks, or series expansions. In practice, nonparametric methods have two drawbacks. They require substantial computational time, and little is known about the sample sizes required for accurate estimation. This paper tries a different approach.

The approach to estimating conditional density is essentially a two-step semi-nonparametric approach. Step one estimates the predictable part of the data parametrically. Step two estimates the remaining unpredictable part nonparametrically. Speed of computation is the primary motivation for doing this in two steps, rather than jointly estimating the parametric and nonparametric parts.[10]

The parametric part in step one deals with the conditional mean and conditional variance of x_t, defined as,

$$\mu_t = E\left(x_t | x_{t-1}, x_{t-2}, \ldots\right),$$

$$\sigma_t = V\left(x_t | x_{t-1}, x_{t-2}, \ldots\right)^{1/2}.$$

For the four currency futures, it will be shown, below, that the conditional mean is zero and that the conditional variance is time varying and depends nonlinearly

---

[8]This finding contradicts those of Hodrick and Srivastava (1987) and McCurdy and Morgan (1987), who find strong autocorrelation in log price changes in currency futures prices using data for which daily price limits were in effect but were not taken into account. Kodres (1988) uses a limited dependent variable method, but fails to take account of the conditional heteroskedasticity, as pointed out by Harvey (1988).

[9]The reader may be concerned with the role of maturity drift in these results using futures data. It is possible that a fixed maturity futures price change is IID, but the distribution of an n-period maturity futures price change is different from that of an $n - 1$ period maturity futures price change. This may induce "spurious" rejection of IID. To check that this is not the case, Appendix A and B (available upon request) provide the BDS statistics and autocorrelation coefficients of the absolute values of daily log price changes of spot currencies, collected by the Board of Governors of the Federal Reserve System, for the same time period. The spot exchange rates (on a two-day forward contract) have essentially the same statistical behavior as the currency futures.

[10]The two-step procedure may suffer from some efficiency loss. However, with the sample size here, the longer computation time of joint estimation is a greater cost than any gain in efficiency.

TABLE 2

Autocorrelations of Price Changes and Their Absolute Values

	BP	DM	JY	SF
Panel A. Autocorrelation Coefficients				
$\rho(1)$	0.032	−0.019	0.024	−0.006
$\rho(2)$	−0.016	−0.009	0.000	−0.013
$\rho(3)$	−0.017	0.042	0.057	0.029
$\rho(4)$	−0.019	−0.043	−0.004	−0.032
$\rho(5)$	−0.005	0.014	0.012	0.009
$\rho(6)$	0.054	0.033	0.021	0.007
$\rho(7)$	−0.045	−0.021	−0.026	−0.017
$\rho(8)$	0.029	0.047	0.051	0.021
$\rho(9)$	−0.016	0.005	0.022	0.008
$\rho(10)$	−0.020	−0.037	−0.005	−0.033
$\rho(11)$	−0.039	−0.009	0.014	−0.011
$\rho(12)$	−0.015	−0.022	0.025	−0.008
$\rho(13)$	0.056	0.018	−0.002	0.034
$\rho(14)$	0.005	0.015	0.042	0.002
$\rho(15)$	0.052	0.056	0.022	0.066
$Q(15)$	20.09	17.12	14.25	12.26
Panel B. Autocorrelation Coefficients of Absolute Values				
$r(1)$	0.107*	0.059	0.118*	0.027
$r(2)$	0.094*	0.038	0.058	0.025
$r(3)$	0.108*	0.079*	0.101*	0.052
$r(4)$	0.112*	0.055	0.041	0.040
$r(5)$	0.081*	0.088*	0.084*	0.084*
$r(6)$	0.096*	0.107*	0.087*	0.097*
$r(7)$	0.088*	0.099*	0.010	0.096*
$r(8)$	0.101*	0.087*	0.088*	0.061
$r(9)$	0.088*	0.063	0.069	0.054
$r(10)$	0.129*	0.128*	0.023	0.113*
$r(11)$	0.047	0.020	0.041	0.038
$r(12)$	0.078*	0.068	−0.005	0.075*
$r(13)$	0.092*	0.086*	0.023	0.088*
$r(14)$	0.116*	0.073*	0.055	0.048
$r(15)$	0.108*	0.115*	0.028	0.103*
$Q(15)$	182.41**	128.85**	79.50**	98.69**

*Significant at the 1-percent level using a two-tailed test.
**Significant at the 1-percent level using a one-tailed test.
$Q(15)$ is the Box-Pierce statistic testing for the first 15 lags to be different from zero. The critical values (marginal significance levels) are: 22.31 (10%), 25.00 (5%), and 27.49 (1%).

on past realizations of x_t. In addition, it is demonstrated that the conditional variance captures most of the predictability of price changes, using the BDS statistic. Therefore, the unpredictable part is modeled as IID,

$$ z_t = (x_t - \mu_t)/\sigma_t. $$

The nonparametric part in step two deals with the density of z_t.

It is important to note that not all nonlinear dependence can be modeled in this way. This method is not appropriate when, for example, there is dependence in higher order moments. Careful diagnostics are therefore needed.

48   Journal of Financial and Quantitative Analysis

A.   Estimating the Conditional Mean Function

The paper now proceeds to characterize the conditional mean function of price changes given its own past, which is defined as,

$$\mu_t = E\left(x_t | x_{t-1}, x_{t-2}, \ldots\right) = f\left(x_{t-1}, x_{t-2}, \ldots\right).$$

Operationally, this means that

$$E\left(x_t - f\left(x_{t-1}, x_{t-2}, \ldots\right) \mid x_{t-1}, x_{t-2}, \ldots\right) = 0.$$

Based on the findings on spot currencies that the conditional mean is zero, it is argued that the same is true for currency futures.

Hsieh (1989) proposes a test of the null hypothesis that the conditional mean function is zero. The test makes use of the fact that, if the conditional mean of x_t is zero, then its bicorrelation coefficients, $E(x_t x_{t-i} x_{t-j})/V(x_t)^{3/2}$, are zero for $i, j \geq 1$.[11] Table 3 provides the estimated bicorrelation coefficients up to the fifth lag. None of them, either individually or jointly, are statistically different from zero. While the bicorrelation test results are consistent with the null hypothesis of a zero conditional mean function, Pemberton and Tong (1981) point out that there exist nonlinear models with zero bicorrelation coefficients and nonzero conditional means. To deal with these types of models, a second approach is turned to using nonparametric methods to directly estimate the conditional mean function.

TABLE 3

Bicorrelation Coefficients

Lags					
i	*j*	BP	DM	JY	SF
1	1	−0.119	−0.059	−0.072	−0.037
1	2	−0.041	−0.011	−0.030	−0.013
2	2	0.232	0.156	0.103	0.185
1	3	−0.024	0.009	0.073	−0.001
2	3	0.125	0.076	−0.003	0.060
3	3	−0.006	−0.097	0.231	−0.035
1	4	0.006	0.000	0.039	−0.012
2	4	−0.012	−0.013	0.034	−0.015
3	4	−0.030	0.021	0.068	0.027
4	4	0.008	−0.016	0.149	0.018
1	5	0.028	−0.020	0.039	−0.005
2	5	−0.007	−0.065	−0.023	−0.045
3	5	0.037	0.037	−0.033	−0.010
4	5	−0.097	−0.027	0.021	−0.005
5	5	0.026	0.015	0.051	0.061
$\chi^2(15)$		15.58	12.42	11.35	12.01

Suppose x_t is generated by the following model,

$$x_t = g\left(x_{t-1}, x_{t-2}, \ldots\right) + \epsilon_t.$$

---

[11]The proof relies on the law of iterated expectations, $E(x_t x_{t-i} x_{t-j}) = E(E(x_t | x_{t-1}, \ldots) x_{t-i} x_{t-j}) = 0.$

where ϵ_t is IID.[12] If $g(\ )$ is sufficiently well behaved, Stone (1977) shows that non-parametric regression methods can be used to estimate $g(\ )$ consistently. There are many ways to implement nonparametric regressions. Diebold and Nason (1990) and Meese and Rose (1990) use the method of locally-weighted regression (LWR) in Cleveland and Devlin (1988).[13] Briefly, LWR can be illustrated in the following way. Suppose it is believed that the conditional mean function $g(\ )$ includes only x_{t-1}.[14] LWR looks at the history of x_t, finds those instances when x_{t-i-1} is close to x_{t-i} by choosing the nearest k neighbors of x_{t-1}, and runs a weighted regression of x_{t-i} on x_{t-i-1} by giving more weights to closer neighbors. This gives a local estimate of $g(\ )$ around the point x_{t-1}. This local estimate can be used to forecast x_t by evaluating it at x_{t-1}.

There are a number of choices to make in this forecasting exercise. The first is the number of nearest neighbors k. Ten percent of all available history, up to 90 percent, is tried in steps of 10 percent. The second is the number of lags of x_{t-1} to include as arguments of $g(\ )$. Lags 1 through 5 are used. The third is the weighting scheme of the local regression. The tricubic weights proposed in Cleveland and Devlin (1988) are used. The length of the out-of-sample forecast is the fourth choice. The last third of this paper's sample is chosen.

Table 4 provides the ratio of the root mean squared errors (RMSE) of the LWR forecasts to that of a random walk model of futures prices (where the predicted x_t is zero). For each currency, there are 45 different RMSEs, corresponding to the five choices of lag lengths and nine sizes of nearest neighborhoods. A ratio larger than one indicates that the RMSE of the LWR is higher than that of the random walk model. In the BP, JY, and SF, LWR performed worse than the random walk model. In the DM, three of the 45 LWR forecasts beat the random walk, but the improvement is less than half a percent. These results are consistent with those in Diebold and Nason (1990) and Meese and Rose (1990), and indicate that there is little evidence of a nonzero conditional mean in price changes in currency futures.[15]

B.   Estimating the Conditional Variance Function

While the conditional mean is statistically not different from zero, the large autocorrelations of the absolute values of price changes suggest that the conditional variance is time varying. The difficulty in modeling the conditional variance is that it is never observed directly. In this paper, two different approaches are taken.

The first approach is motivated by the popularity of the autoregressive conditional heteroskedasticity models of Engle (1982), Bollerslev (1986), and Nelson

---

[12]Note that the restriction that ϵ_t is IID is needed to prove consistency of nonparametric methods to estimate the function $g(\ )$.

[13]Diebold and Nason (1990) and Meese and Rose (1990) found that LWR does not outperform a random walk model in forecasting spot exchange rates in terms of mean squared error or mean absolute error. It is possible that LWR has low power in detecting conditional mean changes. But the simulations in Hsieh (1991) show that LWR can detect all the nonlinear dynamics models most often cited in the time-series literature.

[14]The extension to the case with multiple lags is straightforward.

[15]The significance of day-of-the-week dummies, which turn out not to be a factor in the conditional mean, has also been tested for. These results are available from the author upon request.

50   Journal of Financial and Quantitative Analysis

TABLE 4

Ratio of Root Mean Squared Forecast Errors

No. of Lags	Fraction of Sample	BP	DM	JY	SF
1	0.1	1.0209	1.0081	1.0547	1.0285
1	0.2	1.0254	0.9953	1.0371	1.0325
1	0.3	1.0260	0.9971	1.0323	1.0250
1	0.4	1.0221	0.9996	1.0301	1.0214
1	0.5	1.0188	1.0020	1.0278	1.0196
1	0.6	1.0170	1.0037	1.0263	1.0186
1	0.7	1.0155	1.0051	1.0256	1.0172
1	0.8	1.0141	1.0064	1.0260	1.0154
1	0.9	1.0133	1.0068	1.0260	1.0135
2	0.1	1.0605	1.0312	1.1094	1.0342
2	0.2	1.0548	1.0211	1.0935	1.0121
2	0.3	1.0491	1.0162	1.0831	1.0080
2	0.4	1.0431	1.0102	1.0742	1.0044
2	0.5	1.0370	1.0067	1.0664	1.0019
2	0.6	1.0315	1.0048	1.0593	0.9997
2	0.7	1.0268	1.0041	1.0540	0.9982
2	0.8	1.0232	1.0038	1.0496	0.9973
2	0.9	1.0204	1.0040	1.0459	0.9976
3	0.1	1.1473	1.0777	1.2062	1.0744
3	0.2	1.1019	1.0655	1.1572	1.0305
3	0.3	1.0810	1.0567	1.1323	1.0190
3	0.4	1.0678	1.0477	1.1140	1.0148
3	0.5	1.0582	1.0404	1.0990	1.0112
3	0.6	1.0508	1.0347	1.0855	1.0089
3	0.7	1.0435	1.0303	1.0750	1.0067
3	0.8	1.0375	1.0252	1.0656	1.0048
3	0.9	1.0315	1.0196	1.0590	1.0038
4	0.1	1.3497	1.1755	1.3802	1.1763
4	0.2	1.2435	1.0841	1.2608	1.0698
4	0.3	1.1892	1.0587	1.2091	1.0373
4	0.4	1.1548	1.0472	1.1764	1.0208
4	0.5	1.1302	1.0402	1.1536	1.0125
4	0.6	1.1095	1.0348	1.1362	1.0081
4	0.7	1.0914	1.0291	1.1216	1.0053
4	0.8	1.0742	1.0241	1.1080	1.0049
4	0.9	1.0596	1.0194	1.0958	1.0056
5	0.1	1.4288	1.4386	1.7291	1.3289
5	0.2	1.2553	1.2397	1.4582	1.1802
5	0.3	1.1847	1.1638	1.3585	1.1271
5	0.4	1.1448	1.1182	1.2929	1.0958
5	0.5	1.1162	1.0875	1.2401	1.0739
5	0.6	1.0954	1.0661	1.1983	1.0583
5	0.7	1.0799	1.0507	1.1619	1.0468
5	0.8	1.0673	1.0404	1.1316	1.0382
5	0.9	1.0546	1.0338	1.1077	1.0314

Underlined value represents the lowest ratio in a given currency.

(1991). See Bollerslev, Chow, and Kroner (1990) for a survey. Nelson's (1991) EGARCH model was selected and is given by

$$X_t = \mu + h_t^{1/2}\eta_t,$$
$$\eta_t|\Omega_{t-1} \sim N(0,1),$$

$$\mathrm{Log}\, h_t \;=\; \alpha + \beta\,\mathrm{Log}\, h_{t-1} + \phi\left(|\eta_{t-1}| - (2/\pi)^{1/2}\right) + \gamma\eta_{t-1},$$

where Ω_{t-1} is the information set at time $t - 1$.[16] Since h_t is known at $t - 1$, it is included in Ω_{t-1}. The EGARCH model is chosen over Engle's (1982) ARCH or Bollerslev's (1986) GARCH models for two reasons: a) EGARCH allows the conditional variance to respond differently to a decline versus an advance (by allowing γ to be different from zero), while ARCH and GARCH impose a symmetric response; and b) unlike ARCH and GARCH, EGARCH does not need to impose any constraints on the coefficients of the variance equation to enforce nonnegativity of the variance. This makes estimation much simpler.

The Berndt, Hall, Hall, and Hausman (1974) estimation procedure is used, and the results are given in Table 5. First, the estimates of β are all statistically greater than zero. In fact, those for the BP, DM, and SF are very close to one, which indicates that volatility is highly persistent in currency futures. The much smaller value of β for the JY indicates that its volatility is less persistent. However, the estimates of β for all four currency futures are smaller than one, which means that the distribution is strictly stationary. Secondly, there appears to be no asymmetry in the variance equation, since the estimates of γ are not statistically different from zero. These results are similar to those found in spot exchange rates.

TABLE 5

EGARCH Estimates

$$x_t \;=\; \mu + h_t^{1/2}\eta_t$$

$$\eta_t \;\sim\; N(0, 1)$$

$$\mathrm{Log}\, h_t \;=\; \alpha + \beta\,\mathrm{Log}\, h_{t-1} + \phi\left(|\eta_{t-1}| - (2/\pi)^{1/2}\right) + \gamma\eta_{t-1}$$

	BP	DM	JY	SF
μ	0.000319	0.000377	0.000232	0.000239
	(0.000208)	(0.000214)	(0.000189)	(0.000235)
α	−0.688127	−1.072229	−4.438289	−0.993241
	(0.030088)	(0.041828)	(0.756704)	(0.032479)
β	0.928780	0.889511	0.550707	0.895527
	(0.002995)	(0.004386)	(0.075851)	(0.003508)
ϕ	0.135854	0.187005	0.282167	0.157669
	(0.019961)	(0.028388)	(0.093357)	(0.024013)
γ	−0.110718	0.084173	0.313274	0.129035
	(0.177458)	(0.147279)	(0.201531)	(0.166507)

Bollerslev-Woolridge robust standard errors are in parentheses.

While the EGARCH model can be justified on the grounds that it can approximate variance changes,[17] this paper's main interest is to see if it can capture all the nonlinear dependence in price changes. If it does, the second step of this paper's seminonparametric procedure can be taken. This can be tested as follows. Let $\hat{h}_t$ and $\hat{\mu}$ denote the fitted values of h_t and μ in the EGARCH model. The paper wants

[16] The $(2/\pi)^{1/2}$ is used to center the mean of $|\eta_{t-1}|$ at 0.

[17] See Nelson (1990) for a discussion.

52 Journal of Financial and Quantitative Analysis

to test whether the remaining movements in price changes, called standardized residuals,

$$\hat{\eta}_t = (x_t - \hat{\mu})/\hat{h}_t^{1/2},$$

are IID. This can be done by running the BDS tests on the standardized residuals.

The results are reported in Table 6. There is one important caveat here. The asymptotic distribution of the BDS test cannot be used, as Brock, Hsieh, and LeBaron (1991) show that the BDS test is biased in favor of the null hypothesis of independence and identical distribution when applied to standardized residuals of EGARCH models. Therefore, simulated critical values of the BDS test that are provided in Table 6 are used. They indicate that the standardized residuals still reject independence and identical distribution for the DM and the SF, which means that the EGARCH model cannot capture all the nonlinear dependence in those two currency futures.

TABLE 6

EGARCH Standardized Residuals BDS Test for IID

m	δ	BP	DM	JY	SF
2	0.5	−0.61	−1.10	0.12	−1.34
3	0.5	−0.78	−1.35	0.17	−1.88*
4	0.5	−0.52	−1.08	0.95	−1.71*
5	0.5	−0.09	−0.99	1.90	−1.67
2	1.0	−0.50	−1.65	−0.62	−2.23*
3	1.0	−0.59	−1.77*	−0.69	−2.55*
4	1.0	−0.40	−1.45*	0.32	−2.35*
5	1.0	−0.14	−1.33*	0.89	−2.04*
2	1.5	−0.42	−1.54	−1.03	−2.41*
3	1.5	−0.56	−1.51*	−1.09	−2.59*
4	1.5	−0.50	−1.25*	0.16	−2.29*
5	1.5	−0.31	−1.19*	0.77	−2.08*
2	2.0	−0.42	−1.24	−1.01	−2.05*
3	2.0	−0.54	−1.18	−0.89	−2.07*
4	2.0	−0.41	−0.97	0.33	−1.72*
5	2.0	−0.28	−0.98	0.85	−1.58*

*Statistically significant at the 5-percent two-tailed test based on the simulated critical values of an EGARCH model for 1275 observations with 2000 replications:

m	0.50	1.00	1.50	2.00
			δ	
2.5-Percent Critical Values				
2	−2.04	−1.95	−1.77	−1.62
3	−1.63	−1.39	−1.30	−1.31
4	−1.66	−1.22	−1.14	−1.15
5	−1.66	−1.22	−1.14	−1.15
97.5-Percent Critical Values				
2	1.73	1.58	1.57	1.56
3	1.70	1.45	1.49	1.83
4	1.85	1.47	1.49	2.22
5	1.85	1.47	1.49	2.22

The second approach to modeling volatility is now turned to. The idea is to construct a daily measure of volatility using intraday futures data, which then allows the fitting of a time series model of volatility. As in Kupiec (1990), the paper's daily measure of volatility is the Parkinson (1980) range estimator of the standard deviation.

$$\sigma_{P,t} = (0.361 \times 1440/M)^{1/2} \text{Log} (\text{High}_t/\text{Low}_t),$$

where High_t and Low_t are the high and low transaction prices during each trading day, and M is the number of minutes during a trading day.[18] It should be pointed out that the standard deviation of the trading day in the CME, which is approximately 400 minutes at the end of the sample, is scaled up to a trading day of 24 hours (i.e., 1440 minutes). While this particular scaling is motivated by the fact that the foreign exchange market is open around-the-clock, any scaling factor is innocuous, as the second step of the paper's seminonparametric method will provide the appropriate scaling factor.

It is important to stress here that $\sigma_{P,t}$ is the ex post measure of volatility, while the paper is mainly interested in the ex ante, i.e., conditional, forecast of volatility. To obtain a conditional forecast of volatility, the following model for log price changes, x_t, is posited,

$$x_t = \sigma_{P,t} u_t,$$
$$\text{Log}\, \sigma_{P,t} = \alpha + \Sigma \beta_i \text{Log}\, \sigma_{P,t-i} + \nu_t,$$

where ν_t is IID. This model is called the autoregressive volatility model. It is motivated by the fact that $\sigma_{P,t}$ is autocorrelated.[19] The ex ante volatility can be recovered, as follows. Regress Log $\sigma_{P,t}$ on its own lags and a constant term using ordinary least squares. For simplicity, this is called the "autoregressive volatility" model. The number of lags of Log $\sigma_{P,t}$ is determined by the Schwarz (1978) criterion: eight for the BP, eight for the DM, five for the JY, and eight for the SF. The estimates are given in Table 7. The persistence of volatility is measured by the sum of the β coefficients, which are 0.782 for the BP, 0.760 for the DM, 0.624 for the JY, and 0.736 for the SF. They are statistically less than 1 in all four cases, indicating that log volatility is strictly stationary. When compared to the EGARCH model, the autoregressive volatility model has much less persistence for the BP, DM, and SF. This will have an impact on the simulations in Section V.

As the issue of volatility persistence is important in the distinction between the autoregressive volatility and the EGARCH model, several tests of sensitivity and misspecification of the autoregressive volatility model are performed. First, the lagged values of log volatility up until the 20th lag are included. This does not change the results substantially. In particular, the sums of the β parameters increase slightly, to 0.844 (BP), 0.793 (DM), 0.675 (JY), and 0.779 (SF). But, they

---

[18]For the BP, the trading hours are 7:30 a.m. to 1:24 p.m. from 85/2/22 until 85/10/14, and 7:20 a.m. to 1:24 p.m. from 85/10/15 to 88/10/04. For the DM, the corresponding trading hours are 7:30 a.m. to 1:20 p.m. and 7:20 a.m. to 1:20 p.m. For the JY, they are 7:30 a.m. to 1:22 p.m. and 7:20 a.m. to 1:22 p.m. For the SF, the corresponding trading hours are 7:30 a.m. to 1:16 p.m. and 7:20 a.m. to 1:16 p.m. Since 88/10/05, the trading hours for all currency futures are 7:20 a.m. to 2:00 p.m.

[19]A similar model was identified for the Standard and Poor's 500 cash index in Hsieh (1991).

TABLE 7

Estimates of the Autoregressive Volatility Model Using Parkinson's Standard Deviations

$$\text{Log}\,\sigma_{P,t} = \alpha + \Sigma\beta_i \text{Log}\,\sigma_{P,t-i} + \nu_t$$

	BP	DM	JY	SF
α	−1.037 (0.171)	−1.139 (0.187)	−1.874 (0.199)	−1.219 (0.193)
$\text{Log}\,\sigma_{P,t-1}$	0.192 (0.028)	0.153 (0.028)	0.208 (0.028)	0.115 (0.028)
$\text{Log}\,\sigma_{P,t-2}$	0.134 (0.029)	0.111 (0.028)	0.137 (0.028)	0.106 (0.028)
$\text{Log}\,\sigma_{P,t-3}$	0.062 (0.029)	0.052 (0.028)	0.058 (0.029)	0.068 (0.028)
$\text{Log}\,\sigma_{P,t-4}$	0.069 (0.029)	0.092 (0.028)	0.109 (0.028)	0.091 (0.028)
$\text{Log}\,\sigma_{P,t-5}$	0.137 (0.028)	0.091 (0.028)	0.112 (0.028)	0.118 (0.028)
$\text{Log}\,\sigma_{P,t-6}$	0.027 (0.029)	0.072 (0.028)		0.074 (0.028)
$\text{Log}\,\sigma_{P,t-7}$	0.073 (0.028)	0.110 (0.028)		0.086 (0.028)
$\text{Log}\,\sigma_{P,t-8}$	0.088 (0.028)	0.079 (0.028)		0.078 (0.028)
$\bar{R}^2$	0.274	0.227	0.170	0.193
$\Sigma\beta_i$	0.782 (0.129)	0.760 (0.124)	0.624 (0.165)	0.736 (0.099)
Test of $\Sigma\beta_i = 1$ $F(n_1, n_2)$	36.59 1,1258 [0.0000]	37.27 1,1258 [0.0000]	91.73 1,1264 [0.0000]	55.71 1,1260 [0.0000]

Standard errors in parentheses, p-values in square brackets.

The standard errors and test of $\Sigma\beta_i = 1$ do not change when using a heteroskedasticity-consistent covariance matrix.

are still statistically less than 1, as the $F(1,1234)$ statistics are 15.36 (BP), 21.69 (DM), 38.27 (JY), and 27.43 (SF).

Second, the day-of-the-week dummy variables are added to the model, since the literature has found them to be statistically important in variance changes.[20] While most of the day-of-the-week dummies are statistically different from zero, they add little to the explanatory power. The $\bar{R}^2$s improve only marginally, rising to 0.284 (from 0.274), 0.242 (from 0.227), 0.181 (from 0.170), and 0.208 (from 0.193), respectively, in the BP, DM, JY, and SF. In addition, the Schwarz criterion worsens in three of the four currencies. These dummies also did not change the amount of volatility persistence. The sums of the β coefficients are 0.785 (BP), 0.765 (DM), 0.627 (JY), and 0.740 (SF), which are essentially the same as those without the dummies and remain statistically different from unity in all four cases. Thus, day-of-the-week dummies are excluded from the final model. Third, lags

[20]See Hsieh (1988) for a discussion of day-of-the-week effects in spot currencies.

of the log volatilities of the other currencies are included. They did not appear to be statistically significant, and the Schwarz criterion worsens in all cases. Hence, the specification as reported in Table 7 has been kept.

To ensure that the autoregressive volatility model can capture all the predictability in currency futures, the BDS test is run on the standardized residuals,

$$z_t = x_t/\hat{\sigma}_{P,t},$$

where $\hat{\sigma}_{P,t}$ is the fitted value from the autoregressive volatility model. The results are reported in Table 8. Critical values of the BDS statistics are obtained through simulation, as done in Table 6. Little evidence has been found against the hypothesis that the standardized residuals are IID. For the BP, DM, and JY, there are no rejections of the null, while for the SF, three of the 16 statistics reject the null. Note that this rate of rejection is much lower than that of the EGARCH model in Table 6.

C. Estimating the Density of the Unpredictable Part of Futures Price Changes

The tests indicate that the autoregressive volatility model is appropriately specified and appears to have captured the predictable movements in exchange rates. The second step of the seminonparametric method, which involves modeling $z_t = x_t/\hat{\sigma}_{P,t}$, the unpredictable part of log price changes, is now considered.

Table 8 provides some information about z_t. The mean is close to zero. The standard deviation is close to unity. There is little evidence of skewness, but strong evidence of leptokurtosis. Using the BDS test, it has already been shown that z_t is IID, so its unconditional density can be estimated using standard methods. For example, a parametric density function, such as the Student-t, or a nonparametric density, using kernels or series expansions, can be fitted.

For the purposes of the applications in Section V, the density of z_t does not actually need to be estimated at all. Section V.A requires only the quantiles of z_t, which are provided in Table 8. In Section V.B, future values of x_t are simulated by "bootstrapping" from z_t, as per Efron (1982). These applications are now turned to.

V. Application to Risk Management: Minimum Capital Requirements

There are many uses of the conditional density of price changes. In this section, the minimum capital requirement of a futures position is calculated. First, it is shown that there is a direct method to obtain daily minimum capital requirements and, second, that longer term minimum capital requirements can be obtained via simulation.

A. Daily Minimum Capital Requirements

Suppose a firm holds a long position of L_t units of a foreign currency futures contract. An important question in risk management is: What is the minimum capital, K_t, needed to cover losses of this long position with a 99.5 percent probability?

TABLE 8

Statistical Description of Standardized Residuals of the Autoregressive Volatility Model

	BP	DM	JY	SF
Mean	0.042	0.036	0.037	0.024
Median	0.051	0.000	0.000	0.019
Std. Dev.	0.880	0.853	1.031	0.842
Skewness	−0.035	0.053	0.196	0.025
Kurtosis	5.249	4.360	7.485	4.426
Maximum	5.078	3.389	6.897	3.513
Minimum	−3.560	−3.626	−5.205	−4.000
Quantiles				
0.50%	−3.017	−2.399	−3.623	−2.306
1.00%	−2.474	−2.245	−2.821	−2.080
5.00%	−1.411	−1.319	−1.557	−1.322
10.00%	−0.970	−0.937	−1.046	−0.985
90.00%	1.067	1.135	1.228	1.096
95.00%	1.504	1.487	1.697	1.422
99.00%	2.304	2.220	2.611	2.137
99.50%	2.590	2.418	3.271	2.572

BDS Statistics

m	δ				
2	0.5	−0.61	−0.45	1.69	−1.27
3	0.5	−0.96	−1.09	1.45	−1.64
4	0.5	−0.97	−1.24	1.65	−1.20
5	0.5	−1.01	−1.36	2.04	−1.20
2	1.0	−0.24	−0.91	1.77	−1.80
3	1.0	−0.86	−1.28	1.33	−2.23*
4	1.0	−0.94	−1.17	1.69	−2.07*
5	1.0	−1.02	−1.25	1.77	−1.88
2	1.5	0.42	−0.68	1.48	−1.80
3	1.5	−0.23	−0.83	1.17	−2.04*
4	1.5	−0.32	−0.66	1.91	−1.82
5	1.5	−0.44	−0.73	1.99	−1.73
2	2.0	0.75	−0.40	0.84	−1.42
3	2.0	0.41	−0.32	0.88	−1.52
4	2.0	0.38	−0.11	1.60	−1.31
5	2.0	0.26	−0.20	1.66	−1.34

*Statistically significant at the 5-percent two-tailed test based on the simulated critical values of an autoregressive volatility model for 1275 observations with 2000 replications:

	δ			
m	0.50	1.00	1.50	2.00
2.5-Percent Critical Values				
2	−1.84	−1.86	−1.86	−1.96
3	−1.86	−1.88	−1.85	−1.96
4	−1.86	−1.87	−1.93	−1.96
5	−1.77	−1.89	−1.91	−1.96
97.5-Percent Critical Values				
2	1.90	1.94	1.92	1.96
3	2.01	1.94	2.00	1.96
4	2.01	1.95	2.12	1.96
5	2.04	2.06	2.05	1.96

The minimum capital is the sum of prearranged lines of credit and short-term liquid instruments that can be converted to cash almost instantaneously, e.g., Treasury bills, negotiable certificates of deposits, money market funds, interest bearing checking accounts, etc. Note that 99.5 percent has been selected as the "coverage probability" purely for illustrative purposes.[21]

The capital requirement, K_t, is determined as follows. Let P_{t+1} be the settlement price in the following trading day. The losses of the long position are given by $(P_t - P_{t+1})L_t$. Thus, K_t is wanted to solve the following equation,

$$\Pr\{(P_t - P_{t+1})L_t > K_t\} = 0.005.$$

The left-hand side can be rewritten as follows,

$$\Pr\{\text{Log}(1 - \kappa_t)/\sigma_{t+1|t} > z_{t+1}\} = 0.005,$$

where $\kappa_t = K_t/(P_tL_t)$, $z_{t+1} = x_{t+1}/\sigma_{t+1|t}$, $x_{t+1} = \text{Log}(P_{t+1}/P_t)$, and $\sigma_{t+1|t}$ denotes $\exp\{E_t(\text{Log}\,\sigma_{t+1})\}$. In particular, a rolling regression method can be used to sequentially generate $\sigma_{t+1|t}$. The minimum capital is now expressed as a fraction of P_tL_t.

To solve for κ_t, the quantiles of the distribution of z_{t+1}, which are provided in Table 8, only need to be known. The quantile z_ℓ is the point where

$$\Pr\{z_\ell > z_{t+1}\} = 0.005.$$

In particular, z_ℓ is -3.017 for the BP, -2.399 for the DM, -3.623 for the JY, and -2.306 for the SF. For each currency, then, the minimum capital as a fraction of the market value of the long position is

$$\kappa_t = 1 - \exp\left(\sigma_{t+1|t}\,z_\ell\right).$$

Since z_ℓ is a negative number, an increase in $\sigma_{t+1|t}$ will increase the capital requirement.

As $\sigma_{t+1|t}$ is time varying, so is κ_t. In contrast, the capital requirement using the unconditional density is constant over time. When the conditional variance is larger (smaller) than the unconditional variance, the capital requirement using the conditional density is higher (lower) than that of the unconditional density.

In the second example, suppose the firm is holding a short position of S_t units of currencies in futures contracts. (Shorts are represented by *negative* quantities, i.e., $S_t < 0$.) The capital requirement, K_t, which can cover the losses of the short position with a 99.5-percent probability, is found in an analogous manner. Let $\zeta_t = K_t/(-P_tS_t)$ be the capital requirement as a fraction of $(-P_tS_t)$. Then ζ_t is given by the equation,

$$\zeta_t = \exp\left(\sigma_{t+1|t}\,z_h\right) - 1,$$

where z_h is the quantile of z_t such that,

$$\Pr\{z_h > z_t\} = 0.995.$$

---

[21] A theory of hedging is needed to determine whether "coverage probability" is the appropriate concept for hedging, and what the optimal "coverage probability" should be.

Based on Table 8, z_h equals 2.590 for the BP, 2.418 for the DM, 3.271 for the JY, and 2.572 for the SF. As z_h is positive, an increase in $\sigma_{t+1|t}$ will raise the capital requirement. In contrast, the capital requirement using the unconditional density is constant over time.

In the third example, a futures exchange setting futures margin requirements to protect the capital of its clearing members from defaults by futures traders is considered. There are two types of futures margins: initial margins and maintenance margins. For illustrative purposes, the maintenance margin is concentrated on. Suppose the futures exchange desires to set the maintenance margin to ensure that it is sufficient to cover possible losses of either long or short positions at least 99.5 percent of the time. In other words, the maintenance margin as a percent of the price times the size of the futures contract should be the maximum of the capital requirements for the long and the short sides, i.e., $\max\{\kappa_t, \zeta_t\}$. While there is a 0.5 percent chance that the maintenance margin cannot cover the losses of the futures contract, this should be interpreted as an upper bound of the default probability for a futures contract, since a trader can add funds to his account to cover losses exceeding the maintenance margin.

B. Application to Risk Management: Longer Term Minimum Capital Requirements

So far, the capital requirements for holding a futures position for one trading day have been considered. It would be reasonable to ask how much capital is needed for holding a futures position for longer periods.

This consideration can arise in many contexts. For example, a firm is planning to use a currency futures contract to hedge the exchange rate risk of inflows of British pounds three months from now. The goal of the hedge is to balance gains (losses) in the cash inflow with losses (gains) in the futures position as the exchange rate fluctuates. The problem facing the firm, however, is that a futures position is marked to market, so that gains and losses are settled at the end of each trading day, while the cash position is settled in entirety three months from now. If the exchange rate moves in such a way that the cash position is making profits while the futures position is sustaining losses, the firm may need additional funds to meet margin requirements on the futures position because it cannot use the gains in the cash position to offset these losses. If the firm is unable to meet margin requirements, it will be forced to liquidate the futures position prematurely, which defeats the purpose of hedging. Before the firm commits to the hedging strategy using futures, it must know how much capital (e.g., additional funds) may be needed to maintain this futures position for the next three months.

The answer to this question can be obtained via a simulation study. Start with the conditional density of price changes at the time when the firm initially opens the futures position. For the sake of illustration, take this to be the end of the data sample, March 9, 1990. Simulate the path of the futures price over the course of the next three months. At the end of each trading day, track the value of the futures position, and record its lowest value during the three-month period. This is the maximum "draw down" for this simulated path, which represents the maximum loss sustained by the firm while holding the futures position. If the firm's additional funds are less than this maximum draw down, it would not be able to maintain its futures position. By repeating this for 10,000 simulated paths, an empirical distribution of the maximum draw down is generated. The capital requirement can then be set to the amount that is able to cover a given percentage of the simulated maximum draw downs. The 90-percent coverage probability is used, because 10,000 replications is not accurate enough to measure the extreme tails of a distribution.

The simulation can be done as follows. Recall that the seminonparametric model of futures price changes is given by

$$x_t = \sigma_{P,t} u_t,$$
$$\text{Log } \sigma_{P,t} = \alpha + \Sigma \beta_i \text{ Log } \sigma_{P,t-i} + \nu_t,$$

where $x_t = \text{Log}(P_t/P_{t-1})$. A simulated path of future x_ts is generated recursively, using the estimates of α and βs from the sample, and the values of $\sigma_{P,t}$ at the end of the sample. The u_t and ν_t are drawn randomly, with replacement, from the residuals in a "bootstrap" fashion, per Efron (1982).

Table 9 reports the results of the simulation experiment for the capital requirement needed to hold a futures position with 90-percent probability. The holding period of the futures position is varied over one, five, 10, 15, 20, 25, 30, 60, 90, and 180 trading days. The 95-percent central confidence intervals for these capital requirements are given in Table 10.[22] For comparison, the simulations using the unconditional density and the EGARCH model are also reported. In the case of the unconditional density, the x_ts are drawn randomly, with replacement, from the 1275 observed price changes. In the case of the EGARCH model, the simulated x_ts use the estimated values of α, β, ϕ, and γ, and the value of h_t at the end of the sample. The η_ts are drawn randomly, with replacement, from the standardized residuals, in a way analogous to the autoregressive volatility model.

To understand the results, keep in mind that the simulation was started on March 9, 1990, when the volatility is below the sample average.[23] Thus, the autoregressive volatility model predicts a lower volatility in the near future than the unconditional density.

Consider holding a long futures position in the BP. For a one-day holding period, the capital requirement is 0.73 percent of the initial face value of the contract according to the autoregressive volatility model and 0.91 percent according to the unconditional density. (If the simulation had started on a day that had a higher volatility than the sample average, the capital requirement based on the autoregressive volatility model would have been higher than that based on the unconditional

---

[22]Efron (1982) provides a nonparametric method to estimate the confidence interval for a quantile. Let X be a random variable with distribution F. θ, defined as $\text{Prob}\{X < \theta\} = q$, needs to be estimated. Let $x(1),\ldots,x(n)$ be the ordered data from a sample of size n. A confidence interval for θ, $(x(j),x(k))$, can be found as follows. Observe that $\text{Prob}\{x(j) < \theta \leq x(k)\} = \text{Prob}\{j < Z \leq k\}$, where $Z = \#\{x(i) < \theta\}$ is a binomial distribution. Suppose a 90-percent confidence interval for θ is wanted. J and k can be determined such that $\text{Prob}\{j < Z \leq k\} = 0.95$. If n is small, the exact binomial distribution of Z can be used. Since n is large in this case (i.e., 10,000), the binomial distribution is approximated with a normal distribution.

[23]On that day, the Parkinson volatilities are 12.48 percent, 9.51 percent, 7.90 percent, and 8.90 percent, respectively, for the BP, DM, JY, and SF. Over the entire sample, the averages of the Parkinson volatilities are 16.13 percent, 16.06 percent, 12.68 percent, and 18.01 percent, respectively.

60 Journal of Financial and Quantitative Analysis

TABLE 9

Capital Requirement for 90-Percent Coverage Probability as a Percent of the Initial Value

	No. of Days	Long Position			Short Position		
		AR	Uncond.	EGARCH	AR	Uncond.	EGARCH
BP	1	0.73	0.91	0.93	0.80	0.98	1.05
	5	1.90	2.30	2.61	2.18	2.76	3.00
	10	2.83	3.27	4.19	3.38	4.22	4.88
	15	3.54	3.94	5.72	4.45	5.48	6.67
	20	4.10	4.61	6.96	5.24	6.33	8.43
	25	4.59	5.15	8.25	6.20	7.36	10.46
	30	5.02	5.58	9.08	7.11	8.33	12.06
	60	7.24	7.44	14.50	11.64	12.87	20.71
	90	8.74	8.70	17.91	15.45	16.90	28.03
	180	11.38	10.67	24.25	25.81	27.36	48.02
DM	1	0.72	0.87	0.83	0.89	1.00	0.95
	5	1.89	2.18	2.34	2.23	2.70	2.91
	10	2.77	3.14	3.93	3.40	4.12	5.03
	15	3.52	3.86	5.37	4.36	5.30	6.92
	20	4.05	4.45	6.54	5.19	6.14	8.91
	25	4.55	4.90	7.86	6.14	7.21	10.69
	30	4.93	5.37	8.75	7.02	7.88	12.36
	60	7.16	7.24	13.14	11.36	12.38	20.86
	90	8.87	8.39	16.06	14.68	16.16	27.75
	180	11.38	10.35	21.69	24.25	26.25	45.68
JY	1	0.56	0.74	0.72	0.68	0.87	0.86
	5	1.61	1.99	2.22	1.92	2.36	2.73
	10	2.59	2.82	3.46	3.06	3.53	4.41
	15	3.30	3.46	4.37	4.11	4.60	5.79
	20	3.95	4.10	5.09	5.13	5.45	6.77
	25	4.42	4.58	5.78	5.91	6.30	7.98
	30	4.95	4.92	6.34	6.58	6.85	8.81
	60	6.99	6.84	8.72	10.53	10.74	13.58
	90	8.43	8.00	10.51	13.61	14.00	17.63
	180	10.97	10.27	13.99	21.86	22.21	27.39
SF	1	0.82	0.97	0.89	0.93	1.12	0.98
	5	1.99	2.51	2.48	2.23	2.93	2.98
	10	2.87	3.60	4.12	3.37	4.53	5.09
	15	3.67	4.35	5.60	4.22	5.67	7.03
	20	4.24	5.10	6.82	5.09	6.69	8.86
	25	4.81	5.65	8.12	5.90	7.77	10.93
	30	5.23	6.20	9.12	6.70	8.47	12.50
	60	7.69	8.41	13.73	10.55	13.10	21.27
	90	9.23	9.93	16.89	13.60	17.06	27.80
	180	12.18	12.57	22.92	21.72	27.45	45.47

density.) For a five-day holding period, the capital requirements are, respectively, 1.9 percent and 2.3 percent.

These differences in capital requirements are both statistically and economically significant. In the case of the one-day holding period for the BP, there is a 95-percent probability that the correct capital requirement using the autoregressive model is higher than 0.70 percent and lower than 0.74 percent of the initial face value of the contract. At the same time, there is a 95-percent probability that the correct capital requirement using the unconditional density is higher than 0.85

TABLE 10

Approximate 95-Percent Central Confidence Intervals for Capital Requirement for 90-Percent Coverage Probability as a Percent of the Initial Value

	No. of Days	Long Position			Short Position		
		AR	Uncond.	EGARCH	AR	Uncond.	EGARCH
BP	1	[0.70, 0.74]	[0.86, 0.95]	[0.90, 0.96]	[0.78, 0.82]	[0.96, 0.99]	[1.01, 1.07]
	5	[1.87, 1.95]	[2.26, 2.37]	[2.54, 2.67]	[2.14, 2.25]	[2.70, 2.83]	[2.95, 3.06]
	10	[2.76, 2.91]	[3.19, 3.34]	[4.08, 4.30]	[3.30, 3.48]	[4.15, 4.30]	[4.77, 4.99]
	15	[3.47, 3.61]	[3.87, 4.02]	[5.57, 5.90]	[4.36, 4.53]	[5.38, 5.59]	[6.54, 6.84]
	20	[4.02, 4.20]	[4.52, 4.72]	[6.82, 7.17]	[5.12, 5.34]	[6.22, 6.44]	[8.31, 8.62]
	25	[4.49, 4.70]	[5.03, 5.29]	[8.06, 8.43]	[6.08, 6.33]	[7.22, 7.51]	[10.26,10.64]
	30	[4.94, 5.14]	[5.44, 5.72]	[8.87, 9.32]	[7.00, 7.25]	[8.15, 8.48]	[11.83,12.30]
	60	[7.10, 7.45]	[7.31, 7.58]	[14.21,14.78]	[11.37,11.89]	[12.66,13.08]	[20.41,21.11]
	90	[8.55, 8.94]	[8.57, 8.92]	[17.51,18.25]	[15.22,15.73]	[16.56,17.23]	[27.50,28.62]
	180	[11.15,11.66]	[10.45,10.92]	[23.93,24.74]	[25.33,26.29]	[27.00,27.76]	[47.00,49.05]
DM	1	[0.68, 0.75]	[0.81, 0.90]	[0.78, 0.85]	[0.85, 0.91]	[0.96, 1.08]	[0.93, 0.99]
	5	[1.85, 1.94]	[2.15, 2.23]	[2.28, 2.40]	[2.19, 2.28]	[2.64, 2.75]	[2.86, 2.97]
	10	[2.70, 2.84]	[3.08, 3.22]	[3.86, 4.02]	[3.34, 3.47]	[4.04, 4.22]	[4.92, 5.16]
	15	[3.44, 3.58]	[3.77, 3.93]	[5.28, 5.51]	[4.28, 4.44]	[5.21, 5.40]	[6.80, 7.08]
	20	[3.96, 4.14]	[4.35, 4.55]	[6.41, 6.69]	[5.10, 5.28]	[6.02, 6.26]	[8.70, 9.07]
	25	[4.47, 4.65]	[4.80, 5.00]	[7.71, 8.00]	[6.00, 6.26]	[7.07, 7.38]	[10.47,10.90]
	30	[4.84, 5.06]	[5.24, 5.47]	[8.57, 8.95]	[6.91, 7.16]	[7.73, 8.02]	[12.10,12.65]
	60	[7.03, 7.33]	[7.12, 7.42]	[12.94,13.43]	[11.15,11.59]	[12.18,12.57]	[20.58,21.32]
	90	[8.66, 9.06]	[8.22, 8.60]	[15.77,16.44]	[14.48,15.03]	[15.89,16.46]	[27.17,28.27]
	180	[11.13,11.63]	[10.11,10.59]	[21.31,22.14]	[23.88,24.61]	[25.83,26.64]	[44.81,46.62]
JY	1	[0.56, 0.60]	[0.72, 0.76]	[0.70, 0.75]	[0.68, 0.72]	[0.86, 0.92]	[0.81, 0.89]
	5	[1.60, 1.67]	[1.94, 2.04]	[2.16, 2.28]	[1.89, 1.98]	[2.33, 2.41]	[2.67, 2.81]
	10	[2.45, 2.58]	[2.77, 2.88]	[3.38, 3.53]	[3.06, 3.20]	[3.46, 3.61]	[4.30, 4.51]
	15	[3.23, 3.39]	[3.41, 3.54]	[4.26, 4.46]	[4.03, 4.21]	[4.50, 4.69]	[5.65, 5.93]
	20	[3.84, 4.01]	[4.02, 4.19]	[4.99, 5.18]	[4.93, 5.15]	[5.36, 5.58]	[6.65, 6.93]
	25	[4.33, 4.52]	[4.47, 4.67]	[5.66, 5.91]	[5.75, 6.00]	[6.17, 6.41]	[7.81, 8.13]
	30	[4.79, 4.97]	[4.84, 5.03]	[6.24, 6.46]	[6.50, 6.77]	[6.74, 6.99]	[8.61, 9.05]
	60	[6.90, 7.19]	[6.69, 6.97]	[8.61, 8.92]	[10.33,10.70]	[10.57,10.95]	[13.35,13.87]
	90	[8.29, 8.63]	[7.87, 8.16]	[10.32,10.69]	[13.36,13.91]	[13.81,14.28]	[17.31,17.93]
	180	[10.76,11.23]	[10.09,10.49]	[13.74,14.25]	[21.47,22.26]	[21.79,22.47]	[26.97,27.93]
SF	1	[0.79, 0.84]	[0.95, 1.01]	[0.86, 0.92]	[0.89, 0.96]	[1.10, 1.16]	[0.95, 1.02]
	5	[1.94, 2.04]	[2.45, 2.57]	[2.44, 2.54]	[2.19, 2.29]	[2.86, 3.00]	[2.91, 3.04]
	10	[2.80, 2.94]	[3.51, 3.67]	[4.06, 4.18]	[3.30, 3.45]	[4.43, 4.62]	[4.98, 5.21]
	15	[3.59, 3.75]	[4.28, 4.45]	[5.46, 5.74]	[4.16, 4.32]	[5.57, 5.75]	[6.91, 7.17]
	20	[4.15, 4.33]	[4.99, 5.20]	[6.68, 6.97]	[4.98, 5.18]	[6.57, 6.83]	[8.68, 9.06]
	25	[4.71, 4.93]	[5.54, 5.77]	[7.96, 8.27]	[5.80, 6.02]	[7.60, 7.93]	[10.63,11.12]
	30	[5.11, 5.34]	[6.11, 6.31]	[8.97, 9.29]	[6.58, 6.84]	[8.33, 8.65]	[12.16,12.80]
	60	[7.55, 7.80]	[8.23, 8.57]	[13.48,14.00]	[10.37,10.80]	[12.92,13.37]	[20.88,21.64]
	90	[9.06, 9.42]	[9.72,10.17]	[16.69,17.17]	[13.32,13.89]	[16.83,17.34]	[27.36,28.37]
	180	[11.98,12.43]	[12 27,12.87]	[22.62,23.29]	[21.34,22.09]	[27.01,27.88]	[44.72,46.46]

The first number in the square bracket is the left side of the confidence interval. The second number is the right side of the confidence interval.

percent and lower than 0.95 percent. Furthermore, the difference between capital requirements of 0.73 percent versus 0.91 percent is economically significant, when transactions have face values of several hundred million dollars, such as the case when highly leveraged instruments are involved.

Tables 9 and 10 also provide some information on the convergence behavior of the autoregressive volatility model to the unconditional density. First, it is observed that the capital requirements (and their associated confidence intervals) of the former approach those of the latter as the holding period lengthens. For the BP, this occurs in 90 (trading) days. The DM takes 60 trading days, while

62   Journal of Financial and Quantitative Analysis

the JY takes only 30 days. But the SF takes more than 180 days.[24] However, the convergence is likely to be oscillatory rather than monotonic, as the autoregressive model of volatility has several lags.

In comparison, the EGARCH model produced dramatically different results. Over a one-day holding period, the capital requirements based on the EGARCH model are similar to those based on the unconditional density. However, when simulating into the future, the EGARCH model produces much larger capital requirements than both the autoregressive volatility model and the unconditional density. This phenomenon is due to the high degree of volatility persistence in the EGARCH model. During the simulation period, a large price change (either positive or negative) will cause the conditional variance of the EGARCH model to increase and to remain high for a long period of time.[25] In contrast, there is much less volatility persistence in the autoregressive volatility model and none in the unconditional model. This persistence in volatility also means that the convergence of the EGARCH model to the unconditional density is extremely slow. As many as 500 trading days into the future have been simulated. For the BP, DM, and SF, the capital requirements from the EGARCH model are still twice as high as those from the unconditional density. The exception is the JY. Its capital requirements from the EGARCH model are roughly 50 percent higher than those from the unconditional density. This demonstrates that, while the EGARCH model may produce satisfactory one-day ahead volatility forecasts, it may not be appropriate for multistep ahead volatility forecasts.

Another interesting feature in Table 9 is that a short position requires more capital than a corresponding long position at any given coverage probability. This is due to the fact that the futures price is bounded below by zero, but unbounded above. Even when the logarithmic rate of change of the futures price is symmetric, the change in the futures price itself is asymmetric. Thus, the probability of a one dollar decrease in futures price is less than that of a one dollar increase. This accounts for the difference in the capital requirements between a long and a short position.

VI. Conclusions

This paper demonstrates that when log price changes are not IID, their conditional density may be more accurate than their unconditional density for describing short-term behavior. Using the BDS test of independence and identical distribution, it is shown that daily log price changes in four currency futures contracts are not IID. While there appear to be no predictable conditional mean changes, conditional variances are predictable, and can be described by an autoregressive

---

[24]The SF actually takes about 250 trading days, according to the simulations, which are not reported in Tables 9 and 10.

[25]This explanation is confirmed by the following experiment. The EGARCH model is estimated subject to the constraint that $\beta = 0$ in the variance equation. This allows much less volatility persistence. In the case of the BP, the restricted EGARCH model produced capital requirements of 12.26 percent at the 180-day holding period for long positions, and 31.00 percent for short positions. These are much closer to the capital requirements in Table 9 for the autoregressive volatility model and the unconditional density, and very different from those produced by the unrestricted EGARCH model.

volatility model. Furthermore, this autoregressive volatility model seems to capture all the departures from independence and identical distribution.

Based on this model, daily log price changes can be decomposed into a predictable part and an unpredictable part. The predictable part is described parametrically by the autoregressive volatility model. The unpredictable part can be modeled by an empirical density, either parametrically or nonparametrically. This two-step seminonparametric method yields a conditional density for daily log price changes, which has a number of uses in financial risk management.

In particular, the paper shows how to directly calculate the capital requirement needed to cover losses of a futures position over one trading day, and how to use simulation to obtain the capital requirement over longer holding periods. The paper finds that the conditional density can provide different, and probably more accurate, capital requirements than the unconditional density.

References

Berndt, E. K.; B. H. Hall; R. E. Hall; and J. A. Hausman. "Estimation and Inference in Nonlinear Structural Models." *Annals of Economic and Social Measurement*, 4 (1974), 653–665.

Blattberg, R. C., and N. Gonedes. "A Comparison of the Stable Paretian and Student Distribution as Statistical Model for Prices." *Journal of Business*, 47 (1974), 244–280.

Bollerslev, T. "Generalized Autoregressive Conditional Heteroskedasticity." *Journal of Econometrics*, 31 (1986), 307–327.

Bollerslev, T.; R. Chow; and K. Kroner. "ARCH Modeling in Finance: A Review of the Theory and Empirical Evidence." Working Paper No. 97, Dept. of Finance, Kellogg Graduate School of Management, Northwestern Univ. (1990).

Bollerslev, T., and J. Wooldridge. "Quasi Maximum Likelihood Estimation of Dynamic Models with Time Varying Covariances." Unpubl. Manuscript, Dept. of Economics, MIT (1989).

Boothe, P., and D. Glassman. "The Statistical Distribution of Exchange Rates: Empirical Evidence and Economic Implications." *Journal of International Economics*, 22 (1987), 297–319.

Brock, W.; W. Dechert; and J. Scheinkman. "A Test for Independence Based on the Correlation Dimension." Working Paper, Univ. of Wisconsin at Madison, Univ. of Houston, and Univ. of Chicago (1987).

Brock, W.; D. Hsieh; and B. LeBaron. *Nonlinear Dynamics, Chaos, and Instability: Statistical Theory and Economic Evidence*. Cambridge, MA: MIT Press (1991).

Clark, P. K. "A Subordinated Stochastic Process Model with Finite Variance for Speculative Prices." *Econometrica*, 41 (1973), 135–155.

Cleveland, W. S., and S. J. Devlin. "Locally Weighted Regression: An Approach to Regression Analysis by Local Fitting." *Journal of the American Statistical Association*, 83 (1988), 596–610.

Cornell, B., and M. Reinganum. "Forward and Futures Prices: Evidence from the Foreign Exchange Markets." *Journal of Finance*, 36 (1981), 1035–1046.

Cox, J., and S. Ross. "A Valuation of Options for Alternative Stochastic Processes." *Journal of Financial Economics*, 3 (1976), 145–166.

Dechert, W. "A Characterization of Independence for a Gaussian Process in Terms of the Correlation Dimension." SSRI Working Paper 8812, Univ. of Wisconsin at Madison (1988).

Diebold, F., and J. Nason. "Nonparametric Exchange Rate Prediction?" *Journal of International Economics*, 28 (1990), 315–332.

Efron, B. *The Jackknife, the Bootstrap, and Other Resampling Plans*. Philadelphia, PA: Society for Industrial and Applied Mathematics (1982).

Engle, R. "Autoregressive Conditional Heteroscedasticity with Estimates of the Variance of U. K. Inflations." *Econometrica*, 50 (1982), 987–1007.

Fama, E. "The Behavior of Stock Market Prices." *Journal of Business*, 38 (1965), 34–105.

Gallant, R.; D. Hsieh; and G. Tauchen. "On Fitting a Recalcitrant Series: The Pound/Dollar Exchange Rate, 1974–83." In *Nonparametric and Semiparametric Methods in Econometrics and Statistics, Proceedings of the Fifth International Symposium in Economic Theory and Econometrics*, W. A. Barnett, J. Powell, and G. Tauchen, eds. Cambridge, England: Cambridge Univ. Press (1991).

Harvey, C. "Commentary on Tests of Unbiasedness in the Foreign Exchange Futures Markets: The Effects of Price Limits." *Review of Futures Markets*, 7 (1988), 167–171.

64   Journal of Financial and Quantitative Analysis

Hodrick, R., and S. Srivastava. "Foreign Currency Futures." *Journal of International Economics*, 22 (1987), 1–24.

Hsieh, D. "Statistical Properties of Daily Exchange Rates." *Journal of International Economics*, 24 (1988), 129–145.

_____. "Testing for Nonlinearity in Daily Foreign Exchange Rate Changes." *Journal of Business*, 62 (1989), 339–368.

_____. "Chaos and Nonlinear Dynamics: Application to Financial Markets." *Journal of Finance*, 46 (1991), 1839–1877.

Hsieh, D., and B. LeBaron. "Finite Sample Properties of the BDS Statistic." Unpubl. Manuscript, Univ. of Chicago and Univ. of Wisconsin at Madison (1988).

Kodres, L. "Tests of Unbiasedness in the Foreign Exchange Futures Markets: The Effects of Price Limits." *Review of Futures Markets*, 7 (1988), 139–166.

Kupiec, P. "Futures Margins and Stock Price Volatility: Is There Any Link?" Board of Governors of the Federal Reserve System, Finance and Economics Discussion Paper No. 104 (1990).

LeBaron, B. "The Changing Structure of Stock Returns." Working Paper, Univ. of Wisconsin (1988).

McCurdy, T. H., and I. G. Morgan. "Tests of the Martingale Hypothesis for Foreign Currency Futures." *International Journal of Forecasting*, 3 (1987), 131–148.

Meese, R., and A. Rose. "Nonlinear, Nonparametric, Nonessential Exchange Rate Estimation." *American Economic Review*, 80 (1990), 192–196.

Nelson, D. "ARCH Models as Diffusion Approximations." *Journal of Econometrics*, 45 (1990), 7–38.

_____. "Conditional Heteroskedasticity in Asset Returns: A New Approach." *Econometrica*, 59 (1991), 347–370.

Parkinson, M. "The Extreme Value Method of Estimating the Variance of the Rate of Return." *Journal of Business*, 53 (1980), 61–65.

Pemberton, J., and H. Tong. "A Note on the Distribution of Non-Linear Autoregressive Stochastic Models." *Journal of Time Series Analysis*, 2 (1981), 49–52.

Rogalski, R., and J. Vinso. "Empirical Properties of Foreign Exchange Rates." *Journal of International Business Studies*, 9 (1978), 69–79.

Schwarz, G. "Estimating the Dimension of a Model." *Annals of Statistics*, 6 (1978), 461–464.

Scheinkman, J., and B. LeBaron. "Nonlinear Dynamics and Stock Returns." *Journal of Business*, 62 (1989), 311–337.

Stone, C. J. "Consistent Nonparametric Regressions." *Annals of Statistics*, 5 (1977), 595–620.

Westerfield, J. "An Examination of Foreign Exchange Risk under Fixed and Floating Rate Regimes." *Journal of International Economics*, 7 (1977), 181–200.

[23]

"Chaos" in Futures Markets?
A Nonlinear Dynamical Analysis

Steven C. Blank

INTRODUCTION AND OBJECTIVES

Commodity market analysts constantly seek better explanations of price behavior in the form of economic models. Such models are used for many types of forecasting. However, the various linear models developed to date do not always work very well [Just and Rausser (1981)]. Some cases of short-term forecasting success of time series and econometric models imply that futures and spot prices are not always generated by a "random" process, but the long-term failure of these models to explain price behavior indicates they have not captured the true nature of the underlying generating process. For example, residuals in commodity price models may not be random, as assumed, but the result of a nonlinear process. It may be time to change existing theoretical assumptions and/or empirical approaches.

A new methodology, called nonlinear dynamics (or "chaos"), evolving recently in physics and other natural sciences, may offer an alternative explanation for behavior of economic phenomena [Brock (1988a)]. Based on the assumption that at least part of the underlying process is nonlinear, chaos analysis evaluates whether that process is a deterministic system [Jensen (1987)].[1] Deterministic processes that look random under statistical tests such as spectral analysis and the autocovariance function are called "deterministic chaos" in nonlinear science. In practice, some economists argue that separating deterministic and stochastic processes may be very difficult due to the "noisy" nature of economic data [Mirowski (1990)]. Although applications of chaos analysis in economics are still very rare [examples include Baumol and Benhabib; (1989) Brock (1986); Brock and Sayers (1988); Candela and Gardini (1986); Day (1983); Goodwin (1990); Lorenz (1987); Melese and Transue (1986)], there may be potential for its use in some markets.

In markets for undifferentiated commodities, intuition leads to expectations of multiple sources for chaos or nonlinear feedback [Savit (1988)]. Cyclical and seasonal patterns are often visible in charts of both prices and trade volumes. The futures price-setting process is similar to that in many financial spot markets where

This study was partially funded by a grant from the Center for the Study of Futures Markets, Columbia University. This is Giannini Foundation Research Paper No. 976.

[1]Compared to linear methods, nonlinear dynamics may be a less restrictive approach to modeling economic systems simply because of the assumptions it does *not* make, concerning the distribution, for example, as discussed later.

Steven C. Blank is an extension economist, Department of Agricultural Economics, University of California, Davis.

The Journal of Futures Markets, Vol. 11, No. 6, 711–728 (1991)
© 1991 by John Wiley & Sons, Inc.   CCC 0270-7314/91/060711-18$04.00

evidence of chaos has been found [see Brock (1988b); Frank and Stengos (1989); Hinich and Patterson (1985); Scheinkman and LeBaron (1989); van der Ploeg, (1986]. Also, there are a number of marketing strategies based, at least implicitly, upon behavioral and structural aspects of commodity markets. In sum, futures markets appear to be a logical place to expand the analysis of chaos hypotheses.

Applying a new methodology to any problem raises many questions. The first question is usually "why bother?" It is sometimes claimed that if a model gives a "reasonable approximation" of reality, it is good enough. This implies that the cost of developing a more complex model may not be well spent. Considering the adequate performance of some linear economic models, some analysts may be satisfied to continue using them. But are those models "good enough" only because methods are not yet advanced enough to know that the world is round (nonlinear), not flat (linear)? It may be that BLUE (Best Linear Unbiased Estimate) is not always the relevant "color" for economic models. If the real structure of prices is nonlinear, using linear models may give noisy results; however, a completely deterministic nonlinear function may explain prices with no noise, meaning that forecasting may be possible. While the goal of improving forecasting models through the use of chaotic parameters may seem out of reach at present, the possibility makes studies such as this necessary.

The general objectives of this study are to (i) evaluate commodity futures markets using the methodology of nonlinear dynamics to detect whether there are any signs of a deterministic system underlying prices over time; and (ii) while doing so, to illustrate the empirical procedures and their limitations. Specific objectives of this study are to determine whether (a) there is a difference between chaotic analysis results for cash and futures markets of financials; (b) there is a difference between results for futures markets of financials and agricultural products; and (c) chaos is detectable over a period lengthy enough to justify development of forecasting models. The presentation begins with a summary of related studies. That is followed by a section introducing the basic concepts in chaos analysis. Empirical procedures are outlined then and the results from analyses of two heavily traded futures markets, the S&P 500 index and soybeans, are presented as examples.

SUMMARY OF PREVIOUS WORK

Applying chaos analysis methods to commodity futures prices raises questions ranging from behavioral to structural issues.[2] One motivation for considering chaos as a possible explanation for commodity spot and futures price behavior is the poor results produced by studies using traditional methods. For example, using regression analysis, Roll (1984) explains only 1–3% of the daily variation in orange juice futures prices. If deterministic models can be developed with the assistance of chaos methods, forecasting of futures prices could be improved.

Empirical applications of nonlinear dynamical analysis techniques in economics are few in number. They are concentrated in two areas: assessments of the business cycle [Brock and Sayers (1988); Day (1983); Lorenz (1987)] and financial markets [Hinich and Patterson (1985); Savit (1989); Scheinkman and LeBaron (1989); van

---

[2]For example, "Can nonlinear dynamics explain speculative bubbles?" or "Do trading rules, such as those imposed on futures markets, create price patterns similar to patterns generated by 'strange attractors' (defined in the next section)?" Intuitively, there is reason to believe chaos may contribute to the debate over "bubbles" and structural aspects of commodity trading may provide some of the explanation.

der Ploeg (1986)]. The results are somewhat mixed, possibly due to the nature of data used. Studies of macroeconomic variables, such as the business cycle, do not generate results as strong as micro-level analyses of some specific markets [Barnett and Chen (1988)]. Therefore, evaluating data characteristics should be an early stage of any empirical study.

The first indication that relying on traditional analysis methods alone may be inadequate come from studies evaluating the characteristics of futures market data. Cornew et al. (1984) find that futures prices are not normally distributed, creating error in traditional trading performance measures, all of which are based on the normality assumption. Helms and Martell (1985) also reject the normality assumption concerning the distribution of futures price changes. However, they find that the normal distribution fit their data better than other members of the stable Paretian class of distribution. They note that the underlying generating process does *not* appear to be stationary, possibly being a subordinated stochastic or compound process requiring a more sophisticated approach to determine its exact nature. Garcia et al. (1988) use nonparametric tests and find more "nonrandomness" in livestock futures prices than are found using traditional tests. They suggest that the nonrandomness may be nonlinear in nature. These conclusions are similar to those reached by Hinich and Patterson (1985) regarding stock market returns.

These results are significant because traditional, linear models assume the data are normally distributed [Stevenson and Bear (1970); Kenyon et al. (1987)], while nonlinear dynamics makes no a priori assumptions concerning data distributions. In fact, distributions are hypothesized to change across nonlinear systems of differeing degrees of chaotic behavior.

The usual way of looking for order in a time series entails spectral analysis. [Economic applications are illustrated by Shumway (1988) and Talpaz (1974).] The process involves transforming a series into a number of independent components associated with different frequencies. If the series includes periodic motion, the resulting power spectrum corresponds to the fundamental frequency. At the opposite extreme is white noise; all frequencies contribute equally. Unfortunately, the presence of sharp spectral peaks in a time series does not necessarily indicate a periodic attractor, nor does the absence of such peaks exclude the possibility of deterministic dynamics [Barnett and Hinich (1991)]. Therefore, other methods of analysis must be used to identify chaos in economic time series data.

An intermediate step is illustrated by Ashley and Patterson's (1989) use of the bispectral nonlinearity test. They test for a linear generating mechanism for both an aggregate stock market index and an aggregate industrial production index, rejecting the hypothesis in both cases. They conclude that their results strongly suggest that nonlinear dynamics should be an important feature of any macroeconomic model. The general state-dependent models outlined by Priestly (1988) could be one of the practical ways of pursuing nonlinear modeling in the future.

In microeconomic analysis, one method used to test the speculative efficiency hypothesis is called rescaled range analysis, which is capable of identifying persistent or irregular cyclic dependence in time series data. The hypothesis that respective price changes are independent of previous price changes is rejected in applications of rescaled range analysis to the foreign exchange market [Booth et al. (1982a)], the gold market [Booth et al. (1982b)], and the stock market [Greene and Fielitz (1977)]. Long-term persistent dependence is found in each study. A similar study of soybean futures markets finds nonperiodic cycles (persistent dependence) in both daily and intraday futures prices [Helms et al. (1984)].

Mandelbrot (1977) evaluates cotton prices and finds patterns which match across *scales* of time (daily, monthly). This raises the question, "is scaling a problem or an answer?" [Feigenbaum (1983)]. Economists use different data aggregations in their analyses (annual, quarterly, monthly, weekly, daily, and for futures—intraday). In particular, futures and spot price data for commodities give the appearance of having what Mandelbrot (1977) called *fractal dimensions*. Empirical studies for gold and silver [Frank and Stengos (1989); Scheinkman and LeBaron (1989)] and T-bills [Brock (1988b)] consider only the spot market but the fact that each undifferentiated product tested produces positive results indicates that further investigation is warranted.

CONCEPTS IN CHAOS ANALYSIS

As explained by Brock and Sayers (1988), a data time series (a_t) can be characterized as deterministically chaotic if there exists a system, (h, F, x_0), such that h maps R^n to R, F maps R^n to R^n, $a_t = h(x_t)$, $x_{t+1} = F(x_t)$, and x_0 is the initial condition at time $t = 0$. In this case, the map F is deterministic, the state space is n-dimensional, all trajectories (x_t) lie on an attractor A, and two nearby trajectories on A locally diverge. The variable h is a general function of the unknown state vector x, and F is an unknown dynamic that governs the evolution of the state. Also, x_0 is, in general, unknown. The goal of analysis is to discover information about the system (h, F, x_t) from observations (a_t).

An *attractor*, A, is a subset of the n-dimensional phase space, R^n. Attractors, i.e., collections of points to which initial conditions tend, can be loosely defined as having the following property. Solutions (trajectories) originating at points on the attractor remain there forever; solutions based at points *not* on the attractor, but within a region called the attractor's "basin of attraction," approach the attractor to an arbitrary degree of closeness. In the case of price data, an attractor might be particular (equilibrium?) price levels or patterns.

Chaos theory deals with deterministic processes which appear to be random (stochastic), but whose dimension is finite. Specifically, a "random process" is defined to have a "high" dimension, while a "deterministic process" has a "low" dimension. The object of analysis is to distinguish between the two. To do so, "dimension" must be defined and measured. In chaos analysis, the focus is on *fractal dimensions:* similar patterns across different (time) scalings.

One of the three types of probabilistic fractal dimension[3] is the "correlation dimension" (hereafter CD). It and the Lyapunov exponent (LE) (defined below) have become the most popular measures of nonlinear systems [Abraham et al. (1984); Grassberger and Procaccia (1983); Lorenz (1987)]. It is a measure of the minimal number of nonlinear "factors" needed to describe the data [Brock and Sayers (1988)]. To estimate the correlation dimension it is first necessary to compute the distances between all the points of a time series and then to determine what fraction of those distances are less than a series of predetermined length scales. This gives a measure called the "correlation integral," which is defined for different scale lengths, g, by the equation

$$C(g) = \lim_{N \to \infty} \left[\frac{1}{N(N-1)} \right] \sum_{i \neq j}^{N} (g, X_i, X_j) \tag{1}$$

[3]Probabilistic dimensions explicitly consider the frequency distribution with which points on the attractor are visited.

where N is the sample size, X_i and X_j are (vector-valued) observations in the time series and

$$(g, X_i, X_j) = \begin{cases} 1 \text{ if } |X_i - X_j| < g \\ 0 \text{ if } |X_i - X_j| > g \end{cases}$$

Grassberger and Procaccia (1983) argue that for small g

$$C(g) = \text{Constant} \cdot g^n \qquad (2)$$

where the exponent n is the CD. Empirical procedures used to estimate the CD are discussed in the methodology section later in this paper.

Low-dimensional chaos involves instability and "overshooting," while stochastic processes are infinite dimensional [Brock and Dechert (1991); van der Ploeg (1986)]. The few economic applications of this measure involve a stock returns index and gold and silver spot prices, all of which have CD estimates of about 6 (considered to be low) using weekly data [Frank and Stengos (1989); Scheinkman and LeBaron (1989)], and Treasury bill returns which have a dimension around 2 [Brock (1988b)].

Lyapunov exponents are simply generalized eigenvalues averaged over the entire attractor. They measure the average rate of contraction (when negative) or expansion (when positive) on an entire attractor. They can be positive or negative, but at least one must be positive for an attractor to be classified as chaotic or "strange" [Wolf (1986)]. In the one-dimensional case, where $x_{i+1} = F(x_i)$, the Lyapunov exponent, λ, is defined as

$$\lambda = \lim_{N \to \infty} \left(\frac{1}{N}\right) \sum \log_2 \left|\frac{dF}{dx}\right| \qquad (3)$$

where the derivative is evaluated at each point on the trajectory and logarithms are taken to the base 2. Usually, LEs are reported in units of bits per observation. Positive exponents can be viewed as measuring the rate at which new information is created; specifically, the rate at which unmeasurable (because they are too small) variations are magnified to the point where they can be observed.

In summary, Savit (1988) lists three features a deterministic sequence should have to be chaotic:

1. It should sample all regions of its domain (eventually).
2. It is practically unpredictable in the long term (if there is any indeterminacy in one's knowledge or ability to compute.[4]
3. There are many initial prices, P_o, called periodic points,[5] and the sequence of prices generated by the chaotic map is periodic, i.e., over time the sequence of prices P_t eventually repeats itself.

This list makes it clear that chaos analysis must begin with a detailed description of the data involving a set of statistics new to most market analysts.

GENERAL METHODOLOGY

Empirical methods derived from those applied in previous economic studies of chaotic systems [Brock (1986); Deneckere and Pelikan (1986)] are used here. To ac-

---

[4]For example, rounding errors accumulate rapidly in the calculations involved in estimating fractal dimensions, thus reducing precision in distant forecasts.

[5]The existence of a large number of periodic points is just one example of hidden regularities in a chaotic system.

complish this study's first general objective, this three-step process of dynamical analysis is followed:

1. Calculate the Grassberger-Procaccia correlation dimension for various embedding dimensions [Abraham et al. (1984); Swinney (1983)].
2. Apply a residual test for the presence of deterministic chaos as an alternate for the best-fitting linear model of prices [Brock and Sayers (1988)].
3. Estimate the largest Lyapunov exponent for various embedding dimensions [Abraham et al. (1984); Swinney (1983); Wolf (1986); Wolf and Swift (1984); Wolf et al. (1985)].

Operationally, the correlation dimension [n in eq. (2)] is the slope, k, of the regression: log $C(g)$ versus log g for small values of g. To estimate the CD from a single variable time series, the procedure is as follows:

1. The data are embedded in successively higher dimensions as prescribed by Takens (1985).
2. For each embedding, $C(g)$ is computed and the scaling factor, k, is estimated.
3. The procedure is repeated until the estimates of k converge.

The correlation dimension is therefore expected to equal whatever value at which k remains stable over a number of embedding dimensions.

Lyapunov exponents are local quantities which are averaged over the attractor. To compute the largest LE from a time series, the program by Wolf et al. (1985) is used which suggests choosing a so-called "fiducial" trajectory and estimating the rate at which it and a nearby test trajectory diverge. When the distance between the two points becomes large, a new point is chosen near the fiducial trajectory and the procedure is repeated. The entire time series is stepped through in this way and the stretchings and contractions are averaged.

In practice, estimating Lyapunov exponents in this way requires experimentation on the part of an analyst. Wolf's algorithm requires that the following information be provided:

- an embedding dimension and time lag for the reconstruction of the attractor;
- the time interval over which the two pieces of the trajectory are followed (called the "evolution");
- the minimum acceptable separation between points that are to be followed; and
- the maximum acceptable separation.

As a result of this flexibility in inputs, an analyst must simply experiment. The goal of the experimentation is to find a region in parameter space over which the estimate is approximately constant. Clearly, this portion of the analysis is rough, hence the reluctance of previous authors to report exact LE values for economic data series.

The data used in this study are futures prices for the S&P 500 index and soybeans. These products are selected as examples to represent, respectively, financial and agricultural futures markets because they are traded heavily and each market has been studied previously by analysts using a variety of methods, which provides a base for comparison. The S&P index, in particular, is selected because it is the product traded on futures markets which is closest to the variables studied in earlier chaotic analyses of the cash stock market. This enables direct comparison between results from previous studies of the cash stock market and the results produced here for the futures index. For each product, daily closing price data for recent individual futures contracts and nearby contracts are evaluated. For soybeans, the November 1986 and November 1987 contracts are used. The data for each contract begins during July of the previous calendar year, giving 337 and 335 observations, respectively. The nearby futures price series, constructed from the closing prices of the futures contract closest to its maturity date at each point in time, covers the period from March 1966 through June 1988, with 5823 observations. The December 1986 and December 1987 S&P 500 contracts are used. Each contract has 250 observations covering the previous calendar year. The S&P 500 nearby series begins in May 1982, ends in December 1987, and has 1420 observations.

Before conducting nonlinear dynamical analysis, the data are detrended using ordinary least squares and autoregressive methods, deseasonalized and transformed (if necessary) as described by Baumol and Benhabib (1989). If a time series has a deterministic explanation, fitting a smooth time series model with a finite number of leads and lags will generate a residual series with the same CD and largest LE as the original series. The key is to first make the residuals as close to "white noise" as possible with traditional linear methods. In this way, if nonlinear models find significant traces of a deterministic system in the residuals, the hypothesis of a linear generating system can be rejected.

Brook and Sayers (1988) evaluate the H_o: whiteness tests and diagnostics do not alter chaotic systems and can be used to test residuals from the best linear model. They use a new "W" statistic to test for independence. Based on the correlation integral, the W statistic for embedding dimension m is defined as

$$W_m(g, N) \equiv \sqrt{N}\left(\frac{D_m(g, N)}{b_m(g, N)}\right) \tag{4}$$

where $D_m = C_m - (C_1)^m$, and b_m is an estimate of the standard deviation

$$b_m = (1, -mC_{m-1})' \sum (1, -mC_{m-1}) \tag{5}$$

as discussed by Brock (1988a). The W test detects misspecification caused by a linear model fit to nonlinear data and indicates such by giving a nonzero value. Brock and Dechert (1991) show that $D_m(g, N)$ converges to a nonzero number if evaluated using the residuals from a misspecified model, while the residuals from a correctly fitted linear model are independent and identically distributed and are characterized by $D_m(g, \infty) \equiv D_m(g) = 0$ for all m and all $g > 0$. This means that a W value of 0 indicates a stochastic process and a large W is evidence of a misspecified (nonlinear) model. Statistically significant nonlinearity appears to exist at the 5% level when the W value is greater than 1.96 [Brock and Dechert (1991)]. W statistics are reported below for the data series evaluated.

Due to the weakness of the standard CD empirical processes in some cases, it is desirable to calculate the correlation dimension for "random" numbers generated to provide a basis for comparison and to report the W statistic for those values [Brock (1986)]. The random numbers used are the residuals "scrambled" as described by Scheinkman and LeBaron (1989). If the data are stochastic, the CD estimates for the residuals and the "scrambled" residuals will be identical; if the scrambled data generate higher CD estimates, this is evidence of hidden (nonlinear) structure in the residuals. The scrambled residuals test is conducted in this study.

Also, the small sample distribution of the CD and LE statistics are illustrated here by presenting values calculated from 100 series of random numbers. The series are drawn using random number generators based on the following distributions: normal, log, chi-square, exponential, double exponential, geometric, poisson, F-distribution, T-distribution, and beta. Ten series are drawn from each distribution since no a priori assumption is made concerning which distribution is "best". Each series includes 250 observations. The 100 CD values estimated are averaged to provide a benchmark representing stochastic processes. As in the scrambled residual test, deterministic CD values must be below those estimated from the random numbers. For LEs, two sets of estimates are reported: average values for the 100 series and the highest of the 100 LEs observed for each group of experiments. The average values for the random series can be compared against the values estimated from the actual futures price data to establish the general case for evidence of deterministic processes in the LE values. A qualitative assessment of the degree of significance of actual LE values can be made by a second comparison involving the highest of the 100 random estimates. This means that an LE for futures price data must be both positive and greater than the average LE from the random data to be considered evidence of a chaotic process; but, in addition, it must be greater than the highest of the 100 random LE values to be convincing evidence.

EMPIRICAL RESULTS AND IMPLICATIONS

Estimates of correlation dimensions and Lyapunov exponents are both given below, along with a discussion of the results. First, measures used to "prewhiten" the data are noted.

A generalized autoregressive conditional heteroscedasticity (GARCH) model is used to generate the residuals used in the analysis. The GARCH procedure, developed by Bollerslev (1986), is applied in studies of exchange rates [Hsieh (1989)] and stock market returns using spot market data [Baillie and DeGennaro (1990); Scheinkman and LeBaron (1989)] and futures market data [Cheung and Ng (in press)] as well as in studies of commodity markets [Aradhyula and Holt (1988)]. GARCH methods are found to be useful in detecting nonlinear patterns in variance while not destroying any signs of deterministic structural shifts in a model [Lamoureux and Lastrapes (1990)]. Therefore, it serves as a good filter for studies of chaos.

Brock and Sayers (1988) demonstrate that the power of the W statistic is weak if an autoregressive [AR(q)] model is applied with a high order (q) and, therefore, q should be set as low as possible in GARCH whitening processes. In this study, if conventional criteria finds that a GARCH(1, 1) model produces white noise residuals, it is used. If a GARCH(1, 1) model fails this test, a GARCH(2, 2) model would be fitted next, and so forth until white noise is found.

The data for the two S&P 500 contracts cover years during which prices generally trended. Prices of the December 1986 S&P 500 contract fluctuate around an upward-sloping trendline. As a result, the GARCH(1, 1) model for the December 1986 S&P 500 contract price at time t is

$$x_t = 0.207 - 0.024x_{t-1} + 0.013x_{t-2} + \delta_t \qquad (6a)$$
$$\;\;\;\;\;(0.192)\quad\;\; (0.011)\quad\quad\;\; (0.011)$$

$$h_t = 6.592 + 0.633\delta_{t-1}^2 + 0.566h_{t-1} \tag{6b}$$
$$(0.847) \quad (0.459) \quad\quad (0.490)$$

where the x_t's are first differences, δ is a residual, h is the conditional variance of the residuals, and the standard errors are in parentheses. Stock prices are lower during 1987 due to the "Crash" in October. The uptrend-ending jolt gives the December 1987 S&P 500 contract a model of

$$x_t = 0.008 - 0.252x_{t-2} - 0.120x_{t-4} + 0.109x_{t-5} + \delta_t \tag{7a}$$
$$(0.455) \quad (0.064) \quad\quad (0.064) \quad\quad (0.062)$$

$$h_t = 49.072 + 0.696\delta_{t-1}^2 + 0.752h_{t-1} \tag{7b}$$
$$(33.831) \quad (0.391) \quad\quad (0.359)$$

using the same notation.

The data for the two soybean contracts cover the same two years, but display trends for those years with slopes opposite to those in the S&P 500 data. Whereas stock prices rise during 1986, soybean prices trend downward that year. The GARCH(2, 2) model of the November 1986 soybean contract price at time t is

$$x_t = -0.143 - 0.108x_{t-2} + 0.065x_{t-3} + \delta_t \tag{8a}$$
$$(0.258) \quad (0.055) \quad\quad (0.055)$$

$$h_t = 21.793 + 0.143\delta_{t-1}^2 - 0.541\delta_{t-2}^2 + 0.365h_{t-1} + 0.507h_{t-2} \tag{8b}$$
$$(2.883) \quad (0.343) \quad\quad (0.166) \quad\quad (0.343) \quad\quad (0.182)$$

On the other hand, during 1987 stock prices are lower on the year, while soybean prices rise. The price of the November 1987 soybean contract at time t is

$$x_t = 0.197 - 0.093x_{t-1} - 0.086x_{t-5} + \delta_t \tag{9a}$$
$$(0.349) \quad (0.055) \quad\quad (0.055)$$

$$h_t = 39.964 - 0.738\delta_{t-1}^2 - 0.853\delta_{t-2}^2 - 0.703h_{t-1} - 0.515h_{t-2} \tag{9b}$$
$$(6.867) \quad (0.050) \quad\quad (0.049) \quad\quad (0.080) \quad\quad (0.079)$$

The fact that both soybean models have GARCH(2, 2) processes while both S&P 500 series have GARCH(1, 1) processes may indicate a difference in time series properties of commodity and financial futures.

The two nearby futures contract price series produce models more similar to each other. The price of the nearby S&P 500 contract at time t is

$$x_t = 0.075 + 0.451x_{t-1} - 0.220x_{t-2} - 0.094x_{t-4} + 0.095x_{t-5} + \delta_t \tag{10a}$$
$$(0.240) \quad (0.044) \quad\quad (0.045) \quad\quad (0.045) \quad\quad (0.044)$$

$$h_t = 28.011 + 0.701\delta_{t-1}^2 + 0.773h_{t-1} \tag{10b}$$
$$(18.136) \quad (0.181) \quad\quad (0.159)$$

Stock prices steadily rise during the period covered by the S&P 500 index futures contract data, despite some "corrections." The nearby soybean contract price data have a spiky pattern in which numerous periods of trending prices are evident. As a whole, the GARCH(1, 1) model for the data is

$$x_t = 0.831 - 0.154x_{t-2} + 0.168x_{t-3} + 0.191x_{t-4} - 0.141x_{t-5} + \delta_t \tag{11a}$$
$$(0.415) \quad (0.048) \quad\quad (0.053) \quad\quad (0.054) \quad\quad (0.054)$$

$$h_t = 45.168 + 0.849\delta_{t-1}^2 + 1.107h_{t-1} \tag{11b}$$
$$(13.266) \quad (0.027) \quad\quad (0.013)$$

Correlation Dimension Results

Correlation dimension estimates made from the residuals, δ, of eqs. 6–11 are presented in Table I. Observations which can be made from the results in the table include:

1. Both the S&P index and soybeans have "low" CDs in absolute terms and in comparison to CDs reported in earlier cash stock market studies.
2. Both nearby series have lower CDs than the contract series.
3. All series pass both the "scrambled residuals" and random number tests: their CDs are lower than those of the scrambled and random data.

The general implication of these results is that both the S&P index and soybeans appear to have nonlinearities in their underlying generating processes. More detailed observations are made below before presenting the W statistic results from tests of the nonlinear hypothesis.

Table I presents results for the first ten embedding dimensions to enable the reader to see how the CDs stabilize. The CD estimates are rounded to one decimal point from the regression output for each embedding dimension. Despite this imprecision, it appears that the estimates converge after the fourth or fifth embedding dimension in the case of each data series. Convergence does not occur in most of the scrambled series, nor in the random series.

It appears that the CDs in Table I are lower for soybeans than for the S&P index and that both futures markets evaluated have CDs lower than those Scheinkman and LeBaron (1989) report for cash stock market returns, although no statistic is

Table I
CORRELATION DIMENSION ESTIMATES
FOR S&P 500 AND SOYBEAN FUTURES PRICES

	Embedding Dimension									
	1	2	3	4	5	6	7	8	9	10
Contract Series										
S&P 12/86	1.0	1.5	2.1	2.2	2.4	2.5	2.3	2.7	2.4	2.3
S&P 12/86[a]	1.1	1.9	2.8	3.2	4.1	4.2	4.5	5.3	6.1	5.8
S&P 12/87	1.0	1.6	2.1	2.1	2.3	2.0	2.0	2.3	2.7	2.8
S&P 12/87[a]	1.0	2.0	2.9	3.6	4.3	4.4	4.4	5.1	4.8	4.9
Soybean 11/86	0.9	1.4	1.7	1.9	1.9	2.0	1.6	1.7	1.4	1.4
Soybean 11/86[a]	0.9	1.8	2.8	3.0	3.4	3.7	4.5	4.8	5.3	5.8
Soybean 11/87	0.9	1.3	1.6	1.9	2.0	2.2	1.9	2.1	2.2	2.1
Soybean 11/87[a]	0.9	2.0	2.7	4.0	4.4	4.8	5.1	5.5	5.6	6.2
Nearby Series										
S&P nearby	0.9	1.3	1.4	1.6	1.6	1.7	1.5	1.6	1.5	1.4
S&P nearby[a]	1.0	2.1	3.2	3.8	4.1	5.2	6.0	7.2	7.9	8.3
Soybean nearby	0.9	1.0	1.2	1.2	1.3	1.3	1.3	1.3	1.3	1.3
Soybean nearby[a]	0.9	2.2	3.4	3.9	4.4	5.8	6.4	7.1	8.0	9.2
Random Series[b]	0.9	2.1	3.6	4.5	5.1	6.3	7.8	8.9	9.6	10.3

[a]Results from a "scrambled" series created for comparison.
[b]Average results from 100 series of random numbers generated from various distributions for comparison.

available to aid in determining whether one CD estimate is significantly different than another. The difference between stock and soybean futures results is more apparent for the contract price series than for the nearby series. The general CDs for the November 1986 and 1987 soybean contracts, respectively, seem to be 1.7–2.0 and 1.9–2.2. The CDs for both S&P contracts are 2.3–2.7. The nearby soybean series has a CD of 1.3, while the S&P nearby data have a CD of 1.5–1.7. These values may not be significantly different from each other, but it is expected that they are significantly lower than the CDs of 6–7 which Scheinkman and LeBaron (1989) report.

The level and stability of the CD estimates in Table I give rise to the question of sample size effects. Ramsey and Yuan (1987) show that CDs may be underestimated from small data sets. In this case, estimates are lower and more stable for larger samples. For example, the nearby soybean series is the largest with 5823 observations and it has the lowest, most stable CD estimates across embedding dimensions. This indicates that no conclusions can be reached concerning the relative differences in CDs between the two markets noted above. Nevertheless, the fact that even the smallest data sets (the S&P contract series) generated CDs that are "low," compared to the CDs for the scrambled and random series, supports the hypothesis that nonlinearity exists in all six series. To resolve the question of significance, W statistics are calculated.

Table II presents W statistics for each of the six series, their respective scrambled counterparts, and the random series. For each price series the statistic exceeds the 1.96 value needed (at the 95% confidence level) to reject the null hypothesis of a linear process. For the soybean nearby series, in particular, the results are strong. This indicates that nonlinearities are present in the data. However, although the W statistic can distinguish between a linear and nonlinear generating process, it can-

Table II
W STATISTICS FOR S&P 500 AND SOYBEAN FUTURES PRICE SERIES

		Embedding Dimension		
	Observations (n)	4	5	6
Contract Series				
S&P 12/86	250	4.21	5.81	5.95
S&P 12/86[a]	250	1.27	1.55	1.80
S&P 12/87	250	6.99	7.76	8.12
S&P 12/87[a]	250	3.03	3.62	4.15
Soybean 11/86	335	5.86	6.07	7.23
Soybean 11/86[a]	335	1.17	1.31	1.43
Soybean 11/87	337	4.66	5.40	6.92
Soybean 11/87[a]	337	1.05	1.11	1.31
Nearby Series				
S&P nearby	1420	6.61	7.22	8.10
S&P nearby[a]	1420	0.75	0.99	1.31
Soybean nearby	5823	12.32	13.00	14.26
Soybean nearby[a]	5823	1.27	1.37	1.52
Random Series[b]	250	0.92	1.06	1.15

[a]Results from a "scrambled" series created for comparison.
[b]Average results from 100 series of random numbers.

not detect whether that process is stochastic or deterministic. Therefore, additional evidence, such as LE estimates, is needed to make this distinction.

Lyapunov Exponent Results

Lyapunov exponent estimates for soybean and S&P 500 prices are presented, respectively, in Tables III and IV. In the absence of statistics for use in determining the significance level of these estimates, only qualitative observations can be made, using the random number results presented in Table V, including:

1. Both the S&P index and soybeans have positive, stable LEs across embedding dimensions, implying the presence of chaos.
2. LEs for the S&P nearby series appear to be of similar magnitude to those for S&P contract series and are higher than the random number LEs in many cases, while the LEs for the soybean nearby series are consistently lower than both the soybean contract series' LEs and the highest of the random number LEs.
3. For all series, LE values decline as evolution lengths increase, as expected.

The general conclusion is that these results support those of the correlation dimension analysis: both the S&P index and soybeans appear to have chaotic nonlinearities in their underlying generating processes. More detailed observations are made below.

Tables III and IV present estimates of the largest Lyapunov exponent calculated for different embedding dimensions using different evolution lengths. Dimensions 3, 5, and 9 are selected to illustrate results across the range that has stable CDs. For

Table III
LYAPUNOV EXPONENTS FOR SOYBEAN FUTURES PRICE SERIES

Price Series	Evolution[a]	Embedding Dimension		
		3	5	9
November 1986 Contract	5	0.0430	0.0613	0.0484
	10	0.0401	0.0525	0.0401
	21	0.0308	0.0337	0.0180
	42	0.0112[b]	0.0136	0.0172
	63	0.0109[b]	0.0129[b]	0.0067[b]
November 1987 Contract	5	0.0382[b]	0.0517	0.0410
	10	0.0285	0.0431	0.0402
	21	0.0240	0.0366	0.0180
	42	0.0233	0.0137	0.0126
	63	0.0263	0.0128[b]	0.0122
Nearby Contract	5	0.0002[b]	0.0051[b]	0.0067[b]
	10	0.0001[b]	0.0050[b]	0.0057[b]
	21	0.0000[b]	0.0031[b]	0.0045[b]
	42	−0.0011[b]	0.0039[b]	0.0037[b]
	63	−0.0012[b]	0.0042[b]	0.0035[b]

[a]Number of observations over which the two pieces of the trajectory are followed.
[b]Values fall between the average and highest estimates for the relevant entry in Table V.
Note: The minimum and maximum scale lengths used here are 1 and 45 cents per bushel, respectively.

Table IV
LYAPUNOV EXPONENTS FOR S&P 500 FUTURES PRICE SERIES

Price Series	Evolution[a]	Embedding Dimension		
		3	5	9
December 1986 Contract	5	0.0334	0.0316[b]	0.0339
	10	0.0316	0.0261[b]	0.0317
	21	0.0245	0.0232	0.0168
	42	0.0149	0.0195	0.0097[b]
	63	0.0081[b]	0.0058[b]	0.0183
December 1987 Contract	5	0.0960	0.0978	0.0695
	10	0.0623	0.0930	0.0550
	21	0.0708	0.0647	0.0216
	42	0.0012[b]	−0.0018[b]	0.0100[b]
	63	−0.0027[b]	0.0009[b]	0.0065[b]
Nearby Contract	5	0.0216[b]	0.0465	0.0423
	10	0.0211[b]	0.0336	0.0280
	21	0.0199[b]	0.0120[b]	0.0202
	42	0.0066[b]	0.0077[b]	0.0149
	63	0.0071[b]	0.0129[b]	0.0138

[a]Number of observations over which the two pieces of the trajectory are followed.
[b]Values fall between the average and highest estimates for the relevant entry in Table V.
Note: The minimum and maximum scale lengths used here are 1 and 25 index points, respectively.

Table V
LYAPUNOV EXPONENTS FOR 100 SERIES OF RANDOM NUMBERS

Price Series	Evolution[a]	Embedding Dimension		
		3	5	9
Average Estimates	5	−0.0123	0.0032	−0.0037
	10	−0.0191	0.0006	−0.0112
	21	−0.0265	−0.0069	−0.0131
	42	−0.0281	−0.0080	−0.0143
	63	−0.0254	−0.0101	−0.0162
Highest Estimates	5	0.0238	0.0456	0.0070
	10	0.0223	0.0286	0.0141
	21	0.0185	0.0160	0.0117
	42	0.0140	0.0108	0.0105
	63	0.0152	0.0182	0.0102

[a]Number of observations over which the two pieces of the trajectory are followed.

each of those dimensions, LEs are calculated for evolution lengths equaling one week (five observations), two weeks (ten observations), one month (21 observations), two months (42 observations), and three months (63 observations).

This cross section of LEs is estimated in a "bootstrapping" effort to add robustness to any conclusions reached concerning the presence of chaos and to provide for a preliminary test of the hypothesis that futures prices are detectably deterministic over a long enough time period to make (short-term) price forecasting models possible. As noted by Frank and Stengos (1989, p. 555), "A chaotic system will be quite predictable over very short time horizons. If however the initial conditions are only known with finite precision, then over long intervals the ability to predict the time path will be lost." This means that if chaos can be detected at an evolution interval, the deterministic system generating prices has not been overwhelmed by stochastic noise and the development of forecasting models may be possible. If the largest LE is never positive in experiments across evolution lengths, the system is stochastic. However, if LEs are positive for short evolutions and turn negative at some longer length, the implication is that at that time interval stochastic noise becomes dominant and deterministic forecasting models are not empirically viable, even though the underlying system may be completely deterministic in nature. In summary, experimenting with evolution lengths provides a way in which analysts can assess the potential for developing forecasting models.

Table V provides results for the random numbers for the same cross section of LE experiments. These results illustrate the small sample distribution of the LE statistic and provide a basis for assessing the effects of noise on the estimates. The "Average Estimates" reported in Table V are the mean estimates of the LE from the 100 series of random numbers. The fact that all but two of the values reported are negative indicates that Wolf et al.'s (1985) procedure for calculating LEs does a good job of detecting stochastic processes in general. However, in any particular case there is some chance of mislabeling a stochastic process as being deterministic due to the effects of noise in the small sample (of 250 observations). This is evident in Table V as the "Highest Estimates" are positive for each experiment. In other words, at least one of the 100 random series produces a positive LE for each combination of evolution length and embedding dimension. Therefore, actual data which produce LE estimates falling between the average and highest value reported for the relevant experiment in Table V may or may not have a deterministic generating process.

In Table III all but two LEs are positive, strongly supporting the conclusion that soybean futures prices have a chaotic nonlinear generating process. Also, that process may be predictable over periods as long as the three-month evolutions evaluated here. However, a closer look leads to some interesting issues for future research. For example, the LEs for the two contract price series are very similar across embedding dimensions and evolution lengths, but they differ from LEs for the nearby series. LEs for nearby prices are approximately zero at dimension 3 and, although they stabilize at higher dimensions, no actual estimate exceeds the relevant "Highest Estimate" from Table V. One hypothesis is that the two types of series will have different generating systems because contract series have less noise (possibly indicated by a lower coefficient of variation) and fewer trends, compared to more volatile nearby series which contain multiple trends.

One explanation for this hypothesis comes from expectations concerning the two types of data series. Futures contract price series reflect increasing amounts of information about the relatively few factors known to influence prices expected at one point in time (the contract maturity date). Over the life of a particular contract, trade volume tends to rise as information changes become easier to interpret, making the market more liquid and, hence, more efficient in its reaction to information flows. On the other hand, nearby futures contract prices reflect a liquid market's interpretation of information concerning many supply and demand factors for different points in time. Trading volume in whatever contract is "nearby" at the moment tends to remain high and be closely correlated with spot prices of the commodity [Blank et al. (1991)].

The results in Table III indicate that compared to contract series, nearby soybean futures prices have a more complex generating system requiring analysis at a higher embedding dimension before the effects of chaos (if any) can be captured. The differences in LEs between dimensions may also mean that more complex models will be required for forecasting, making successful specification of those models less likely.

Table IV presents LE estimates for S&P 500 futures prices which, in general, are surprisingly similar to those for soybeans, but which have two subtle differences raising additional issues for future research. First, the LEs for the December 1986 contract and the nearby series are similar to the soybean contracts' LEs. One hypothesis for this phenomenon is that the S&P nearby series is like many contract series in that the data have a single trend around which prices demonstrate relatively low levels of noise (at least at higher embedding dimensions). If multiple trends are present, the S&P nearby series might produce a more complex set of results, as in the case of soybeans.

Second, the LE results for the December 1987 S&P contract are unique compared to the other three contract series studied, drawing attention to the effects of the sharp market correction in October 1987. The LE values for all embedding dimensions are noticeably higher than those of any other series at evolution lengths of 5–21 days, yet for evolutions of 42 and 63 days the LEs are low and occasionally negative. It is hypothesized that the strong uptrend in S&P prices prior to the "crash" had so little noise in it that forecasting was quite possible for periods of up to one month (21 trading days), but longer forecasts necessitate more complex models to account for the effects of "Black Monday," which are interpreted as noise by simple models. This illustrates the frustration which will no doubt continue to face modelers: even if a system such as that underlying stock prices is deterministic, forecasting models cannot be expected to detect every trend or turning point. As long as initial conditions are not perfectly identified, analysts will not know whether a model is correctly specified until it fails. In other words, no matter how complex a deterministic model is, additional complexity may be required to avoid forecasting errors so large as to question the modeling effort's value.

SUMMARY AND CONCLUDING COMMENTS

This study provides results of nonlinear dynamical analysis of two commodity futures markets. It illustrates what type of methodological and empirical procedures must be used to evaluate these markets. It also raises and attempts to address issues concerning identification and measurement of nonlinear generating systems in economic data, providing a guide for research in the future. Although chaos analyses in economics are still very rare, the results presented here and elsewhere give reason for expecting use of these methods to expand, but with difficulty.

Results from analyses of a financial, the S&P 500 index, and an agricultural product, soybeans, are presented as examples. All empirical results in this study are consistent with those of markets with underlying generating systems characterized by deterministic chaos. Comparing results for the stock index and soybean futures reveals surprising similarity, yet the CDs for the index are noticeably different than those reported in earlier stock market studies which use cash price data. Both futures markets are shown to have a "low" correlation dimension of about two, while CDs are slightly lower for soybeans and for nearby series compared to contract series. The statistical significance of this difference in CDs between product types is unclear, but statistical tests do indicate the presence of nonlinearities in both markets. Estimates of Lyapunov exponents indicate that these nonlinearities are (at least partially) deterministic, rather than stochastic in nature. However, the absence of any tests for the statistical significance of estimated LEs makes the results of this study necessary, but not sufficient conditions to prove the existence of deterministic chaos.

Although providing just an introduction to the study of nonlinear dynamics in future markets, the results of this analysis may be useful for commodity market analysts in industry, academia, and government. The fact that futures prices appear to have a nonlinear generating process of a type not recognized previously raises the possibility that short-term forecasting models may be improved by incorporating these new factors. This, in turn, has significant implications for resource allocation and marketing strategies for firms trading in these product markets. Ultimately, the discovery of a nonlinear, nonrandom process in commodity futures markets could raise the level of debate in the economic literature concerning "random walk" hypotheses and definitions of pricing efficiency. However, from a practical viewpoint, chaos analysis procedures provide another test for (deterministic) nonlinearity, but do not easily lend themselves to direct applications in forecasting model construction.

Bibliography

Abraham, N., Gollub, J., and Swinney, H. (1984): "Testing Nonlinear Dynamics," *Physica*, 11D:252–264.

Aradhyula, S., and Holt, M. (1988): "GARCH Time-Series Models: An Application to Retail Livestock Prices," *Western Journal of Agricultural Economics*, 13:365–374.

Ashley, R., and Patterson, D. (1989): "Linear Versus Nonlinear Macroeconomies: A Statistical Test," *International Economic Review*, 30:685–704.

Baillie, R., and DeGennaro, R. (1990): "Stock Returns and Volatility," *Journal of Financial and Quantitative Analysis*, 25:203–214.

Barnett, W., and Chen, P. (1988): "The Aggregation-Theoretic Monetary Aggregates Are Chaotic and Have Strange Attractors: An Econometric Application of Mathematical Chaos," in *Dynamical Econometric Modeling*, Barnett, Berndt, and White (eds.). Cambridge: Cambridge University Press, pp. 199–246.

Barnett, W., and Hinich, M., (1991): "Has Chaos Been Discovered with Economic Data?" in *Evolutionary Dynamics and Nonlinear Economics*, Chen and Day (eds.), Oxford University Press.

Baumol, W., and Benhabib, J. (1989): "Chaos: Significance, Mechanism, and Economic Applications," *The Journal of Economic Perspectives*, 3:77–105.

Blank, S., Carter, C., and Schmiesing, B. (1991): *Futures and Options Markets: Trading Commodities and Financials*. Englewood Cliffs, NJ: Prentice Hall, Chapter 3.

Bollerslev, T. (1986): "Generalized Autoregressive Conditional Heteroscedasticity," *Journal of Econometrics* 31:307–327.

Booth, G., Kaen, F., and Koveos, P. (1982a): "R/S Analysis of Foreign Exchange Rates under Two International Monetary Regimes," *Journal of Monetary Economics*, 10:407–415.

Booth, G., Kaen, F., and Koveos, P. (1982b): "Persistent Dependence in Gold Prices," *Journal of Financial Research*, 85–93.

Brock. W. A. (1986): "Distinguishing Random and Deterministic Systems: Abridged Version," *Journal of Economic Theory,* 40: 168–195.

Brock, W. A. (1988a): "Introduction to Chaos and Other Aspects of Nonlinearity," in *Differential Equations, Stability, and Chaos in Dynamic Economics,* Brock, W., and Malliaris, A., New York: North Holland.

Brock, W. A. (1988b): "Nonlinearity and Complex Dynamics in Economics and Finance," in *The Economy as an Evolving Complex System,* Addison-Wesley Publishing Company: New York.

Brock, W., and Dechert, W. (1991): "Theorems on Distinguishing Deterministic from Random Systems," in *Dynamic Econometric Modeling,* Barnett, Berndt, and White (eds.). Cambridge: Cambridge University Press.

Brock, W., and Sayers, C. (1988): "Is the Business Cycle Characterized by Deterministic Chaos?" *Journal of Monetary Economics,* 22:71–90.

Candela, G., and Gardini, A. (1986): "Estimation of a Non-Linear Discrete-Time Macro Model," *Journal of Economic Dynamics & Control,* 10:249–255.

Cheung, Y., and Ng, L. (in press): "The Dynamics of S&P 500 Index and S&P 500 Futures Intraday Price Volatilities," *The Review of Futures Markets.*

Cornew, R., Town, D., and Crowson, L. (1984): "Stable Distributions, Futures Prices, and the Measurement of Trading Performance," *The Journal of Futures Markets,* 4:531–557.

Day, R. H. (1983): "The Emergence of Chaos from Classical Economic Growth," *The Quarterly Journal of Economics,* 98:201–213.

Deneckere, R., and Pelikan, S. (1986): "Competitive Chaos," *Journal of Economic Theory,* 40:13–25.

Feigenbaum, M. J. (1983): "Universal Behavior in Nonlinear Systems," *Physica,* 7D:16–39.

Frank, M., and Stengos, T. (1989): "Measuring the Strangeness of Gold and Silver Rates of Return," *Review of Economic Studies,* 56:553–567.

Garcia, P., Hudson, M., and Waller, M. (1988): "The Pricing Efficiency of Agricultural Futures Markets: An Analysis of Previous Research Results," *Southern Journal of Agricultural Economics* 20:119–130.

Goodwin, R. (1990): *Chaotic Economic Dynamics.* Oxford: Oxford University Press.

Grassberger, P., and Procaccia, I. (1983): "Measuring the Strangeness of Strange Attractors," *Physica,* 9D:189–208.

Greene, M., and Fielitz, B. (1977): "Long Term Dependence in Common Stock Returns," *Journal of Financial Economics,* 4:339–349.

Helms, B., and Martell, T. (1985): "An Examination of the Distribution of Futures Price Changes," *The Journal of Futures Markets,* 5:259–272.

Helms, B., Kaen, F., and Rosenman, R. (1984): "Memory in Commodity Futures Contracts," *The Journal of Futures Markets,* 4:559–567.

Hinich, M., and Patterson, D. (1985): "Evidence of Nonlinearity in Daily Stock Returns," *Journal of Business and Economic Statistics,* 3:69–77.

Hsieh, D. (1989): "Testing for Nonlinear Dependence in Daily Foreign Exchange Rate Changes," *Journal of Business,* 62:339–368.

Jensen, R.V. (1987): "Classical Chaos," *American Scientist,* 75:168–181.

Just, R., and Rausser, G. (1981): "Commodity Price Forecasting with Large Scale Econometric Models and the Futures Market," *American Journal of Agricultural Economics,* 63:197–208.

Kenyon, D., Kling, K., Jordan, J., Seale, W., and McCabe, N. (1987): "Factors Affecting Agricultural Futures Price Variance," *The Journal of Futures Markets,* 7:73–91.

Lamoureux, C., and Lastrapes, W. (1990): "Persistence in Variance, Structural Change, and the GARCH Model," *Journal of Business and Economic Statistics,* 8:225–234.

Lorenz, H.-W. (1987): "Strange Attractors in a Multisector Business Cycle Model," *Journal of Economic Behavior & Organization,* 8:397–411.

Mandelbrot, B. (1977): *The Fractal Geometry of Nature.* New York: Freeman.

Melese, F., and Transue, W. (1986): "Unscambling Chaos through Thick and Thin," *The Quarterly Journal of Economics,* 101:419–423.

Mirowski, P. (1990): "From Mandelbrot to Chaos in Economic Theory," *Southern Economic Journal,* 57:289–307.

Priestly, M. B. (1988): *Non-Linear and Non-Stationary Time Series Analysis,* San Diego: Academic Press.

Ramsey, J., and Yuan, H. (1987): "The Statistical Properties of Dimension Calculations Using Small Data Sets." New York: C. V. Starr Center for Applied Economics, New York University.

Roll, R. (1984): "Orange Juice and Weather," *American Economic Review,* 74:861–880.

Savit, R. (1988): "When Random is Not Random: An Introduction to Chaos in Market Prices," *The Journal of Futures Markets,* 8:271–289.

Savit, R. (1989): "Nonlinearities and Chaotic Effects in Options Prices," *The Journal of Futures Markets,* 9:507–518.

Scheinkman, J., and LeBaron, B. (1989): "Nonlinear Dynamics and Stock Returns," *Journal of Business* 62:311–337.

Shumway, R. H. (1988): *Applied Statistical Time Series Analysis.* Englewood Cliffs, NJ: Prentice-Hall.

Stevenson, R., and Bear, R. (1970): "Commodity Futures: Trends or Random Walks?" *Journal of Finance,* 25:65–81.

Swinney, H. L. (1983): "Observations of Order and Chaos in Nonlinear Systems," *Physica,* 7D:3–15.

Takens, F. (1985): "On the Numerical Determination of the Dimension of an Attractor," in *Dynamical Systems and Bifurcations,* Braaksma, N., Broer, H., and Takens, F. (eds.). Berlin: Springer-Verlag, pp. 99–106.

Talpaz, H. (1974): "Multi-Frequency Cobweb Model: Decomposition of the Hog Cycle," *American Journal of Agricultural Economics* 56:38–49.

van der Ploeg, F. (1986): "Rational Expectations, Risk and Chaos in Financial Markets," *Economic Journal,* 96:151–161.

Wolf, A. (1986): "Quantifying Chaos with Lyapunov Exponents," in *Nonlinear Science: Theory and Applications,* Holden, A. (ed.) Manchester: Manchester University Press.

Wolf, A., and Swift, J. (1984): "Progress in Computing Lyapunov Exponents from Experimental Data," in *Statistical Physics and Chaos in Fusion Plasmas,* Horton, C., and Reichl, L. (eds.). New York: John Wiley & Sons.

Wolf, A., Swift, J., Swinney, H., and Vastano, J. (1985): "Determining Lyapunov Exponents from a Time Series," *Physica,* 16D:285–317.

J ECO BUSN
1992; 44:63-74

Testing for Nonlinear Dependence in Daily Stock Indices

Thomas Willey

This article presents the results of tests for nonlinear dependence in the daily prices of the Standard & Poor's Index and the National Association of Securities Dealers Automated Quotations System 100 Stock Index. Deterministic chaos is rejected by two of three recently developed empirical tests. The methodology for implementing these diagnostic tests for financial time series is discussed, along with a route for future research to follow.

I. Introduction

Is the current market price of an asset the best estimate to the future price, making all attempts at forecasting price movements a useless exercise? Or is it possible to develop a model to fully explain day-to-day price fluctuations? The answer probably lies somewhere between these two extremes, in improving existing examples of short-term forecasting successes. Many empirical studies have shown that stock returns follow a white noise model and are unable to be forecast successfully (Fama 1970), but new evidence has been presented that shows that these results may be supplemented, and perhaps replaced, by a new hypothesis of an underlying nonlinear process.

Nonlinear processes are the focus of research in many scientific areas. Although the beginnings of these new techniques have been in the natural sciences of physics and chemistry, they are now being applied to finance and economics. Interest in these techniques is based on the assumption that highly complex behavior that appears to be random is actually generated by an underlying nonlinear process. Typically, standard statistical tests, such as spectral analysis and autocorrelation functions, are used to test for randomness and may fail to detect this hidden order.

Empirical evidence of this phenomenon has been shown by various researchers. Brock and Sayers (1988) found nonlinearity in the U.S. labor market and investment. Barnett and Chen (1988) discovered low dimensionality in some U.S. monetary measures. Frank et al. (1988) indicated nonlinearities were present in Japan's quarterly real GNP. Strong nonlinear dependence was also found in daily price changes of five foreign exchange rates by Hsieh (1989) and in financial and agricultural futures by

Address reprint requests to Thomas Willey, Department of Finance, Central Missouri State University, Warrensburg, Missouri 64093.

0148-6195/92/$05.00

Blank (1990). Scheinkman and LeBaron (1989) found that a significant part of the variation in weekly Center for Research in Security Prices (CRSP) stock index returns is due to nonlinearities instead of randomness. Other studies in this area include Frank and Stengos (1988), Hinich and Patterson (1985), and Savit (1988), (1989).

This nonlinear process, termed *deterministic chaos*, is the focus of this research. Specifically, the purpose of this article is to test for the presence of deterministic chaos in the daily prices of two time series: the Standard & Poor's 100 Stock Index (OEX) and the NASDAQ (NAS) 100 Stock Index.

II. Research Methodology

The methodology follows the lead of Brock (1986), Brock, Dechert, and Scheinkman (1987; hereafter BDS), Hsieh (1989), and Frank et al. (1988) by estimating the correlation dimension. The correlation dimension is used to differentiate between deterministic chaos and stochastic systems. Dimensionality is a measure of the complexity of an object. Brock and Sayers (1988) describe the dimension of an object as a rough indication of the number of nonlinear "factors" that describe the data. For example, a single point has zero dimension. A line has one dimension. A solid has three dimensions. A white noise process is completely disorderly and has infinite dimension. Similarly, a purely random process has infinite dimension. A chaotic system has a positive but finite dimension (Frank et al. 1988).

One method to test for nonlinear dependence involves the "correlation integral," $C(e)$. For a time series $\{Y_t: t = 1, \ldots, T\}$ of D-dimensional vectors, the correlation integral measures the fraction of the pairs of points of $\{Y_t\}$ that are within a distance of e from each other. This value is:

$$C(e) = \lim_{T \to \infty} \frac{2}{T(T-1)} \sum_{i<j} I_e(Y_i, Y_j), \tag{1}$$

where $I_e(x, y)$ = indicator function that equals unity if $\|x - y\| < e$, and zero otherwise; $\|x - y\|$ = the norm as measured by the Euclidian distance.

A form of the correlation integral is used by Grassberger and Procaccia (1983) and Swinney (1985) to define the "correlation dimension" of $\{Y_t\}$: Calculate this value by

$$C_m(e, T) = \#\{(t, s), 1 < t, s < T \mid |x_t^m - x_s^m| < e\}/T_m^2, \tag{2}$$

where

$\# S$ = the cardinality of set S;

$T_m = T - (m - 1)$ = the number of m-histories $x_t^m = (x_t, \ldots, x_{t+m-1})$

constructed from the sample of length T;

m = embedding dimension.

Theoretically, $T \to \infty$ but actually it is determined by the number of observations available for the analysis. This places limits on possible values for e and m. For a given m, e cannot be too small because $C_m(e, T)$ will contain too few observations.

Also, e cannot be too large because $C_m(e, T)$ will contain too many observations. Barnett and Choi (1989) suggest selecting a small value for e, without allowing it to reach zero. This implementation of a lower limit guards against noise in the data. Hsieh (1989) defines e in terms of multiples of the series standard deviation. These multiples are 1.50, 1.25, 1.00, 0.75, and 0.50. For this study, e is defined by the same multiples of the standard deviation of the data. For small values of e it has been shown that $C_m(e, T) \sim e^D$ so that D is the system's dimensionality (Frank et al. (1988). The series dimension is estimated by

$$D^m = \lim_{e \to 0} \left[\log C_m(e, T) / \log e \right], \text{ if the limit exists.} \tag{3}$$

The correlation dimension is used to differentiate between deterministic chaos and stochastic systems. If chaos is present, as D^m is estimated for increasingly larger values of the embedding dimension, the dimension estimate will stabilize at some value. If this stabilization does not occur, the system is considered "high-dimensional" or stochastic.

Brock's Residual Test

The first procedure creates the data for use in Brock's Residual Rest (Brock 1988). Baumol and Benhabib (1989) suggest, prior to analyzing a time series for nonlinear dynamics, that the series be transformed by ordinary least squares (OLS) and/or autoregressive techniques. The first task is to remove any linear structure in the data. This filtering, or *pre-whitening*, is done by fitting an autoregressive model to the transformed series. This process allows for a nonlinear test for the presence of a deterministic system and, if accepted, enables the rejection of a linear generating process. The dimension of the residuals is estimated and compared with the dimension of the original data. If a nonlinear process is present, these values will be undisturbed. However, the results for this diagnostic must be interpreted with caution. A bias has been shown when the relatively smaller (100 to 2,000 observations) data sets available to economic researchers are used compared with the series in the natural sciences (10,000 to 30,000 observations). This bias results in estimation errors in the dimension estimates that lead to rejection of deterministic chaos, even when it is present (Brock 1988; Hsieh 1989; Ramsey et al. 1988).

Shuffling and Bootstrapping Procedure

Another diagnostic has been presented by Scheinkman and LeBaron (1989). They suggest taking the time series and randomly sampling from it with replacement. This "shuffled" series will be a new series of the same length as that of the original series. The estimated dimension of the shuffled residuals is compared with the estimated dimension of the original residuals. If the original series was chaotic, the underlying order would be upset. This would result in a higher value of estimated dimensionality for the shuffled series than for the original series. This procedure is repeated 50 times for each level of e, to carry out the bootstrapping aspect of the test.

BDS Test

BDS (1987) have presented a hypothesis test using the W statistic. This test is based on the correlation integral. The null hypothesis is that the data are independently and identically distributed (IID); this test is applied instead of an attempt to determine if the data are stochastic or chaotic. BDS have shown that tests based on the W statistic have a higher power for tests of stochastic or chaotic independence than other statistical techniques.

BDS show that under the null hypothesis (x_t) is IID with a nondegenerate density F (Hsieh 1989),

$$C_m(e, T) \to C_1(e)^m \text{ with probability equal to unity, as } T \to \infty,$$

for any fixed m and e. Furthermore, they show that $T^{1/2}[C_m(e, T) - C_1(e, T)^m]$ has a normal limiting distribution with zero mean and variance equal to

$$\sigma_m^2(e) = 4\left[K^m + 2\sum_{j=1}^{m-1} K^{m-j}C^{2j} + (m-1)^2 C^{2m} - m^2 KC^{2m-2} \right], \qquad (4.1)$$

where:

$$C = C(e) = \int \left[F(z + e) - F(z - e) \right] dF(z),$$

$$K = K(e) = \iint \left[F(z + e) - F(z - e) \right]^2 dF(z).$$

Since $C_1(e, T)$ is a consistent estimate of $C(e)$, and

$$K(e, T) = \frac{6}{T_m(T_m - 1)(T_m - 2)} \sum_{t<s<r} I_e(x_t, x_s)I_e(x_s, x_r) \qquad (4.2)$$

is a consistent estimate of $K(e)$. Therefore $\sigma_m(e)$ can be estimated by $\sigma_m(e, T)$, which uses $C_1(e, T)$ and $K(e, T)$ instead of $C(e)$ and $K(e)$. The W statistic has a standard normal limiting distribution and is calculated by

$$W_m(e, T) = T^{1/2}[C_m(e, T) - C_1(e, T)^m]/\sigma_m(e, T). \qquad (4.3)$$

BDS show that, under the null of IID, $W_m \to N(0, 1)$, as $T \to \infty$. If the residuals from the estimated linear (or nonlinear) model are actually IID, the W statistics should be asymptotically $N(0, 1)$. Large values would indicate strong evidence for nonlinearity in the data.

III. Application to the Stock Indices

The data consist of the daily closing values of the respective stock indices. For the OEX, the observations begin on January 4, 1982, and end on December 30, 1988 ($n = 1,769$). For the NASDAQ series the period begins on October 7, 1985, and ends on June 20, 1989 ($n = 945$ observations). To ensure that the data are stationary, the first difference of the log of each series is taken. Let x_t = [(log of the OEX index on day t) − (log of the OEX index on day $t − 1$)] and y_t = [(log of the NAS index on day t) − (log of the NAS index on day $t − 1$)]. Figures 1 and 2 contain the plots of x_t and y_t. Brock and Sayers (1988) have shown that the power of the BDS statistic declines as higher-order AR(x) models are applied, leading to a need to set x as low as possible. An autoregressive model of order 3 [AR(3)] was fit to the OEX series and an AR(4) was fit to the NAS data to generate the white noise residuals used in the analysis:

$$x_t = 0.13 x_{t-1} - 0.08 x_{t-2} - 0.02 x_{t-3} + \delta x_t; \tag{5.1a}$$
$$ (5.6) \qquad (-3.5) \qquad (-0.8)$$

$$R^2 = 0.004, \, SSR = 0.281, \, SEE = 0.013, \, NOBS = 1764, \, DW = 1.99,$$

$$\sigma_x = 0.0126, \, \sigma_{\delta x} = 0.0126, \, \sigma_x / \sigma_{\delta x} = 1.00,$$

$$sk_x = -3.725, \, sk_{\delta x} = -4.022,$$

$$k_x = 74.266, \, k_{\delta x} = 78.279. \tag{5.1b}$$

$$y_t = -0.73 y_{t-1} - 0.13 y_{t-2} + 0.13 y_{t-3} + 0.08 y_{t-4} + \delta y_t; \tag{5.2a}$$
$$ (-22.53) \qquad (-3.12) \qquad (3.11) \qquad (2.37)$$

$$R^2 = 0.142, \, SSR = 0.288, \, SEE = 0.018, \, NOBS = 939, \, DW = 1.99,$$

$$\sigma_y = 0.019, \, \sigma_{\delta y} = 0.017, \, \sigma_y / \sigma_{\delta y} = 1.08,$$

$$sk_y = -4.239, \, sk_{\delta y} = -3.458,$$

$$k_y = 124.245, \, k_{\delta y} = 61.557. \tag{5.2b}$$

The numbers in parentheses are t statistics, SSR is the sum of squared residuals, SEE is the standard error of the estimate, $NOBS$ is the number of observations and DW is the Durbin–Watson statistic. The symbols σ_z, sk_z, k_z represent the standard deviation of z, the skewness of z, and kurtosis of z.

Figures 3 and 4 contains plots for the residuals for both series. Table 1 contains the results of the autocorrelation tests for the unwhitened and whitened series. All linear structure has been removed by the AR(3) process for the OEX series. The AR(4) model fits the NAS series well, taking away all significant autocorrelations, except those at lags 7 and 26.

As a further test for structure in the residuals of both series, two diagnostics were applied. First, the series were tested for the presence of an autoregressive conditional heteroskedasticity (ARCH) process (Engle 1982). The test results for the OEX series were 32.71 (order = 1), 42.65 (order = 2), 45.91 (order = 3) and 45.89 (order = 4). The results for the NAS series were 215.93, 217.04, 285.33, and 306.20. The critical values follow a chi-square distribution with the chosen ARCH order as the degrees of freedom. In every case, the test statistic exceeded the critical value, indicating evidence of an ARCH process in the residuals.

Next, the Ljung–Box Q statistic for general serial correlation was employed (Ljung and Box 1978). Testing the OEX residuals for lags up to 126 days resulted in a Q statistic of 160.85 (p value = .014), indicating the series may have significant autocor-

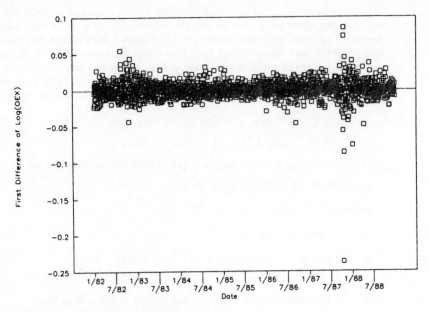

Figure 1. First difference of log (OEX).

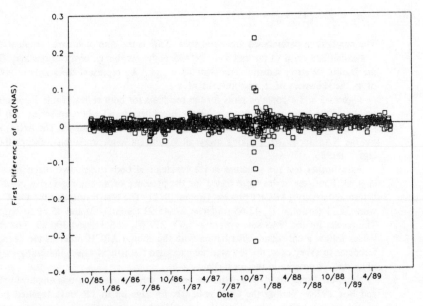

Figure 2. First difference of log (NAS).

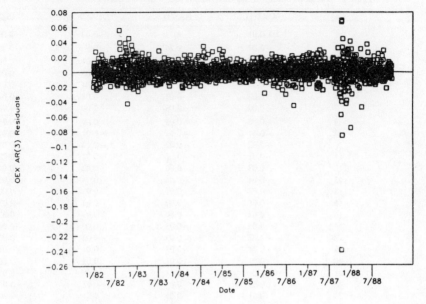

Figure 3. OEX (AR3) residuals.

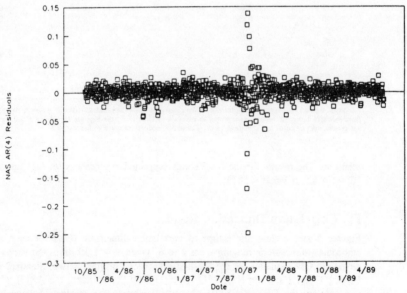

Figure 4. NAS AR(4) residuals.

Table 1. Autocorrelations of the Unwhitened and Whitened Series

Lag	OEX(1)	NAS(1)	OEX(2)	NAS(2)
1	0.01	− 0.31	− 0.00	− 0.00
2	− 0.07	0.24	− 0.00	− 0.00
3	− 0.02	0.03	0.01	0.00
4	− 0.04	0.01	− 0.05	0.01
5	0.04	− 0.00	0.04	0.01
6	0.02	0.01	0.02	− 0.04
7	− 0.00	− 0.08	− 0.00	− 0.08
8	− 0.00	0.03	− 0.00	0.02
9	− 0.01	− 0.01	− 0.01	0.02
10	− 0.02	− 0.02	− 0.03	− 0.01
11	− 0.01	− 0.02	− 0.02	− 0.02
12	0.03	− 0.00	0.02	− 0.02
13	− 0.04	− 0.04	− 0.04	− 0.03
14	0.02	0.02	0.02	0.00
15	− 0.01	− 0.05	− 0.01	− 0.03
16	0.03	0.04	0.03	0.03
17	0.00	− 0.03	0.00	− 0.00
18	− 0.02	0.03	− 0.02	0.02
19	− 0.04	− 0.03	− 0.04	− 0.03
20	0.01	0.01	0.01	− 0.00
21	0.01	− 0.01	0.00	− 0.01
22	− 0.02	− 0.02	− 0.02	− 0.02
23	0.01	0.01	0.01	− 0.00
24	0.02	0.00	0.02	− 0.01
25	− 0.03	− 0.01	− 0.03	0.00
26	− 0.02	0.06	− 0.02	0.07
27	0.04	0.03	0.04	0.04
28	0.03	− 0.00	0.03	− 0.00
29	0.03	0.05	0.03	0.04
30	− 0.00	0.02	0.01	0.02
Sample size	1768	944	1764	939
Critical values	0.05	0.06	0.05	0.06

Note: Index(1) = logged first difference of the closing value of stock index; index(2) = linear structure removed from index(1) using AR process as reported in equation (5.1) or (5.2); the lags are significant if the reported values are greater than or equal to the critical value. The underlined values are significant at 5% level.

relations. The results for the NAS series supported randomness for lags up to 90 days ($Q = 74.82$, p value = .875).

IV. Correlation Dimension Results

Figures 5 and 6 show the estimated correlation dimension (CD) for each series for embedding dimensions ranging from 2 to 6, given $e = 1.50$ times the series standard deviation. CD estimates for the log-first-differenced original series, Standard & Poor's Index [OEX(1)] and the NASDAQ [NAS(1)] 100 Stock Index, the AR(3) white noise residuals for the OEX [OEX(2)], the AR(4) white noise residuals for the NASDAQ

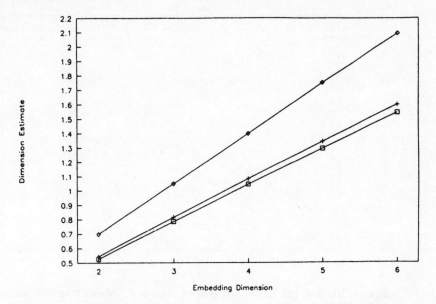

Figure 5. Standard & Poor's 100. □ first differenced log: OEX(1); +, whitened: OEX(1); ◊, average of shuffles: OEX(3).

[NAS(2)], and the 50 scrambled white noise residuals [OEX(3) and NAS(3)] are contained in Table 2. The CDs for the OEX(1) range from 0.53 to 1.65, while the estimates for the NAS(1) series are from 0.17 to 0.95. Estimates for the CDs for the OEX(2) series from 0.54 to 1.69, while the NAS(2) observations vary between 0.37 and 1.34. Both series of white noise residuals have CDs that are similar to those of about 2 reported for Treasury bill returns by Brock (1988) and for the S & P 500 and the soybean nearby futures contract by Blank (1990), but are lower in terms of the absolute value than the previously reported CD of around 6 for another cash stock index (Scheinkman and LeBaron 1989).

At the present time, no statistical test has been developed to distinguish if two CD estimates are significantly different from each other. The OEX series passes Brock's Residual Test for low-dimension chaos, since there is no apparent difference between the CDs of the original series and the AR(3) white noise residuals. The NASDAQ series fails this same test: A noticeable increase is present between the two estimates. Another indication that points to the lack of chaos in both series is that the estimated dimensions of both series continue to increase. CD estimates for chaotic systems stabilize at some value of the embedding dimension. In summary, these events imply that the two series are stochastic, not chaotic.

The CD estimates for the OEX(3) series range from 0.70 to 1.94 and for the NAS(3) data the values from 0.47 to 1.60. This increase in the dimensionality estimates of the shuffles, compared to the residuals of the whitened data indicates that both series are chaotic. However, convergence of the dimension estimates occurs under this technique either, which indicates a nonchaotic series.

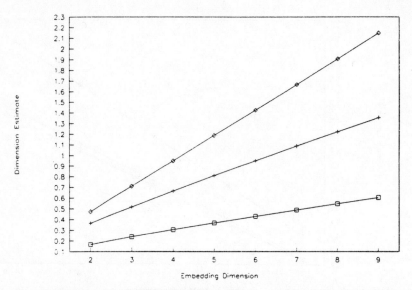

Figure 6. NASDAQ 100. □, first differenced log: NAS(1); +, whitened: NAS(2); ◊, average of shuffles: NAS(3).

The nonconvergence of the CD estimates may be attributed to the potential small sample size bias. Other researchers (Brock 1988; Hsieh 1989; Ramsey et al (1988)) have shown that CD estimates are lower and more stable as the number of observations increase. Evidence of this bias may be present in the mixed results of this study. On the one hand, the low CDs indicate the presence of nonlinearity; on the other hand, the lack of stability of the CDs leads to the conclusion of of a stochastic process.

The added audit of the BDS Test for IID conditions in the data is applied to each of the six series and the results are presented in Table 3. The critical value for the test is 1.96 with a 5% level of significance. The values of the test statistic for the first-differenced NASDAQ series approach the critical value in 4 of a possible 45 cases. The conclusion is to reject the IID null hypothesis for this series. This is an indication that the series is generated by a nonlinear, as opposed to a linear, process. Applying the same test to the AR(3) and AR(4) residuals, as well as the two scrambled residual series, the null hypothesis is retained, because all BDS test values are less than the critical value. The significance of this test is that no underlying dependence, chaotic or otherwise, is present in the data.

V. Conclusion

This study presents three tests for the existence of deterministic chaos, or controlled randomness, in the daily prices of two cash stock indices. Also, the techniques and procedures used to implement these tests are discussed in relation to financial time series.

Table 2. Correlation Dimension Estimates

e	m	Standard & Poor's 100			NASDAQ 100		
		OEX(1)	OEX(2)	OEX(3)	NAS(1)	NAS(2)	NAS(3)
1.50	2	0.5257	0.5443	0.6977	0.1654	0.3651	0.4728
1.50	3	0.7858	0.8151	1.0471	0.2376	0.5159	0.7105
1.50	4	1.0419	1.0808	1.3963	0.3039	0.6633	0.9479
1.50	5	1.2934	1.3411	1.7468	0.3662	0.8075	1.1857
1.50	6	1.5443	1.5989	2.0947	0.4275	0.9487	1.4251
1.50	7	1.7889	1.8534	NA	0.4872	1.0873	1.6681
1.50	8	2.0312	2.1010	NA	0.5459	1.2229	1.9073
1.50	9	2.2759	2.3450	NA	0.6042	1.3552	2.1485
1.50	10	2.5353	2.6041	NA	0.6614	1.4807	NA
1.25	2	0.5834	0.6012	0.7494	0.2154	0.4271	0.5353
1.25	3	0.8726	0.9005	1.1246	0.3114	0.6069	0.8041
1.25	4	1.1571	1.1957	1.5004	0.4014	0.7822	1.0727
1.25	5	1.4370	1.4840	1.8755	0.4872	0.9550	1.3419
1.25	6	1.7143	1.7707	2.2594	0.5717	1.1249	1.1629
1.25	7	1.9770	2.0434	NA	0.6541	1.2929	1.8331
1.25	8	2.2317	2.3251	NA	0.7352	1.4599	2.1538
1.25	9	2.4790	2.5711	NA	0.8163	1.6236	NA
1.25	10	2.7391	2.8357	NA	0.8952	1.7840	NA
1.00	2	0.6520	0.6692	0.8105	0.2816	0.5008	0.6075
1.00	3	0.9765	1.0013	1.2158	0.4089	0.7159	0.9128
1.00	4	1.2944	1.3320	1.6222	0.5312	0.9277	1.2179
1.00	5	1.6060	1.6594	2.0337	0.6484	1.1401	1.5240
1.00	6	1.9135	1.9732	NA	0.7644	1.3495	1.8301
1.00	7	2.2202	2.2801	NA	0.8781	1.5538	2.1381
1.00	8	2.4968	2.5509	NA	0.9905	1.7521	NA
1.00	9	2.7561	2.8125	NA	1.1034	1.9465	NA
1.00	10	3.0070	3.0059	NA	1.2160	2.1510	NA
0.75	2	0.7298	0.7467	0.8799	0.3714	0.5908	0.6930
0.75	3	1.0944	1.1186	1.3189	0.5425	0.8503	1.0417
0.75	4	1.4646	1.4931	1.7575	0.7101	1.1040	1.3902
0.75	5	1.8354	1.8666	2.1994	0.8738	1.3614	1.7408
0.75	6	2.2049	2.2383	NA	1.0365	1.6231	NA
0.75	7	2.6147	2.7626	NA	1.1949	1.8805	NA
0.75	8	2.9122	NA	NA	1.3526	2.1391	NA
0.75	9	NA	NA	NA	1.5036	2.3286	NA
0.75	10	NA	NA	NA	1.6518	2.5153	NA
0.50	2	0.8304	0.8441	0.9684	0.4939	0.7035	0.7989
0.50	3	1.2441	1.2656	1.4515	0.7261	1.0196	1.2005
0.50	4	1.6538	1.6873	1.9380	0.9537	1.3416	1.6017
0.50	5	2.0623	2.1055	NA	1.1805	1.6572	NA
0.50	6	2.4293	2.5389	NA	1.3966	1.9327	NA
0.50	7	2.8131	2.8122	NA	1.6116	2.2543	NA
0.50	8	NA	NA	NA	1.8263	2.7399	NA
0.50	9	NA	NA	NA	2.0060	NA	NA
0.50	10	NA	NA	NA	2.1542	NA	NA

Note: e = multiples of index standard deviation; m = embedding dimension; index(1) = logged first difference of the closing value of stock index; index(2) = linear structure removed from index(1) using AR process as reported in equation (5.1) or (5.2); index(3) = average of 50 scrambles of index(2) series.

Table 3. BDS Statistics

e	m	Standard & Poor's 100			NASDAQ 100		
		OEX(1)	OEX(2)	OEX(3)	NAS(1)	NAS(2)	NAS(3)
1.50	2	0.0734	0.0665	−0.0055	0.5150	0.5909	0.0043
1.50	3	0.0588	0.0422	−0.0014	1.0559	0.9579	−0.0034
1.50	4	0.0430	0.0326	0.0000	1.5119	0.8928	−0.0039
1.50	5	0.0277	0.0217	0.0002	1.8091	0.7056	−0.0036
1.50	6	0.0145	0.0119	0.0002	1.9100	0.5157	−0.0034
1.50	7	0.0077	0.0060	0.0001	1.9020	0.3601	−0.0027
1.50	8	0.0038	0.0030	0.0001	1.8136	0.2456	−0.0017
1.50	9	0.0017	0.0014	0.0000	1.6751	0.1652	−0.0011
1.50	10	0.0006	0.0006	0.0000	1.5197	0.1121	−0.0006
1.25	2	0.0473	0.0422	−0.0028	0.4703	0.4833	0.0046
1.25	3	0.0323	0.0237	−0.0004	0.8798	0.6786	−0.0014
1.25	4	0.0218	0.0150	0.0000	1.1259	0.5517	−0.0016
1.25	5	0.0123	0.0092	0.0001	1.2075	0.3767	−0.0013
1.25	6	0.0058	0.0043	0.0000	1.1491	0.2378	−0.0010
1.25	7	0.0031	0.0022	0.0000	1.0342	0.1433	−0.0005
1.25	8	0.0015	0.0009	−0.0000	0.8939	0.0835	−0.0002
1.25	9	0.0007	0.0004	−0.0000	0.7456	0.0482	−0.0002
1.25	10	0.0003	0.0002	−0.0000	0.6154	0.0277	−0.0001
1.00	2	0.0271	0.0225	−0.0022	0.3900	0.3544	0.0041
1.00	3	0.0137	0.0133	0.0002	0.6457	0.4139	−0.0012
1.00	4	0.0091	0.0058	0.0002	0.6942	0.2748	−0.0012
1.00	5	0.0047	0.0024	0.0002	0.6394	0.1503	−0.0005
1.00	6	0.0019	0.0012	0.0001	0.5228	0.0770	−0.0003
1.00	7	0.0007	0.0005	0.0000	0.4049	0.0385	−0.0003
1.00	8	0.0003	0.0003	0.0000	0.3016	0.0191	−0.0001
1.00	9	0.0001	0.0001	0.0000	0.2159	0.0094	−0.0000
1.00	10	0.0001	0.0001	−0.0000	0.1512	0.0043	0.0000
0.75	2	0.0176	0.0113	−0.0014	0.2638	0.2233	0.0023
0.75	3	0.0051	0.0045	0.0004	0.3607	0.2017	−0.0014
0.75	4	0.0001	0.0008	0.0002	0.2999	0.1061	−0.0005
0.75	5	−0.0002	0.0002	0.0001	0.2138	0.0442	0.0000
0.75	6	−0.0001	0.0000	0.0000	0.1366	0.0165	0.0001
0.75	7	−0.0001	−0.0001	−0.0000	0.0849	0.0061	0.0000
0.75	8	0.0000	−0.0000	0.0000	0.0504	0.0021	−0.0000
0.75	9	−0.0000	−0.0000	−0.0000	0.0303	0.0011	−0.0000
0.75	10	−0.0000	−0.0000	−0.0000	0.0179	0.0005	0.0000
0.50	2	0.0085	0.0101	−0.0009	0.1393	0.1098	0.0020
0.50	3	0.0021	0.0020	0.0001	0.1346	0.0684	−0.0006
0.50	4	0.0006	0.0003	0.0000	0.0801	0.0216	−0.0002
0.50	5	0.0001	0.0001	0.0000	0.0386	0.0063	−0.0002
0.50	6	0.0001	0.0000	0.0000	0.0189	0.0022	0.0000
0.50	7	0.0000	0.0000	0.0000	0.0085	0.0005	0.0000
0.50	8	−0.0000	−0.0000	−0.0000	0.0036	0.0000	−0.0000
0.50	9	−0.0000	−0.0000	−0.0000	0.0019	−0.0000	−0.0000
0.50	10	−0.0000	−0.0000	−0.0000	0.0011	−0.0000	−0.0000

Note: e = multiples of index standard deviation; m = embedding dimension; index(1) = logged first difference of the closing value of stock index; index(2) = linear structure removed from index(1) using AR process as reported in equation (5.1) or (5.2); index(3) = average of 50 scrambles of index(2) series.

The results from an analysis of Standard & Poor's Index and the NASDAQ 100 Stock Index are used in the study. The results for both market indicators are very similar to each other, but they are lower than those found for a cash index in an earlier study. Both series have a correlation dimension of about 2. The existence of an underlying nonlinear relationship was indicated for the OEX by Brock's Residual Test and for both series by the Scrambled Residual Test. However, these results are not conclusive, because the estimated correlation dimension failed to stabilize at any single value. In an attempt to resolve this question, the results from another test using the BDS statistic, led to the overall conclusion that changes in the price level of the two series were not deterministic, but are instead independent of past changes.

A primary purpose of this study was to apply current techniques to search for nonlinearities in a financial time series. While no strong nonlinear relationship was found in the data, perhaps the existence of such a condition in other assets may improve forecasting models by uncovering dependence in stock returns and aid in the unresolved debate about market efficiency.

The author would like to thank W. D. Dechert for providing access to his BDS computer program. Also, this article benefited from the comments of an anonymous reviewer. Any errors or misinterpretations are solely mine.

References

Barnett, W., and Chen, P. (1988) The aggregation–theoretic monetary aggregates are chaotic and have strange attractors: An econometric application of mathematical chaos. In *Dynamic Econometric Modelling* (W. Barnett, E. Berndt, and H. White, eds.). Cambridge: Cambridge University Press, pp. 199–246.

Barnett, W., and Choi, S. (1989) A comparison between the conventional econometric approach to structural inference and the nonparametric chaotic attractor approach. In *Economic Complexity: Chaos, Sunspots, Bubbles and Nonlinearity* (W. Barnett, J. Geweke, and K. Shell, eds.). Cambridge: Cambridge University Press, pp. 141–212.

Baumol, W., and Benhabib, J. (1989) Chaos: Significance, mechanism, and economic applications. *Journal of Economic Perspectives* 3:77–105.

Blank, S. (1990) 'Chaos' in future markets? A nonlinear dynamic analysis. *Center for the Study of Futures Markets*, CSFM # 204, Columbia Business School, New York.

Brock, W. A. (1986) Distinguishing random and deterministic systems: Abridged version. *Journal of Economic Theory* 40:168–195.

Brock, W. A. (1988) Nonlinearity and complex dynamics in economics and finance. In *The Economy as an Evolving Complex System* (P. Anderson, K. Arrow, and D. Pines, eds.). New York: Addison-Wesley, pp. 77–97.

Brock, W. A., Dechert, W. D., and Scheinkman, J. (1987) A test for independence based on the correlation dimension. *SSRI Working Paper*, no. 8702, Department of Economics, University of Wisconsin, Madison, Wisconsin.

Brock, W. A., and Sayers, C. (1988) Is the business cycle characterized by deterministic chaos? *Journal of Monetary Economics* 22:71–90.

Engle, R. F. (1982) Autoregressive conditional heteroskedasticity with estimates of the variance of United Kingdom inflation. *Econometrica* 50:987–1007.

Fama, E. (1970) Efficient capital markets: A review of theory and empirical work. *Journal of Finance* 25:383–417.

Frank, M. Z., Gencay, R., and Stengos, T. (1988) International chaos? *European Economic Review* 32:1569–1584.

Frank, M. Z., and Stengos, T. (1988) Some evidence concerning macroeconomic chaos. *Journal of Monetary Economics* 22:423-438.

Grassberger, P., and Procaccia, I. (1983) Measuring the strangeness of strange attractors. *Physica* 9D:189-208.

Hinich, M., and Patterson, D. (1985) Evidence of nonlinearity in daily stock returns. *Journal of Business and Economic Statistics* 3:69-77.

Hsieh, D. (1989) Testing for nonlinear dependence in daily foreign exchange rates. *Journal of Business* 62:339-368.

Ljung, G. M., and Box, G. E. P. (1978) On a measure of lack of fit in time series models. *Biometrika* 65:67-72.

Ramsey, J., Sayers, C., and Rothman, P. (1988) The statistical properties of dimension calculations using small data sets: Some economic applications. C.V. Starr Center for Applied Economics, New York University, New York.

Savit, R. (1989) Nonlinearities and chaotic effects in option prices. *Journal of Futures Markets* 9:507-518.

Savit, R. (1988) When random is not random: An introduction to chaos in market prices. *Journal of Futures Markets* 8:271-290.

Scheinkman, J., and LeBaron, B. (1989) Nonlinear dynamics and stock returns. *Journal of Business* 62:311-337.

Swinney, H. (1985) Observations of order and chaos in nonlinear systems. *Physica* 5D:1-3, 3-15.

[25]

INTERNATIONAL ECONOMIC REVIEW
Vol. 31, No. 4, November 1990

THE STATISTICAL PROPERTIES OF DIMENSION CALCULATIONS USING SMALL DATA SETS: SOME ECONOMIC APPLICATIONS*

By James B. Ramsey, Chera L. Sayers, and Philip Rothman[1]

Several recent attempts have been made to test for chaos in economic time series through dimension calculations. Relative to the large data sets used in the natural sciences, economic time series are small. Using a procedure developed by Ramsey and Yuan, the authors show that with the techniques available to date, and for the time series examined so far, there is virtually no evidence for the presence of simple chaotic attractors.

1. INTRODUCTION

Recently there has been an increase in the resources invested in the study of nonlinear dynamics. Originating in the natural sciences, applications of the theory have spread through various fields including brain research, optics, meteorology, and economics. The revived interest in nonlinear dynamics was sparked by the discovery in the natural sciences of processes characterized by deterministic chaos, that is, highly complex behavior that is generated by relatively simple nonlinear functions. Observed time series generated by chaotic processes appear to be random utilizing conventional time series methods such as time series plots, autocorrelation functions, and spectral analysis.

However, while empirical studies in the natural sciences are characterized by large data sets, often numbering in the tens of thousands, data sets in economic applications usually consist of less than one thousand observations. Consequently, statistical procedures designed in the former context may not be appropriate in the latter.

The correlation dimension, a measure of the relative rate of scaling of the density of points within a given space, permits a researcher to obtain topological information about the underlying system generating the observed data without requiring a prior commitment to a given structural model. If the time series is a realization of a random variable, the correlation dimension estimate should increase monotonically with the dimensionality of the space within which the points are contained. By contrast, if a low correlation dimension is obtained, this provides an indication that additional structures exists in the time series—structure that may be useful for forecasting purposes. In this way, the correlation dimension estimates may prove

* Manuscript received March 1988; final revision May 1990.

[1] Technical support by the C. V. Starr Center for Applied Economics at New York University is gratefully acknowledged. Helpful comments were provided by William Brock and Charles Dale. The authors wish to thank William Barnett for providing a copy of Fayyad's work and for pointing out numerous errors in our references. The following individuals kindly provided detailed information about their work: William Brock, Ping Chen, Salam Fayyad, Blake Le Baron and Thanasis Stengos. We thank all for helping to improve our paper.

useful to economists wishing to scrutinize uncorrelated time series or the residuals from fitted linear time series models for information on possible nonlinear structure. Furthermore, potentially the correlation dimension can provide an indication of the number of variables necessary to model a system accurately.

Three terms that are frequently used in this literature are "attractor," "embedding dimension," and "orbit" and should be at least intuitively defined in this paper; a more complete discussion is contained in the Appendix. An "attractor" in the context of dynamical analysis is that subset of points towards which any dynamical path will converge; that is, the dynamical path is "attracted" to a subspace of the space containing the paths of the dynamical system from any initial condition. "Embedding dimension" is the topological dimension of the space in which the attractor is situated; loosely stated the embedding dimension is the number of axes needed to portray the attractor. Topological dimension specializes in vector spaces to the usual notion of Euclidian dimension. "Orbit" is essentially a synonym for the dynamical path, but also implies the notion that the dynamical path revisits any given part of the attractor infinitely often.

Recent economic empirical applications of the correlation dimension include Barnett and Chen (1988a, 1988b), Brock (1986), Brock and Sayers (1988), Frank and Stengos (1988, forthcoming), Gennotte and Marsh (1986), Sayers (1986, 1987) and Scheinkman and LeBaron (1987, 1989). By the standards set in the physical sciences, the sizes of the data sets used for these analyses have been minuscule.

A rough guide to orders of magnitude is easily obtained and very enlightening. The minimal possible embedding dimension for simple smooth manifolds is $(n + 1)$ for a manifold of dimension n. Even a simple geometric shape with observational errors would require at least 10 points per embedding dimension to be delineated with any usefulness; although many physicists, Alan Wolf, for example, argue that at least 30 points per embedding dimension are needed. Even with only 10 points per embedding dimension, a simple 2-dimensional figure would require 1000 data points of 3-tuples, and a five dimensional figure would require 1,000,000 points; or to view the matter the other way around, 1000 points on a five dimensional figure in a six dimensional space yields an average of 3.16 points per dimension.

But many attractors have a "fractal" structure, like the Cantor set, which would require considerably more data points than for simple geometric shapes. Consequently, one can easily see that the procedures to be discussed in this paper are by economic standards very, very data extensive.

There is increasing concern over the application of the correlation dimension procedure to small data sets, even within the physics community, see for example, Ramsey and Yuan (1989a, 1989b) and associated references. Furthermore, no finite sample distributional theory yet exists for the correlation dimension estimator, although the authors have some preliminary results. However, Brock, Dechert and Scheinkman (BDS) (1988) provide asymptotic results for the distribution of the standardized correlation integral when the observed points are generated by an independently and identically distributed set of random variables. Hsieh and LeBaron (1988) show that the BDS statistic, that is, the standardized correlation integral, has good power against the null hypothesis of independence; the alternative hypothesis is very broad as it includes not only attractors, but also linear and nonlinear stochastic processes. Brock (1988a) has shown that the statistic is usefully applied to the residuals of estimated times series.

The work of Ramsey and Yuan (1989a, b), which examines the statistical properties of dimension estimates and their variances, provides some insight into the finite sample properties of correlation dimension estimators. They have estimated empirical relationships between the conditional mean of correlation dimension estimates, the embedding dimension, and the sample size in order to evaluate the small sample biases in these estimators and to verify the asymptotic normality of the estimates.

The purpose of this paper is to reevaluate the calculation of dimension utilized in a few recent economic empirical applications in light of the results of Ramsey and Yuan (1989a, b) and to present some cautionary remarks for researchers attempting application of the correlation dimension algorithms. In particular, it will be argued that biases are created in the dimension estimation process due largely to small sample size and incorrect assumptions about the distribution of the "error term." These biases are dependent on the embedding dimension and the sample size as well as the region used to estimate the relative rate of scaling; all of which must be carefully chosen if highly misleading results are not to be obtained.

Section 2 summarizes the theory of correlation dimension and its estimation, together with a brief summary of the difficulties that are inherent in dimension calculations. Section 3 presents the models that were examined and the results of our reexamination of previous research. Section 4 contains our conclusions.

For the impatient reader, the main conclusion is that while there is abundant evidence for the presence of nonlinear stochastic processes and some evidence for nonlinear dynamical processes, there is virtually no evidence at the moment for the presence of simple chaotic attractors of the type that have been discovered in the physical sciences; at least with the tools used to date. The reader should recognize that finding an attractor in economic or financial data is particularly difficult in that attractors are, in fact, long term steady state dynamical paths, even if the steady state paths are wild. Finding a nonlinear, evolutionary dynamical path, possibly subjected to sporadic shocks, is a much more feasible task.

2. CORRELATION DIMENSION: DEFINITION AND ESTIMATION

Reviews of the correlation dimension procedures that are written with the economist in mind include Brock (1986), Brock, Dechert, and Scheinkman (1987), Brock and Sayers (1988), Barnett and Chen (1988a, 1988b), and a more detailed evaluation of the details with a guide to the relevant physics literature is Ramsey and Yuan (1989a, b). The basic idea underlying the calculation of dimension is relatively easily stated.

The Grassberger-Procaccia (1983a, b, c) algorithm will be utilized throughout this paper. Let the ordered sequence $\{X_t\}$, $t = 1, \ldots, N$, represent the observed time series. Then, for a given embedding dimension d, create a sequence of d-histories,

$$(2.1) \qquad \{(x_t, x_{t+\tau}, \ldots, x_{t+(d-1)\tau})\}.$$

Here, τ stands for the time delay parameter. The sample correlation integral is given by,

$$(2.2) \qquad C_r^N = N^{-2} \sum_{i,j} \theta(r - |X_i - X_j|), \quad r > 0, \quad X_i = (x_i, x_{i+1\tau}, \cdots, s_{i+(d-1)\tau}).$$

$\theta(\cdot)$ is the Heaviside step function which maps positive arguments into one, and nonpositive arguments into zero. Thus, $\theta(\cdot)$ counts the number of points which are within distance r from each other. "r" is the scaling parameter. The calculation of C_r^N is useful because:

$$(2.3) \qquad\qquad\qquad \lim_{\substack{N \to \infty \\ r \to 0^+}} C_r^N \to C,$$

and $d \ln C / d \ln r = D_2$, whenever the derivative is defined, Guckenheimer (1984). In the rest of the paper, D_2 will be designated dc to stand for correlation dimension. The dc is a measure of pointwise dimension, dp. Pointwise dimension, see for example, Farmer, Ott, and Yorke (1983), measures the relative rate of change in the number of points on the attractor as the diameter of the covering sets is decreased. A brief introduction to these concepts is provided in the Appendix.

Correlation dimension is usually estimated from experimental data by a linear regression of the observed values of $\ln C_r^N$ on $\ln r$ over a suitably chosen subinterval of the range of r, $(0, 1)$. The estimated slope coefficient of this regression, designated hereafter as $d\hat{c}$, is the usual estimator of correlation dimension cited in the literature and is the basic variable used in this paper. There are a number of important qualifications to this seemingly simple procedure, see Ramsey and Yuan (1989a).

One of these problems involves the extended "maintained hypothesis" that is needed in economic analysis. In the problems examined to date in physics and chemistry, the simple dichotomy of: "either an attractor, or the data are merely (high dimensional) noise" has been considered to be appropriate. But this is not the case in economics. The extended maintained hypothesis must include as alternatives the options that the data come from ARIMA or nonlinear stochastic processes.

Even more damaging to a simplistic version of dimension calculation is the realization that some researchers mistakenly perform dimension analysis on data that are highly autocorrelated. This procedure vitiates any conclusions that might possibly be made.

The problem for all experimental data, even if there were a perfectly well defined and recoverable attractor, is that at small enough scales the dimension is that of noise. Thus, the practical problem of trying to distinguish between attractors, autocorrelated processes, and nonlinear stochastic processes is a real one.

The main difficulty in estimating dimension is an incorrect assumption about the nature of the regression to be used. The traditional model assumes,

$$(2.4) \qquad\qquad\qquad \ln C = a + b \ln (r) + u$$

where b is an estimate of dc, and u is an independently and identically distributed normal error term that is distributed independently of r. Thus, the variance of u generates the variance in estimating the dimension as represented by the coefficient "b." Ramsey and Yuan (1989a) present an alternative and more appropriate random coefficient regression model of the following form,

$$(2.5) \qquad \ln C = a(e|N, ED) + b(e|N, ED) \ln(r) + u$$

where the variance of u is very small relative to the variance of e for small N and large ED. "e" represents an experimental error term whose distribution is dependent on the sample size, N, and the embedding dimension, ED; e seems to be distributed independently of u, but u is itself autocorrelated.

Ramsey and Yuan demonstrate empirically that the conditional mean of the estimate of dc depends both upon the sample size and the embedding dimension in the following manner,

$$(2.6) \qquad \ln(k + \bar{dc}) = \gamma_1 + \gamma_2 N^{\gamma_3} + \gamma_4 N^{\gamma_5} [\exp(\gamma_6/ED^{\gamma_7}) - 1.0],$$

where $\bar{dc}$ is the mean of the estimator $\hat{dc}$.

This equation is not as parameter extensive as it would appear. The parameter k is set to zero or one. Its purpose is to improve the approximation for very low dimensional attractors and to allow γ_1 to be strictly positive for attractors. It could easily be set to 0 for all data sets with little serious impact on the overall results; this is the case in this study. The right-hand side of equation (2.6) can be considered in two parts:

$$(2.6') \qquad \text{(a)} \qquad (\gamma_1 + \gamma_2 N^{\gamma_3})$$

$$\qquad \text{(b)} \qquad (\gamma_4 N^{\gamma_5} [\exp(\gamma_6/ED^{\gamma_7}) - 1.0]).$$

The expression $(\gamma_1 + \gamma_2 N^{\gamma_3})$ indicates the main effect of small sample size on the expected value of the estimator $\hat{dc}$. For random variables that scale monotonically in ED, $\gamma_1 = 0$ and both γ_2 and γ_3 are positive; that is, the limit towards which the term (2.6'b) is approaching is given by $\gamma_2 N^{\gamma_3}$; the larger N, the larger the limiting value for $\bar{dc}$ expressed as a function of ED. Both γ_2 and γ_3 depend on the properties of the distribution of the random variable. The higher the entropy of the distribution for equivalent ranges of the support of the distribution, the larger the values of γ_2 and γ_3. The entropy of the distribution is defined by:

$$\text{ent} = -\int_{-\infty}^{\infty} \ln(f) f\, dx,$$

where f is the density function.

If, however, one has an attractor, then $\gamma_1 > 0$ and $\gamma_3 < 0$, so that as $N \to \infty$ the small sample bias provided by the term $\gamma_2 N^{\gamma_3}$ goes to zero; one would expect γ_3 to be -1.0 for attractors with low dimension. The asymptote as both N and $ED \to \infty$, but such that $\lim_{N \to \infty} ED/N \to 0$ is given by γ_1.

$$\lim_{\substack{N \to \infty \\ ED \to \infty}} \ln (1 + d\bar{c}) = \gamma_1, \quad \text{or} \quad \lim_{\substack{N \to \infty \\ ED \to \infty}} d\bar{c} = e^{\gamma_1} - 1.$$

The second part of the expression shown in (2.6'b) models the bias effect due to the embedding dimension. For both random and attractor generated data, one expects γ_6 to be negative, but γ_7 to be positive so that the approach to the limit is a sigmoid shape. The factor $\gamma_4 N^{\gamma_5}$ modifies the ED bias effect. γ_5 seems to be negative for attractors and zero for random variables. Thus, for low dimensional attractors the effect of a downward bias on $d\bar{c}$ due to small values for ED declines as N increases. γ_4 depends on the units of measurement chosen for ED and the relative weight of the ED effect to sample size, N.

The functional class, defined up to parameter values in equation (2.6), seems to be sufficiently general so as to be able to describe the bias scaling effects of a wide variety of alternative models, including simple attractors and random numbers. The equation would seem to be sufficiently general as to provide at least useful guidance for other, and perhaps less simple, attractors. It is to be hoped that while the coefficient values of equation (2.6) are clearly model specific, the form of the equation is invariant to a wide class of attractors and a wide class of distribution functions. The basic properties of the function discussed above parametrize what is by now widely known qualitatively about dimension estimates for both attractors and noise. The authors found that dimension estimates for random signals are downward biased, while for chaotic signals the dimension estimate is upward biased for all, but very small values of ED.

The distribution of the estimates about the biased mean values is well approximated by the Normal for sample sizes above 1000; the variance, however, is heteroskedastic, being a function of both sample size and embedding dimension.

This relationship contains a potential test for differentiating between low dimensional processes and random phenomena. If the underlying model is a random variable, then $\gamma_1 = 0$, and γ_2, $\gamma_3 > 0$. If the observed sequence of observations is being generated by a low dimensional process, then $\gamma_1 > 0$, and $\gamma_3 < 0$.

One of the implications of equation (2.5) is that the usual formula for the variance of the estimator of the parameter "b" is inappropriate; indeed, the usual estimate is a gross underestimate of the true variance as has been documented by Ramsey and Yuan (1989a). The equation that expresses the relationship between the actual standard deviation and the design parameters, N and ED is:

(2.7) $\ln (\text{Std}) = \alpha_1 + \alpha_2 \ln N + \alpha_3 \ln ED + \alpha_4 ED/N.$

In general, the standard deviation increases in embedding dimension, and decreases in sample size. However, the relative effect of ED is much greater than that for N; that is, small increases in ED must be offset by proportionately much larger increases in N in order to maintain a given variance. Ramsey and Yuan (1989a) obtained estimates of the parameters in equation (2.7) by calculating dc for multiple repetitions of a given sample size, N, and for each value of ED.

However, given the very small sample sizes involved in the studies examined in this paper we are unable to use this approach. This is a serious deficiency. Ramsey and Yuan (1989a) found that the OLS estimate is a small fraction of the actual variance; the ratio varied anywhere from only a fifth to a low of 0.006 for the models studied in Ramsey and Yuan (1989a).

3. THE ECONOMIC DATA AND THE ESTIMATION OF EQUATION (2.6)

We chose to examine the data sets utilized in Barnett and Chen (1988a, 1988b[2]), Sayers (1986, 1987), and Scheinkman and LeBaron (1989).

Barnett and Chen assert evidence of chaos in the demand Divisia monetary aggregates. Our efforts concentrated on the demand Divisia *M*2. This choice was dictated in part by our wish to concentrate on the more important results of Barnett and Chen and in part because we discovered very little difference between the Divisia demand indices for *M*2 and *M*3; why there is almost an exact linear relationship between Divisia demand *M*2 and *M*3 we have not discovered. The sample period is "weekly" from January 1969 to July 1984, *N* = 807. The data source is Fayyad (1986). The basic procedure that Fayyad seems to have followed is to apply the Divisia procedure to the components of monthly *M*2, or monthly *M*3, data series as published by the Federal Reserve, and then to generate a weekly series by spline interpolation at an approximate period of 0.23 to represent a week's fraction of a month. Consequently, only a very few of the original monthly data points are contained in the constructed "weekly" data series; the corresponding number of monthly data points is about 200. Some of the weights used in creating the Divisia index were from weekly observations.

Sayers (1986, 1987) used man-days idle due to work stoppages, monthly figures from January 1928 to December 1981, *N* = 648, as published by The Bureau of Labor Statistics.

Scheinkman and LeBaron utilize Center for Research in Security Prices (CRSP) data. They have indicated finding a dimension of about 4.5. These data are value weighted daily stock returns, with a sample size of 5200 daily returns. Weekly returns were obtained by simple compounding of the daily returns; the details are contained in Scheinkman and LeBaron (1989). This procedure yields 1227 weekly observations.

Our analytical procedure with respect to each data set was as follows. The first step was to replicate each author's published results. Except for minor errors due to differences in algorithms or computer word size, we were able in all cases to duplicate the original results: given the experience of one of the authors of this paper, this is a testimony to the care taken by all of the above mentioned researchers.

The next step was to split each sample into subsamples of 200, 400, 600, 800, etc. observations in order to attempt to estimate equation (2.6). The original idea was to obtain subsamples by random sampling of the initial starting value. However,

[2] This statement is not quite correct. We used the working papers that preceded the published versions. To our knowledge, this difference in source has no effect on our results or conclusions. We restricted ourselves to these data sets purely on the basis of availability at the time the analysis was started.

problems that we encountered with the Scheinkman data led us back to a sampling procedure that was more systematic for that data set. The problem that we encountered is of considerable interest and will be discussed below. For each set of subsets of data, we estimated dc in the standard manner, for $ED = 2, 3, \ldots, 25$, if the data set could sustain such a high embedding dimension. Our practical decision rule was to stop increasing the embedding dimension as soon as the estimated dimension, $\hat{dc}$ fell sharply indicating that the extreme limits of the data had been exceeded. In particular cases, the highest sustainable dimension was as low as 8. The final step was to regress the estimated dc on N, sample size, and ED, embedding dimension, as discussed with respect to equation (2.6). The estimated equation was then analyzed in accordance with the discussion above in order to try to resolve the issue of whether the observed time series indicated the presence of a chaotic attractor. In addition the data were randomized in terms of their time order and the whole procedure repeated with the randomized data.

4. RESULTS

Before presenting the results using economic data, it is informative to consider briefly the simulation results obtained in Ramsey and Yuan (1989a, b) that are to serve as a benchmark of comparison. While it is obvious that computer simulated data are actually data from some attractor, the extensive and numerous tests that we have done demonstrate clearly that the simulated data can usefully be regarded for our purposes and at the scales that we are using as "random variables"; that is, these are attractors at sufficiently high dimension that their attractor origin can be ignored.

Figures 1 to 3 together with Table 1 demonstrate in a striking manner the difference in the relationship between the estimated dimension, sample size, and embedding dimension that was discovered in the context of a known attractor and a known distribution. There is in fact a characteristic sequence of shapes to the plots for attractors that differs significantly from the sequence of shapes of plots for noise generated data. The characteristic sequence of shapes for randomized attractor data matches that for random data.

The reader should note that the "k" defined in equation (2.6) has been set to 0 identically for all runs in this paper.

In Ramsey and Yuan (1989b) it was found with respect to the models examined there that the assumption of asymptotic normality for the conditional distribution of $d\hat{c}$ given sample size and embedding dimension was reasonable at sample size on the order of 1000. No Monte Carlo sampling check was carried out for the specific models cited in this section. However, the cited "student-t ratios" are useful in giving the reader an idea of the relative precision of estimate; coefficients that are at least three "standard deviations" from zero can be safely assumed to be nonzero.

Sayer's Work Stoppage Data.   Figures 4 to 7 and Table 2 summarize the results of applying the procedures discussed in this paper to the work stoppage data. These data provide the clearest impression of structure that might have low dimension.

The dimension calculations were performed at a lag of 5 which represents the lowest lag with zero autocorrelation. However, one must be extremely cautious about any conclusions, because the number of data points is so limited. Nevertheless, the results are intriguing.

A comparison of Figures 6 and 7, together with an examination of Table 2, indicates that there is apparently more evidence of structure in the raw data than in the randomized data. However, with real as opposed to simulated data, especially when using strictly limited data sets, difficulties with estimating the coefficients occur. Examine the estimates for γ_1 and γ_3 for the randomized data. By the analysis in Ramsey and Yuan (1989a) γ_1 should be zero and γ_3 should be positive, whereas the estimated values are 4.97 for γ_1 and -0.06 for γ_3. But both estimates have t-ratios that are about .1; that is, the standard deviations are about 10 times the size of the coefficients. In addition, the limited extent of the data produces very elongated confidence ellipsoids. Consequently, the randomized Sayers' data produces an estimate of γ_1 that is very large and offsets that with an estimated value of γ_3 that is negative, instead of the theoretically predicted values of $\gamma_1 = 0$ and $\gamma_3 > 0$.

The results for the raw data indicate an estimated asymptotic value for the dimension of the data of 0.214, but the actual value could easily be as high as 1.68 at an approximate 95 percent confidence level; a value of 1.6 to 1.8 seems to be a common finding in economic data. But the reader is warned that the estimated standard errors are usually fractions of those indicated by the standard analysis, see Ramsey and Yuan (1989a). The remaining coefficient estimates seem to have reasonable values; for example, the power on the additive term in N is approximately -0.5 (actual value is -0.62), which agrees with the usual square root law of asymptotic convergence.

The results for the randomized data are plausible, notwithstanding the "positive asymptotic estimate" of dimension; at a value of 148, we can safely conclude that the randomized data are not indicating a low dimensional result.

The original dimensional estimates by Sayers were in a range of about 5.0 to 10.0, depending on subsampling size and scaling region used. While these results would indicate the probability at least of a low dimensional result, one cannot conclude from these results alone that one has an attractor. However, one can conclude that these data are neither random, nor simple ARMA processes.

The results produced in this paper can be regarded as a modest improvement in the determination of dimension using these work stoppage data.

Scheinkman and LeBaron Stock Market Data. The results are summarized in Figures 8 to 13 and Table 3. The τ lag used to generate the dimension calculations was 2. While we were able to reproduce the results quoted by Scheinkman and LeBaron, it soon became clear that there were difficulties with the inferences drawn by the authors. First, a careful examination revealed that even with the procedure used by Scheinkman and LeBaron, there is slight, but perceptible, evidence of continued scaling of dimension estimates as embedding dimension increases. Secondly, our initial subsampling procedures produced some surprising anomalies that were for some time quite puzzling, until we discovered the key; see Figure 13.

1000   JAMES B. RAMSEY, CHERA L. SAYERS, AND PHILIP ROTHMAN

Essentially, the authors cited an attractor dimension of less than 6.0. But this conclusion is in fact driven by approximately 25 observations. In the second panel of the time series plot for these data at about 625 observations, the reader will observe that the range of the data suddenly doubles; the data are in fact nonstationary. The effect of the presence of these observations in the series is to lower the entropy of the whole data set dramatically; these data, when normalized to facilitate the analysis, have a long thin tail of values in the histogram plot with a heavy concentration of points in the narrow range defined by the bulk of the data. The implication of low entropy for random data is that it slows, often dramatically, the rate at which estimated dimension increases with embedding dimension. Consequently, such data can easily give the appearance of a low dimensional attractor.

We discovered that the elimination of 25 consecutive data points in this region led to slightly different estimates for the whole sample, but removed all our anomalous results with the subsamples. The 25 observations that we dropped were 626 to 650; these observations cover the period from July 1974 to the beginning of January 1975. Figures 11 and 12 were produced with the "purged" data. The corresponding plots for the unpurged data behave wildly from subsample to subsample, depending on whether the 25 observations are, or are not included as is illustrated in Figure 13.

We are not advocating the dropping of these data in order to facilitate the analysis, but merely to indicate that the original results were in large part driven by these few data points. While these data may well have systematic nonlinear components, and while the dropped data may contribute to that conclusion, the dropping of such a set should still reveal an attractor if there were one; in fact, such a procedure would enhance the discovery of an attractor if the "anomalous data" represented a period during which the dynamical path might have been kicked off the attractor. Consequently, we conclude that there is no clear evidence of an attractor in these plots as is confirmed by the regression estimates for the raw and randomized data sets. The estimated asymptotic limits for the dimension are respectively about 60 and 200; these estimates do not provide persuasive evidence for the existence of an attractor.

Let us repeat that while the evidence for an attractor is weak, these results do not preclude the existence of nonlinear dynamical components in these data. Indeed, Brock (1988b), Gennotte and Marsh (1986), and LeBaron (1988a, 1988b) seem to find evidence of time varying nonlinearities in stock market data.

Barnett and Chen's Filtered Divisia Money Demand (M2) Data. The results of our efforts are summarized in Figures 14 to 21 and Table 4. Before proceeding, we should warn the reader that the procedures used to generate the "weekly" data involved spline interpolations from about 200 original data points, not 807 original observations as might be inferred by a careless reader. A greater difficulty with the original approach used by Barnett and Chen is that the first zero of the autocorrelation function for the data series that they used to calculate dimension is at a lag of approximately 180. As we have seen from the discussion in Ramsey and Yuan (1989a), it is crucial to a useful interpretation of dimension calculations that the calculations be carried out at a zero autocorrelation lag, or at least at the first minimum of the mutual information, Fraser (1986). With only 807 splined data points, the standard procedure was clearly impossible. We were able, as mentioned above, to reproduce all of Barnett and Chen's results, including the graphs.

However, we had previously generated strikingly similar graphs by plotting the phase diagrams of simulated autoregressive data with long autocorrelated lags. In order to facilitate this comparison Figure 15 shows the phase diagram for Barnett and Chen's Divisia money demand data, M2 definition, calculated exactly as in their Figure 1, Case 3, Barnett and Chen (1988b) that shows the phase diagram for the Divisia money demand, M3 definition; the plots for M2 and M3 are very similar as the two data sets are almost exactly linearly related. In contrast, the phase diagram for a simulated data set based on an autoregressive model using Normal deviates and parameter values obtained by estimating a sixth order AR process for Barnett and Chen's data is shown in Figure 16; the choice of τ for the phase plot is the same as that chosen by Barnett and Chen. We believe that it is difficult to distinguish the two plots on qualitative grounds; especially when one recognizes the substantial smoothing effect of using splines; the Barnett and Chen data are splined, but our simulation data are not.

Because of the extraordinarily long autocorrelation lag in these data, we were compelled to transform the original data into a stationary low correlated series before beginning the attempt to estimate correlation dimensions. We did so by subtracting from the original series a 19 point double sided moving average filter in order to eliminate from the series the trend and some of the lowest frequency variation; the corresponding transfer function is shown in Figure 18 and the autocorrelation function of the transformed data are shown in Figure 17. In effect, the output of this filter can be regarded as the residuals from a smoothing filter of the data. The chosen τ lag was 6, see Figure 17.

The objective of our procedure was to remove, without curve fitting, the trend and lowest frequency components of the data that contributed to the very long autocorrelation lag and to the more obvious aspects of nonstationarity; what remains in the higher frequency components is one or more elements of noise, nonlinear stochastic process, nonlinear dynamical process, or an attractor, if one exists. With these data if a low dimensional result were to be obtained, one would be justified in examining the data more intensively for further evidence of an attractor. Unfortunately, with the original data one cannot distinguish an attractor from the dimensional results that one gets from a highly autocorrelated linear process.

The raw, but filtered, Barnett data show the least indication of any structure of the three sets of data examined in this paper; compare Figures 19 and 20, the plots of the dimensional estimates on N and ED for the raw filtered and randomized filtered data, with Figures 1 to 3. While the sign of γ_2 using the randomized data is incorrect, the corresponding t-ratio is less than 0.03, so that little confidence can be placed in the value of its estimate. The estimated asymptotic limit for dimension for the raw data is 22.9 and for the randomized data is 446. The difficulty in obtaining these estimates precludes placing much reliance on the numbers obtained. Nonetheless, the very fact that the estimates are so imprecise indicates that there is no strong evidence for the presence of an attractor as a review of Figures 1 to 3 will demonstrate.

The Barnett and Chen data demonstrate an important lesson that we have mentioned several times; namely, the distinction between an attractor and a nonlinear dynamical system; especially one that is subjected to exogenous shocks. Figure 21 plots a segment of the phase diagram for the filtered data in which we see that the period from October, 1979 to October, 1982 is a relatively smooth process, while the periods before and after are not. The smooth period corresponds quite closely to the period of the Volcker experiment. We have been reluctant to reproduce this figure until now as we wished first to verify that it is not an artifact of our processing, nor is it due to splining and the use of the Divisia index, nor is it an isolated special case. The analysis of such diagrams is the subject of a future paper.

5. CONCLUSIONS

The main question of burning interest is whether or not there is any evidence of the presence of a strange, or of a chaotic, attractor. The short answer is no. That does not mean that other procedures, or that the use of new data, will produce evidence of attractors; but the current evidence based on minuscule data sets does not provide any indication of an attractor. A possible exception to this general statement is the work stoppage data whose plots begin to show the characteristic shapes exhibited by attractors and their randomized values. However, even this modest claim must be severely hedged by the fact that there are only 648 observations.

There is evidence of varying persuasiveness of nonlinearity in all of these data. The effect of randomization is clear, even when applied to data points that are plotted at the zero autocorrelation lags. The phase diagram of the filtered Barnett and Chen data is most intriguing in this regard.

The second major pair of lessons is that the calculation of dimension with small data sets is delicate to say the least and that the procedures proposed in Ramsey and Yuan (1989a, b) do provide some relief from the stringency of small sample sizes. By capitalizing on the implicit structure of the bias relationship between the conditional mean of the dimension estimate, sample size, and the embedding dimension, one can improve the quality of one's inferences about the topological structure of nonlinear stochastic processes, if not about the topological structure of chaotic attractors.

One final important insight is that economic data seem to show definite signs of nonstationarity, even when in differenced form or when low frequency components have been removed. A typical structure is that of noise components, or seemingly random variation, that are interspersed with periods of very high amplitude at low frequency.

New York University, U.S.A.
University of Houston, U.S.A.
University of Delaware, U.S.A.

BIAS IN DIMENSION CALCULATIONS   1003

APPENDIX

The objective of this Appendix is to provide a succinct, but intuitive, introduction to some dimension concepts with which economists may not be familiar.

A dynamical system may be characterized as either a map, or a flow. Maps are discrete, flows are continuous. In either case, an orbit, or path, of the dynamical system is defined by the solution of the system to yield the sequence:

$$\{x_1, x_2, x_3, x_4, \ldots\}, \qquad \text{for maps,}$$

$$\{x(t)\}, \qquad \text{for flows.}$$

The sequences $\{x_i\}$, or $\{x(t)\}$, can be scalars or vectors. If x is a scalar, then the Takens extension of the Whitney Embedding Theorem can be used to justify the use of only one component in the vector at each t to represent the flow of the dynamical system; from observations of the one component over time many of the topological and dynamical properties of the flow can be obtained; this is the justification for using a single "variable" within a dynamical system to represent that system.

An attractor is a compact set, A, such that the limit set of the orbit, $\{x_n\}$, or $\{x(t)\}$, as n, or t, $\rightarrow \infty$ is A for almost all initial conditions within a neighborhood of A. An attractor is the set of points of the path that represents the long term behavior of the dynamical system. Attractors can be very simple sets such as single points that represent equilibria, or limit cycles, such as the Cob-web cycle. But attractors can be much more complex. An attractor can be quasiperiodic, chaotic, or strange. All but the last can be defined on a manifold. An example of a quasiperiodic attractor is an orbit on a torus, (a doughnut generated by the cosines of a pair of incommensurate frequencies). A chaotic attractor is characterized by exponential divergence away from any point within the attractor. Because the attractor is compact, the exponential divergence means that the path is constantly folded over onto the attractor. Strange attractors have a fractal component, that is, at least along one axis of the attractor, the set is like a Cantor set. An attractor can be both chaotic and strange. Indeed, most of the examples with which economists are by now familiar are both strange and chaotic.

Dynamical orbits have dynamical properties and attractors have topological properties. For strange attractors we can define also measure theoretic properties. Dimension is mainly a topological concept, but some concepts of dimension have measure theoretic components.

Dimension concepts indicate:

the amount of information needed to specify the position of a point on an attractor;

the lower bound on the number of essential variables that are needed to model the attractor, or rather, the dynamical system within the attractor;

the relative density of the points on the attractor.

The natural probability measure of an attractor is the relative frequency with which the different regions of an attractor is visited by the orbit. There are many definitions of dimension used in the literature on nonlinear dynamics. The reader should be warned that sometimes "dimension" is used in its purely topological sense, that is, dimension is merely a generalization of the Euclidian notion with which all economists are very familiar. In this sense the dimension is always an integer and represents the "number of degrees of freedom," or "the number of axes needed to represent the attractor."

The other definitions of dimension can be put into three classes of concepts; those that are purely "metric," those based on the natural probability measure of the attractor, and those based on the dynamical properties of the orbit within the attractor. Our discussion will be restricted to the first two classes of concepts.

The purely metric concepts include the notion of capacity, d_c, and Hausdorff dimension, d_h. The capacity measure is formally defined by:

$$d_c = \lim_{\varepsilon \to 0} \frac{\ln N(\varepsilon)}{\ln (1/\varepsilon)},$$

where $N(\varepsilon)$ is the minimum number of ε diameter cubes needed to cover the attractor. d_c is nothing more than a measure of the relative rate of increase in the number of coverings of an attractor to the number of coverings needed to cover the unit interval. For a fixed point, an equilibrium point, $d_c = 0$; for a simple cycle $d_c = 1$; but for strange attractors d_c can be noninteger to represent the fractal structure of strange attractors. For example, the capacity measure of the Cantor set created by deleting middle thirds is $(\ln 2)/\ln 3 = 0.63$. Hausdorff dimension is defined with respect to the concept of Hausdorff measure, which in turn is a generalization of Lebesgue measure. Hausdorff measure enables one to assign a nonnegative number to many nonempty sets that under Lebesgue would have zero measure.

The Hausdorff α measure of a set A is:

$$HM_\alpha = \lim_{\varepsilon \to 0} (\inf) \sum_{\{A_i\}} \delta(A_i)^\alpha, \quad A \subset \cup A_i$$

where the A_i are covering sets, $\delta(\cdot)$ is the diameter of the set, and α is a scale factor on the diameter. If a set has a nonzero Lebesgue measure, then the Hausdorff measure will be the same and the choice of α will be the same as the topological dimension of the set. For example, the Lebesgue measure of a plane figure is obtained by adding up the "area" of rectangles, a two dimensional covering; the corresponding Hausdorff measure will have a value for α of two and the Hausdorff α measure will equal the value obtained from the Lebesgue concept. Hausdorff dimension is given by α_0, where α_0 is defined by:

$$\alpha_0 = \inf \{\alpha : HM_\alpha(A) = 0\}$$

α_0 is merely that scale variable such that the sum of "volumes" to cover the attractor is finite and nonzero. If $\alpha > \alpha_0$, then $HM_\alpha = 0$, and if $\alpha < \alpha_0$, then $HM_\alpha \to \infty$. If the attractor is not strange, say, for example, that it is a simple cycle, then α_0 will be an integer. Whenever Lebesgue measure is positive, Hausdorff dimension will be an integer; Hausdorff dimension will be noninteger when the attractor is strange and has Cantor set characteristics.

The problem with these purely metric concepts is that they treat all parts of the attractor equally, no matter how infrequently some part of the attractor is visited by the orbit. Such measures are enormously data extensive. Two measures that incorporate the relative frequency of visit by the orbit are information dimension, d_I, and pointwise dimension, d_p. We will assume in the sequel that there exists a natural probability measure in that any probability measure defined on the attractor is invariant to the initial conditions.

Information dimension, d_I, is defined by:

$$d_I = \lim_{\varepsilon \to 0} \frac{I(\varepsilon)}{\ln (1/\varepsilon)},$$

where $I(\varepsilon)$ is Shannon's Information measure and is formally defined by:

$$I(\varepsilon) = - \sum_{i=1}^{N(\varepsilon)} P_i \ln (P_i).$$

$N(\varepsilon)$ is the same measure of the number of coverings of the attractor as occurred in the definition of capacity; P_i is the relative frequency of occurrence of points on the orbit that lie in the ith cell. If all coverings are equally likely, that is, $P_i = N(\varepsilon)^{-1}$, then $d_I = d_c$; in general, d_I is not greater than d_c.

To define pointwise dimension, d_p, we have to define $\mu(B_\varepsilon)$ as the natural probability measure of a "ball" of radius ε; $B_\varepsilon(x)$ is a hypersphere of radius ε centered at X. Pointwise dimension at x is then:

$$d_p(x) = \lim_{\varepsilon \to 0} \frac{\ln \mu(B\varepsilon(x))}{\ln (\varepsilon)}.$$

If $d_p(x)$ is independent of x for almost all x on the attractor, then the common value of d_p is the pointwise dimension of the attractor. Pointwise dimension is that concept of dimension that the Grassberger-Procaccia procedure measures. Pointwise dimension measures the relative rate of scaling of the probability measure of a ball of diameter of radius ε as the diameter approaches zero; compare this measure with that of capacity.

TABLE 1
REGRESSION RESULTS TO FITTING
$$\ln (k + \bar{dc}) = \gamma_1 + \gamma_2 N^{\gamma_3} + \gamma_4 N^{\gamma_5} [\mathrm{Exp}\,(\gamma_6/m^{\gamma_7}) - 1]$$
TO SEVERAL EXAMPLES

Examples (Preset Coefficients)	(γ)	Coefficient Estimates	Estimated "Student-t Ratios"	R^2 Value/Asymptotic $\bar{dc}$ Estimate
Henon	1	0.802	105.3	$R^2 = 0.9992$
($k = 1$,	2	0.235	4.8	Asympt. $\bar{d}_c = 1.23$
$\gamma_3 = -1$)	4	0.264	5.3	
	5	−0.930	−36.0	% Error = 1.7
	6	−3.012	−17.4	89 degrees of freedom (DOF)
	7	2.104	5.3	
Normal	2	4.246	4.8	
($k = 0$,	3	0.016	4.5	$R^2 = 0.9993$
$\gamma_1 = 0$,	4	5.290	2.1	90 DOF
$\gamma_5 = 0$)	6	−0.540	−7.7	
	7	0.465	2.3	
Randomized Henon	2	4.968	2.6	
($k = 0$,	3	0.006	2.3	$R^2 = 0.9993$
$\gamma_1 = 0$,	4	7.565	1.0	83 DOF
$\gamma_5 = 0$)	6	−0.478	−2.3	
	7	0.367	1.3	

N is in thousands; m is in tens.

The estimated "student-t ratios" are quoted for reader's convenience in interpreting the results. This is in part justified by the approximate normality of the $\bar{dc}$ estimates for large samples discovered in the Monte Carlo simulations quoted in Ramsey and Yuan (1989b)

TABLE 2
REGRESSION RESULTS FROM FITTING
$$\ln (\bar{dc}) = \gamma_1 + \gamma_2 N^{\gamma_3} + \gamma_4 N^{\gamma_5} [\mathrm{Exp}\,(\gamma_6/ED^{\gamma_7}) - 1]$$
TO SAYERS "WORK STOPPAGE DATA"

Data	(γ)	Coefficient Estimates	Estimated "Student-t Ratios"	R^2 Value
Original	1	−1.543	−1.495	$R^2 = 0.983$
	2	4.069	3.772	
	3	−0.621	−4.423	
	4	2.882	4.313	
	5	−0.806	−11.358	60 degrees of freedom (DOF)
	6	−1.066	−4.921	
	7	0.537	4.495	
Randomized	1	4.967	0.084	$R^2 = 0.988$
	2	5.310	0.089	
	3	−0.055	−0.086	
	4	11.872	0.995	
	5	−0.032	−0.601	54 DOF
	6	−1.192	−1.658	
	7	0.298	1.189	

The estimated "student-t ratios" are quoted for reader's convenience in interpreting the results. This is in part justified by the approximate normality of the $\bar{dc}$ estimates for large samples discovered in the Monte Carlo simulations quoted in Ramsey and Yuan (1989b).

BIAS IN DIMENSION CALCULATIONS 1007

TABLE 3

$$\ln (\bar{dc}) = \gamma_1 + \gamma_2 N^{\gamma_3} + \gamma_4 N^{\gamma_5} [\text{Exp} (\gamma_6 ED^{\gamma_7}) - 1]$$

TO SCHEINKMAN "COMPUTED STOCK RETURNS DATA"; PURGED DATA USED

Data	(γ)	Coefficient Estimates	Estimated "Student-t Ratios"	R^2 Value
Original	1	4.018	1.585	$R^2 = 0.981$
	2	4.060	0.524	
	3	−0.121	−1.499	
	4	11.255	0.850	
	5	−0.079	−5.269	268 DOF
	6	−0.893	−5.815	
	7	0.160	0.833	
Randomized	1	5.340	8.651	$R^2 = 0.998$
	2	0.646	1.560	
	3	0.267	1.690	
	4	7.690	9.211	
	5	0.032	4.340	165 DOF
	6	−0.715	−19.288	
	7	0.378	8.540	

The estimated "student-t ratios" are quoted for reader's convenience in interpreting the results. This is in part justified by the approximate normality of the $\bar{dc}$ estimates for large samples discovered in the Monte Carlo simulations quoted in Ramsey and Yuan (1989b).

TABLE 4

REGRESSION RESULTS FOR FITTING

$$\ln (\bar{dc}) = \gamma_1 + \gamma_2 N^{\gamma_3} + \gamma_4 N^{\gamma_5} [\text{Exp} (\gamma_6 / ED^{\gamma_7}) - 1]$$

TO FILTERED BARNETT "MONEY DIVISIA DEMAND (M^2) DATA"

Data	(γ)	Coefficient Estimates	Estimated "Student-t Ratios"	R^2 Value
Original	1	3.133	1.669	$R^2 = 0.986$
	2	3.848	0.750	
	3	3.003	1.156	
	4	7.683	0.916	
	5	1.153	7.478	57 DOF
	6	−1.294	−2.338	
	7	0.293	1.001	
Randomized	1	6.10	0.122	$R^2 = 0.982$
	2	−1.042	−0.029	
	3	−0.069	−0.034	
	4	8.029	0.138	
	5	0.014	0.216	23 DOF
	6	−0.515	−0.460	
	7	0.310	0.140	

The estimated "student-t ratios" are quoted for reader's convenience in interpreting the results. This is in part justified by the approximate normality of the $\bar{dc}$ estimates for large samples discovered in the Monte Carlo simulations quoted in Ramsey and Yuan (1989b).

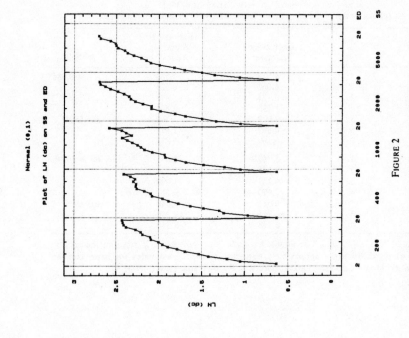

FIGURE 2

THIS SET OF 5 PLOTS SHOWS THE RELATIONSHIP BETWEEN ln (dc) AND SS, ED, WHEN THE UNDERLYING DATA WERE GENERATED BY A SEQUENCE OF INDEPENDENT $N(0, 1)$ RANDOM VARIABLES. IN (20), THE MAXIMUM ED, = 2.995. SO THE SUBSTANTIAL DOWNWARD BIAS IS CLEAR.

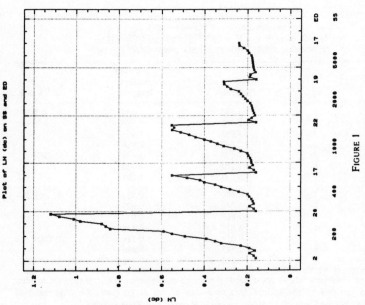

FIGURE 1

THIS SET OF 5 PLOTS SHOWS THE GRAPH OF ln (dc), THE MEAN dc ESTIMATES, AGAINST SAMPLE SIZES SS AND EMBEDDING DIMENSION ED. THE CORRECT VALUE FOR ln (dc) IS 0.19. THE SUBSTANTIAL BIAS THAT OCCURS WITH EVEN MODEST LEVELS OF ED IS STRIKING. IN THIS CASE, A SAMPLE SIZE OF 5000 IS BEGINNING TO YIELD REASONABLE ESTIMATES. THESE DATA POINTS ARE FITTED BY EQUATION (2.6).

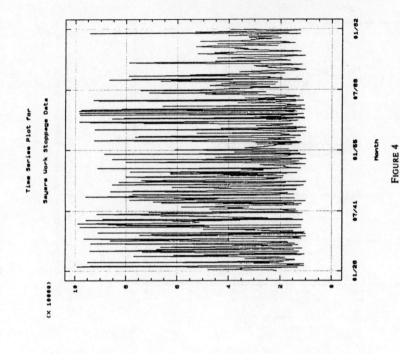

FIGURE 4

THIS IS A TIME SERIES OF MONTHLY MAN-DAYS IDLE DUE TO WORK STOPPAGES FROM JANUARY 1928 TO DECEMBER 1981, AS PUBLISHED BY THE BUREAU OF LABOR STATISTICS.

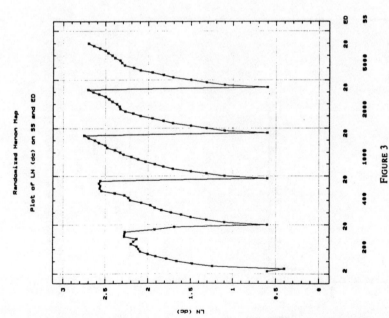

FIGURE 3

THIS SET OF 5 PLOTS SHOWS THE RELATIONSHIP BETWEEN ln (dc) AND SS, ED, WHEN THE UNDERLYING DATA WERE GENERATED BY A HENON MAP WHOSE TIME SEQUENCE OF POINTS WERE THEN RANDOMLY PERMUTED. COMPARE THIS FIGURE WITH FIGURE 2 FOR THE NORMAL DISTRIBUTION AND FIGURE 1 FOR THE NONPERMUTED HENON DATA POINTS.

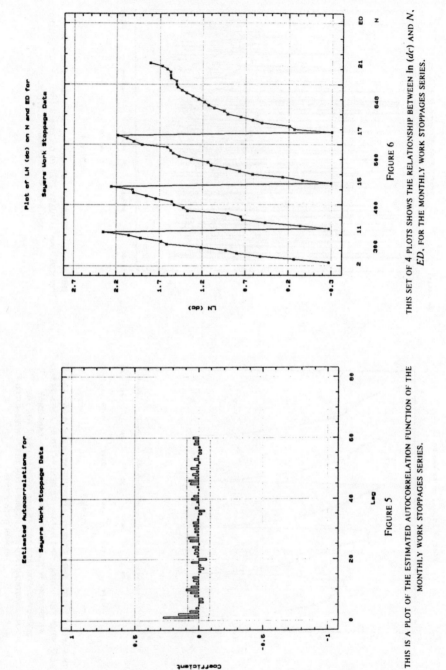

FIGURE 6

THIS SET OF 4 PLOTS SHOWS THE RELATIONSHIP BETWEEN ln (dc) AND N, ED, FOR THE MONTHLY WORK STOPPAGES SERIES.

FIGURE 5

THIS IS A PLOT OF THE ESTIMATED AUTOCORRELATION FUNCTION OF THE MONTHLY WORK STOPPAGES SERIES.

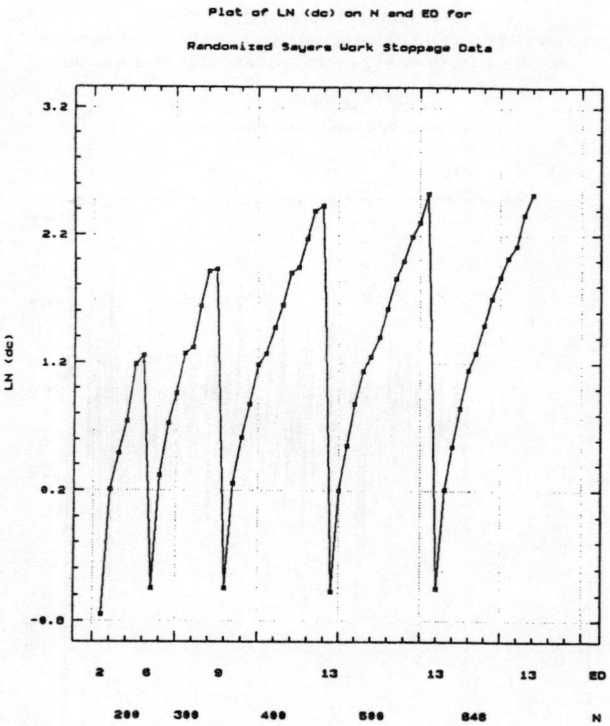

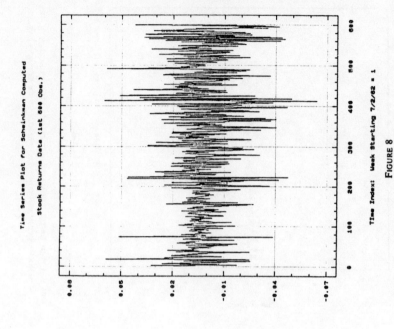

Time Series Plot For Scheinkman Computed

Stock Returns Data (1st 600 Obs.)

FIGURE 8

THIS IS A TIME SERIES PLOT OF THE FIRST 600 OBSERVATIONS OF THE SCHEINKMAN/LEBARON COMPUTED WEEKLY STOCK RETURNS BASED ON DAILY CRSP STOCK RETURNS DATA.

Plot of LN (dc) on N and ED For

Randomized Square Work Stoppage Data

FIGURE 7

THIS SET OF 5 PLOTS SHOWS THE RELATIONSHIP BETWEEN $\ln (dc)$ AND N. ED, WHEN THE UNDERLYING DATA WERE GENERATED BY A RANDOM PERMUTATION OF THE MONTHLY WORK STOPPAGES SERIES.

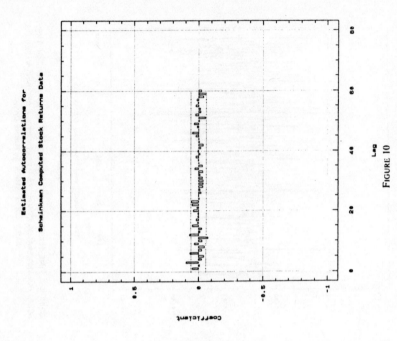

FIGURE 10

THIS IS A PLOT OF THE ESTIMATED AUTOCORRELATION FUNCTION OF THE
SCHEINKMAN/LEBARON COMPUTED WEEKLY STOCK RETURNS DATA.

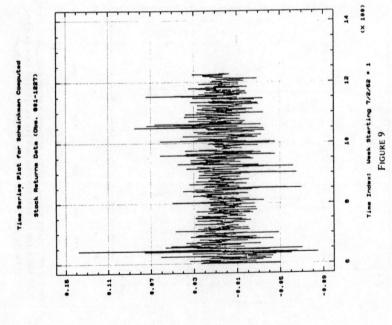

FIGURE 9

THIS IS A TIME SERIES OF THE LAST 627 OBSERVATIONS OF THE
SCHEINKMAN/LEBARON COMPUTED WEEKLY STOCK RETURNS BASED ON
DAILY CRSP STOCK RETURN DATA.

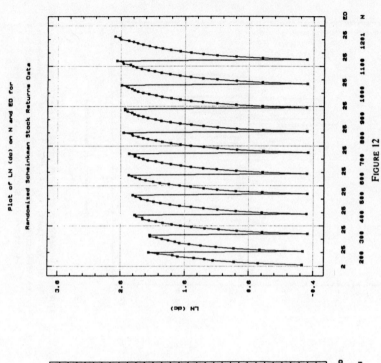

FIGURE 12

THIS SET OF 11 PLOTS SHOWS THE RELATIONSHIP BETWEEN $\ln (dc)$ AND N, ED WHEN THE UNDERLYING DATA WERE GENERATED BY A RANDOM PERMUTATION OF THE PURGED SCHEINKMAN/LEBARON COMPUTED WEEKLY STOCK RETURNS DATA.

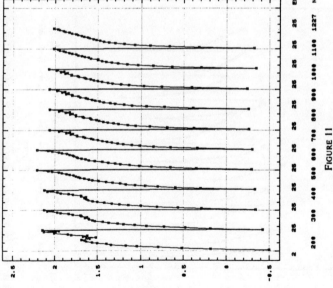

FIGURE 11

THIS SET OF 11 PLOTS SHOWS THE RELATIONSHIP BETWEEN $\ln (dc)$ AND N, ED FOR THE PURGED SCHEINKMAN/LEBARON COMPUTED WEEKLY STOCK RETURNS DATA.

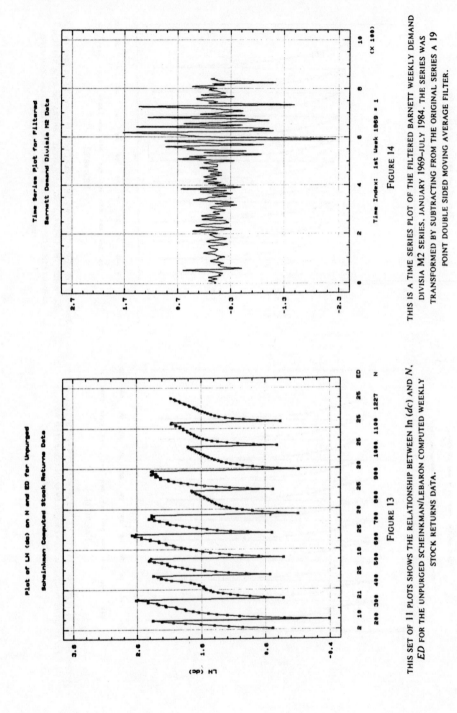

FIGURE 14

THIS IS A TIME SERIES PLOT OF THE FILTERED BARNETT WEEKLY DEMAND DIVISIA M2 SERIES, JANUARY 1969–JULY 1984. THE SERIES WAS TRANSFORMED BY SUBTRACTING FROM THE ORIGINAL SERIES A 19 POINT DOUBLE SIDED MOVING AVERAGE FILTER.

FIGURE 13

THIS SET OF 11 PLOTS SHOWS THE RELATIONSHIP BETWEEN $\ln(dc)$ AND N, ED FOR THE UNPURGED SCHEINKMAN/LEBARON COMPUTED WEEKLY STOCK RETURNS DATA.

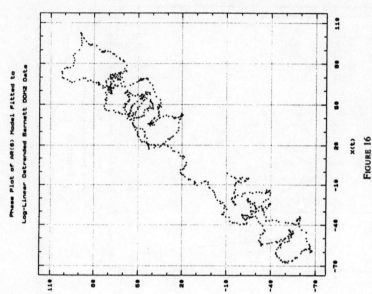

Phase Plot of AR(6) Model Fitted to
Log-Linear Detrended Barnett DDM2 Data

x(t)

FIGURE 16

PHASE PLOT OF A SIMULATED AR(6) MODEL WITH COEFFICIENTS OBTAINED
FROM ESTIMATING AN AR(6) MODEL ON THE BARNETT LOG-LINEAR
DETRENDED DDM2 SPLINED SERIES.

Phase Plot of Log-Linear Detrended
Barnett Demand Divisia M2 Data

DDM2(t)

FIGURE 15

PHASE PLOT OF LOG-LINEAR DETRENDED BARNETT DEMAND DIVISIA M2
SPLINED DATA.

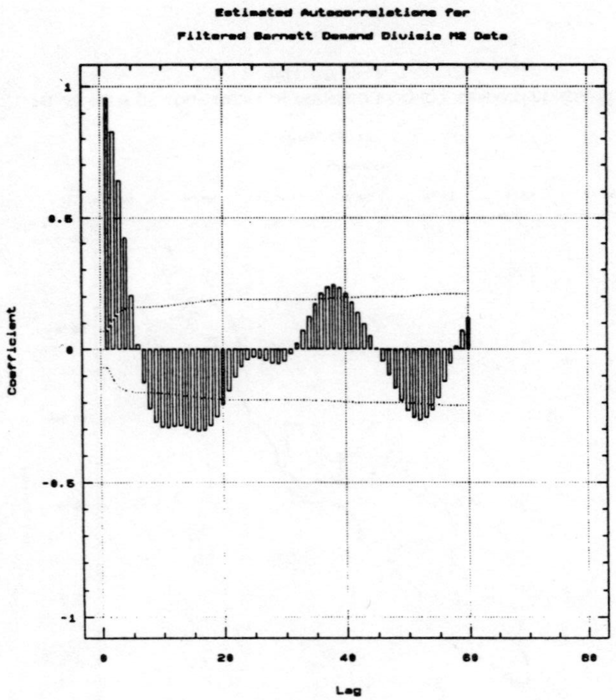

1016   JAMES B. RAMSEY, CHERA L. SAYERS, AND PHILIP ROTHMAN

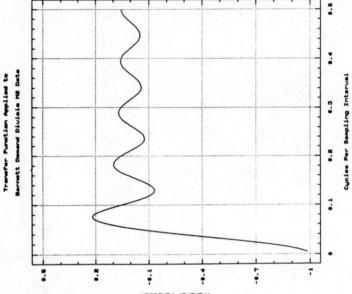

FIGURE 18

THIS IS A PLOT OF THE TRANSFER FUNCTION FOR THE DIGITAL FILTER
APPLIED TO THE RAW BARNETT WEEKLY DEMAND DIVISIA M2 SERIES.

FIGURE 17

THIS IS A PLOT OF THE ESTIMATED AUTOCORRELATION FUNCTION OF THE
FILTERED BARNETT DEMAND DIVISIA M2 SERIES. BARNETT AND CHEN
WORKED WITH A SERIES FOR WHICH THE FIRST ZERO OF THE
ESTIMATED AUTOCORRELATION FUNCTION IS AT A LAG OF
APPROXIMATELY 180.

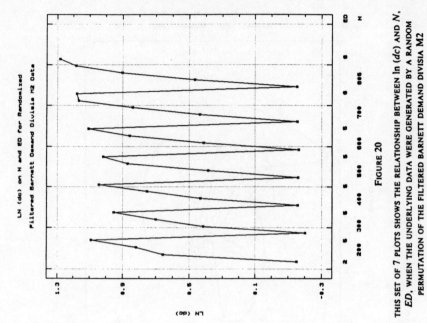

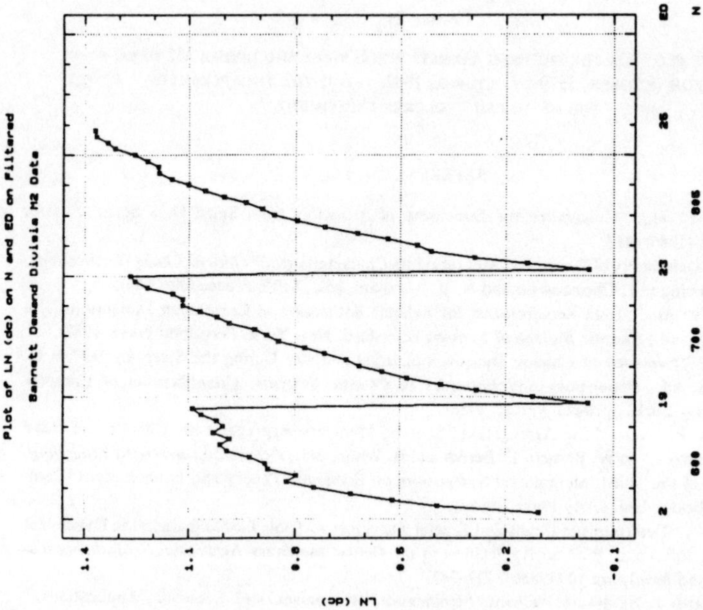

FIGURE 19

THIS SET OF PLOTS SHOWS THE RELATIONSHIP BETWEEN ln (dc) AND N, ED, FOR THE FILTERED WEEKLY BARNETT DEMAND DIVISIA M2 SERIES.

FIGURE 20

THIS SET OF 7 PLOTS SHOWS THE RELATIONSHIP BETWEEN ln (dc) AND N, ED, WHEN THE UNDERLYING DATA WERE GENERATED BY A RANDOM PERMUTATION OF THE FILTERED BARNETT DEMAND DIVISIA M2 SERIES.

1018   JAMES B. RAMSEY, CHERA L. SAYERS, AND PHILIP ROTHMAN

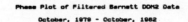

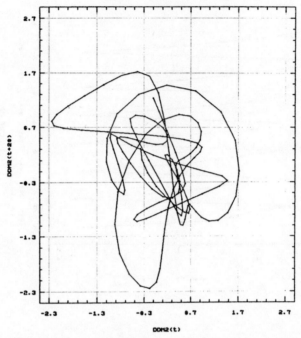

FIGURE 21

PHASE PLOT FOR THE FILTERED BARNETT WEEKLY DEMAND DIVISIA M2 DATA
FROM OCTOBER, 1979 TO OCTOBER, 1982. THIS IS THE TIME PERIOD OF
THE SO-CALLED "VOLCKER EXPERIMENT."

REFERENCES

ABRAHAM, N.B., ET AL., "Calculating the Dimension of Attractors from Small Data Sets," *Physics Letters* 114A (1986), 217.

———, ET AL., "Definitions of Chaos and Measuring its Characteristics," *Optical Chaos* (forthcoming) (also forthcoming in J. Chrostowski and N. B. Abraham, eds., SPIE Proceedings 667).

ALBANO, A. M., ET AL., "Data Requirements for Reliable Estimation of Correlation Dimensions," in A. V. Holden, ed., *Chaotic Biological Systems* (Elmsford, New York: Pergamon Press, 1987).

BABLOYANTZ, A., "Evidence of Chaotic Dynamics of Brain Activity During the Sleep Cycle," in G. Mayer-Kress, ed., *Dimensions and Entropies in Chaotic Systems, Quantification of Complex Behavior* (New York: Springer-Verlag, 1986).

BARNETT, W. AND P. CHEN, "The Aggregation-Theoretic Monetary Aggregates are Chaotic and Have Strange Attractors," in W. Barnett, E. Berndt and H. White, eds., *Dynamic Econometric Modelling*, Proceedings of the Third International Symposium on Economic Theory and Econometrics (Cambridge: Cambridge University Press, 1988a).

——— AND ———, "Deterministic Chaos and Fractal Attractors as Tools for Nonparametric Dynamical Econometric Inference: With an Application to the Divisia Monetary Aggregates," *Mathematical Computing and Modelling* 10 (1988b), 227–242.

BAUMOL, W. J. AND J. BENHABIB, "Chaos: Significance, Mechanism, and Economic Applications,"

Journal of Economic Perspectives 3 (1987), 77–105.

BEN-MIZRACHI, A., ET AL., "Characterization of Experimental (Noisy) Strange Attractors," *Physical Review A* 29 (1984), 975–986.

BRANDSTATER, A. AND H. L. SWINNEY, "A Strange Attractor in Weakly Turbulent Couette-Taylor Flow," mimeo, Department of Physics and the Center for Nonlinear Dynamics, University of Texas, 1986.

BROCK, W. A., "Distinguishing Random and Deterministic Systems: Abridged Version," *Journal of Economic Theory* 40 (1986), 168–195.

————, "Hicksian Nonlinearity," SSRI Working Paper No. 8815, Department of Economics, University of Wisconsin-Madison, 1988a.

————, "Nonlinearity and Complex Dynamics in Economics and Finance," in P. Anderson, K. Arrow and D. Pines, eds., *The Economy as an Evolving Complex System*, SFI Studies in the Sciences of Complexity (Reading, MA: 1988b).

————, "Introduction to Chaos and Other Aspects of Nonlinearity," in W. A. Brock and A. G. Malliaris, eds., *Differential Equations, Stability, and Chaos in Dynamic Economics* (New York: North Holland, forthcoming).

————, W. D. DECHERT AND J. A. SCHEINKMAN, "A Test for Independence Based on the Correlation Dimension," in W. Barnett, E. Berndt and H. White, eds., *Dynamic Econometric Modelling*, Proceedings of the Third International Symposium on Economic Theory and Econometrics (Cambridge: Cambridge University Press, 1988).

———— AND C. SAYERS, "Is the Business Cycle Characterized by Deterministic Chaos?" *Journal of Monetary Economics* 22 (1988), 71–90.

CAPUTO, J. G., ET AL., "Determination of Attractor Dimension and Entropy for Various Flows: An Experimentalist's Viewpoint," in G. Mayer-Kress, ed., *Dimensions and Entropies in Chaotic Systems, Quantification of Complex Behavior* (New York: Springer-Verlag, 1986).

FARMER, J. D., E. OTT AND J. A. YORKE, "The Dimension of Chaotic Attractors," *Physica* 7D (1983), 153–180.

FAYYAD, SALAM, "Monetary Asset Component Grouping and Aggregation: An Inquiry into the Definition of Money," Ph.D. Dissertation, Department of Economics, University of Texas at Austin, 1986.

FRANK, M. AND T. STENGOS, "Some Evidence Concerning Macroeconomics Chaos," *Journal of Monetary Economics* 22 (1988), 423–438.

———— AND ————, "Measuring the Strangeness of Gold and Silver Rates of Return," Department of Economics, University of British Columbia and University of Guelph, *Review of Economic Studies* (forthcoming).

FRASER, A. M., "Using Mutual Information to Estimate Metric Entropy," in Gottfried Mayer-Kress, ed., *Dimensions and Entropies in Chaotic Systems* (New York: Springer-Verlag, 1986).

GENNOTTE, G. AND T. MARSH, "Variations in Ex Ante Risk Premiums on Capital Assets," mimeo, Berkeley Business School, University of California, 1986.

GRASSBERGER, P., "Generalizations of the Hausdorff Dimension of Fractal Measures," *Physics Letters* 107A (1985), 101–123.

———— AND I. PROCACCIA, "Characterization of Strange Attractors," *Physical Review Letters* 50 (1983a), 346–349.

———— AND ————, "Estimation of the Kolmogorov Entropy from a Chaotic Signal," *Physical Review A* 28 (1983b), 2591–2603.

———— AND ————, "Measuring the Strangeness of Strange Attractors," *Physica* 9D (1983c), 189–208.

GREBOGI, C., ET AL., "Strange Attractors That Are Not Chaotic," *Physica* 13D (1984), 261–268.

GREENSIDE, H. S., ET AL., "Impracticality of a Box-counting Algorithm for Calculating the Dimensionality of Strange Attractors," *Physical Review A* 25 (1982), 3453–3467.

GUCKENHEIMER, J., "Dimension Estimates for Attractors," *Contemporary Mathematics* 28 (1984), 357–372.

HALSEY, T. C., ET AL., "Fractal Measures and their Singularities: The Characterization of Strange Sets," *Physical Review A* 33 (1986), 1141–1153.

HOLZFUSS, J. AND G. MAYER-KRESS, "An Approach to Error-free Estimation in the Application of Dimension Algorithms," in G. Mayer-Kress, ed., *Dimensions and Entropies in Chaotic Systems, Quantification of Complex Behavior* (New York: Springer-Verlag, 1986).

HSIEH, D., AND B. LEBARON, "Finite Sample Properties of the BDS Statistics," mimeo, Department of

1020   JAMES B. RAMSEY, CHERA L. SAYERS, AND PHILIP ROTHMAN

Economics, University of Chicago and University of Wisconsin-Madison, 1988.

KURTHS, J. AND H. HERZEL, "An Attractor in a Solar Time Series," *Physica* 25D (1987), 165–184.

LEBARON, B., "Nonlinear Puzzles in Stock Returns," mimeo, Department of Economics, University of Wisconsin-Madison, 1988a.

——, "Stock Return Nonlinearities: Some Initial Tests and Findings," Ph.D. Dissertation, Department of Economics, University of Chicago, 1988b.

LOVEJOY, S. AND D. SCHERTZER, "Scale Invariance, Symmetries, Fractals, and Stochastic Simulations of Atmospheric Phenomena," *Bulletin of the American Meteorological Society* 67 (1986), 344–362.

PRIESTLY, M. B., *Spectral Analysis and Time Series*, Volumes I and II (New York: Academic Press, 1981).

RAMSEY, J. B. AND H. YUAN, "Bias and Error Bars in Dimension Calculations and their Evaluation in some Simple Models," *Physics Letters A* 134 (1989a), 287–297.

—— AND ——, "The Statistical Properties of Dimension Calculations Using Small Data Sets," *Nonlinearity* (1989b).

SAYERS, C. L., "Work Stoppages: Exploring the Nonlinear Dynamics," mimeo, Department of Economics, University of Houston, 1986.

——, "Diagnostic Tests for Nonlinearity in Time Series Data: An Application to the Work Stoppages Series," mimeo, Department of Economics, University of Houston, 1987.

SCHEINKMAN, J. A. AND B. LEBARON, "Nonlinear Dynamics and GNP Data," in W. Barnett, J. Geweke and K. Shell, eds., *Economic Complexity, Chaos, Sunspots, Bubbles, and Nonlinearity* (Cambridge: Cambridge University Press, 1987).

—— AND ——, "Nonlinear Dynamics and Stock Returns," *Journal of Business* 62 (1989), 311–337.

WOLF, A., ET AL., "Determining Lyapunov Exponents from a Time Series," *Physica* 16D (1985), 285–317.

[26]

European Economic Review 32 (1988) 1569–1584. North-Holland

INTERNATIONAL CHAOS?

Murray FRANK*

University of British Colombia, Vancouver, BC, Canada V6T 1Y8

Ramazan GENCAY

Queen's University, Kingston, Ont., Canada K7L 3N6 and Middle East Technical University, Ankara, Turkey

Thanasis STENGOS

University of Guelph, Guelph, Ont., Canada N1G 2W1

Received February 1988, final version received April 1988

Tests are conducted on quarterly macroeconomic data for Italy, Japan, the United Kingdom and West Germany to check for the presence of deterministic chaos. Deterministic chaos is rejected using a number of fairly recently developed empirical tools. In the process we found surprisingly strong evidence of nonlinearities in the case of Japan. The evidence indicates that Japan is also the most stable of the countries studied. A satisfactory modelling of Japanese data will need to allow for suitable nonlinearity.

1. Introduction

The appropriate interpretation of business fluctuations is a frequent topic of debate amongst economists. It is common to distinguish Keynesians from New Classicals, however quite a few distinct perspectives are represented even in the serious literature. The perspective of interest here is based on the mathematical theory of 'chaos'. According to the chaos perspective business fluctuations are endogenous to the system. They reflect the presence of important nonlinearities in the behavioral relationships of the economic system. This view differs sharply from the more familiar log linear macro models with Gaussian error terms. Examples of the theoretical models based on chaos include Grandmont (1985), Boldrin and Montrucchio (1986) and Farmer (1986). These models are reviewed by Frank and Stengos (1988a).

Serious researchers have proposed that chaos may be important to an understanding of macroeconomics. It is natural to ask whether there is empirical evidence of such phenomena. Brock and Sayers (1988) examine a

---

*We would like to thank W. Dechert for providing us with access to his excellent computer program to compute BDS statistics. The comments and suggestions of an anonymous referee were very helpful. Of course any errors or misinterpretations remain ours alone.

variety of American time-series. They found significant evidence of nonlinearity in the labor market and in investment. They did not obtain clean evidence of chaos. Frank and Stengos (1988c) examine Canadian macroeconomic time-series. No evidence of chaos was found. Barnett and Chen (1988) found evidence of low dimensionality in certain American monetary aggregates.

Consideration of these findings caused us to be concerned about the extent to which North America might be atypical amongst the industrialized countries. It is often suggested that Europe and Japan have quite different economic structures from North America. Most often cited are differences in the labor market conditions, see Blanchard and Summers (1986) and Tachibanaki (1987). There are also important differences in the product markets and in the industrial policies, see de Jong and Shepherd (1986).

In this study we examine several of the leading industrial nations.[1] The issue is whether evidence of chaos might be found for these countries. Such evidence would place important restrictions on acceptable approaches to modelling business cycles. There are of course substantial real differences among the countries. Are these differences reflected at the macroeconomic level? Japan is frequently cited as a particularly unusual case. The balance of the paper is organized as follows. Section 2 briefly introduces the testing procedures. Empirical findings are set out in section 3, while conclusions are drawn in section 4. An appendix describes the data and collects some details.

2. Testing for chaos

In this section we introduce the methods to be used in looking for evidence of chaos. Our introduction will be heuristic. For more formal treatments, see Brock and Dechert (1988), Eckmann and Ruelle (1985) and Mayer-Kress (1986). There are two basic classes of measurements to be used, the correlation dimension of Grassberger and Procaccia (1983) and the Lyapunov exponent.

The basic set up for each measurement is the same. Begin by assuming that the system under investigation consists of a time-series that is dense on an attractor. An attractor is a compact set A with a neighborhood such that almost all initial conditions in the neighborhood have A itself as their forward-limit set. Attractors may be distinguished according to whether they are well behaved or whether they are chaotic. For an attractor that is well behaved a small change to the initial conditions will remain small as time

---

[1] We wanted to include France in the group of countries we examined. However, French GNP was only available to us after 1970 quarterly. Therefore, the French GNP series would not have been of comparable length as the other series and the empirical analysis could not have been carried out in the same way.

goes on. A strange (or chaotic) attractor exhibits 'sensitive dependence on initial conditions'. Hence small deviations get magnified locally as time proceeds.

A slightly more precise statement of the concept is as follows. Let Ω be a space with a metric d and let $f:\Omega \to \Omega$ be a continuous mapping defined on Ω. A discrete dynamical system (Ω, f) is said to be chaotic (or strange) if there exists a $\delta > 0$ such that for all $\omega \in \Omega$ and all $\varepsilon > 0$ there is an $\omega' \in \Omega$ and a k such that $d(\omega, \omega') < \varepsilon$ but $d(f^k\omega, f^k\omega') \geqq \delta$. Here $f^k\omega$ denotes the k-fold iteration of the point ω by the map f. There are other approaches to defining chaos, our usage is consistent with Eckmann and Ruelle (1985). In this definition nearby points get stretched apart over time. This can be checked directly by estimation of the largest Lyapunov exponent which will be positive in the case of chaos. It can be checked indirectly by estimation of the system's correlation dimension.

For both approaches one must create an 'embedding'. Consider a time-series of scalar observations X_t, $t = 1, 2, \ldots, T$ which are assumed to have been generated by an orbit that is dense on an attractor. Using these observations create a series of 'M-histories' as $X_t^M = (X_t, X_{t+1}, \ldots, X_{t+M-1})$. This converts the T scalars into $T - M + 1$ vectors with overlapping entries. All analysis is carried out using the M-histories. The formal justification of this approach is due to Takens (1981). Suppose that the true, but unknown, system that generated the observations is n-dimensional. Then provided $M \geqq 2n + 1$ generically the M-histories recreate the dynamics of the process that generated the data. In other words there is a diffeomorphism between the M-histories and the original data generating process.

2.1. Correlation dimension

Dimensionality measures how complicated an object is. A point is zero dimensional. A line is one dimensional. A white noise is completely disorderly (stochastic) and so is infinite dimensional. A chaotic process has positive but finite dimensionally. A random process is infinite dimensional.

The next step in the analysis is to measure the spatial correlations among the points (M-histories) on the attractor. To do this one calculates the correlation integral $C^M(\varepsilon)$

$$C^M(\varepsilon) = \{\text{the number of } (i, j) \text{ for which } \|X_i^M - X_j^M\| \leq \varepsilon\}/T^2. \tag{1}$$

Here $\|\cdot\|$ denotes the distance induced by the selected norm. We use the Euclidean distance. In principal $T \to \infty$ but in practice T is determined by data availability. This places constraints on the useable values for ε and M. For small values of ε one can demonstrate that $C^M(\varepsilon) \sim \varepsilon^D$ so that D is the system's dimensionally, see Grassberger and Procaccia (1983).

$$D^M = \lim_{\varepsilon \to 0} \{\ln C^M(\varepsilon)/\ln \varepsilon\}. \tag{2}$$

If the system is chaotic then as one evaluates D^M for successively larger M the measured values will stabilize at some value D. If the system does not saturate then the system is regarded as 'high dimensional' or stochastic.

Processes that have a near unit root can cause trouble in finite samples. As a result Brock (1986) and Brock and Sayers (forthcoming) have recommended pre-whitening the data. To do this one fits a linear-time series model to the data. If the series is chaotic then the estimated dimensionality will be unaffected by the linear transformation. A unit root process will be drastically affected. We refer to this procedure as Brock's Residual Test.

Scheinkman and LeBaron (1986) have proposed another diagnostic. Take the time series and randomly sample from it with replacement. In this manner one creates a new series of the same length as the original series. If the original series was chaotic then the shuffled series will have had the coherence of the underlying structure seriously disrupted. As a result the shuffled series will have a higher value of estimated dimensionality than will the original series, if the original series was chaotic. By bootstrapping the shuffle one can obtain an empirical confidence interval.[2]

2.2. Lyapunov exponent

The existence of a positive Lyapunov exponent is often used as a definition of chaos, see for example Deneckere and Pelikan (1986). It quantifies the notion of local instability that is fundamental to chaos. The dimensionality may be thought of as an estimate of the degree of complexity of the system. The Lyapunov exponent measures whether adjacent trajectories converge, or whether they separate. If they converge then the economy will be stable in reaction to small perturbations. If they separate then the system will be chaotic. The Lyapunov exponent is an explicitly dynamic concept. The algorithm that we employ is due to Kurths and Herzel (1987).

Start by constructing M-histories in order to reconstruct the system. From amongst the M-histories select all nearby pairs. Select all (X_i^M, X_j^M) satisfying

---

[2]As pointed out by a referee there is an important issue concerning the asymptotic properties of this approach, see Bickel and Friedman (1981) and Lee (1985). To formally deal with this question is beyond the scope of the present paper. In computer experiments on systems with known properties the bootstrap seems to work pretty well. As will be shown below, on our data the Brock, Dechert and Scheinkman (1987) alternative approach leads to essentially the same inferences.

$$r_0(M; i, j) = \left\| X_i^M - X_j^M \right\| < \varepsilon. \tag{3}$$

Now ε is a small positive number and $\|\cdot\|$ is a metric. We will use the Euclidean measure of distance. In eq. (3) we have selected the nearby points in the M-space. Next follow the original nearby points a further n steps forward in time. Calculate

$$r_n(M; i, j) = \left\| X_{i+n}^M - X_{j+n}^M \right\|. \tag{4}$$

Now take the ratio

$$d_n(M; i, j) = r_n(M; i, j)/r_0(M; i, j). \tag{5}$$

If the nearby points have separated then $d_n(M; i, j)$ will be larger than one. Finally one aggregates over the $d_n(M; i, j)$ to get an aggregate statistic.

$$L(M, n) = \sum_{i \neq j} \ln d_n(M; i, j)/N(N - 1). \tag{6}$$

Certain features of $L(M, n)$ are discussed in Frank and Stengos (1988b). It might be better to refer to $L(M, n)$ as a 'stretching factor' rather than as a Lyapunov exponent estimate. It is only a lower bound on the true concept of a Lyapunov exponent, see Mayer-Kress (1986). Accordingly chaos does not require $L(M, n) > 0$ since one only requires a positive Lyapunov exponent in one direction to satisfy the usual definition of chaos. The attempts to isolate the direction of most rapid expansion leads to empirically fragile results, see Brock and Sayers (1988). In general if the economy is stable we expect negative values for $L(M, n)$. If the economy is unstable we might anticipate positive values for $L(M, n)$.

3. Empirical findings

In order to use common statistical procedures one needs to ensure that the data being analyzed is stationary. The issue of the stationarity of macroeconomic time series is currently an area of active research, see Nelson and Plosser (1982), Blanchard and Summers (1986), Campbell and Mankiw (1987) and Perron (1987) for differing perspectives on this issue. In this paper we will induce stationarity by using first differences. The reason for this approach is that using a time trend imposes trend-reversions on the data. As shown by Frank and Stengos (1988c) a simple application of the correlation dimension may then misidentify a stochastic series as being chaotic.

The chosen GNP series are described in the appendix. Having first differenced the logs of each series, we then attempt to find a reasonable

Table 1

	Japan	Italy	U.K.	Germany
1st lag	0.149	0.322	−0.032	−0.019
(S.E.)	(0.107)	(0.094)	(0.098)	(0.099)
2nd lag	0.348	0.333	0.120	0.006
(S.E.)	(0.095)	(0.094)	(0.097)	(0.099)
3rd lag	0.233	–	–	–
(S.E.)	(0.100)			
4th lag	0.111	–	–	–
(S.E.)	(0.041)			
SSR	0.010	0.017	0.024	5.179
S.E.	0.011	0.013	0.015	0.224
$\log L$	252.831	305.611	296.343	−76.085
NOBS	82	104	104	105
L.L.F.	252.831	305.611	287.421	9.000

linear fit. As shown in table 1 the United Kingdom and Italy both seem to be well fit by an AR-2 specification. These are consistent with American data, see Brock and Sayers (1988). For Japan it was necessary to use an AR-4 specification.

The case of Germany poses a bit of a problem. As may be seen in table 1 the AR structure does not appear to fit well. The reason for this may be understood by considering table A.1 in the appendix. The seasonally adjusted German time series is already white according to the autocorrelation function. There is no linear structure left to be picked up by an AR process. We also tried unsuccessfully to fit an ARCH process to the series, see Engle and Bollerslev (1986).[3] In the end we used the AR-2 specification as the linear filter for Brock's Residual Test. In the appendix we present the autocorrelation function for the whitened and the unwhitened series. As is evident from the results, filtering the series through an appropriate AR process has succeeded in removing from the series any linear structure.

In figs. 1–4 the estimated correlation dimension for each series at embedding dimensions ranging up to $M = 15$ are depicted. For embedding dimensions 5, 10 and 15 the numerical values are reported in table 2.

What would a chaotic system look like in the figures? The seasonally adjusted series would be roughly horizontal as the system does not utilize the extra freedom associated with the increasing embedding dimension. A chaotic series should pass Brock's Residual Test. Accordingly the estimated dimensionality of the whitened series should be negligibly different from the seasonally adjusted series. Finally the shuffles destroy structure thereby

---

[3]We tested for the presence of an ARCH(1), ARCH(2), ARCH(3) and ARCH(4) process. The test statistics obtained were 0.008, 0.015, 0.073, 0.131. The test statistic for an ARCH(q) process was obtained as is TR^2 from the artificial regression $l_t^2 = \alpha_0 + \alpha_1 l_{t-1}^2 + \cdots + \alpha_q l_{t-q}^2 + \varepsilon_t$ where l_t^2 are the squared residuals from the AR fit. The test statistic is distributed as χ_q^2.

M. Frank, R. Gencay and T. Stengos, International chaos? 1575

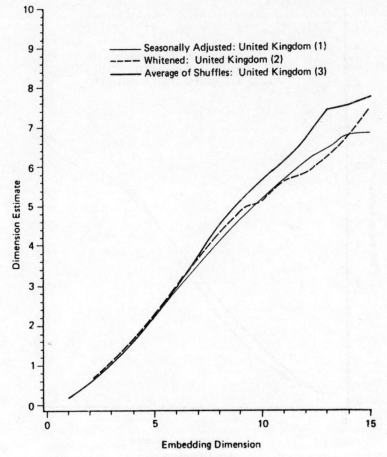

Fig. 1. United Kingdom.

causing a substantial increase in the dimensionality estimates. Accordingly the average of the shuffles should lie above the other two series.

Even with just a casual examination it is apparent that the Japanese case is quite different from the others. The evidence depicted in fig. 4 is quite consistent with nonlinear structure in the case of Japan. Table 3 provides further evidence supporting this finding. We present the proportion of 50 shuffled series that produce dimension estimates that lie above the estimated dimensionality of the original whitened series. As argued above, if the whitened series has little or no structure, the shuffling with replacement will produce a series with similar dimension estimate. However, if there is still substantial structure in the whitened series, then the shuffled series will produce a substantially higher dimension estimate. We created 50 shuffled

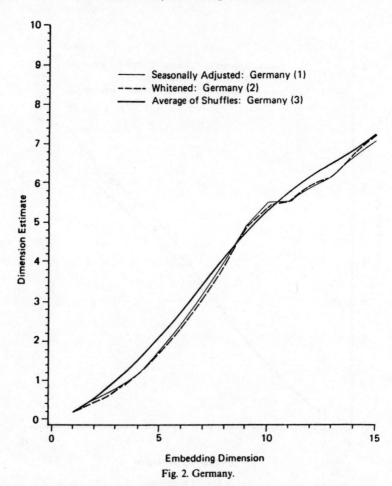

Fig. 2. Germany.

series and looked at the proportion of the dimension estimates above the original whitened series estimate for $M = 5$, 10 for the different series. Clearly, the results obtained for Japan indicate that there is still quite a lot of structure in the whitened series, whereas no such evidence was found for the other series.

Brock, Dechert and Scheinkman (1987) have proposed an interesting approach to hypothesis testing based on the correlation dimension. They take the hypothesis of independently distributed data (iid) to be the null hypothesis. Under the null, the correlation integral at embedding dimension M will equal the correlation integral at embedding dimension one raised to the power M (i.e.: $C^M = (C^1)^M$). With an appropriate rather complicated normalization one obtains a test statistic that is distributed asymptotically as

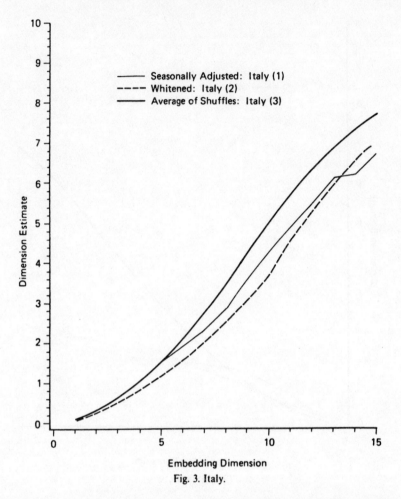

Fig. 3. Italy.

$N(0, 1)$, see the discussion of Brock and Sayers (1988). As an added check we tried this approach for both the unwhitened and the whitened versions of each of our series. Neither Germany nor the U.K. were close to rejecting the iid hypothesis. Italy offered ambiguous borderline results whose interpretation would depend upon the particular choices of ε and M. The Japanese results were quite different. For wide ranges of ε and for embedding dimensions ranging from 3 to 10 the data rejects the null hypothesis. One gets numerical values of the test statistic typically about 5 while the critical value at 5% significance is 1.96. This was true both for the whitened and the unwhitened versions of the Japanese data. The inferences from the Brock, Dechert and Scheinkman (1987) approach agree with the inferences from the bootstrapping approach.

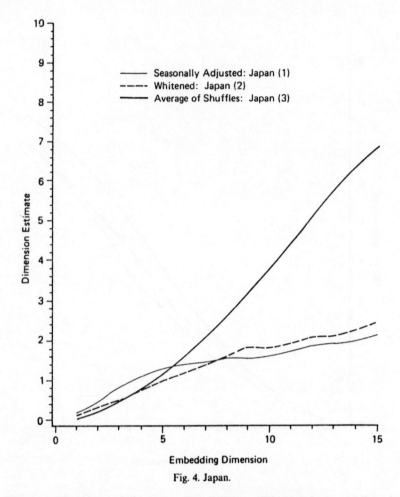

Fig. 4. Japan.

Given the evidence of added structure in the whitened Japanese data it is natural to wonder if it might represent some form of linear misspecification. Accordingly we examined a variety of different linear models for Japan.[4] While our emphasis is on differenced data, we also considered the use of time trends. In every case that we tried, the Brock, Dechert and Scheinkman (1987) tests continued to indicate the presence of added structure in the residuals. Perhaps the most interesting of these tests follows Perron (1987) in allowing for structural change in 1973. A plot of Japanaese GNP against time certainly appears to indicate some sort of shift in the early 1970s. On

---

[4]Japanese data is actually slightly better fit as an MA-4 than as an AR-4. However MA residuals and ARMA residuals continue to provide evidence of additional structure according to Brock, Dechert and Scheinkman (1987) tests.

Table 2

Correlation dimension estimates for selected embedding dimensions.[a]

	$M=5$	$M=10$	$M=15$
Italy (1)	1.5	4.2	6.7
Italy (2)	1.2	3.7	7.0
Italy (3)	1.5	5.0	7.7
Japan (1)	1.3	1.6	2.1
Japan (2)	1.0	1.8	2.4
Japan (3)	1.2	3.8	6.8
United Kingdom (1)	2.2	5.2	6.8
United Kingdom (2)	2.2	5.1	7.4
United Kingdom (3)	2.2	5.7	7.7
West Germany (1)	1.7	5.5	7.1
West Germany (2)	1.7	5.4	7.2
West Germany (3)	2.1	5.3	7.2
Random numbers	3.6	5.4	7.1

[a]M = embedding dimension. Country (1) = logged differenced seasonally adjusted national income series of the particular nation. Country (2) = linear structure removed from the Country (1) series using the AR process as reported in table 1. Country (3) = a typical example of the reshuffled values from reshuffling the Country (2) series. The 'random number's are a computer generated series with 100 observations. The series was created to have the same mean and variance as the Japan (1) series.

Table 3

Proportion of the 50 shuffles which lie above the estimated dimensionality of the original whitened series.

Embedding dimension	Italy	Japan	United Kingdom	West Germany
5	0.62	0.80	0.48	0.42
10	0.64	1.00	0.68	0.46

logged time detrended data one does obtain statistically significant evidence of a trend shift. However taking the shift into account had no noticeable effect on the Brock, Dechert and Scheinkman (1987) tests on the residuals. As far as we can tell, the findings for Japan do not represent a simple linear misspecification.

In order to check whether the nonlinear structure found for Japan is chaotic we estimate the lower bound on the largest Lyapunov exponent (L). Recall the interpretation of L. A positive value for L would imply local instability. If the economy is stable then we expect to find a negative value for L. Some estimates are reported in table 4. The reported values of L correspond to a value of ε determined as follows. First calculate the

Table 4

Estimated Lyapunov exponents (L) at selected embedding dimensions (M).[a]

	M	$n=1$	$n=2$	$n=3$
Italy (1)	5	−0.0051	−0.0079	−0.0116
Italy (1)	10	−0.0042	−0.0066	−0.0091
Italy (1)	15	−0.0016	−0.0041	−0.0078
United Kingdom (1)	5	−0.0026	−0.0045	−0.0065
United Kingdom (1)	10	−0.0027	−0.0038	−0.0043
United Kingdom (1)	15	−0.0020	−0.0032	−0.0049
West Germany (1)	5	0.0026	0.0046	0.0079
West Germany (1)	10	−0.0025	−0.0061	−0.0099
West Germany (1)	15	−0.0037	−0.0076	−0.0112
Japan (1)	5	−0.0573	−0.0713	−0.0843
Japan (1)	10	−0.0537	−0.0681	−0.0829
Japan (1)	15	−0.0524	−0.0719	−0.0924
Japan (2)	5	−0.0154	−0.0156	−0.0157
Japan (2)	10	−0.0137	−0.0139	−0.0141
Japan (2)	15	−0.0192	−0.0201	−0.0203
Japan (3)	5	0.0035	0.0038	0.0039
Japan (3)	10	0.0026	0.0028	0.0028
Japan (3)	15	0.0012	0.0013	0.0014
Random numbers	5	0.0085	0.0086	0.0086
Random numbers	10	0.0077	0.0078	0.0078
Random numbers	15	0.0090	0.0091	0.0093

[a] n = time step number. Country (1) = logged differenced seasonally adjusted national income series of the particular nation. Country (2) = linear structure removed from the the Country (1) series using the AR process as reported in table 1. Country (3) = a typical example of the reshuffled values from reshuffling the Country (2) series.

arithmetic mean for each entry in the set of M-histories to obtain the mean M-history $(\mu_1, \mu_2, \ldots, \mu_M)$. Then compute

$$\varepsilon \equiv \left[\sum_{j=1}^{T-M+1} \sum_{i=1}^{M} (x_{ji} - \mu_i)^2 \right]^{1/2} \bigg/ 2(T - M + 1). \tag{7}$$

Certain practical drawbacks to L should be noted. As pointed out by Frank and Stengos (1988b) for iid data and $n < M$ the measure L has a positive bias. This bias reflects the fact that initially one selected nearby points which are therefore closer together than two average points. A second drawback is that as yet no statistical theory exists for L. To develop such a theory is important but beyond the scope of this paper, see Brock and Baek (1987) for some related developments.

In order to partially alleviate these problems we calculated some comparison series. A computer-generated series of random numbers with similar length and the same first two moments as Japan resulted in small positive values. Shuffled versions of the whitened Japanese data [Japan (3)] also result in positive values for L. We regard these series as indicative of the probable degree of positive bias. The fact that the bias is positive strengthens the interpretation that the GNP series are stable (i.e.: $L < 0$).

The empirical estimates of L alter the manner in which one might have been inclined to interpret the earlier tests. Again Japan is empirically distinct. However it appears that Japan is the most stable of all the countries being investigated. Consideration of the dimensionality estimates alone might have left one inclined to interpret the findings as evidence of chaos for Japan. The results of the Lyapunov exponent estimates caution against such an interpretation. The structure of the Japanese economy may have induced nonlinearities into its time series, but those linearities do not appear to be of the chaotic variety.

4. Conclusion

Our findings can be given a fairly succinct summary. None of these countries' national income would appear to be well interpreted as being chaotic. The end of the use of stochastic models is not in sight. The Japanese case is empirically distinct from the others. Japan does seem to offer evidence of important nonlinear structure. However, Japan also appears to be the most stable of the countries investigated. When interpreting the findings one must be cautious given the shortness of the series. With longer time series matters could change.

There are many real differences among the countries we studied and so there are a number of possible interpretations of the results. One aspect that we regard as important was also noted by Hall and Taylor (1988): 'actual GNP for Japan behaves much like smoothly trending potential GNP for the United States.' We view this as suggestive of a high signal to noise ratio for Japanese data. The signal to noise ratio matters a great deal for such short time series as are under investigation here.

What then produced the evidence of a nonlinear 'signal'? Brock and Sayers (1988) have discussed the possibility of asymmetric adjustment costs for capital and labor in response to positive and negative shocks. Such an interpretation is consistent with some of the evidence discussed by Tachibanaki (1987). Many Japanese firms are less willing than their Western counterparts to shed labor in response to a downturn. Another possibility is that we have found a reflection of some aspect of a governmental policy rule. Each of these could potentially have had a large enough impact to have been empirically discernible. In any case, a satisfactory model of the Japanese economy will probably need to come to grips with the evidence of nonlinearity in the data.

Appendix

I.

Data	Description:
Germany	Real GNP, seasonally adjusted, quarterly since 1960. Series 1000.182 OECDMEI from I.P. Sharp data base.
Italy	Real GNP, seasonally adjusted quarterly since 1960. Series 3000.102 OECDMEI from I.P. Sharp data base.
Japan	Real GNP, seasonally adjusted, quarterly since 1965. Series 1000.012 OECDMEI from I.P. Sharp data base.
U.K.	Real GDP, seasonally adjusted, quarterly since 1960. Series 3000.172 OECDMEI from I.P. Sharp data base.

II. Autocorrelation functions of the unwhitened series

Table A.1.[a]

Lag	U.K.	Germany	Japan	Italy
1	−0.21	−0.02	−0.07	0.24
2	−0.01	0.00	0.01	0.24
3	−0.07	−0.03	0.12	−0.02
4	0.03	−0.02	0.12	−0.06
5	−0.06	−0.01	0.05	−0.07
6	0.19	0.01	0.02	−0.05
7	0.01	−0.02	0.06	0.05
8	−0.14	−0.00	0.02	−0.05
9	−0.02	−0.01	0.11	0.03
10	−0.07	−0.01	0.05	0.11
11	0.01	−0.01	0.08	0.14
12	−0.01	−0.01	0.05	0.07
13	0.09	−0.01	0.08	0.06
14	−0.05	−0.02	0.15	0.05
15	0.08	−0.01	−0.01	−0.06
16	−0.22	−0.01	0.07	−0.00
17	0.04	−0.02	0.02	−0.04
18	−0.04	−0.02	0.11	−0.03
19	0.12	−0.01	0.01	−0.04
20	0.09	−0.02	−0.00	0.14
Sample size	107	108	87	107
Critical values	0.19	0.19	0.21	0.19

[a]The lags are significant if the values in each cell are greater than or equal to the critical value given on this row for each country. The underlined values are significant at a 5% level.

III. Autocorrelation functions of the whitened series

Table A.2.[a]

Lag	U.K.	Germany	Japan	Italy
1	−0.00	−0.15	−0.05	−0.06
2	−0.01	−0.14	−0.06	−0.07
3	−0.02	−0.03	−0.09	−0.14
4	−0.02	0.00	−0.01	−0.13
5	−0.01	−0.05	−0.05	−0.07
6	0.01	0.19	−0.09	−0.02
7	−0.02	−0.01	−0.04	0.10
8	−0.00	−0.13	−0.38	−0.10
9	−0.01	−0.03	0.01	−0.04
10	−0.01	−0.07	0.06	0.09
11	−0.01	−0.02	0.15	0.10
12	−0.01	0.04	−0.03	−0.02
13	−0.01	0.07	0.16	0.02
14	−0.02	−0.01	−0.08	0.04
15	−0.02	0.06	−0.03	−0.09
16	−0.01	−0.20	0.09	0.02
17	−0.02	−0.01	0.04	−0.01
18	−0.02	−0.00	0.04	−0.07
19	−0.01	0.12	−0.03	−0.11
20	−0.02	0.09	−0.03	0.11
Sample size	105	104	82	104
Critical values	0.20	0.20	0.22	0.20

[a]The lags are significant if the values in each cell are greater than or equal to the critical value given on this row for each country. The underlined values are significant at a 5% level.

References

Barnett, W. and P. Chen, 1988, The aggregation-theoretic monetary aggregates are chaotic and have strange attractors, in: W. Barnett, E. Berndt and H. White, eds., Dynamic econometric modelling (Cambridge University Press, Cambridge) forthcoming.

Bickel, P.J. and D.A. Friedman, 1981, Some asymptotic theory for the bootstrap, Annals of Statistics 9, 1196–1217.

Blanchard, O. and L.H. Summers, 1986, Hysteresis and the European unemployment problem, in: S. Fischer, ed., NBER macroeconomics annual 1986 (MIT Press, Cambridge, MA).

Boldrin, M. and L. Montrucchio, 1986, On the indeterminacy of capital accumulation paths, Journal of Economic Theory 40, 26–39.

Brock, W. and E. Baek, 1987, The theory of statistical inference for nonlinear science: Gauge functions, complexity measures, and instability measures, Mimeo. (University of Wisconsin, Madison, WI).

Brock, W. and W. Dechert, 1988, Theorems on distinguishing deterministic from random systems, in: W. Barnett, W. Berndt and H. White, eds., Dynamic econometric modelling (Cambridge University Press, Cambridge).

Brock, W. and C. Sayers, 1988, Is the business cycle characterized by deterministic chaos?, Journal of Monetary Economics 22, 71–90.

Brock, W., W. Dechert and J. Scheinkman, 1987, A test for independence based on the correlation dimension, Discussion paper no. 8702 (University of Wisconsin, Madison, WI).

Campbell, J. and N.G. Mankiw, 1987, Are output fluctuations transitory?, The Quarterly Journal of Economics 52, 857–880.

deJong, H.W. and W.G. Shepherd, eds., 1986, Mainstreams in industrial organization, book 1 and book 2 (Nijhoff, Dordrecht).

Deneckere, R. and S. Pelikan, 1986, Competitive chaos, Journal of Economic Theory 40, 13–25.

Eckmann, J. and D. Ruelle, 1985, Ergodic theory of chaos and strange attractors, Reviews of Modern Physics 57, 617–656.

Engle, R. and T. Bollerslev, 1986, Modelling the persistence of conditional variances, Econometric Reviews 5, 1–50.

Farmer, R., 1986, Deficits and cycles, Journal of Economic Theory 40, 77–88.

Frank, M. and T. Stengos, 1988a, Chaotic dynamics in economic time-series, Journal of Economic Surveys 2, 103–133.

Frank, M. and T. Stengos, 1988b, The stability of Canadian macroeconomic data as measured by the largest Lyapunov exponent, Economics Letters, forthcoming.

Frank, M. and T. Stengos, 1988c, Some evidence concerning macroeconomic chaos, Journal of Monetary Economics 22, forthcoming.

Grandmont, J.M., 1985, On endogenous competitive business cycles, Econometrica 50, 1345–1370.

Grassberger, P. and I. Procaccia, 1983, Measuring the strangeness of strange attractors, Physica D 9, 189–208.

Hall, R. and J. Taylor, 1988, Macroeconomics, 2nd ed. (Norton, New York).

Kurths, J. and H. Herzel, 1987, An attractor in a solar time series, Physica D 25, 165–172.

Lee, A.J., 1985, On estimating the variance of a U-statistic, Communications in Statistics A: Theory and Methods 14, 289–301.

Mayer-Kress, G., ed., 1986, Dimensions and entropies in chaotic systems (Springer-Verlag, Berlin).

Nelson, C. and C. Plosser, 1982, Trends and random walks in macroeconomic time-series: Some evidence and implications, Journal of Monetary Economics 10, 139–162.

Perron, P., 1987, The great crash, the oil price shock and the unit root hypothesis, Mimeo. (Université de Montréal, Montréal).

Scheinkman, J. and B. LeBaron, 1986, Nonlinear dynamics and stock returns, Journal of Business, forthcoming.

Tachibanaki, T., 1987, Labour market flexibility in Japan in comparison with Europe and the U.S., European Economic Review 31, 647–684.

Takens, F. 1981, Detecting strange attractors in turbulence, in: D. Rand and L. Young, eds., Dynamical systems and turbulence, Warwick 1980 (Springer-Verlag, Berlin).

Journal of Monetary Economics 22 (1988) 423–438. North-Holland

SOME EVIDENCE CONCERNING MACROECONOMIC CHAOS*

Murray Z. FRANK and Thanasis STENGOS

University of British Columbia, Vancouver, BC, Canada V6T 1Y8
University of Guelph, Guelph, Ont., Canada N1G 2W1

Received March 1987, final version received April 1988

An empirical assessment of a linear-stochastic perspective for Canadian macroeconomic time series is presented. The methods used are based on the mathematics of 'chaos'. Present evidence suggests that low-order deterministic chaos does not provide a satisfactory characterization of the data. The absence of significant nonlinear structure for the investment and unemployment series is of particular note in light of past findings with American data. The degree to which the use of a time trend can impose a pseudo-structure on the data is illustrated.

1. Introduction

An assumption of linearity often provides considerable analytical simplification. Both in theoretical and empirical economic research such an assumption is extremely common. Such a simplification comes at a cost. There are phenomena which can only arise in nonlinear systems. In assuming linearity one is ignoring the possibility of these phenomena. This paper tries to assess empirically whether a linear (stochastic) perspective might be rejected for some macroeconomic time series.

The fact that very irregular looking time series can be generated even by extremely simple, deterministic nonlinear difference equations, has been attracting increasing attention in macroeconomics. Such trajectories are termed 'chaotic' or 'strange'; see Devaney (1986) and Guckenheimer and Holmes (1986). Applications of chaos in economic theory appears to have been initiated by Stutzer (1980) and Benhabib and Day (1981, 1982). Since then theoretical interest by economists has progressed rapidly; see Grandmont (1985, 1986) as well as the references cited there.

There is starting to be an interest in investigating economic data for evidence of chaos. Brock (1986), Brock and Dechert (1987), and Brock,

*This research was partly supported by a grant from the Research Excellence Program of the University of Guelph. We would like to thank William Brock, Roger Farmer, Chera Sayers, and Jose Scheinkman for helpful discussions about chaos. The suggestions of an anonymous referee were quite useful. Our intellectual debt to William Brock is especially large and is gratefully acknowledged. Any deficiencies remain our responsibility.

Dechert, and Scheinkman (1987) are concerned with the theory of testing for chaos. Barnett and Chen (1987) find evidence of low dimensionality in certain monetary aggregates. Scheinkman and LeBaron (1986) find evidence of chaos in the stock market, while Frank and Stengos (1986) find similar results for gold and silver rates of return.

This paper reports results of tests of Canadian macroeconomic time series. This parallels Brock and Sayers (1988) examination of American time series. They did not find clear evidence of deterministic chaos, however the possibility of noisy chaos remains open. Similarly Sayers (1986) found mixed evidence of chaos in American workstoppage data.

This study differs from Brock and Sayers (1988) in several respects. In terms of implementation there are two main differences. Brock and Sayers (1988) did consider a number of different embedding dimensions, but their reported results focus on a particular embedding dimension. We report results for embeddings up to 20 in order to check for saturation. An absence of saturation provides evidence against significant chaotic structure. A chaotic system would be expected to saturate as the embedding dimension is increased. A second major difference concerns the approach to hypothesis testing. We did not use the Brock, Dechert, and Scheinkman (1987) method. In its place we use a method based on 'bootstrapping'; see Efron (1982) and Lee (1985). We find the bootstrapping approach particularly simple to implement and to interpret.

The use of Canadian data rather than American data may account for the differences in the empirical findings. Canadian data is available in a seasonally unadjusted form. We did our own seasonal adjustment.[1] The findings differ most noticeably for private investment and unemployment. In each case the Canadian data did not offer evidence of significant nonlinear structure. Both studies consider both trend stationary and difference stationary approaches. We report the implications of the differences between these two methods for correlation dimension estimation. This difference highlights the importance of Brock's Residual Test and of the shuffle diagnostic.

Section 2 discusses the role of chaos in macroeconomics briefly and reviews some of the past empirical results. Section 3 defines and informally discusses the test procedures to be used. More formal treatments are provided by Eckmann and Ruelle (1985) and Brock (1986). An informal discussion is provided by Frank and Stengos (1987b). Empirical results are reported in section 4. Section 5 concludes the paper. Considerable numerical detail is available as Frank and Stengos (1987a).

---

[1] This aspect of available Canadian data does not seem to have been adequately recognized. Those interested in issues such as Miron (1986) might find Canadian data to be of use.

2. Chaos and macroeconomics

Present interest concerns what has been termed a 'Frisch-type' perspective by Blatt (1980). The reference is to fundamental work by Frisch (1933). The Frisch-type view is of an economy that is basically a stable (growing) system subject to recurrent random shocks. From this perspective the economy may be modelled as a system of linear stochastic difference equations with no internal oscillations. It is the propagation of the stochastic shocks which we know as the business cycle. If there were no random shocks, then the economy would settle back into a smoothly growing time path. There would be no noticeable cycles. Influential examples of such models are Lucas (1975) and Prescott (1986). Lucas and Sargent (1979) discuss the issue of linearity.

An alternative perspective is that business cycles are generated endogenously from the internal dynamics of the system. Business cycles will occur whether or not there are random shocks. This view has roots amongst both Classical and Keynesian economists; see Zarnowitz (1985). Particularly influential examples of such economies are provided by Grandmont (1985) and Boldrin and Montrucchio (1986). Chaotic dynamics are quite possible in well specified theoretical models. The question then arises whether there is evidence of such phenomena.

Certain previous studies are particularly relevant. Blatt (1980) attempts a direct refutation of the Frisch-type perspective. He examined several microeconomic time series rather than looking at aggregated series such as GNE. After first detrending the data he found a lack of symmetry between the ascending and descending phases of the cycle. This asymmetry he takes to be inconsistent with all models of the Frisch-type. Neftci (1984) provides evidence that the American unemployment rate behaves asymmetrically over the cycle. Recessions tend to be steeper and shorter than recoveries. Falk (1986) extends Neftci's methods to American macroeconomic series other than the unemployment rate. He also considered industrial production in several countries. The evidence is mixed, but Falk's findings are considerably less favourable to the idea of significant asymmetries than were Neftci's findings.

Brock and Sayers (1988) is the study most similar to this paper. They examine American data on the unemployment rate, employment rate, real GNP, gross domestic investment, and pig iron production. Their evidence does not support low-dimensional deterministic chaos (a finding which would have refuted the Frisch-type perspective). However, they do find evidence of nonlinearity for detrended employment and detrended gross private domestic investment. Scheinkman and LeBaron (1987) consider annual U.S. per capita GNP (1872–1986). Their interest was primarily to explore issues arising in the implementation of the Brock, Dechert, and Scheinkman (1987) test. Their findings do seem supportive of there being significant nonlinearities.

Since the past empirical findings are not all consistent, a grand synthesis is not possible. They did leave us inclined to view the labor market as a likely place to find evidence of nonlinearity. Overall GNE seemed a less likely candidate.

3. Testing procedures

The usual parametric techniques are not well equipped to test for chaos. The reason is that the analyst is required to prespecify the functional form. An apparent rejection of chaos could well simply indicate that the maintained hypothesis concerning the functional form is false. An alternative approach is available. We define the methods here, but do not formally establish their properties. The reader interested in more depth is directed to Brock (1986) and Eckmann and Ruelle (1985). The basic concept is the correlation dimension due to Grassberger and Procaccia (1983).

Consider a time series of observations x_t, $t = 1, \ldots, T$. Use this series of scalars to create an 'embedding'. In other words construct a series of 'M-histories' as $x_t^M = (x_t, x_{t+1}, \ldots, x_{t+M-1})$. This converts the series of scalars into a slightly shorter series of vectors with overlapping entries. One uses this stack of vectors to carry out the analysis. Suppose that the true, but unknown, system which generated the observations is n-dimensional. Then provided $M \geq 2n + 1$ generically the M-histories recreate the dynamics of the underlying system (there is a diffeomorphism between the M-histories and the underlying data generating system). This result, due to Takens (1981), permits one to use the M-histories to analyze the system's dynamics.

Next measure the spatial correlations amongst the points (M-histories) by calculating the correlation integral, $C^M(\varepsilon)$. For a given embedding dimension M, the correlation integral is given as

$$C^M(\varepsilon) = \lim_{T \to \infty} \left\{ \text{the number of } (i, j) \text{ for which } \|x_i^M - x_j^M\| \leq \varepsilon \right\}/T^2.$$

$$(1)$$

Here $\| \cdot \|$ denotes the distance induced by the selected norm. By theorem 2.4 of Brock (1986) the correlation dimension is independent of the choice of norms. We use the Euclidean distance. In principal $T \to \infty$, but in practice T is limited by the length of the available time series of data. This will in turn place important limitations on the range of ε and M values to be considered. For small values of ε one has $C^M(\varepsilon) \sim \varepsilon^D$ and D is the dimension of the system; see Grassberger and Procaccia (1983). To compute the correlation dimension D^M:

$$D^M = \lim_{\varepsilon \to 0} \left\{ \ln C^M(\varepsilon)/\ln \varepsilon \right\}.$$

$$(2)$$

If the values of D^M stabilize at some value D as M increases, then D is the correlation dimension estimate. If as M increases D^M continues to rise, then the system is regarded as high-dimensional or stochastic. For such a system as one increases the available degrees of freedom by increasing M, the system uses the extra freedom. If instead a stable low value for D^M is obtained, then there is evidence that the system is essentially deterministic, even if fairly complicated.

Associated with the limited length of the available data sets are practical problems involved in implementation of (2). With a finite data set it will almost always be possible to take ε sufficiently small that any two distinct points will not lie within ε of each other. At the other end, if ε is too large, then all of the points will lie within ε. Two approaches may be taken to this difficulty.

One approach is to plot $\ln C^M(\varepsilon)$ against $\ln \varepsilon$ for various levels of ε. By eye one selects an intermediate range over which a straight segment is found for this plot (if such a linear segment exists). One then uses OLS on the points in that segment to calculate the slope. Another approach is conceptually similar but may be easier to recreate. Define

$$SC^M = \frac{\left\{\ln C^M(\varepsilon_i) - \ln C^M(\varepsilon_{i-1})\right\}}{\left\{\ln(\varepsilon_i) - \ln(\varepsilon_{i-1})\right\}} \tag{3}$$

Now SC^M is a local estimate of the slope of the plot using adjacent values of ε. For each embedding dimension take the arithmetic average of the three highest values of SC as an estimate of D^M. The reason for using three values of SC may be seen by considering the many tables found in Frank and Stengos (1987a). It reflects the size of the intervals between the ε_i that were used. For the present data sets the two approaches lead to the same economic inferences. For more about correlation dimension estimation with small data sets see Ramsey and Yuan (1987).

There are several ways in which to consider the estimates. The first is to compare them to computer-generated (pseudo-)random numbers. Chaotic data should exhibit lower dimensionality than computer-generated random numbers. This is a fairly weak test since computer-generated random numbers really are fairly random.

Brock (1986) has pointed out that a linear or smooth nonlinear transformation of chaotic data will leave the estimated dimensionality unchanged. To implement Brock's Residual Test fit an AR to each time series and check whether the D^M remains the same. If not, then this is evidence against chaos. This is particularly useful to guard against misidentification of a unit root process as chaos; see Brock and Sayers (1988).

The shuffle diagnostic is due to Scheinman and LeBaron (1986). Treat the original series like an 'urn' and sample from it with replacement. By this sampling create a shuffled series with the same length as the original data series. If there was a chaotic process in the data, then the shuffling should destroy its coherence and hence will raise the estimated dimensionality. If there was no chaotic structure in the first place, then there will not be much impact on the dimensionality estimates.

Motivated by the literature on bootstrapping [see Efron (1982)] we perform fifty of these shuffles for each series at various embedding dimensions for both whitened and unwhitened series. We than ask what fraction of the shuffles lie below the original series. If only 5% or 10% of the shuffles lie below the original data, then there is evidence of structure. If the original data is truly stochastic, then one might expect half of the shuffles to lie below the original data.

4. Empirical results

The first issue confronting the empirical researcher is that, due to economic growth, the Canadian national accounts are nonstationary. A simple adjustment for nonstationarity is to use a linear time detrending. Nelson and Plosser (1982) have severely criticised such a procedure. Given that one only sees the ex post outcomes, a detrended series will necessarily tend to revert to trend. If one is interested in the presence or absence of structure in the data, then forcing the data to be trend-reverting potentially presupposes the answer. We follow Campbell and Mankiw (1987) in making the primary focus of attention the first difference of the log of each series. This at least has the merit of not imposing trend reversions. There are more sophisticated approaches to making a time series stationary; see Nelson and Plosser (1982) and Watson (1986). Many of these procedures have stochastic trend components. If the trend is itself assumed to be stochastic, then the issue of determinism versus stochasticity naturally does not arise.

Since our primary motivation is to see whether we can reject the presence of chaos we proceed as follows. We do not focus on time detrended data since that imposes trend reversions. The data is 'made stationary' by examining the first differences of the logs. If the resultant series do not permit rejection of deterministic chaos, then one might be concerned that the process by which the data is pretreated has somehow imposed the chaos. The use of more sophisticated detrending procedures would constitute the natural next step. Since our findings appear to reject deterministic chaos we do not examine whether the finding of chaos is sensitive, since we did not find chaos.

4.1. National income accounts

In this part we consider the results for the national income accounts. Unemployment will be discussed separately since the data set is somewhat different. After differencing the logs of the various series, the data is seasonally

M.Z. Frank and T. Stengos, Macroeconomic chaos 429

Table 1

Removing linear structure.

X =	$Y(2)_t$	$C(2)_t$	$G(2)_t$	$I(2)_t$	$BI(2)_t$	$GI(2)_t$	$U(2)_t$
X_{t-1}	−0.3512	−0.2926	−0.1889	0.1862	0.2089	−0.0299	0.0615
(S.E.)	(0.0830)	(0.0810)	(0.0761)	(0.0840)	(0.0850)	(0.0780)	(0.0686)
X_{t-2}	−0.1435	0.1148	0.0890	−0.2382	−0.2565	−0.1312	−0.0776
(S.E.)	(0.0850)	(0.0830)	(0.0759)	(0.0840)	(0.0850)	(0.0750)	(0.0686)
X_{t-3}	−0.1963	−0.0008	−0.1095	0.8635	0.1376	0.0487	—
(S.E.)	(0.0840)	(0.0791)	(0.0750)	(0.0863)	(0.0870)	(0.0754)	
X_{t-4}	0.3684	0.2911	0.3523	0.2175	0.2217	0.4225	—
(S.E.)	(0.0850)	(0.0760)	(0.0750)	(0.0860)	(0.0880)	(0.0750)	
X_{t-5}	−0.0519	−0.1713	—	−0.0958	−0.0724	−0.1064	—
(S.E.)	(0.0860)	(0.0790)		(0.0869)	(0.0883)	(0.0750)	
X_{t-6}	−0.2715	−0.2453	—	−0.0967	−0.1105	−0.0304	—
(S.E.)	(0.0840)	(0.0770)		(0.0899)	(0.0905)	(0.0730)	
X_{t-7}	−0.1877	—	—	−0.1729	−0.1726	−0.2219	—
(S.E.)	(0.0870)			(0.0880)	(0.0890)	(0.0720)	
X_{t-8}	0.1915	—	—	0.2116	0.1757	0.2854	—
(S.E.)	(0.0830)			(0.0880)	(0.0890)	(0.0750)	
SSR	0.0830	0.0454	0.2452	0.1520	0.1889	0.2285	0.4714
SER	0.0244	0.0179	0.0414	0.0331	0.0369	0.0405	0.0470
$\bar{R}^2$	0.795	0.28	0.29	0.395	0.35	0.46	0.09
NOBS	147	147	147	147	147	147	217
F	81.92	11.43	19.58	14.62	11.22	17.01	2.19

adjusted. The associated autocorrelation functions show that the data still possesses structure. The issue is whether all of that structure which is empirically relevant takes a linear form. In order to remove linear structure ('whiten') each series is fit with an AR process. We tried different AR processes and then tested for the most parsimonious representation for each series by successive log likelihood tests. Table 1 reports the results for the most parsimonious AR representations. According to the ACFs the resulting residuals appear to be white. As far as one can determine from the ACF values, all linear structure has been removed. For purposes of comparison we also report results for detrended GNE.[2] For numerical details on the above steps see Frank and Stengos (1987a).

For ease of reading we make the following notational definitions. Let X_t be a generic representation of any series at date t. $X(1)$ is the logged differenced series X. $X(2)$ is the seasonally adjusted series $X(1)$. $XS(2)$ is an average of the shuffles for series $X(2)$. $X(3)$ is a whitened version of $X(2)$ as shown in

[2]An ordinary linear time trend was used. For the numerical values see Frank and Stengos (1987a).

Table 2

Correlation dimension estimates at embedding dimensions of $M = 5, 10, 15, 20$.[a]

$M =$				5	10	15	20
Random numbers (R147)				3.7	5.3	6.3	6.7
Random numbers (R217)				3.7	5.7	6.7	7.1

$M =$	5	10	15	20	$M =$	5	10	15	20
$Y(2)$	2.6	3.3	3.4	3.6	$Y(3)$	3.5	4.9	5.5	5.9
$I(2)$	3.3	4.7	5.2	5.8	$I(3)$	3.5	4.8	5.8	6.2
$GI(2)$	3.3	4.0	4.4	4.7	$GI(3)$	3.5	5.0	5.9	6.3
$BI(2)$	3.6	5.0	5.5	5.9	$BI(3)$	3.5	4.9	5.8	6.5
$G(2)$	3.0	3.7	4.2	4.4	$G(3)$	3.2	4.8	5.8	6.3
$C(2)$	3.3	4.5	5.4	5.7	$C(3)$	3.3	5.1	5.9	6.0
$YT(2)$	2.3	2.4	2.5	2.6	$YT(3)$	3.3	4.8	5.1	5.4
$U(2)$	3.5	5.3	6.2	6.7	$U(3)$	3.5	5.3	6.2	6.7

[a] The random numbers (R147) were computer-generated and constructed to have the same mean and variance as the differenced log GNE. The length of the random number series was 147, the same as the actual data. The random numbers (R217) correspond to the unemployment data.

table 1. Finally $X(4)$ is an average of the shuffles of series $X(3)$. These terms are explained more fully below.

The typical series has a flat slope ($SC = 0$) both for the very small values of ε as well as the very large values. In between there are segments for which positive slope is obtained. Our values of ε are such that for most of these series about three or four values of ε have SC values in the positively sloped segment. In order to simplify interpretation we imposed the rule that the arithmetic mean of the three highest SC values for each series at each embedding dimension would be taken to be the dimensionality estimate. As previously indicated the usual 'eyeball followed by OLS' alternative approach leads to the same inferences.

Table 2 provides the correlation dimension estimates for selected embedding dimensions. The real data routinely exhibits lower dimensionality than do computer generated random numbers. Of course computer-generated 'random numbers' are actually generated in a deterministic manner. Interestingly it is the most aggregated level which offers the lowest dimensionality estimate, $Y(2) = 3.6$ at $M = 20$. However GNE clearly fails Brock's Residual Test as may be seen in fig. 1 by comparing $Y(2)$ and $Y(3)$.

The estimated dimensionality of the detrended GNE is below that of the differenced log GNE. On its own one might have been inclined to conclude from the detrended data that GNE had dimensionality of about 2.4, a rather remarkable result. However, the detrended data clearly fails Brock's Residual Test. The apparently correct interpretation is that the detrending in fact

Table 3

Shuffle diagnostic results at embedding dimensions of $M = 5, 10, 15, 20$.[a]

$M =$	5	10	15	20	$M =$	5	10	15	20
$Y(3)$	3.47	4.89	5.50	5.93	$G(3)$	3.21	4.80	5.77	6.26
H	4.07	5.31	6.33	7.12	H	3.99	5.18	6.22	7.32
M	3.61	4.95	5.62	6.03	M	3.44	4.83	5.75	6.25
L	3.03	4.62	5.11	5.66	L	3.10	4.55	5.41	5.90
P	0.44	0.55	0.45	0.52	P	0.30	0.55	0.53	0.52
$I(3)$	3.53	4.83	5.76	6.23	$C(3)$	3.26	5.11	5.90	6.03
H	4.21	5.18	6.44	7.45	H	4.11	5.31	6.25	6.95
M	3.73	4.90	5.90	6.30	M	3.51	5.00	5.90	6.10
L	3.12	4.55	5.35	5.82	L	3.07	4.67	5.45	5.90
P	0.42	0.60	0.51	0.55	P	0.32	0.62	0.53	0.48
$GI(3)$	3.50	5.03	5.93	6.26	$YT(3)$	3.26	4.82	5.08	5.36
H	4.15	5.25	6.53	7.51	H	4.05	5.25	5.88	6.85
M	3.58	4.95	5.88	6.33	M	3.61	4.85	5.55	5.70
L	3.13	4.58	5.48	5.91	L	3.11	4.58	4.90	5.19
P	0.41	0.65	0.57	0.56	P	0.30	0.52	0.32	0.35
$BI(3)$	3.47	4.94	5.80	6.46	$U(3)$	3.52	5.26	6.21	6.68
H	4.12	5.22	6.18	7.35	H	3.93	5.62	6.63	7.61
M	3.60	4.90	5.77	6.40	M	3.50	5.15	6.18	6.78
L	3.16	4.61	5.45	6.11	L	3.11	4.71	5.69	6.25
P	0.38	0.52	0.56	0.68	P	0.50	0.55	0.55	0.45

[a]After $X(3)$ the table lists the calculated dimensionality for the whitened values of series $X = Y$, I, GI, BI, G, C, YT, U. For each of these series fifty replications of the shuffle were carried out at embedding dimensions $5, 10, 15, 20$. H = highest dimensionality estimated obtained from the 50 replications, L = lowest value obtained, and M = the arithmetic mean value of the replications. Following the P we report the proportion of the dimension estimates of the shuffled series which lie below the dimension estimates of series $X(3)$.

imposed a kind of structure on the data.[3] That structure is consistent with a low correlation dimension estimate. An imposed structure is quite different from an endogenous chaos. This finding appears to bolster the Nelson and Plosser (1982) criticism of using detrended data for this type of work.

The next step in the analysis is to carry out the shuffle diagnostic on the residuals of the whitened series. As discussed in section 3, shuffling will presumably destroy any structure that might have been present. Each series was shuffled fifty times at each embedding dimension. For each shuffled series the dimensionality was calculated in the same manner as for the unshuffled data. Table 3 provides results for selected embedding dimensions. These results are rather damaging to the idea that these series were generated by low-order deterministic chaos. Had chaos been present one would have

---

[3]If one uses the 'eyeball followed by OLS' approach then the estimated correlation dimension was still lower at 2.1. The failure of Brock's Residual Test was just as stark however.

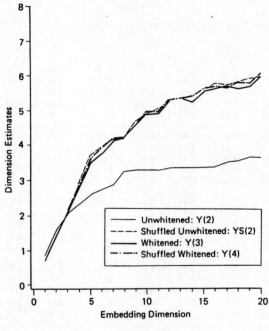

Fig. 1. GNE.

expected that most of the shuffles would have higher dimensionality than the unshuffled series. Instead, the shuffled series are about as likely to be lower as to be higher-dimensional.

An overall sense of the results may be obtained by consideration of figs. 1–4. In the figures a chaos in series X would have $X(2)$ rising at first until a saturation level is obtained. Beyond the saturation point an approximately horizontal line would be seen. The system no longer exploits the extra degrees of freedom being made available. To pass Brock's Residual Test, at least beyond the saturation level, the series $X(3)$ should lie almost together with $X(2)$. The average of the shuffled whitened series $X(4)$ should be expected to lie clearly above series $X(2)$ and $X(3)$ if chaos were present. We also depict results from the average of fifty shuffles of the unwhitened series $XS(2)$. The $X(4)$ and the $XS(2)$ series yield very similar results which on the whole are indistinguishable from the whitened $X(3)$ series. This provides evidence against chaos. Numerical details as well as figures for the other series may be found in Frank and Stengos (1987a).

The real data highlights the usefulness of Brock's Residual Test. Without this test one might have been inclined to believe that saturation had occurred

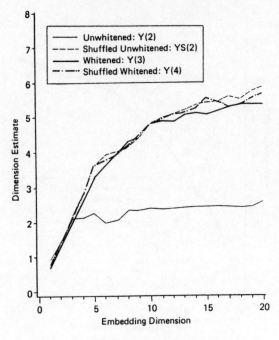

Fig. 2. Detrended GNE.

for detrended GNE and perhaps also for some of the other series. However, none of the series which even approximately saturates pass the Residual Test. On the other side, without worrying about saturation, one might have been inclined to suspect that consumption and perhaps investment pass the Residual Test. The shuffle diagnostic considerably strengthens the lack of saturation findings. To the extent that these series have passed the Residual Test, they did so at a level at which they were already indistinguishable from stochasticity. As one puts together the evidence depicted in the figures one does not appear to have evidence in favor of deterministic chaos for any of the national income accounts series.

4.2. Labor market

Empirical work on the American economy cited earlier suggested that the labor market might be a likely candidate for evidence of chaos. American studies have often found support for the idea that there are nonlinearities in the labor market.

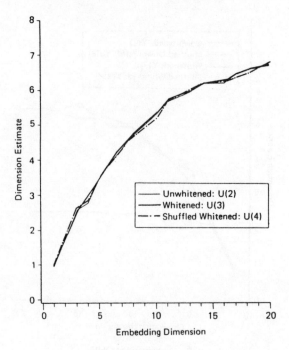

Fig. 3. Unemployment.

In this section we consider the monthly unemployment rate in Canada. At a 95% level of confidence, three of the twenty ACFs are significantly different from zero. Since the seasonally adjusted unemployment rate is already close to white noise it is a bit difficult selecting an appropriate linear filter in order to carry out Brock's Residual Test. As reported in table 1 we eventually settled on an AR-2 specification. Following Engle (1982) we also tried a variety of ARCH (Autoregressive conditional heteroskedastic) specifications. We were unable to find a reasonable fit using ARCH. Since the fit obtained is not all that good, one might expect that the data will pass Brock's Residual Test, but for the wrong reason.

Consideration of fig. 3 indeed indicates that the unemployment data passes Brock's Residual Test. However, saturation was not obtained. Furthermore, the actual data is also close to 'passing the Residual Test' with respect to the computer generated random numbers. The shuffle diagnostic results in about half of the estimates below and half above the unshuffled series. A simple linear filter of a white noise will leave the correlation dimension unaffected. That is what seems to have happened in this case. The results depicted in fig. 3 reject chaos for the Canadian unemployment time series. This failure to find

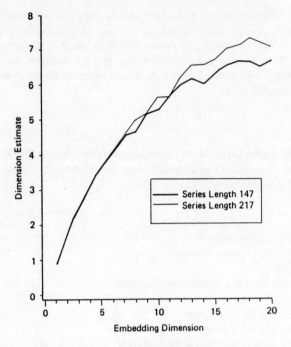

Fig. 4. Random number series.

evidence of significant nonlinearity in the labor market came as a surprise. In light of past American studies it was anticipated that evidence of nonlinearity would be found for this series.

5. Conclusion

Several Canadian macroeconomic time series have been analyzed to see if evidence of deterministic chaos might be found. The reason for doing so is that there have been many recent papers in which business cycles are modelled as deterministic chaos. A line of theoretical research that has attracted so much serious effort deserves a chance to confront the data. The attempt has been to distinguish the applicability of a linear-stochastic perspective from a chaotic perspective.

For none of the time series was it possible to reject the null hypothesis of linear stochasticity. For the labor market in particular this result came as a surprise. The tests were potentially capable of rejecting the linear underpinnings of much theoretical and empirical research in macroeconomics. Empirically we did not reject. On present evidence it appears that low-order deterministic chaos does not provide a satisfactory characterization of these time series. Accordingly the proponents of chaos in macroeconomics have yet to make a case that is empirically persuasive. This result is not as negative as it might seem. For general discussion of this line of research see Frank and Stengos (1987b). The natural next step would seem to be an investigation of more disaggregated series.

Appendix

Apart from unemployment, the data is quarterly starting in 1947 measured in millions of 1971 dollars unadjusted for seasonal variations. The series were taken from CANSIM matrix 525 as follows:

Name	Abbreviation(X)	Number
1. Gross national expenditure	Y	D40561
2. Personal expenditure on consumer goods and services	C	D40562
3. Government current expenditure on goods and services	G	D40568
4. Gross fixed capital formation	I	D40569
5. Gross fixed capital formation by government	GI	D40570
6. Gross fixed capital formation by business	BI	D40575

Series 5 and 6 are components of series 4, while series 2, 3 and 4 are components of series 1.

The unemployment data is monthly beginning in January 1966 taken from CANSIM matrix 2074:

7. Unemployment both sexes 15 years and over	U	D767287

We denote by $X(i)$ a series X at step i in the analysis. $X(1)$ is the first differences of the log of the various series.

References

Barnett, W. and P. Chen, 1987, The aggregation-theoretic monetary aggregates are chaotic and have strange attractors, in: W. Barnett, E. Berndt, and H. White, eds., Dynamic econometric modelling (Cambridge University Press, Cambridge).

Benhabib, J. and R. Day, 1981, Rational choice and erratic behavior, Review of Economic Studies 48, 459–471.

Benhabib, J. and R. Day, 1982, A characterization of erratic dynamics in the overlapping generations model, Journal of Economic Dynamics and Control 4, 37–55.

Blatt, J.M., 1980, On the Frisch model of business cycles, Oxford Economic Papers 32, 467–479.

Boldrin, M. and L. Montrucchio, 1986, On the indeterminacy of capital accumulation paths, Journal of Economic Theory 40, 26–39.

Brock, W., 1986, Distinguishing random and deterministic systems: Abridged version, Journal of Economic Theory 40, 168–195.

Brock, W. and W.D. Dechert, 1987, Theorems on distinguishing deterministic from random systems, in: W. Barnett, E. Berndt, and H. White eds., Dynamic econometric modelling (Cambridge University Press, Cambridge).

Brock, W., W.D. Dechert, and J. Scheinkman, 1987, A test for independence based on the correlation dimension, SSRI working paper no. 8702 (Department of Economics, University of Wisconsin, Madison, WI).

Brock, W. and C. Sayers, 1988, Is the business cycle characterized by deterministic chaos?, Journal of Monetary Economics 22, 71–90.

Campbell, J.Y. and N.G. Mankiw, 1987, Are output fluctuations transitory?, Quarterly Journal of Economics 52, 857–880.

Devaney, R.L., 1986, An introduction to chaotic dynamical systems (Benjamin/Cummings Publishing, Menlo Park, CA).

Eckmann, J.P. and D. Ruelle, 1985, Ergodic theory of chaos and strange attractors, Reviews of Modern Physics 57, 617–656.

Efron, B., 1982, The jackknife, the bootstrap, and other resampling plans, SIAM Monograph no. 38 (Society for Industrial and Applied Mathematics, Philadelphia, PA).

Engle, R.F., 1982, Autoregressive conditional heteroscedasticity with estimates of the variance of U.K. inflation, Econometrica 50, 987–1008.

Falk, B., 1986, Further evidence on the asymmetric behavior of economic time-series over the business cycle, Journal of Political Economy 94, 1096–1109.

Frank, M.Z. and T. Stengos, 1986, Measuring the strangeness of gold and silver rates of return, Discussion paper no. 1986-13 (Department of Economics, University of Guelph, Guelph).

Frank, M.Z. and T. Stengos, 1987a, Some evidence concerning macroeconomic chaos, Discussion paper no. 1987-2 (Department of Economics, University of Guelph, Guelph).

Frank, M.Z. and T. Stengos, 1987b, Chaotic dynamics in economic time-series, Journal of Economic Surveys, forthcoming.

Frisch, R., 1933, Propagation problems and impulse problems in dynamic economics, Economic essays in honour of Gustav Cassel (George Allen and Unwin, London).

Grandmont, J.M., 1985, On endogenous competitive business cycles, Econometrica 50, 1345–1370.

Grandmont, J.M., ed., 1986, Nonlinear economic dynamics, Special issue of the Journal of Economic Theory 40, 1–195.

Grassberger, P. and I. Procaccia, 1983, Measuring the strangeness of strange attractors, Physica D 9, 189–208.

Guckenheimer, J. and P. Holmes, 1986, Nonlinear oscillations, dynamical systems, and bifurcations of vector fields, 2nd rev. ed. (Springer-Verlag, New York).

Lee, A.J., 1985, On estimating the variance of a U-statistic, Communications in Statistics A: Theory and Methods 14, 289–301.

Lucas, R.E., Jr., 1975, An equilibrium model of the business cycle, Journal of Political Economy 83, 1113–1144.

Lucas, R.E., Jr. and T. Sargent, 1979, After Keynesian macroeconomics, reprinted in: R.E. Lucas, Jr. and T. Sargent, eds., Rational expectations and econometric practice (University of Minnesota Press, Minneapolis, MN).

Miron, J.A., 1986, Seasonal fluctuations and the life cycle–permanent income model of consumption, Journal of Political Economy 94, 1258–1279.

Neftci, S., 1984, Are economic time series asymmetric over the business cycle?, Journal of Political Economy 92, 307–328.

Nelson, C.R. and C.I. Plosser, 1982, Trends and random walks in macroeconomic time-series: Some evidence and implications, Journal of Monetary Economics 10, 139–162.

Prescott, E., 1986, Theory ahead of business cycle measurement, Carnegie–Rochester Conference Series on Public Policy 25, 11–44.

Ramsey, J. and H. Yuan, 1987, The statistical properties of dimension calculations using small data sets (C.V. Starr Center for Applied Economics, New York University, New York).

Sayers, C., 1986, Workstoppages: Exploring the nonlinear dynamics, Mimeo. (Department of Economics, University of Wisconsin, Madison, WI).

Scheinkman, J.A. and B. LeBaron, 1987, Nonlinear dynamics and GNP data (Department of Economics, University of Chicago, Chicago, IL).

Scheinkman, J. and B. LeBaron, 1986, Nonlinear dynamics and stock returns, Journal of Business, forthcoming.

Stutzer, M.J., 1980, Chaotic dynamics and bifurcation in a macro-model, Journal of Economic Dynamics and Control 2, 253–276.

Takens, F., 1981, Detecting strange attractors in turbulence, in: D. Rand and L.Young, eds., Dynamical systems and turbulence (Springer-Verlag, Berlin).

Watson, M., 1986, Univariate detrending methods with stochastic trends, Journal of Monetary Economics 18, 49–75.

Zarnowitz, V., 1985, Recent work on business cycles in historical perspective: A review of theories and evidence, Journal of Economic Literature 23, 523–580.

[28]

On Nonlinear Dynamics: The Case of the Pork Cycle

Jean-Paul Chavas and Matthew T. Holt

New methods for analyzing nonlinear dynamic processes are used to evaluate the hog-corn price ratio. The results present evidence of nonlinear dynamics in the pork cycle. Moreover, while GARCH processes account for some of the nonlinearities, the pork cycle is apparently characterized by more complex dynamic forms. The empirical analysis provides some evidence of the presence of chaos in the pork cycle. The results also indicate that the dynamic process generating the pork cycle is nonlinear and cannot be adequately characterized by a small number of state variables.

Key words: business cycle, chaos, GARCH, nonlinear dynamics.

The pork market has been viewed by economists as a clear example of a business cycle. Beginning with Coase and Fowler, an extensive body of research has focused on identifying the source and nature of the pork cycle (e.g., Breimyer, Larson, Jelavich, Jameson). For example, Harlow proposed to explain a four-year hog cycle in the context of the cobweb theorem and a delayed supply response to market price. Using harmonic analysis, Talpaz argued that hog prices follow several different cycles, each with a different period and magnitude. Using linear time-series models, Wallis, Shonkwiler and Spreen, Bessler and Kling, and Kaylen presented empirical evidence on the existence and nature of the pork cycle. Although the results often vary according to the period analyzed and/or the methodology used, the existence of a pork cycle has been strongly supported by the empirical evidence.

In many respects, the continuing presence of any price cycle is disturbing for economists. If a predictable price cycle exists, then producers responding in a countercyclical fashion could earn larger than "normal" profits over time (Hayes and Schmitz). Such profits could occur even with lags in the production process because predictable price movements would still influence pro-

duction decisions. Eventually, countercyclical production response would smooth out price fluctuations at the market level, causing the cycle to disappear.

The implication is that predictable price cycles are incompatible with rational producer behavior. Hence, the continuance of a business cycle could imply that producers are not behaving rationally and are ignoring important information. The assumption of naive producer behavior, while dating back to Ezekiel and others, still is a basic premise in much of the literature on livestock supply response.

An alternative explanation for the existence of a business cycle is that the cycle itself is not perfectly predictable. The law of motion underlying the business cycle may be a deterministic nonlinear relationship that generates unpredictable patterns (e.g., Grandmont and Malgrange). In recent years, examples of nonlinear, deterministic dynamic systems that produce seemingly random behavior have been reported in both the physical and social sciences (May, Grandmont and Malgrange). Such systems, usually called "chaotic," are necessarily associated with nonlinear dynamics (Hao, Baumol and Benhabib).

Until recently, economists have not considered that unpredictable patterns could result from deterministic, nonlinear dynamics. Recent work by Day; Brock; Scheinkman and LeBaron; Brock and Sayers; Frank, Genzay, and Stengos and others has, however, begun to examine the prospect that observed economic events could result from deterministic chaos. This research

Jean-Paul Chavas and Matthew T. Holt are a professor and an assistant professor, Department of Agricultural Economics, University of Wisconsin.

Financial support was provided by a Hatch grant from the College of Agriculture and Life Sciences, University of Wisconsin.

The authors would like to thank two anonymous reviewers for helpful comments on an earlier draft of this paper.

820 *August 1991*

Amer. J. Agr. Econ.

has resulted in a set of tools and statistical tests useful for investigating deterministic nonlinear dynamics in economic analysis.

The objective of this paper is to consider whether a particular business cycle, the pork cycle, may be characterized by a deterministic nonlinear dynamic process, and hence may not be fully predictable. In so doing, we present some of the analytical tools currently available for nonlinear dynamic analysis and illustrate their application to the pork cycle. In the next section deterministic nonlinear dynamic systems are briefly reviewed. Methods for detecting nonlinear dynamics in economic data are discussed, and the dynamics of the hog-corn price ratio in the United States is investigated.

Nonlinear Dynamics

The focal point of most dynamic analysis is a system of difference equations which dictate how a vector of state variables, y_t, evolves over time, t.[1] In general form, a system of n first-order difference equations can be written as

$$(1) \qquad y_{t+1} = f(y_t),$$

where y_t is an n-vector of state variables and the function f consists of n separate linear or nonlinear component functions. The system of first-order difference equations in (1) provides a basis for analyzing any discrete-time dynamic system; any system of second- or higher-order difference equations can always be reformulated as an equivalent first-order system (Luenberger, p. 96).

Linear State Equations

The properties of the state equations (1) are best understood in the context of linear models where $f(y_t) = Ay_t$, and A is an $(n \times n)$ matrix. In this situation, an analytical solution to the time path of the state variables can be obtained (Chow). It is well known that linear models result in state trajectories that can exhibit several types of behavior: trajectories that converge to a steady state, trajectories that become arbitrarily large over time, or periodic trajectories that oscillate or cycle.

For linear systems, the type of behavior can be deduced from the characteristic roots of the system matrix, A. Complex roots imply oscillations and cyclical patterns (e.g., Luenberger, p. 158). The system will also be stable (unstable) whenever the modulus of the dominant characteristic root is less than (greater than) one.

Because linear models exhibit well-known analytical properties and are empirically tractable, they have been used extensively to investigate dynamic behavior in economics. Indeed, time-series analysis and the analysis of distributed lags in econometrics have mostly used linear models. Also, most studies of pork market dynamics have used linear models (e.g., Wallis, Shonkwiler and Spreen, Bessler and Kling, Kaylen).

Linear models can provide useful insights into the dynamic properties of economic systems. But, are economic models always best characterized with linear state equations? Many economists would agree that dynamic relationships in economics are often fundamentally nonlinear, but that linear systems provide a useful "first-order" approximation to the true (but unknown) laws of motion. This argument is consistent with the methods frequently used to analyze the stability of nonlinear systems. That is, according to Lyapunov's first method, any system of nonlinear differentiable state equations can be linearized at a point (Luenberger, p. 324). The analytical results for inferring "global" stability in linear systems can then be used to infer "local" stability in nonlinear systems.[2] Several implications of using linear systems to approximate nonlinear systems are discussed below.

Nonlinear State Equations

By comparison, relatively little research has focused on nonlinear dynamics in economics. Unlike linear models, tractable methods for solving and analyzing nonlinear systems are not generally available. When analyzing nonlinear models, it is often necessary to obtain results numerically. Consequently, recent progress in computer technology has created new opportunities for investigating the dynamic properties of nonlinear state equations.

Quantitative predictions can differ between

---

[1] The discussion is limited to discrete-time dynamic systems. Similar results could be obtained for continuous-time systems. In this case, the dynamic equations (1) would take the form of first-order differential equations instead of difference equations.

[2] The term local is used when evaluating the stability of nonlinear systems because the results hold only in some neighborhood of the point of approximation.

systems of linear and nonlinear state equations. "Approximation errors" are introduced if a linearized model is used to represent a nonlinear system. Such considerations arise in policy analysis or in forecasting when dynamic simulations are used to predict values for the state variables that are well beyond the observed range of the data.

Moreover, nonlinear state equations can exhibit dynamic behavior that is qualitatively different from that of linear state equations. Nonlinear state equations can exhibit dynamic patterns that cannot, under any circumstances, be generated or reproduced by a system of linear state equations. These new and different patterns have been grouped in the literature under the general term "chaos."

In the early 1960s, Lorenz first identified chaotic patterns in the context of a dynamic weather model. He discovered that a deterministic system of three differential equations could generate nonperiodic but bounded solutions. In 1975, Li and Yorke introduced the term "chaos" to denote the apparently random output of certain nonlinear dynamic systems. In 1976, May cited the complicated dynamics generated by simple population models. Over the last fifteen years, there has been growing interest across disciplines (e.g., physics, climatology, ecology, economics) in nonlinear deterministic models and the highly irregular trajectories they can generate.

The word "chaos" refers to "unpredictability" in completely deterministic dynamic systems. The concept is at odds with the more traditional view that accurate predictions are always possible from a deterministic model. Chaos means, for example, that apparently random fluctuations in some state variables are not necessarily associated with a stochastic process or with errors in measuring the model's parameters (e.g., Brock). The potential for chaos warns us of the dangers of extrapolation and of the difficulties of economic forecasting. It also suggests a need for a careful reevaluation of the traditional way of thinking about stochasticity in modeling. Finally, chaos should not be equated with disorder. Rather, chaos is considered a kind of order without periodicity.

Unfortunately, few analytical results are available for characterizing the potential for, and nature of, chaos associated with a general system of state equations as in (1). Most analytical results have been obtained using particular specifications of (1) (e.g., Hao). Apparently, nonlinearities can appear in so many ways that it is difficult to develop a general criterion or classification scheme for characterizing chaos. Nonetheless, chaos occurs in a variety of nonlinear dynamic models that are often relevant in explaining a fairly wide class of observable events (Hao).

Deterministic Chaos, an Example

The above discussion suggests that chaos is best illustrated in the context of specific models. One useful example is given by the deterministic state equation

$$(2) \qquad y_{t+1} = \alpha y_t (1 - y_t),$$

where y_t is a scalar and α is a positive "tuning" parameter. Equation (2) is the logistic difference equation discussed by May. It is one of the simplest nonlinear state equations possible: it is a first-order quadratic difference equation with a single state variable. However, as shown by May, this simple deterministic state equation can generate complex dynamics. The time path of y_t in (2) is determined completely by the parameter α and by the initial condition, y_0. The logistic equation (2) is unstable for any $y_0 < 0$ or $y_0 > 1$. We focus on the case where $0 < y_t < 1$ and $0 < \alpha < 4$. In these intervals, the dynamic properties of (2) depend entirely on the value of the tuning parameter, α.

For $0 < \alpha < 3$, model (2) is stable and converges to a unique steady state for any initial condition y_0, $0 < y_0 < 1$. For $3 < \alpha < 3.5699$, the logistic equation exhibits cyclical patterns. For any initial condition, $0 < y_0 < 1$, the state variable converges on stable cycles of period 2^n, where n is an integer that depends on α. For example, if $3 < \alpha < 3.4495$, then $n = 1$ and the model would exhibit a two-period cycle. As α increases from 3.4495 to 3.5699, n takes on successively the values of 2, 3, 4, ..., each value corresponding to a stable cycle of period 4, 8, 16, ... (see May). In other words, as α increases from 3 to 3.5699, first there is one stable two-period cycle; then a four-period cycle emerges; then an eight-period cycle appears, and so on, ad infinitum. Given $0 < \alpha < 3.5699$, model (2), therefore, exhibits either stable or cyclical patterns in the interval $0 < y_t < 1$. That is, the state variable y_t would eventually converge to its "attractor": the point or set of points (e.g., limit cycle) describing the stable equilibrium of the system. Such predictable patterns can be found in linear models and are not specific to nonlinear models.

822   *August 1991*   *Amer. J. Agr. Econ.*

The dynamic properties of (2) are of particular interest, however, when $3.5699 < \alpha < 4$.
In this region, model (2) exhibits "chaotic" behavior. Chaos implies that "small" changes in
the initial condition, y_0, can give rise to time
paths that eventually diverge. Such divergence
has been called "sensitive dependence to initial
conditions" and is illustrated numerically by
Baumol and Benhabib (pp. 93–95) for the logistic equation (2). Sensitivity to initial conditions shows that long-term predictions from a
chaotic system are virtually impossible. This is
the point first made by Lorenz, who argued that
weather patterns are deterministic but chaotic,
implying the impossibility of accurate long-term
weather predictions.[3]

The divergence of neighboring paths does not
preclude the convergence of the state variables
to a bounded set of points. This bounded set of
points is called a "chaotic attractor." More specifically, a chaotic attractor is an uncountable
set of points attracting all paths starting within
the neighborhood of the set, where such paths
are aperiodic. Aperiodicity here means the existence of an infinite number of different periodic cycles that never repeat themselves. Thus,
under chaos, an uncountable number of initial
points y_0 gives totally aperiodic (although
bounded) trajectories.

One implication of nonlinear dynamics is that
a chaotic deterministic system can generate a time
series that appears completely random. This, in
turn, raises the issue of distinguishing between
a random process and a chaotic deterministic
process.[4] For example, standard statistical tests
relying on the spectrum or on the autocovariance function may suggest that a chaotic trajectory is indistinguishable from a trajectory generated by a "white noise" stochastic process
(Brock and Sayers). In this case, standard tests
for "randomness" could not discriminate between a stochastic explanation and a deterministically chaotic explanation of a time series. This
indicates an important weakness of the traditional linear statistical approach to time-series

analysis. It also suggests a need for different
methods in the analysis of nonlinear dynamic
processes.

Tools for Nonlinear Dynamic Analysis

Nonlinear dynamic analysis is fairly new; it has
received serious attention in the scientific community only during the last fifteen years. Consequently, the analytical tools for investigating
nonlinear dynamic systems are still being developed. In this section, we briefly review some
of the tools currently available and discuss their
potential for empirical analysis.

Consider a univariate time-series of length T,
represented by the scalar x_t. We wish to investigate the nonlinear dynamics of x_t, where

$$(3a) \qquad\qquad x_t = h(y_t),$$

$$(3b) \qquad y_{t+1} = f(y_t), \quad t = 1, 2, \ldots, T.$$

Here, (3a) is the observer equation, (3b) is the
equation of motion, and y_t is an $(n \times 1)$ vector
of state variables characterizing the dynamics of
x_t. Assume that the x_t's are observed but the state
variables y_t are not. The problem then is how to
use observations on the x_t's to investigate the
underlying dynamic structure of the state variables. We assume that the functions $h(.)$ and
$f(.)$ in (3) are differentiable and that the process
$y_{t+1} = f(y_t)$ possesses an unique attractor. Three
questions related to the equation of motion (3b)
are of interest: (a) how can one tell whether the
dynamic properties of x_t are chaotic? (b) how
can one uncover the dimension, n, of the state
vector y_t that underlies the dynamic properties
of x_t? And (c) how can one test for the existence
of nonlinearities? Each issue is addressed in turn.

Identifying Chaos

Chaos is associated with the local divergence of
neighboring paths in the attractor. Given this local property, consider the linearized version of
model (1) around some resting point, $\bar{y}$:

$$y_{t+1} = \bar{y} - A(\bar{y})\,\bar{y} + A(\bar{y})y_t,$$

where $A(\bar{y}) = \partial f / \partial y(\bar{y})$. In principle, the modulus of the characteristic roots of $A(\bar{y})$ could be
averaged over a trajectory to obtain a set of global
measures.[5] Such measures are called "Lyapu-

---

[3] Using his simple three-equation nonlinear deterministic model,
Lorenz discovered that long-term simulations were extremely sensitive to the initial conditions, thus implying the unpredictability of
long-term weather patterns.

[4] To the extent that random variables are used to represent part
of the real world we do not understand well, the issue may not be
to choose between a random versus a deterministic explanation of
observable phenomena. Rather, the motivation should be to obtain
better explanations for the seemingly "unpredictable" events that
often occur in the real world. Chaotic models may help improve
understanding of certain phenomena beyond that which is possible
for stochastic models.

[5] The characteristic roots of $A(\bar{y})$ determine the local stability of
the state equation (1). The system is locally stable (unstable) if the
modulus of the dominant root of $A(\bar{y})$ is less than (greater than)
one.

nov exponents": they are generalizations of the modulus of characteristic roots along general forward trajectories. In the case of a single state system, $n = 1$, $A(\bar{y})$ is a scalar, and there is only one Lyapunov exponent defined as

$$\lambda = \lim_{T \to \infty} \frac{1}{T} \sum_{t=1}^{T} \ln(|A(y_t)|).$$

From the above discussion, $\lambda > 0$ corresponds to chaotic trajectories ($|A(.)| > 1$ identifying local divergence) while $\lambda < 0$ corresponds to nonchaotic trajectories ($|A(.)| < 1$ identifying local stability). In the general case of n state variables, there exist n Lyapunov exponents, λ_1, λ_2, ..., λ_n.[6] Supposing that $\lambda_1 \geq \lambda_2 \geq ... \geq \lambda_n$, then λ_1 denotes the largest Lyapunov exponent. For inferring chaos, it follows then that a positive largest exponent, $\lambda_1 > 0$, corresponds to chaotic trajectories, while $\lambda_1 < 0$ corresponds to nonchaotic trajectories. Thus, an empirical estimate of the largest Lyapunov exponent λ_1 will provide a measure of the existence of chaos in dynamic analysis.

Wolf et al. proposed a numerical algorithm for calculating the Lyapunov exponents of a time series. While the statistical properties of their estimator are not yet known, the Wolf et al. es-

is given in part by Takens' theorem, which states that the dynamics of m-histories x_t^m is equivalent to the dynamics of y over its attractor when $m \geq 2n + 1$ (Takens). This indicates that the smallest unit useful for dynamic analysis is given by x_t^m in (4) with $m \geq 2n + 1$.

Second, if the unobserved state equation (1) is identifiable, one way to measure the "dimension" of the attractor of y_t is to use the generalized definition of dimension proposed by Hausdorff. (See Grassberger and Procaccia for details.) In general, the Hausdorff dimension D of the attractor of y_t is at most equal to n, the dimension of the state vector y_t. However, the Hausdorff dimension D of a chaotic attractor could be a non-integer and smaller than n. An often cited example of a non-integer dimension (also called fractal dimension) is the Cantor set which has dimension $D = .6309$.[7]

Although the Hausdorff dimension D has received much attention in the literature, it is difficult to compute empirically. Consequently, Grassberger and Procaccia (GP) proposed the "GP correlation dimension" α as an alternative measure

$$(5) \qquad \alpha = \lim_{\epsilon \to 0} \ln (C_m(\epsilon))/\ln (\epsilon),$$

where

$$(6) \qquad C_m(\epsilon) = \lim_{T \to \infty} \{\text{number of pairs } (i, j) \text{ whose distance,}$$
$$\|x_i^m - x_j^m\|, \text{ is less than } \epsilon, i \neq j\}/(T^2 - T).$$

timator of λ_1 does provide a basis for detecting the presence of chaos in a given time series.

The Dimension of the Attractor

Noting from (3) that $y_{t+2} = f(f(y_t)) = f^2(y_t)$ and $y_{t+k} = f(f^{k-1}(y_t)) = f^k(y_t)$, $k = 1, 2, ...$, consider the m-history

$$(4) \quad \begin{aligned} x_t^m &= (x_t, x_{t+1}, ..., x_{t+m-1}) \\ &= (h(y_t), h(f(y_t)), ..., h(f^{m-1}(y_t))) \\ &= J_m(y_t), \end{aligned}$$

where $J_m(y_t)$ is a mapping from R^n to R^m. Because x_t is observed but y_t is not, the first question addresses the minimum number of observations on x_t that are needed to recover the unobserved state equations in (3). The answer

Grassberger and Procaccia show that the GP correlation dimension α is a lower bound estimate of the Hausdorff dimension, where $\alpha \leq D$. They also argue that, in most cases, $\alpha \cong D$, implying that α can provide a useful measure of the underlying structure of the attractor of y_t. The empirical estimation of the GP correlation dimension is also computationally convenient and has several nice properties (Brock). Even though the statistical properties of this estimator are unknown at this time, the GP measure α is a useful method for identifying the minimum number of state variables needed in the dynamic analysis of a time series.

---

[6] See Benettin, Galgani, and Strelcyn for a general definition of Lyapunov exponents and for a proof of their existence.

---

[7] To see this, consider a Cantor set on the interval (0, 1) obtained by deleting the central 1/3, i.e., the interval (1/3, 2/3). Then repeat this operation with respect to the remaining segments an infinite number of times. In this case, increasing the linear size of the interval (0, 1/3) by a factor of 3 yields 2 copies of the same object. The resulting dimension is $D = \ln 2/\ln 3 = .6309$. This indicates that the volume of a Cantor set increases by 63.09% given a doubling of each of its spatial dimensions.

824   *August 1991*   *Amer. J. Agr. Econ.*

A Whiteness Diagnostic Test

As discussed in the second section, traditional statistical tests may not distinguish between a random process and a deterministic chaotic process. However, Brock proposed a statistical test (the BDS test) to empirically analyze this distinction. The BDS test statistic is

$$(7) \qquad W = T^{1/2}[C_m - (C_1)^m]/b_m,$$

where C_1 and C_m are given in (6) and b_m is the asymptotic variance of $[C_m - (C_1)^m]T^{1/2}$ (see Brock). Under the null hypothesis that x_t is an independent identically distributed (white noise) random variable, as $T \to \infty$, the W statistic in (7) converges to a standard normal variable with mean zero and variance one. Thus, the BDS test provides a statistical foundation for obtaining evidence against the null hypothesis that x_t is a white noise random process. Given the inability of more traditional statistical tests to distinguish between white noise and a deterministic but chaotic process, the BDS test can help uncover evidence of nonlinear dynamics. In particular, it can help detect misspecifications from using a linear model fit to nonlinear data.

The Residual Test Theorem

The results just discussed can be applied to any observable time-series x_t satisfying some weak regularity conditions. In applied work, the time series x_t is often assumed to follow a linear process that can be represented by an $AR(q)$ model of the form:

$$(8) \qquad \beta_0 + B(L)x_t = e_t,$$

where $B(L) = \beta_1 L + \ldots + B_q L^q$, L is a lag operator such that $L^s x_t = x_{t-s}$, β_0 is an intercept, and e_t is an innovation with mean zero and finite variance, h_t. Of particular interest here is Brock's theorem on the dynamic properties of the residual e_t in (8). Brock's residual test theorem states that, given a set of regularity conditions, the GP correlation dimension and the largest Lyapunov exponent of x_t and e_t are the same. This result suggests that the tools for analyzing nonlinear dynamics can be applied to the original data x_t, as well as to the innovations e_t associated with standard time-series models. This attractive characteristic increases the range of applications of the results discussed earlier. An empirical illustration of these tests and procedures is presented next.

An Application to the Pork Cycle

Here we investigate the nature of the U.S. pork cycle by analyzing the dynamics of the hog–corn price ratio. Quarterly observations on the U.S. hog–corn price ratio were obtained from various issues of *Livestock and Meat Statistics* for the period 1910–84. We first consider a typical linear time-series model where x_t, the hog-corn price ratio at time t, is assumed to follow an $AR(q)$ process as in (8), where e_t is normally distributed with mean zero and variance h_t. The order q of the AR process (8) was evaluated using Akaike's information criterion.

Equation (8) was estimated by the maximum likelihood method under two specifications: first, assuming that e_t is a homoscedastic white noise process where $h_t = h$, a scalar; and second, assuming e_t follows a GARCH(1, 1) process where $h_t = a_0 + a_1 e_{t-1}^2 + a_2 h_{t-1}$ (Bollerslev).[8] The Akaike criterion was minimized at $q = 20$. Table 1 presents the parameter estimates for an AR(20) (where $h_t = h$), and for an AR(20) with a GARCH(1, 1) error process. The estimates of $B(L)$ are similar in both instances. However, using a likelihood ratio test, the null hypothesis that $a_1 = a_2 = 0$ is rejected at the 5% level. Thus, statistical evidence indicates that the error term e_t is not homoscedastic and that its variance h_t is changing over time.

Following Luenberger (p. 96), the expected value of (8) can be expressed as an equivalent system of first-order difference equations: $X_t = HX_{t-1}$. The characteristic roots of the companion matrix, H, provide useful information about the dynamics of the estimated model (8). Details about the characteristic roots for both the estimated AR(20) and the AR(20)-GARCH(1, 1) models are presented in table 2. The results in table 2 indicate that both estimated models are dynamically stable and have cycles with periods ranging from one to five years. These results are consistent with previous research on cycles in the pork market (e.g., Wallis, Bessler and Kling, Kaylen). Moreover, the presence of multiple cycles is also consistent with the results obtained by Talpaz.

To check the validity of the estimated versions of model (8), several standard tests were performed on the estimated residuals, e_t. The Box-Pierce test examines the estimated resid-

---

[8] GARCH stands for "generalized autoregressive conditional heteroscedasticity."

Table 1. Parameter Estimates for the AR(20) and AR(20)-GARCH(1, 1) Models

| | AR(20) | | AR(20)-GARCH(1, 1) | |
	Coefficient	Standard Error	Coefficient	Standard Error
Intercept	.5909	.0528	.4874	.5439
β_1	1.1046***	.0613	1.1032***	.0667
β_2	-.3542***	.0915	-.3446***	.0969
β_3	.0501	.0936	.0806	.0966
β_4	-.0152	.0931	-.0844	.0920
β_5	-.2339***	.0931	-.1942**	.0898
β_6	.1506	.0938	.1437*	.0915
β_7	.0629	.0942	.0562	.0934
β_8	-.0083	.0941	.0246	.0936
β_9	-.1804**	.0933	-.2105**	.0922
β_{10}	.1573*	.0940	.1500*	.0960
β_{11}	-.0639	.0940	-.0437	.0910
β_{12}	.1959**	.0936	.1734**	.0940
β_{13}	-.1131	.0944	-.0824	.0938
β_{14}	-.0549	.0948	-.0691	.0918
β_{15}	.1898**	.0945	.1829**	.0916
β_{16}	.0568	.0944	.0603	.0903
β_{17}	-.1850**	.0943	-.1757**	.0893
β_{18}	.2040**	.0951	.2038**	.0907
β_{19}	-.2021**	.0938	-.1725**	.0879
β_{20}	.2043***	.0642	.1714***	.0612
GARCH, a_0	2.5088***	.0555	.4016	.3156
GARCH, a_1			.1065*	.0709
GARCH, a_2			.7378***	.1652
Log likelihood	-264.482		-260.711	
	$R^2 = .844$		$R^2 = .928^a$	

Note: Asterisks indicate significance levels: *** = 1%, ** = 5%, * = 10%.
[a] The R^2 for the AR(20)-GARCH(1, 1) model was computed using the standardized residuals.

uals for white noise.[9] The white noise test proposed by Ljung and Box is a modification of the first test.[10] Last, McLeod and Li proposed a test for white noise which is based on the squared-residual autocorrelations of e_t.[11] This test is use-

---

[9] The Box-Pierce Q_a and the Ljung-Box Q_a^* tests are based on the residual autocorrelation function:

$$r_a(k) = \sum_{t=k+1}^{T} \hat{e}_t \hat{e}_{t-k} \Big/ \sum_{t=1}^{T} \hat{e}_t^2,$$

where the $\hat{e}_t$ are the innovations associated with equation (8). Under the null hypothesis that the residuals are white-noise, the Box-Pierce statistic

$$Q_a = T \sum_{i}^{m} r_a^2(i)$$

is distributed approximately as a $\chi^2(m - q)$.
[10] Ljung and Box proposed to use the statistic

$$Q_a^* = T(T + 2) \sum_{i=1}^{m} r_a^2(i)/(T - i),$$

which is approximately distributed as a $\chi^2(m - q)$ under the null-hypothesis of white noise.
[11] The squared-residual autocorrelation function is given by

$$r_{aa}(k) = \sum_{t=k+1}^{T} (\hat{e}_t^2 - \sigma^2)(\hat{e}_{t-k}^2 - \sigma^2) \Big/ \sum_{t=1}^{T} (\hat{e}_t^2 - \sigma^2)^2,$$

where

Table 2. Dynamics Associated with the Characteristic Roots of H

| AR(20) | | AR(20)-GARCH(1, 1) | |
Modulus	Period[a]	Modulus	Period
.992	[b]	.970	3.00
.966	[b]	.960	[b]
.951	4.51	.950	[b]
.941	2.29	.949	1.82
.935	1.88	.945	2.27
.931	2.95	.929	1.44
.924	1.01	.924	5.14
.921	1.43	.917	1.05
.916	1.38	.900	4.67
.911	4.55	.885	1.34
.831	1.12	.794	1.05

Note: The roots are ordered according to their modulus.
[a] The period is denoted in years.
[b] These are real roots and hence do not exhibit cyclical behavior.

$$\sigma^2 - \sum_{t=1}^{T} \hat{e}_t^2/T.$$

McLeod and Li show that, under white noise, the statistic

$$Q_{aa} = T(T + 2) \sum_{i=1}^{m} r_{aa}^2(i)/(T - i)$$

is asymptotically distributed as a $\chi^2(m)$.

826 *August 1991* *Amer. J. Agr. Econ.*

ful for detecting certain types of nonlinear statistical dependence in time-series residuals.

The above tests were used to determine whether the AR(20) residuals in (8) are white noise for $m = 40$. The test statistics were 23.34 and 26.49 for the Box-Pierce and Ljung-Box tests, respectively. Given a critical value of 31.41 from the asymptotic chi-square distribution at the 5% level, the null hypothesis that the residuals of (8) are white noise cannot be rejected in either case. Alternatively, the test statistic for the McLeod-Li test was 40.06. Given a critical value of 55.76 from the asymptotic chi-square distribution at the 5% level, the hypothesis that second-order autocorrelation is present in the residuals, e_t, also is rejected. Similar results were obtained for the standardized residuals from the AR(20)-GARCH(1, 1) model.[12] These tests suggest that the linear model (8) (with either homoscedastic errors or with GARCH errors) appropriately represents price dynamics in the hog market.

Now consider the BDS test. Choosing $m = 40$, the W statistics (7) were calculated for the original data x_t, for the AR(20) residuals in (8), and for the standardized residuals of the AR(20)-GARCH(1, 1) model. The results are reported in table 3 for selected values of ϵ. Recall that under the null hypothesis of white noise, W converges asymptotically to $N(0, 1)$. Thus, the critical value of the W test at the 5% level is 1.96.

The results in table 3 indicate that the null hypothesis that x_t is white noise is strongly rejected. The W statistics also provide statistical evidence that the AR(20) residuals are not, in fact, white noise. Given the results of the more

[12] The standardized residuals for the AR(20)-GARCH(1, 1) model are given by $e_t h_t^{-1/2}$, where h_t is the conditional variance.

traditional tests for white noise, it follows that obtaining significant W statistics for the residuals of (8) provides important evidence of model misspecification caused by fitting a linear model to data generated by a nonlinear process. Moreover, these results are consistent with those of Brock and Sayers in their analysis of business cycles.

The BDS test applied to the standardized residuals from the AR(20)-GARCH(1, 1) model is also of interest. First, the evidence against white noise is not as strong as for the AR(20) residuals (see table 3). This result indicates that the GARCH specification is perhaps capturing some of the nonlinearities of the dynamic process. Second, for high values of ϵ, the BDS test still indicates that the standardized AR(20)-GARCH residuals are not white noise. Thus, the existence of nonlinear dynamics in the pork cycle cannot be fully explained by the GARCH error process. Importantly, this evidence for nonlinearities indicates that fundamental asymmetries may exist between the expansion phase and the contraction phase of the hog cycle.

Given that the hog–corn price ratio is associated with nonlinear dynamics, evidence on the nature of the underlying dynamic process also can be obtained by measuring the GP correlation dimension and the largest Lyapunov exponent. Brock and Sayers proposed using

$$(9) \quad SC_m(\epsilon_i) = (\ln C_m(\epsilon_i) \\ - \ln C_m(\epsilon_{i-1}))/(\ln (\epsilon_i) - \ln (\epsilon_{i-1}))$$

as an empirical estimate of the GP correlation dimension where C_m is defined in (6). The dimension estimates, SC_m, are reported in table 3 (using $m = 40$) for the hog-corn price ratio x_t,

Table 3. Dimension Estimates (SC_m) and BDS White Noise Test Statistics (W)

ϵ	x_t		e_t from AR(20)		Standardized e_t from AR(20)-GARCH(1, 1)	
	SC_m	W	SC_m	W	SC_m	W
$.9^2$	.009	51.50	.431	8.329	.126	2.305
$.9^1$	.218	41.85	1.181	5.300	.341	6.070
$.9^4$	.724	25.90	1.924	2.463	.996	1.659
$.9^5$	1.115	17.41	3.557	1.398	1.802	.215
$.9^6$	1.391	16.03	4.077	.851	3.023	−.298
$.9^7$	1.615	18.27	6.210	1.604	4.553	−.262
$.9^8$	2.330	24.85	8.501	2.040	6.365	−.387
$.9^9$	3.948	42.21	11.058	2.227	9.095	−.279
$.9^{10}$	4.977	78.47	14.756	2.081	12.921	−.427
$.9^{11}$	5.591	184.59	25.603	2.035	21.582	−.926
$.9^{12}$	9.115	554.04			25.911	−.909
$.9^{13}$	9.339	161.970				

Note: All results are obtained for $m = 40$.

for the AR(20) residuals in (8), and for the standardized residuals of the AR(20)-GARCH(1, 1) model. The dimension estimates for x_t are rough: they can be as high as 9. The dimension estimates for both e_t form the AR(20) model and $e_t h_t^{-1/2}$ for the AR(20)-GARCH(1, 1) model are also rough but tend to be higher: they can be as high as 25. Based on the GP dimension estimates, the underlying dynamic process appears complex and would probably not be adquately represented by just a few state variables.

Last, given the evidence of nonlinearity provided by the BDS test, is there any evidence of chaotic behavior in the pork cycle? This question is investigated by calculating the largest Lyapunov exponent, λ_1, using Wolf et al.'s algorithm.[13] The estimates of λ_1 were positive: .0041 for x_t and .0038 for the AR(20) residuals. Thus, the estimates of λ_1 are in the chaotic region. Their small magnitude indicates that the rate of divergence of neighboring paths is low. Thus, the pork cycle may still be predictable in the short- and intermediate-run, even if chaotic. Only in the longer run may neighboring paths diverge and, hence, become unpredictable. Finally, the estimates of λ_1 are close to the nonchaotic region ($\lambda_1 < 0$). Because the statistical properties for the estimator of λ_1 are currently unknown, we cannot conclude there is strong evidence of chaos in the dynamics of the hog–corn price ratio.[14]

Conclusions

The results provide clear evidence that the dynamic process generating the pork cycle is, in fact, nonlinear; however, the evidence in favor of "chaos" is less conclusive. The results of this study also suggest that linear time-series models commonly used to analyze pork market dynamics (e.g., Wallis; Shonkwiler and Spreen; Bessler and Kling; Kaylen) may fail to fully capture economic dynamics. Furthermore, while GARCH error processes can account for some of the nonlinearities, the pork market appears to be characterized by other forms of nonlinear dynamics. In addition, the empirical estimates of the GP correlation dimension show that the nature of nonlinear dynamics in the pork market are complex and cannot be represented by a few state

variables. Although little a priori information is available about the exact source of these nonlinearities, fundamental asymmetries likely exist between the expansion and contraction phases of the pork cycle. Consequently, structural models are needed to provide useful information on this issue. The dynamics of entry and exit in the pork industry and its implications for supply response are promising topics for future research.

Finally, if the existence of the pork cycle requires that the cycle is not perfectly predictable (as argued in the introduction), the source of this unpredictability remains unclear. Although our results present some evidence in favor of chaos that could explain the unpredictability of the pork cycle, this evidence is not definitive. Further work is needed to assess whether chaos can help us better understand the dynamics of agricultural markets.

[Received May 1990; final revision received October 1990.]

References

Akaike, H. "Information Theory and an Extension of the Maximum Likelihood Principle." *Second International Symposium on Information Theory*, ed. B. N. Petrov and F. Csàki. Budapest: Academiai Kiado, 1973.

Baumol, J. William, and Jess Benhabib. "Chaos: Significance, Mechanism, and Economic Applications." *J. Econ. Perspectives* 3(1989):77–106.

Benettin, Giancarlo, Luigi Galgani, and Jean-Marie Strelcyn. "Kolmogorov Entropy and Numerical Experiments." *Physical Rev. A* 14(1976):2338–45.

Bessler, David A., and John L. Kling. "Forecasting Vector Autoregression with Bayesian Priors." *Amer. J. Agr. Econ.* 68(1986):143–51.

Bollerslev, Tim. "Generalized Autoregressive Conditional Heteroscedasticity." *J. Econometrics* 31(1986):307–27.

Box, G. E. P., and D. A. Pierce. "Distribution of Residual Autocorrelations in Autoregressive Integrated Moving Average Time Series Models." *J. Amer. Statist. Assoc.* 64(1970):1509–26.

Breimyer, Harold F. "Emerging Phenomenon: A Cycle in Hogs." *J. Farm Econ.* 41(1959):760–68.

Brock, William A. "Distinguishing Random and Deterministic Systems: Abridged Version." *J. Econ. Theory* 40(1986):168–95.

Brock, William A., and Chera L. Sayers. "Is the Business Cycle Characterized by Deterministic Chaos?" *J. Monetary Econ.* 22(1988):71–90.

Chow, Gregory C. *Analysis and Control of Dynamic Economic Systems*. New York: John Wiley & Sons, 1975.

Coase, R. H., and R. F. Fowler. "The Pig-Cycle in Great Britain: An Explanation." *Economica* 4(1937):55–82.

Day, Richard H. "The Emergence of Chaos from Classical Economic Growth." *Quart. J. Econ.* 98(1983):201–13.

---

[13] Recall that positive Lyapunov exponents indicate chaos.

[14] The results obtained for λ_1 are consistent with those obtained by Brock; Brock and Sayers; and Frank, Genzay, and Stengos, in that the numerical estimates of λ_1 are, in general, small in magnitude.

828   *August 1991*   *Amer. J. Agr. Econ.*

Ezekiel, Mordecai. "The Cobweb Theorem." *Quart. J. Econ.* 53(1938):255–80.

Frank, Murray, R. Genzay, and T. Stengos. "International Chaos." *Eur. Econ. Rev.* 32(1988):1569–84.

Grandmont, Jean-Michel, and P. Malgrange. "Nonlinear Economic Dynamics: Introduction." *J. Econ. Theory* 40(1986):3–12.

Grassberger P., and I. Procaccia. "Characterization of Strange Attractors." *Physical Rev. Letters* 50(1983): 448–51.

Hao, Bai-Lin. *Chaos.* Singapore: World Scientific Publishing Co., 1984.

Harlow, Arthur A. "The Hog Cycle and the Cobweb Theorem." *J. Farm Econ.* 42(1960):842–53.

Hayes, Dermot J., and Andrew Schmitz. "Hog Cycles and Countercyclical Production Response." *Amer. J. Agr. Econ.* 69(1987):762–70.

Jameson, Melvin H. "Rational Expectations and the U.S. Hog Cycle: Statistical Tests in a Linear Model." *New Directions in Econometric Modeling in Agriculture,* ed. Gordon C. Rausser. Amsterdam: North-Holland Publishing Co., 1983.

Jelavich, Mark S. "Distributed Lag Estimation of Harmonic Motion in the Hog Market." *Amer. J. Agr. Econ.* 53(1973):223–24.

Kaylen, Michael S. "Vector Autoregression Forecasting Models: Recent Developments Applied to the U.S. Hog Market." *Amer. J. Agr. Econ.* 70(1988):701–12.

Larson, Arnold B. "The Hog Cycle as Harmonic Motion." *J. Farm Econ.* 46(1964):375–86.

Ljung, G. M., and G. E. P. Box. "On a Measure of Lack of Fit in Time Series Models." *Biometrika* 65 (1978):297–303.

Lorenz, E. N. "Deterministic Non-Periodic Flow." *J. Atmospheric Sci.* 20(1963):130–41.

Luenberger, David G. *Introduction to Dynamic Systems: Theory, Models and Applications.* New York: John Wiley & Sons, 1979.

McLeod, A. I., and W. K. Li. "Diagnostic Checking ARMA Time-Series Models Using Squared-Residuals Autocorrelations." *J. Time Series Anal.* 4(1983):269–73.

May, R. M. "Simple Mathematical Models with Complicated Dynamics." *Nature* 261(1976):459–67.

Scheinkman, J., and B. LeBaron. "Nonlinear Dynamics and Stock Returns." Econ. Dep. Work. Pap. No. 181, University of Chicago, 1986.

Shonkwiler, J. Scott, and Thomas H. Spreen. "A Dynamic Regression Model of the U.S. Hog Market." *Can. J. Agr. Econ.* 30(1982):37–48.

Talpaz, Hovav. "Multi-Frequency Cobweb Model: Decomposition of the Hog Cycle." *Amer. J. Agr. Econ.* 56(1974):38–49.

Takens, F. "Detecting Strange Attractors in Turbulence." *Dynamic Systems and Turbulence,* ed. D. Rand and L. Young. Lecture Notes in Mathematics No. 898. Berlin: Springer-Verlag, 1980.

U.S. Department of Agriculture, Economic Research Service. *Livestock and Meat Statistics.* Statist. Bull. No. 552 and annual supplements. Washington DC, various issues 1973–83.

Wallis, Kenneth F. "Multiple Time Series Analysis and the Final Form of Econometric Models." *Econometrica* 45(1977):1481–97.

Wolf, Alan, Jack B. Swift, Harry L. Swinney, and John A. Vastano. "Determining Lyapunov Exponents from a Time Series." *Physica* 16D(1985):285–317.

CHAOS THEORY AND MICROECONOMICS: AN APPLICATION TO MODEL SPECIFICATION AND HEDONIC ESTIMATION

Steven G. Craig, Janet E. Kohlhase, and David H. Papell*

Abstract—This paper is the first to apply the theory of deterministic chaos to a microeconomic problem. Previous applications of chaos theory to time series data, while successful in uncovering nonlinearities, have not provided guidelines for resolving uncovered misspecification problems. In contrast, we show that a modified test statistic from chaos theory is an extremely valuable tool in microeconomic model specification because it shows when excluded information is correlated with included information. This test, applied to hedonic estimation of marginal housing prices, is able to distinguish among alternative regression specifications and assists in discovering a parsimonious specification devoid of nonlinear effects.

I. Introduction

INTEREST in the theory of deterministic chaos has recently exploded. Although the theory originated in the hard sciences, applications of chaos theory to economics, as described by Grandmont (1985), Brock (1988), and Baumol and Benhabib (1989), are becoming more common. All of the empirical applications to date, however, have used macroeconomic or financial time series data. Even though researchers have been successful in detecting evidence of nonlinear structure, they have not yet used chaos theory to provide guidelines for model specification to purge nonlinearities from the data. Our application of chaos theory to microeconomic data offers a natural way to attempt to resolve the presence of nonlinear structure through an examination of model specification.

In this paper we present an innovative statistical test, based on the BDS test of Brock, Dechert, and Scheinkman (1987), to detect the presence of

nonlinear structure in microeconomic data. The essence of our test is to examine the residuals of a regression for systematic patterns. In a time series context, the data follow a natural order. With cross section data, the choice by which variable to order the data becomes important. We demonstrate that our modified BDS test examines whether there is information omitted from the regression that is correlated with the variable by which the residuals are ordered. Omitted information correlated with included variables can either be truly omitted variables, or can be a nonlinear combination of the information already included in the regression. While there are no systematic methods for finding excluded variables, it is possible to explore nonlinear combinations of included variables as alternative regression specifications.

To illustrate the importance of chaos theory to microeconomic research, we apply the test for nonlinear structure to a hedonic housing price regression. This application is particularly important since model specification is a crucial issue without clear theoretical guidance in the housing literature.[1] We show that the residuals from standard specification typically exhibit nonlinearities; that is, the residuals are not independently and identically distributed (iid). For some of the cases that we examine, we are able to purge the nonlinearities from the system by examining alternative specifications of the regression model.

There are two separate aspects of specification in applied economics that are highlighted in the hedonic housing literature. One is to find the best overall fit of a regression equation. The second is to determine whether the central coefficient of the model is correctly estimated. While the econometric literature has recently proliferated with new specification tests that address the first of these problems, no test exists that is focused

Received for publication September 1, 1989. Revision accepted for publication August 9, 1990.

* University of Houston and Hunter College and Graduate Center, CUNY; University of Houston and Hunter College and Graduate Center, CUNY; and University of Houston, respectively.

We would like to thank Dee Dechert for unravelling some of the complexities of chaos theory and the BDS test for us. We have also benefited from discussions with Chera Sayers, the comments of two excellent referees, and from seminars at the Dallas Federal Reserve Bank, the University of Houston, Hunter College, and Wayne State University. Partial research support for Craig and Kohlhase was provided by Texas Advanced Research Program Grant 003652-113.

[1] Applications in labor economics, such as the specification of earnings equations (Murphy and Welch, 1990), may also benefit from our approach.

upon a single variable in order to address the second of these problems. The modified BDS test is applied with respect to a single variable in the equation and does not rely on the overall goodness of fit of the regression model.

Complicated functional forms are often needed to obtain the highest possible goodness of fit measures. Achieving the best overall goodness of fit sacrifices, however, the parsimonious specification needed to make precise statements about single regression coefficients. The problem, as discussed in Cassel and Mendelsohn (1985), is that complicated functional forms can make it difficult to calculate marginal prices and standard errors of specific housing characteristics. We find that the modified BDS test gives valuable information when applied to the analysis of individual variables in hedonic housing regressions.

We apply the modified BDS test to the specification of a hedonic housing price equation used in Kohlhase (1991). We search for the existence of systematic nonlinearities in the error term of a regression. If systematic nonlinearities are found, we can conclude that the error term is not independently and identically distributed and that the regression specification needs to be explored further. We apply the test and show how it leads to a parsimonious specification with ease of interpretation of the coefficients of a single variable.

The test is described in section II. We show that ordering by one of the right hand side variables of the regression allows the BDS test to detect correlations between the included variable and information excluded from the regression. Section III discusses the application of the modified BDS test to the hedonic housing equation. This application shows that a parsimonious specification, which allows straightforward analysis of the effects of a single variable and relatively uncomplicated calculation of the resulting standard errors, retains some of the desirable features of more complex functional forms. Section IV offers conclusions and suggestions for further research.

II. A One Variable Specification Test

The problem we analyze is to determine the correct specification of a hedonic housing price equation such as:

$$g(P) = f(X) + e \tag{1}$$

where P is the price of a residential dwelling, and X represents a vector of characteristics of the house, the neighborhood characteristics of the area, and its location. Goodness of fit tests, such as Box and Cox (1964), examine the overall specification of (1) and maximize an appropriately defined likelihood function. As pointed out in Cassel and Mendelsohn (1985), however, if the true specification of (1) is

$$\ln(P) = \sum_i a_i \ln(X_i) + b_j X_j + e \tag{2}$$

then goodness of fit tests will prefer a log-log[2] specification over all others. This is in spite of the fact that X_j is not specified correctly in the log-log form. Such a misspecification may be crucial if X_j is the variable of interest. The modified BDS test developed here is the first diagnostic test capable of examining the error structure with respect to a single variable.

A. Outline of the Basic BDS Test

The BDS test developed in Brock et al. (1987) examines the pattern of a series of data. Compare the ith observation to the $(i + 1)$th observation. There is some positive probability that this pair of observations is within a known distance (d) of each other. Now consider a third observation. Again there is a probability that it is within the same distance of the second. If these three observations are from an iid series, the probability that each pair is within d is well defined. The BDS test compares how often a series of data points are actually within d of each other to the expected value if the series were distributed iid.

Define an Indicator function I, where $I = 1$ if the absolute value of the difference between two points is less than or equal to d, and $I = 0$ otherwise. The embedding dimension m defines the number of points that are compared in a series.[3] The function C depends on the sum over the product of the indicator functions for each m

---

[2] Here we define log-linear to mean $\ln(P)$ is a function of linear X's, linear to mean a linear specification, and log-log to indicate logs of both the left and right hand side variables.

[3] The embedding dimension defines the "m dimensional cube" that would be filled by the data if the data are truly random. If the data are deterministic, then a function of the data would show a relationship in m dimensional space. For our purposes, the embedding dimension simply represents a parameter to be specified, where m can be specified larger the larger is the data set.

as

$$C(m, n, d)$$

$$= C\left[\sum_{1 \le i \le j \le n} \left(\prod_{k=0}^{m-1} I_d(X_{i+k}, X_{j+k}) \right) \right] \quad (3)$$

where m is the embedding dimension, n is the number of observations minus m, d is the distance between two points that causes the indicator function to equal one, and X represents a data point. The expression in parentheses will equal one if all $m - 1$ pairs of points are within d of each other, and it will equal zero if even one of the pairs of points is farther apart than d. The summation shows how many times in an entire data series there is a succession of $m - 1$ pairs that are close (within d).

The BDS test relies on a proof that $C(m, n, d)$ asymptotically approaches C^m in probability when the data series is independent and identically distributed. Brock et al. (1987) use this result to derive a statistic, called a C statistic, that depends on comparing the actual calculation of $C(m, n, d)$ to the calculation of $[C(1, n, d)]^m$. If the data are independent and identically distributed, this difference should approach zero. Asymptotically, the difference between the two functions divided by the standard error approaches a standard normal distribution. Dechert (1987) has written a computer program to calculate the BDS statistic defined as

$$BDS = n^{1/2} \{ C(m, n, d) - [C(1, n, d)]^m \} / b_m \quad (4)$$

where the numerator is called the C statistic and b_m is the standard deviation of the C statistic.[4] If there are more (or less) points close together than would be expected from iid data, where $[C(1, n, d)]^m$ is the number of times a series of iid points would be expected to be close, then the BDS statistic indicates the likelihood that those points could have been generated by an iid series.

B. Application of the BDS test to Micro Data

The BDS test described in (4) has been applied to macroeconomic time series data to search for

[4] This is the C test based on Corollary 2 of Theorem 2 of Brock et al. (1987), rather than the S test which relies on the ratio of C functions.

occurrences of systematic nonlinearities (for example Brock and Sayers, 1988). In a time series context, the data have a natural order. In the microeconomic context we must impose sequencing on the data by sorting on the variable of interest. What further differentiates our application of the BDS test from the time series context is that application to micro data allows consideration of why a series of residuals might or might not be "close" to one another. If the observations are ordered randomly, it would be expected that the BDS statistic would be zero, as the error term should be iid. On the other hand, assume the data are ordered by one of the right hand side variables. If there is a misspecification error, either through incorrect functional form or an omitted variable that is correlated with the included variables, then the BDS statistic will be significantly different from zero.

Brock and Dechert (1988) have proven that the BDS test is a good specification test for time series data provided the residuals of the estimated regression can be written as a function of the current and lagged values of the residuals of the true relation. In the case of omitted variables for micro data, the intuition works the same way because the estimated residuals are a function of the omitted variables. This can be seen by assuming the true model is

$$g(P) = f(X) + h(Z) + u \quad (5)$$

where u is independently and identically distributed. Assume the equation is estimated omitting the Z terms:

$$g(P) = f(X) + v \quad (6)$$

so that the error term of the estimated regression is

$$v = h(Z) + u. \quad (7)$$

If the excluded information (Z) from the true regression (5) is correlated with the included information (X) in the actual regression (6), then equation (7) can be rewritten to depend upon only the included information:

$$v = w(X) + e + u = g(P) - f(X) \quad (8)$$

where e is an iid error term independent of u and $w(X)$ describes how the excluded information is correlated with the included information.

Brock and Dechert (1988) show that if $g(P) - f(X)$ is independent of X, then v is iid. The modification to the BDS test that we propose involves ordering the data by X, the included variable of interest. If there is a relation such as $w(X)$, then sorting by X will uncover the fact that $g(P) - f(X)$ will depend on the size of X. Thus the indicator function in the BDS test will capture the relationship in $w(X)$ by showing that the error terms do not have equal probability of being close to each other. We therefore are able to use the BDS test as a specification test to look for the importance of excluded information from the regression.

To see why the pattern of residuals reflects the information omitted from the regression, consider a set of residuals sorted by X and the probability that a given pair of residuals will be within, in absolute value terms, d of each other. If the series of residuals are iid, the probability that one pair of residuals is close to each other is unaffected by whether the previous pair of residuals is close or not. If the residuals reflect the omitted information $w(X)$, however, then the probability that they are within d of each other can be predicted based on knowledge of whether the previous residuals are close to each other. The prediction is possible only because the previous pair reflects the impact of the omitted information. That is, the BDS test will show a significantly greater probability than independence of finding residuals close to each other when the residuals have been ordered by an included variable. Therefore the probability that the BDS statistic is significantly different from zero depends on the probability that there is an omitted variable that is correlated with the included variable.

The key to the test we propose is how the excluded information impacts the included variables. When the functional form of a regression is not correct, it is quite likely that the excluded information is related to the included information. Even in the case of truly omitted variables, however, the BDS test will detect the influence of omitted information if it is correlated with the included information. This poses a potential problem for the applied researcher, in that a significant value of BDS (showing a lack of iid) may mean more than one problem exists. On the other hand, a BDS value insignificantly different from zero shows that excluded information does not have any significant effect on the estimated

parameters of interest. Thus our modified BDS test has the advantage of providing a stopping rule in the search for an appropriate specification.

III. Empirical Application of the Modified BDS Test

We apply the modified BDS test to the residuals from the housing price equation used in Kohlhase (1991). Hedonic estimation to find marginal prices of various housing attributes provides a particularly useful application because there is no theoretically preferred functional form and the correct functional form is likely to be rather complicated. For many purposes, however, what is of interest is the marginal price of a specific housing attribute. We focus here on the marginal price of square feet of living area ($SQFT$) for illustrative purposes.

The data set consists of 1366 cross sectional observations on housing prices in Houston in 1985. There are three types of variables differentiated by geographic level.[5] The first type differs by observation and includes housing characteristics such as $SQFT$. The second and third types vary by geographic area, Keymap number and census tract level.[6] The second and third type of variables may have systematic measurement error due to geographic aggregation bias, so we concentrate on discussing the specification of a house-specific variable $SQFT$, and report other specifications for comparison. Variables that are truly constant over geographic area, however, should not pose a problem for the modified BDS test.

Our goal is to find an estimate of the marginal price of $SQFT$ where we are confident that we have captured any nonlinearities in the specification of this variable. We proceed in two steps.

[5] Variables included in the regression are of 4 types: (1) house-specific—square feet, lotsize, parking, bedrooms, fireplaces, baths, condition, age, central air, range, dishwasher, (2) Keymap number specific—distance to toxic waste site, (3) census tract specific—distance to employment, % owner occupied, % with high school education, income, poor, blue collar, black, hispanic, % under 19 years, and (4) time period—dummies for quarter. A data appendix is available from the authors.

[6] There are 286 keymap letter areas and 155 census tract areas in the data set. A Keymap letter area is about 0.56 square miles and the average census tract is about 3.44 square miles.

First we examine three primary simple specifications, linear, log-log, and log-linear to find a preferred basic functional form. Because the preferred log-linear specification does not pass the modified BDS test, we examine alternative interaction and higher order terms. This allows us to find a relatively parsimonious specification where the marginal price of *SQFT* and its standard error are straightforward to calculate, but which still meets the requirements of statistical reliability as identified by an iid error structure.

A. Evidence for Systematic Nonlinearities

Table 1 presents the *C* statistics, their standard errors, and the resulting BDS statistics for the three alternative hedonic housing price equation specifications with the data ordered by *SQFT*.[7] There are two basic results presented in table 1. First, there is considerable evidence of nonlinear structure, as the BDS statistics are all over 4.[8] Second, table 1 shows that the log-linear functional form is clearly preferred to the linear, and is weakly preferred to the log-log. This can be seen because the log-linear specification has a *C* statistic significantly below that of the linear model, and a *C* statistic lower than that of the log-log model.[9] We will therefore use the log-linear specification in the remainder of the paper.[10]

We find the BDS test to have considerably more power for detecting complex patterns in the error structure than do commonly used tests for functional form. We perform two standard functional form tests: MacKinnon, White and David-

TABLE 1.—MODIFIED BDS TEST RESULTS
FOR ALTERNATIVE FUNCTIONAL FORMS

Basic Model[b]	C^a (Standard Error)	BDS Statistic[c]
Linear	1.57 (0.15)	10.61
Log-Log	0.43 (0.09)	4.84
Log-Linear	0.29 (0.07)	4.06

[a] Calculated from the regression residuals sorted by *SQFT*.
[b] See text.
[c] Significance test from zero.

son's (1983) PE test and Kmenta's (1986) Durbin-Watson (DW) statistic test. Neither provides any clear guidance about which functional form of the regression is preferred and the inconclusive results in the DW test do not even warn the researcher of the nonlinearity problem.

We also estimate an autoregressive moving average (ARMA) model on the basic residuals ordered by *SQFT* for the log-linear regression, and find that, based on the Ljung-Box *Q* Statistic, the appropriate specification for our data is an ARMA (1, 1). We then apply the modified BDS test to the residuals from the ARMA model. Purging the linear structure from the residuals, however, appears to have little effect. The *C* statistic falls insignificantly from 0.29 (0.07) for the basic model residuals to 0.27 (0.07) on the ARMA residuals. Further, the resulting BDS statistic of 3.82 indicates that significant nonlinear structure remains.

B. Respecification of the Basic Model

While the preference for the log-linear specification is consistent with results elsewhere, the BDS statistics in table 1 indicate that further model specification is needed. There is statistical evidence that the regression residuals vary systematically, but nonlinearly, with the size of *SQFT*. When the regression residuals are ordered randomly, the BDS statistic falls to 0.003 with a standard error of 0.06. It is therefore because of ordering by *SQFT* that we uncover a pattern in the residuals through the BDS test.

Possible causes of a significant BDS statistic include omitted unobserved variables, higher order terms, or interaction terms. Clearly, it is not

---

[7] We use an embedding dimension (*m*) of 5 and a distance (*d*) of the standard deviation of the data divided by the range. The results are robust for values of *m* between 3 and 10 and for values of *d* between 0.5 and 1.5 times that chosen.
[8] We use standard normal tables to calculate probabilities. Hsieh and LeBaron (1988) show that small sample properties of the BDS statistic only become important for sample sizes less than 500.
[9] The test of significance is approximate only and is based on comparing the statistic $z = (C1 - C2)/(\text{Var}(C1 - C2))^{.5}$ to a standard normal distribution, where $C1$ is the *C*-statistic in model 1. This calculation is approximate because the covariance between $C1$ and $C2$ has not yet been theoretically derived and is assumed here to be zero. *z* equals 7.73 comparing the linear model to the log-linear, and *z* equals 1.21 comparing the log-log to the log-linear model.
[10] Both the linear and the log-linear specification include *SQFT* squared as in the basic Kohlhase model. The BDS statistic without the squared term is significantly higher under both of these specifications, but the relative results are unchanged.

possible to include unobserved variables. We therefore first search higher order terms of the included variables. While squared terms have a theoretical basis, to capture variation in marginal effects for example, further higher order terms are not very appealing theoretically. Including terms up to *SQFT* to the sixth power, however, reduce the BDS to 3.12 which is still significantly different from zero. We conclude that simple nonlinearities are not the explanation for the observed pattern of the regression residuals.

To refine the model further, we desire a parsimonious set of interaction terms that will still allow a relatively straightforward calculation of the marginal price of *SQFT*. There is no clear guidance as to which interaction terms, or how many interaction variables, might be appropriate. Table 2 presents BDS results when each of the house-specific characteristics, and two region-specific variables, is used as an interaction variable with all of the other variables in the regression model. In all cases, we ordered the data by *SQFT* to calculate the BDS statistic. We find that an interaction with the number of bedrooms (*BED*) passes the BDS test.[11] The BDS statistic of 0.92 shows that the hypothesis of iid residuals cannot be rejected at the 5% level. This specification has the further attraction that the marginal price of *SQFT* calculation only involves *SQFT*, the squared term, and the interaction of these two variables with BED.

Choosing a specification with *BED* as the interaction variable is attractive on a priori grounds. The interaction allows the marginal price of *SQFT* to vary by the number of bedrooms. Table 3 presents the marginal price of *SQFT* and its standard error under the two alternative specifications. In the basic model, a marginal price of a square foot of living area is estimated to cost $52.49 irrespective of other house characteristics. Under the interactive and correctly specified model, however, the marginal price varies from $33.42 for a two bedroom house to $85.95 for five bedrooms. The modified BDS test allows a certain confidence that the interaction specification

---

[11] The *BED* interaction specification is not the only possible specification that passes the modified BDS test, for example, additional interaction variables also pass. Brock and Dechert (1988) conclude their paper by speculating on whether the BDS test is a unique test for specification error. Our empirical results indicates that it is not.

TABLE 2.—MODIFIED BDS TEST RESULTS WITH VARIOUS INTERACTION TERMS

	C^a (Standard Error)	BDS statistic[b]
Interaction Variable		
SQFT	.18 (.07)	2.66
Lotsize	.24 (.06)	4.16
Bedrooms	.06 (.07)	0.92
Fire	.23 (.07)	3.30
Bath	.15 (.07)	2.18
Cond	.29 (.07)	4.08
Age	.30 (.07)	4.11
Air	.24 (.07)	3.60
Range	.30 (.07)	4.54
Toxic	.21 (.08)	2.77
CBD	.41 (.08)	5.16
Other Specifications		
No Sqft Squared	.44 (.07)	5.97
With Higher Order Sqft Terms	.23 (.07)	3.12

[a] Calculated from the regression residuals sorted by SQFT.
[b] Significance test from zero.

TABLE 3.—MARGINAL PRICE OF A SQUARE FOOT OF LIVING AREA[a]

Basic Model	$52.49 (2.34)
Bedroom Interaction	
—Two Bedrooms	33.42 (4.06)
—Three Bedrooms	50.93 (2.32)
—Four Bedrooms	68.44 (3.64)
—Five Bedrooms	85.95 (6.33)

[a] Asymptotic standard errors are in parentheses.

has captured any systematic nonlinearities with respect to square feet. In addition, the advantage of the parsimonious specification is shown because the marginal prices of *SQFT* calculated under the interaction model are still estimated relatively precisely.

Because of the success of the *BED* interaction model, we examine other housing characteristics

TABLE 4.—MODIFIED BDS TEST RESULTS WITH INTERACTION TERMS

	Basic Model		Bedroom Interaction	
	C^a (Standard Error)	BDS statistic[b]	C^a (Standard Error)	BDS statistic[b]
Sorted Variable				
SQFT	.29 (.07)	4.06	.06 (.07)	0.92
Lotsize	.32 (.07)	4.44	.28 (.07)	4.25
Bedrooms	.51 (.07)	7.09	.25 (.07)	3.78
Fire	.34 (.07)	4.69	.14 (.07)	2.12
Bath	.28 (.07)	3.98	.11 (.07)	1.64
Cond	.29 (.07)	4.08	.11 (.07)	1.65
Age	.53 (.07)	7.44	.32 (.07)	4.76
Air	.37 (.07)	5.18	.11 (.07)	1.66
Range	.44 (.07)	6.15	.20 (.07)	3.01
Toxic	.71 (.07)	9.87	.55 (.07)	8.26
CBD	.82 (.07)	11.42	.49 (.07)	7.40

[a] Calculated from the regression residuals sorted by indicated variable.
[b] Significance test from zero.

and their performance on the BDS test. Table 4 presents the results. The first two columns show BDS test results for the basic model when the residuals are ordered by each of the housing specific characteristics, plus the Keymap variable *TOXIC* as well as the Census tract variable *CBD*.[12] None of the variables that we use to sort the residuals show an insignificant BDS statistic. The second two columns show the residuals of the *BED* interaction model when ordered by each of the variables. In addition to *SQFT*, three other variables now show BDS statistics insignificantly different from zero at the 5% level: the number of baths, condition of the house, and the presence of air conditioning. In fact, with the exception of lotsize, all of the variables in the model show a significant improvement in the *C* statistics. Thus the number of bedrooms appears to be an important source of nonlinearities with respect to many of the housing characteristics.

[12] We omitted from table 4 two house-specific characteristics, dishwashers and number of parking spaces, because the coefficient estimates in the basic model were quite low and imprecise (*t*-statistics less than 0.1).

One of the most valuable aspects of the modified BDS test is that unlike many other tests, the BDS test provides a stopping rule in the search for an appropriate specification. When the residuals are found to be iid, information excluded from the regression is not correlated with the ordering variable. For example, the BDS test shows that the residuals from the basic model augmented by bedroom interactions are iid when ordered by *SQFT*. In contrast, a standard *F*-test about the inclusion of more variables, such as *CBD* or *TOXIC* interactions, would lead the researcher to add unnecessary complexity.

We have shown that the modified BDS test is an important diagnostic tool when examining the specification of a regression equation with respect to a single variable. There are, however, important limitations to using the modified BDS test. As discussed earlier, when variable measurement exhibits geographic aggregation bias, the BDS test may show significant nonlinearities for all specifications. Further, we found several specifications where the BDS statistic is larger using three interactive variables than one.[13] This may be because some interaction variables induce nonlinearities into the data rather than control for them. Even more important, perhaps, is that in addition to incorrect functional form, another source of significant BDS statistics can be omitted variables. The finding that the BDS statistic when the regression residuals are ordered by lotsize do not fall with the *BED* interaction is not very reassuring. The BDS statistic using the basic log-linear model is 4.44. With the *BED* interaction, it fell slightly to 4.25. With three interaction variables, it is still 4.46. In fact, we failed to discover a specification for lotsize that provides a significant improvement in, much less passes, the modified BDS test. As with all diagnostic tests, the test is able to indicate where more work is needed without being very specific about how to correct the problem.

IV. Summary and Conclusions

This paper has shown that an application of chaos theory provides an excellent tool for investigating microeconomic model specification. The modified BDS test proposed here provides an important diagnostic test for the presence of nonlinear structure in microeconomic data, and provides an important indication about whether a particular variable in a regression is correctly specified. The modified BDS test examines whether the residuals of a regression equation exhibit a systematic pattern when ordered by the right hand side variable of interest. The test therefore determines whether excluded information from the specified regression is correlated with the variable of interest; a determination of no correlation indicates that the resulting parameter estimates are unbiased. The modified BDS test applied to micro data is an important specification test with respect to a single variable because possible sources of excluded information consist of alternative functional forms employing included variables.

Specification tests for a single variable are especially important in applications where a precise coefficient on a specific variable is desired. We have applied the modified BDS test to a hedonic housing price regression, and are able to find a

relatively parsimonious specification where the residuals are iid when ordered by square feet of living area. Thus we offer the first attempt to mediate the trade-off between a complex specification of the overall equation and ease of manipulation for a particular regression coefficient.

The test for nonlinear structure, when used on macroeconomic data, can give evidence about whether the residuals are iid, but does not indicate how the model can be transformed to purge the systematic component from the residuals. In the microeconomic context, the modified BDS test is an excellent signpost about potential errors in modelling because ordering by the variable of interest provides a method for uncovering systematic nonlinearities in the residuals.

REFERENCES

Baumol, William J. and Jess Benhabib, "Chaos: Significance, Mechanism, and Economic Applications," *The Journal of Economic Perspectives* 3 (Winter 1989), 77–106.

Box, G. E. P. and D. R. Cox, "An Analysis of Transformations," *Journal of the Royal Statistical Society Series B*, 26 (1964), 211–252.

Brock, William A., "Introduction to Chaos and Other Aspects of Nonlinearity," in W. A. Brock and A. G. Malliaris, *Differential Equations, Stability and Chaos in Dynamic Economics* (New York: North-Holland, 1988).

Brock, William A., and W. Davis Dechert, "A General Class of Specification Tests: The Scalar Case," *Proceedings of the Business and Economic Statistics Section*, American Statistical Association (1988), 70–79.

Brock, William A., W. Davis Dechert, and Jose A. Scheinkman, "A Test for Independence Based on the Correlation Dimension," SSRI Working Paper #8702, University of Wisconsin-Madison, 1987.

Brock, William A., and Chera L. Sayers, "Is the Business Cycle Characterized by Deterministic Chaos?" *Journal of Monetary Economics* 22 (1988), 71–90.

Cassel, Eric, and Robert Mendelsohn, "The Choice of Functional Forms for Hedonic Price Equations: Comment," *Journal of Urban Economics* 18 (Sept. 1985), 135–42.

Dechert, W. Davis, "A Program to Calculate BDS Statistics for the IBM PC," University of Houston, 1987.

Grandmont, Jean-Michel, "On Endogenous Competitive Business Cycles," *Econometrica* 53 (Sept. 1985), 995–1045.

Hsieh, David A. and Blake LeBaron, "Finite Sample Properties of the BDS Statistic I: Distribution Under the Null Hypothesis," University of Chicago mimeo, May 1988.

Kmenta, Jan, *Econometrics* (New York: Macmillan, 1986).

Kohlhase, Janet E., "The Impact of Toxic Waste Sites on Housing Values," *Journal of Urban Economics* 30 July 1991), 1–26.

MacKinnon, J. G., H. White, and R. Davidson, "Tests for Model Specification in the Presence of Alternative Hypotheses: Some Further Results," *Journal of Econometrics* 21 (Jan. 1983), 53–70.

Murphy, Kevin M. and Finis Welch, "Empirical Age-Earnings Profiles," *Journal of Labor Economics* 8 (Apr. 1990), 202–229.

[13] For example, interactions with *BED*, *TOXIC*, and *CBD* produce a BDS statistic of 0.93, despite the fact that *BED* only as an interaction variable produces a BDS of 0.92.

Name Index

The International Library of Critical Writings in Economics

The Foundations of Public Finance (Volumes I and II)
Peter Jackson

The Economics of Communication and Innovation
Donald M. Lamberton

The Economics of Uncertainty
John D. Hey

International Finance
Robert Z. Aliber

Welfare Economics
William J. Baumol and Janusz A. Ordover

The Theory of the Firm
Mark Casson

The Economics of Inequality and Poverty
A.B. Atkinson

The Economics of Housing
John M. Quigley

Population Economics
Julian L. Simon

The Economics of Crime
Isaac Ehrlich

The Economics of Integration
Willem Molle

The Rhetoric of Economics
Deirdre McCloskey

Migration
Oded Stark

The Economics of Defence
Keith Hartley and Nicholas Hooper

Consumer Theory
Kelvin Lancaster

Law and Economics
Richard A. Posner and Francesco Parisi

The Economics of Business Policy
John Kay

Microeconomic Theories of Imperfect Competition
Jacques Thisse and Jean Gabszewicz

The Economics of Increasing Returns
Geoffrey Heal

The Balance of Payments
Michael J. Artis

Cost-Benefit Analysis
Arnold Harberger and Glenn P. Jenkins

The Economics of Unemployment
P.N. Junankar

Mathematical Economics
Graciela Chichilnisky

Economic Growth in the Long Run
Bart van Ark

Gender in Economic and Social History
K.J. Humphries and J. Lewis

The Economics of Local Finance and Fiscal Federalism
Wallace Oates

Privatization in Developing and Transitional Economies
Colin Kirkpatrick and Paul Cook

Input-Output Analysis
Heinz Kurz and Christian Lager

The Economics of Global Warming
Tom Tietenberg

Political Business Cycles
Bruno Frey

The Economics of the Arts
Ruth Towse

The Economics of Energy
Paul Stevens

The Economics of Intellectual Property
Ruth Towse

Ecological Economics
Robert Costanza, Charles Perrings and Cutler Cleveland

The Economics of Tourism
Clem Tisdell

The Economics of Productivity
Edward Wolff

The Economics of Organization and Bureaucracy
Peter Jackson

Independent Central Banks and Economic Performance
Sylvester Eijffinger

The Economics of the Commodity Markets
David Greenaway and Wyn Morgan

Realism and Economics: Studies in Ontology
Tony Lawson

Women in the Labor Market
Marianne A. Ferber

New Developments in Game Theory
Eric S. Moskin

Economic Demography
T. Paul Schultz